CORPORATE GOVERNANCE IN AUSTRALIA *and* NEW ZEALAND

John Farrar

OXFORD

OXFORD

UNIVERSITY PRESS

253 Normanby Road, South Melbourne, Victoria 3205, Australia

Oxford University Press is a department of the University of Oxford.
It furthers the University's objective of excellence in research, scholarship,
and education by publishing worldwide in

Oxford New York

Auckland Bangkok Buenos Aires Cape Town Chennai
Dar es Salaam Delhi Hong Kong Istanbul Karachi Kolkata
Kuala Lumpur Madrid Melbourne Mexico City Mumbai Nairobi
São Paulo Shanghai Singapore Taipei Tokyo Toronto

OXFORD is a trade mark of Oxford University Press
in the UK and in certain other countries

National Library of Australia
Cataloguing-in-Publication data:

Farrar, John H. (John Hynes), 1941-
    Corporate Governance in Australia and New Zealand

    Bibliography.
    Includes index
    ISBN 0 19 551314 2.

    1. Corporate governance—Australia. 2. Corporate Governance—New Zealand.
    3. Directors of corporations—Australia. 4.Directors of corporations—New Zealand.
    5. Corporations law—Australia. 6. Corporations law—New Zealand.

356.940664

Typeset by Desktop Concepts
Printed through Bookpac Production Services, Singapore

Coventry University

Contents

PART 3 THE SELF-REGULATION PENUMBRA AND OTHER CONTEMPORARY ISSUES IN CORPORATE GOVERNANCE   301

APPENDICES

Preface

This book is about corporate governance in general but with particular reference to Australia and New Zealand. The book has grown out of LLM classes on Corporate Governance and the Duties of Directors that I have taught at the University of Melbourne since 1992, and Bond University since 1994. At Bond I have sometimes taught a mixed class of LLM and MBA students. In the Melbourne seminars since 1995 I have taught with my friend Doug Branson of the University of Pittsburgh and author of the leading American treatise on the law of corporate governance. Both Doug and I have learned a lot from our students and also from Henry Bosch. Henry and I drafted the Code of Conduct for Company Directors for the Australian Institute of Company Directors in 1994 and prepared a report that led to the present system of training, conduct and discipline for the institute.

I am grateful to Doug and Henry for sharing their knowledge with me. I have also learned much over the years from my friends Mel Eisenberg of the University of California, Berkeley and Columbia Law Schools, Harold Ford and Bob Baxt. In the last few years I have profited from the discussions with my Bond colleagues Jim Corkery, John Lessing, Bernard McCabe and Ken Moores, the research of my colleagues at Melbourne notably Ian Ramsay, Geof Stapledon, Elizabeth Boros, Helen Bird, Sally Sievers, Pamela Hanrahan and George Gilligan, and my friends in Sydney, Jennifer Hill and Saul Fridman. To all these I owe intellectual debts.

Chapter 31 is based substantially on 'Corporatisation, Corporate Governance and Deregulation of the Public Sector Economy' (1995) PLR 24, which I wrote jointly with Bernard McCabe.

Chapter 7 on Meetings in part relies on the lucid analysis of the *Company Law Review Act 1998* changes by Brian Burnett and I am grateful to him for his permission to do so.

I would also like to acknowledge and thank two of my former students, Lara Lukich and Alan Bulman, for letting me draw on excellent research papers they wrote under my supervision, for substantial parts of Chapters 22 and 23, and Catherine Flynn and Trinity McGarvie for some research assistance.

I am grateful to Korn/Ferry International for permission to quote from their annual surveys, to the Business Council of Australia for permission to set out part of *Corporate Practices and Conduct, 3rd edn*, to the Investment and Financial Services Association for permission to set out their Guidelines, and to the Institute of Directors in New Zealand (Inc.) for permission to set out their 'Code of Proper Practice for Directors'.

I would like to thank Kerri Nancarrow for the cheerful and efficient way in which she has typed my often messy manuscript and the staff of the Bond Law library for help in checking references.

I have benefited over the years from my membership of the Legal Committee and Corporate Governance Committee of the Australian Institute of Company Directors. Earlier I had a good working relationship with the New Zealand institute.

While my training is in law I have practised corporate law in different roles in the United Kingdom, New Zealand and Australia and served on law reform bodies in all three countries. I have also some familiarity with the corporate laws of Canada and the USA. Increasingly I am interested in the problems of developing corporate governance in China through my association with the University of Hong Kong and visits to Taiwan and Beijing. I worked in a public listed group early in my career and have served on boards and I have an interest in economics and empirical data about companies, which began at the time. As a result I hope that this book reflects more than just a narrow legal perspective. Corporate governance is too important a subject to be left to the lawyers.

The text was originally written as at 1 October 2000. During the production of this book major cases were noted, but at a very late stage of production agreement was reached between the Commonwealth and the states, and the Corporations Law was replaced by the *Corporations Act 2001* and the *Australian Securities and Investments Act 1989* by a new act of 2001. Both commenced on 15 July 2001, although hard copy arrived on 6 August 2001 after this book had gone to press.

On 23 August 2001 the Financial Services Reform Bill was passed by the Senate. This adds yet more detail to the legislation. The Bill extends the insider trading provisions to cover any financial products traded on a financial market. The new provisions will be financial services civil penalty provisions with their own regime. Another significant amendment is the removal of the objective knowledge test, which will make proof very difficult (see the new Division 3, Part 7.10, ss 1042A to 1044A, which will replace ss 1002 to 1002u).

John Farrar

List of Figures

List of Tables

Table of Cases

Table of Statutes

GENERAL CONCEPTS

CHAPTER 1

The Concept of Corporate Governance

This book is about corporate governance. The etymology of 'governance' comes from the Latin words *gubernare* and *gubernator*, which refer to steering a ship and to the steerer or captain of a ship. This is the origin of the word 'governor'. The word 'governance', which has a rather archaic ring to it, comes from the old French word 'gouvernance' and means control and the state of being governed. According to the *Oxford Dictionary*, it also means good order. Thus we have from the etymology of the word a useful metaphor—the idea of steering or captaining a ship. We have references to control and also to good order, which is more than simply being on course: it is also being shipshape and in good condition.

'Corporate governance' is a term that has been in circulation for the last twenty years and its present use emanates from the USA although it is now truly international. 'Corporate governance' was used, probably for the first time, in 1962, by Richard Eells of Columbia Business School in his book *The Government of Corporations*.[1] 'The Study of Corporate Governance' was the subject of Chapter 1. Now it is a fashionable concept, and like many fashionable concepts, it is somewhat ambiguous[2] and a bit of a cliché. In its narrower, and most usual, sense it refers to control of corporations and to systems of accountability by those in control. It refers to the companies legislation but it also transcends the law because we are looking not only at legal control but also de facto control of corporations. We are also looking at accountability, not only in terms of legal restraints but also in terms of systems of self-regulation and the norms of so called 'best practice'. Self-regulation starts off as a simple concept but becomes progressively more

---

1   Richard Eells, *The Government of Corporations*, Free Press of Glencoe, New York, 1962.
2   For a discussion of this ambiguity see K. Keasey, S. Thompson and M. Wright in the introduction to *Corporate Governance—Economic, Management and Financial Issues*, Oxford University Press, Oxford, 1997, p. 2.

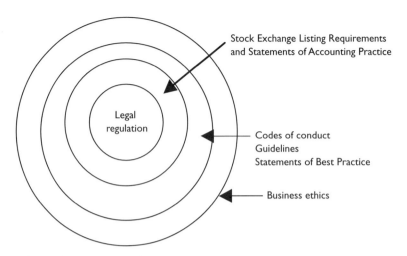

Figure 1.1 The structure of corporate governance

complex. Added to this we have business ethics. The relationship can be represented as in Figure 1.1.

The subject of corporate governance, therefore, covers: the Australian Corporations Act; the New Zealand *Companies Act 1993*; and the case law decided by the courts. It also includes the listing rules of the Australian Stock Exchange (ASX) and New Zealand Stock Exchange and Statements of Accounting Practice, which are hybrids or what we can call hard soft law; soft law in the sense of codes such as *Corporate Practices and Conduct*, the Guidelines of the Australian Investment Managers Association, now the Investment and Financial Services Association (IFSA) and the *Code of Proper Practice* of the New Zealand Institute of Directors; and last we have attempts to formulate business ethics. All of these have some place in an analysis of corporate governance.

Within the concept of legal regulation we shall concentrate on the role of the board of directors and the general meeting, directors' duties, the conduct of general meetings, shareholders' rights and remedies, and the role of auditors and the Australian Securities and Investments Commission (ASIC) and the New Zealand Securities Commission. We shall normally refer to the Corporations Act and the New Zealand *Companies Act 1993*.

It is impossible to understand Australian and New Zealand corporate governance without some basic knowledge of its historical origins. UK law and practice have influenced both countries from their colonial origins to modern times. However, both countries are now increasingly subject to North American influences. In the case of Australia this influence has tended to be direct whereas in the case of New Zealand it has been through exposure to the Canadian experience of assimilating English and US corporate laws and practices.

To understand corporate governance we must first focus on certain key concepts in the remainder of Part 1. We first examine the concept of the corporation and see how the traditional legal model of British Commonwealth corporate law, which treats the corporation as a separate legal person, provides a rather technical and increasingly inadequate basis for corporate governance. Alternative models are the associational model, the corporation as a fund of capital model and the corporation as a firm model. Recent law-and-economics scholarship sees the corporation as an elaborate standard form contract or nexus of contracts, in a sense, a surrogate market. Linked with the concept of the corporation is the idea of the purpose of the corporation and the questions of whose interests it serves or should serve. The two main theories here are, on the one hand, the primacy of the shareholder interest and the enhancement of shareholder value and, on the other hand, the stakeholder theory, which maintains that corporations exist to serve a number of different interests and not just shareholders. Thus creditors, employees, consumers and even local communities have a 'stake' in the corporation. This does not, however, necessarily mean that they have or should have enforceable rights.

Ownership and control of corporations are also vital questions to be considered. Control in respect of what, for what purpose? Control is thus ultimately a relative term and control questions differ greatly between listed public and proprietary companies.

The corporation, since it is a legal fiction, must act by human hands and the questions arise of whose hands bind the corporation and when the individuals will be personally liable for acts done on behalf of the corporation. These are complex questions of agency, attribution and risk-bearing.

After consideration of these key concepts we move to the law and practice of corporate governance in Parts 2 and 3. First, the roles of the general meeting and board of directors as corporate organs must be considered. We shall see how the role of both of these has changed over time and is continuing to change. The relationship of the board to individual directors and executives has also to be considered.

The law relating to the duties of directors is a complex amalgam of case law and statute law in both jurisdictions and it is necessary to explore this in some detail. The remedies of the corporation and the possibility of individual and collective shareholder redress need to be considered.

The law emphasises the responsibility of the company and its directors to keep proper accounts and to monitor solvency. Accounts are subject to audit except in the case of most small proprietary companies. The role of auditors and accounting standards are important issues. In the background is a system of administrative regulation by the Australian Securities and Investments Commission and the New Zealand Securities Commission. Issues of insider trading and serious fraud raise even more complex questions, which threaten to undermine the whole system of corporate governance, and cast considerable doubt on our capacity to deal adequately with abuse of the corporate form.

Increasingly the law seems a blunt instrument to deal with corporate governance and many new developments are variations on the theme of self-regulation. We deal with these in Part 3. Institutional investors play an important role in developing standards of self-regulation. Among the matters of self-regulation, key topics include the role of the non-executive or independent directors, specialist board committees, and procedures for dealing with executive remuneration, and risk management.

Different entities necessitate consideration of different perspectives and priorities on corporate governance so we must consider bodies such as corporatised enterprises and not for profits and see what rules and practices apply to them.

In a wide sense, corporate governance includes 'the entire network of formal and informal relations involving the corporate sector and their consequences for society in general'.[3] It is capable of subsumption under broader concepts of contractual and social governance. Every country approaches corporate governance from the background of its own distinctive culture. New Zealand has tended in the past towards a pragmatic adaptation of the UK model but has recently adopted a more North American approach. In the case of Australia one sometimes has the impression that this is based on either Ned Kelly or his jailer. We love a larrikin but we are inclined to come down heavily on 'tall poppies' and be excessively penal in our approach. The attitude to the excesses of the 1980s and their aftermath reflects this. We also have a tendency to over-legislate and the result is obese and user-unfriendly legislation. Meanwhile the tendency globally is in the opposite direction—towards greater accountability through emerging norms of self-regulation promoted by the private sector and backed by economic sanctions from the international financial community. In any study of corporate governance we must, therefore, look at other systems and consider the evolving norms of 'global' corporate governance.

In studying the evolving norms of global corporate governance we must necessarily think new thoughts about the whole subject. Is the Anglo-American model of the corporation a durable model for the twenty-first century? Are we correct in concentrating on corporate governance when increasingly the emphasis is on contracts through strategic alliances, networks and joint ventures? Is there some convergence of divergent systems in global corporate governance or is this an illusion or wishful thinking?

These are some of the interesting questions we shall address, if not answer, in this book.

---

3   *ibid.*, p. 2.

CHAPTER 2

A Brief Thematic History of Corporate Governance

The use of history is to explain the present by reference to the past. In this respect there are arguably two rival schools of thought. One, the traditional view of common lawyers, is to emphasise and perhaps to overemphasise the lessons we can learn from the past. The other—the radical view of Jeremy Bentham in the early nineteenth century—is that it is from the folly not the wisdom of our ancestors that we have so much to learn. Whichever school one subscribes to, there is no denying the facts of historical change and the importance of the emergence of the corporate form. As the Oxford legal historian, C. A. Cooke, wrote in 1950, 'In less than three hundred years the social institution connoted by the words "company" and "corporation" has undergone mutations in form and application that have placed it among the most influential of social groupings'.[1] It is currently fashionable to talk about the history of corporate governance in terms of path dependence[2] and to assume that, as in the natural sciences, complex systems can be reduced to a few simple rules. Corporate structures, it is said, depend in part on the structures a country had in earlier times, in particular the structures with which the economy started.[3] These structures also bias the legal rules in terms of what is efficient in any given country and the interest group politics that determine which rules are chosen.[4] To some extent this is an elaborate statement of the obvious, and to

---

1   C. A. Cooke, *Corporation, Trust and Company—An Essay in Legal History*, Manchester University Press, Manchester, 1950, p. 7.
2   See for example M. Roe, 'Chaos and Evolution in Law and Economics' (1996) 109 Harvard L Rev 641; L. A. Bebchuk and M. J. Roe, 'A Theory of Path Dependence in Corporate Ownership and Governance' (1999) 52 Stanford L Rev 127; G. Walker, 'Reinterpreting New Zealand Securities Regulation', in G. Walker, B. Fisse and I. Ramsay (eds), *Securities Regulation in Australia and New Zealand*, 2nd edn, LBC Information Services, North Ryde, 1998, p. 88. The chapter by Gordon Walker gives a useful overview at p. 89. See further for the scientific background, R. Lewin, *Complexity—Life on the Edge of Chaos*, Phoenix, London, 1997.
3   Bebchuk and Roe, *op. cit.*, p. 127.
4   *ibid.*

some extent it is the application to law and economic phenomena of a metaphor taken from science and offered as an alternative analytical perspective for economics.[5] Justice Cardozo many years ago warned us of the dangers of seduction by metaphors.[6] One of the dangers is a tendency to reductionism. The interplay of historical forces that lead to any given state of affairs is often complex. This is particularly true of economic history and the relationship of law and economics.[7]

It has sometimes been said that economic history is the major part of Australian history. This is no doubt true since European settlement.[8] The same is probably true of New Zealand except for the Maori wars and Maori dimension.

In this chapter we will examine some dominant themes in the history of corporate governance. This will necessarily be of an international nature since Australian and New Zealand owe much to their colonial inheritance and are currently influenced by North American ideas and yet do business with South-East Asia where many of the legal systems are of a different background and history. Having identified major themes we shall see how they are relevant to Australia and New Zealand. In doing so we shall consider path dependence among other things.

The public law privilege model[9]

The earliest form of incorporation in the common law was by papal bull or royal charter. Rights of association and corporate status sprang from the Church or the Crown. Later the same result could be achieved by specific legislation. Implicit in this approach is that incorporation is a privilege, which exists for a public purpose. Early grants were for charitable purposes or for the extension of the power and interests of the Crown.

Abuse of defunct charters and other excesses led to the *UK Bubble Act* (1720) which set back the development of the modern corporation for some time. The legislation, as Maitland said,[10] screams at us from the statute book. Much business continued to be

---

5   See Roe, *op. cit.*, p. 641; S. J. Liebowitz and S. E. Margolis, 'Path Dependence, Lock-In and History' (1995) 11 *Journal of Law, Economics and Organization* 205.

6   *Berkey v. Third Avenue Railway Co.* 244 NY 84 (1926) at 94–5 'Metaphors in law are to be narrowly watched, for starting as devices to liberate thought, they often end by enslaving it'.

7   See W. Samuels, 'The Idea of the Corporation as a Person: On the Normative Significance of Juridical Language', in W. J. Samuels and A. S. Miller (eds), *Corporations and Society: Power and Responsibility*, Greenwood Press, New York, 1987, 124; Liebowitz and Margolis, *op. cit.*, pp. 223–4.

8   S. J. Butlin, *Foundations of the Australian Monetary System 1788–1851*, Melbourne University Press, Melbourne, 1953, p. 1. See too P. Groenewegan and B. McFarlane, *A History of Australian Economic Thought*, Routledge, London, 1990, p. 12.

9   See J. W. Hurst, *The Legitimacy of the Business Corporation*, University Press of Virginia, Charlottesville, 1970, p. 2; P. Davies, *Gower's Principles of Company Law*, 6th edn, Sweet & Maxwell, London, 1997, ch. 2; J. H. Farrar and B. Hannigan, *Farrar's Company Law*, 4th edn, Butterworths, London, 1998, ch. 2; S. Berns and P. Baron, *Company Law and Governance: An Australian Perspective*, Oxford University Press, Melbourne, 1998, ch. 2.

10   F. W. Maitland, *Collected Papers*, Vol. 3, 'Trust and Corporation', Cambridge University Press, Cambridge, 1911, p. 390.

run as sole traders or partnerships until the late nineteenth century. Canals and railways were the subject of specific legislation because of the large sums of capital involved.[11] International trade developed originally through the grant of royal charters to companies such as the East India Company, the Africa Company, the Virginia Company and the Hudson's Bay Company.[12]

The term 'director' was first used generally at the end of the seventeenth century. It was used by the Bank of England and Bank of Scotland.[13]

Despite these restrictive trends entrepreneurs and their lawyers managed to evade the Bubble Act by deed of settlement companies and many of our modern principles and problems in the law spring from that source.[14] The deed of settlement company was built on a foundation of trust and partnership and was at best an inchoate corporation.

From the seventeenth century, using all three methods of charter, statute and deed of settlement, people began to employ the concept of joint stock, the pooling of investment capital.[15]

When the first general UK Companies Act was passed in 1844 it provided for incorporation by registration of Deeds of Settlement. It did not confer limited liability, which came in 1855. Incorporation began to change from an ad hoc privilege to be granted on certain terms for the public benefit to a right to be granted with relatively few conditions.[16] Freedom of contract began to take over. The legislation became increasingly facilitative.[17] As such it was soon adopted by entrepreneurial capitalism. Australia and New Zealand followed the UK model.

Banking capitalism[18]

Colonial and post-colonial systems suffer from a lack of capital.[19] Few immigrants bring much capital. There is a need for investment capital.[20] The state needs capital to provide for infrastructure. Some it raises through taxation but from a small base. The rest is raised through debt capital.

---

11 Farrar and Hannigan, *op. cit.*, p. 19.
12 Davies, *op. cit.*, p. 22.
13 R. R. Formoy, *The Historical Foundations of Company Law*, Sweet & Maxwell, London, 1923, p. 21.
14 Davies, *op. cit.*, p. 29.
15 Farrar and Hannigan, *op. cit.*, p. 17.
16 *ibid.*, p. 21.
17 *ibid.*, p. 21 and ch. 9.
18 See L. van den Berghe and L. de Ridder, *International Standardisation of Good Corporate Governance*, Kluwer Academic Publishers, Boston, 1999, ch. 4.
19 See for instance G. Blainey, *A Shorter History of Australia*, Mandarin, Melbourne, 1994, p. 119 *et seq.* On the history of banking and banking issues in Australia see C. D. W. Goodwin, *Economic Enquiry in Australia*, Duke University Press, Durham, NC, 1966. See too R. Ma and R. D. Morris, *Disclosure and Bonding Practices of British and Australian Banks in the Nineteenth Century*, Monograph No. 4, University of Sydney Accounting Research Centre, Sydney, March 1982.
20 For a fascinating account see T. Sykes, *Two Centuries of Panic—A History of Corporate Collapses in Australia*, Allen & Unwin, Sydney, 1988, chs 1, 3, 5, 7 and 9.

This results in the next phase of banking capitalism[21] which characterised the history of the USA, Australia and New Zealand in the nineteenth century and into the twentieth century, at least until the 1930s.

Unlike UK banks of the time, most Australian and New Zealand banks were incorporated with limited liability on formation either by charter or private act or later under the Companies Acts, of the respective colonies.[22] The first Australasian bank was the Bank of New South Wales[23] formed in 1817. It had an inauspicious start. Opposed by Whitehall it ran into difficulties in 1826 and had to be rescued by the Governor. Technically its charter was null and void. Fortunately the Governors proceeded on the assumption of its validity, renewed it and weathered the storm. There were fifty-one trading and savings banks formed in Australia between 1817 and 1851 and fifty-three operating between 1851 and 1900.[24] There were also a number of land banks in the 1880s and 1890s. These were a species of land mortgage company that competed for deposits.[25] The imperial government and the colonies attempted, unsuccessfully, to regulate the activities of the banks.[26] The colonies were subject to cycles of boom and bust.[27] The worst crisis was the banking collapse of 1891–93 when fifty-four out of sixty-four banks closed their doors, thirty-four never to open them again.[28] The response to the crash was the *Bank Issue Act 1893* and the *Current Account Depositors Act 1893*. The first limited legal tender.[29] The first Commonwealth note was issued in 1910. Another crisis came in the Depression with the collapse of the Government Savings Bank of New South Wales and the bitter medicine prescribed by the Bank of England to deal with the Depression.[30]

Bank finance of business was usually debt finance although some investment or merchant banks took equity interests as well. Intensive investment in equity has been restricted by banking rules such as capital adequacy and other prudential regulation.

This mode of banking capitalism has survived in the universal banks in countries such as Germany.[31]

Banks have traditionally been conservative lenders but abandoned their natural caution in the 1980s with disastrous results in Australia and New Zealand.[32]

21 See van den Berghe and de Ridder, *op. cit.*
22 Ma and Morris, *op. cit.*, p. 20.
23 *ibid.*
24 *ibid.*, p. 21.
25 ibid.
26 ibid.
27 See e.g. Sykes, *op. cit. passim.*
28 A. Tyree, *Banking Law in Australia*, Butterworths, Sydney, 1998, p. 2.
29 *ibid.*
30 See M. Clark, *History of Australia*, abridged by M. Cathcart, Melbourne University Press, Melbourne, 1993, p. 535 *et. seq.*
31 van den Berghe and de Ridder, *op. cit.*
32 See T. Sykes, *Bold Riders*, Allen & Unwin, St Leonards, NSW, 1994, ch. 17.

Imperialism and the imperial model

Many of the early businesses in Australia and New Zealand were branches of UK companies. Later they were subsidiaries. Imperial commerce dominated the economies and the local statutes were based on the UK companies legislation.[33] By the turn of the century the larger local banks were often owned by or affiliated with UK banks.

As a system this worked tolerably well while the interests of the UK coincided with those of Australia and New Zealand but increasingly they did not and there were crises and friction, particularly in the Depression.[34] When the UK joined the European Union in 1973 there was a final parting of the ways and the two countries looked more and more to North America for reform ideas.

A legacy of this dependence survives in the fact that a significant number of Australian and New Zealand listed companies are owned by other companies, the ultimate ownership of which is often in foreign hands.[35]

Managerial capitalism

As companies adapted to the corporate form some needed further equity capital and went public. Disclosure regimes developed, backed with a degree of self-regulation by the securities industry. Many English companies in the late nineteenth century issued preference shares in order for the owners to retain control.[36] Later, ordinary shares were floated and there began the development of the separation of ownership and control which had been foreshadowed by Marx[37] and Lenin[38] and was documented by Adolf Berle Jr of Columbia Law School and Gardiner Means[39] of Harvard in respect of the USA. This era marks the ascendancy of professional management in the absence of ownership blocs large enough to represent a countervailing power. It created the agency problem as Adam Smith had anticipated.[40] Management, in the absence of a

---

33   For an interesting account see R. McQueen, 'Limited Liability Corporate Legislation—The Australian Experience' (1991) 1 Australian J of Corp L 22. See also J. Waugh, 'Company Law and the Crash of the 1890s in Victoria' (1992) 15 UNSWLJ 356; R. McQueen, 'An Examination of Australian Corporate Law and Regulation 1901–1961' (1992) 15 UNSWLJ 1.

34   Clark, *op. cit.*

35   See G. Stapledon, 'Share Ownership and Control in Listed Australian Companies' (1999) 2 *Corporate Governance International* 17 and the earlier work in respect of New Zealand by J. H. Farrar in 'Ownership and Control of Listed Public Companies—Revising or Rejecting the Concept of Control' in B. Pettet (ed.), *Company Law in Change*, Stevens & Sons, London, 1987, p. 39.

36   See Farrar and Hannigan, *op. cit.* footnote 9 supra, p. 226.

37   *Das Kapital.*

38   *Essay on Imperialism.*

39   *The Modern Corporation and Private Property*, revised edn, Harcourt Brace, New York, 1968.

40   *An Inquiry into the Nature of Causes of the Wealth of Nations*, 3 Vols, Strahan, London, 3rd edn, 1784 (v.i.e.). The highly critical account of joint stock companies was added to this edition. See I. S. Ross, *The Life of Adam Smith*, Clarendon Press, Oxford, 1995, p. 283.

countervailing power, have a tendency to pursue their own self-interest at the expense of the corporation.[41]

There is a need then to monitor management to prevent shirking and other opportunistic behaviour.[42] One way to achieve this is by the law. The law developed fiduciary restraints[43] which were supplemented by legislation so that modern directors' duties are an amalgam of common law, equity and statute. Another way is by economic forces or markets.[44] The company is in the market for products. There is no future in producing bad widgets. The company needs investment capital. Investors will not support badly managed companies but to some extent companies protect themselves by ploughing back profits. The management themselves are a marketable commodity. They need to have a good profile. Ultimately there is the market for corporate control. Underperformance may lead to a takeover bid by more aggressive managers.

The periods from 1960 until the 1980s represented the supremacy of management. The management of larger corporations were, to some extent, the masters and not the servants of finance.[45] However, the stock market crash of 1987 precipitated the collapse of confidence and heralded a number of changes.[46]

To ward off the increasing politicisation of reform of corporate law, to combat increased shareholder activism, and simply out of self-protection, management of leading companies, through their interest groups and in cooperation with institutional investors, began to give serious attention to the development of self-regulation or corporate governance in the 1990s. This led to a number of reports and codes of guidelines on corporate governance.

Institutional investor capitalism[47]

Since World War II a number of factors have led to increased investment by institutional investors in public corporations. There has been the use of superannuation and pension schemes, and an increase in insurance-linked investment products and other forms of indirect investment. Also, trustee investment rules have been relaxed, enabling trustees to invest in equities.[48]

---

41   See the law and economics literature cited by Farrar in Pettet, *op. cit.*, pp. 44–7.
42   *ibid.* See also F. H. Easterbrook and D. R. Fischel, *The Economic Structure of Corporate Law*, Harvard University Press, Cambridge, Mass, 1991, ch. 4.
43   Easterbrook and Fischel, *op. cit.*
44   *ibid.*
45   See Sykes, *op. cit.* footnote 32 supra.
46   *ibid.*
47   van den Berghe and de Ridder, *op. cit.* See generally G. Stapledon, *Institutional Shareholders and Corporate Governance*, Clarendon Press, Oxford, 1996; C. K. Brancato, *Institutional Investors and Corporate Governance*, Irwin, Chicago, 1997.
48   See Farrar and Hannigan, *op. cit.* footnote 9 supra, p. 579.

The result is that in Australia, New Zealand, the USA and the United Kingdom more than 50 per cent of all equities are held by institutional investors and the tendency is to increase. Add to this the traditional domination by institutions of the bond market and we have the beginning of the growth of a significant countervailing power if the economic strength is harnessed to a common cause. Listed corporations are becoming the servants of global financial activity rather than its masters.[49]

Peter Drucker argued that this led to a quiet revolution—'The Unseen Revolution … The US is the first truly Socialist country'.[50] This was simply reflecting what Berle in his later workings identified and his research student Paul Harbrecht called 'The Para-proprietal Society'—the evolution of a new form of property.[51]

Until the late 1980s the tendency of the institutions was to be a sleeping giant. There were instances of discreet intervention but by and large the institutions voted with their feet and followed the Wall Street Walk — if in doubt, sell.[52]

Institutions themselves came under attack and we see two developments. First, the involvement by them in promotion of improved corporate governance and second the use of specialist funds managers. The latter makes it more unlikely for institutions to become activists in particular companies although there have been exceptional cases where a group of funds managers has taken action.[53]

Institutions are primarily focused on profit and liquidity and have been attacked for short-termism in their approach to companies.[54] There is also a problem of lack of coincidence between the interests of institutions and other smaller shareholders in takeover situations. Often institutions collectively have strategically significant holdings.[55]

Institutions sometimes encounter legal problems in increased shareholder activism.[56] We deal with this in Chapter 26.

It is sometimes argued that public sector pension funds are more likely to take a long-term strategic view and certainly the US and the UK public sector funds have had a tendency at least to mouth the appropriate rhetoric.[57]

---

49   P. Warburton, *Debt and Delusion*, Penguin Books, London, 1999.

50   P. Drucker, *The Unseen Revolution: How Pension Fund Socialism Came to America*, Harper Row, New York, 1976, p. 1.

51   See J. H. Farrar and M. Russell, 'The Impact of Institutional Investment on Company Law' (1984) 5 Co Law 107. See J. Gates, *The Ownership Solution—Towards a Shared Capitalism for the Twenty-First Century*, Penguin Books, London, 1998.

52   See Farrar and Russell, *op. cit.* and Brancato, *op. cit.*, pp. 23, 108.

53   See Stapledon, *op. cit.* footnote 47, pp. 189 *et seq.*

54   See EPAC, *Short-Termism in Australian Investment*, Proceedings of an EPAC Workshop held in Canberra, 10 November 1994, AGPS, 1995; Stapledon, *op. cit.*, pp. 212–37.

55   See Farrar and Russell, *op. cit.*, p. 110.

56   *ibid.*, p. 110 *et seq.* See also G. P. Stapledon, 'Discentives to Activism by Institutional, Investors in Listed Australian Companies' (1996) 18 Sydney LR 152.

57   See Brancato, *op. cit.*, pp. 11, 26–31, 122.

Reference shareholdings

In their book *International Standardisation of Good Corporate Governance*,[58] Professor Lutgart van den Berghe and Liesbeth de Ridder use the term reference shareholdings to signify the presence of a significant shareholder that has a long-term relationship with the corporation, and as a result, a close involvement in and contribution to the strategic development of the company. This is common in countries such as France, Belgium and Italy.[59] Surprisingly, it is common in Australia and New Zealand[60] as we shall see in Chapter 5. In Australia, New Zealand and Canada a significant number of companies are under majority or minority control.

The governance problems with such shareholdings are excessive power positions and potential conflict of interest in group transactions.[61]

The impact of globalised standards of corporate governance is to promote equal treatment of shareholders, and to dismantle elaborate crossholdings and interlocking directorships.[62] With countries such as Japan this is virtually impossible due to the Keiretsu system. A Keiretsu is a spider's web of cross shareholdings and interlocking directorships clustered around one or more banks.[63]

The evolution of multinational and transnational corporations[64]

The evolution of the multinational and transnational corporation represents the latest stage of development of the traditional corporate group. However, the more recent evolution begins to transcend the corporate and group form, as we shall see in Chapters 34 and 35.

The complexity of structure and the economic strength of such entities present a challenge to nation states and international institutions. One of the most common concerns involves income shifting through transfer pricing, which raises problems of conflict of interest for directors of subsidiaries. These are most acute where there are minority shareholders or creditors in the host state. Even without them there are the economic interests of the host state itself which may be affected.

58 See van den Berghe and de Ridder, *op. cit.*
59 *ibid.*
60 See Stapledon, *op. cit.* footnote 35 above and the earlier work in respect of New Zealand by J. H. Farrar in Pettit, *op. cit.* and R. Daniels and R. Morck (eds), *Corporate Decision-Making in Canada*, University of Calgary Press, 1995.
61 See Farrar and Hannigan, *op. cit.*, pp. 569 *et seq.*
62 See J. H. Farrar, 'The New Financial Architecture and Effective Corporate Governance' (1999) *The International Lawyer* 927.
63 See K. Miyashita and D. Russell, *Keiretsu—Inside the Hidden Japanese Conglomerates*, McGraw-Hill, New York, 1996.
64 See Farrar and Hannigan, *op. cit.*, ch. 44 for a more detailed discussion on which this is based.

Attempts have been made to regulate such entities at national, bilateral, regional and international levels. All have failed. Some argue that the answer lies in international institutional investment but this in its way simply adds to the complexity and the question arises as to whom the institutions themselves are accountable.

Recent research emphasises the myth of the genuinely multinational and transnational corporation, stressing the significance of the home state.[65]

The relationship of corporate governance to such entities and the development of a new financial architecture are dealt with in Chapter 34.

Modernisation and reform

Both Australian and New Zealand have faced the breakdown of the imperial model, the international financial revolution and the forces of globalisation but have handled change in different ways.

In 1961–62 Australia adopted uniform companies legislation which was substantially based on the *Victorian Companies Act 1958*.[66] This followed the UK *Companies Act 1948* but contained some differences including the statutory statement of the basic directors' duties, breach of which was foolishly made the subject of criminal penalties. This provided the model for Singapore and Malaysia which still have the legislation in force as amended. In the late 1970s the New Zealand National government favoured this model but by 1981 Australia had opted for the more complex Companies Code. Corporate governance had become a political football.

The incoming Labour government in New Zealand rejected this as an appropriate model in spite of the Closer Economic Relations Agreement between the two countries and instead favoured the Canadian models of the Canada Business Corporations Act and Ontario Business Corporations Act which represent a halfway house between the UK and US models.[67] This legislation was finally adopted in 1993, after a thorough, if at times seemingly endless debate. The result was that business and its advisers knew what they were getting and supported the reforms. The preamble to the *Companies Act 1993* provides that the objects of the legislation are to reform the law and in particular:

(a) To reaffirm the value of the company as a means of achieving economic and social benefits through the aggregation of capital for productive purposes, the spreading of economic risk, and the taking of business risks;

(b) To provide basic and adaptable requirements for the incorporation, organisation, and operation of companies;

(c) To define the relationships between companies and their directors, shareholders, and creditors;

---

65 P. N. Doremus et al., *The Myth of the Global Corporation*, Princeton University Press, Princeton, 1998.

.66 For the history see the material by McQueen, *op. cit.* and H. A. J. Ford, R. Austin and I. Ramsay, *Ford's Principles of Corporations Law*, 10th edn, Butterworths, Sydney, 2001, para. 2.170 *et seq.*

67 See J. H. Farrar, 'Closer Economic Relations and Harmonisation of Law Between Australia and New Zealand', in P. A. Joseph (ed.), *Essays on the Constitution*, Brookers, Wellington, 1995, p. 158.

(d) To encourage efficient and responsible management of companies by allowing directors a wide discretion in matters of business judgment while at the same time providing protection for shareholders and creditors against the abuse of management power; and

(e) To provide straightforward and fair procedures for realising and distributing the assets of insolvent companies.

The New Zealand model, which was substantially based on the Canadian models, abolished the distinction between public and private companies and yet took as its underlying prototype the private company, leaving more substantial regulation to the *Securities Act 1978* with its under-financed Securities Commission and a weak stock exchange. Otherwise faith was put in private enforcement, which was somewhat naïve given the absence in New Zealand of institutional support for such litigation.

Australia meanwhile in endless pursuit of national legislation despite the narrow interpretation of the Constitution by the High Court, adopted the *Corporations Act 1989*, which became known as the Corporations Law. This was subsequently amended and now has been replaced as a result of constitutional challenge. The *Corporations Act 2001* stands as an obese monument to complexity and confused thinking about modernisation.

The complexity was the subject of the Simplification Task Force, which succeeded in further complicating the law, particularly the law of corporate governance.[68] This was followed by the Corporate Law Economic Reform Program (CLERP).[69] The reform program is well intentioned and pursues the following fundamental economic principles:

• market freedom

Competition plays a key role in driving efficiency and enhancing community welfare. However, free markets do not always operate in a sufficiently competitive, equitable or efficient manner. Business regulation can and should help markets work by enhancing market integrity and capital market efficiency. At the same time, the regulatory framework needs to be sufficiently flexible so that it does not impede market evolution (for example, new products and technologies) and competition.

• investor protection

With an increasing number of retail investors participating in the markets for the first time, business regulation should ensure that all investors have reasonable access to information regarding the risks of particular investment opportunities. Regulations should be cognisant of the differences between sophisticated and retail investors in access to information and the ability to analyse it.

---

68   See M. Whincop, 'Trivial Pursuit: A Theoretical Perspective on Simplification Initiatives' (1997) 7 Aust Jnl of Corp Law 250.

69   See R. Baxt, K. Fletcher and S. Fridman, *Afterman and Baxt's Cases and Materials on Corporations and Associations*, 8th edn, Butterworths, Sydney, 1999, p. 173 *et seq.*

- information transparency

    Disclosure is a key to promoting a more efficient and competitive marketplace. Disclosure of relevant information enables rational investment decision-making and facilitates the efficient use of resources by companies. Disclosure requirements increase the confidence of individual investors in the fairness and integrity of financial markets and, by fostering confidence, encourage investment. Different levels of disclosure may be required for sophisticated and retail investors.

- cost effectiveness

    The benefits of business regulation must outweigh its associated costs. The regulatory framework should take into account the direct and indirect costs imposed by regulation on business and the community as a whole. What Australia must avoid is outmoded business laws that impose unnecessary costs through reducing the range of products or services, impeding the development of new products or imposing system-wide costs.

    The regulatory framework for business needs to be well targeted to ensure that the benefits clearly exceed the costs. A flexible and transparent framework will be more conducive to innovation and risk-taking, which are fundamental elements of a thriving market economy, while providing necessary investor and consumer protection.

- regulatory neutrality and flexibility

    Regulation should be applied consistently and fairly across the marketplace. Regulatory distinctions or advantages should not be conferred on particular market structures or products unless there is a clear regulatory justification. The regulatory framework should also avoid creating incentives or opportunities for regulatory arbitrage. The regulatory framework should be sufficiently flexible to permit market participants to respond to future changes in an innovative, timely and efficient manner. Regulation should be designed to facilitate predictability and certainty.

- business ethics and compliance

    Clear guidance regarding appropriate corporate behaviour and swift enforcement if breaches occur are key elements in ensuring that markets function optimally ... Fostering an environment that encourages high standards of business practice and ethics, will remain a central objective of regulation, as will effective enforcement.

The policy is sound; the implementation unsound, lacking a coherent *modus operandi* and still relying on piecemeal reforms and an overtechnical style of drafting. The result has been further complication with some sporadic attention paid to the clearer and simpler New Zealand reforms that were more comprehensive in scope. CLERP continues now as the latest reform juggernaut in Australia, trampling other reform proposals in its path but jeopardised by recent doubts in the High Court about the constitutional basis of the present system. It is only a capacity for endurance by the business and professional communities and an ability to cope with endless, often gratuitous, change and uncertainty that makes a poor system work with moderate efficiency but at considerable expense. The result is a shaky foundation for coping with the challenges of modernisation and globalisation in what is increasingly regarded as a postmodern era, characterised by disillusionment with lawyers and the legal system.

Obese legislation like the Corporations Act and the tendency to prolixity of Australian courts, particularly the High Court, do not serve the community well. More attention needs to be paid to principle instead of the endless proliferation of rules. Modern developments, particularly in computer science, point towards the overriding principles of incompatibility and flexibility or user friendliness and a presumption in favour of freedom of transactions.[70] The principle of incompatibility was described by Professor L. A. Zadeh of Berkeley in the following terms:[71]

> The closer one looks at a 'real world' problem the fuzzier becomes its solution. Stated informally, the essence of this principle is that as the complexity of a system increases, our ability to make precise and yet significant statements about its behaviour diminishes until the threshold is reached beyond which precision and significance (or relevance) become almost mutually exclusive characteristics.

Analogous arguments can be made about legal complexity. In an age of revolution in communications it is also necessary to be user friendly and globalisation seems to entail freedom of transactions. There is thus a need for a legal Occam's razor—unnecessary technicalities should not be encouraged.

The development of a new model of democratic capitalism

So much for history but what about the future? Van den Berghe and de Ridder[72] argue for the evolution of a democratic model of corporate governance. This will be characterised by:

(a) the knowledge worker empowered as a result of the communications revolution
(b) the power shift from shareholders towards the knowledge worker
(c) a sense of shared values.[73]

Something that is immediately noticeable about this model is, first how it differs from the current model in Anglo-American systems including Australia and New Zealand, second how much it reflects European Union and Japanese ideas, third how much it resembles in (b) and (c) an earlier model of labour relations in Australia and

---

70 See J. H. Farrar, 'Fuzzy Law, the Modernisation of Corporate Laws and the Privatisation of Takeover Regulation', in J. H. Farrar (ed.), *Takeovers, Institutional Investors and the Modernisation of Corporate Laws*, Oxford University Press, Auckland, 1993, ch. 1.

71 L. A. Zadeh, 'Outline of a New Approach to the Analysis of Complex Systems and Decision Processes', IEEE Trans Syst Man Cybern, SMC-1, 28–44.

72 See van den Berghe and de Ridder, *op. cit.*, ch. 4.

73 *ibid.*

New Zealand last seen in the Accord of the Hawke government in Australia, and last how much it is now based on the communications revolution. The discussion of stakeholder capitalism is the beginning of a new debate in Anglo-American countries.[74] This type of theory breaks away from the shareholder/manager focus of earlier corporate governance debate and turns the spotlight on the neglected role of employees, particularly in the knowledge-based industries. It necessarily involves study of the formal and informal ways in which employees are currently involved in governance in different systems and why this has occurred.[75] Here there is much emphasis on path-dependent explanations.[76]

Any development along these lines involves revisiting our traditional conceptions of the corporation and private property and the development of some sense of the corporation as a firm in the real world.[77] This may entail some reconsideration of the role of contract in relation to corporation and some downplaying of the significance of ownership or reinterpretation of the concept.[78]

Nevertheless, as we move into this new era we must not forget the historical significance of property to the development of the rule of law and the modern system of democracy.[79] Both of these may be under threat by globalisation.

The history of corporate governance shows a process of change and adaptation to change but the contemporary triumph of democracy and capitalism. The interesting questions are whether these can survive their own success or whether both must inevitably mutate and what form the mutation will take. Can they coexist indefinitely? Does one depend on the other? How can they adapt to the communications revolution that both empowers and enslaves us all?

In this brief chapter we have attempted to sketch the major historical themes. In the rest of the book we shall return to them from time to time to explain the present and later, to attempt to predict the future development of corporate governance.

---

74   See J. H. Farrar, 'Frankenstein Incorporated or Fools' Parliament—Revisiting the Concept of the Corporation in Corporate Governance' (1998) 10 Bond LR 142 and material cited.

75   See M. M. Blair and M. J. Roe (eds), *Employees and Corporate Governance*, Brookings Institution Press, Washington, DC, 1999.

76   *ibid*, Introduction.

77   See ch. 3 of this book.

78   See J. Child and D. Faulkner, *Strategies of Cooperation*, Oxford University Press, Oxford, 1998, ch. 14. See also J. Aoi, 'To Whom Does the Company Belong? A New Management Mission for the Information Age', in D. H. Chew (ed.), *Studies in International Corporate Finance and Governance Systems*, Oxford University Press, New York, 1997, p. 244. Joichi Aoi is Chairman of the Board of Toshiba Corporation.

79   See R. Pipes, *Property and Freedom*, The Harvill Press, London, 1999, *passim*, especially p. 281.

The Concept of the Corporation[1]

Fundamental to corporate governance is the concept of the corporation. Corporation in its broadest sense is a legal concept that, through the conferment of separate legal personality, provides legal recognition to bodies of persons, associated together, as distinctive holders of rights under a collective name, with distinct legal consequences.[2] This is not simply a matter of form and fiction. It is the way in which law defines and regulates economic reality. The relationship between law and economic reality is not simple although there is a natural desire to make it so. If the corporation is regarded as a separate legal person, the questions arise: what is its nature as a legal person; how is this to be ascertained; and what does it entail in terms of institutional frameworks for decision-making.[3] These are troublesome questions of legal and political philosophy as well as economics and they represent a kind of intellectual no man's land where warring parties venture from time to time to do battle in the night. Some interpret the phenomenon in realist terms,[4] others favour a positivist reduction of the problem to relationships between different sets of rules,[5] or sets of contracts,[6] while others seek a solution

---

1   This chapter is based to some extent on an earlier article, 'Frankenstein Incorporated or Fools' Parliament? Revisiting the Concept of Corporation in Corporate Governance' (1998) 10 Bond LR 142. See too M. Whincop, 'Overcoming Corporate Law: Instrumentalism, Pragmatism and the Separate Legal Entity Concept' (1997) 15 C&SLJ 411.

2   See The Case of Sutton Hospital, 10 Coke Rep. 1, 32 (1613). Cf. W. Hohfeld, 'The Nature of Stockholders' Individual Liability for Corporation Debts' (1909) 9 Colum. L. Rev 285; E. Freund, The Legal Nature of Corporations, Burt Franklin, New York, 1897, p. 9. It is now possible to have single person corporations.

3   Freund, op. cit., pp. 10 et seq.

4   See e.g. F. W. Maitland, Introduction to O. Gierke, Political Theories of the Middle Ages, Cambridge University Press, Cambridge, 1900; Sir F. Pollock, First Book of Jurisprudence, Stevens, London, 1896, pp. 108–9.

5   H. L. A. Hart, 'Definition and Theory in Jurisprudence' (1954) 70 LQR 37; Meridian Global Funds Management Asia Ltd v. Securities Commission [1995] 2 AC 500.

6   See the law-and-economics scholars discussed later in this chapter at footnotes 69 to 95.

in more utopian terms.[7] Lurking in the shadows is anthropomorphism,[8] to which the courts resort on occasion.

In 1931 an American law professor, Maurice Wormser of Fordham University, who was an able corporate law scholar in his day, wrote a polemic work which he entitled '*Frankenstein, Incorporated*'.[9] He wrote at the time of the Depression and echoed the views of the early US judges when he said, 'Corporations, the creature of the state, owe a deep duty to the state'.[10] Works like this and Berle and Means' *Modern Corporation and Private Property*[11] reflected popular wariness of corporations[12] and influenced the development of administrative regulation of corporations in the New Deal period.[13] Recently with the election of the New Labour government in the United Kingdom there has been a renaissance of the stakeholder concept and a stakeholder analysis of society and the place of corporations within it.[14] Although this has been effective election rhetoric and occasioned new literature it is essentially a recycling of ideas from the 1960s, which has a tendency to reduce the corporation to a fools' parliament if it moves from the indisputable proposition of legitimate interests to enforceable legal rights in the corporation by different factors. The recycling has been prompted by the wave of so-called 'constituency statutes' in the USA which have broadened the range of interests that directors can take into account[15] and which have prompted a more principled but as yet inconclusive debate in Canada about amendment of the Business Corporations legislation.[16] Measured against these public and welfarist conceptions of the corporation is the traditional approach of Anglo-Australian Corporate Law of persistent equivocation between treating the corporation as a separate legal person and equation of the

---

7   See the developing modern literature on stakeholders e.g. J. Plender, *A Stake in the Future: The Stakeholding Solution*, Nicholas Brearley Publishing, London, 1997, and on communitarianism e.g. L. Mitchell (ed.), *Progressive Corporate Law*, Westview Press, Boulder, Colorado, 1995.

8   See D. Wishart, *Company Law in Context*, Oxford University Press, Auckland, 1994, p. 144; Lord Cooke of Thorndon, *Turning Points of the Common Law*, Sweet & Maxwell, London, 1997, p. 27.

9   Whittlesey House, New York (1931).

10 *ibid.*, Preface, p. viii.

11 A. Berle Jr and G. Means, *The Modern Corporations and Private Property*, revised edn, Harcourt Brace & World, New York, 1968, original edn, 1932. See too A. Berle Jr, 'Corporate Powers as Powers in Trust' (1931) 44 Harv L Rev 1949; E.M. Dodd Jr, 'For Whom are Corporate Managers Trustees?' (1932) 45 Harv L Rev 1145; E.M. Dodd Jr, 'Is Effective Enforcement of the Fiduciary Duties of Corporate Managers Practicable?' (1935) 2 Univ of Chicago L Rev 194. Cf A. Berle Jr, 'For Whom Corporate Managers Are Trustees' (1932) 45 Harv L Rev 1365.

12 See J. W. Hurst, *The Legitimacy of the Business Corporation*, University of Virginia Press, Charlottesville, 1970, p. 106.

13 *ibid.*, pp. 108, 130 *et seq.*

14 See W. Hutton, *The State We're In*, Vintage, London, 1995; S. Wheeler, 'Inclusive Communities and Dialogical Stakeholders—a Methodology for Authentic Corporate Citizenship' (1998) 9 Aust Jnl of Corp Law 1 and J. Hill, 'Public Beginnings, Private Ends—Should Corporate Law Privilege the Interest of Shareholders?' (1998) 9 Aust Jnl of Corp Law 21.

15 See the list in 'Other Constituency Statutes: Potential for Confusion' (1990) 45 *Business Lawyer* 2253 at 2261.

16 See the Special Issue of the *Toronto Law Journal* on Corporate Stakeholder Debate: The Classical Theory and its Critics (1993) 43 UTLJ No. 3, Summer 1993.

corporation with its shareholders.[17] In the middle somewhere lie German law and German influence on the European Union which have recognised the corporation as a social institution that accommodates the interest of employees[18] and the practice of Japanese corporations which ultimately sees the corporation in terms of social relations and gives low priority to shareholders but high priority to social, employee and consumer interests.[19] These are complex questions of culture and cannot be accounted for simply by taking over metaphors from the natural sciences such as path dependence and the like.

In this chapter we will examine the development of the concept of the corporation as a separate legal person and the legal and economic consequences of the development before considering the ultimate inadequacy of the concept and its ethnocentrism. Then we will briefly review how the courts have attempted to deal with manifest injustices in its application, inevitably resulting from the lack of coherent principle and policy behind its adoption as orthodox legal doctrine. We will then attempt a conclusion in which we point to a need to reformulate the basic doctrine and outline how this can be done. Essentially the argument will be that *Salomon v. Salomon & Co Ltd*, the origin of the modern doctrine, was inadequately justified in terms of principle and policy, likewise in its extension later to corporate groups. This tipped the balance too much in favour of equity investors at the expense of general and particularly involuntary creditors. It and its aftermath also frustrated the development of a more sophisticated and flexible doctrine of the business corporation as a firm which requires a balancing of competing interests, a position which equates more closely to management's conception of their role and the mission of many major corporations. Law-and-economics and stakeholder ideas will be reviewed to consider whether and to what extent they can contribute to the development of such doctrine.

The development of the concept of the corporation as a separate legal person

Roman law[20] recognised certain types of body as having corporate status and these ideas influenced canon law.[21] Roman and canon law ideas influenced the development of the common law ideas of corporations.[22] The question of limited liability of members of corporations came later although it was often assumed.[23]

---

17   See F. Rixon (1986) 49 MLR 446.
18   See J. Charkham, *Keeping Good Company*, Oxford University Press, Oxford, 1994, ch. 2.
19   *ibid*, ch. 3.
20   Digest 3.4.1.
21   H. R. Hahlo and J. H. Farrar, *Hahlo's Cases and Materials on Company Law*, 3rd edn, Sweet & Maxwell, London, 1986, p. 1.
22   *ibid.*, ch. 1.
23   In *Banco Regis Edmunds against Brown and Tillard* (1668) 1 Lev. 237; 83 ER 385.

Early forms of corporation were eleemosynary, existing to pursue the charitable objects of their founder.[24] Some of these were incorporated by papal bull or royal charter. In the case of ancient corporations there was a presumption of a lost grant.[25]

The corporations existed for the public benefit.[26] There was also a notion of public benefit in the incorporation of early trading corporations such as the Muscovy Company, the East India Company, and the Africa Company. Such bodies existed for mixed public and private purposes.[27]

This tendency was followed in the early history of the USA.[28] Corporations were social organisations 'midway between the state and the individual, owing their existence to the latter's need of organisation and the former's inability to supply it'.[29]

John P. Davis in his massive work *Corporations: A Study of the Origin and Development of Great Business Combinations and of Their Relation to the Authority of the State*[30] 1909, wrote that corporations have changed from divisions of society to associations of individuals.

The early theory of incorporation, as we have seen, was predicated on the idea of privilege to be granted on certain terms.[31] With the development of the modern company registration system from the *UK Companies Act 1844* and its Australasian counterparts, there is the development of an alternative theory based on the corporation as a contract.[32] This was reflected in increasing latitude with regard to choice of corporate constitutions.

Salomon

The concept of the corporation as a separate legal person was not clearly recognised until 1897 with the House of Lords' decision in *Salomon v. Salomon & Co. Ltd*.[33]

The early companies' legislation merely referred to the subscribers forming themselves into an incorporated company and did not spell out the consequences in any detail. As a learned commentator in the *Law Quarterly Review* of 1897 stated: 'Our

---

24 Hahlo and Farrar, *op.cit.*, ch. 1.
25 See P. L. Davies, *Gower's Principles of Modern Company Law*, 6th edn, Sweet & Maxwell, London, 1997, p. 18.
26 See generally J. W. Hurst, *The Legitimacy of the Business Corporation*, University of Virginia, Charlottesville, Virginia, 1970, chs I and II.
27 Davies, *op. cit.*
28 Hurst, *op. cit.*
29 J. P. Davis, *Corporations: A Study of the Origin and Developments of Great Business Combinations and of Their Relation to the Authority of the State*, B. Franklin, New York, 1909, p. 264. See too Dodd, *op. cit.* especially (1932) 45 Harv L Rev at 1148–9.
30 Davis, *op. cit.*, p. 246. But cf. W. J. Samuels and A. S. Miller, *Corporations and Society: Power and Responsibility*, Greenwood Press, New York, 1987, p. 3.
31 See e.g. J. H. Farrar and B. Hannigan, *Farrar's Company Law*, 4th edn, Butterworths, London, 1998, p. 19.
32 *ibid.*, pp. 19, 93 *et seq.*
33 [1897] AC 22 (HL).

Legislature … delivered itself on the Companies Acts in its usual oracular style, leaving to the courts the interpretation of its mystical utterances'.[34]

The facts of *Salomon v. Salomon & Co. Ltd* were as follows: Aron Salomon was a boot and shoe manufacturer trading as a successful sole trader in the East End of London for over thirty years. There was pressure by members of the family to give them a share in the business and he wished to extend the business. He therefore formed a company and sold his business to the company. At the time the legislation required a company to have a minimum of seven members. A. Salomon and Co. Ltd had Salomon himself and six members of his family who held one share each as nominees. Thus the company was in reality a 'one-man company'. The price paid by the company for the transfer of the business was on paper over £39 000, 'which',[35] Lord Macnaghten said, 'represented the sanguine expectations of a fond owner rather than anything that can be called a businesslike or reasonable estimate of value'. Although worthy of comment, this fact ultimately had no bearing on the case in the House of Lords. The purchase price of £30 000 was to be paid out of money as it came in, which Salomon immediately returned to the company in exchange for fully paid shares, £10 000 in debentures and the balance (except for £1000) to be used to pay the debts. The debentures were an acknowledgment of indebtedness by the company secured on its property and effects. At the end of the day Salomon received about £1000 in cash, £10 000 in debentures and half the nominal capital of the company in issued shares. The company fell upon hard times. There was a great depression in the trade and strikes by workmen. In view of the latter, contracts with public bodies on which the company relied were farmed out among a number of different firms. Salomon attempted various strategies to get the company back on its feet. He and his wife lent it money. He mortgaged his debentures to obtain the necessary funds, which he loaned to the company. The mortgagee was registered as the holder of the debentures. Still the company did not prosper and it went into receivership and then liquidation. There was a forced sale of its assets. There was enough to enable the liquidator, if he wished, to pay the mortgagee but not enough to repay the debentures in full or the unsecured creditors. In the course of the liquidation the mortgagee of the debentures brought a claim under the debentures against the company. The liquidator attempted to resist the claim by arguing that the debentures were invalid on the ground of fraud.

At first instance Mr Justice Vaughan Williams, a bankruptcy expert, looked upon the case with a jaundiced eye. He disapproved of the one-man company, which was then a new practice, and thought he detected fraud. He held that the company was merely acting as Salomon's nominee and agent and therefore Salomon as principal had to indemnify the company's creditors himself.

---

34 (1897) 13 LQR 6. It is assumed that this was the editor Sir Frederick Pollock. See P. Ireland, 'Triumph of the Company Legal Form 1856–1914' and G. R. Rubin, 'Aron Salomon and His Circle', in J. Adams (ed.), *Essays for Clive Schmitthoff*, Professional Books, Abingdon, 1983, pp. 29 *et seq.* and pp. 99 *et seq.* See too the interesting discussion by Lord Cooke in *Turning Points of the Common Law*, Sweet & Maxwell, London, 1996, and in 'Corporate Identity' (1998) 15 C&SLJ 160.

35 [1897] AC at 49.

Salomon appealed to the Court of Appeal, which turned down his appeal, but largely on the different ground that Salomon was a trustee for the company which was his mere shadow.[36] Both the first instance judge and the Court of Appeal thought that a one-man company was an abuse of the Companies Act.

Salomon appealed to the House of Lords, which totally rejected the rulings in the courts below.[37] A one-man company was not an abuse of the Companies Act, all the relevant formalities had been complied with and the Act was silent on the question of beneficial interests and control. A. Salomon and Co. Ltd was different from Salomon as an individual. In deciding this, the clarity of its decision was not matched by the articulation of a coherent basis in either principle or policy. Indeed the speeches of the law lords give different bases for the decision.

Lord Halsbury LC[38] saw the view of the Court of Appeal as involving a logical contradiction. Sometimes it regarded A. Salomon and Co. Ltd as a company and sometimes it did not. Lord Watson[39] mentioned a new point, namely that the creditors of the company could have searched the Companies Register to find out the name of the shareholders and their failure to do so should not impute a charge of fraud against Salomon. Lord Herschell[40] largely based his speech on the intention of the statute to protect shareholders by limiting their liability. The speech of Lord Macnaghten,[41] which is more comprehensive, is regarded as a legal classic. He states quite firmly that:

> The company is at law a different person altogether from the subscribers to the Memorandum and, although it may be that after incorporation the business is precisely the same as it was before, and the same persons are managers, and the same hands receive the profits, the company is not in law the agent of the subscribers or trustee for them. Nor are subscribers as members liable, in any shape or form, except to the extent and in the manner provided by the Act. That is, I think, the declared intention of the enactment.[42]

Although regarded as a legal classic by undiscriminating lawyers it is largely tautologous and question-begging reasoning. Lord Davey[43] was more pragmatic. He considered that it was possible that the result would not have been contemplated by the legislature and might have been due to a defect in the legislation. He also mentioned that it was not argued that there was no association. He was impressed with the absence of a trust and rejected the arguments based on fraud. Lord Morris[44] simply agreed with the others.

---

36 See Lindley LJ at [1895] 2 Ch. 323 at 336. Lindley LJ was an expert on partnership and company law and learned in jurisprudence. He translated a work on German legal theory.
37 [1897] AC 22.
38 [1897] AC at 31.
39 [1897] AC at 40.
40 [1897] AC at 45.
41 [1897] AC at 51.
42 *ibid.*
43 [1897] AC at 54.
44 [1897] AC at 54.

The excesses of *Salomon* and the political reaction

Initial reaction

The stark recognition of separate legal personality of what was in effect a one-man firm to the prejudice of creditors startled contemporary commentators who found inadequate justification in terms of principle and policy. Thus both Sir Fredrick Pollock in a note in the *Law Quarterly Review*[45] and the Hon. Walter Lindley editing the sixth edition of his father's *Treatise on the Law of Companies*,[46] wrote that such actions were never contemplated by the legislature. Nevertheless the concept became firmly established and was extended to corporate groups in due course, again without any adequate reasoning in terms of principle and policy other than a dogmatic application of *Salomon* itself.

The House of Lords' decision in *Salomon* has been criticised as going too far. The contemporary comment of Pollock in the *Law Quarterly Review*[47] was that the House of Lords had recognised that one trader and six dummies would suffice and that the statutory conditions were mere machinery. 'You touch the requisite button and the company starts into existence, a legal entity, an independent *persona*'. There was nothing startling in that. Once limited liability was recognised the creditors must look at the capital—the limited fund—and that only. Nevertheless, from the point of view of statutory construction it was thought that such a decision would have been impossible twenty or thirty years earlier. The reference in the Act to the persons being 'associated' would then have predicated a partnership.

Drastic criticism

A more drastic criticism was that of the late Professor Sir Otto Kahn-Freund[48] who thought that the decision was 'calamitous'. The courts, while developing fiduciary principles to protect shareholders, had failed to mitigate 'the rigidities of the "folklore" of corporate entity in favour of the legitimate interests of the company's creditors'. Not only this but the incongruity permeated the whole of legal business life. He thought that the answer lay in:

1   raising the cost of incorporation
2   the introduction of minimum capital for all companies not exempted by the Department of Trade and a minimum subscription on incorporation
3   the abolition of private companies
4   a general clause deeming those companies under the control of ten persons to be the agents of those persons.

---

45   [1897] 13 LQR 6. Pollock was editor and is assumed to have been the author of the case note.
46   W. Lindley, *A Treatise on the Law of Companies Considered as a Branch of the Law of Partnership*, 6th edn, Sweet & Maxwell, London, 1902, Vol. I, p. 160.
47   [1897] 13 LQR 6.
48   (1944) 7 MLR 54.

A minimum capital has now been introduced for public companies in the United Kingdom as a result of the Second European Union Directive[49] but undercapitalisation does not feature in the piercing the veil cases.[50]

A more general criticism of the decision rests on fundamental principle and policy. If we adopt Justinian[51] as a convenient starting place on principle—that the purposes of the law are to cause a person to live honestly, not to harm another and give to each his or her due—then *Salomon* is potentially deficient on each count. With its extension to corporate groups it facilitates fraud or at least dishonest conduct. Tort claimants can be left without effective redress and it facilitates undercapitalised businesses. In terms of policy it fails to identify the legitimate ends of incorporation and provides the basis of a massive shift of risk to creditors including involuntary creditors who have no choice in the matter.

The legal and economic justifications put forward by the law lords in *Salomon* were formalistic and simplistic. The practical *effects* of their decision were:

1   to legitimate the one-person company.
2   to allow a corporate controller to escape personal liability and to succeed as a secured creditor where he or she held security even though this was validated substantially by the corporate controller.

The results were to encourage the incorporation of small business that effectively transfers some of the risk to general and involuntary creditors since finance creditors insist on personal collateral. Also it eliminated the potentially complex questions of liability to creditors for corporate debts which had bedevilled the earlier law. These aspects were simply not discussed in *Salomon*.

The extension to groups
Since *Salomon* the concept has been extended to corporate groups. Thus we have limited liability within a system of limited liability; an idea that was never intended by the legislature and that has led to abuse.

Political reaction
In practice, however, as a result of persistent abuse and political reaction to the most patent abuses we see this gradually eroded by:

1   personal liability of directors for failing to prevent insolvent trading
2   the extension of this to parent companies for failing to prevent insolvent trading by subsidiaries

---

49   77/91/EEC; 20 OJL 26, 31 January 1977.
50   See e.g. Farrar and Hannigan, *op. cit.* footnote 31 supra, ch. 7.
51   *Institutes* Book I-1-3.

3   in New Zealand the possibility of discretionary contribution and pooling orders by the courts which are under consideration by the Australian Companies and Securities Advisory Committee

4   the new Australian Commonwealth legislation linking insolvent trading to asset stripping to the detriment of employees.

From this it can be seen that there have been and are successful assaults on the models of separate legal personality and limited liability. These are largely politically inspired reforms without adequate attention to fundamental principle.

The inadequacy of the concept as legal doctrine

In spite of the dogmatic clarity of *Salomon* the courts have found that the separate legal personality of the corporation was inadequate on crucial occasions to perform the tasks set for it. Agency and organic approaches have been used to fill the gap and more recently there has been a frank statement that a corporation is only a legal fiction and represents nothing as such but only the relevant legal rules.[52] To accommodate a corporation into the rest of the law is simply an elaborate exercise in rule interpretation and application.[53] This approach, although elegant, is reductionist. While there is some justification for it as a legal proposition it scarcely stands as a proposition of social or political philosophy or social fact. Even the justification as a legal proposition rests on tautology, and the courts have found it necessary to supplement it with other doctrine on occasion. Thus the axiomatic duty of directors and of shareholders at the general meeting is to act for the good of the company but what is the company for this purpose?[54] The abstraction and fiction do not help. They seem to beg the question in the absence of a conception of the corporation as a firm.

As a result in four key areas, namely directors' duties,[55] constitutional change,[56] takeover defences,[57] and share capital[58] the courts have found the necessity to go beyond the fiction. In the first and second cases this has led them to consider the interests of the shareholders as a general body.[59] In a sense, a corporation is a personified fund of capital—the corporation is the capital—as Sir George Jessel suggested in

---

52   *Meridian Global Funds Management Asia Ltd v. Securities Commission* [1995] 3 WLR 413, 418. See further Farrar and Hannigan, *op. cit.* footnote 31 supra, ch. 12; L. S. Sealy, 'The Corporate Ego and Agency Untwined' [1995] CLJ 507; S. Robert-Tissot, 'A Fresh Insight Into the Corporate Criminal Mind: *Meridian Global Funds Management Asia Ltd v. The Securities Commission*' (1996) 17 Co Law 99; C. Wells, 'A Quiet Revolution in Corporate Liability for Crime' (1995) NLJ 1325; G. R. Sullivan, 'The Attribution of Culpability to Limited Companies' [1996], CLJ 515 (1995) 15 OJLS 281; C. M. V. Clarkson, 'Kicking Corporate Bodies and Damning Their Souls' (1996) 59 MLR 557.

53   *Meridian v. Securities Commission ibid.*

54   See F. Rixon, 'Competing Interests and Conflicting Principles' (1986) 49 MLR 446.

55   See e.g. H. A. J. Ford, R. P. Austin, I. M. Ramsay, *Ford's Principles of Corporations Law*, 10th edn, Butterworths, Sydney, 2001, para [8-070] et seq.

56   *ibid.*, ch. 11.

57   *ibid.*, para [8.070] et seq.

58   See *Re Exchange Banking Co, Flitcroft's Case* (1882) 21 ChD 519, 533–4 per Jessel MR.

59   *ibid.*

1882.[60] Recently it has been recognised that in the case of insolvency or near insolvency this gives way to the creditor interest.[61] In the case of takeovers there has generally been an equation of the corporation with its shareholders but on rare occasions the recognition of the corporation as a firm which potentially takes in a broader range of stakeholders.[62] The main problem has been to identify the basis on which the term 'stakeholder' is being used. Is it a legal concept, a moral concept or simply a loose term of managerial theory?

In the USA the junk bond financed asset stripping tender offers of the 1980s led to a number of state constituency statutes that have authorised the directors to consider as a matter of law a broad range of specified corporate stakeholders.[63]

As the American Bar Association (ABA) Committee on Corporate Laws stated in its report *Other Constituencies Statutes: Potential for Confusion* in 1990:[64]

All the statutes incorporate one or more of the following provisions:

1   The directors may consider the interest of, or the effects of their action on, various non-stockholder constituencies.
2   These constituencies may include employees, customers, creditors, suppliers, and communities in which the corporation has facilities.
3   The directors may consider the national and state economies and other community and societal considerations.
4   The directors may consider the long-term as well as the short-term interests of the corporation and its shareholders.
5   The directors may consider the possibility that the best interests of the corporation and its stockholders would best be served by remaining independent.
6   The directors may consider any other pertinent factor.
7   Officers may also be covered.

In most of the state statutes, the relevant wording is qualified by words such as 'in considering the best interests of the corporation'.[65]

In the case of the Connecticut statute the Act *mandates* directors to take the specified interests into account but this is unusual. Other states tend to simply allow directors to do so.[66]

In the United Kingdom the *Companies Act 1980* introduced a more limited provision which is now section 309 of the *Companies Act 1985*. This provides:

1   The matters to which the directors of a company are to have regard in the performance of their functions include the interests of the company's employees in general as well as the interests of its members.

---

60   See *Flitcroft's Case, op. cit.*
61   Ford et al., *Ford's Principles*, 10th edn, *op. cit.* para [8.100].
62   *ibid.*, para [8.070] *et seq.*
63   See *inter alia* the special issue of the *Stetson Law Review* devoted to this question: 21 Stetson L Rev (1991).
64   [1990] *Business Lawyer* 2253, 2261.
65   *ibid.* 2265.
66   Conn Gen Stat Ann sections 33–313(c).

   2   Accordingly, the duty imposed by this section on the directors is owed by them to the company (and the company alone) and is enforceable in the same way as any other fiduciary duty owed to a company by its directors.

The ABA Committee states:

Several aspects of this (UK) formulation are noteworthy. First, it makes it mandatory for directors to take into account the interests of employees. However, by providing that the duty is 'owed by (the directors) to the company (and the company alone) ...', it was apparently intended that the duty could be enforced only by the company or in the limited circumstances permitted in England in a derivative suit brought by a share-holder; there is no right on the part of any employee, as an employee, to enforce the duty put upon directors to consider the interests of employees.[67]

In spite of the wording of section 309 the assumption in the United Kingdom is that this merely legitimates consideration of the interests of employees. They can be considered along with the interests of members. Directors are in effect mandated to perform a balancing act. It is to be noted also that there is no reference to creditors in the section.[68]

The law and economics literature

In the last thirty years there has been a growth of the law and economics literature on companies which provides a sharp contrast to legal reasoning about corporations and provides some useful insights into policy debates. The origins of this approach lie in Ronald Coase's paper on the 'Nature of the Firm' in *Economica*[69] in 1937. Henry Manne developed some ideas about management[70] and the different corporate systems[71] and invented the idea of the market for corporate control.[72] Today it is perhaps true to say that there is a reasonably consistent school of thought that is built upon Coase's idea of the firm as a team method of production; Alchian and Demsetz's explanation of the separation of ownership and control in terms of specialisation;[73] Fama and Jensen's explanations of control systems in different types of organisation;[74] economic theories

---

67   [1990] *Business Lawyer* 2253, 2263.

68   See D. Prentice, *Companies Act 1980*, Butterworths, London, 1980, p. 138.

69   (1937) 4 *Economica* (NS) 386.

70   'Higher Criticisms of the Modern Corporation' (1962) 62 Colum L Rev 399 Cf. Adolf Berle's reply 62 Colum L Rev 433.

71   'Our Two Corporation Systems: Law and Economics' (1967) 53 Va L Rev 259.

72   'Mergers and the Market for Corporate Control' (1965) 73 J Pol Econ 100.

73   A. A. Alchian and H. Demsetz, 'Production Information Costs and Economic Organization' 62 Am Econ Rev 777; A. A. Alchian, 'Corporate Management and Property Rights' in H. Manne (ed), *Economic Policy and the Regulation of Corporate Securities*, American Enterprise Institute for Public Policy Research, Washington, 1969.

74   E. F. Fama and M. C. Jensen, 'Separation of Ownership and Control' (1983) 26 *Journal of Law and Economics* 301; Fama and Jensen, 'Agency Problems and Residual Claims' (1983) 26 *Journal of Law and Economics* 327. See also M. C. Jensen and W. H. Meckling, 'Theory of the Firm: Managerial Behaviour, Agency Costs and Ownership Structure.' (1976) 3 *Journal of Financial Economics* 305.

of voting;[75] economic theories of the monitoring role of markets;[76] and theories of the efficiency of markets as elaborate information systems.[77] Let us consider the main ideas of this school.[78]

The corporation is clearly recognised as a species of firm.[79] It is a characteristic of modern Western economies that production is typically carried out by firms, not by individuals although logically this is not a necessary consequence of the price system. It is theoretically possible for all production to be carried out by individuals but as society and technology become more complex this becomes difficult and costly. The firm then represents to some extent an alternative to the price system and, instead of a host of market transactions, the defining characteristic of a firm is in a 'team use of inputs and a centralised position of some party in the contractual arrangements of other inputs'.[80] The firm produces economies in transaction costs.[81]

The corporation evolved as a distinct species of firm primarily as a method of solving problems encountered in raising substantial amounts of capital.[82] As such it is a kind of standard form contract.[83] The capital raised enables an elaborate organisation to be set up with professional management. Instead of a series of separate investment contracts and contracts with the various factors in production there is substituted the nexus of contracts constituted by the company.[84] This and the existence of limited liability facilitate the growth of corporate firms.

The corporate constitution cannot and does not attempt to cover everything. Some things are left to a vote of the shareholders in general meetings. Voting can thus be seen as an aspect of contracting and the right to vote is vested in those with the residual claim to the firm's income.[85]

The separation of shareholding and management is due to specialisation.[86] Decision management is separate from risk bearing, and with limited liability and the

---

75   H. G. Manne, 'Some Theoretical Aspects of Share Voting,' (1964) 64 Colum L Rev 1427; F. H. Easterbrook and D. R. Fischel, 'Voting in Corporate Law' (1983) 25 *Journal of Law and Economics* 395.
76   H. G. Manne, 'Mergers and the Market for Corporate Control,' (1965) 73 J Pol Econ 110; (1967) 53 Va L Rev 259; E. F. Fama, 'Agency Problems and the Theory of the Firm' (1980) 88 J Pol Econ 288.
77   R. A. Posner and K. E. Scott, *Economics of Corporation Law and Securities Regulation*, Little Brown & Co, Boston, 1980, ch. 6 and the materials cited; D. R. Fischel, 'Efficient Capital Market Theory, The Market for Corporate Control, and the Regulation of Cash Tender Offers' (1978) 57 *Texas Law Review* 57.
78   See R. A. Posner, *Economic Analysis of Law*, 5th edn, Little Brown & Co, Boston, 1998, ch. 14; Posner and Scott, *op. cit.*; H. G. Manne (ed.), *Corporate Governance; Past and Future*, KCG Productions, New York, 1982; N. Wolfson, *The Modern Corporation—Free Markets vs Regulation*, Free Press, New York, 1984.
79   R. Coase, 'The Nature of the Firm' (1937) 4 *Economica* (NS) 386; N. S. Buchanan, *The Economics of Corporate Enterprise*, H Holt, New York, 1940, p. 15.
80   Alchian and Demsetz, *op. cit.*, p. 777.
81   Coase, *op. cit.*
82   Manne, (1964) 53 Va L Rev 1427; Easterbrook and Fischel, (1983) 26 *Journal of Law and Economics* 195.
83   Posner, *op. cit.*, p. 369. However, for recent emphasis on the property aspects see H. Hansmann and R. Kraakman 'The Essential Role of Organizational Law' (2000) 110 Yale LJ 387.
84   Fama and Jensen, *op. cit.*, p. 302.
85   Manne, (1964) 64 Colum L Rev 1427; Easterbrook and Fischel, (1983) 26 *Journal of Law and Economics* 195.
86   Fama and Jensen, *op. cit.*, pp. 327 *et seq.*

possibility of diversified investment, risk bearing itself is reduced.[87] The diversified shareholder is not usually skilled in management nor even necessarily interested in the detailed operations of the companies in which he or she invests. The growth of institutional investment is a further step on the road of diversification.[88]

The separation of ownership and control gives rise to agency costs because of the opportunities for conflict of interest. Agency costs are, however, limited by the separation of decision management (the initiation and implementation of decisions) from decision control (the ratification and monitoring of decisions). The board of directors of a listed company in this scheme of things controls top level managers. This is a system of internal control.[89] To some considerable extent this is monitored externally by the markets in which the company operates. First, there is the product market. Management inefficiencies will affect the survival or competitiveness of the company. Second, the public listed company competes in the market for investment capital. A well-run company will be more likely to obtain investment funds on better terms than one that is less well run. The share prices reflect all knowledge available to the market. Third, the company and its management participate in the market for management itself. Management is a specialised form of labour and is a marketable commodity. The fourth market in which the company operates is the market for corporate control. Larger and more efficient companies will be constantly on the look-out for companies to take over where the existing management is making inefficient use of the corporate assets.[90]

Management shirking is also policed by the system of auditors and by the case law fiduciary duties that have been augmented by statute.[91] These duties are regarded by writers of this school as an elaborate standard form contract that avoids the need for a host of individual management bonding contracts.[92] The generality of the case law principles is seen as an advantage.

Some law and economics scholars[93] criticise the US constituency statutes on the grounds first that they conflict with the underlying premise of corporate laws that fiduciary duties should only be owed to the firm's residual claimants, second that they require directors to serve too many masters, and third that they fail to recognise the need to protect the residual claimants as the group which faces the most difficult contracting problems with respect to defining the duties owed to them by the directors.[94]

---

87   *ibid.*, p. 332.

88   *ibid.*, pp. 337 *et seq.*

89   Fama and Jensen, 'Separation of Ownership and Control' (1983) 26 *The Journal of Law and Economics* 301, 303 *et seq*; Fama, 'Agency Problems and the Theory of the Firm' (1980) 88 J Pol Econ 288.

90   Manne (1965) 73 J Pol Econ 110; Fama and Jensen, *op. cit.*, pp. 312 *et seq*; Fama *op. cit.*, pp. 292 *et seq.*

91   Fama and Jensen, *op. cit.*, p. 314; D. Fischel, 'The Corporate Governance Movement' (1982) 35 Va L Rev 1259.

92   Fischel, 'Efficient Capital Market Theory ...', *op. cit.*

93   J. R. Macey, 'An Economic Analysis of the Various Rationales for Making Shareholders the Exclusive Beneficiaries of Corporate Fiduciary Duties' (1991) 21 Stetson L Rev 23.

94   *ibid.*, p. 36.

On the other hand an experienced US corporate counsel, Morey McDaniel,[95] has argued:

> With Pareto efficiency as the economic goal, it is possible to derive objective standards for interpreting constituency statutes. The most important standard is a dual goal:
> * maximise stockholder gain
> * minimise stakeholder loss
>   Statutes that enable directors to eliminate or mitigate losses to other constituencies help assure that a transaction in fact produces net gains in social wealth.

Separate legal personality: anthropomorphism as ethnocentrism

The rigour of the Anglo–Australian concept of the corporation as a separate legal person and its traditional equation since the mid nineteenth century with its shareholders, have been distinctly ethnocentric phenomena.

Civil law based jurisdictions including Japan have never recognised fully the two aspects of the doctrine. German company law from the Weimar period recognised a broader range of stakeholders in the corporation and Japanese corporate governance emphasises the corporation as a social institution with shareholders ranking lowest in the scheme of things.[96]

If we take Germany, article 14(2) of the Federal Constitution states 'Property imposes duties. Its uses should also serve the public good'.[97]

The objectives of German companies do not stop at profit maximisation but recognise a broader concept of the interest of the company as a whole.[98] Institutionally this broader conception of the company is reflected in works councils and worker directors on the supervisory boards in the two-tier board system.[99]

The two-tier board system dates back to the beginning of the modern German corporation law. It was intended as a substitute for a state charter and continuous state control. It linked persons other than the owners with the enterprise.[100]

It is obligatory for all *aktiengesellschaften* (public companies) but not for GmbHs (Gesellschaften mit beschränkter Haftung), which are the equivalent of proprietary

---

95 See M. W. McDaniel, 'Stockholders and Stakeholders' (1991) 21 Stetson L Rev 121, 161–2.
96 See *generally* Charkham *op. cit.* footnote 18 supra. See M. Bradley et al, 'The Purposes and Accountability of the Corporation in Contemporary Society: Corporate Governance at a Crossroad' (1999) 62 *Law and Contemporary Problems* 9.
97 Charkham *op. cit.* footnote 18 supra, p. 10.
98 *ibid.*, pp. 10–11.
99 *ibid.*, pp. 12 *et seq.*
100 See K. J. Hopt, 'The German Two-Tier Board (Aufsichtsrat): A German View on Corporate Governance', in K. J. Hopt and E. Wymeersch, *Comparative Corporate Governance*, Walter de Gruyter, Berlin, 1997, pp. 3, 6.

companies. Nevertheless a number of GmbHs have informal advisory boards. Even a GmbH which normally employs at least 500 employees must have a supervisory board under the co-determination provisions of the *Works Constitution Act 1952*.[101]

The Japanese system, although influenced by German and US laws, is marked by underlying social concepts of obligation, family and consensus.[102] In this system shareholders tend to rank lowest in the list of stakeholders and a corporation is seen as a complex form of relational contract in which the primary enforcement system is social rather than legal. This has been described in the following way by a leading Japanese commentator:[103]

> The Japanese concept of a corporation, based on this commune or village concept, is fundamentally different from the Western model, which sees the stockholders as the owners of the corporation and the work force as employed labor.
>
> Many Japanese chief executives, when asked what they consider their main responsibility, will say that they work for the well-being of their people. Stockholders do not rank much higher than bankers in their list of concerns.

In an interesting recent study by Dr Ivor Francis entitled *Future Direction—The Power of the Competitive Board*,[104] Australian directors were asked to rank in priority, the following:

- shareholders
- employees
- the community
- customers
- the future
- the company
- suppliers
- lenders
- the nation
- other

The results are shown in percentage terms in Figure 3.1 along with the corresponding results for Japanese and US directors. These show that Australian directors, like their US counterparts, overwhelmingly (74 per cent) give first priority to *shareholders*, notwithstanding the fact that the law states unequivocally that a director's first duty is to the *company*.[105] This contrasts strongly with the results for Japanese directors where the company and customers ranked highest, followed closely by employees.[106]

101 *ibid.*, p. 7.
102 Charkham, *op. cit.* footnote 18 supra, p. 70.
103 K. Ohmae, *The Mind of the Strategist*, McGraw-Hill, New York, 1982, pp. 218–19.
104 FT Pitman Publishing, Melbourne, 1997, p. 354.
105 *ibid.*, p. 354.
106 *ibid.*, pp. 353–4.

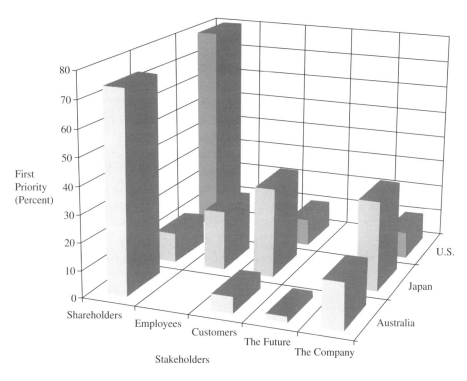

Figure 3.1 Comparative ranking of stakeholders by directors

Source: Adapted from *Future Direction: The Power of the Competitive Board*, FT Pitman Publishing, Melbourne, 1997.

The courts' unprincipled approaches to the injustice of the concept[107]

Given the lack of a coherent basis for *Salomon* in principle and policy it is perhaps inevitable first that injustice can arise in its application and second that the courts' departures from it have not been easy to explain and justify in terms of principle and policy. We lack a clear idea of the legitimate ends of incorporation.

The orthodox approach to the application of *Salomon* is that the company is a separate legal person[108] and, in the case of a group of companies, the parent company and each subsidiary are separate legal persons.[109] Each, as a necessary consequence, is solely responsible for its own debts.

---

107 See Farrar and Hannigan, *op. cit.* footnote 31 ch. 7 and J. H. Farrar, 'Legal Issues Involving Corporate Groups' (1998) 16 C&SLJ 184 on which this is based.

108 *Salomon v. Salomon & Co Ltd* [1897] AC 22 (HL).

109 Farrar and Hannigan, *op. cit.* footnote 31 supra, p. 185.

There are some exceptional cases where the courts have pierced the veil.[110] In a number of these this has been on the basis of the corporations as a facade[111] or on the basis of what they conceive to be the reality of a group enterprise as a single economic entity.[112] The facade cases have usually been at one end of the spectrum and the enterprise cases at the other. Facade is used as a category of illusory reference to express the court's disapproval of the use of the corporate form to evade obligations, although the courts have failed to identify a clear test based on pragmatic considerations such as undercapitalisation or domination.[113] The main group enterprise cases have been compulsory acquisition cases where the court sees no harm in the arrangements and it would be unjust for the court to rely too heavily on technicalities.[114] Whereas the facade cases, which represent no clear principle, have generally won approval, the group enterprise cases, which are clearer, although unorthodox, now represent a backwater.[115]

The orthodox modern approach is reflected in the English Court of Appeal decision in *Adams v. Cape Industries Plc.*[116] in 1990, where the piercing of the veil argument was used to attempt to bring an English public company, which was the parent company of a group that included subsidiaries in the USA, within the jurisdiction of the courts of the USA. The Court of Appeal rejected the single group entity argument, and held that it was a legitimate use of the corporate form to use a subsidiary to insulate the remainder of the group from tort liability. There was no evidence to justify a finding of agency or facade. The Court of Appeal followed the House of Lords in the Scottish appeal in *Woolfson v. Strathclyde Regional Council,*[117] which had rejected the earlier reasoning in the English Court of Appeal in *DHN Food Distributors Ltd v. Tower Hamlets LBC.*[118] However, the court felt that earlier authorities provided sparse guidance as to the principles which should guide the court in determining whether or not the arrangements of a corporate group involved a facade.

Counsel had argued that the court should lift the veil where the corporate structure attempts to evade: (1) limitations imposed on conduct by the law; (2) such rights of relief as third parties already possess; and (3) such rights of relief as third parties might in the future require. On the basis of the authorities, it would be safe only to accept (1) and (2); (3) seems to go beyond the present law.

110　See e.g. Farrar and Hannigan, *op. cit.* footnote 31 supra, ch. 7; H. A. J. Ford, R. Austin and I. Ramsay, *Ford's Principles of Corporations Law,* 10th edn, Butterworths, Sydney, 2001, para [4.350] *et seq.*

111　See e.g. *Adams v. Cape Industries* [1990] Ch 433.

112　See *Ford's Principles of Corporations Law op. cit.,* para [4.140] *et seq.*

113　Farrar, *op. cit.* footnote 107 supra, 185.

114　See *Smith, Stone & Knight Ltd v. Birmingham Corporation* [1939] 4 All ER 116; *DHN Food Distributors Ltd v. Tower Hamlets LBC* [1976] 1 WLR 852.

115　Farrar, *op. cit.* footnote 107 supra, p. 185.

116　[1990] Ch. 433.

117　(1978) 38 P&CR 521.

118　[1976] 1 WLR 852.

By contrast, in two cases involving the granting of injunctions, the courts have been inclined to take a more flexible approach. Thus in *Aiglon Ltd and L'Aiglon SA v. Gau Shan Co. Ltd*[119] the court granted an injunction against a company in connection with a liability owed by its affiliate where there was evidence of transactions at undervalue. Also, in *TSB Private Bank International SA v. Chabra*,[120] Justice Mummery was prepared to countenance that a company was the alter ego of its controlling shareholder and granted an injunction against it in respect of a claim by the shareholder.

Australian authority has generally followed the mainstream UK authorities in spite of the increasing awareness of judges, such as Andrew Rogers, of the need to reform to bring the law into contact with commercial reality. Thus in *Pioneer Concrete Services Ltd v. Yelnah Pty Ltd*[121] we have a useful review by Justice Young of the English, New Zealand and Australian authorities in the context of construction of a complex commercial agreement.

In *Briggs v. James Hardie & Co Pty Ltd*[122] Acting Justice of Appeal Rogers referred to the unity of enterprise theory in cases such as *DHN*, and thought that its adoption may have been foreclosed to Australian courts below the High Court as a result of the decision in *Industrial Equity Ltd v. Blackburn*.[123] In the case of the High Court it held that, where a parent company had full and effective control over the funds of a subsidiary and the way they dealt with them, the profits to which it could look for the purposes of the declaration of dividends were confined to those already within the parent company. Similarly, in *Walker v. Wimborne*[124] Justice Mason emphasised the principle of separate legal personality of members of a group and the need for directors of each company to consult its interests and its interests alone in deciding whether to make payments to other companies.

There have been similar conservative trends in New Zealand[125] and Canadian[126] case law which stand in stark contrast to the greater willingness of US courts to pierce the veil on a number of different policy bases, including domination, unity of enterprise and undercapitalisation.[127]

---

119 [1993] BCLC 1321.
120 [1992] 1 WLR 231.
121 (1986) 5 NSWLR 254.
122 (1989) 16 NSWLR 549.
123 (1977) 137 CLR 567.
124 (1976) 137 CLR 1 at 6–7.
125 *Re Securitibank Ltd (No 2)* [1978] 2 NZLR 136.
126 See B. Welling, *Corporate Law in Canada—The Governing Principles*, 2nd edn, Butterworths, Toronto, 1991, pp. 122 *et seq.*
127 See for example, *Gibraltar Savings v. LD Brinkman* 860 F 2d 1275 (USCA 5ᵗʰ Circuit) 1286–1289 (1988). See generally P. Blumberg, *The Multinational Challenge to Corporation Law*, Oxford University Press, New York, 1993, ch. 4, and his magisterial five volume treatise, *The Law of Corporate Groups*, Little Brown, Boston, 1987. For a simple overview of the US position see T. W. Cashel, 'Groups of Companies—Some US Aspects', in C. Schmitthoff and F. Wooldridge (eds), *Groups of Companies*, Sweet & Maxwell, London, 1991, ch. 2.

In US corporations law, according to Professor Phillip Blumberg,[128] a leading US scholar, traditional piercing the veil jurisprudence has been on the doctrinal bases of instrumentality, *alter ego* and identity. The instrumentality doctrine is based on:

- control by shareholders so that the corporation has no separate existence of its own;
- use of a corporation to perpetrate some fraudulent or wrongful act; and
- conduct resulting in loss to creditors.

The alter ego doctrine is similar, but is used in the case of affiliated corporations when:

- there is such unity of ownership and control that the corporations have ceased to be separate, so that one is the alter ego of the other; and
- application of separate legal personality would sanction fraud or otherwise produce an inequitable result.

The identity doctrine is basically the same. Professor Blumberg has argued strongly[129] for the development of an enterprise doctrine in respect of corporate groups but, as in the British Commonwealth, this is not yet established.

Conclusion

We have seen above that *Salomon* represented a development which was inadequately justified in terms of principle and policy and shocked contemporaries, and that this trend was continued in its extension to corporate groups. The policy behind the shift of the law from a privilege approach to incorporation, to a freedom of contract approach, was never adequately addressed. The public benefit or prejudice in this transition was never considered by the House of Lords, to the detriment of ordinary and involuntary creditors. At the same time the concept has proved at key times to be heuristically inadequate as a matter of fundamental legal doctrine. Resort has been had to the earlier conception of the company as the association of shareholders in the absence of a more sophisticated concept of the corporation as a firm. Comparative corporate governance also shows the ethnocentrism of the Anglo-Australian concept. By contrast a number of states in the USA legitimate consideration by management of a broader range of stakeholders. German and Japanese corporate governance systems embrace a broader, more flexible concept of the corporation. Added to all this is the lack of a coherent approach in principle or policy by the British Commonwealth courts in departing from *Salomon* where there is manifest injustice. Any advance from this unsatisfactory state of affairs must return to basics and take into account the fact that the corporation is in no real sense a person but simply and more abstractly a human agency operating a pool of capital devoted to distinct purposes pursued under definite conditions—certainly a

---

128   See P. I. Blumberg, *The Multinational Challenge to Corporation Law—The Search for a New Corporate Personality*, Oxford University Press, New York, 1993, pp. 84–8.

129   *ibid.*, ch. 5.

holder of rights but not a person in the sense of distinctive individuality.[130] A corporation is more than a fictional bracket round its shareholders and represents some sense of a firm which is a social institution characterised by unity, distinctiveness and continuity.[131] Given that the latter characteristics are more typically present in a listed public corporation than in a small incorporated firm this may entail some separate legislative treatment of the latter[132] or indeed some fundamental legislative reappraisal of the facts and actual decision in *Salomon v. Salomon & Co. Ltd*[133] in the light of modern insolvency law.[134] These are serious questions to be addressed and they cannot be answered by mindless repetition of *Salomon's* so-called principle as some kind of mantra or in equally mindless denigration of the corporation as a form of 'Frankenstein Incorporated'. Nor does the answer simply lie in a glib resort to the stakeholder concept, which is merely a fashionable doctrine that begs this and many other questions which go beyond the focus of this chapter and this book.

The law and economics depiction of the corporation as a nexus of contracts provides some useful insights once it is recognised that contract does not mean contract in the legal sense but an individual exchange relationship.[135] This helps to explain the basis of the various 'stakes' in a way which escapes the dogma of an analysis in terms of legal rights or the uncertainties of an ethical basis. It is suggestive of possible solutions in terms of institutional framework but perhaps needs to be supplemented by broader policy objectives.[136] In particular the arguments against the constituency statutes seem overstated[137] and it seems possible to accommodate them within Paretan optimality. As we have seen, constituency statutes which enable directors to minimise losses to other constituencies help to achieve an overall net gain in social wealth.[138] The agency theory of the firm is less helpful for our purpose and suffers from an innate reductionism.[139] A corporation is a more complex social institution than a principal and agent relationship although there are similarities and historical connections.

Doctrine and reform based on the idea of the corporation as a firm would involve:

1   a reconsideration of the scope of directors' authority and shareholder power in general meetings[140]

---

130 See Freund, *The Legal Nature of Corporations*, New York, 1897, p. 81.
131 *ibid.*
132 Cf. H. Manne, 'Our Two Corporation Systems: Law and Economics', (1967) 53 Virginia L Rev 259.
133 [1897] AC 22 (HL).
134 For a brilliant reappraisal of the case in the light of modern insolvency law see L. S. Sealy, 'Modern Insolvency Laws and Mr Salomon' (1998) 16 C&SLJ 176.
135 See M. Eisenberg, 'The Structure of Corporation Law' (1989) 89 Colum L Rev 1461; R. C. Clark, 'Agency Costs versus Fiduciary Duties', in J. W. Pratt and R. J. Zechhauser (eds), *Principals and Agents: The Structure of Business*, Harvard Business School Press, Cambridge 1985, p. 55.
136 See P. Milgram and J. Roberts, *Economics, Organization and Management*, Prentice Hall, Englewood Cliffs, NJ, 1992, chs 16 and 17.
137 See e.g. Macey, *op. cit.* footnote 93 supra, and cf. McDaniel, *op. cit.* footnote 95 supra, pp. 161–2.
138 See McDaniel, *op. cit.* footnote 95 supra, p. 162.
139 See Eisenberg, *op. cit.*, and Clark *op. cit.*, pp. 196 et seq.
140 See McDaniel, *op. cit.* footnote 95 supra, pp. 152–3.

2   some institutional recognition of employees in the structure of the corporation[141]

3   some sense of basic capitalisation and legislative recognition of the legitimacy of consideration of the creditor interest by directors even before insolvency[142]

4   As a result of 1 to 3 the articulation of some sense of the legitimate ends of incorporation.[143]

Above and beyond that lies the need to re-educate a whole generation to the fact that corporations exist in society as an important source of rights but with that comes some concomitant social obligations as the price to be paid for recognition of those rights.[144] This is a projection, into the corporate universe, of an approach to the rights and duties of individuals in society that is predicated on a basic principle of reciprocity.[145]

As Adam Smith wrote in *The Theory of Moral Sentiments*,[146] 'All the members of the human society stand in need of each other's assistance … where the necessary assistance is reciprocally afforded … the society flourishes and is happy'. This was the moral background to his concept of the 'invisible hand of the market' which needs to be emphasised for the sake of balance and accurate depiction of his ideas in view of his classical status.[147] Without the underlying social order resulting from reciprocity, markets cannot function effectively.[148] The relationship of law to social order and economic systems is complex.

Professor Warren Samuels, a US economist, wrote in 1987,[149] 'The doctrine of the affirmation of the corporation as a person is part of the matrix of legal concepts, principles, and lines of reasoning through which the legal system, as both dependent and independent variable, relates to the power structure and belief system of the economy. In adopting fundamental conceptions, such as the idea of the corporation as a person, the courts *pro tanto* define and legislate economic reality, determining the normative structure of the economy.'

The particularly complex question is the link between the law's role as the definer of social and economic reality and the law's role as ratifier of existing social and economic reality.[150] *Salomon's* recognition of the concept of the corporation as a legal

---

141   See Farrar and Hannigan, *op. cit.*, footnote 31 supra, ch. 3. For valuable recent discussion see M. M. Blair and M. Roe, *Employees and Corporate Governance*, Brookings Institution Press, Washington, DC, 1999.

142   See *Ford's Principles of Corporations Law*, 8th edn, *op. cit.*, [para 8–100].

143   See Farrar and Hannigan, *op. cit.* footnote 31 supra, p. 78.

144   Cf. D. Selbourne, *The Principle of Duty*, Sinclair Stevenson, London, 1994.

145   See e.g. R. H. Campbell and A. S. Skinner, *Adam Smith*, Croom Helm, London, 1982, ch. 9; I. S. Ross, *The Life of Adam Smith*, Clarendon Press, Oxford, 1995, pp. 175–6. Cf. R. Dworkin, *Law's Empire*, Fontana Press, London, 1986, p. 216.

146   Pt 3, Sec. 3, Para. 7 and Pt 2, Sec. 2, Ch. 3, Para. 1.

147   See G. Goyder, *The Just Enterprise*, Adamantine Press, London, 1987, ch. 4.

148   See for instance R. Dahrendorf, *Law and Order*, Stevens, London, 1985; E. Gellner, *Conditions of Liberty— Civil Society and its Rivals*, Penguin, London, 1996.

149   'The Idea of the Corporation as a Person: On the Normative Significance of Judicial Language', in W. J. Samuels and A. S. Miller, *Corporations and Society: Power and Responsibility*, Greenwood Press, New York, 1987, p. 119.

150   *ibid.*, pp. 124 *et seq.*

person is formal reasoning with value and policy consequences that were not adequately addressed and that need to be fully aired and reconsidered.

A corporation is the legal personification of a firm that is a social institution. This legal personification should not distort the underlying social reality. Sir Samuel Griffiths CJ in *Miles v. Sydney Meat Preserving Co. Ltd*,[151] an early case in the High Court, put it negatively in the following terms: 'The law does not require the members of a company to … maintain the character of the company as a soulless and bowelless thing, or to exact the last farthing in its commercial dealing or forbid then to carry on its operations in a way which they think conducive to the best interests of the community as a whole …'

To refer to *Salomon's* principle in discussing corporate theory is simply to recognise it as a starting point for reasoning rather than a statement of comprehensive doctrine. A century after *Salomon* we need to address these questions about the nature of the corporation as a firm in society,[152] which the House of Lords failed to do in 1897. As Dean Roscoe Pound once said, 'Law must be stable and yet it cannot stand still'.[153]

---

151 (1912–13) 16 CLR 50, 66.
152 Cf. Dodd *op. cit.* footnote 11 supra. Cf. Berle *op. cit.* footnote 11 supra. For a recent reappraisal see A. Von Tunzelmann, *Social Responsibility and the Company: A New Perspective on Governance, Strategy and the Community*, Institute of Policy Studies, Wellington, 1996.
153 R. Pound, *Interpretations of Legal History*, The Macmillan Co., New York, 1923, p. 1.

The Concept of Corporate Control and its Relevance

Corporate control, like corporate governance itself, is another of those concepts that start from a legal base but ultimately transcend law.[1] It is fundamental to the law of meetings, to minority shareholders rights and to takeovers. Indeed one could argue that, together with the possibility of diffused ownership, corporate control is the essence of the modern corporation.

Corporate control is thus crucial to corporate law and corporate governance and yet it suffers from considerable ambiguity. The problem is made worse by the fact that different statutory provisions use different definitions of control for different purposes. Section 50AA(1) of the Corporations Act defines control in general terms as the capacity to determine the outcome of decisions about financial and operating policies. The American Law Institute's *Principles of Corporate Governance* paragraph 1.08 defines it as:

> The power, directly or indirectly, either alone or pursuant to an arrangement or understanding with one or more other persons to exercise a controlling influence over the management or policies of a business organisation through the ownership of or power to vote equity interests through one or more intermediary persons, by contract, or otherwise.

This is more explicit.

Clearly ownership of all the voting shares in a corporation and a majority on the board of directors gives complete control. While this will be the characteristic pattern in a small incorporated firm which in Australia is a proprietary company, it will not be the pattern in a listed company. Here the shares are likely to be dispersed among a large

---

1   See generally J. H. Farrar, 'Ownership and Control of Listed Public Companies—Revising or Rejecting the Concept of Control', in B. Pettet (ed.) *Company Law in Change*, Stevens, London, 1987, p. 39.

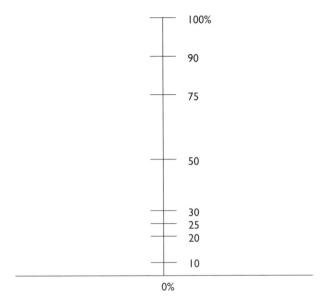

Figure 4.1   Voting power and control

number of shareholders and effective control may well rest for the moment with the board of directors. However, control is a relative term. Control in respect of what in which circumstances? One can, therefore, analyse basic corporate control in terms of Figure 4.1.

A hundred per cent of the voting power gives absolute control, at least if one controls the board of directors, which is likely. If one does not, one can remove the existing directors under section 203D(1) of the Corporations Act in the case of a public company by requisitioning the board to call a general meeting under section 249D or calling a meeting at one's own expense under section 249F of the Corporations Act. Section 203D contains a similar but simpler provision to section 203C applicable to proprietary companies. This is a replaceable rule. The equivalent sections in the New Zealand Act are sections 156(1) and 121(a)(ii) and (b).

Ninety per cent is the figure for compulsory acquisition under Part 6A.2 of a dissenting majority after a successful takeover scheme.

Seventy-five per cent is the figure needed for passing a special resolution under section 9 of the Corporations Act and section 2 of the New Zealand Act. This is needed for constitutional change under section 136(2) of the Corporations Act and section 32(1) of the New Zealand Act.

More than 50 per cent is the figure needed for passing an ordinary resolution. It is also one of the criteria for the definition of subsidiary under section 46 of the Corporations Act and section 5 of the New Zealand Act. Ownership or control of more than 50 per cent of the voting shares or control of the board also make a company a parent or holding company.

Thirty per cent is simply mentioned because under the City of London Takeover Code it triggers a compulsory bid for the remainder of the shares; 20 per cent is the percentage referred to in Australia under Chapter 6 of the Corporations Act for the purposes of restrictions on acquisitions.

Ownership of more than 25 per cent gives negative control in the sense that one can block a special resolution. The American Law Institute treats this as a presumption of control in the absence of any larger interest (paragraph 1.08(b)).

Ten per cent is sometimes mentioned to indicate that, in the absence of a significant ownership bloc, with this percentage, management have de facto control of the company.

The Berle and Means hypothesis of the separation of ownership and control

Adolph Berle Jr, a law professor at Columbia University, and Gardiner Means, an economist at Harvard, published their classic work, *The Modern Corporation and Private Property*[2] in 1932. This has been referred to in Chapter 2. Their central thesis, based on US empirical data, was that as publicly listed corporations grew their shareholdings tended to become dispersed so that there was a separation of ownership and control. In this hiatus management power increased and the question was one of devising effective safeguards or counterveiling power. Berle and Means saw it being developed in the equitable jurisdiction of the courts yet their book contributed to a political movement in the New Deal period which led eventually to legislation setting up the Securities and Exchange Commission (SEC).

Berle and Means' thesis of separation of ownership and control of the modern corporation rested on three foundations:

1   the dispersal of stockholdings so that no one stockholder typically owned a significant fraction of the stock
2   the small holdings of management
3   the divergence of interests of stockholders and management

Statistical support was provided for hypotheses 1 and 2 but 3 rested on conjecture. Built upon this conjecture was the remaining third of the book, which dealt with the fiduciary obligations of control. This latter part of the book was written in an oddly discursive way, making selective use of legal history and arguing the corporate powers as powers in trust thesis. The corporate powers in trust thesis was put by Berle and Means in these terms:

> that all powers granted to a corporation or to the management of a corporation, or to any group within the corporation, whether derived from statute or charter or both, are

---

2   Revised edn, Harcourt, Brace, New York, 1968.

necessarily and at all times exercisable only for the rateable benefit of all the shareholders as their interest appears. That, in consequence, the use of the power is subject to equitable limitation when the power has been exercised to the detriment of their interest, however absolute the grant of power may be in terms, and however correct the technical exercise of it may have been.[3]

Berle and Means regarded control as something apart from ownership on the one hand and management on the other. They adopted as the core of their concept of control the actual power to select the board of directors (or its majority) either by controlling a majority of votes directly or through some legal device or by exerted pressure which influences their choice.[4] Although they recognised that a measure of control was also exercised through dictation to management, in most cases they thought if one could determine who does actually have the power to select the directors one had located the group of individuals who, for practical purposes, could be regarded as 'the control'.[5] Having adopted this as a working definition of control, Berle and Means then enumerated a number of species. These were:

- Control through almost complete ownership;
- Majority control;
- Control through a legal device;
- Minority control;
- Management control.[6]

We will consider each of these in turn in the context of Australian and New Zealand company law.

Control through almost complete ownership[7]

This was a straightforward category which resembled the position in proprietary companies in which a single individual or small group of associates owned all or practically all of the shares. In such a company ownership and control are in the same hands.

Majority control[8]

Berle and Means regarded this as the first step in the separation of ownership and control. It consisted of ownership of a majority of the company's issued shares. In the ordinary case this gives the group holding such a majority virtually all the legal powers of control. The extent of the control, however, depends on the extent of the majority in our systems. Seventy-five per cent will be needed to have control in the sense of ability

---

3   *ibid.*, p. 220.
4   *ibid.*, p. 212.
5   *ibid.*, p. 213.
6   *ibid.*, ch. V.
7   *ibid.*, p. 67.
8   *ibid.*, pp. 67–8.

to pass special as opposed to ordinary resolutions and thus to be able to effect constitutional change. Since much of the time the interests of a minority shareholder will run parallel to the controlling majority, the minority will not seriously be affected. However, there will of course be occasions when the interests will differ. The position in many listed companies today is such that it is relatively rare that any single group of shareholders has majority control. The largest shareholders in the largest listed companies are often institutional investors who individually hold less than 10 per cent.

Control through a legal device[9]

This separate category was more appropriate to the USA in 1932 than British Commonwealth company law systems then or now. The practice of elaborate pyramiding and the use of voting trusts and shareholder agreements were much more common in the USA than in our systems. The problem of pyramiding in particular was acute at the time when Berle and Means published their book in 1932. Pyramiding involves the owning of stock of one company which in turn holds stock in another—a process that is repeated a number of times. It may, but usually does not, involve a group relationship. The problem was particularly acute in the USA in respect of public utilities and eventually led to corrective legislation which defines control in a broad way. Another legal device is the use of non-voting shares, which again is quite rare in our systems. It is interesting to note in passing that close study of Berle and Means' third species in practice reveals financial control in the sense of control by financial institutions in many cases.

Minority control[10]

This exists when an individual or small group holds a sufficient interest to be in a position to dominate a company *through their share interest*. Berle and Means thought that this form of control rests upon an ability to attract from their owners proxies sufficient when combined with their substantial minority interest to control a majority of the votes at the annual elections and conversely that no other shareholding is sufficiently large to act as a nucleus around which to gather a majority of the votes. The larger the company the easier it is to have minority control but everything depends on the situation in the particular company. Berle and Means took ownership of between 20 and 50 per cent as generally necessary for minority control although in a number of cases they accepted a smaller holding.

Management control[11]

This category of control is characterised by shares initially being so widely distributed that no individual or small group has even a minority interest large enough to dominate

---

9   *ibid.*, pp. 69–75.
10   *ibid.*, pp. 75–8.
11   *ibid.*, pp. 78–84.

the affairs of the company. Berle and Means regarded this as a residual category and this approach has been much criticised by later writers. However, it is only fair to say that Berle and Means did recognise that the dividing line between control by minority interest and control by the management was not clear.

Joint control[12]

In addition, Berle and Means accepted that some corporations were jointly controlled but instead of treating this as a separate category they divided the corporations into two 'half companies'. One of these was classified as, say, management controlled, the other as minority controlled. This seems a very artificial way of interpreting the data.

Immediate and ultimate control[13]

Berle and Means distinguished between immediate and ultimate control. Where immediate control of a corporation was exercised by a second corporation which was management controlled, they classified the first as under ultimate management control. There are problems with this approach and it has the effect of increasing the number of corporations which Berle and Means thought were under management control.

Berle and Means then applied their categories of control to the 200 largest companies in the USA at the beginning of 1930 and their results were as follows:[14]

Table 4.1   Berle and Means' categories of control applied to the 200 largest companies in the USA in 1930

	By number		By wealth	
	(ultimate)	*(immediate)*	*(ultimate)*	*(immediate)*
Management control	44%	32.5%	58%	44%
Legal device	21%	10.5%	22%	12%
Minority control	23%	36.5%	14%	32%
Majority ownership	5%	5%	2%	2%
Private ownership	6%	6%	4%	4%
Joint control	-	8%	-	6%
In hands of receiver or special	1%	1.5%	-	negligible
	100%	100%	100%	100%

As can be seen they found even at this date that 32.5 per cent of such companies were under immediate management control and 44 per cent were under ultimate management control.

12   *ibid.*, p. 84.
13   *ibid.*, p. 109.
14   *ibid.*, p. 109.

Later US writings

Zeitlin

Although many later writers adopted the Berle and Means hypotheses and produced further data to support them,[15] there has been an attack on the findings by both Marxist and law and economics writers. The most articulate Marxist criticism was by Maurice Zeitlin in 1973.[16] Zeitlin regarded the separation of ownership and control as a 'pseudo fact which has inspired incorrect explanations, inferences and theories'. He argued that although Berle and Means classified seventy-three of the top two hundred companies as being under management control, they claimed to have 'reasonable definite and reliable information' on, at most, two-thirds of such companies and a detailed study of their sources reveals that many of their findings rest upon surmise. Zeitlin argued that the empirical question is still open and that at the end of the day the concept of control is 'essentially relative and relational: how much power, with respect to whom?' This is a useful insight. He did not, however, do any modern research.

Herman

Detailed research in the USA was carried out by Edward Herman in *Corporate Control, Corporate Power*:[17] *A Twentieth Century Funds Study*, in 1981. Herman puts forward a theory of control based on the importance of strategic position. In this respect he took certain basic structural facts and broadened and elaborated upon Berle and Means' concept of control. His overall tentative conclusions, however, supported the Berle and Means hypothesis while at the same time recognising the ways in which ownership persists as a powerful influence and constraint on managerial behaviour. He identified the financial power of institutions as real but presently exercised as a constraint and ideological influence rather than a form of direct control. Management control is often a constrained control.

Herman's overall results were that proximate management control accounted for 81 per cent in number of the two hundred largest non-financials and ultimate management control accounted for 82.5 per cent of the number of the two hundred largest non financials and 78 per cent in number of the hundred largest industries in the mid 1970s. This represented an increase from an ultimate management control of 23.8 per cent in 1900–01 and 40.5 per cent in 1929. The shift towards management control since 1929 (that is, since Berle and Means) was as dramatic as the shift between 1900 and 1929. He also identified a sharp decline between 1929 and 1975 in director ownership control

---

15 See Farrar in Pettet, *op. cit.* footnote 1 supra, p. 43.
16 'Corporate Ownership and Control: the Larger Corporation and the Capitalist Class' (1973–74) 79 *American Journal of Sociology*, 1073.
17 Cambridge University Press, New York, 1981, ch. 3.

which had changed little between 1900 and 1929.[18] However, he acknowledged that these figures understated the influence of ownership interests on corporate behaviour through constraints and pressures. His researches also revealed the decline of financial control over the large corporation. This is *control* as opposed to ownership.

More recent studies[19]

Later studies have identified a regrouping of ownership interest, particularly through the rise of institutional investment which we consider in Chapter 26.

The law and economics literature

As we saw in Chapter 3 the modern law and economics scholarship concentrating on agency theory of the firm has been critical of the Berle and Means hypothesis and tended to bypass it. The corporation is regarded as an elaborate standard form contract and the role of markets in monitoring management is emphasised.

Thus we have seen in Chapter 3 how management is monitored by:

• the product market
• the market for investment capital
• the market for management
• the market for corporate control.

If the corporation produces a poor product it is unlikely to prosper in a trading environment characterised by increasing competition. This will cause the shareholder to take action or the board to put pressure on the CEO.

If the corporation needs to raise funds externally it will be subject to the disciplines of the capital markets. For this reason many boards finance new initiatives out of retained earnings.

Management itself is a marketable commodity and managers will want to look good for future job prospects.

Last, an underperforming corporation is likely to attract the attention of other corporations, which may consider making a takeover bid.

To this extent the management of a corporation is subject to the disciplines of the market place which curb managerial excesses.

---

18 *ibid.*, pp. 65 *et seq.*
19 See the material cited in Farrar in Pettet, *op. cit.* footnote 1 supra, pp. 48 *et seq.* For recent Australasian data see G. P. Stapledon, 'Share Ownership and Control in Listed Companies' (1999) 2 *Corporate Governance International* 17. See his earlier chapter on 'Australian Sharemarket Ownership' in G. Walker, B. Fisse and I. Ramsay (eds), *Securities Regulation in Australia and New Zealand*, 2nd edn, LBC, North Ryde, 1998, ch. 8. See also M. Fox and G. Walker, 'New Zealand Sharemarket Ownership', ch. 9, *ibid.*

Ownership and control of listed companies in Australia and New Zealand

In a recent article Dr Geof Stapledon[20] of the University of Melbourne surveyed share-ownership and control in listed Australian companies. His main findings were:

1   Local industrial and commercial companies held 12 per cent of listed equities in Australia compared with 1 per cent in the United Kingdom. Using 1996 ASX data he found that 33.5 per cent of listed companies had a substantial shareholder holding 30 per cent or more, 11.5 per cent had a substantial shareholder holding of 20–30 per cent, 18 per cent had a substantial shareholder with 5–20 per cent and 33.8 per cent had an institution as their largest or only substantial shareholder. This is similar to research findings by Mark Fox and Gordon Walker[21] for New Zealand using 1996 data. Their findings were 46.7 per cent under majority control and 44.4 per cent under minority control.[22] A recent survey by the present author, based on the *New Zealand Investment Year Book 1999*, of the top forty listed companies, showed 30 per cent under majority control, and 57.5 per cent under minority control, using Berle and Means categories of control.[23]

2   A high proportion of the Australian equity market (32 per cent) is held by foreigners. A proportion of this is held by overseas institutions. According to the *ASX Fact Book 1999*, the percentage increased from 29.3 per cent in 1991 to 31.7 per cent in 1998. New Zealand also had a very high percentage of foreign ownership. According to Fox and Walker's survey using 1996 data, this was 46.7 per cent. Australia held the highest percentage of foreign ownership of New Zealand equities.

3   The average holding of Australian equities by local institutional investors is less than in the United Kingdom.

Dr Stapledon[24] argued on the basis of these findings that the Berle and Means hypothesis of separation of ownership and control does not represent the position in Australia and, as we have seen, it does not apply to New Zealand. Institutions are more active than they used to be but the rise of funds management creates a disincentive to shareholder activism by institutions.[25] This is coupled with the presence of significant non-institutional shareholders in a large proportion of companies. The latter may improve the chance of active monitoring of management since the significant shareholder may cooperate with institutions in this respect[26] unless of course it is responsible for the poor corporate governance in the first place.

---

20   Stapledon, 'Share Ownership and Control', *op. cit.*
21   See Fox and Walker, *op. cit.*, p. 265.
22   See also the earlier research in respect of the United Kingdom and New Zealand in Farrar, in Pettet, *op. cit.* footnote 1 supra, pp. 48 *et seq.*
23   The differences can probably be accounted for to some extent on the basis of the sampling techniques used.
24   Farrar in Pettet, *op. cit.* footnote 1 supra, p. 28.
25   *ibid.*, p. 29.
26   *ibid.*, p. 30.

Control and takeovers

Issues of ownership and control come to a head with takeovers. Takeovers are to be distinguished from reconstructions and amalgamations. Reconstructions are transactions where one company transfers the whole of its undertaking and property to a new company in consideration of the issue of shares by the new company to the shareholders of the old company. Amalgamations are mergers of at least two companies, usually characterised by the formation of a third company which acts as a holding company. Takeover is a loose term used to describe the situation where one company ('the bidder') makes an offer to the shareholders of another company ('the target'). A takeover bid can be made over the head of existing management in which case it will be a hostile takeover.

In Australia takeovers are dealt with by Chapter 6 of the Corporations Act. Section 602 states that the purposes of Chapter 6 are to ensure that:

(a) the acquisition of control over:
  (i) the voting shares in a listed company, or an unlisted company with more than 50 members; or
  (ii) the voting shares in a listed body; or
  (iii) the voting interests in a listed managed investment scheme; takes place in an efficient, competitive and informed market; and
(b) the holders of the shares and interests and the directors:
  (i) know the identity of any person who proposes to acquire a substantial interest in the company, body or scheme; and
  (ii) have a reasonable time to consider the proposal; and
  (iii) are given enough information to enable them to assess the merits of the proposal; and
(c) as far as practicable, the holders of the relevant class of voting shares or interests all have a reasonable and equal opportunity to participate in any benefits accruing to the holders through any proposal under which a person would acquire a substantial interest in the company, body or scheme; and
(d) an appropriate procedure is followed as a preliminary to compulsory acquisition of voting shares or interests or any other kind of securities.

The Corporations Act sets out detailed rules on disclosure of ownership of shares, prohibiting acquisitions of voting shares above a threshold of 20 per cent subject to certain exemptions, which include acceptance of an offer under a takeover bid that complies with the Act and compulsory acquisition and buyouts after a takeover bid.

Takeover bids under the law are either off market or market bids. Section 632 sets out an overview of steps in an off market bid and section 633 gives a table setting out the detailed steps. Section 634 sets out an overview of steps in a market bid and sections 635 gives a table setting out the detailed steps. These are useful guides.

Until recently New Zealand operated with the *Companies Amendment Act 1963*, which was based on earlier Australian law. The *Takeovers Act 1993*, which provides for a panel and a code, came into force on 1 July 2001.[27] The code is in the form of a statutory regulation.

The purpose of this book is to deal with corporate governance in general and no detailed discussion of takeovers is included. However, the matter is referred to in Chapter 11 when we deal with the duty of directors to act for a proper purpose and in Chapter 28 when we deal with takeover defence strategies.

Ownership and control of small and medium-sized firms

In proprietary companies and other small or medium-sized firms there will not usually be a separation of ownership and control. There will rarely be investment by members of the public although there may be minority shareholders. If there are no minority shareholders there is simply the question of creditors and the public interest. Fiduciary and other duties under the case law and the legislation act as a restraint on corporate control in proprietary companies. Such companies are also monitored by the product market but not usually by the other markets we have mentioned. We examine the corporate governance problems of such companies in Chapter 29.

Corporate governance in not for profits

Not for profits exist for a purpose other than distributed gain. As such they lack the discipline of a market for members' interests. There is a need for alternative monitoring devices. We examine these in Chapter 30.

Corporate governance in corporatised enterprises

Corporatised enterprises are either statutory corporations or companies under the Corporations Act or New Zealand Act, the shares of which are held by the appropriate minister or ministers.

Again, the lack of private ownership presents a gap in the scheme of governance. Modern governments seek to fill that gap by simulating the governance regimes of the private sector. We examine this in Chapter 31.

---

27   See D. Quigg, J. Horner and D. Baker, 'The New Takeover Regime for New Zealand' (2001) 12 Aust. Jnl of Corp. Law 282.

CHAPTER 5

The Corporation as Legal Actor: Questions of Risk, Authority and Liability

Since a corporation is normally, in a sense, a kind of association of persons, it needs a constitution setting out appropriate rules of governance. There is, however, a recent tendency in both Australia and New Zealand to try to make the statute serve as a basic or residual source of constitutional rules.

The constitution historically had both an external and an internal effect. It specified the capacity of the company, its name and initial nominal capital and the basis of liability of its members. It also provided the rules for internal governance. The question of the capacity of the company affected third parties who dealt with the company because of the doctrines of *ultra vires* and constructive notice. Similarly, the rules for internal governance were capable of prejudicing third parties because of the doctrine of constructive notice. *Ultra vires* and constructive notice of constitutional restraints have now been abolished and the rules of internal governance have been reformed and restated.

A major matter with which a corporate constitution still has to deal is the basic line of authority in decision making, which can affect the outside world, although much less than previously. Other major matters concern the allocation of risk and return for investors, and the asymmetrical distribution of information about the enterprise and its prospects, which separates management and investors, with consequent risks of opportunism and conflict of interest. These require constitutional provisions that deal with due process, shareholder rights, monitoring by the board of directors, financial reporting, and appropriate incentive arrangements.

Speaking generally, risk is the possibility of suffering harm or loss. There are many types of risk that corporate governance needs to address—market risks, credit risks, operational risks and legal risks. Efficient contracts balance the costs of risk bearing against the gains which result. Some risks can be insured against and the premiums are a business expense. The corporation is a useful device for pooling resources and spreading and shifting risks. How this is done is partly determined by provisions of the corporate constitution and partly by the general laws. How the corporation is capitalised determines how risk and return are ultimately shared among investors and financiers. Here we are more concerned with the threshold question of the liability of the corporation itself and its management to outsiders. True, the corporation is a legal actor but it must act by human hands. What this entails can sometimes seem almost gratuitously complex in practice, and yet effective corporate governance needs to deal with it.

The evolution of the modern corporate constitution

The modern corporate constitution evolved out of the Deed of Settlement, which was a trust deed combining trust with association. In 1844 when the first Companies Act was enacted in the United Kingdom the constitution which had to be registered was still in this archaic form. This changed in 1856 to the Memorandum and Articles of Association form with a model set of articles which has survived but is gradually being phased out in Australia. It has been phased out in New Zealand. The Memorandum and Articles of Association form was adopted one year after limited liability of members was introduced. The legislation contained a transitional provision which recognised that the changed form still took effect as if it were some kind of elaborate contract executed under seal by each member. A remnant of this remains in section 140 of the Corporations Act, which provides that a company's constitution has effect as a contract:

(a) between the company and each member; and
(b) between the company and each director and company secretary; and
(c) between a member and each other member;

under which each person agrees to observe and perform the constitution and rules so far as they apply to that person.

In 1998 in Australia there was a further transition from the memorandum and articles form to a new form of constitution consisting of one document and a system of replaceable rules set out in the Corporations Act which replace Table A for post-1998 companies and those pre-1998 companies which choose the new form. A table of replaceable rules appears in section 141 of the Corporations Act.

New Zealand adopted a new form of constitution in 1993 but this simply has statutory effect and has abandoned the contractual model. Section 31(2) of the New Zealand *Companies Act 1993* provides that 'Subject to this Act, the constitution of a company is binding as between:

(a) the company and each shareholder; and
(b) each shareholder in accordance with its terms'.

There are no references to the directors or secretary.

Fiction and contradiction in the law

Corporate constitutions and the companies legislation do not exist in a vacuum. They have to fit into the framework of the common law and other statute law. The common law has developed its principles of liability on the basis of individualism and personal responsibility with limited recognition of the social group personality and liability. Where recognition of the group has taken place it has been done on the basis of analogy, metaphor or fiction. As we shall see in Chapter 21 the problem is compounded when we introduce the concept of the corporate group.

Sir John Salmond, the distinguished New Zealand judge and jurist, summed this up with his usual lucid dogmatism in the following passages from the last edition of his *Jurisprudence*, which he wrote in 1924:[1]

> A society is not a person, but a number of persons. The so-called will of a company is in reality nothing but the wills of a majority of its directors or shareholders. Ten men do not become in fact one person, because they associate themselves together for one end, any more than two horses become one animal when they draw the same cart. The apparent absurdity of holding that a rich and powerful joint-stock company is a mere fiction of the law, and possesses no real existence, proceeds not from the fiction-theory, but from a misunderstanding of it. No one denies the reality of the company (that is to say, the group of shareholders). What is in truth denied is the reality of its personality. A group or society of men is a very real *thing*, but it is only a fictitious *person*.
>
> … Although corporations are fictitious persons, the acts and interests, rights and liabilities, attributed to them by the law are those of real or natural persons, for otherwise the law of corporations would be destitute of any relation to actual fact and of any serious purpose.

A company is thus a potentially complex organisation which is assimilated into the pre-existing individualistic framework of the law by pursuit of fiction and analogy with a natural person.[2] This approach is at the risk of ignoring its distinctive social and legal characteristics.[3] As Sir John Salmond stated, a company must act by human hands in the real world. This raises questions such as whose acts are regarded as the acts of the company. Normally this is solved by reference to the constitution and the rules of agency and vicarious liability. In the case of criminal law the approach has been first to

---

1   7th edn, Sweet & Maxwell, London, 1924, pp. 342–3. These passages were dropped by more recent editors. Salmond was Professor of Law at the University of Adelaide and published the first edition of this book while he held that chair. He was later Solicitor General of New Zealand and then judge of the Supreme Court. For an interesting study see A. Frame, *Salmond—Southern Jurist*, Victoria University Press, Wellington, 1995.

2   H. L. A. Hart, 'Definition and Theory in Jurisprudence' (1954) 70 LQR 37.

3   M. Dan-Cohen, *Rights, Persons and Organisations—A Legal Theory for Bureaucratic Society*, Stanford University Press, Stanford, 1986, p. 14. For a useful modern survey see C. Wells, *Corporations and Criminal Responsibility*, Oxford University Press, Oxford, 1993.

deny corporate criminal liability then to base it on identification of certain persons as the alter ego of the company. In some offences this is mitigated by excuses based on lack of fault. Most recently this has been subsumed under a general concept of attribution which provides a path through the mists of metaphysics of fictitious personality. Other approaches are based on the ideas of aggregation and organisational liability.

Lord Hoffmann, in the New Zealand appeal to the Judicial Committee of the Privy Council in *Meridian Global Funds Management Asia Ltd v. Securities Commission*,[4] echoes some of Salmond's dogmatic views and engages in the following general analysis:

> A company exists because there is a rule (usually in a statute) which says that a *persona ficta* shall be deemed to exist and to have certain of the powers, rights and duties of a natural person. But there would be little sense in deeming such a persona ficta to exist unless there were also rules to tell one what acts were to count as acts of the company. It is therefore a necessary part of the corporate personality that there should be rules by which acts are attributed to the company. These may be called 'the rules of attribution'.
>
> The company's primary rules of attribution will generally be found in its constitution, typically the articles of association, and will say things such as 'for the purpose of appointing members of the board, a majority vote of the shareholders shall be a decision of the company' or 'the decisions of the board in managing the company's business shall be in the decision of the company'. There are also primary rules of attribution which are not expressly stated in the articles but implied by company law, such as 'the unanimous decision of all the shareholders in a solvent company about anything which the company under its memorandum of association has power to do shall be the decision of the company': see *Multinational Gas and Petrochemical Co. v. Multinational Gas and Petrochemical Services Ltd* [1983] 2 All ER 563, [1983] Ch. 258.

His Lordship recognised the limits of corporate law to provide in itself a comprehensive framework. He continued:

> These primary rules of attribution are obviously not enough to enable a company to go out into the world and do business. Not every act on behalf of the company could be expected to be the subject of a resolution of the board or a unanimous decision of the shareholders. The company therefore builds upon the primary rules of attribution by using general rules of attribution which are equally available to natural persons, namely, the principles of agency. It will appoint servants and agents whose acts, by a combination of the general principles of agency and the company's primarily rules of attribution, count as the acts of company. And having done so, it will also make itself subject to the general rules by which liability for the acts of others can be attributed to natural persons, such as estoppel or ostensible authority in contract and vicarious liability in tort.[5]

---

4   [1995] 2 AC 500, 506 [1995] 3 WLR 413, 418. Followed by Heerey J in *ACCC v. J McPhee & Son (Aust) Pty and Others* (1997) ATPR 41-570. See also *State of South Australia v. Peat Marwick Mitchell & Co.* (1997) 24 ACSR 231; *DPP (Victoria) Reference No. 1 of 1996)* (26 September 1997) (Unreported Court of Appeal) per Callaway JA.

5   *ibid.*, p. 418.

His Lordship then made the following interesting philosophical remark pointing to the implausibility of the law's characteristic mode of approaching companies:

> Judges sometimes say that a company 'as such' cannot do anything; it must act by servants or agents. This may seem an unexceptionable, even banal remark. And of course the meaning is usually perfectly clear. But a reference to a company 'as such' might suggest that there is something out there called the company of which it can be meaningfully said that it can or cannot do something. There is in fact no such thing as the company as such, no '*ding an sich*', only the applicable rules. To say that a company cannot do something means only that there is no one whose doing of that act would, under the applicable rules of attribution, count as an act of the company.[6]

This approach, which at this last point is somewhat narrower than that of Sir John Salmond, contrasts with that of Professor Meir Dan-Cohen in his interesting monograph, *Rights, Persons and Organisations*.[7] Dan-Cohen refers to the limits of the traditional approaches and the legal personality of corporation when confronted by the reality of the separation of ownership and control in large companies. He sees such entities as examples of organisations, characterised by large, goal-oriented, permanent, complex, formal, decision making, functional structures. The problem is that whole areas of law such as contract, tort and criminal law have been built up on the premise of individual autonomy. Dan-Cohen attempts to resolve the problem by treating organisations such as corporations as entities for ontological purposes but aggregates for regulatory purposes. This is a problematic compromise. The advantage of Lord Hoffmann's speech is that it enables us to deal with this case by case through a flexible rule-based approach,[8] and to overcome some but not all of the problems which the law has sought to face using either the agency or organic approach to organisations. Let us examine each of the traditional approaches before considering Lord Hoffmann's approach and the gaps which remain and how they might be filled.

Traditional approaches to the problem

Agency rules applicable to companies

The basic principles of agency apply, with some modifications, to companies. These principles are:

1   a principal is bound by the contracts of an agent acting within the scope of express, implied or apparent (or ostensible) authority

---

6   *ibid.*, at 506–7.
7   Dan-Cohen, *op. cit.* For a penetrating review of this book see R. B. Stewart 'Organisational Jurisprudence' (1987–88) 101 Harv L Rev 371 especially at 344 for the ontological/normative distinction. See Wells, *op. cit.* ch 7. For another interesting approach see G. Teubner, 'Enterprise Corporation: New Industrial Policy and the "Essence" of the Legal Person', in S. Wheeler (ed.), *A Reader on the Law of the Business Enterprise*, Oxford University Press, Oxford, 1994, p. 51.
8   Consistently with Hart, *op. cit.*

2   a principal may also be vicariously liable for torts committed by an agent in certain circumstances.

Authority presupposes corporate capacity and while the doctrine of *ultra vires* applied in its full vigour the question of *ultra vires* had to be resolved first. Next, there was the doctrine of constructive notice whereby the public were deemed to have notice of constitutional restraints. This led in turn to the so-called indoor management rule which protected bona fide third parties from internal irregularities not verifiable by reference to the public file. This rule known as the Rule in *Royal British Bank v. Turquand* (1856) 6 E&B 327 overlapped with the agency principles in a confusing way until relatively recently. The judicial attempt to clarify the law has now been partially superseded by statutory reform but a few ghostly relics of the old law remain to haunt and confuse us.

It is now provided that a company has the legal capacity and powers of an individual and, to avoid doubt, these include some distinctly corporate powers (section 124(1) of the Corporations Act and section 16 of the New Zealand Act). Although the constitution can limit these powers the limits generally only have internal effect and do not prejudice third parties dealing with the company (section 125(1) and (2) of the Corporations Act and section 17 and 18 of the New Zealand Act).

In place of the indoor management rule and agency rules we now have a statutory statement of the assumptions that people dealing with companies are entitled to make. These can be relied on in spite of fraud or forgery unless the third party knew or suspected that the assumption was incorrect (section 128(3) and (4) and section 18(1) and (2) of the New Zealand Act).

Section 129 of the Corporations Act sets out the assumptions. These are:

1   that the constitution and replaceable rules have been complied with
2   that persons appearing from the information available to the public at ASIC to be directors or secretary have been validly appointed and have the requisite authority
3   that persons held out by the company to be officers or agents of the company have been validly appointed and have the requisite authority
4   that officers and agents will properly perform their duties to the company
5   that documents have been properly executed without seal
6   that documents executed under seal have been validly executed
7   that officers or agents having authority to issue a document also have authority to warrant its genuineness or that it is a true copy.

Constructive notice of constitutional matters has been abolished (section 130). There are similar rules in sections 18(1) and 19 of the New Zealand Act.

The *alter ego* approach

An alternative approach to corporate liability based on agency principles is the organic or alter ego approach which has been mainly applied in criminal law and tort. The leading case is *Lennard's Carrying Co. Ltd v. Asiatic Petroleum Co. Ltd*[9] in 1915 which concerned a cargo claim that Lennards sought to defend by arguing section 502 of the *Merchant Shipping Act 1894* which exonerated the owner from losses arising without his actual fault. The House of Lords held that they could not rely on that defence since the fault of the appropriate organ such as the board of directors or managing director could be attributed to the company. Viscount Haldane, drawing on his knowledge of German law and philosophy, said:[10]

> My Lords, a corporation is an abstraction. It has no mind of its own any more than it has a body of its own; its active and directing will must consequently be sought in the person of somebody who for some purposes may be called an agent, but who is really the directing mind and will of the corporation, the very ego and centre of the personality of the corporation. That person may be under the direction of the shareholders in general meeting; that person may be the board of directors itself, or it may be, and in some companies it is so, that the person has the authority co-ordinate with the board of directors given to him under the articles of association, and is appointed by the general meeting of the company, and can only be removed by the general meeting of the company.

The doctrine attributes to the company the mind and will of the natural person or persons who manage and control its affairs. As Justice Millett said in *El Ajou v. Dollar Land Holdings Plc* [1993] BCLC 735 at 760: 'Their minds are its mind; their intention its intention; their knowledge its knowledge.'

It is nevertheless necessary, not to consider management in the round, but to identify the natural person or persons having actual management and control in relation to the act or omission in question. The formal constitutional position, though highly relevant, is not necessarily conclusive and the question is to some extent pragmatic—what is the actual practice in the particular company?

In the Court of Appeal in the same case Lord Justice Hoffmann said:[11]

> It is well known that Viscount Haldane derived the concept of the 'directing mind; from German law (see Gower, *Principles of Modern Company Law* (5th edn, 1992) p. 194, footnote 36) which distinguishes between the agents and organs of the company. A German company with limited liability (GmbH) is required by law to appoint one or more directors (*Geschäftsführer*). They are the company's organs and for legal purposes represent the company. The knowledge of any one director, however obtained, is the knowledge of the company (Scholz, *Commentary on the GmbH Law* (7th edn, 1986), section 35). English law has never taken the view that the knowledge of the director is *ipso facto* imputed to the company: *Powles v. Page* (1846) 3 CB 16, 136

---

9   [1915] AC 705 HL.
10   *ibid.*, at 713.
11   [1994] 1 BCLC 464. There are, however, limits to this see for example *Deutsche Genossenschaftsbank v. Burnhope* [1995] 4 All ER 717, 727, HL.

ER 7; *Re Carew's Estate Act* (1862) 31 Beav 39, 54 ER 1051. Unlike the German *Geschäftsführer*, an English director may as an individual have no powers whatever. But English law shares the view of the German law that whether a person is an organ or not depends upon the extent of the powers which in law he has express or implied authority to exercise on behalf of the company.

An employee who acts for the company in the course of his or her employment will usually bind the company and his or her knowledge will be attributed to the company because he or she is the company for the purpose of the transaction in question.

This is so even if the employee is acting dishonestly or against the interests of the company or contrary to orders but it is not so where the company is the victim.[12] This is to avoid the obvious contradiction.

Practical problem of identification

In *Tesco Supermarkets Ltd v. Nattrass* in 1972,[13] the defendant company was charged under section 11(2) of the *Trade Descriptions Act 1968* with advertising goods at a price less that that at which they are in fact available. The store branch had run out of specials and had replaced them by similar items at the normal price. The employee in question should have notified the store manager but had failed to do so. The manager therefore failed to discharge his responsibilities. The defendant company had in place an extensive system designed to ensure compliance with the Act. Section 20 of the Act provided:

> Where an offence under this Act which has been committed by a body corporate is proved to have been committed with the consent and connivance of ... any director, manager, secretary or other similar officer of the body corporate ... he as well as the body corporate shall be guilty of that offence ...

Section 24 of the Act provided the following defence:

> In any proceedings for an offence under this Act it shall ... be a defence for the person charged to prove—(a) that the commission of the offence was due to ... the act or default of another person ... and (b) that he took all reasonable precaution and exercised all due diligence to avoid the commission of such an offence ...

The defendant company successfully pleaded the defence. Lord Reid said:[14]

> Normally the board of directors, the managing director and perhaps the other superior officers of a company carry out the functions of management and speak and act as the company. Their subordinates do not. They carry out orders from above and it can make no difference that they are given some measure of discretion. But the board of directors may delegate some part of their functions of management giving to their del-

---

12   *R v. Roziek* [1996] 3 All ER 281, 286, CA.
13   [1972] AC 153, [1971] 2 All ER 127, HL.
14   [1972] AC at p 170.

egates full discretion to act independently of instructions from them. I see no difficulty in holding that they have thereby put such a delegate in their place so that within the scope of the delegation he can act as the company. It may not always be easy to draw the line but there are cases in which the line must be drawn.

Not only is the line drawn but also the law has hitherto avoided liability based on the *aggregation* of individual faults into a concept of organisational liability or responsibility.

Vicarious liability

Vicarious liability is an extension of individual liability based on the responsibility to meet losses because of control over the employee's acts and the benefits derived from them.

Vicarious liability requires three things:

1 a tortious act or omission
2 some relationship between the wrongdoer and the defendant
3 a nexus between the act and the relationship.[15]

Vicarious liability developed at the same time as the growth of corporations.[16]

There is a need to distinguish vicarious from personal liability. Using the organic theory a company can be liable personally for acts by its 'controlling mind and will'. Vicarious liability is in addition to such liability but it is only in criminal law that the distinction has much significance.

In general, excepting the common law offences of public nuisance and criminal libel, criminal law in the United Kingdom and the Commonwealth has rejected vicarious liability on the basis that it would be unjust to impose such liability in the absence of personal fault. However, statute law has made inroads into this on occasion and a different rule applies in the US federal courts and in South Africa.[17]

The policy basis of corporate liability

The late Professor Glanville Williams[18] stated that the liability of corporations exemplifies utilitarian theory in the criminal law and is based not on the theory of justice but upon the need for deterrence. It may help to keep the company as an organisation up

---

15 P. Atiyah, *Vicarious Liability in the Law of Torts*, Butterworths, London, 1967, p. 3.
16 *ibid.*, p. 38.
17 See E. Colvin, 'Corporate Personality and Criminal Liability' (1995) 6 *Criminal Law Forum* 1.
18 *Textbook of Criminal Law*, Sweet & Maxwell, London, 1978, p. 950. See also the important article by John Coffee Jr, '"No Soul to Damn: No Body to Kick": An Unscandalized Inquiry into the Problem of Corporate Punishment' (1981) 79 *Michigan L Rev* 386 and the recent work by Wells, *op. cit.* footnote 3 supra; G. Sullivant, 'Kicking Corporate Bodies and Damning Their Souls' C. Clarkson, (1996) 59 MLR 557.

to the mark. It is arguable that strict liability does not create the same problem of justice as with human defendants and it may help to overcome the problem of tracing the individual in the organisation ultimately responsible or the problem of aggregating individual actions or states of mind.

Nevertheless some offences allow exemptions to strict liability based on 'passing on' the blame to someone else including an employee or on proving due diligence. Indeed in many areas of regulation today there is often a due diligence defence that exonerates the company where it can prove that it used all due diligence to secure compliance. This usually involves proof of having a workable system in place to ensure compliance. However, in the absence of such a defence, steps taken to prevent a prohibited matter are only a matter of mitigation, not excuse. This even extends to the law of contempt. Thus *Re Supply of Ready Mixed Concrete (No 2) Director-General of Fair Trading v. Pioneer Concrete (UK) Ltd,*[19] the House of Lords held the respondent companies in contempt for giving effect to an agreement registrable under the *Restrictive Trade Practice Act 1976* which had not been registered. The actions were actions of local managers without express or ostensible authority and without the knowledge of the respondent companies' management.

The new basis of attribution

A fresh approach to corporate liability based on attribution was adopted as we saw earlier by the Judicial Committee of the Privy Council in *Meridian Global Funds Management Asia Ltd v. Securities Commission* in 1995.[20] In that case two employees of Meridian, Koo, a former management director but presently its chief investment officer, and Ng, a senior portfolio manager, had improperly used their authority to purchase in the name of the company a substantial interest in Euro-National Corp. Ltd (ENC), a New Zealand listed company. Under the New Zealand *Securities Amendment Act 1988*, Meridian was required to give notice of its acquisition to ENC and the Stock Exchange. Koo and Ng knew this but the board and the managing director of Meridian did not. No notice was given. The Privy Council upheld the New Zealand court in ruling that Meridian had contravened the law, holding that the knowledge of Koo was to be attributed to Meridian.

Lord Hoffmann, delivering the opinion of the board, said:[21]

> The company's primary rules of attribution together with the general principles of agency, vicarious liability and so forth are usually sufficient to enable one to determine its rights and obligations. In exceptional cases, however, they will not provide an answer. This will be the case when a rule of law, either expressly or by implication, excludes attribution on the basis of the general principles of agency or vicarious liabil-

---

19   [1995] 1 All ER 135, especially at 142 per Lord Templeman.
20   [1995] 2 AC 500, [1995] 3 All ER 918.
21   *ibid.,* 507.

ity. For example, a rule may be stated in language primarily applicable to a natural person and require some act or state of mind on the part of that person 'himself', as opposed to his servants or agents. This is generally true of rules of the criminal law, which ordinarily impose liability only for the *actus reus* and *mens rea* of the defendant himself. How is such a rule to be applied to a company?

His Lordship then considered the potentially complex situations where the law may be ambiguous in its application to companies. He continued:

> One possibility is that the court may come to the conclusion that the rule was not intended to apply to the companies at all; for example, a law which created an offence for which the only penalty was community service. Another possibility is that the court might interpret the law as meaning that it could apply to a company only on the basis of its primary rules of attribution, that is, if the act giving rise to liability was specifically authorised by a resolution of the board or a unanimous agreement of the shareholders. But there will be many cases in which neither of these solutions is satisfactory; in which the court considers that the law was intended to apply to companies and that, although it excludes ordinary vicarious liability, insistence on the primary rules of attribution would in practice defeat that intention. In such a case, the court must fashion a special rule of attribution for the particular substantive rule. This is always a matter of interpretation: given that it was intended to apply to a company, how was it intended to apply? Whose act (or knowledge, or state of mind) was *for this purpose* intended to count as the act, etc., of the company? One finds the answer to this question by applying the usual canons of interpretation, taking into account the language of the rule (if it is a statute) and its content and policy.[22]

The advantage of this analysis[23] is that it provides a comprehensive approach to corporate liability which is aware of the complications of applying law often premised on individual autonomy to companies and other organisations.

Another new basis

A corporate culture leading to non-compliance

In recognition of these complexities, there is an increasing tendency in some jurisdictions to consider law reform imposing liability, particularly criminal liability, on

---

22 *ibid.*, p. 418.
23 See L. S. Sealy, 'The Corporate Ego and Agency Untwined', [1995] CLJ 507; S. Robert-Tissot, 'A Fresh Insight into the Corporate Criminal Mind: *Meridian Global Funds Management Asia Ltd v. The Securities Commission*', (1996) 17 Co Law 99; G. R. Sullivan, 'The Attribution of Culpability to Limited Liability Companies', [1996] CLJ 515; C. M. V. Clarkson, 'Kicking Corporate Bodies and Damning their Souls', (1996) 59 MLR 557; R. Grantham, 'Attributing Responsibility to Corporate Entities: A Doctrinal Approach' (2001) 19 C&SLJ 168. For economic arguments against the very concept of corporate criminal liability see D. R. Fischel and A. O. Sykes, 'Corporate Crime' (1996) 25 J Legal Stud 319 and V. S. Khanna, 'Corporate Criminal Liability: What Purpose Does it Serve?' (1996) 109 Harv L Rev 1477. For a useful comparative study see H. de Doelder and K. Tiedemann, *Criminal Liability of Corporations*, Kluwer Law International, The Hague, 1996.

institutions for having a corporate culture which directed, encouraged, tolerated or led to non-compliance with the law. This is a form of organisational responsibility. This has arisen out of dissatisfaction with derivative forms of criminal liability in the aftermath of disasters such as the sinking of the *Herald of Free Enterprise*, where organisational sloppiness was insufficient because corporate liability depended on an individual's criminal liability.[24] The need has been felt for some kind of organisational liability. The English Law Commission in its draft Involuntary Homicide Bill introduces the new offence of corporate killing. Clause 4 of the draft bill provides *inter alia*:

(1) A corporation is guilty of corporate killing if:
  (a) a management failure by the corporation is the cause or one of the causes of a person's death; and
  (b) that failure constitutes conduct falling far below what can reasonably be expected for the corporation in the circumstances.
(2) For the purposes of subsection (1) above:
  (a) there is a management failure by the corporation if the way in which its activities are managed or organised fails to ensure the health and safety of persons employed in or affected by those activities; and
  (b) such a failure may be regarded as a cause of person's death notwithstanding that the immediate cause is the act or omission of an individual.
(3) A corporation guilty of an offence under this section is liable on conviction on indictment to a fine.
(4) No individual shall be convicted of aiding, abetting, counselling or procuring an offence under this section but without prejudice to an individual being guilty of any other offence in respect of the death in question.[25]

There are special provisions extending these rules to cases where injury takes place on a British ship or aircraft.

The court is to be given power to make remedial orders and a failure to comply will give rise to a fine.

Similar general provisions now appear in Australia in the *Criminal Code Act 1995* (Cwth), which is not yet in force.[26] 'Corporate culture' is defined by section 12.3(6) of that Act in broad terms. It is 'an attitude, policy, rule, course of conduct or practice

24 See *R v. HM Coroner for East Kent* (1987) 88 Cr App Rep 10; *Re v. P&O European Ferries (Dover) Ltd* (1990) 93 Cr App Rep 72. See also *Seaboard Offshore Ltd v. Secretary of State for Transport* [1992] 2 All ER 99. But see *R v. Kite and OLL Ltd* (9 December 1994, unreported), Winchester Crown Court; *R v. Tam Ping-Cheong and Kwong Tim-yau* (1996) Hong Kong High Court, Crim Action No 355 of 1995, 12 June for recent successful prosecutions of corporations for manslaughter. See the useful articles by C. Wells, 'Corporate Manslaughter: A Cultural and Legal Form', (1995) 6 *Criminal Law Forum* 45 and M. Pritchard, 'Corporate Manslaughter: The Dawning of a New Era?', (1997) 27 Hong Kong LJ 40.
25 See now B. Sullivan, 'Corporate Killing—Some Government Proposals' (2001) *Criminal Law Review* 31.
26 See B. Fisse, 'The Attribution of Criminal Liability to Corporations: A Statutory Model' (1991) 13 Syd LR 277; and T. Woolf, 'The Criminal Code Act 1995 (Cth): Towards a Realistic Vision of Corporate Liability' (1997) 21 *Criminal Law Journal* 257.

existing within the body corporate generally or within the area of the body corporate in which the relevant activities take place'. Two specific factors are mentioned as being relevant: whether authority or permission to commit a similar offence had previously been given by a high managerial agent of the body corporate; and whether the person who actually committed the offence reasonably believed that a high managerial agent would have authorised or permitted the commission of the offence. 'High managerial agent' is defined as a person whose role in the body corporate is such that his or her conduct can be taken to represent corporate policy.[27]

The residual question of personal liability of officers

Lennard's, *Tesco* and *Meridian* were all concerned with establishing the existence of liability on the part of the defendant company, not with providing the *absence* of liability of the company employee. In the case of the tort of negligence, for example, an individual tort feasor is essential to establish corporate liability. But it is difficult to argue that a liability based on identification with another can at the same time be treated as inconsistent with the liability of that other.[28] The doctrine of identification has been no more than a fiction for establishing the state of mind of the company. It does not address the state of mind of the director or his or her personal liability. Whether the courts should go behind the separate legal personality of the company and hold an individual director liable is a question of policy assuming that factors such as proximity and foreseeability are established. Into the policy analysis will enter factors such as control, identification and assumption of responsibility. In the New Zealand Court of Appeal decision in *Trevor Ivory Ltd v. Anderson*[29] in 1992, the plaintiffs contracted with Ivory, the principal shareholder of Trevor Ivory Ltd, for expert advice in the management of a raspberry orchard. There was no conduct with Ivory personally. Ivory gave negligent advice about spraying which led to destruction of the plants. The trial judge held both the company and Ivory liable. The Court of Appeal overturned the finding that Ivory was personally liable. Each of the three judges held that Ivory had not assumed responsibility for the advice given. Assumption of the responsibility, however, like intentional wrong doing, will lead to personal liability. It will not be enough simply to trade as a one-person company or directly or indirectly to direct or procure the act or omission. The test is the

27   For a very useful discussion on these trends see Colvin, *op. cit.* footnote 17 supra. See also *Legislating the Criminal Code—Involuntary Manslaughter* (Law Com No 237), Parts VI and VIII (recommending the new offence of corporate killing).

28   See also S. M. D. Todd, 'Duties of Care: the New Zealand Jurisprudence: Part I: General Principles of Duty' (1993) 9 PN2, 54; M. Simpson, 'The Tort Liability of Corporate Participants', LLM thesis at the University of Canterbury (NZ).

29   [1992] 2 NZLR 517. See G. Fridman, 'Personal Tort Liability of Company Directors', (1992) 5 Cant L Rev 41; D. Wishart, 'Overseas Notes', (1992) 10 C&SLJ 363; M. Simpson, 'Directors' Liability in Tort' [1995] NZLJ 6. *Trevor Ivory* was followed by the House of Lords in *Williams v. National Life Health Food Ltd* [1998] 2 All ER 577. Noted by R. Grantham, 'Company Directors and Tortious Liability', [1997] CLJ 259.

degree and kind of personal involvement by which the director or officer makes the tortious act his or her own.[30] The state of mind of the director or officer might be relevant where it is a necessary ingredient in proving the commission of the particular wrong but different considerations may apply where the state of mind of the tort feasor is not relevant.[31] In the case of some torts such as trespass or nuisance there is no question that the employee of officer is personally liable and the company subject to vicarious liability. However, an officer is not vicariously liable for the torts of the company. In areas other than negligence the courts have applied the tests of whether the director directed or procured the act or omission in question or whether the director made the tort his or her own.[32] The first seems inappropriate and the second question begging. In conclusion it must be said that the law of torts has failed to provide clear rules and principles applicable to companies and their officers.[33]

Risk management in corporate governance

Risk management for corporations and their officers is an increasingly important aspect of corporate governance. We deal with the question of waiver of liability and insurance in respect of directors and other officers in Chapter 16 and risk management as such in Chapter 28.

---

30 See *Fairline Shipping Corpn v. Adamson* [1975] QB 180; *Mentmore Merchandising Co. Ltd v. National Merchandising Manufacturing Co. Ltd* (1978) 89 DLR (3d) 195; *C. Evans & Sons Ltd v. Spritebrand Ltd* [1985] 2 All ER 415, CA.

31 *C. Evans & Sons Ltd v. Spritebrand Ltd* [1985] 2 All ER 415, 424d–e.

32 See *Australiasian Performing Right Association Ltd v. Valamo Pty Ltd* (1990) 18 IPR 216; *Kalamazoo (Aust) Pty Ltd v. Compact Business Systems Pty Ltd* (1985) 5 IPR 213 at 240–241; *Martin Engineering Co. v. Nicaro Holdings Pty Ltd* (1991) 100 ALR 358; *Microsoft Corporation v. Auschina Polaris Pty Ltd* (1996) 71 FCR 231; *Autocaps (Aust) Pty Ltd v. Pro-Kit Pty Ltd* (1999) 46 IPR 339; and *Root Quality Pty Ltd v. Root Control Technologies Pty Ltd* [2000–1] 177 ALR 231.

33 See J. H. Farrar, 'The Personal Liability of Directors for Corporate Torts' (1997) 9 Bond LR 102; J. Payne, 'The Attribution of Tortious Liability between Director and Company' [1998] JBL 153; J. H. Farrar, 'Bypassing the Corporate Veil' (1999) 19 *Proctor* 22. For an interesting recent analysis by Finkelstein J see *Root Quality Pty Ltd v. Root Control Technologies Pty Ltd*, supra, where he held that directors and officers are not generally liable for procuring the corporation's unlawful interference with another's rights.

Part 2

THE LEGAL CORE

CHAPTER 6

Division of Power between the Board of Directors and the General Meeting

The two principal organs of power in a corporation are the board of directors and the general meeting. The main statutory role of the general meeting is to appoint and remove the directors, approve their remuneration and to change the constitution. The basic role of the board of directors is to manage or direct the management, although we shall say more about that in Chapter 8.

The nineteenth-century position

In the nineteenth century the law regarded the general meeting as the dominant body. It could intervene in management. It was the company and the directors were its agents. This is illustrated by section 90 of the United Kingdom *Companies Clauses Consolidation Act 1845* which contained wording that the exercise of the board's powers 'shall be subject also to the control and regulation of any general meeting specially convened for the purpose but not so as to render invalid any act done by the directors prior to any resolution passed by such general meetings'.

Thus in *Isle of Wight Railway Co. v. Tahourdin*[1] Lord Justice Cotton said, 'It is a very strong thing indeed to prevent shareholders from holding a meeting of the company, when such a meeting is the only way in which they can interfere, if the majority of them think that the course taken by the directors, in a matter which is *intra vires* of the directors, is not for the benefit of the company.'

---

1   (1883) ChD 320 at 329.

69

The development of the modern position

In the 1900s the wording of Table A was changed and this more clearly delegated the management power to the board of directors. This was first recognised by the English Court of Appeal in *Automatic Self-Cleansing Filter Syndicate Co. v. Cunninghame*,[2] where it held that the new ruling gave the power to the board and it could not be interfered with except by alteration of the articles. This was followed in Australia in *NRMA Ltd v. Parker*.[3] Section 198A(1) of the Corporations Act now clearly provides (as a replaceable rule) that the business of the company is to be managed by or under the direction of the directors, and section 128(1) of the New Zealand Act provides that the business and affairs of a company must be managed by, or under the direction or supervision of, the board of the company.

Nevertheless certain residual powers of management still rest in the general meeting. These are:

- where there is deadlock on the board
- where there is no effective board
- ratification
- where there is refusal to litigate by the board
- alteration of the constitution
- removal of directors.

Let us deal with each of these in turn.

Deadlock

Where there is an even split on the board and no casting vote in the chairman the general meeting can act. In *Barron v. Potter*[4] an attempt to convene a board meeting failed due to the reluctance of Canon Potter to attend a board meeting with Barron of whom he strongly disapproved. The court held that the general meeting could intervene.

No effective board

This may arise where all or the majority of the board have a conflict of interest and in the case of a public company in Australia under section 195(1) of the Corporations Act they cannot attend and vote at the meeting. Here again the general meeting can act.[5]

Ratification

Ratification properly so called is an agency doctrine and means supplying a lack of authority. Here it is used in an extended sense to cover not only that but also waiver or

---

2   [1906] 2 Ch 34.
3   (1986) 4 ACLC 609.
4   [1914] 1 Ch 895.
5   s. 195(4).

condonation of at least some breaches of directors' fiduciary duties. Thus the general meeting can ratify an honest exercise of power for an improper purpose such as issuing shares as a takeover defence.[6] Ratification can be effective even if given in the form of prior authorisation.

There must be full and frank disclosure in the notice convening the meeting. The leading authority in Australia is the New South Wales Court of Appeal decision in *Winthrop Investments Ltd v. Winns*[7] where the earlier authorities were thoroughly reviewed. Ratification of a breach of statutory duty is not possible, at least where it constitutes a criminal offence.[8]

Litigation

Where the board, motivated by self-interest, refuse to sue on a cause of action, the general meeting may intervene.[9] Where there is no conflict of interest, the position is less clear.[10] Where the directors have instituted proceedings and the general meeting object the general meeting cannot intervene.[11]

Under the statutory minority shareholders' remedy in section 233(1)(g) of the Corporations Law the court may authorise an action in the company's name and it is now possible to bring a statutory derivative action with leave of the court under sections 236–242 of the Corporations Act and section 165 of the New Zealand Act. Sections 169 to 175 of the New Zealand Act allow personal actions by shareholders.

Alteration of the constitution

Under section 136(2) of the Corporations Act and section 32(2) of the New Zealand Act the company in general meeting is given the power to alter or amend the constitution.

Removal of directors

In both countries companies are given power to remove directors in general meeting by ordinary resolution. In Australia this is dealt with in section 203D for public companies. Proprietary companies are also usually given this power by their constitution and this is now a replaceable rule in Australia under section 203C.

In New Zealand where the distinction between public and private companies has been abolished there is a general provision in section 156 of the 1993 Act.

---

6   *Howard Smith Ltd v. Ampol Petroleum Ltd* [1974] AC 821.
7   [1975] 2 NSWLR 666.
8   *Miller v. Miller* (1995) 16 ACSR 73.
9   *Marshall's Valve Gear Co. Ltd v. Manning Wardle & Co. Ltd* [1909] 1 Ch 267.
10   *Kruus Pty Ltd v. JG Lloyd Pty Ltd* [1965] VR 232; *Breckland Group Holdings Ltd v. London & Suffolk Properties Ltd* [1989] BCLC 100.
11   *Shaw & Sons (Salford) Ltd v. Shaw* [1935] 2 KB 113.

CHAPTER 7

Meetings

The constitution of a company, read in conjunction with the legislation, envisages that the main decisions of the company will be taken in meetings of the board of directors and shareholders by majority rule. There are exceptions to this basic proposition but by and large it is the case. The board of directors acts as a collegiate body although it is usually given power to delegate functions to a managing director or a committee of the board. We must, therefore, consider first the procedure at board meetings.

Meetings of the board of directors[1]

Board meetings are usually called by the company secretary but any director can call a directors' meeting under section 248C of the Corporations Act. Reasonable notice of the meeting must be given to each director unless it is waived: section 248C; *Petsch v. Kennedy* [1971] 1 NSWLR 494. In Australia the notice need not specify the nature of the business to be transacted unless the constitution so requires.[2] The rule is otherwise in New Zealand. The notice need not be in writing or substantially in advance but mere coincident physical presence of all directors does not constitute a formal directors' meeting. They need to be aware that the occasion is to be a directors' meeting and to assent to it being so. This assent can be implied from staying at the meeting and amicably proceeding to business.[3]

It is now provided by section 248D that a directors' meeting may be called or held using any technology consented to by all the directors. The consent may be a standing

---

1   See H. A. J. Ford, R. P. Austin and I. M. Ramsay, *Ford's Principles of Corporations Law*, 10th edn, Butterworths, Sydney, 2001, para. [7.310].

2   *Tool v. Flexihire Pty Ltd* (1992) 10 ACLC 190. Cf. *Companies Act 1993* (NZ), Third Schedule, para. 2(2).

3   For further discussion of recent dicta see Ford, Austin and Ramsay, *op. cit.*, para. [7.350].

one. A director may only withdraw their consent within a reasonable period before the meeting.

A quorum at the meetings must be two directors present at all times during the meeting unless the board determines otherwise: section 248F.

A chairperson must be elected from those present at the meeting unless the board has previously elected a chairperson. In the latter case a person may be appointed for a fixed period: section 248E(1) and (2). This is a replaceable rule.

Business is decided by majority (section 248G(1)) and in the event of an evenly divided vote the chairperson has a casting vote in addition to any vote as director: section 248G(2).

Section 191 sets out rules for disclosure of and voting on matters involving material personal interests.[4] All self-interested directors must declare their interest in any matter that relates to the affairs of the company.

Section 194 sets out a replaceable rule for voting and completion of transactions in the case of directors of proprietary companies. This allows him or her to vote if disclosure has been made.

This section is to be contrasted with section 195 which applies to public companies. This disqualifies the director from voting or being present while the matter is being discussed. However, there is a massive escape route in section 195(2) if non-self-interested members of the board pass a resolution indicating that they are satisfied that the interest should not disqualify the director from considering or voting on the matter. ASIC can allow participation in certain circumstances under section 196 and the general meeting can deal with the matter under section 195(4) if there is no quorum. The relevant sections in New Zealand are sections 139–144 of the 1993 Act. These sections will be discussed in Chapter 12.

Directors are allowed to appoint alternates to act in their place under section 210K and they can delegate their powers to a managing director under section 210J or to committees under section 198D(1)(a). Sections 210K and 210J are replaceable rules. Section 198D is not.

Section 248B provides that a director of a proprietary company that has only one director can pass a resolution by recording and signing the record. It also provides that a single director of a proprietary company can make a declaration by recording it and signing the record. This will satisfy any requirement of the Corporations Act that the declaration was made at a directors' meeting.

In New Zealand, section 160 of the *Companies Act 1993* provides that, subject to the constitution, the provisions set out in the Third Schedule to that Act govern the proceedings of the board. The Third Schedule sets out the following rules:

1 Chairperson

1   The directors may elect one of their number as chairperson of the board.

---

4   See ch. 12.

2   The director elected as chairperson holds that office until he or she dies or resigns or the directors elect a chairperson in his or her place.

3   If no chairperson is elected, or if at a meeting of the board the chairperson is not present within 5 minutes after the time appointed for the commencement of the meeting, the directors present may choose one of their number to be chairperson of the meeting.

2 Notice of meeting

1   A director or, if requested by a director to do so, an employee of a company, may convene a meeting of the board by giving notice in accordance with this clause.

2   Not less than 2 days' notice of a meeting of the board must be sent to every director who is in New Zealand, and the notice must include the date, time, and place of the meeting and the matters to be discussed.

3   An irregularity in the notice of a meeting is waived if all directors entitled to receive notice of the meeting attend the meeting without protest as to the irregularity or if all directors entitled to receive notice of the meeting agree to the waiver.

3 Methods of holding meetings

A meeting of the board may be held either:

1   By a number of the directors who constitute a quorum, being assembled together at the place, date, and time appointed for the meeting; or

2   By means of audio, or audio and visual, communication by which all directors participating and constituting a quorum, can simultaneously hear each other throughout the meeting.

4 Quorum

1   A quorum for a meeting of the board is a majority of the directors.

2   No business may be transacted at a meeting of directors if a quorum is not present.

5 Voting

1   Every director has one vote.

2   The chairperson does not have a casting vote.

3   A resolution of the board is passed if it is agreed to by all directors present without dissent or if a majority of the votes cast on it are in favour of it.

4   A director present at a meeting of the board is presumed to have agreed to, and to have voted in favour of, a resolution of the board unless he or she expressly dissents from or votes against the resolution at the meeting.

6 Minutes

The board must ensure that minutes are kept of all proceedings at meetings of the board.

7 Unanimous resolution

1   A resolution in writing, signed or assented to by all directors then entitled to receive notice of a board meeting, is valid and effective as if it had been passed at a meeting of the board duly convened and held.

2   Any such resolution may consist of several documents (including facsimile or other similar means of communication) in like form each signed or assented to by one or more directors.

3   A copy of any such resolution must be entered in the minute book of board proceedings.

8 Other proceedings
Except as provided in this Schedule, the board may regulate its own procedure.

General meetings[5]

In Australia the main provisions on the law of meetings are set out in Part 2G.2 of the Corporations Act. A number of these are replaceable rules. A few provisions are made mandatory for public listed companies and there is a general requirement in section 249Q that a meeting must be held for a proper purpose. This requirement, which was introduced on 1 July 1998 as a general requirement, does not introduce any new substantive law, although it may have an effect as far as standing and procedure are concerned.[6]

In New Zealand, section 124 of the *Companies Act 1993* provides that the provisions of the First Schedule to that Act govern proceedings and meetings of shareholders 'except to the extent that the constitution of the company makes provision for the matters that are expressed in that schedule to be subject to the constitution of the company'.

In New Zealand it is possible to have postal votes but with the new technology it may be possible in the future to devise a scheme for direct electronic voting. These developments throw into question the age-old assumption that it should always be necessary for public listed companies to hold physical meetings to pass shareholder resolutions.

The subject of shareholder meetings has recently been addressed by the Corporations and Securities Advisory Committee (CASAC) in Australia in its discussion paper, *Shareholder Participation in the Modern Listed Public Company*, September 1999 and Final Report, June 2000.[7]

Who can convene a meeting?

Meetings of the members are normally called by the directors. Under section 249C there is a replaceable rule that a director may call a meeting of the members. Section 249CA contains a mandatory rule to the same effect for ASX listed companies incorporated in Australia.

---

5   Ford, Austin and Ramsay, *op. cit.*, para. [7.370] *et seq.*
6   *Howard v. Mechtler* (1999) 17 ACLC 632, 639 per Austin J. Presumably His Honour is referring to this as an aspect of directors' duties or the equitable obligations on majority shareholders as a result of *Gambotto v. WCP Ltd* (1995) 182 CLR 432. Good faith and proper purpose have always been relevant to requisitioning the meeting under s. 249D. See *Humes Ltd v. Unity APA Ltd* (1987) 5 ACLC 15.
7   See also *Company General Meetings and Shareholder Communications—A Consultation Document from the Company Law Review Steering Group*, October 1999 (UK).

Section 249D provides that the directors must call a meeting on the request of

(a) members with at least 5 per cent of the votes that may be cast at the general meeting; or

(b) at least 100 members who are entitled to vote at the general meeting. Regulations may provide a different number of members (section 249D(1A).

The Corporations Amendment Regulations 2000 (No. 4) provided for a change to at least 5 per cent of the total number of members of the company. The CASAC Discussion Paper had favoured abolition of the 100 member alternative and possible increase of the percentage.[8] The statutory regulation, however, was opposed by the Opposition and disallowed.

It has been held that the power to requisition a meeting must be exercised in good faith for the purpose for which it is conferred and not to harass the company and its directors. It is, however, legitimate to pursue one's own interests provided that the reason for the meeting is bona fide: *Humes Ltd v. Unity APA Ltd* (1987) 5 ACLC 15.

Under section 249E members with more than 50 per cent of the votes of all the members who make a request under section 249D may call a meeting if the directors refuse within 21 days of the request. The power to call a general meeting is not a personal proprietary right; it is simply a right to act in place of the directors: *Adams v. Adhesives Pty Ltd* (1932) 32 SR (NSW) 398; *Re Ariadne Australia Ltd* (1990) 2 ACSR 791. The shareholder must act for the good of the company as a whole.

In addition under section 249F members with at least 5 per cent of the votes may call and arrange a meeting at their own expense.

Under section 249G the court has power to order a meeting of the members to be called if it is impracticable to call the meeting in any other way. Directors and members entitled to vote have got *locus standi* to apply to the court.

Section 121 of the New Zealand *Companies Act 1993* simply provides:

A special meeting of shareholders entitled to vote on an issue:

(a) May be called at any time by:

  (i) The board; or

  (ii) A person who is authorised by the constitution to call the meeting;

(b) Must be called by the board on the written request of shareholders holding shares carrying together not less than 5 per cent of the voting rights entitled to be exercised on the issue.

Notice of meetings[9]

Under section 249H(1) the general rule is that at least twenty-one days' notice must be given of a meeting of members. However, a company's constitution can specify a longer

---

8   *ibid.* Issue 2, p. 18. See also the Final Report, Recommendation 2, p. 15.

9   See Ford, Austin and Ramsay, *op. cit.*, paras [7.470] *et seq*; B. Burnett (ed.), *Australian Corporations Law*, CCH Australia Ltd, Sydney, 2000, ch. 9; B. Burnett, *A Resource Book in Company Law*, Burnett, Sydney, 2001 edition, p. 146.

minimum period of notice. Section 249J states that notice must be given individually to each member entitled to vote and to directors; joint members only need be given notice to the one named first on the register (section 249J(2) (replaceable rule)).

Under section 249H(2) a company may call an AGM on shorter notice if all members entitled to attend and vote agree beforehand. Any other general meeting can be called on shorter notice if members with at least 95 per cent of the votes that may be cast at the meeting agree beforehand.

The period of at least twenty-one days' notice must be given if the resolution is moved under section 203D to remove a director of a public company or to appoint a director in place of a director removed under that section (section 249H(3)). The twenty-one days' notice rule also applies to removal of an auditor under section 329. (section 249H(4)). These cannot be shortened.

Under section 249HA twenty-eight days' notice must be given if the meeting being called is a meeting of a company incorporated in Australia and included in an official list of the ASX. This is mandatory (section 249HA(3)).

A company must give the auditor of the company the same notice as members in regard to a general meeting, and any other communications the members are entitled to receive (section 249K).

Section 249L sets out the basic details required for a notice of meeting. This includes the general nature of the business but where a special resolution is to be proposed it must be set out in the notice (section 249L(b) and (c)). The directors have a fiduciary duty to disclose all relevant information on which members can make a properly informed decision (*Fraser v. NRMA Holdings Ltd* (1995) FCR 452; 13 ACLC 132). The duty is to provide such material information as would fully and fairly inform members of what is to be considered at the meeting to enable them to judge for themselves whether to attend and vote. This has to be tempered by the need for intelligibility.

A meeting must be held at a reasonable time and place (section 249R). It may be reasonable to hold an extraordinary general meeting to remove directors at 6 p.m. on 30 December.[10] This seems debatable.

Paragraph 2 of the First Schedule of the New Zealand *Companies Act 1993* simply provides:

1   Written notice of the time and place of a meeting of shareholders must be sent to every shareholder entitled to receive notice of the meeting and to every director and an auditor of the company not less than ten working days before the meeting.

2   The notice must state:
    (a) The nature of the business to be transacted at the meeting in sufficient time to enable a shareholder to form a reasoned judgment in relation to it; and
    (b) The text of any special resolution to be submitted to the meeting.

---

10   *Howard v. Mechtler* (1999) 17 ACLC 632.

3   An irregularity in notice of a meeting is waived if all the shareholders entitled to attend and vote at the meeting attend the meeting without protest as to the irregularity, or if all such shareholders agree to the waiver.

3A Subject to the constitution of the company, the accidental omission to give notice of a meeting to, or the failure to receive notice of a meeting by, a shareholder does not invalidate the proceedings at that meeting.

4   Subject to the constitution of the company, if a meeting of shareholders is adjourned for less than thirty days it is not necessary to give notice of the time and place of the meeting other than by announcement at the meeting which is adjourned.

Quorum[11]

A quorum is the minimum number of persons who are qualified to attend and who must be present at a meeting to constitute a valid meeting.

Under section 249T(1) of the Corporations Act there is a replaceable rule that the quorum for a meeting of members is two. This applies both to public and to proprietary companies except for single-person companies. The quorum must be present at all times during the meeting. In determining whether a quorum is present, proxies and corporate representatives can be counted but a member cannot constitute a meeting by sending more than one proxy or representative (section 249T(2)).

If a quorum is not present within thirty minutes after the time set for the start of the meeting, the meeting is to be adjourned to a date, time and place to be specified by the directors. If the directors do not specify the date the meeting is to be adjourned to the same day in the next week. Unless otherwise specified the time and place remain the same (section 249T(3)).

Under section 249T(4) if no quorum is present at the resumed meeting within thirty minutes after the time of meeting, the meeting is dissolved. The whole of section 249T is a replaceable rule.

Paragraph 4 of the First Schedule to the New Zealand Companies Act provides:

1   Subject to subclause (3) of this clause, no business may be transacted at a meeting of shareholders if a quorum is not present.

2   Subject to the constitution of the company, a quorum for a meeting of shareholders is present if shareholders or their proxies are present or have cast postal votes who are between them able to exercise a majority of the votes to be cast on the business to be transacted at the meeting.

Subclause (3) deals with the situation where a quorum is not present within thirty minutes. In the case of a meeting called under section 121(b) it is dissolved. In any other case, it is adjourned.

---

11   See Ford, Austin and Ramsay, *op. cit.*, para. [7.500]; Burnett, *Resource Book, op. cit.*, p. 149.

Voting[12]

Matters under the Corporations Act are determined by a show of hands, unless a poll is demanded (section 250J(1)). Before the vote is taken the chair must inform the meeting whether proxy votes have been received and how the proxy votes are to be cast (section 250J (1A)). These are replaceable rules.

Under section 250E(1) subject to any class rights in the case of a company with a share capital each member has one vote on a show of hands and one vote per share on a poll. Where the company does not have a share capital a member has one vote both on a show of hands and a poll (section 250E(2)). The chair has a casting vote in addition to any vote as a member (section 250E(3)). These are all replaceable rules. On a show of hands a declaration by the chair is conclusive evidence of the result, provided that the declaration reflects the show of hands and votes of the proxies received (section 250J(2)). However, under section 250L(3) members entitled under section 250L(1) may demand a poll before a vote is taken or before the voting on a show of hands is declared or immediately after the vote on a show of hands goes against them.

A poll may be demanded by:
(a) at least five members entitled to vote on the resolution
(b) members with at least 5 per cent of votes that may be cast on the resolution on a poll
(c) the chair (section 250L(1)).

If a company has a constitution it may provide that a poll cannot be demanded on any resolution concerning the election of a chairman of a meeting or the adjournment of a meeting (section 250K(1), (2)). Where there is a right to a poll on such matters a poll must be taken immediately (section 250M(2)) otherwise it is in the discretion of the chair (section 250M(1)).

IFSA Guideline 11–12.12.4 provides that voting should be by poll only on the conclusion of discussion of each item of business and appropriate forms of technology used to facilitate proxy voting. The Australian Shareholders Association is opposed to this and believes that voting in the first instance should be by way of a show of hands.

Paragraph 12.12.5 of Guideline 11 deals with disclosure of voting results to the ASX. The note explains the difficulties that institutional investors have in exercising their votes and how the steps which they take are not reflected on a vote on a show of hands.

Apart from a few specific mentions of the chair, the duties of the chair are largely left to the common law of meetings and the constitution[13] and could usefully be the

---

12   Ford, Austin and Ramsay, *op. cit.*, para. [7.520]; Burnett, *Resource Book, op. cit.*, p. 147.
13   See *John J Starr (Real Estate) Pty Ltd v. Robert Andrew (A'Asia) Pty Ltd* (1991) 9 ACLC 1372 at 1389 per Young J; Ford, Austin and Ramsay, *op. cit.*, para. [7.510].

subject of general principles of self-regulation or a revised ASIC Practice Note. CASAC did not favour a statutory formulation and has also raised the question of alternative voting arrangements such as cumulative voting.[14]

In New Zealand paragraph 5 of the First Schedule to the *Companies Act 1993* provides:

1 In the case of a meeting of shareholders held under clause 3(a) of this Schedule, unless a poll is demanded, voting at the meeting shall be by whichever of the following methods is determined by the chairperson of the meeting:
   (a) Voting by voice; or
   (b) Voting by show of hands.

2 In the case of a meeting of shareholders held under clause 3(b) of this Schedule, unless a poll is demanded, voting at the meeting shall be by the shareholders signifying individually their assent or dissent by voice.

3 A declaration by the chairperson of the meeting that a resolution is carried by the requisite majority is conclusive evidence of that fact unless a poll is demanded in accordance with subclause 4 of this clause.

4 At a meeting of shareholders a poll may be demanded by:
   (a) Not less than five shareholders having the right to vote at the meeting; or
   (b) A shareholder or shareholders representing not less than 10 per cent of the total voting rights of all shareholders having the right to vote at the meeting; or
   (c) By a shareholder or shareholders holding shares in the company that confer a right to vote at the meeting and on which the aggregate amount paid up is not less than 10 per cent of the total amount paid up on all shares that confer that right.

5 A poll may be demanded either before or after the vote is taken on a resolution.

6 If a poll is taken, votes must be counted according to the votes attached to the shares of each shareholder present in person or by proxy and voting.

7 Subject to the constitution of the company, the chairperson of a shareholders' meeting is not entitled to a casting vote.

8 For the purpose of this clause, the instrument appointing a proxy to vote at a meeting of a company confers authority to demand or join in demanding a poll and a demand by a person as proxy for a shareholder has the same effect as a demand by the shareholder.

Proxies[15]

• A member of a company who is entitled to attend and cast a vote at a meeting of a company's members may appoint a person as the member's proxy to attend and vote

---

14 CASAC Final Report, pp. 82, 92 *et seq.*
15 Ford, Austin and Ramsay, *op. cit.*, para. [7.560]; Burnett, *Resource Book*, p. 148; IFSA Guideline 11-12.12.2 Form of Proxies. See also the Model Form of Proxy in Appendix B to the Guidelines.

at the meeting (section 249X—replaceable rule for proprietary company and a mandatory rule for a public company).

- At a meeting a person appointed as a proxy has the same rights as a member to speak, vote and join in a demand for a poll at the meeting. The constitution may provide that a proxy will not be able to vote on a show of hands (section 249Y(1) and (2)).
- Unless the company's constitution provides otherwise, when a member who has given a proxy attends a meeting, the proxy's authority to speak and vote for the member at the meeting is suspended while the member is present at the meeting (section 249Y(3)).
- If a member requests a proxy form, copies must be sent to all who request them, otherwise all members must be sent them (section 249C2).
- A proxy appointment is valid if signed by the member and if it meets the requirements set out in section 250A (1).
- An appointment of a proxy may specify the way the proxy is to vote on a particular resolution (section 250A(4)). Section 250A(4) sets out some basic rules which rather oddly apply if the appointment specifies the way a proxy is to vote.
- Proxy documents can be posted to or faxed to the company, but must be received at least forty-eight hours before the meeting. The company's constitution or the notice of the meeting may reduce the period (section 250B(1), (3), (5)).
- Listed companies incorporated in Australia must specify in a notice of meeting, a place, fax number and electronic address for the purposes of receipt of proxy appointments (section 250BA).
- A proxy vote is valid even if the member dies, revokes the appointment or is mentally incapacitated or transfers the shares unless the company has written notice of the matter before the start or resumption of the meeting (section 250C(2)—replaceable rule).
- Section 251AA requires listed Australian companies to record in the minutes proxy voting details and disclose them to the ASX.
- Proxy solicitation is very common in North America and is increasingly used in Australia. CASAC considers that some regulation of this and disclosure of proxy voting details prior to and at the meeting may be necessary in Australia. The question of voting by institutional investors should be left to self-regulation and best practice. This view is increasingly difficult to justify.
- Recent research carried out by the Centre for Corporate Law and Securities Regulation and Corporate Governance International showed that proxy voting by institutional investors is much lower in Australia than in the USA and United Kingdom. The research also showed that a number of listed companies failed to comply adequately with the statutory disclosure requirements in section 251A of the Corporations Act.[16]

---

16   G. Stapledon, S. Easterbrook, P. Bennett and I. Ramsay, *Proxy Voting in Australia's Largest Companies*, Centre for Corporate Law and Securities Regulation, University of Melbourne and Corporate Governance International, Melbourne, 2000.

• IFSA Guideline 2 provides that investment managers should vote on all material issues at all Australian company meetings where they have the voting authority and responsibility to do so. This seems to be honoured in the breach by a number of institutional investors. The note states that institutions should support boards by positive use of their voting power unless they have good reason for doing otherwise. Where the board has received steady support in the past and it is withdrawn it should be a matter of concern for the board.

• In New Zealand paragraph 6 of the First Schedule to the *Companies Act 1993* provides:

1 A shareholder may exercise the right to vote either by being present in person or by proxy.

2 A proxy for a shareholder is entitled to attend and be heard at a meeting of shareholders as if the proxy were the shareholder.

3 A proxy must be appointed by notice in writing signed by the shareholder and the notice must state whether the appointment is for a particular meeting or a specified term not exceeding twelve months.

4 No proxy is effective in relation to a meeting unless a copy of the notice of appointment is produced before the start of the meeting.

5 The constitution of the company may provide that a proxy is not effective unless it is produced by a specified time before the start of a meeting if the time specified is not earlier than forty-eight hours before the start of the meeting.

Paragraph 7 sets out detailed rules for postal votes.

The board of directors in both countries are entitled to seek proxies and may circulate completed proxy forms but the power must be exercised in good faith in the best interests of the company.[17]

Corporate representatives

Section 250D provides for the appointment of an individual as a representative by a member who is a body corporate. The appointment may be a standing one. Under section 250D(4) unless otherwise specified in the appointment the representative may exercise all the powers that the body corporate could exercise at a meeting or in voting on a resolution.

Paragraph 10 of the First Schedule to the New Zealand *Companies Act 1993* contains a similar provision.

---

17 *Campbell v. AMP* (1906) 7SR (NSW) 99, Affirmed JCPC (1903) 24 TLR 623; Cf. *Capital Energy NL v. Stirling Resources NL* (1996) 20 ACSR 704. *Advance Bank Australia Ltd v. FAI Insurances Ltd* (1987) 12 ACLR 118, 136–7

Resolutions

Format of resolutions

IFSA Guideline 11–12.12.1 provides that separate issues should not be combined and presented as a single motion for shareholder vote and is aimed against bundling what are separate issues into a composite resolution.

Ordinary resolutions

These are not defined in section 9 of the Corporations Act but are defined in section 105(1) of the New Zealand *Companies Act 1993*.

They are passed by a simple majority of those present in person or by proxy and voting at the meeting for the resolutions.

Special resolutions

Section 9 of the Corporations Law defines a special resolution as one:

(i) of which notice as required in section 249L(c), has been given; and,
(ii) that has been passed by at least 75 per cent of the votes cast by members entitled to vote on the resolution.

Section 2 of the New Zealand Act defines it as a resolution approved by a majority of 75 per cent or, if a higher majority is required by the constitution, that higher majority, of the votes of those shareholders entitled to vote and voting on the question.

Members' rights to put resolutions

Under section 249N of the Corporations Act certain members may give notice to the company of a resolution that they propose to move at a general meeting. The members proposing the resolution must have at least 5 per cent of the votes that may be cast on the resolution or the notice of the resolution must be given by at least a hundred members who are entitled to vote at a general meeting. Regulations may prescribe a different number (section 249N(1A)). In addition, under section 249P the members can require the company to give all its members a statement dealing not only with the resolution but any other matter that may be properly considered at a general meeting. If the material is received in time the company bears the cost of distribution (249P(7)).

CASAC, which is heavily weighted towards representation of corporate interests, considered some curtailment of these rights. One way is to codify the common law relating to the board's power to deal with resolutions out of left field. Another way is to delete the hundred members alternative and possibly increase the percentage or specify a minimum value for holding. A third way is to follow US law and have some explicit grounds for exclusion. Whichever is favoured, some exclusion of defamatory, frivolous or vexatious material can be justified.

CASAC in Chapter 3 of its Final Report did not favour non-binding resolutions concerning corporate management such as are allowed in New Zealand. In New Zealand any shareholder can put forward proposals including resolutions under paragraph 9 of the First Schedule to the Companies Act 1993.

Minutes

A company must keep minute books in which it records within one month, proceedings and resolutions of meetings of directors and of the company's members. In addition resolutions passed by members or directors without a meeting and in the case of a proprietary company with only one director, the making of declarations by the director must also be recorded (section 251A(1)).

The company must ensure that the minutes of the meeting are signed within a reasonable time after the meeting by the chairperson of the meeting or the chairperson of the next meeting (section 251A(2)). The company must ensure that the minutes of the passing of a resolution without a meeting are signed by a director within a reasonable time after the resolution is passed (section 251A(3)). The director of a one-director company must sign the minutes within a reasonable time after the declaration has been made (section 251A(4)).

Normally, minute books must be kept at the registered office of the company or principal place of business (section 251A(5)) and a minute so recorded and signed is evidence of the proceeding, resolution or declaration to which it relates, unless the contrary is proved (section 251A(6)).

A company must ensure that minute books for its meetings of members and copies of resolutions passed without meetings are open for inspection by members free of charge. If a member asks in writing for a copy of the minutes or an extract, this must be provided within fourteen days (section 251B). IFSA Guideline 11–12.12.6 provide that a shareholder should be able to authorise an agent to inspect or obtain copies of the minutes. (See also section 247D, under which directors or a general meeting may authorise this (replaceable rule) and section 247A (court order).)

Listed companies incorporated in Australia must record in the minutes of a meeting the total number of proxy votes exercisable by all validly appointed proxies and how they were in fact exercised. This information must be supplied to the ASX (section 251AA).

Resolutions of proprietary companies without meetings

Section 249A deals with the passing of resolutions of proprietary companies without holding a general meeting. The procedure requires a document signed by all members of the company stating that they are in favour of the resolution set out in the document. When the last member signs the document, the resolution is said to be passed. It must be recorded in the minute book (section 251A(1)(c)). This procedure does not apply to a resolution under section 329 to remove an auditor.

Section 122 of the New Zealand Act provides for written resolutions in lieu of meetings for all companies if they are signed by not less than 75 per cent of the shareholders holding not less than 75 per cent of the votes entitled to be cast on the resolution.

Annual general meetings

The Cadbury Report said that too many AGMs represented an opportunity for shareholder communications that is wasted because shareholders do not make the most of them and in some cases, boards do not encourage them to do so.[18] The City of London/Industry Working Group chaired by Paul Myners in their report *Developing a Winning Partnership* said that virtually all of the participants in their consultation exercise viewed the AGM as presently constituted an expensive waste of time and money. Reference was made to poor attendance by institutional investors and proceedings being hijacked by special interest groups or individuals. The group favoured a revamping of the procedure to make the AGM more relevant. One of the suggestions was for questions to be submitted in advance for operational managers to make presentations. In the United Kingdom the matter is now the subject of consultation by the Company Law Review Steering Group.[19]

In Australia AGMs are now only required for public companies (section 250N(1)). The AGM must be held at least once in each calendar year and within five months after the end of the financial year (section 250N(2)). ASIC is given power to extend the period under section 250P.

The business to be transacted may include the following even if not listed in the notice of meeting:

(a) consideration of the accounts, directors' report and auditor's report (section 250R);
(b) election of directors;
(c) appointment and remuneration of the auditor.

In New Zealand annual general meetings are compulsory for all companies under section 120 of the *Companies Act 1993* unless they have passed a resolution in lieu under section 122(4). Section 120(1) provides:

> Subject to subsection 2 of this section [which refers to the first meeting of new companies], the board of a company must call an annual meeting of shareholders to be held—
>
> (a) Once in each calendar year; and
> (b) Not later than six months after the balance date of the company; and
> (c) Not later than fifteen months after the previous annual meeting.

---

18 Report of the Committee on the Financial Aspects of Corporate Governance, Gee, London, 1992, para. 6.7.

19 *Company General Meetings and Shareholder Communication*, DTI, London, October 1999.

In Australia the members as a whole must be given a reasonable opportunity to ask questions or make comments on the management of the company (section 250S) and to ask questions of the auditor (section 250T). There is no legal obligation to answer the questions according to the *Explanatory Memorandum to the Company Law Review Bill 1997*.

This is to be contrasted with the more wide ranging provision for management review by shareholders by question, discussion, comment or resolution recognised by New Zealand law under section 109 and the right to put forward a shareholder proposal under paragraph 9 of the First Schedule to the *Companies Act 1993*. Again CASAC, whose membership is heavily weighted towards corporate interests, did not favour this kind of reform.[20] It thought that the AGM already provided an opportunity for shareholders to express their views in the form of questions or comments on the management. This seems somewhat unrealistic and is out of line with the North American approach to shareholder relations. On the other hand it seems to be supported by most of the submissions received.

Use of technology

Section 249S of the Corporations Act provides for the use of technology to hold meetings at two or more venues provided that the members as a whole have a reasonable opportunity to participate. Paragraph 3(b) of the First Schedule to the New Zealand *Companies Act 1993* is more specific. It provides that a meeting of shareholders may be held by means of audio, or audio and visual communication by which all shareholders participating and constituting a quorum, can simultaneously hear each other throughout the meeting.[21]

Procedural irregularities and the court's powers

In Australia the courts are given general powers to deal with procedural irregularities under section 1322 of the Corporations Act. Procedural irregularity includes the absence of a quorum, defects, irregularities or deficiency of notice or time (section 1322(1)(b)). This is not exhaustive (*Jordan v. Avram* (1998) 16 ACLC 867). Accidental irregularities do not necessarily invalidate meetings unless the court declares the proceedings at the meeting to be void under section 1322(3).

The basis of the court's power is set out in section 1322(6). The court shall not make an order unless it is satisfied:

(a) that the act was essentially of a procedural nature
(b) that the person or persons concerned acted honestly

---

20   CASAC, *op. cit.*, p. 37.
21   See *further* E. Boros, *The Online Corporation—Electronic Corporate Communications*, Discussion Paper, CCLSR, University of Melbourne, December 1999.

(c) that it is in the public interest that the order be made and

(d) no substantial injustice has been or is likely to be caused to any person.

'Substantial injustice' has been considered in a number of cases to mean any real prejudice.[22]

In New Zealand irregularities in notices of meeting can be waived under paragraph 2(3) of the First Schedule to the *Companies Act 1993*. Paragraph 2(3A) further provides that, subject to the constitution, the accidental omission to give notice of a meeting to, or failure to receive notice of a meeting by, a shareholder does not invalidate the proceedings at that meeting. There is no equivalent of section 1322 of the Corporations Act.

---

22   See *for example, Re Canberra Labor Club Ltd* (1987) 5 ACLC 84; *NRMA Ltd v. Gould* (1995) 13 ACLC 1518; *Jordan v. Avram* (1998) 16 ACLC 867.

CHAPTER 8

The Legal Role of the Board of Directors and Delegation and Reliance

The role of the board

The historic role of the modern board of directors was to manage. This was dealt with in the model regulations in Table A of the legislation. Now this has been amended to include the alternative of supervision or direction of management. Thus section 128(1) of the New Zealand *Companies Act 1993* provides that: 'The business and affairs of a company must be managed by, or under the direction or supervision of, the board of the company'. The new section 198A(1) of the Australian Corporations Act first enacted in 1998 provides: 'The business of a company is to be managed by or under the direction of the directors'. This is a replaceable rule. Section 198E sets out special rules for single director/shareholder companies where the single director can also exercise all the powers of the company.

Notice that neither section 128(1) nor section 198A uses the word 'monitor' although, as we shall see, that word appears in section 130(2)(b) of the New Zealand Act which deals with delegation and it was referred to by Justice Thomas in *Dairy Containers Ltd v. NZI Bank Ltd*[1] in 1995 as the 'primary duty' of the directors. It was also mentioned by Justice Rogers at first instance[2] and the majority of the New South Wales Court of Appeal in *Daniels v. Anderson*[3] when they referred to US case law. It does not appear in section 192 of the New Zealand Act or section 189 of the Corporations Act which deal with reliance.

The concept of monitoring appeared in the early 1998 draft of the Corporate Law Economic Reform Bill Clause 11 of the New Directors' Duties and Corporate Governance Provisions which was based on section 130 of the New Zealand Act. The wording

---

1   [1995] 2 NZLR 30, 79 l. 20–24.
2   (1992) 10 ACLC 933, 1012–3.
3   (1995) 13 ACLC 614, 662, 664.

met with some resistance from the Legal Committee of the Australian Institute of Company Directors who favoured the present wording of the draft, notwithstanding that the majority of the New South Wales Court of Appeal in *Daniels v. Anderson*[4] referred to the monitoring role of the board.

In fact the modern trend in the USA is increasingly to recognise the monitoring role of boards.[5] This was developed in the last two decades and influenced the *Revised Model Business Corporations Act* and the American Law Institute's *Principles of Corporate Governance.*[6]

An important practical question is whether such an obligation or indeed references to supervision predicate some information gathering or other monitoring device such as compliance systems. In *Graham v. Allis-Chalmers Manufacturing Co.*[7] the Delaware Supreme Court thought not but in 1996 the Delaware Chancellor in *Re Caremark International, Inc. Derivative Litigation*[8] disagreed. Times had changed and he said:

> Can it be said today that, absent some ground giving rise to suspicion of violation of law, that corporate directors have no duty to assure that a corporate information gathering and reporting system exists which represents a good faith attempt to provide senior management and the board with information respecting material acts, events or conditions within the corporation, including applicable statutes and regulations? I certainly do not believe so.
>
> Thus, I am of the view that a director's obligation includes a duty to attempt in good faith to assure that a corporate information and reporting system, which the board concludes is adequate, exists, and that failure to do so under some circumstances may, in theory at least, render a director liable for losses caused by non-compliance with applicable legal standards.

The efficacy of Chancellor Allen's dicta is potentially undermined by the technicalities of the Business Judgment Rule and its impact on derivative litigation in the USA. Professor Deborah DeMott[9] has written:

---

4   *ibid.*

5   See M. A. Eisenberg, *The Structure of the Corporation—A Legal Analysis*, Little Brown & Co., Boston, 1976, pp. 162 *et seq.* Professor Eisenberg, a strong advocate of this model, later became Chief Reporter of the ALI Principles of Corporate Governance project. See too D. Branson, *Corporate Governance*, The Michie Co., Charlottesville, 1993, ch. 5, 'The Monitoring Model for Publicly Held Corporations'. Both these works are a valuable source of thought and references on this topic.

6   For criticism of this aspect of the ALI's principles see W. J. Carney, 'The Monitoring Board, Duties of Care and the Business Judgment Rule', in P. D. Mink (ed.), *The American Law Institute and Corporate Governance—An Analysis and Critique*, National Legal Centre for the Public Interest, Washington, DC, 1987, p. 111.

7   186 A2d 125, 129 (Del 1963).

8   1996 WL 549894 slip op at 9–13 (Del Ch 1996). See too *Miller v. Schreyer*, 683 NYS 2d 51, 55 (AD 1999). See too Norman Veasey CJ, in 'The Defining Tension in Corporate Governance in America', in I. M. Ramsay (ed.), *Corporate Governance and the Duties of Directors*, Centre for Corporate Law and Securities Regulation, University of Melbourne, 1997, pp. 16, 18 20.

9   'Organisational Incentives to Care About the Law' (1997) 60 *Law and Contemporary Problems* 39, 66; cf. Branson, *op. cit.*, 1999 Cumulative Supplement, pp. 30–1 and other materials cited.

The pitfall of a duty to monitor that is largely aspirational is that the duty is likely to be taken seriously by directors who are suitably receptive to advice about their duties, but less likely to be taken seriously by directors who are not so inclined.

Compliance programs have been developed in Australia in such areas as trade practices law.

Delegation and reliance[10]

The New Zealand Companies Acts 1955 and 1993 were the first to contain express provisions on delegation and reliance.

Thus section 130 of the 1993 Act which deals with delegation provides:

1 Power to delegate

Subject to any restrictions in the constitution of the company, the board of a company may delegate to a committee of directors, a director or employee of the company, or any other person, any one or more of its powers other than its powers under any of the sections of this Act set out in the Second Schedule to this Act.

2 Board's responsibility

A board that delegates a power under subsection 1 of this section is responsible for the exercise of the power by the delegate as if the power had been exercised by the board, unless the board:

(a) Believed on reasonable grounds at all times before the exercise of the power that the delegate would exercise the power in conformity with the duties imposed on directors of the company by this Act and the company's constitution; and

(b) Has monitored, by means of reasonable methods properly used, the exercise of the power by the delegate.

The interesting things to note about this section are:

1   Only certain powers are delegable. Those that cannot be delegated are set out in the Second Schedule. This is an odd list, largely concerned with share capital.

2   The reference to 'subject to any restrictions in the constitution of the company' in section 130(1) envisages the possibility of curtailment of the power to delegate in the constitution.

3   The fact that the board's responsibility continues unless (a) the board believed on reasonable grounds that the delegate would faithfully exercise the power and (b)

---

10   On this see A. Comerford and L. Law, 'Directors' Duty of Care and the Extent of "Reasonable" Reliance and Delegation' (1998) 16 C&SLJ 103. This deals with the earlier CLERP draft. The wording on delegation has changed in what is now sections 198D and 190 of the Corporations Act. For a useful earlier discussion see Justice Alex Chernov, 'The Role of Corporate Governance Practices in the Development of Legal Principles Relating to Directors', in Ramsay, *op. cit.* footnote 8 supra, ch. 3.

the board has 'monitored, by means of reasonable methods properly used', the exercise of the power. There is no reference to good faith, which appears in section 138(2) and the Australian sections on delegation and reliance.

Section 138 of the 1993 Act deals with reliance on information and advice. It provides:

1   Power to rely on certain persons

Subject to subsection (2) of this section, a director of a company, when exercising powers or performing duties as a director, may rely on reports, statements, and financial data and other information prepared or supplied, and on professional or expert advice given, by any of the following persons:

(a) An employee of the company whom the director believes on reasonable grounds to be reliable and competent in relation to the matters concerned;

(b) A professional adviser or expert in relation to matters which the director believes on reasonable grounds to be within the person's professional or expert competence;

(c) Any other director or committee of directors upon which the director did not serve in relation to matters within the director's or committee's designated authority.

2   Good faith, etc.

Subsection (1) of this section applies to a director only if the director:

(a) Acts in good faith; and

(b) Makes proper inquiry where the need for inquiry is indicated by the circumstances; and

(c) Has no knowledge that such reliance is unwarranted.

The Australian Corporations Act contains a rather stark delegation power in the replaceable rule in the new section 226D. This provides:

1   Delegation of powers

Unless the company's constitution provides otherwise, the directors of the company may delegate any of their powers to:

(a) a committee of directors; or

(b) a director; or

(c) an employee of the company; or

(d) any other person.

Delegation to a committee and to a managing director were formerly dealt with in regulations 76 and 81 of Table A. Delegation is also envisaged in the defence to a failure to prevent insolvent trading under section 588H(3) (information as to solvency from another person).

Sections 190 and 198 set out more explicit provisions on responsibility and reliance which have been influenced by sections 130 and 138 of the New Zealand Act.

Section 190 provides:

Responsibility for actions of delegate

1 If the directors delegate a power under section 198D, a director is responsible for the exercise of the power by the delegate as if the power had been exercised by the directors themselves.

2 A director is not responsible under subsection (1) if:

(a) the director believed on reasonable grounds at all times that the delegate would exercise the power in conformity with the duties imposed on directors of the company by this Act and the company's constitution (if any); and

(b) the director believed:

(i) on reasonable grounds; and

(ii) in good faith; and

(iii) after making proper inquiry if the circumstances indicated the need for inquiry;

that the delegate was reliable and competent in relation to the power delegated.

As can be seen section 190 does not specify which powers can be delegated and section 190 (2)(b) differs from section 130(2)(b) of the New Zealand Act and reflects the older case law. It also uses three tests—reasonable grounds, good faith and proper inquiry. While each of these is well known they are not free from doubt and it may create unnecessary complication by requiring directors to satisfy all three.[11] As we shall see the same tests apply in the case of reliance.

Section 189 deals with reliance on information and advice and provides as follows:

Reliance on information or advice provided by others

If:

(a) a director relies on information, or professional or expert advice, given or prepared by:

(i) an employee of the corporation whom the director believes on reasonable grounds to be reliable and competent in relation to the matters concerned; or

(ii) a professional adviser or expert in relation to matters that the director believes on reasonable grounds to be within the person's professional or expert competence; or

(iii) another director or officer in relation to matters within the director's or officer's authority; and

(b) the reliance was made:

(i) in good faith; and

(ii) after making an independent assessment of the information or advice, having regard to the director's knowledge of the corporation and the complexity of the structure and operations of the corporation; and

---

11 See Comerford and Law, *op. cit.,* p. 119.

(c) the reasonableness of the director's reliance on the information or advice arises in proceedings brought to determine whether a director has performed a duty under this Part or an equivalent general law duty;

the director's reliance on the information or advice is taken to be reasonable unless the contrary is proved.

Section 189 is very similar to but not identical with section 138 of the New Zealand Act. The wording of section 189(b)(ii) was changed by opposition amendment late in the day from the draft bill which read 'after making proper inquiry if the circumstances indicated the need for inquiry'. The new wording is more onerous and fundamentally inconsistent with how boards actually operate. Directors act as members of a collegiate body and rely on each other. They do not act as Lone Rangers. The wording is also inconsistent with section 190(2)(b)(iii), which retains the original wording. It is, however, more consistent with the idea of the monitoring role of the board as a whole and section 130(2) of the New Zealand Act, which as we have seen above provides for the responsibility of the board to monitor 'by means of reasonable methods properly used', the exercise of the power by the delegate. The criticism which has been made about the three separate tests in relation to section 190 also applies here. These two new sections appear to be of general effect and are not limited to section 180. They are thus relevant to compliance with the common law and equitable duties. At the time of writing, sections 181 and 189 have been referred to CASAC for consideration and advice.

CHAPTER 9

Definition of Director and Officer: Appointment, Retirement and Removal of Directors

Definition

In this chapter we are concerned with some basic rules about directors that are largely, but not exclusively, the subject of statutory rules. Section 9 of the Corporations Act sets out a dictionary of terms. These include 'director' and 'officer'.

Director

Section 9 provides

'**director**' of a company or other body means:
(a) a person who:
  (i) is appointed to the position of a director; or
  (ii) is appointed to the position of an alternate director and is acting in that capacity; regardless of the name that is given to their position; and
(b) unless the contrary intention appears, a person who is not validly appointed as a director if:
  (i) they act in position of a director; or
  (ii) the directors of the company or body are accustomed to act in accordance with the person's instructions or wishes.

Subparagraph (b)(ii) does not apply merely because the directors act on advice given by the person in the proper performance of functions attaching to the person's professional capacity, or the person's business relationship with the directors of the company or body.

The old wording which used to appear in section 60 was longer and more complicated.

There are a number of things to notice about this new wording. These are:

1   It applies to persons who are validly appointed directors or alternate directors.
2   It applies to persons who have not been validly appointed directors but who occupy or act in the position of a de facto director by whatever name called.
3   It covers shadow directors.
4   It excludes persons who merely act in a professional or business relationship to the company.

The old section 60(3) provided that where nobody has been appointed director it referred to the controllers or controlling shareholder. This has been dropped from the amendment by the *Corporate Law Economic Reform Program Act 1999*.

For what is a reasonably simple and clear statute the New Zealand Act contains a verbose definition of director in section 126. This is similar to the old section 60 but limits the extended definition to specific sections of the Act. These deal with the major directors' duties, setting aside transactions and charges and return of property (section 126(1)(b)). The section refers to 'directions or instructions'. Shareholders may be deemed directors (section 126(2) and (3)). Acting only in a professional capacity does not make a person a director. There is no reference to acting in a business relationship (section 126(4)).

Shadow directors[1]

Unlike the UK *Companies Act 1985*, the Corporations Act and the New Zealand Act do not use the term shadow director but nevertheless they recognise the concept. The wording of section 9(b) includes a person in accordance with whose directions other directors are accustomed to act. This refers to 'instructions or wishes'. The old wording referred to 'directions or instructions' and section 126 of the New Zealand Act still does. The old wording seems to involve an element of compulsion so that the recipient does not exercise any discretion in the decision making process. Nevertheless it seems that a formal direction or instruction need not always be shown.[2] Formal commands are not necessary. There must nevertheless be an intention to 'call the tune' and the directors must dance to it.[3] The directors must perform positive acts, not simply forebear to act or desist from acting.[4]

---

1   See M. Markovic, 'The Law of Shadow Directorships' (1996) 6 Aust Jnl of Corp Law 232; P. M. C. Koh, 'Shadow Director, Shadow Director, Who Art Thou?' (1996) 14 C&SLJ 240; M. D. Hobson, 'The Law of Shadow Directorships' (1998)10 Bond LR 184.
2   *ASC v. AS Nominees Ltd* (1995) 13 ACLC 1822, 1838. See now *Secretary of State for Trade and Industry v. Deverell* [2000] 2 All ER 365 (CA).
3   *Harris v. S* (1976) 2 ACLR 51, 64; *ASC v. AS Nominees Ltd*, supra.
4   *Harris v. S*, supra.

Next there is the impact on the board as a whole. It is not sufficient that a minority of the board follow the direction or instruction.[5]

The directors must be accustomed to act on the directions or instructions. This suggests a pattern of behaviour but not necessarily all-embracing directions.[6] Rather it only requires that as and when they are directed or instructed, they are accustomed so to act.[7]

The instructions must go beyond merely acting in a professional or business relationship in Australia. In New Zealand the section simply refers to acting in a professional capacity. Thus merely giving advice as a solicitor or accountant would not make one a shadow director. Neither would insisting on performance of a contract by the company in Australia. The position of the latter is less certain in New Zealand.

Where a bank was a shareholder which held 49.9 per cent of the voting shares of a company and had three out of seven of the directors as nominees this did not necessarily make the bank a shadow director.[8] However, where one company held 42 per cent, had nominated three out of the eleven directors and had management and financial control and imposed its own financial reporting system on another company this was sufficient to make the former a shadow director of the latter.[9]

Thus a body corporate, incapable of being *appointed* a director, can be deemed to be a director for these purposes.

The significance of being held to be a director under section 9 is that the Corporations Act applies to the person, with all its draconian consequences. In particular the civil penalty provisions will apply. There are also extensive disclosure obligations. Thus by a tortuous and technical path Australia has potentially imposed more severe penalties on controlling shareholders than US corporation laws which recognise fiduciary duties on controlling shareholders. The position is similar in New Zealand except that it does not have a civil penalty regime.

The new definition of officer

Section 9 of the Corporations Act now contains a new definition of 'officer'. This provides:

'officer' of a corporation means:

(a) a director or secretary of the corporation; or

(b) a person:

---

5   *Re Lo-Line Electric Motors* (1988) 4 BCC 415.

6   *ASC v. AS Nominees Ltd*, supra; *Secretary of State for Trade and Industry v. Deverell*, supra.

7   Cf. *Re Hydrodam (Corby) Ltd* [1994] 2 BCLC 180, 183; *ASC v. AS Nominees Ltd* (1995) 13 ACLC 1822, 1838.

8   *Kuwait Asia Bank v. National Mutual Life Nominees Ltd* [1991] 1 AC 187 (JCPC).

9   *Standard Chartered Bank v. Antico* (1995) 13 ACLC 1381.

(i) who makes, or participates in making, decisions that affect the whole, or a substantial part, of the business of the corporation; or

(ii) who has the capacity to affect significantly the corporation's financial standing; or

(iii) in accordance with whose instructions or wishes the directors of the corporation are accustomed to act (excluding advice given by the person in the proper performance functions attaching to the person's professional capacity or their business relationship with the directors or the corporation); or

(c) a receiver, or receiver and manager, of the property of the corporation; or

(d) an administrator of the corporation; or

(e) an administrator of a deed of company arrangement executed by the corporation; or

(f) a liquidator of the corporation; or

(g) a trustee or other person administering a compromise or arrangement made between the corporation and someone else.

The points to be noted here are:

1 It differs from the former wording in that it absorbs some of the definition of executive officer in section 9 which now disappears. This is in section 9 (b)(i) which is expanded by (ii) and (iii) and now introduces the concept of shadow officer as well as shadow director. Thus a person who is not appointed an officer but acts in the ways described will attract the full range of statutory duties.

2 It drops a reference to employees as such.

3 It now covers all receivers, receivers and managers, administrators and liquidators.

Appointment of directors

Section 201A of the Corporations Act provides that a proprietary company must have at least one director, a public company at least three. At least one proprietary company director must ordinarily reside in Australia and at least two in the case of a public company. Section 201B(1) states that only an individual who is at least eighteen may be appointed as a director. Thus a body corporate cannot be appointed a director.

To be appointed a director a person must:

(a) be an individual

(b) be at least eighteen years old and in the case of a public company or its subsidiaries not over seventy-two unless section 201C is complied with

(c) not be disqualified

(d) consent in writing.

Section 201F(2) provides for appointment of a new director on the death, mental incapacity or bankruptcy of a single director/shareholder of a proprietary company.

Power to appoint directors vests in the company under section 201G and the board under section 210H(1). Both are replaceable rules. In the case of appointments by the board they must be later confirmed by the general meeting (sections 201H(2) and (3)).

Appointment of directors of a public company must be voted on individually unless the general meeting has resolved otherwise and no votes were cast against the resolution (section 201E).

Section 201K provides for the appointment of alternate directors. This is a replaceable rule.

Acts of a director are valid notwithstanding a defect in their appointment (section 201M).

New Zealand companies must have at least one director (section 150). Appointment procedures are similar to the above. (See sections 150–155.)

Vacation of office by and disqualification of directors

The office of director is vacated by:

(a) resignation
(b) removal
(c) death
(d) disqualification

A director is automatically disqualified if:

(a) they become an undischarged bankrupt or have executed a deed of arrangement or composition with creditors which have not been fully complied with (sections 206B(3) and (4)).
(b) they are convicted of an offence mentioned in section 206B
(c) they become subject to a disqualification order under Part 2D.6
(d) they become subject to a civil penalty disqualification (section 206C(1)).

In New Zealand section 157 deals with vacation of office and resignation and section 151(2) with disqualification. These are similar to the above except that there is no civil penalty regime in New Zealand.

We deal with disqualification in detail in Chapter 20.

Removal from office of directors

Section 203D sets out a procedure for a public company to remove a director by ordinary resolution in general meeting of which special notice has been given.

Notice of an intention to move the resolution must be given to the company at least two months before the meeting (section 203D(2)).

A copy of the notice must be sent to the director, who must be given the right to be heard at the meeting, irrespective of whether they are a member (section 203D(3)). The director can also require copies of their representations to be circulated to every member (section 203D(4)).

The wording of section 203D appears to assume a meeting requisitioned by members rather than being called by the other directors. It is not happily worded.[10] The statutory procedure and the constitution are concurrent and alternative procedures with the result that if one is followed the other is not relevant.[11]

Removal is without prejudice to any claim for damages for breach of contract.[12]

It is possible to remove the whole board under section 203D.[13]

Section 203C provides a replaceable rule for proprietary companies which states that the company:

(a) may by resolution remove a director from office; and

(b) may by resolution appoint another person as a director instead.

This is a much simpler procedure.

Section 156 of the New Zealand Act simply states that subject to the constitution, a director may be removed by ordinary resolution passed at a meeting called for the purpose or for purposes that include removal of the director. The notice of meeting must state the purpose is to remove the director. There is now no provision for special notice or written representations by the director. However, it should be noted that the constitution may restrict and even exclude the right. This seems undesirable in principle.[14]

---

10   *Dick v Comvergent Telecommunications Ltd* (2000) 34 ACSR 86, 90.
11   *Link Agricultural Pty Ltd v Shanahan* (1998) 28 ACSR 498, 516 et seq.
12   *Carrier Australasia Ltd v. Hunt* (1939) 61 CLR 534; *Southern Foundries Ltd v. Shirlaw* [1940] AC 701
13   *Claremount Petroleum NL v. Indosuez Nominees Pty Ltd* (1986) 4 ACLC 315.
14   See *Bushell v. Faith* [1970] 2 WLR 272 (HL).

CHAPTER 10

Duties of Directors and Officers: Overview

The overall scheme

Figure 10.1 shows how the duties of directors arise under the general law in Australia and New Zealand.

From Figure 10.1 it can be seen that the general law basically subdivides into the fiduciary duties of loyalty and good faith on the one hand and the non-fiduciary duties of care, diligence and skill on the other.

Figure 10.2 shows how the general law and statute relate in Australia and Figure 10.3 shows the New Zealand position.

Apart from specific legislation, the statutory duties of directors and officers are contained in the Australian Corporations Act and the New Zealand *Companies Act 1993*.

The basic fiduciary duty is a duty to act bona fide for the good of the company. Closely linked with this is the duty to act for a proper purpose. In addition there is the duty not to fetter one's discretion and the duty to avoid conflict of interest or a conflict of duty and duty. These give rise to remedies available to the company under the general law.

In addition in Australia there is a separate remedial regime of civil and criminal penalties where ASIC has *locus standi*. These necessitate some duplication of the general law duties in Part 2D.1. Section 181 provides for a duty on directors and officers to act in good faith in the best interests of the corporation and for a proper purpose and sections 182 and 183 for duties on directors, other officers and employees to avoid improper use of information or position. These are supplemented by the disclosure provisions in sections 191–196.

The basic non-fiduciary duty is a duty of care, diligence and skill which is actionable by the company in equity and now at common law. In addition in Australia there is

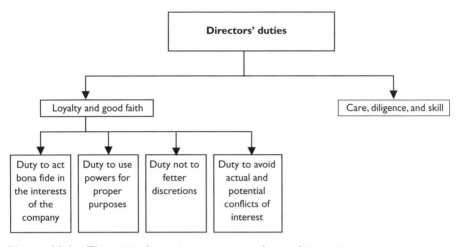

Figure 10.1 The original position at common law and in equity

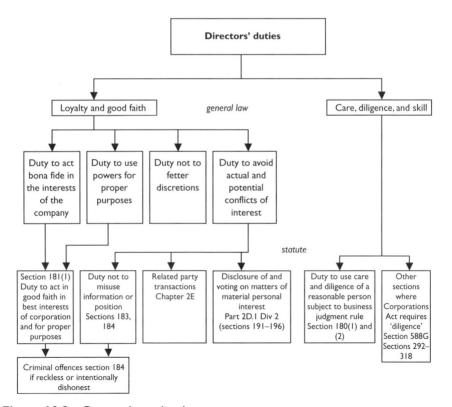

Figure 10.2 Current Australian law

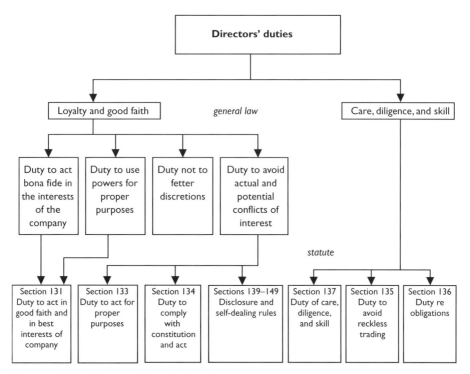

Figure 10.3 Current New Zealand law

the statutory duty of care and diligence but not skill under section 180 for the purposes of the civil remedy regime. These are subject to a Business Judgment Rule in section 180(2) but are supplemented by section 588G which imposes a duty to prevent insolvent trading, and other provisions which impose due diligence obligations. The latter fall outside the protection of the Business Judgment Rule.

New Zealand has the same general law remedies but the statutory duties are sometimes different and exist for a different purpose. The statutory duties are the duty on directors to act in good faith and in the best interests of the company (section 131), to exercise powers for a proper purpose (section 133), to comply with the Act and constitution (section 134), to avoid reckless trading (section 135), to avoid obligations which the company will be unable to perform (section 136), and a duty of care, diligence and skill (section 137). These are supplemented by the self-interested transaction rules in sections 139–149.

New Zealand has codified the general law remedies in Part IX but does not have a civil penalty regime and the relationship of the above sections to the general law is not completely clear. Presumably they codify and restate the law. As in the Canadian model which they follow, the position has not been made clear. [1]

---

1   See *Taurus Transport v Taylor* High Court, Napier CP33/99 22 May 2000, Master Thomson.

CHAPTER 11

The Basic Duties to Act in Good Faith and for a Proper Purpose

The duty to act bona fide for the good of the company and the duty to act for a proper purpose are basic fiduciary duties which are closely related and probably overlap.

The requirement of good faith is a fundamental principle of equitable jurisdiction although Australian and New Zealand law does not recognise a general duty to act in good faith in all situations. It is recognised here because directors and senior officers are fiduciaries. Nevertheless recognition is one thing, proof is another.

A medieval judge, Brian CJ, once said, 'it is common knowledge that the intention of a man will not be investigated for the Devil does not know man's intention'.[1] An analysis of object, view or purpose of a person or body of persons necessarily opens up the possibility of an almost infinite analysis of the fears and desires, proximate and remote, which form the compound motives usually animating human behaviour.[2]

The powers of directors are necessarily more complex than for example a special power of appointment. They are also exercised in a business situation which is often fast moving.[3] The courts must, therefore, take a more robust line and tend to approach the matter in the negative in practice, outlawing conduct in bad faith and for an improper purpose, rather than seeking to impose an optimal obligation.[4]

---

1   YB 17 Ed IV, of 2 (1477).
2   See Dixon J in *Mills v. Mills* (1938) 60 CLR 150, 185.
3   See J. H. Farrar, 'Abuse of Power by Directors' [1974] CLJ 221.
4   However, compare Perry J in *State of South Australia v. Marcus Clark* (1996) 14 ACLC 1019, 1042–3 which shows some confusion over the issue of whether the absence of good faith is the same as bad faith. Bad faith is clear evidence of the absence of good faith but good faith can be absent in cases where there is honesty and no bad faith. The relationship is thus ultimately not one of a simple dichotomy. See also *Mills v. Mills* (1938) 60 CLR 150; *Howard Smith Ltd v. Ampol Petroleum Ltd* [1974] AC 821

Scope of the duty to act in good faith

The first duty was stated by Chief Justice Latham in the High Court case of *Mills v. Mills*[5] when he said:

> It is clear that, if it established that the directors did not act bona fide in the interests of the company, the court in a properly constituted action will set aside their resolution. Thus, if directors issue shares only for the purpose of conserving their own power, the resolution creating the shares will be set aside or an injunction will be granted to prevent the holding of a proposed meeting … But before the exercise of a discretionary power by directors will be interfered with by the court it must be proved by the complaining party that they have acted from an improper motive or arbitrarily and capriciously …

Directors are often shareholders. Does this stop them from ever considering their own interests as shareholders? The answer is no. Chief Justice Latham explained the matter as follows:[6]

> It must … be recognised that as a general rule, though not invariably, directors have an interest as shareholders in the company of which they are directors. Most sets of articles of association actually require the directors to have such an interest, and it is generally desired by shareholders that directors should have a substantial interest in the company so that their interests may be identified with those of the shareholders of the company. Ordinarily, therefore, in promoting the interests of the company, a director will also promote his own interests. I do not read the general phrases which are to be found in the authorities with reference to the obligations of directors to act solely in the interests of the company as meaning that they are prohibited from acting in any matter where their own interests are affected by what they do in their capacity as directors.

This shows a refreshing degree of pragmatism but probably only applies where there is a coincidence of interest between the company and its directors. Where there is a conflict of interest the rule is strict.[7]

Apart from this, the courts are reluctant to second guess honest business judgment. As Barwick CJ, McTiernan J and Kitto J said in their joint judgment in 1968:[8]

> Directors in whom are vested the right and the duty of deciding where the company's interests lie and how they are to be served may be concerned with a wide range of

---

5   (1938) 60 CLR 150, 162–3. For a useful discussion see Chief Justice David Malcolm, 'Directors' Duties: The Governing Principles', in I. M. Ramsay (ed.), *Corporate Governance and the Duties of Directors*, Centre for Corporate Law and Securities Regulation, University of Melbourne, 1997, ch. 5.
6   (1938) 60 CLR 150, at 163.
7   *Howard Smith Ltd v. Ampol Petroleum Ltd* [1974] AC 821.
8   *Harlowes Nominees Pty Ltd v. Woodside (Lakes Entrance) Oil Co* (1968) 121 CLR 483 at 493D–E.

practical considerations, and their judgment, if exercised in good faith and not for irrelevant purposes, is not open to review in the courts.

To this can now be added the protection of the Business Judgment Rule which we consider in Chapter 13.

The duty to act bona fide for the good of the company is sometimes thought to be axiomatic—the fundamental duty from which all other fiduciary duties of directors flow. In the New Zealand Law Commission there was originally a proposal to make it expressly the fundamental duty. The wording of clause 101 of the draft Bill read:

> The fundamental duty of every director of a company, when exercising powers or performing duties as a director, is to act in good faith and in a manner that he or she believes on reasonable grounds is in the best interests of the company.[9]

This designation as fundamental was dropped from what became section 131(1) of the *Companies Act 1993*.

The duty was transcribed into the Australian legislation originally in the *Victorian Companies Act 1958* as a duty to act honestly, which was far too reductionist and its meaning had to be interpreted by the courts as encompassing both duties in the context of a new criminal offence.[10]

Now section 181 provides that a director or other officer of a corporation must exercise their powers and discharge their duties:

(a) in good faith in the best interests of the corporation; and

(b) for a proper purpose.

This is substantially the same as sections 131(1) and 133 of the New Zealand Act except that section 131(1) reads 'in good faith and in what the director believes to be the best interests of the company'. The original wording of the Corporate Law Economic Reform Program Act 1999 (CLERP) read 'in good faith in what they believe to be the best interests of the corporation'.[11] It is arguable whether the new wording of section 181 is more objective and, together with the amendment to the reliance provision in section 189(b)(ii), may conflict with the Business Judgment Rule in section 180(2).

Section 181(1) is a civil penalty provision. As such it is supplemented by sections 182 which deals with improper use of position and section 183 which deals with improper use of information. These extend to officers and employees and section 182 also to the company secretary.

Section 184 makes these criminal offences if there is an extra element of recklessness or intentional dishonesty.

---

9   See Report No. 9 Company Law Reform and Restatement, p. 241
10 See *Byrne v. Baker* [1964] VR 443; *Marchesi v. Barnes* [1970] VR 434, 437; *Southern Resources Ltd v. Residues Treatment & Trading Co.* (1990) 3 ACSR 207. See CLERP Bill Explanatory Memorandum para. 6.77.
11 Clause 181(1)(a).

Section 187 relaxes the rules in respect of directors of wholly owned subsidiaries if:

(a) the constitution of the subsidiary authorises the director to act in the best interests of the subsidiary, and
(b) the director acts in the best interests of the holding company; and
(c) the subsidiary is not insolvent at the time the director acts and does not become insolvent because of the director's act.

The New Zealand Act section 131(3) and (4) also contains similar provisions in respect of not wholly owned subsidiaries and joint venture companies which do not appear in the Corporations Act. There is no reference to solvency in any of the New Zealand provisions but simply a general provision in section 135 to avoid reckless trading. New Zealand does not have a civil and criminal penalty regime.

Whose interests are to be considered?

In *Mills v. Mills*[12] Chief Justice Latham recognised the inability of the test to settle disputes between different classes or groups of shareholders. He said:

> Directors are required to act not only in matters which affect the relations of the company to persons who are not members of the company but also in relation to matters which affect the rights of shareholders *inter se*. Where there are preference and ordinary shares a particular decision may be of such a character that it must necessarily affect adversely the interests of one class of shareholders and benefit the interests of another class. In such a case it is difficult to apply the test of acting in the interests of the company. The question which arises is sometimes not a question of the interests of the company at all, but a question of what is fair as between different classes of shareholders.

He repeated this idea in *American Delicacy Co. Ltd v. Heath* (1939) 61 CLR 457.

Directors do not, however, normally owe duties to shareholders direct. Their duty is to the company in the absence of special facts giving rise to a fiduciary relationship with particular shareholders.[13] The company here means the shareholders as a general body, not the company as a firm.[14]

Where a company is insolvent or nearly insolvent the interests of creditors must be taken into consideration and given priority.[15]

---

12   (1938) 60 CLR 150.
13   *Coleman v. Myers* [1977] 2 NZLR 225; *Brunninghausen v. Glavanics* (1999) 17 ACLC 1247.
14   See J. H. Farrar and B. Hannigan, *Farrar's Company Law*, 4th edn, Butterworths, London, 1998, pp. 125 *et seq.*
15   See for example, *Walker v. Wimborne* (1976) 137 CLR 1, 6–7; *Nicholson v. Permakraft (NZ) Ltd* [1985] 1 NZLR 242; *Kinsela v. Russell Kinsela Pty Ltd* (1986) 10 ACLR 395.

This does not necessarily mean that the directors owe creditors a duty of care or fiduciary duty. Such duties are owed to the company.[16] Creditors, however, may have *locus standi* in Australia to apply for an injunction or damages under section 1324 of the Corporations Act.[17]

The duty to act for a proper purpose

This duty seems to have developed out of equitable supervision of the exercise of powers of appointment which are necessarily a simpler and more precise setting.[18] In the modern law it is similar to some principles in administrative law.[19]

The scope of this duty and its link with the duty to act bona fide for the good of the company was addressed by Justice Isaacs in the High Court in *Australian Metropolitan Life Assurance Co. Ltd v. Ure* (1923) 33 CLR 199 at 217 when he said of a power to refuse to register transfers 'although it is a power which necessarily involves some discretion, it must be exercised, as all such powers must be, bona fide, that is, *for the purpose for which it was conferred*, not arbitrarily or at the absolute will of the directors, but honestly in the interest of the shareholders as a whole'.

In *Howard Smith Ltd v. Ampol Petroleum Ltd*[20] Lord Wilberforce, speaking for the Judicial Committee of the Privy Council on appeal from New South Wales, made some useful remarks about proper purpose in terms of the parameter of the powers and the question of abuse of power by acts within the parameter but done for a collateral purpose. He said:[21]

> To define in advance exact limits beyond which directors must not pass is, in their Lordships' view, impossible. This clearly cannot be done by enumeration, since the variety of situations facing directors of different types of company in different situations cannot be anticipated. No more, in their Lordships' view, can this be done by the use of a phrase such as 'bona fide in the interest of the company as a whole', or 'for some corporate purpose'. Such phrases, if they do anything more than restate the general principle applicable to fiduciary powers, at best, serve negatively, to exclude from

16   For a useful analysis see Gummow J in *Re New World Alliance Pty Ltd; Sycotex Pty Ltd v. Baseler* (1994) 122 ALR 531 at 550; *Fitzroy Football Club Ltd v. Bondborough Pty Ltd & Ors* (1997) 15 ACLC 638; and the recent High Court decision in *Spies v. The Queen* [2000] 18 ACLC 727 per Gaudron, McHugh, Gummow and Hayne JJ.
17   *Allen v. Atalay* (1993) 11 ACSR 753.
18   See Dixon J in *Mills v. Mills* (1938) 60 CLR 150 at 185. As to the distinction between purpose and motive see *Hancock Prospect Pty Ltd v. Estate of Hancock* (1999) 17 ACLC 681, 693.
19   See generally Chief Justice David Malcolm in Ramsay, *op. cit.* footnote 5 supra; R. C. Nolan, 'The Proper Purpose Doctrine and Company Directors', in B. Rider (ed.), *The Realm of Company Law*, Kluwer Law, London, 1998, p. 1; S. Fridman, 'An Analysis of the Proper Purpose Rule' (1998) 10 Bond LR 164.
20   [1974] AC 821.
21   *ibid.*

the area of validity cases where the directors are acting sectionally, or partially, that is, improperly favouring one section of the shareholders against another.[22]

He said that it is necessary to start with a consideration of the power whose exercise is in question, in this case a power to issue shares. 'Having ascertained, on a fair view, the nature of this power, and having defined as can best be done in the light of modern conditions the, or some, limits within which it may be exercised, it is then necessary for the court, if a particular exercise of it is challenged, to examine the substantial purpose for which it was exercised, and to reach a conclusion whether that purpose was proper or not'. In doing so the courts will necessarily give credit to the bona fide opinion of the directors, if such is found to exist, and will respect their judgment as to matters of management; 'having done this, the ultimate conclusion has to be as to the side of a fairly broad line on which the case falls'.[23]

In that case the Judicial Committee of the Privy Council said that at the end of the day the question was what the dominant purpose or moving cause of the directors' decision was. In the later High Court case of *Whitehouse v. Carlton Hotel Pty Ltd*[24] this was followed but in the case of more than one dominant purpose the test was whether the power would not have been exercised in the particular way 'but for' the improper purpose.

Some commentators regard the proper purpose test as redundant and logically presupposed by the duty to act in good faith for the benefit of the company.[25] Although there is some overlap in the cases there is not complete identity. An attempt to omit it by the New Zealand Law Commission was defeated by the Justice Department.[26]

The cases deal with a number of powers but most controversy has arisen over the issue of shares as a takeover defence strategy. If the dominant or primary purpose is to retain control then this is an exercise of powers for an improper purpose. In the USA the courts do not apply this test but the Business Judgment Rule qualified by a proportionality test. In other words they leave it to the business judgment of directors if the conditions of the relief are available and the takeover defence is not disproportionate to the threat posed by the bid. It is arguable because of the reference to proper purpose in section 180(2) of the Corporations Act that Australian law will remain the same on this notwithstanding the adoption of a Business Judgment Rule. New Zealand has not adopted a Business Judgment Rule.

Difference in significance between the Australian and New Zealand sections

Whereas the general law is basically the same with the same remedial consequences the role of the statutory provisions is different. The Australian sections are simply there for

22   *ibid.* 825 C–E.
23   *ibid.* 835 F–H.
24   (1987) 162 CLR 285.
25   See for instance Fridman, *op. cit.*, but compare the vigorous defence of a separate rule by Nolan, *op. cit.*
26   See s. 133 of the *Companies Act 1993*.

the purposes of civil and criminal penalties. It is not completely clear whether the New Zealand provisions codify the common law and equity and what the consequence of this is. It seems that they do codify and occasionally reform and restate the case law. Thus the detailed rules on self-dealing have been reformed and restated as we shall see in the next chapter.

CHAPTER 12

The Duty to Avoid Self-dealing

The basic rule

The basic equitable rule is very strict. Directors must not enter into a contract with their company even though the terms are fair and reasonable. If they do the contract is voidable.[1]

Business people found this rule too strict and the practice developed in the nineteenth and early twentieth centuries of drafting articles which tempered the rigours of the law or even attempted to exclude the rule. A director was allowed to attend the board meeting and vote in many instances.[2]

The statutory regimes

Parliament in the United Kingdom stepped in and provided for a compulsory disclosure regime and introduced a criminal penalty for non-compliance. The old equitable rule survived in tandem with this provision.[3] This was followed in Australia and New Zealand.

In Australia the statutory disclosure regime only applied to proprietary companies between 1993 and 2000 but now there is a reinstatement of a common rule in section 191 which requires disclosure of material personal interest in matters that relate to the

---

1   *Aberdeen Railway Co. v. Blaikie* (1854) 1 Macq 461.
2   See P. Davies, *Gower's Principles of Modern Company Law*, 6th edn, Sweet & Maxwell, London, 1997, pp. 611–12. For a recent comparative study see D. A. DeMott, 'The Figure in the Landscape: A Comparative Sketch of Directors' Self-Interest Transactions' (1999) 62 *Law and Contemporary Problems* 243.
3   *Hely Hutchinson v. Brayhead Ltd* [1965] 1 QB 549.

affairs of the company. This is not limited to contracts. It does not apply to single-director companies. The wide definition of 'affairs' in section 53 does not apply to this section but section 191(2) sets out an extensive list of interests which do not require disclosure. The subsection is drafted in a verbose fashion but the main situations where a director need not give notice are where the interest:

(a) arises because the director is a member of the company and is held in common with other members;

(b) arises in relation to remuneration as a director; or

(c) relates to a contract which the company is proposing to enter into subject to approval by the members; or

(d) relates to an insurance contract which insures the director against liability incurred as an officer of the company (provided that the company or a related body corporate is not the insurer); or

(e) arises in a proprietary company and the other directors are fully aware of it; or

(f) has already been disclosed.[4]

Section 192 provides for directors to give a standing notice about an interest.

A key concept is materiality of the interest. This is something which raises a real sensible possibility of conflict.[5]

Section 193 makes it clear that sections 191 and 192 are in addition to the general law and any provisions in the constitution and do not derogate from them. Indeed the fiduciary obligation in the circumstances of a particular case may require proactive conduct which in its turn may give rise to a conflict of duty and duty where a person is an interlocking director.[6]

Section 140 of the New Zealand Act provides for disclosure of an interest in a transaction but there is no reference to the general law or the constitution.

There is an elaborate definition of interest in section 139. This provides that a director is only interested in a transaction to which the company is a party if:

(a) the director is a party to or may derive a material financial benefit from it;

(b) the director has a material financial interest in another party to the transaction; or

(c) the director is a director, officer or trustee of a party to or person who may derive a material financial benefit from the transaction; or

---

4   See P. Lipton and A. Herzberg, *Understanding Company Law*, 10th edn, LBC Information Services, Sydney, 2001, p. 335.

5   See *Boardman v. Phipps* [1967] AC 46 at 124 per Lord Upjohn. See also *Queensland Mines Ltd v. Hudson* (1978) 18 ALR 1; *Hospital Products Ltd v. United States Surgical Corp.* (1984) 156 CLR 41. As to the amount of detail of disclosure see Justice Santow in *Camelot Resources Ltd v. MacDonald* (1994) 14 ACSR 437.

6   See *Permanent Building Society v. Wheeler* (1994) 12 ACLC 674; *State of South Australia v. Marcus Clarke* (1996) 14 ACLC 1019; *Duke Group Ltd (in liq.) v. Pilmer* (1999) 17 ACLC 1329 reversed on other points by the High Court sub. no. *Pilmer v The Duke Group Ltd* [2001] HCA 31.

(d) the director is the parent, child, or spouse of a party to or person who may derive a material financial benefit from the transaction; or

(e) is otherwise directly or indirectly materially interested in the transaction.

Section 139A(2) provides that:

> For the purposes of the Act, a director of a company is not interested in a transaction to which the company is a party if the transaction comprises only the giving by the company of a security to a third party which has no connection with the director, at the request of the third party, in respect of a debt or obligation of the company for which the director or another person has personally assumed responsibility in whole or in part under a guarantee, indemnity, or by the deposit of a security.

As with the Corporations Act, a key concept is materiality of the interest.[7]

New Zealand law is relatively lax on self-interested transactions. Section 141 of the New Zealand Act provides a transaction with the company in which a director is interested can be avoided by the company before the expiration of three months after disclosure to all the shareholders. However, there can be no avoidance where the company receives fair value under the transaction (section 141(1) and (2)). Under section 141 (4) there is a presumption of fair value where the transaction is in the ordinary course of business and on usual terms and conditions.

Section 144 of the New Zealand Act allows a self-interested director to attend and vote.

The onus of proof of fair value is normally on the person seeking to validate the transaction and who knew of or ought to have known the director's interest at the time of the transaction (section 141(5)).

Bona fide purchasers of the property without notice are protected where the transaction is avoided (section 142).

The Australian procedures are now lenient for proprietary companies and stricter for public companies.

Section 194 of the Corporations Act sets out a replaceable rule dealing with voting and completion of transactions involving directors of proprietary companies. If there has been disclosure under section 191:

(a) the director may vote

(b) the transaction may proceed

(c) the director may retain benefits

(d) the company cannot avoid the transaction.

Section 195 provides for restrictions on voting in the case of directors of public companies. Such a director must not be present at the meeting or vote unless a majority of non-self-interested directors have resolved to allow the interested director to participate. In addition ASIC may allow it under section 195(3), and a general meeting under

---

7   See A. Beck et al. (ed.), *Morison's Company and Securities Law*, Butterworths, vol. 2, para. 24.23.

section 195(4) may likewise allow it where it is not possible to get a quorum of disinterested directors, and the director can attend and vote as a shareholder. The powers of ASIC to make specific declarations or class orders are dealt with in section 196 and are limited to the situation of the need for a quorum and the matter is urgent or there is some other compelling reason to deal with the matter at the board rather than in a general meeting. [8]

A contravention does not affect the validity of the transaction (section 195(5)).

The extension of the basic rule

The basic rule of the general law has been extended to cover directors making off with a corporate opportunity, that is, taking advantage of an opportunity of a contract which should have gone to the company.

The rationale of this rigour was explained by Justice Laskin in the Canadian Supreme Court case of *Canadian Aeroservices Ltd v. O'Malley*[9] where he said:

> What these decisions indicate is an updating of the equitable principle whose roots lie in the general standards that I have already mentioned, namely loyalty, good faith and avoidance of conflict of duty and self-interest. Strict application against directors and senior management officials is simply recognition of the degree of control which their positions give them in corporate operations, a control which rises above day (sic) accountability to shareholders and which comes under some scrutiny only at annual general or special meetings. It is a necessary supplement, in the public interest, of statutory regulation and accountability which themselves are, at one and the same time an acknowledgment of the importance of the corporation in the life of the community and of the need to compel obedience by it and by its promoters, directors and managers to norms of exemplary behaviour.

This approach has been followed in Australia and New Zealand and in Australia has been reinforced by statute in sections 182 and 183. These are civil penalty provisions but there is also the possibility of criminal liability under section 184(2) and (3) where the additional mental elements are present.

The extension of the basic rule can be justified on four different conceptual grounds:[10]

1   *Property in equity*
     The benefit of the contact has been held to belong in equity to the company.[11]

---

8   For more detailed discussion see J. H. Farrar, 'A Note on Dealing with Self-interested Transactions by Directors' (2000) 11 Bond LR 106.
9   (1974) 40 DLR (3d) 371 at 384.
10   For a useful general discussion see R. B. Austin, 'Fiduciary Accountability for Business Opportunities', in P. D. Finn (ed.), *Equity and Commercial Relationships*, LBC, Sydney, 1987, ch. 6.
11   *Cook v. Deeks* [1916] 1 AC 554.

2 *Strict approach based on trustee principles*

In the House of Lords case of *Regal (Hastings) Ltd v. Gulliver*[12] the trustee principle was applied and it was held that the directors were liable to account to the company for a secret profit made on a sale of the shares of a subsidiary which they had subscribed for because the company itself was unable to subscribe due to lack of funds. This provided an unmerited windfall gain to the purchaser of the shares in the company and its subsidiary.

3 *A more lenient approach based on full disclosure and consent*

Where directors have made full disclosure and the company has consented to the profit made by the director there will be no breach of duty.[13]

4 *Modern use of confidential information*

Modern cases tend also to plead confidential information since the courts have developed a number of principles regarding the granting of injunctions to restrain a breach.[14]

In Australia these case law rules are supplemented by sections 181, 182 and 183. Section 181, as we have seen, imposes a duty to act in good faith in the best interests of the company and for a proper purpose. Section 182 provides that a director, secretary, other officer or employee must not improperly use their position to (a) gain an advantage for themselves or someone else or (b) cause detriment to the corporation. Section 183 provides that such persons must not improperly use information gained in that capacity to (a) gain and advantage for themselves or someone else or (b) cause detriment to the corporation.[15]

Sections 182 and 183 overlap with section 181 and the general law but arguably go beyond the general law in that the officer can be liable for causing a detriment to the company without making a corresponding gain to himself or herself.[16] The information used need not necessarily be confidential information.[17] Also where there is a criminal intent or recklessness there can be an offence under section 184(1), (2) and (3).

---

12 [1942] 1 All ER 378.

13 *Peso Silver Mines Ltd v. Cropper* (1966) 58 DLR (2d) 1; *Queensland Mines Ltd v. Hudson* (1978) CLC 40–389 (PC).

14 *Pacifica Shipping Co. v. Anderson* [1986] 2 NZLR 328.

15 As to impropriety see *R v. Byrnes* (1995) 13 ACLC 1488; *R v. Cook* (1996) 14 ACLC 947. For its use in an insolvency see *Jeffree v. NCSC* (1989) 7 ACLC 556. On propriety see M. Whincop, 'Directors' Statutory Duties of Honesty and Propriety', in I. M. Ramsay, *Corporate Governance and the Duties of Directors*, Centre for Corporate Law and Securities Regulation, Melbourne, 1997, ch. 8.

16 The sections are to be given a purposive construction—*Chew v. R* (1992) 10 ACLC 816 and *R v. Donald* (1993) 11 ACLC 712.

17 The judiciary seem rather confused on this question. The better view is that of Justice Young in *Rosetex Co. Pty Ltd v. Licata* (1994) 12 ACLC 269, namely that the information is that of a type which equity would restrict the director from using for his personal profit. See also *McNamara v. Flavel* (1988) 6 ACLC 802 but cf. *Esme Pty Ltd v. Parker* [1972] WAR 52.

Nominee and interlocking directors[18]

Complicated questions can arise where people are appointed nominee or interlocking directors.

A nominee director is a person nominated by another person to be a director. Usually they will be appointed by the company itself. The process is thus:

Nominator

↓

Nominee

↓

Company

The nominee must always act for the good of the company[19] but the Australian and New Zealand case law is flexible about the practice provided that there is no actual conflict of interest.[20] These cases recognise the fact that people can be appointed to protect a commercial interest.

A nominator may possibly be regarded as a director under section 9 of the Corporations Act or section 126 of the New Zealand Act in appropriate circumstances.

An interlocking directorship is where the same person is director of two different companies. Thus A is director of X Ltd and Y Ltd (see Figure 12.1).

There is no problem unless X Ltd and Y Ltd have competing interests and there is actual conflict.[21] Here A is not so much in a conflict of interest situation as a conflict of duty situation since he owes duties to both companies.[22] In Australia one must also bear in mind sections 182 and 183.

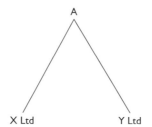

Figure 12.1   An interlocking directorship

---

18   For valuable discussion see Justice E. W. Thomas, 'The Role of Nominee Directors and the Liability of their Appointors', in Ramsay, *op. cit.*, ch. 9; R. Austin, 'Representatives and Fiduciary Responsibilities: Notes on Nominee Directorship and Like Arrangements' (1995) 7 Bond LR 19; CASAC, *Corporate Groups*, Final Report, 2000, Recommendations, pp. 5–8.

19   *Scottish Cooperative Wholesale Society Ltd v. Meyer* [1959] AC 324.

20   *Levin v. Clark* [1962] NSWR 686; *Re Broadcasting 2 GB Pty Ltd* [1964–65] NSWR 1648; *Berlei Hestia Ltd v. Fernyhough* [1980] 2 NZLR 150. However, there may be a conflict of duty and duty; see for instance *Duke Group Ltd (in liq.) v. Pilmer* (1999) 17 ACLC 1329, 1437; S. Seivers, 'Finding the Right Balance: The 2GB Case Revisited' (1993) 3 Aust Jnl of Corp Law 1,

21   *London and Mashonaland Co. v. New Mashonaland Exploration Co.* [1891] WN 165. See, however, R. Carroll, B. Stening and K. Stening, 'Interlocking Directorships and the Law in Australia' (1990) 8 C&SLJ 290.

22   *Duke Group Ltd (in liq.) v. Pilmer* (supra). Reversed on other points [2001] HCA 31.

Financial benefits to related parties[23]

In the late 1980s the stock market crash exposed a number of cases of self-dealing where the basic rules had been breached or circumvented using members of the family or related companies. The transactions included loans to directors, inter company loans, excessive remuneration and service charges and other uncommercial arrangements. As the evidence to the Australian House of Representatives Standing Committee on Legal and Constitutional Affairs in 1991 demonstrated in certain companies there had been 'significant transfers of wealth from shareholders to management'.[24] There had been a failure of the law to restrict and compel adequate disclosure in respect of self-interested deals between a company and parties related to companies.

The legislation prior to 1993 contained a section which merely prohibited loans to directors subject to certain exceptions. The new regime adopted in 1993, in what is now Chapter 2E, is limited to public companies and proprietary companies which are controlled entities of public companies. This was originally enacted as part of the *Corporate Law Reform Act 1992* and amended by the *Company Law Reform Act 1998* and the *Corporate Law Economic Reform Act 1999*. It came into force from 1 February 1994.

The aim is to protect creditors and minority shareholders.

The structure of Chapter 2E

The old structure was rational and was as follows:

Parts 2E.1 and 2 dealt with objects, structure and definition of key terms.
Part 2E.3 set out the basic prohibitions.
Part 2E.4 dealt with the general exceptions.
Part 2E.5 provided for shareholder approval.
Part 2E.6 dealt with enforcement.

Now this has been rewritten in the *Corporations Law Economic Reform Program Act 1999* in a less logical fashion as follows:

Section 207	Purpose
Sections 208–209	Need for member approval
Sections 210–216	Exceptions
Sections 217–227	Procedure for member approval
Section 228	Related parties

---

23 For a useful survey see I. M. Ramsay and G. Stapledon, *Directors' Conflicts: An Empirical Survey*, University of Melbourne Law School Public Law Research Paper No 04 (2000). The largest categories in director-related transactions were goods or services supplied by the director or a director-related entity. For a review of the United Kingdom provisions see the Law Commission's Report (Law Com No 261), *Company Directors: Regulating Conflicts of Interest and Formulating a Statement of Duties*, HMSO, London, 1999.

24 See *Report on Corporate Practices and the Right of Shareholders*, November 1991, AGPS, Canberra, para. 4.7.8.

Section 229   Giving a financial benefit

Section 230   General law duties still apply.

The style of the original provisions was postmodern and feminist with familiar examples.[25] All this has now disappeared.

The basic prohibition is that a *public company* or an *entity* controlled by a public company must not give a *financial benefit* to a *related party* (each of the italicised terms is defined) UNLESS:

(a) the transaction is properly disclosed and approved by the shareholders in general meeting; or

(b) the transaction is within one of the general exceptions.

The purpose of Chapter 2E

Section 207 sets out the purpose of the chapter. The rules are designed to protect the interests of a public company as a whole, by requiring member approval for giving financial benefits to related parties that could endanger those interests.

Key terms

The key terms are: public company, entity, controlling entity, control, related party and financial benefit.

Public company

Public company under section 9 basically means a company which is not a proprietary company and includes certain listed companies not formed under the Corporations Act.

Entity

Entity is defined in section 9 as any of the following:

(a) a body corporate

(b) a partnership

(c) an unincorporated body

(d) an individual

(e) for a trust that has only one trustee—the trustee

(f) for a trust that has more than one trustee—the trustees together.

There is now no longer any cross reference to the definition in accordance with AASB 1017.

---

25   For a valuable discussion of this see P. Hanrahan, 'Transactions with Related Parties by Public Companies and Their "Child Entities" under Pt 3.2A of the *Corporations Law*' (1994) 12 C&SLJ 138.

Control

Section 228 deals with related parties and a key definition is that of control. Control is now defined in section 50AA. This provides that an entity (A) controls a second entity (B) if A has the capacity to determine the outcome of decisions about B's financial and operating policies. The test is now less obviously based on personnel.

In determining whether A has this capacity:

(a) the practical influence that A can exert (rather than the rights it can enforce) is the issue to be considered; and

(b) any practice or pattern of behaviour affecting B's financial or operating policies is to be taken into account (even if it involves a breach of an agreement or a breach of trust) (section 50AA(2)).

A does not control B merely because A and a third entity (C) jointly have the capacity to determine the outcome or decisions about B's financial and operating policies (section 50AA(3)).

If A:

(a) has the capacity to influence decisions about B's financial and operating policies; and

(b) is under a legal obligation to exercise that capacity for the benefit of someone other than A's members;

A is taken not to control B (section 50AA(4)).

Related parties

Related parties are dealt with in section 228. Section 228(1) deals with controlling entities of a public company. These are related parties of the public company. Section 228(2) and (3) states that the following persons are also related parties:

(a) the directors

(b) directors or other persons of a controlling entity

(c) spouses and de facto spouses of the above

(d) relatives of the above in the sense of parents or children

(e) entities controlled by the related party unless it is also controlled by the public company

(f) entities acting in concert with the related party.

Financial benefit

The giving of a financial benefit is dealt with in section 229. Under section 229(1) in determining whether a financial benefit is given for the purposes of the chapter:

(a) one should give a broad interpretation to financial benefits being given, even if criminal or civil penalties may be involved; and

(b) the economic and commercial substance of conduct is to prevail over its legal form; and

(c) one should disregard any consideration that is or may be given for the benefit, even if the consideration is adequate.

Under section 229(2) 'Giving a financial benefit' includes the following

(a) giving a financial benefit indirectly, for example, through one or more interposed entities

(b) giving a financial benefit by making an informal agreement, oral agreement or an agreement that has no binding force

(c) giving a financial benefit that does not involve paying money (for example by conferring a financial advantage).

The following are examples of giving a financial benefit to a related party:

(a) giving or providing the related party finance or property

(b) buying an asset from or selling an asset to the related party

(c) leasing an asset from or to the related party

(d) supplying services to or receiving services from the related party

(e) issuing securities or changing an option to the related party

(f) taking up or releasing an obligation of the related party.

General exceptions[26]

There are seven general exceptions. These are:

1   indemnities, exceptions and insurance premiums or payments in respect of legal costs (section 212).

2   the payment of *reasonable remuneration* of officers (section 211).

3   financial benefits given on arm's length terms or less favourable than arm's length terms (section 210).

4   *advances* of less than $2000 to directors and spouses and de facto spouses of such directors (section 213).

5   financial benefits given within a *closely held group* (for example, a holding company/wholly owned subsidiary) (section 214).

6   financial benefits given to related parties *as members* of a public company, as long as the benefits are given on a non-discriminatory basis (for example, dividends, rights and bonus issues and other member-type privileges) (section 215).

7   financial benefits given under a *court order.*

Members' approval[27]

Even if the transaction is a financial benefit and falls outside the seven general exceptions it is possible to get shareholder approval in general meeting provided that the rigorous disclosure regime is followed and the special disinterested majority is obtained in the meeting. This is covered by sections 208–209 and 217–227.

---

26   Some of what follows is based on a seminar paper by Malleson Stephen Jaques, Brisbane 1993, adapted in the light of the recent changes.

27   Members' approval is also generally required for termination payments under Ch. 2D.2 Division 2.

Section 208 provides that a financial benefit may be given by a public company or child entity of the public company if:

(a) approval of the public company's members is obtained in accordance with sections 217–227;

(b) the benefit is given within fifteen months after the approval;

The mechanics of shareholder approval

1 A prohibited financial benefit may be given if three conditions are met:
   (a) a resolution of the public company must permit the giving of the benefit
   (b) the benefit must be given within fifteen months of the passing of the resolution
   (c) the prescribed disclosure conditions must be satisfied.
2 When a public company that is a controlled entity of another public company proposes to give a financial benefit to a related entity of the parent company, both public companies must comply with the approval provisions (it is not enough for the parent company to approve the giving of the benefit).
3 Approval is a six-stage process:
   (a) Prescribed documents must be lodged with ASIC at least fourteen days before the meeting.
   (b) Within fourteen days of lodgment ASIC may give written comments.
   (c) A notice of meeting must be given to the shareholders which must include the documents given to ASIC and no other documents.
   (d) A resolution in the same terms as that given to ASIC must be passed by a majority of disinterested shareholders.
   (e) Notice that the resolution has been passed must be lodged with AISC within fourteen days of it being passed.
   (f) If a poll is demanded, detailed records of the manner in which each shareholder voted must be made and kept for seven years.
4 The prescribed documents lodged with ASIC include:
   (a) the meeting notice and the text of the resolution
   (b) a proposed explanatory statement
   (c) other documents proposed to accompany the notice
   (d) any other documents from the company, a related party or an associate of either that can reasonably be expected to be material to a member in deciding how to vote.
5 The explanatory memorandum must set out:
   (a) the related parties who are the subject of the proposed benefit
   (b) the nature of the financial benefits
   (c) each director's recommendations and reasons
   (d) if a director was not available to consider the proposed resolution, reasons why not

(e) whether any director has an interest in the outcome of the proposed resolution and if so, the nature of the interest

(f) any other information that can reasonably be expected to be material to a member in deciding how to vote and is known to the company or to any of its directors (section 219(1)).

(g) in looking at the director's interest, opportunity costs, tax consequences, and benefits foregone need to be considered. (section 219(2)).

6   Restrictions on voting

(a) The following persons cannot vote on a proposed resolution:

(i)   a related party of the public company who will be receiving the benefit

(ii) an associate of such a related party (section 224(1)).

(b) The restriction does not prohibit the person voting as proxy for another as long as the proxy is appointed in writing and the proxy form specifies how the proxy is to vote (section 224(2)).

(c) Votes passed in contravention of this provision will not invalidate the resolution. The resolution will be taken to be passed if it would have been passed, disregarding the invalid votes (section 224(8)).

7   Substantial compliance—the court may declare compliance with the disclosure and meeting provisions where there has been substantial compliance (section 227).

Enforcement

Enforcement is dealt with in section 209.

A related party and any person who is involved in the contravention of section 208 by a public company or entity is liable to a civil penalty (sections 209(2) and (3) and 79). This does not include the public company or entity (section 209(1)(b)). The consequences are civil penalties up to $200 000, disqualification of directors or officers for up to five years and a possible liability for damages to a person who has suffered loss.

Criminal liability can ensue if the conduct is dishonest (section 209(3)).

New Zealand has no equivalent of these provisions. For the New Zealand rules on self-dealing see the earlier discussion under the Statutory Regimes at the beginning of this chapter.

CHAPTER 13

Duties of Care and Business Judgment[1]

Having a number of non-executive company directorships was once compared by Lord Boothby with having a nice warm bath.[2] It was not exactly an onerous activity. The law was prepared to tolerate a surprising amount of inactivity, absenteeism and incompetence. However, the modern tendency is the other way, towards greater business professionalism, more responsibilities, more matters to consider, more time demanded.

There are many reasons for this: monitoring by markets characterised by aggressive competition; adverse economic conditions; technological change; global financial markets with an array of sophisticated financing methods that often carry stings in their tails and the increasing activism of institutional investors.[3] To the rigours of monitoring by markets has been added the threat of potential takeover, the so-called market for corporate control.[4] In addition, the power of the regulatory regimes has been increased in recent years and ASIC and the courts have shown an increasing willingness in the post-crash period to police directors' misconduct. Thus, at a time when professions are becoming more like businesses, businesses are becoming more professional.[5] This is part of an increasing trend towards greater accountability, which even extends to

---

1   This is based to some extent on the Finlayson Lecture the author gave at the University of Adelaide in 1992.

2   Lord Boothby, a Conservative peer, was member of a number of boards in the United Kingdom. See R. Rhodes-James, *Bob Boothby—a Portrait*, Hodder & Stoughton, London, 1991.

3   See F. Hilmer and B. Tricker, 'An Effective Board', in A. Yeomans (ed.), *Company Directors' Manual*, Prentice Hall, Sydney, 1990, ch. 21, 2.2.

4   See, for example, H. Manne, 'Mergers and the Market for Corporate Control' (1965) 73 J Pol Econ 110; J. H. Farrar, 'Ownership and Control of Listed Public Companies: Revising or Rejecting the Concept of Control' in B. Pettet (ed.), *Company Law in Change*, Sweet & Maxwell, London, 1987.

5   See C. W. Mills, *White Collar: The American Middle Classes*, Oxford University Press, Oxford, 1951. This was a theme of this book.

university professors; more is being expected, perhaps to an unrealistic degree and in a bureaucratic manner.

Risk-taking and directors' duties

In our enthusiasm for making company directors accountable, we must not lose sight of the significance of risk-taking in entrepreneurism and the innate diversity of business enterprise. Any attempt to professionalise business must take account of these factors.[6]

In the 1872 case of *Overend and Gurney Co. v. Gibb*, Lord Hatherley, the Lord Chancellor, stated:

> It would be extremely wrong to import into the consideration of the case of a person acting as a mercantile agent in the purchase of a business concern, those principles of extreme caution which might dictate the course of one who is not at all inclined to invest his property in any ventures of such a hazardous character … men were chosen by the company as their directors, to act on their behalf in the same manner as they would have acted on their own behalf as men of the world, and accustomed to business, and accustomed to speculation, and having a knowledge of business of this character.[7]

In other words, the basic test to be applied in corporations law is not that of the risk-averse person but that of the person of the world accustomed to business and in some cases accustomed to speculation. Neglect of this simple truth is the source of much error in the contemporary debate in many of the jurisdictions of the Commonwealth but not the USA. The difficult question is how to reconcile this test with ordinary concepts of fiduciary obligations and the duties of due care. The public issue is how to provide a balance between appropriate regulation and control on the one hand and the freedom necessary to permit the risk-taking and innovation needed for economic growth on the other.

New Zealand and Australia share the confused inheritance of UK law with regard to the duty and standard of care of company directors.[8] Historically the duty arose as an equitable duty which preceded the development of the modern law of negligence. Recently there has been a tendency to subsume it under common law negligence. Even now as we have seen there is lack of clarity in the legal conception of the role of the board of directors, a question which arguably logically precedes any discussion of duty of care. However, unlike the United Kingdom, both countries for different reasons and with different consequences have now opted for some clarification of the role of the board and the basic duties by statutory restatement and, in doing so, have considered the enactment of a US style of Business Judgment Rule which immunises directors from negligence liability for business decisions taken in good faith and without

---

6   See J. H. Farrar, *Report on Modernising Australian Corporations Law*, Australian Institute of Company Directors and the Business Council of Australia, August 1992.

7   (1872) LR 5 HL 480 at 495. See too *Daniels v Anderson* (1995) 13 ACLC 614 at 644–5.

self-interest.[9] Australia has now adopted its own version of the Business Judgment Rule. The structure of this chapter will be: first a review of the case law; second a discussion of the statutory provisions on care; and third a discussion of the Business Judgment Rule.

The case law

As a prelude to a discussion of the director's duties of care it is as well to bear in mind the admonition of Justice Isaacs and Justice Rich in the High Court of Australia case of *Gould v. The Mount Oxide Mines Ltd (in liq.)*[10] in 1916 when they said:

> No rule of universal application can be formulated as to a director's obligation in all circumstances. The extent of his duty must depend on the particular function he is performing, the circumstances of the specific case, and the terms on which he has undertaken to act as director.

An equitable duty

Both the duty and standard of care of directors were initially developed in equity, before the evolution of the modern tort of negligence. This is often forgotten. Although one does not wish to be obsessed with the peculiarities of UK legal history, the distinction may have continuing relevance as regards defences.[11] Added to this is the Australian complication of an attempt to state the duty in statutory form and to criminalise it and, then, recently, to decriminalise it but to impose upon the decriminalisation a level of criminality which has now been abolished. The result, like many aspects of Australian corporate law, is gratuitously complex. New Zealand law is a little simpler.

The *locus classicus* on the duty and standard of care has long been the judgment of Justice Romer in the English case of *Re City Equitable Fire Insurance Co. Ltd* in

---

8   This part is based to some extent on the author's article 'The Duty of Care of Company Directors in Australia and New Zealand' [1998] 6 Cant LR 228. For further reference see H. A. J. Ford, R. P. Austin and I. M. Ramsay, *Ford's Principles of Corporations Law*, 9th edn, Butterworths, Sydney, 1999, para. 8.330; S. Seivers, 'Farewell to the Sleeping Director' (1993) 21 *Australian Business Law Review* 111; J. H. Farrar, 'Corporate Governance, Business Judgment and the Professionalism of Directors (1993) 6 *Corporate and Business Law Journal* 1. As for New Zealand, see J. H. Farrar and M. Russell, *Company Law and Securities Regulation in New Zealand*, Butterworths, Wellington, 1985, p. 233 *et seq*.; D.O. Jones, *Company Law in New Zealand: A Guide to the Companies Act*, Butterworths, Wellington, 1993, p. 108 *et seq*.; The Hon Justice Tompkins, 'Directing the Directors: The Duties of Directors under the *Companies Act 1993*' (1995) 2 *Waikato Law Review* 13. See also *CCH New Zealand Company Law and Practice Commentary*, vol. 1 at para. 10-835. For a useful review of English law, see V. Finch, 'Company Directors: Who Cares About Skill and Care?' (1992) 55 *Modern Law Review* 179.

9   See J. H. Farrar, 'Corporate Governance, Business Judgment and the Professionalism of Directors' (1993) 6 *Corporate and Business Law Journal* 1.

10   (1916) 22 CLR 490 at 531.

11   For example, laches (equitable delay), acquiescence, 'clean hands' and possibly contributory negligence.

1925.[12] This predates *Donoghue v. Stevenson*.[13] *Re City Equitable* was a long judgment involving a case of investigation of fraud in the winding up of an insurance company. The company had been defrauded by its managing director, Bevan, who was convicted and sentenced. A misfeasance summons was brought by the liquidator to make the other directors liable for negligence in respect of losses occasioned by investments, loans and the payment of dividends out of capital. Justice Romer found that the directors were guilty of negligence but were exonerated by a provision in the articles in the absence of 'wilful neglect or default'. Such clauses have since been outlawed. Justice Romer laid down a number of propositions of law which were accepted by the Court of Appeal and later followed but which have increasingly been called into question.

Proposition 1

'In discharging the duties of his position … a director must, of course, act honestly; but he must also exercise some degree of both skill and diligence.'[14]

The precise meaning of honesty gave rise to problems in the Australian legislation but we will pass over that now and concentrate on the duty of care.[15]

In *Re Brazilian Rubber Plantations and Estates Ltd*, Justice Neville said of a director of a rubber company:

> He is not, I think, bound to take any definite part in the conduct of the company's business, but so far as he does undertake it he must use reasonable care in its dispatch. Such reasonable care must, I think, be measured by the care an ordinary man might be expected to take in the same circumstances on his own behalf.[16]

This seems to lay down an objective test for the standard of care but there is no reference to risk. It is clear from the other three propositions laid down by Justice Romer that some characteristics of the particular director could be taken into account. Note also the equivocation between care, skill and diligence in the judicial usage.

Proposition 2

A director need not exhibit in the performance of his duties a greater degree of skill than may reasonably be expected from a person of his knowledge and experience. A director of a life insurance company, for instance, does not guarantee that he has the

---

12 [1925] Ch 407 (at first instance, affirmed on appeal). However, for an earlier more objective appraisal in the High Court of Australia see Isaacs and Rich JJ in *Gould v. The Mount Oxide Mines Ltd (in liq.)* (1916) 22 CLR 490 at 529. See Sievers, 'Farewell to the Sleeping Director—The Modern Judicial and Legislative Approach to Directors' Duties of Care, Skill and Diligence' (1993) 21 ABLR 111.

13 [1932] AC 562.

14 *Re City Equitable* at 427.

15 For a full discussion, see B. Fisse, 'The Criminal Liability of Directors: Honesty and Dishonesty and Law and Corporate Law Reform' (1992) 2 *Journal of Banking and Finance Law and Practice* 151.

16 [1911] 1 Ch 425 at 437.

skill of an actuary or a physician ... [D]irectors are not liable for mere errors of judgment.[17]

It is difficult, if not impossible, to formulate a single objective duty of skill for company directors as there is no common body of knowledge shared by company directors. It is difficult to regard company directorships as a separate calling.

One final point on the question of skill. A director acts as a member of a group, the board. What is required is not so much a skilful director as a skilful board. Different members may be chosen for different skills and, in some cases, their personal qualities of integrity, common sense and judgment, which are not skills as such.

Proposition 3

A director is not bound to give continuous attention to the affairs of his company. His duties are of intermittent nature to be performed at periodical board meetings, and of meetings of any committee of the board upon which he happens to be placed. He is not, however, bound to attend all such meetings, though he ought to attend whenever, in the circumstances, he is reasonably able to do so.[18]

Although this proposition indicated a lax standard it did in fact tighten up existing law. Nevertheless the interpretation of what constitutes a reasonable excuse for non-attendance was quite liberal. Thus in *Re City Equitable* one of the directors had not attended board meetings for a number of years due to serious illness and another had attended only rarely because they lived and carried on business in Aberdeen. Yet Justice Romer held that they were not liable for breach of duty.

Proposition 4

'In respect of all duties that, having regard to the exigencies of business, and the articles of association, may properly be left to some other official, a director is in the absence of grounds for suspicion, justified in trusting that official to perform such duties honestly.'[19]

This is a maxim of common sense but the extent of delegation depended on the type of company and the nature of the business.[20] The extent of delegation had to be reasonable and there seem to be some duties which a director cannot delegate.[21]

A common law duty of care

The AWA case[22]

This case clearly recognised that common law negligence also applies to directors.

---

17 *Re City Equitable* at 428–9.
18 *Re City Equitable* [1925] Ch 407 at 429.
19 *Re City Equitable* [1925] Ch 407 at 429. See also *ASC v. Gallagher* (1993) 11 ACLC 286; 10 ACSR 43.
20 See *Re City Equitable* at 426–7. For a New Zealand discussion see *Jagwar Holdings Ltd v. Julian* (1992) 6 NZCLC 68 040 at 68 075ff.
21 *Drincqbier v. Wood* [1899] 1 Ch 393 at 406; *Re Majestic Recording Studios Ltd* [1987] BCLC 601.
22 *AWA Ltd v. Daniels* (1992) 10 ACLC 933; *Daniels v. Anderson* (1995) 13 ACLC 614.

The facts
In this leading Australian case, AWA Ltd, a listed company, engaged in foreign exchange dealings to hedge against risks of foreign currency fluctuations. These were managed by a young employee, Koval, who was inadequately supervised, and proper records were not kept. The company made heavy losses in 1986 and 1987 which Koval concealed. The company was audited twice by Deloitte Haskins and Sells, and the auditing partner warned the company of inadequacies in internal controls but failed to warn the board. Instead he wrote a letter suggesting improvements. The board did not become aware of the extent of the losses until the end of March 1987.

The company sued the auditors for negligence. The auditors counterclaimed for contributory negligence.

First instance decision[23]
Justice Rogers, Chief Judge of the Commercial Division of the Supreme Court of New South Wales, at first instance held that the auditors were negligent but that the company was also liable for contributory negligence.

He made some sensible remarks about the relationship between non-executive directors and executive directors and management. He then applied the *Re City Equitable* principles to the non-executive directors and delegation by the board but applied a more rigorous standard to Hawke, the chief executive officer.

The decision of Justice Rogers was well received by the business community. It was followed in later cases although criticised by the Royal Commission into the Tricontinental Group of Companies. The decision was subsequently appealed.

The NSW Court of Appeal Decision[24]
The majority of the Court of Appeal allowed the appeal of the chief executive officer and allowed the auditors' appeal in part and AWA's appeal in part.

The court held that the auditors were negligent and had failed to comply with the then Companies Code in respect of the foreign exchange operations.

The duties of the auditors and the AWA board and management had to be considered in the context of the duties owed by the others. Management was responsible for ensuring that adequate internal controls were put in place and operating. The duty of auditors was to report the absence of proper records and weaknesses in internal controls to management. In the absence of appropriate response by management, auditors should then report to the board.

While paying lip service to business judgment Justices Clark and Sheller held that the directors were negligent because:

1   The law had developed since *Re City Equitable.*
2   Directors are now required to take reasonable steps to place themselves in a position to guide and monitor the management of the company.

---

23   *AWA Ltd v. Daniels* (1992) 10 ACLC 933.
24   *Daniels v. Anderson* (1995) 13 ACLC 614. See R. Baxt, 'The Duty of Care of Directors—Does it Depend on the Swinging of the Pendulum?' Centre for Corporate Law and Securities Regulation, University of Melbourne, 1997, in I. Ramsay (ed.), *Corporate Governance and the Duties of Directors*, ch. 7.

3   The duty of care was not merely subjective, limited by the directors' knowledge and experience. Ignorance and inaction were no excuse.

4   Following US authorities, they held that while delegation was possible, the test of grounds for suspicion formulated in *Re City Equitable* and repeated by Chief Judge Rogers was too low. A director may not rely on the judgment of others especially when there is notice of mismanagement. Certainly, when an investment poses an obvious risk, a director cannot rely blindly on the judgment of others. The test was whether the director had actual or constructive knowledge of any facts which would awaken suspicion and put a prudent man on his guard. Directors must devote a sufficient amount of time and energy to oversee the company's affairs.

5   The directors were not only under an equitable and statutory duty of care. They were also under a common law duty of care, and were tortfeasors under section 5(1)(c) of the *NSW Law Reform (Miscellaneous Provisions) Act 1946*.

6   Executives and non-executive directors were under the same duty and standard of care.

The law of negligence can accommodate different degrees of duty owed by people with different skills but that does not mean that a director can safely proceed on the basis that ignorance and failure to inquire are a protection against liability for negligence.

Justice Powell[25] dissenting said that the duty of care was equitable and statutory and an insufficient case had been made out to extend common law negligence on the facts.

The decision of the majority thus overturned Justice Rogers' views on a number of important points affecting directors. Whereas Justice Rogers' judgment was practical and clearly expressed the majority judgment was somewhat academic and theoretical and not very clearly expressed in a number of crucial passages. Hence the confusion in the business community and an increased demand for the introduction of a Business Judgment Rule.

In particular the refusal of the majority in the Court of Appeal to see a distinction between executive and non-executive directors seems to ignore the significance of employment law[26] and the possible dangers of an overactive non-executive enclave on the board, substituting their judgment for that of management.

As the Supreme Court of Iowa said in *Rowen v. Le Mars Mutual Insurance Company of Iowa*[27] in 1979, one of the few cases anywhere which properly addresses the role of independent directors, outside directors should not take a position adversary to management and should not substitute their judgment for those in active control of decision making. At least until they have reason to suspect impropriety, they should be allowed within reasonable limits to rely on those who have primary responsibility for

---

25   (1995) 13 ACLC 743 *et seq.*

26   Under employment law there is an implied warranty of competence and skill by executives. See also the recent case of *Sheahan v Verco* (2001) 37 ACSR 117.

27   (1979) 282 NW 2d 639 at 653.

the corporate business. The balancing of these factors must be on a case to case basis, depending on the circumstances at the time the action is taken that is challenged.

The statutory duty of care in Australia

Section 180(1) of the Corporations Act imposes on the directors and other officers of corporations a statutory duty to exercise a reasonable degree of care and diligence. This provision had its origin in section 107 of the *Companies Act (Vic) 1958*. The original section provided that:

1   A director shall at all times act honestly and use reasonable diligence in the discharge of the duties of his office.
2   Any officer of a company shall not make use of information acquired by virtue of his position as an officer to gain an improper advantage for himself or to cause detriment to the company.
3   Any officer who commits a breach of the foregoing provisions of this section shall be guilty of an offence against this Act and shall be liable to a penalty of not more than £A500 and shall in addition be liable to the company for any profit made by him for any damage suffered by the company as a result of the breach of any such provisions.
4   Nothing in this section shall prejudice the operation of any other enactment or rule of law relating to the duty or liability of directors or officers of the company.

The Victorian provision was the model for the uniform companies legislation of 1961 and those provisions, as supplemented by subsequent amending legislation, are now restated in section 180(1) of the Corporations Act. It is interesting, therefore, to see the paucity of debate which led to their adoption in the first place in the Victorian legislation.

It was thought at the time that the two provisions merely reflected the scope of the case law and that their reduction to statutory form would serve an educative function. There seems to have been no real debate as to the criminal aspects of the provision, nor adequate debate on the section as a whole. It should be noted that the duty of care provision originally only applied to directors whereas the improper advantage provision applied to officers in general.

The provisions seem to have been inadequately thought out from their inception and the attribution of criminal liability, for what in other jurisdictions is a civil matter, was arguably misguided.

Although it is clear that section 107 of the *Companies Act (Vic) 1958* intended to impose an objective test, the Full Court of the Supreme Court of Victoria applied something of a subjective test in *Byrne v. Baker*.[28] The court noted the omission of the word

---

28   [1964] VR 443.

'skill'; that the legislature demanded diligence only; that the degree of the diligence demanded was what was reasonable in the circumstances and no more. The test to be applied is what could reasonably be expected of that director in the circumstances. This measure of subjectivity has been subject to increasing criticism.

In the light of the general comments made in the insolvent trading cases and the decision of Justice Rogers at first instance in *AWA Ltd v. Daniels*,[29] the section was amended in 1992.

The new wording of what was then section 232(4) of the Corporations Act read as follows:

> In the exercise of his or her powers and the discharge of his or her duties, an officer of a corporation must exercise the degree of care and diligence that a reasonable person in a like position in a corporation would exercise in the corporation's circumstances.

The objective standard and the circumstances of the case

The Explanatory Memorandum stated[30] that the government considered that the new section 232(4) did not change the law but merely confirmed the present position expounded in recent decisions such as *Hussein v. Good*,[31] *Heide Pty Ltd v. Lester*,[32] *Statewide Tobacco Services Ltd v. Morley*,[33] *Commonwealth Bank of Australia v. Friedrich*[34] and *AWA Ltd v. Daniels*.[35] The reference to 'reasonable person' was intended to confirm that the required standard of care and diligence was to be determined objectively.

The wording was similar to that of paragraph 8.30(a)(2) of the *Model Business Corporation Act* (USA) which refers to 'the care an ordinarily prudent person in a like position would exercise under similar circumstances'. The commentary to the *Model Business Corporation Act* (USA) states that the phrase 'in a like position' recognises that the care under consideration is that which would be shown by the ordinarily prudent person if they were a director of the particular corporation. The combined phrase 'in a like position ... under similar circumstances' is intended to recognise: that the nature and extent of responsibilities will vary, depending upon such factors as the size, complexity, urgency, and location of activities carried on by the particular corporation; that decisions must be made on the basis of the information known to the directors without the benefit of hindsight; and that the special background, qualifications and manage-

---

29   (1992) 10 ACLC 933.
30   Corporate Law Reform Bill 1992 (Cth) Explanatory Memorandum para. 83.
31   (1990) 8 ACLC 390; 1 ACSR 710.
32   (1990) 8 ACLC 958; 3 ACSR 159.
33   (1990) 8 ACLC 827; 2 ACSR 405.
34   (1991) 8 ACLC 946; 5 ACSR 115.
35   (1992) 10 ACLC 933; 7 ACSR 463.

ment responsibilities of a particular director may be relevant in evaluating his compliance with the standard of care.

Even though the phrase takes into account the special background, qualifications and management responsibilities of a particular director, it does not excuse a director lacking business experience or particular expertise from exercising the common sense, practical wisdom, and informed judgment of an ordinary prudent person. The Explanatory Memorandum stated that Australian law recognised that the special background, qualifications and management responsibilities of the particular officer may be relevant in evaluating their compliance with the standard of care. At the same time, Australian law also recognised that decisions must be made on the basis of the circumstances at the time and without the benefit of hindsight. This mirrored the US commentary. Similarly the Explanatory Memorandum stated that the new subsection recognised that what constitutes the proper performance of the duties of a director of a particular corporation will be influenced by matters such as the state of the corporation's financial affairs, the size and nature of the corporation, the urgency and magnitude of any problem, the provisions of the corporation's constitution and the composition of its board.[36]

Duty, risk and business judgment

The Explanatory Memorandum stated that in the case of a business corporation, the standard reflected the fact that corporate decisions involve risk-taking.[37] In the *Report on Modernising Australian Corporations Law*, prepared by the author for the Business Council of Australia and the Australian Institute of Directors in 1992, the significance of risk-taking in entrepreneurism and the diversity of business enterprise was emphasised. The government gave some recognition to these facts. Reference was made to the fact that directors or officers are not liable for honest errors of judgment and that the courts have shown a reluctance to review business judgment made in good faith.[38] In addition the courts have exercised their discretion under section 1318 of the Corporations Act to excuse directors who have acted honestly and fairly. The government endorsed this approach and did not intend any change in the law by the revised wording of the section.[39] However, no attempt was made in the Bill to enact a US style of Business Judgment Rule. The reason given was that no State in the USA had adopted a legislative statement of the rule but left the matter to the courts to develop.[40] Similarly, the memorandum stated that the government considered that the development of such

---

36   Corporate Law Reform Bill 1992 (Cth) Explanatory Memorandum para. 86.
37   Para. 87.
38   Para. 87.
39   Para. 89.
40   For the need for caution in attempting such a legal transplant see DeMott, 'Directors' Duty of Care and the Business Judgment Rule: American Precedents and Australian Choices' (1993) 4 Bond LR 1.

principles in Australia was better left to the courts. The wording of the Explanatory Memorandum, although of dubious legal status in the absence of an ambiguity, seemed to provide some green light to the Australian courts to develop a case law equivalent of the Business Judgment Rule.

The wording of the section was further amended, this time in minor respects, by the *Corporate Law Economic Reform Program Act 1999.* It now reads:

Care and diligence—civil obligation only

180(1) Care and diligence—directors and other officers

A director or other officer of a corporation must exercise their powers and discharge their duties with the degree of care and diligence that a reasonable person would exercise if they:

(a) were a director or officer of a corporation in the corporation's circumstances; and

(b) occupied the office held by, and had the same responsibilities within the corporation as, the director or officer.

The Explanatory Memorandum paragraph 6.75 said that doubt had been expressed about whether the section enabled the courts to have regard for the circumstances of the particular officer as well as their position in the corporation. As someone who drafted the 1992 wording relying on the US precedent, the writer finds that doubt surprising.

Now section 180(1) is accompanied by section 180(2) which provides for a statutory Business Judgment Rule compliance with which satisfies the duties under section 180(1) and the general law. We shall return to this later.

Civil penalties

The other major amendment in 1992 was the introduction of civil penalty provisions. Section 180(1) is one of those provisions. While this leads to a measure of decriminalisation, its major impact on the duty of care is in fact to increase the consequences of a breach. A breach of the original section resulted in a maximum penalty of $5000 with a criminal standard of proof. Under the civil penalty provisions the maximum penalty increased to $200 000 with a civil standard of proof and, in addition, the court may disqualify an officer for acting as a director for such period as is set out in the order.[41] Prior to 2000, if the breach was committed with dishonest intent there could be a fine of up to $200 000 and/or imprisonment for a maximum period of five years. The Law Council of Australia, in its submissions to the Attorney-General on the reports of the Senate Standing Committee on Legal and Constitutional Affairs and the Companies and Securities Law Review Committee, advocated that the provision for payment of fines to the

---

41   See sections 1317E *et seq.* and 206C. As to the standard of proof see also Briginshaw v. Briginshaw (1938) 60 CLR 336 at 362–3.

Commonwealth for breaches of the duty of care should be withdrawn. The Australian Institute of Company Directors also opposed civil penalties and favoured more thorough decriminalisation. The thinking in the Attorney-General's Department, however, was that there should be a range of sanctions from civil liability through to civil penalty, conceived as equivalent to punitive damages, and then disqualification, and ultimately criminal penalties for dishonesty. The criminal penalty was intended to be dropped by the CLERP Act but despite the note to section 180(1), the wording of section 1311(5) still seems capable of catching it except that there is now no criminal penalty specified in Schedule 3.

The statutory duty of care in New Zealand

Section 137 of the New Zealand Act now provides:

> A director of a company, when exercising powers or performing duties as a director, must exercise the care, diligence and skill that a reasonable director would exercise in the same circumstances taking into account, but without limitation,
>
> (a) the nature of the company; and
> (b) the nature of the decision; and
> (c) the position of the director and the nature of the responsibilities undertaken by him or her.[42]

Section 137 must now be read in conjunction with sections 128, 135 and 136.[43] Section 128 sets out the role of the board of directors to manage or supervise management. Section 135 deals with reckless trading and section 136 deals with the duty in relation to incurring obligations in general. The latter provisions have no counterpart in the Australian legislation with the exception of section 588G of the Corporations Act, which deals with preventing insolvent trading. All are limited to directors and do not apply to officers unless they behave as directors. Justice Tompkins,[44] in a valuable lecture given in 1994 at the University of Waikato, said that the test is an objective test of a reasonable director judged in the same circumstances. The new section states expressly that there is to be taken into account the nature of the company, the nature of the decision, the position of the directors and the nature of the responsibilities undertaken by him or her.

His Honour referred to a change which had occurred in the Select Committee hearings.[45] The Law Reform Division had inserted into the Bill a considerably higher standard of care by requiring that a director in a professional occupation or possessing special skills of knowledge must exercise the care, diligence and skill that a reasonable director 'in that profession or occupation or possessing those special skills or

---

42   See Jones, *op. cit.*, footnote 8, supra at 108 *et seq.*
43   See Jones, footnote 8, supra and Tompkins, supra.
44   Tompkins, footnote 8, supra at 28.
45   *ibid.* at 29.

knowledge would exercise in the same circumstances'. This requirement has been deleted. In its place there is to be taken into account the particular matters which have been referred to above. The nature of the company allows one to consider factors such as the size and status of the company, whether it is a publicly listed company or a small incorporated firm. The nature of the decision allows one to consider the significance of the decision or its routine nature. Clearly the greater the significance the greater the need for care. The reference to the position of the director and the nature of the responsibilities undertaken by him or her allows one to consider the executive or non-executive nature of the appointment, although this will not necessarily be conclusive on the standard of care.

The relationship of section 137 to the common law and equity is unclear. On the face of it it seems to restate the case law, not necessarily to supersede it. Unlike the Australian section, it is not the subject of a separate remedial regime.

The relationship of section 137 to the earlier sections also seems somewhat problematic because of the degree of overlap and the reforms to the reckless trading provisions seem to render what was a reasonably clear and graduated law in the old section 320 of the Companies Act 1955[46] now rather obscure. For further discussion of sections 135 and 136 see Chapter 14.

The juridical nature of the duty and its significance

Australia has three duties of care: equitable; statutory; and now, common law. The position in New Zealand at the moment is less clear.

Section 137 of the New Zealand Act, unlike section 185 of the Australian Act, does not clearly preserve the common law and equity. Nevertheless the assumption is that the case law survives.

The question arises as to why any of this is still relevant in the modern law. The judgment in the West Australian case of *Permanent Building Society v. Wheeler*[47] shows that these questions are still relevant because that case showed a distinction between the common law and equity on the question of causation in the case of breach of fiduciary duty. Strict liability ensues from breach of a fiduciary duty in equity. This is not so at common law nor in respect of any equitable duty which is non-fiduciary. Other possible significances of the distinction are the impact of equitable delay, limitation and waiver. The question of whether equitable negligence is covered by contributory negligence legislation is also problematic although the modern tendency in the cases is to assume that it is covered.[48] Clearly it should be even if it is not.

46   On which see J. H. Farrar, 'The Responsibility of Directors and Shareholders for Company Debts' (1989) 4 *Canterbury Law Review* 12.
47   (1994) 12 ACLC 674.
48   See, for example, *Daniels v. Anderson Ltd* (1995) 13 ACLC 614.

Recent cases have shown that if directors are negligent this will enable the company to sue them for damages in common law or equity for breach and their breach may constitute the company's breach for the purpose of contributory negligence. This is of particular significance with regard to claims against auditors. In addition in Australia there is the risk of liability for a civil penalty.

The Business Judgment Doctrine and the new Business Judgment Rule

British Commonwealth corporate laws have long recognised the Business Judgment Doctrine, that the courts should not second guess business judgments by directors taken in good faith. As the High Court of Australia said in *Harlowe's Nominees Pty Ltd v. Woodside (Lakes Entrance) Oil Co*[49] in 1968, 'directors in whom are vested the right and the duty of deciding where the company's interests lie and how they are to be served may be concerned with a wide range of practical considerations, and their judgment, if exercised in good faith or not for irrelevant purposes, is not open to review by the courts'. However, the Business Judgment Doctrine which states a general judicial policy is to be distinguished from the Business Judgment Rule which creates a rule or presumption of no liability.[50]

In the lead up to the Australian reforms of 1992 and the enactment of the New Zealand *Companies Act 1993* there were calls by the business community in both countries for the enactment of a US style of Business Judgment Rule. There was considerable confusion as to what exactly was the nature of such a rule but the work of the American Law Institute in its *Principles of Corporate Governance* provided some clarification of the concept. The Institute formulated the basic Business Judgment Rule as follows:

> A director or officer who makes a business judgment in good faith fulfils the duty under this section if the director or officer (1) is not interested in the subject of the business judgment; (2) is informed with respect to the subject of the business judgment to the extent to which the director or officer reasonably believes to be appropriate under the circumstances; and (3) rationally believes that the business judgment is in the best interests of the corporation.[51]

Such a rule exists under the case law of the various US jurisdictions and now has been codified to some extent in the *Virginia Stock Corporations Act*, section13.1-690A which provides that 'A director shall discharge his duties as a director ... in accordance with his good faith business judgment of the best interests of the corporation'. In the

---

49 (1968) 121 CLR 483, 493.
50 For a discussion of the distinction see J. H. Farrar, 'Business Judgment and Defensive Tactics in Hostile Takeover Bids', in Farrar (ed.), *Takeovers, Institutional Investors and the Modernisation of Corporate Laws*, Oxford University Press, Auckland, 1993, ch. 11.
51 Part IV para. 4.01(a).

American Law Institute's formulation the rule gives an immunity from liability for negligence to directors who satisfy the three prerequisites.

According to a leading US commentator,[52] there are at least five policy bases for the rule. First, there is the judicial concern that persons of reason, intellect and integrity will not serve as directors if the law expects from them a degree of prescience not possessed by people of ordinary knowledge. Even without pressing liability, qualified persons will not serve if their decisions can be second guessed at every turn. The second rationale is to encourage the type of informed risk-taking with which corporate enterprise is undertaken especially in an increasingly global economy. Third, on a more mundane level, courts are ill equipped to exhume and examine business decisions. Corporate officers and directors make many decisions on the basis of incomplete information, and intangibles such as experience or intuition and wide ranging general considerations such as consumer preferences, local and regional economic trends and competitive outlook. Even if courts were able to assemble before them sufficient data on these topics, most courts would feel ill at ease in re-evaluating the data. Fourth, the rule represents a well-established judicial policy of leaving management to managers and a reluctance to undertake or second guess business decisions. Last, the rule is a means whereby courts are aided in the management and allocation of their own resources. The Business Judgment Rule is a device courts use to cut off unmeritorious but complex cases at the motion or other pre-trial stage. The Business Judgment Rule is thus a standard of judicial review consciously or unconsciously used as a tool for achieving judicial economy.

In Practitioners' Forums on the Corporate Law Reform Bill 1992, Allan Rose,[53] then Secretary of the Attorney-General's Department, did not consider the above policy arguments, but attacked a statutory version of the Business Judgment Rule on five more technical grounds. First, he said that the rule is a creature of the US common law and that it may not be wise to introduce one aspect of the US law in isolation from the very different company law regime in Australia. The answer is that the Business Judgment Rule is compatible with existing company law as the courts have already paid some attention to the Business Judgment Doctrine and under section 1318 of the Corporations Act exercised a discretionary jurisdiction in respect of business judgment. Second, Rose noted that attempts by the American Law Institute and the American Bar Association to codify the rule had broken down. This is no longer the case and some of the states have adopted statutory versions of the Business Judgment Rule. Third, Rose argued that Australia should not lose sight of the fact that the Australian company law already includes a rule which embodies some of the Business Judgment Rule. This is not so. We have the Business Judgment Doctrine but not a Business Judgment Rule. Fourth, Rose argued that there is section 1318 and this is sufficient. The answer to this

---

52   See D. M. Branson, *Corporate Governance*, The Mitchie Co., Charlotteville, 1993, pp. 338–41

53   See J. H. Farrar, 'Towards a Statutory Business Judgment Rule in Australia' (1998) 8 Aust Jnl of Corp Law 237, pp. 241–2.

is that it is not sufficient since it is a judicial discretion rather than a presumption of safe harbour. Last, Rose argued that the advocates of the Business Judgment Rule sometimes failed to articulate what it is intended to achieve. The answer is that this is not so and the points have been made clearly that what is intended is a safe harbour for honest business decisions that turn out badly providing they satisfy certain specified criteria. Rose added that if it intended mainly to reflect the current standard of care and diligence, why is it necessary? The answer is that it is not quite doing this and it is converting the judicial discretion in section 1318 into a matter of safe harbour. Rose argued that if it is meant to lower the standard of care and diligence then how can this be appropriate? It is submitted that because of the policies stated above and others considered below there is sufficient justification for an amendment to the law along the lines suggested. This does not equate to a call for lowering of directors' standards, but for a realistic application of them in a business context.

Professor Paul Redmond, of the University of New South Wales, in a paper given to both the Law Council of Australia and the Corporate Law Teachers Association Conference opposing the introduction of a Business Judgment Rule, repeated some of these arguments.[54] In addition he raised further arguments. The first relates to the limited protection afforded by the Business Judgment Rule. The argument seems to be that it is a safe harbour from duty of care liability and not from other distinct fiduciary responsibilities. This is true. He also emphasises the preconditions of relief. There is no need to argue about these points. He adds another reason based on 'some realism about shareholder litigation risk', by which he means there is little risk of shareholder litigation in practice. This underemphasises the fact that section 180(1) is a civil penalty section under the Corporations Act.

Neither the Australian Federal Parliament in 1992 nor the New Zealand Parliament in 1993 decided to enact a Business Judgment Rule. We have seen above how the Australian Parliament dealt with the matter by adopting amendments which clarified the law and included material in the Explanatory Memorandum which gave a green light to the courts to develop a case law Business Judgment Rule in Australia. At the same time there was a tightening up of related party transactions in the Corporations Act.

However, corporate law reform in Australia was transferred from the Commonwealth Attorney-General's Department to the Treasury and with this came a change of approach. The Treasurer, Peter Costello, always supported the concept of a Business Judgment Rule and has promoted the Corporate Law Economic Reform Program. The wording of the section 180(2) now includes a Business Judgment Rule as a corollary to the slightly revised statutory duty of care. It also applies to the equivalent duty under common law and in equity. The wording provides as follows:

---

54   See 'Safe Harbour or Sleepy Hollows: Does Australia Need a Statutory Business Judgment Rule?', in I. Ramsay (ed.), *Corporate Governance and the Duties of Company Directors*, Centre for Corporate Law and Securities Regulation, University of Melbourne, Melbourne, 1997, p. 185.

Business Judgment Rule

2 A director or other officer of a corporation who makes a business judgment is taken to meet the requirements of subsection (1), and their equivalent duties at common law and in equity, in respect of the judgment if they:

(a) make the judgment in good faith for a proper purpose; and

(b) do not have a material personal interest in the subject matter of the judgment; and

(c) inform themselves about the subject matter of the judgment to the extent they reasonably believe to be appropriate; and

(d) rationally believe that the judgment is in the best interests of the corporation.

The director's or officer's belief that the judgment is in the best interests of the corporation is a rational one unless the belief is one that no reasonable person in their position would hold.

The note states:

This subsection only operates in relation to duties under this section and their equivalent duties at common law or in equity (including the duty of care that arises under the common law principles governing liability for negligence). It does not operate in relation to duties under any other provision of this Law or under any other laws.

Section 180(3) provides:

business judgment means any decision to take or not take action in respect of a matter relevant to the business operations of the corporation.

There are a number of points to be made about this subsection.[55] These are:

1 Like section 180(1) it applies to officers, not just directors.

2 It applies to the duty of care and diligence under the Corporations Act and the general law but not to any other breach of statutory duty.

3 Conditions (a) to (d) in section 180(2) have to be fulfilled. These are based on the American Law Institute (ALI) draft but differ in the reference to 'proper purpose' and the use of the term 'material personal interest'. The retention of proper purpose probably means that the rule cannot be used in takeover defence cases, unlike US law.

4 There has to be a business judgment. Unlike the ALI draft which leaves it undefined, this is defined in section 180(3) to mean 'any decision to take or not to take action in respect of a matter relevant to the business operations of the corporation'. This seems to predicate an actual decision, not mere inactivity.

5 There has to be a reasonably informed decision. This springs from both a fiduciary[56] and a tortious basis.[57]

55 Farrar, *op. cit.* footnote 50 supra, pp. 242–3.
56 *Smith v. Van Gorkom* 488 A2d 585 (Supreme Court of Delaware).
57 *Daniels v. Anderson* (1995) 13 ACLC 614.

6 The need for rationality in (d) excludes decisions that cannot be coherently explained or are reckless or represent equitable waste of the corporate assets.[58] It is likely that this will cause difficulty in the Australian courts since rationality is an alien concept.[59]

7 The note makes it clear that the rule is not intended to exonerate the officer from the liability under any other section of the Corporations Act or any other act or regulation.

8 Paragraph 6.1 of the Explanatory Memorandum, using US language, refers to the rule as a safe harbour and its operation as a rebuttable presumption in favour of directors (sic). This ought to have been spelt out expressly in the legislation.

9 The rule is not intended to apply to insolvent trading[60] or misstatements in a prospectus or takeover document.

The immediate economic effect of the new rule will be to prevent the company from suing. This will impose the loss on the company and hence on its shareholders who presumably will take more care in the appointment of directors. The inability of the company to sue will not stop the conduct being relevant for the purposes of contributory negligence. It is thought by the Australian Treasury that the adoption of the statutory Business Judgment Rule ought to encourage entrepreneurism by facilitating legitimate business decisions and risk-taking.[61] The adoption of a statutory Business Judgment Rule will certainly not be a panacea for Australia's economic problems nor a convenient refuge for unprincipled corporate executives. The requirements of absence of self-interest, and being properly informed in particular, are strict. The Business Judgment Rule is mainly used in the USA in respect of related-party transactions, takeover defences and derivative suits. In Australia we have express rules on the first and third and the use of proper purpose in the new wording seems to exclude its use in takeover defences. This reduces its utility in Australia. However, quite apart from the immediate legal effect of the change, there is the cultural effect of the change. It will be a step in the direction of encouraging wealth creation through innovation and responsible risk-taking.

No doubt some corporate lawyers and judges influenced by the Ralph Nader approach to big business do not like it. They argue that it will give further licence to corporate frauds and other abuses, which is nonsense. They are on stronger ground when they ask how business judgment justifies this special treatment. It is arguable that in addition to the US policy arguments justifying such a rule there is a qualitative difference between business decisions and professional decision making, although not

58 See W. Cary and M. A. Eisenberg, *Corporations—Cases and Materials*, 7th edn, unabridged, pp. 603–4. For detailed discussion on the US law see D. J. Block, N. E. Barton and S. A. Radin, *The Business Judgment Rule—Fiduciary Duties of Corporate Directors*, 4th edn, Aspen Law and Business, Englewood Cliffs, NJ, 1993.

59 See for instance Hodgson CJ in Eq. in *Talbot v. NRMA Ltd* (2000) 18 ACLC 600, 606–7.

60 On this see R. Langford, 'The New Statutory Business Judgment Rule: Should it Apply to the Duty to Prevent Insolvent Trading?' (1998) 16 C&SLJ 533.

61 Farrar, *op. cit.* footnote 50 supra, p. 243.

necessarily in the subject matter of the decision. Professional decision making takes place in a more focused situation with specified norms of behaviour which help to define the scope of legitimate risk-taking. Professionals have, by law, to have particular qualifications and experience. These seem significant differences.

Conversely, the directors of publicly listed companies are subject to the disciplines of the market for investment capital. As Frank Easterbrook and Daniel Fischel state in *The Economic Structure of Corporate Law*, 'managers have better incentives to make correct business decisions than do judges'.[62] In the case of proprietary and non-listed public companies this argument has less force. Nevertheless, such companies are still in the product market at least and their directors generally stand to lose more personally from making bad business decisions.

In New Zealand the approach has been different. The only reference to a Business Judgment Rule in the 1993 Act is in the long title in paragraph (d) which provides that an object of the Act is 'to encourage efficient and responsible management of companies by allowing directors a wide discretion in matters of business judgment while at the same time providing protection for shareholders and creditors against the abuse of management power'. New Zealand opted for the rather loosely worded Canadian model of self-interested transactions in section 141 which turns ultimately on fair value. In both Australia and New Zealand there have been increasing pressures on the courts to expect more of company directors. At the same time the Australian courts have begun to recognise the legitimacy of some degree of risk-taking in business judgment. In the words of the majority in *Daniels v. Anderson*:[63]

> The courts have recognised that directors must be allowed to make business judgments and business decisions in the spirit of enterprise untrammelled by the concerns of a conservative investment trustee. Any entrepreneur will rely upon a variety of talents in deciding whether to invest in a business venture. These may include legitimate but ephemeral, political insights, a feel for future economic trends, trust in the capacity of other human beings. Great risks may be taken in the hope of commensurate rewards. If such ventures fail, how is the undertaking of it to be judged against an allegation of negligence by the entrepreneur?

Consistent with their view of the duty as a common law duty their Honours thought that the law of negligence could accommodate differing degrees of duty subject to the ultimate test resting 'upon a general public sentiment of moral wrongdoing for which the offender must pay'. Business people unfortunately do not share the enthusiasm of some of the judiciary for common law negligence.

The recent trend in Antipodean case law in insolvent trading cases has been increasingly rigorous and many of the cases have contained general statements which have been used by the courts in tightening the law on the duty of care. Such rigour is in

---

62   Harvard University Press, Cambridge, Mass., 1991, p. 243
63   (1995) 13 ACLC 614, at 644–5.

fact potentially inconsistent with an increased recognition of the legitimacy of risk-taking and a US style of Business Judgment Rule.[64] However, judging by the US experience, the introduction of a Business Judgment Rule, without tightening up on disclosure requirements and the effective policing of self-interested transactions, could be disastrous for investors.[65] The USA pursues more coherent corporate law policies of latitude for business error balanced by rigorous policing of self-interested transactions. In New Zealand the matter of business judgment has been left to the courts. Their task is to strike the appropriate balance against a background of differing approaches to the regulation of self-interested transactions and a pretty slack approach to insider trading. This is not any easy task for the courts and there is the risk that, like the old English War Office, they will always be busy preparing for the previous war.

Australia now has the Business Judgment Rule and what impact it will have on the courts remains to be seen. There are dangers in legal transplants[66] but globalisation and the economic strength of the USA make it the dominant model in international corporate governance today.[67] It is paradoxical that it should be Australia rather than New Zealand that has enacted a statutory Business Judgment Rule since Australia has generally chosen to go its own way in corporate law reform since 1981 with results which have often misfired and contributed to the excessive complexity of the legislation. New Zealand, by contrast, apart from this, has indicated a greater willingness to borrow from the North American model and to produce modern and intelligible legislation.

---

64   See Farrar, *op. cit.* footnote 1 supra. See p. 122 above.

65   D. A. DeMott, 'Directors' Duty of Care and the Business Judgment Rule: American Precedent and Australian Choices' (1992) 4 *Bond Law Review* 133; M. I. Steinberg, 'The Corporate Law Reform Act 1992: A View from Abroad' (1993) 3 Aust Jnl of Corp Law 154; Farrar, supra n 2.

66   See A. Watson, *Legal Transplants: An Approach to Comparative Law*, Scottish Academic Press, Edinburgh, 1974, ch. 2.

67   See J. H. Farrar, 'The New Financial Architecture and Effective Corporate Governance' (1999) 33 *The International Lawyer* 927.

CHAPTER 14

Directors' Duties and Corporate Governance in Troubled Companies

Corporate governance in a troubled company provides the acid test of management skills. By troubled company is meant a company which is suffering a liquidity crisis and is insolvent or nearly insolvent. This topic raises questions of directors' fiduciary duties in a near insolvency situation and their statutory duties faced with insolvency and the various options open to them. These options will require cooperation with an insolvency practitioner who will look critically at their previous conduct with the advantage of perfect hindsight.

Prediction of business failure

Management, because of its strategic position, has a greater opportunity to forecast insolvency than investors. Investors can, however, by diversification reduce some of the risks for them of company failure. Nevertheless, they have to rely on financial data provided by companies which will fall short of all the information in the hands of management. Finance creditors will depend on either security or higher interest charges and careful monitoring. Trade creditors will often rely on knowledge of the company's business and adjust their credit terms accordingly.

Attempts have been made to develop formulas or ratios for predicting business failure to aid all three groups but most of the empirical work has been based on a population of failed companies, which gives an immediate bias to the findings. The early work was based on univariate analysis whereas the later work such as that of Edward Altman[1] makes use of multivariate analysis. Using this technique Altman concentrates on the following ratios:

---

1 E. Altman, *Corporate Bankruptcy in America*, Heath, Lexington, 1971; *Corporate Financial Distress*, John Wiley & Sons, New York, 1983, p. 339.

- working capital/total assets;
- retained earnings/total assets;
- earnings before interest and taxes/total assets;
- market value of equity/book value of long-term debt;
- sales/total assets.

To these he assigned weights to give an overall score known as the Z factor. A variation on this theme has been produced in the United Kingdom by R. J. Taffler.[2]

Without going into the detailed operation of these ratios or the resulting analysis, the following general points can be made. First, there is no unanimity among the studies as to which ratios offer the best guide. Second, the predictive accuracy of the models improves as the failure approaches. Third, there seems to be a time about one or two years ahead of the predicted failure after which management is unlikely to be able to reverse the decline. Fourth, while they provide information the models do not necessarily aid the decision on the appropriate strategy. They are based on static or comparatively static, not dynamic, calculations but Altman argues that this is because the science is underdeveloped.[3]

The causes of business failure

Apart from such work, the causes of business failure have been inadequately studied. Most insolvency practitioners have their own theories but there is usually little settled consensus.

It is interesting to note that the first *Report of the United Kingdom Select Committee on Joint Stock Companies* in 1844 divided what it described as 'bubble companies' into three categories:

1   Those which, being faulty in their nature, in as much as they are founded on unsound calculations, cannot succeed by any possibility;

2   Those which, let their object be good or bad, are so ill constituted as to render it probable that the miscarriages or failures incident to management will attend them; and

3   Those which are faulty, or fraudulent in their object, being started for no other purpose than to create shares for the purpose of jobbing in them, or to create, under pretence of carrying on a legitimate business, the opportunity, and means of raising funds to be shared by the adventurers who start at the company.

---

2   Finding those firms in danger using discriminate analysis and financial ration data: a comparative UK-based study, City University Business School Working Paper 4; R. J. Taffler and H. J. Tisshaw, 'Going, Going, Gone: Four Factors Which Predict' (1977) 88 *Accountancy* 50. For a very detailed technical study see P. B. Alexander, 'The Failure of Corporate Failure Models to Classify and Predict: Aspects and Refinements', M Comm thesis, University of Canterbury, 1991. See also J. Argenti, *Corporate Collapse*, McGraw-Hill, New York, 1976.

3   J. Freear, *The Management of Business Finance*, Pitman, London, 1980, ch. 14.

We may regard this as an apt description of business failure before the introduction of the modern form of incorporation. Remarkably little seems to have changed with the introduction of incorporation under general Companies Acts and limited liability.

Clearly, inadequate capital is a common failing. Many businesses are started up with insufficient working capital. Bank finance, which is usually sought, has its drawbacks. The interest has to be found whether or not the company makes profits, unlike dividends on ordinary shares which are only paid out of profits. Bank surveillance and the changes in banking policy from time to time can inhibit the company's freedom to manoeuvre. Buying goods on hire purchase is a great temptation but the true cost of such goods is rarely taken into account. Another factor is inadequate control over working capital. Imprudent business judgment in some form is another common failing which in fact covers a multitude of sins. One has only to walk regularly through any shopping mall in any town to see the rise and fall of small businesses.

Fraud is another factor although its incidence is often exaggerated. Some businesses are fraudulent by nature, others are basically lawful but are carried on fraudulently. Others again are lawful and are carried on in a lawful manner but there are management frauds committed against the company.

In a survey carried out in the USA, Dun and Bradstreet,[4] the commercial intelligence specialists, identified 'management inexperience and incompetence' as the major cause of failures. Fraud accounted for a mere 2 per cent. In a survey of a hundred UK private companies that had been wound up and almost all of which were small incorporate businesses, 71 per cent failed due to mismanagement. A high proportion had a low share capital—£100 or less in 52 per cent of the cases, and £1000 or less in 78 per cent of the cases.[5]

The most interesting and thorough analysis of company failure in the United Kingdom was done by a financial journalist and management consultant, John Argenti, in his book *Corporate Collapse.*[6] Argenti listed the following causes or symptoms: management shortcomings; lack of accountancy information; failure to respond to change; constraints; recession; big expensive projects; 'creative' (that is, cosmetic) accountancy; and excessive gearing. Let us examine each of these in turn.

Under management shortcomings, Argenti listed: one-man rule; a non-participating board; unbalanced top team; lack of management depth; weak financial function; and a combined office of chairman/chief executive. He instances the former Rolls-Royce as having five out of six of these shortcomings. These are all pretty self-explanatory.

As examples of accountancy failings he instanced lack of budgetary control, cash flow forecasts, and costing systems, and unrealistic valuation of properties.

---

4   *ibid.,* p 349.

5   R. Brough, 'Business Failure in England and Wales', (1967) *Business Ratios* 8.

6   Argenti, *op. cit.* See also S. Slatter and D. Lovett, *Corporate Turnaround—Managing Companies in Distress,* Penguin Books, London, 1999, p. 49. For an Australian study based on Argenti see A. McRobert and R. Hoffman, *Corporate Collapse,* McGraw Hill, Sydney, 1997.

He gave five examples of change: competitive trends; political change; economic change; social change; and technological change. A company must be capable of responding to change. Included under economic and social change would now be changes in industrial relations.

'Constraints' covers a wide range of things. Some matters such as monopolies and restrictive practices are caught by legal and administrative mechanisms. Some corporate activities may be penalised by tax provisions. Trades unions also represent a powerful constraint on a company's freedom of manoeuvre. Again, public opinion, especially through the media or in the form of organised pressure groups, operates as an increasingly powerful check on companies. This is particularly true in the area of the environment. Recession and inflation both represent considerable threats to business. The big project often brings a company down. It is frequently accompanied by little or no realistic costing of research and development. Rolls-Royce was a classic case. Royston Industries, manufacturers of the Midas black box for aeroplanes, was another. In both cases, profitable aspects of the group were brought down by overambitious research projects.

Creative accounting is usually a symptom rather than a cause. It has frequently occurred in the past with the overvaluation of properties or work in progress. The accountancy profession is seeking to establish controls over this kind of activity.

Excessive gearing, that is, excessive loan capital in relation to share capital, again is usually a symptom rather than a cause. In some cases the blame can be laid at the door of the banks for encouraging this kind of improvidence, but for small incorporated businesses, it can be the only available source of finance.

In a survey published in the *Bank of England Quarterly Bulletin* [7] two other factors are mentioned: low and declining profitability often marked by historic cost accounts which may show a steady, but in reality inadequate, return; and increased import penetration of home markets.

In the useful recent work *Corporate Collapse—Regulatory, Accounting and Ethical Failure*, Professors F. L. Clarke, G. W. Dean and K. G. Olivier review the failures of the accounting profession in Australia to monitor creative accounting and the abuse of group structures in Australia. Their book covers the 1960s, 1970s and 1980s as three separate periods and includes case studies of the major collapses. As such it is valuable reading for all those concerned with corporate governance.

The onset of trouble

In a solvent situation directors owe their fiduciary duties to the company, which is normally equated with the shareholders as a general body.[8] The duties are not owed to individual shareholders in the absence of special facts or express statutory provision.[9] The

---

7   (1980) 20 *Bank of England Quarterly Bulletin* 430.
8   See ch. 11 of this book.
9   *ibid.*

company is not equated with its creditors until insolvency but it has been held in recent years that in a near insolvency situation directors must also consider the creditor interest.[10] One unorthodox view is that this engenders a duty of care in negligence to creditors but the weight of authority is against this.[11]

To this extent the directors are obliged to serve two masters and will also be concerned to protect themselves from potential personal liability. The introduction of the Business Judgment Rule in Australia will not protect them here if their action or inaction fails to prevent insolvent trading.[12] It is arguable that more is expected of directors who serve on the audit committee because of the nature of an audit committee and general concepts of the duty of care.[13]

When insolvency occurs it has an impact on the company's assets and the directors' authority to manage the company. We will consider this later.

Let us now examine in some detail the impact of insolvency. First, we must consider whether the directors are personally liable for failing to prevent insolvent trading. Second, we shall consider the impact of voluntary administration and a formal scheme of arrangement, and third, we shall consider the impact of receivership and winding up. Since the laws of Australia and New Zealand differ we shall deal with them separately.

The Australian position

Failing to prevent insolvent trading[14]

The present law dates back to the UK *Companies Act 1929* when it was limited to fraudulent trading.[15] This was adopted in Australia and New Zealand and still survives in section 592(6) of the Corporations Act. The main provision of the present law in Australia

---

10   *ibid.*
11   *Nicholson v. Permakraft (NZ) Ltd* [1985] 1 NZLR 242. Cf. *Kinsela v. Russell Kinsela Pty Ltd (in liq.)* (1986) 4 ACLC 215; *Spies v. The Queen* [2000] 18 ACLC 727.
12   See ch. 13 of this book.
13   *Syracuse Television Inc. v. Channel 9 Syracuse Inc.* 273 NYS 2d 16, 27 (1996); *Feit v. Leasco Data Processing Equipment Corporation* 332 F Supp 544, 477–8 (1971); *Goldstein v. Aldoex Corp.* 409 F Supp 1201, 1203 (1976).
14   There is a growing literature on this. See for instance, J. Dabner, 'Trading Whilst Insolvent—A Case for Individual Creditors' Rights Against Directors' (1994) 17 UNSW LJ 546; J. Dabner, 'Insolvent Trading—Recent Developments in Australia, New Zealand and South Africa' (1994) 6 Bond LR 1; J. Dabner, 'Insolvent Trading: An International Comparison' (1994) 7 CBLJ 49; J. Dabner, 'Insolvent Trading—Recent Developments in Australia, New Zealand and South Africa [1995] JBL 282; R. Goode, 'Insolvent Trading Under English and Australian Law' (1998) 16 C&SLJ 170; A. Herzberg, 'Insolvent Trading' (1991) 9 C&SLJ 285; A. Herzberg, 'Why Are There So Few Solvent Trading Cases?' (1998) 6 Insolvency LJ 77; R. Lyons, 'Insolvent Trading—When Should Directors be on Guard?' (1999) 7 Insolvency LJ 45; B. H. McPherson, 'The Liability of Directors for Company Debts' (1996) 1 Insolvency LJ 133; B. Mescher, 'Personal Liability of Company Directors for Company Debts' (1996) 70 ALT 837; B. Mescher, 'Company Directors' Knowledge of Insolvent Trading Provisions' (1998) 6 Insolvency LJ 186; J. Mosley, 'Insolvent Trading: What is a Debt and When is One Incurred?' (1996) 4 Insolvency LJ 155; I. Ramsay (ed.) *Company Directors' Liability for Insolvent Trading*, CCLSR, Melbourne, 2000.
15   See J. H. Farrar, 'Fraudulent Trading' [1980] JBL 336.

is contained in section 588G under which a director has a duty to prevent insolvent trading by his or her company. Subject to four defences which are reasonably generous, a director who contravenes the section can be made personally liable to pay compensation to the company and may face a civil penalty. There is also criminal liability if the additional criminal intent can be proved.

The onus of proof rests on the person seeking to make the director liable and the standard of proof in civil penalty and compensation proceedings is the civil standard of proof on a balance of probabilities. The same standard applies to proof of defences but here the onus obviously rests on the director. In the criminal proceedings the ordinary standard of criminal law applies.

The meaning of 'director'

Unlike section 592 and its predecessors, section 588G is limited to directors, but 'directors' as widely defined by section 9. This includes validly appointed directors as well as de facto and shadow directors as we have seen in Chapter 9.

Incurring a debt

Section 588G(1) focuses on incurring a debt when the company is insolvent or will become insolvent as a result of incurring that debt. This raises the question of what is meant by incurring a debt and when a debt is incurred.

In *Hawkins v. Bank of China*[16] the Court of Appeal of New South Wales said that the meaning depended on the context and the purpose of the statute. In *Russell Halpern Nominees Pty Ltd v. Martin*[17] it was held that a company must do a positive act.

On the question of when a debt is incurred there are a number of cases dealing with different kinds of debts and section 588(1A) sets out an operative table which deals with a number of examples concerning share capital. Giving a guarantee also constitutes incurring a debt since the concept includes a contingent liability.[18]

Insolvency

This is defined by section 95A in terms of commercial insolvency in the sense of company's inability to pay all its debts as and when they became due and payable. In 1997 in *Metropolitan Fire Systems Pty Ltd v. Miller*[19] the court stressed the need to consider all the company's resources including its access to credit and current and future debts. Apart from this it is largely a matter of cash flow and the timing of when debts fall due

---

16   (1992) 10 ACLC 588. See also *Credit Corp Pty Ltd v. Atkins* (1999) 17 ACLC 756.
17   (1986) 4 ACLC 393.
18   *Hawkins v. Bank of China* (supra).
19   (1997) 23 ACSR 699. See also *Sycotex Pty Ltd v Baseler & others* (1994) 12 ACLC 494.

and when the company's debtors are likely to pay.[20] Thus lack of liquidity, while relevant, may not be conclusive.[21]

Section 588E(3) and (4) sets out two rebuttable presumptions of insolvency: winding up where the company was insolvent during the twelve months ending with the filing of the winding up application and contravention of sections 286(1) and (2). Section 286(1) deals with the failure to keep adequate financial records and section 286(2) deals with a failure to retain them.

Having reasonable grounds for suspecting that the company is insolvent

Section 588G(1)(c) requires that there were reasonable grounds for suspecting that the company was insolvent or would become so at the time the debt was incurred.

The phrase 'reasonable grounds for suspecting' has been the subject of judicial analysis. In *Queensland Bacon Pty Ltd v. Rees*[22] Justice Kitto held that suspicion requires positive feeling of actual apprehension, amounting to a slight opinion but without sufficient evidence. A reason to suspect that a fact exists is more than a reason to consider or look into the possibility of its existence.

In *Metropolitan Fire Systems Pty Ltd v. Miller*[23] it was held that the test of reasonable grounds was objective which seems obvious from the wording and a similar view was expressed in *Quick v. Stoland*.[24]

Just what this means in practical terms is less clear. In *Quick v. Stoland*[25] and the unreported Victorian case of *Fabric Dyeworks (Australia) Pty Ltd v. Benaharon*[26] the courts seem to consider balance sheet insolvency, then cash flow and then the trading relationship between the plaintiff creditor and the defendants.[27] It has been suggested that directors should query solvency on a daily basis.[28]

What constitutes contravention?

Section 588G(2) defines 'contravention' as failing to prevent the company from incurring the debt if (a) the person is aware at that time that there are grounds for suspecting insolvency or (b) that a reasonable person in a like position in a company in the company's circumstances would be so aware.

---

20 *Melbase Corporation Pty Ltd v. Seganoe Ltd* (1995) 13 ACLC 823, 832. See also *Cuthbertson & Richards Sawmills Pty Ltd v. Thomas* (1999) 17 ACLC 670, 676.
21 *Re Timbatec Pty Ltd* (1974) 4 ALR 12.
22 (1966) 115 CLR 266 at 303.
23 (1997) 23 ACSR 699.
24 (1998) 157 ALR 615. See also *Credit Corp Pty Ltd v. Atkins* (1999) 17 ACLC 756.
25 (1998) 157 ALR 615, 622.
26 Smith J, Supreme Court of Victoria, 29 May 1998.
27 See D. A. Hope, 'The Duty of Directors to Prevent Insolvent Trading', unpublished LLM research paper, University of Melbourne, 1999, p. 20.
28 R. Lyons, 'Insolvent Trading—When Should Directors be on Guard?' (1999) 7 Insolvency LJ 50.

The extension to asset stripping and failure to pay employee entitlements

The *Corporations Law Amendment (Employee Entitlements) Act 2000* makes the entering into of an uncommercial transaction (as defined in section 588FB)[29] a debt for the purposes of section 588G. The test is objective. In addition there is a new section 596AB which creates an offence of entering into agreements or transactions to avoid employee entitlements. The aim is to prevent asset stripping to the detriment of employees. There has been a strident objection by business interest groups but it should be noted that there are more draconian provisions in force in Canada,[30] and the *US Uniform Fraudulent Conveyances Act* sections 4, 5 and 6 seem equally stringent.[31] The United Kingdom deals with the matter by a redundancy payments fund with rights of subrogation against the company.

Defences

Section 588H sets out four defences. These are:

1 having reasonable grounds to expect that the company is solvent
2 delegation and reliance on another person for information as to solvency
3 not taking part in management
4 taking all reasonable steps to prevent the incurring of the debt.

Let us look at each in turn.

Reasonable grounds to expect solvency
Section 588H(2) uses the word 'expect' solvency which is to be contrasted with 'suspect' insolvency in section 588G(1)(C).

In *Metropolitan Fire Systems Pty Ltd v. Miller*[32] it was held that to expect something is a higher test than to suspect something. It suggests a measure of confidence in the company's solvency that is objectively justifiable. This involves taking into account the facts about the debtors and creditors ascertainable by enquiry and facts actually known to any of the directors.[33] This defence predicates action by the director[34] and it is not enough to rely on creditors' indulgences. [35]

Delegation and reliance
Section 588H(3) states that it is a defence if it is proved at the time the debt was incurred that

---

29   For a useful recent decision on the meaning of this see Austin J in *Lewis v. Cook* (2000) 18 ACLC 490.
30   See e.g. *Ontario Business Corporations* Act, s. 131, directors jointly and severally liable for all debts not exceeding six months wages of employees. See too the New Zealand Employee Relations Bill, clause 245, to similar effect.
31   See R. C. Clark, *Corporate Law*, Little Brown & Co, Boston, 1986, para. 2.2.
32   (1997) 23 ACSR 699. See too *Tourprint International Pty Ltd v. Bott* (1999) 17 ACLC 1543.
33   *Standard Chartered Bank v. Antico* (1995) 18 ACSR 1.
34   B. Mescher, 'Company Directors' Knowledge of the Insolvent Trading Provisions' (1998) 6 Insolvency LJ 191.
35   *Powell and Duncan v. Fryer, Tonkin and Perry* (2000) 18 ACLC 480

(a) the director had reasonable grounds to believe and did believe:
    (i) that a competent and reliable person was responsible for providing adequate information about solvency and
    (ii) that the other person was fulfilling that responsibility; and
(b) the director expected that the company was and would remain solvent on the basis of information so provided.[36]

This links with our previous discussion of delegation and reliance in Chapter 8. The delegation must be reasonable and to a competent and reliable person who must be monitored.

Non-participation in management

Section 588H(4) provides a defence if the director did not take part in the management of the company because of illness or some other good reason.[37] Presumably attendance at a funeral of a relation would constitute an example of a good reason.

Taking all reasonable steps to prevent the incurring of the debt

Section 588H(5) provides that it is a defence if it is proved that the person took all reasonable steps to prevent the company from incurring the debt and section 588H(6) states that in determining whether that defence has been proved the court will take into account any action to appoint an administrator, when that was taken, and what was the result.

This is a crucial defence and highlights the necessity for a director to get the board to consider this procedure, to minute this and to resign if necessary if the advice is not followed. Merely expressing reservations and not agreeing to further debt is not enough.[38]

Consequences of contravention

The contravention of section 588G(2) gives rise to the possibility of

(a) civil penalty proceedings under Part 9.4B.
(b) criminal proceedings under section 1317P if the additional criminal intent required by section 588G(3) is proved. (This requires a dishonest failure to prevent the incurring of the debt.)
(c) compensation orders under section 588M(1) in respect of losses resulting from insolvent trading whether or not (a) and (b) have been brought.

---

36 See *Metropolitan Fire Systems Pty Ltd v. Miller* (1997) 23 ACSR 699.
37 See *Tourprint International Pty Ltd v. Bott* (1999) 17 ACLC 1543 where concentrating on sales and debt collection was held not enough.
38 *Byron v. Southern Star Group Pty Ltd* (1997) 15 ACLC 191 (NSWCA on the old wording).

Compensation orders can be brought by a liquidator and in certain circumstances by a creditor but the proceedings must be brought within six years after the beginning of a winding up (section 588M(2), (3) and (4)).

Voluntary administration[39]

If the company goes into voluntary administration the administrator takes over the affairs of the company with a view to developing a deed of company arrangement. The object of this procedure is stated by section 435A to be:

(a) the maximisation of the chances of the company or as much as possible of its business to continue in existence.
(b) If this is not possible, a better return for creditors and members than would result from an immediate winding up.

This raises the question of the role of the directors in the process.[40]

In an insolvency the creditors' interest assumes greater significance. The directors will be worried about potential liability under section 588G and may have received a notice requiring them to initiate voluntary administration or be liable for unremitted tax deductions. They will also be worried about personal liability on guarantees.

Unlike the US Chapter 11 procedure where control remains with the management subject to supervision by the court, administration represents a loss of control, the investigation of their affairs by an outside insolvency practitioner and thus something of a threat. On the other hand it also represents the possibility of salvaging the company.

During administration, directors are not removed but their powers are suspended (section 437C(2)). They can only act if authorised by the administrator under section 437C(1). If they act without authority the act is void and they can be prosecuted for an offence under section 437D(5) and may be liable for compensation under section 437E(1).

The administrator can remove them and appoint others in their place (section 442A).

In case the relationship between the administrator and the directors is too cosy ASIC and the creditors have powers to apply to the court to terminate the administration or to protect creditors' interests (section 447A and B).

Directors must assist the administrator under Part 5.3A.

The directors' powers may revive in whole or in part under a deed of company arrangement. The procedure is flexible and allows a number of possibilities.

---

39   See H. A. J. Ford, R. P. Austin and I. M. Ramsay, *Ford's Principles of Corporations Law*, 10th edn, Butterworths, Chatswood, 2001, ch. 26.
40   For a very useful survey see A. Keay, 'Corporate Governance During Administration and Reconstruction Under Part 5.3A of the *Corporations Law* (1997) 15 C&SLJ 145 on which this relies.

Obviously much depends on the creditors' perception of the conduct of directors prior to the administration and the good sense and professionalism of the administrator in the carrying out of the administration. It is possible for companies to survive troubled times by the use of this procedure. New Zealand does not currently have this procedure although it has been under consideration for some time.

A formal scheme of arrangement[41]

If the company is a large public company it may consider a more formal scheme of arrangement under Part 5.1 of the Corporations Act. This enables a company to enter into compromise with creditors as an alternative to winding up, vary its share capital, transfer its assets to a new company in consideration for the issue of shares in the new company to members, or amalgamate with one or more companies.

The procedures necessitate application to the Supreme Court which is given wide powers provided certain safeguards are in place. Much depends on whether the scheme involves a solvent or an insolvent situation.

From the point of view of corporate governance the significance of the procedures lies in the necessity for management to work closely with specialist legal and accounting advisers to produce a scheme and documentation which will satisfy the court. Schemes are less common since the introduction of the administration procedure but are still useful to large companies for reasons other than insolvency. The breadth of order that the court can make can be useful in mergers and their aftermath.

Receivership[42]

Receivership is normally a debenture holder's remedy to enforce the security under a debenture or a debenture stock trust deed. Receivers can be appointed by the court but more usually are appointed by the debenture holder, or trustee, under an express power in the charge.

The appointment of a receiver usually takes the form of appointment as receiver and manager.

As with the appointment of an administrator, the appointment of a receiver and manager puts the powers of the directors in suspense during the receivership. From the point of view of corporate governance, the position is similar to an administration.

Winding up[43]

Winding up can be for reasons of solvency or insolvency. There are two types: winding up by the court under section 461 and section 459A; and voluntary winding up. Volun-

---

41 See Ford, Austin and Ramsay, *op. cit.*, paras 24.020 *et seq.*
42 *ibid.*, ch. 25.
43 *ibid.*, ch. 27.

tary winding up can be either creditors' voluntary winding up or members' voluntary winding up.

A winding up order by the court does not remove an officer from office (section 471A(3)). However, their powers are suspended during the winding up and the liquidator assumes control of the company. The officers are required to help the liquidator under section 530A.

In a voluntary winding up, all the powers of the directors cease except so far as their continuance is approved by a any committee of inspection, or in the absence of any committee of inspection, by the creditors (section 499(4)). The company is to cease to carry on business except so far as required for the beneficial winding up of the company (section 493(1)).

Winding up is not the corporate equivalent of death. This comes with deregistration under Chapter 5A.

The New Zealand position

There is no exact equivalent of section 588G of the Corporations Act. Sections 135 and 136 of the *Companies Act 1993* deal with reckless trading and incurring obligations.

Reckless trading

Section 135 provides that directors must not:

a   agree to the business of the company being carried on in a manner likely to create a substantial risk of serious loss to the company's creditors; or

b   cause or allow the business to be carried on in a manner likely to create a substantial risk of serious loss to the company's creditors.

The section departs from the Law Commission's draft which would have given protection for business judgment in cases of reasonable risk-taking and seems to be based on statements in the case law interpreting the old section 320 of the *Companies Act 1955*. Section 320 only applied in winding up whereas section 135 applies before winding up. Recklessness as such only appears in the heading to the section, which is a bit odd.

In *Thompson Innes*[44] Justice Bisson said:

---

44   (1985) 2 NZCLC 99, 463 at 99 472. See also the very interesting discussion by Justice Sian Elias, 'Company Law After Ten Years of Reform' and R. B. Perkins, 'Corporate Governance and the Companies Act of 1993' in *The Company Law Conference of the New Zealand Law Society* (1997). See pages 1–12 and in particular pages 9–10 for Justice Elias's paper and pages 77–91, especially 79–81, for Perkins' paper. Justice Elias shows how the final version differs from the Law Commission's draft and Perkins shows how it is inconsistent with a Business Judgment Rule.

Was there something in the financial position of this company which would have drawn the attention of an ordinary prudent director to the real possibility not so slight as to be negligible risk, that his continuing to carry on the business of the company would cause the kind of serious loss to creditors which [the former section 320(1)(b) of the Companies Act 1955] was intended to prevent?

As regards the interpretation of 'substantial risk' and 'serious loss', Mike Ross in his useful recent work *Corporate Reconstructions: Strategies for Directors*[45] states:

The first phrase, 'substantial risk', requires a sober assessment by directors as to the company's likely future income stream. Given current economic conditions, there are reasonable assumptions underpinning the directors' forecasts of future trading revenues. If future liquidity is dependent upon one large construction contract or a large forward order for the supply of goods or services, how reasonable are the directors' assumptions regarding the likelihood of the company winning the contract? Even if the company wins the contract, how reasonable are the prospects of performing the contract at a profit?

Creditors are likely to suffer 'serious losses' if future cash outflows exceed cash inflows during the same period. If there is no profit margin on goods being sold or services provided, the company will reach a stage where shareholders' risk capital has been exhausted and directors are instead continuing to trade at a time when the company cannot meet all creditors' claims. Those creditors who are paid get preferential treatment, to the exclusion of others. In these circumstances, the company should have stopped trading: to continue is to risk creditors' money.

Duty in relation to obligations

Section 136 provides that a director must not agree to the company incurring an obligation unless the director believes at that time, on reasonable grounds that the company will be able to perform the obligation when it is required to do so.

Whereas section 135 deals with debts on revenue account, section 136 deals with obligations on capital account such as major investments.[46]

In *Re Wait Investments Ltd (in liq.); McCallum v. Webster*[47] a shell company was used to enter into an unconditional contract for the purchase of a building for $NZ1.6 million. The company defaulted, the vendor resold and claimed the shortfall. The directors were held liable.

Defences

There are no separate defences, only those contained in the statutory wording.

---

45 CCH New Zealand Ltd, Auckland, 1999, p. 40.
46 *ibid.*, p. 44.
47 (1997) 3 NZLR 96.

Criminal offences

There are no equivalent civil and criminal penalties under these sections but a general power in the court under section 301 to order repayment of money or return of property, and this is effective even though the conduct may constitute an offence.

Voluntary administration

This has not yet been introduced in New Zealand.

A formal scheme of arrangement

New Zealand now has more modern provisions for compromises with creditors in Part XIV, amalgamations in Part XIII, and court approval under Part XV of the 1993 Act. These are based on Canadian legislation.

Receiverships

New Zealand has modern provisions in the *Receiverships Act 1993*.

Statutory management

The *Corporations (Investigation and Management) Act 1989* makes provision for a form of statutory receivership and management and enables swift intervention by government in cases of major corporate collapses. This was used in the case of the Development Finance Corporation and Equiticorp collapses.

Liquidations

There are simplified provisions for liquidations in Part XVI of the *Companies Act 1993*. These are similar to Australian law.

CHAPTER 15

Shareholder Rights and Duties

The changing role of shareholders

The modern company is historically based on the idea of an association of persons who contribute to a common stock for the purposes of a business and who share the profit.[1] The proportion of capital contributed is the share or shares. A share is a bundle of legal and economic rights in the company. This is a relatively simple idea which perhaps belies the complexities of the modern corporation. Ownership of the shares is not necessarily ownership and control of the company.

Professor Jennifer Hill in a characteristically thoughtful recent paper[2] has pointed to seven visions and revisions of the concept of shareholder. These are as:

1   Owner/principal
2   Beneficiary
3   Bystander
4   Participant in a political entity
5   Investor
6   Cerberus
7   Managerial partners

Let us look at each in turn.

  1   'Owner/principal' is historically justifiable and is implicit in Lindley's analysis in 1891. Modern company law grew out of partnership law. Today it is an increasingly artificial notion with the fact that share ownership is of a bundle of rights,

---

[1]   Sir Nathaniel Lindley, *A Treatise of the Law of Companies Considered as a Breach of the Law of Partnership*, 5th edn, Sweet & Maxwell Ltd, London, 1891, p. 1
[2]   J. Hill, 'Visions and Revisions of the Shareholder' (2000) 48 American J of Comp Law 39 (an earlier version of this appeared as 'Changes in the Role of the Shareholder', in R. Grantham and C. Rickett (eds), *Corporate Personality in the 20th Century*, Hart Publishing, Oxford, 1998, ch. 10. Cf. J. Charkham and A. Simpson, *Fair Shares*, Oxford University Press, Oxford, 1999, pp. 31–3.

not ownership of the company, with the increasing separation of ownership and control and diffused ownership. It is thus becoming an empty shell or myth.

2   'Beneficiary' is not legally accurate but conveys some of the sense of shareholders (through the intermediation of the company) being the beneficiaries of the directors' fiduciary duties.

3   'Bystander' emphasises the increasing powerlessness of the smaller shareholders in public listed companies.

4   'Participant in a political entity' again is historically justifiable. Corporations were often thought of as political bodies and sometimes performed political functions, and there were at least some strong analogies between them and the state.

5   'Investor' represents the modern reality with the ordinary shareholder being a residual claimant after prior charges have been met.

6   'Cerberus' refers to the mythical watch dog, and to the guardian or monitoring role of shareholders.

7   'Managerial partners' is put forward by Professor Hill to reflect a scheme of shared power but is a slight exaggeration in listed companies except possibly in relation to institutional investors.

Her analysis helps to convey the complexity of the modern role of shareholder and its many aspects. A difficult question in corporate governance is to work out what should be the appropriate modern role.

The classification of shareholders

While shareholders in proprietary companies are often owner/managers, shareholders in listed companies can be broadly classified into three categories:

1   significant shareholders
2   institutional investors
3   individual investors.[3]

Substantial holding under section 9 of the Corporations Act refers to one entitled to 5 per cent or more of the voting shares. Here we are using 'significant shareholder' to refer to situations where a shareholder, usually another company, owns a majority or minority holding which is likely to give corporate control.[4] The term 'reference

---

3   On the question of classification of shareholders see A. Berle Jr and G. Means, *The Modern Corporation and Private Property*, revised edition, Harcourt Brace, New York, 1968; J. H. Farrar, 'Ownership and Control of Listed Public Companies and Revising or Rejecting the Concept of Control', in B. Pettet (ed.), *Company Law in Change*, Sweet & Maxwell, London, 1987, p. 39; G. Stapledon, 'Share Ownership and Control in Listed Australian Companies' (1999) 3 *Corporate Governance International* 17.

4   Cf. the more relativist approach of J. Charkham and A. Simpson, *Fair Shares, op cit,* ch. 21.

shareholder' which was used in Chapter 2 normally refers to a majority shareholder. A number of Australian and New Zealand listed companies have a corporate shareholder or shareholders with majority or minority control.

'Institutional investors' refers to investors such as insurance companies, investment trusts, unit trusts and banks, which manage other people's savings. Usually they delegate the function to a specialist funds manager.

'Individual investors' refers to individuals. Australia has the highest proportion of the population owning shares in the world. In Australia 53 per cent of the population own shares compared with 48 per cent in the USA.[5]

Shareholder rights

Shareholders have a number of rights under the companies legislation. The main rights are:

1 the right to information and accounts under Chapter 2M of the Corporations Act and Part XII of the New Zealand Act
2 the right to vote under Chapter 2G of the Corporations Act and Part VII of the New Zealand Act
3 the right to requisition and call general meetings and propose resolutions under Chapter 2G of the Corporations Act and Part VII of the New Zealand Act
4 the right to appoint and remove directors under Chapter 2D of the Corporations Law and Part X of the New Zealand Act.

In addition shareholders have the following remedies:

(a) a minority shareholder remedy under the personal right exception to the rule in *Foss v. Harbottle* in Australia.
(b) statutory minority shareholder remedies under Chapter 2F of the Corporations Act and Part IX of the New Zealand Act. Chapter 2F covers the remedy for unfairly prejudicial conduct and oppression, derivative actions, class rights and the remedy of inspection of books. Part IX covers all of these except class rights, which are dealt with in Part VII of the New Zealand Act.

Economically shareholders are residual claimants after creditors and employees have been paid. Holders of ordinary shares are the ultimate residual claimants after preference shareholders have received their due. It can be argued that this status as residual claimant justifies the right to vote.[6]

---

5 See the editorial in the *Australian Financial Review* of 12–13 February 2000, p. 20.
6 See F. Easterbrook and D. Fischel (1983) 26 *Journal of Law and Economics* 395, 403.

Shareholder duties

Individual shareholders do not owe duties to other shareholders[7] although they owe duties to the company to pay for their shares. Collectively the majority owe a duty to act within the constitution and without oppression and, where there is an alteration of the constitution involving an expropriation of shares held by the minority, there is a duty to act for a proper purpose and fairly.[8]

Apart from this and exceptional cases where a majority shareholder acts as a shadow director there is no fiduciary duty on controlling shareholders such as we find in US corporate laws.[9]

Modern corporate governance is still trying to formulate appropriate duties as a matter of self-regulation.

Shareholder relations

Just as shareholders themselves fall broadly into three groups, so the question of shareholder relations and communications needs to reflect these realities. Relations with a significant shareholder will reflect the nature and extent of the ownership. If the significant shareholder has majority control then there will be a group relationship. If the relationship is minority control then much will depend on the way the shareholder views the investment.

Turning to institutional investors, the UK Cadbury Report[10] recommended regular, systematic contact at senior executive level to exchange views and information on strategy, performance, broad membership and quality of management. It thought that institutional investors should make positive use of their voting rights unless they had good reason to do otherwise. They should also disclose their voting policies. It also thought that institutional investors should take a positive interest in the composition of boards.

These views were generally supported by the joint City of London/ Industry working group in its report *Developing a Winning Partnership* in 1995 and by the Final Report of the Hampel Committee in 1998[11] although it emphasised that institutions are not normally experienced business managers and cannot substitute for them. Similar views are expressed in the IFSA Guidelines.[12]

---

7   See J. H. Farrar and B. Hannigan, *Farrar's Company Law*, 4th edn, Butterworths, London, 1998, ch. 11, pp. 126, 128.
8   *Gambotto v. WCP Ltd* (1995) 13 ACLC 342.
9   See Farrar and Hannigan, *op. cit.*, pp. 569 *et seq.*
10   *Report of the Committee on the Financial Aspects of Corporate Governance*, Gee, London, 1 December 1992, para. 6.11.
11   Committee on Corporate Governance, *Final Report*, Gee, London, January 1998.
12   See IFSA Guidance Note No 2.00, Part 2.

The special treatment of significant and institutional investors raises awkward questions about parity between shareholders. The Cadbury Committee thought that boards must ensure that any significant statements concerning their companies are made publicly and so are equally available to all shareholders, and in Australia we now have the system of continuous disclosure as well as ASX listing rules. The other concern is to avoid liability for insider trading by passing price-sensitive information relative to the securities of the company.[13]

The annual general meeting

The UK Hampel Committee Report in 1998 recognised that the annual general meeting is often the only opportunity for the small shareholder to be fully briefed on the company's activities and to question senior executives on both operative and governance matters.[14]

It recommended:[15]

1   the practice of mounting a business presentation with a question and answer session
2   companies should announce the total proxy votes for and against each resolution once it has been dealt with on a show of hands.

Disclosure of proxy votes to the ASX is now obligatory in Australia in respect of listed companies under section 251AA(2) of the Corporations Act.

It considered whether all resolutions should be put to a postal vote but thought that this might be seen as a move to stifle debate and thought the time was not right for a change of this kind.

It favoured making presentations to institutional investors available to a wider audience through the Internet.[16]

For a comment on the CASAC Final Report *Shareholder Participation in the Modern Listed Public Company*, see Chapter 7 above.

The myth or reality of shareholder democracy

In the last fifty years, from time to time, the ideas of shareholder democracy and people's capitalism have been floated.

---

13   *ibid.*, 11.2.6.
14   Committee on Corporate Governance, *Final Report*, Gee, London, January 1998, para. 5.13.
15   *ibid.*, para. 5.14. For a recent Australian discussion see CASAC, Discussion Paper, *Shareholder Participation in the Modern Listed Public Company*, September 1999, and the Final Report, 2000.
16   Hampel Report, para. 5.24.

The concept of shareholder democracy was described by Bayless Manning, a leading US commentator, in 1958 as 'a shimmering conception fusing good old American free enterprise with good old American Jacksonianism'.[17]

Here he was referring to President Andrew Jackson, first frontier President, who came to office with great popular support. He said that the nostrums of corporate democracy had a vaguely familiar quality because they were based on the ideas of the municipal reformers of the turn of the century: more disclosure; greater attendance at shareholders' meetings; more policy issues on the ballot paper for shareholder vote; cumulative voting; more before, during and after meeting reports; more shareholder proposals to vote; and more representation of women.

Manning, however, made the point that it was not shareholder democracy at work but the work of the SEC which had monitored management. He argued that the most serious charge against the myth of shareholder democracy is that it creates the illusion in people's minds that a degree of shareholder supervision exists which in fact does not.

Since Manning wrote that, there has been a massive growth of institutional investment and involvement by institutional investors in the development of corporate governance as a self-regulatory system. This, and the market for corporate control, have probably contributed more to effective monitoring of management than a broader based shareholder democracy concept in the past. Nevertheless the recent growth in the Australian Shareholders' Association shows that there is interest by minority shareholders in seeking an effective voice.

It is, however, arguable that the new technology, especially email and the Internet, will create more opportunities for effective communications and more flexible methods of meeting and voting without the necessity for physical presence.[18] Postal voting is allowed in New Zealand and computerised voting will no doubt come. It may be that this will lead to virtual meetings and virtual shareholder communities in the future.[19] Whether it will redefine the role of the shareholder remains to be seen.

---

17   Book review (1958) 67 Yale LJ 1477, 1486. See also J. Hetherington, 'Fact and Legal Theory: Shareholders, Managers and Corporate Responsibility' (1969) 21 Stanford L Rev 248; L. Getz, 'The Structure of Shareholder Democracy', in J. Ziegel (ed.), *Studies in Canadian Company Law*, vol. 2, Butterworths, Toronto, 1973, p. 239.

18   See the interesting discussion paper: E. Boros, 'The Online Corporate: Electronic Corporate Communications', Centre for Corporate Law and Securities Regulation, University of Melbourne, Melbourne, December 1999, ch. 3.

19   UK Company Law Review Steering Group, *Modern Company Law for a Competitive Economy: Company General Meetings and Shareholder Communications*, Department of Trade and Industry, London, October 1999, para. 30.

CHAPTER 16

Excusing Directors

In this chapter we shall consider various ways in which the law allows directors to be excused for acting without authority, or committing a breach of duty, or to be compensated for defending proceedings against them. We shall consider:

1 Ratification
2 The court's discretionary powers to grant relief under sections 1318 and 1317S of the Corporations Act.
3 Indemnity under section 199A of the Corporations Act and section 162 of the New Zealand Act.
4 Insurance under section 199B of the Corporations Act and section 162(5) and (6) of the New Zealand Act.

Ratification

We have already considered ratification in Chapter 6. The general meeting can remedy a lack of authority and condone at least some breaches of duty. The ratification must not itself be part of a campaign of oppression or unfairly prejudicial conduct. Ratification of a breach of statutory duty is not possible, at least where it constitutes a criminal offence.

The court's discretionary powers

Section 1318 provides that if in any civil proceedings against an officer for negligence, default, breach of trust or breach of duty, it appears to the court that the person is or may be liable but has acted honestly and that, having regard to all the circumstances of the case, the person ought fairly to be excused, the court may relieve the officer wholly or partly from liability.[1]

---

1   *Re Claridge's Patent Asphalte Co. Ltd* [1921] Ch 543.

Honesty does not require proof that the person acted on competent advice.[2] It is subjective.[3] The general conduct of the officer must be honest.[4] The onus is on the officer to prove honesty.[5] The court is unlikely to find in the officer's favour if he or she has benefited from the breach.[6]

The section covers proceedings by the company[7] and probably also proceedings by a third party[8] but it does not apply to criminal proceedings.[9]

Section 1317S contains similar provisions in respect of contravention of a civil penalty provision.

There is a similar provision to section 1318 in section 468 of the New Zealand *Companies Act 1955* but no equivalent provision in the *Companies Act 1993*. This seems to have been omitted by mistake. There is no equivalent to section 1317S as there are no civil penalties in New Zealand.

Indemnity under sections 199A and 162

At common law it was possible to exclude liability for breach of duty and to give indemnities. This is outlawed by what is now section 199A(1).

Under section 199A(2) indemnities (other than for legal costs) are prohibited for the following liabilities incurred as officer or auditor of the company:

- liability owed to the company or a related body corporate
- liability for a pecuniary civil penalty order or compensation order
- liability arising out of conduct which is not in good faith owed to someone other than the company or a related body corporate.

Section 199A(3) deals with restrictions on indemnities in respect of legal costs. Such indemnities are not allowed if the costs were incurred:

- in defending proceedings where they are found liable in circumstances that would not be covered by section 199A(2)
- in defending criminal proceedings in which they are found guilty
- in defending proceedings by ASIC or a liquidator if the grounds for making an order are established

---

2   See *Dominion Insurance Co. of Australia Ltd (in liq.) v. Finn* (1989) 7 ACLC 25, 34 and cases cited.
3   *ibid.*, p. 33.
4   *ibid.*, p. 34.
5   *ibid.*, p. 33; *Selangor United Rubber Estates Ltd v. Cradock* [1968] 2 All ER 1073, 1154-5; cf. *State Bank of South Australia v. Clark* (1996) 11 ACLC 1019.
6   *Re Lasscock's Nurseries Ltd (in liq.)* [1940] SASR 251.
7   *Customs and Excise Commissioners v. Hedon Alpha Ltd* [1981] 2 All ER 697.
8   *Daniels v. Anderson* (1995) 13 ACLC 614.
9   *Lawson v. Mitchell* [1975] VR 579. Cf. *Pascoe Ltd (in liq.) v. Lucas* (1998) 16 ACLC 1247. See R. Baxt, K. Fletcher and S. Fridman, *Afterman and Baxt's Cases and Materials on Corporations and Associations*, 8th edn, Butterworths, Sydney, 1999, p. 515.

• in proceedings for relief where the court denies relief.

It is now possible to get a loan from the company pending the outcome of a case but this must be repaid, if unsuccessful.

Under section 162 of the New Zealand Act there is also a basic prohibition which even extends to employees. However, there are the following exceptions:

• proceedings with a favourable outcome;
• liability to a third party.

The first concerns indemnities for legal costs which are allowed by the constitution and where the outcome is favourable in the sense of obtaining judgment, acquittal or discontinuance.

The second concerns indemnities in respect of liability to a third party (that is, not the company or a related company) for act or omission. It must be authorised by the constitution and not extend to criminal liability or liability for breach of duty to act in good faith and in the best interests of the company (section 162(4)).

Insurance under sections 199B and 162(5) and (6)

A company or a related body must not pay premiums for insurance of a person who is or has been an officer or auditor against liability for:

• wilful breaches of duty; or
• contraventions of sections 182 and 183.

Any such contract of insurance is void (section 199C(2)).

It is, however, possible to insure the officers against:

(a) non-wilful breaches (other than breaches of sections 182 and 182) and
(b) the costs of defending proceedings whether civil or criminal and apparently whatever their outcome (section 199B).

The scope of (b) seems too wide and should be limited to acquittal or a successful defence or settlement of a civil claim.

Under section 162(5) of the New Zealand Act it is possible to insure against:

(a) non-criminal liability
(b) costs in defending or settling a civil claim
(c) costs incurred in defending criminal proceedings where there is acquittal.

The purchase of insurance must be expressly authorised by the constitution and approved by the board beforehand. The board must certify that the cost is fair to the company (section 162(b)).

Holding Directors Accountable: Remedies of the Company

Assuming the directors are in breach of duty and have not been excused, the company has a number of remedies against them. These are in addition to civil and criminal penalties in Australia. It may be that the wrongdoers are in control and the company will not sue. Here the minority shareholders may take action as we will see in the next chapter. If the company goes into liquidation a liquidator may take action and in any event in Australia ASIC may intervene as we shall see in Chapters 18 and 20. New Zealand has opted for a system of private enforcement. In this chapter we shall mainly concentrate on the company's remedies that are equitable.[1] This means that they are ultimately discretionary and affected by equitable considerations.

Equitable considerations

The courts in exercising equitable jurisdiction have regard to clean hands of the parties but since in this kind of case the company is an injured party in the hands of wrongdoers this point will often be somewhat academic.

The directors may have equitable defences. For instance, where there has been delay or acquiescence or where it is impossible to restore the parties to their original positions, relief may be denied. However, where a third party is in complicity with a wrongdoing director, the third party may be liable as a constructive trustee.

---

1   H. A. J. Ford, R. P. Austin and I. M. Ramsay, *Ford's Principles of Corporations Law*, 10th edn, Butterworths, Sydney, 2001, para. 9.350; P. Lipton and A. Herzberg, *Understanding Company Law*, 9th edn, LBC Information Services, Sydney, 2000, pp. 325 et seq.

Equitable remedies

The company in both Australia and New Zealand has the following remedies:

• rescission or avoidance of a contract
• account of a secret profit
• equitable damages or compensation
• constructive trust
• injunction
• tracing

These are in addition to possible remedies in tort or restitution or in respect of voidable transactions in winding up.

Rescission or avoidance

In Australia the old law on rescission still applies. Lord Cairns LC said in *Tennent v. City of Glasgow Bank*:[2]

> The law upon this subject is contained in three propositions. In the first place, a contract induced by fraud is not void, but only voidable at the option of the person defrauded; second, this does not mean that the contract is void till ratified, but it means that the contract is valid till rescinded; and thirdly, the option to avoid the contract is barred where innocent parties have, in reliance on the fraudulent contract, acquired rights which would be defeated by its recission.

He was talking there about rescission of a contract to take shares but the same principles apply here.

Where a third party is involved it depends on their innocence but to some extent they may be protected by the presumption in section 129(4) that officers have properly performed their duties to the company.

In New Zealand as we have seen in Chapter 12, section 141 of the *Companies Act 1993* expressly deals with avoidance of contracts with a director and this section and the constitution replaces rescission in equity (section 141(b)). Section 142 protects bona fide purchasers for value without notice. A transaction cannot be avoided if the company receives fair value under it (section 141(2)). This is different from the equitable principles which are stricter but follows the US trends.

Account of secret profits

Lord Porter in *Regal (Hastings) Ltd v. Gulliver*[3] said, 'The legal proposition may, I think, be broadly stated by saying that one occupying a position of trust must not make a profit

---

2   (1879) 4 App Cas 615, 620–1.
3   [1942] 1 All ER 387, 395C–D. See *Furs Ltd v. Tomkies* (1936) 54 CLR 583, 592 per Rich, Dixon and Evatt JJ.

which he can acquire only by use of his fiduciary position, or, if he does, he must account for the profit so made'. The undisclosed profit belongs in equity to the company.

In the case of a sale to the company at overvalue the company cannot approbate and reprobate, that is, rescind the contract and sue for the secret profit. It can merely rescind the contract.[4] It cannot force on the director a contract to sell at another price.

The court may, in a suitable case, award some reasonable remuneration where the director has acted openly but mistakenly and the company's gain is by the director's skill and judgment.[5]

Equitable damages or compensation

The court has inherent power to award equitable compensation for loss caused by breach of fiduciary duty.[6] This is akin to equitable damages.

This is different from common law damages on matters such as the liability, which is strict, and the date when loss is assessed, which is the date of restoration of the property or its value. The liability of the director may thus increase with appreciation in value of the property misapplied.[7]

The company may also claim compound interest as compensation for loss of use of the money.[8]

This remedy is in addition to statutory compensation for contravention of a civil penalty provision.[9]

Constructive trust

Where a director retains a corporate asset he or she may be liable as a trustee of the asset: similarly where the asset has been replaced.[10]

Where a director makes off with a corporate opportunity, the director holds the benefit on trust for the company.[11]

Third parties with knowledge, who receive funds in breach of duty, are also liable as constructive trustees.[12]

---

4   *Burland v. Earle* [1902] AC 83. *Re Cape Breton Co.* (1885) 29 Ch D 795. See also *Re Lord Chesham* (1886) 31 Ch D 466, 473 per Chitty J as to the principle of election.
5   *Phipps v. Boardman* [1967] 2 AC 46 per 104 E–G, Lord Cohen, 112 D per Lord Hodson.
6   *Catt & Ors v. Marac Australia Ltd* (1986) 9 NSWLR 639; 9 ACLC 450.
7   *Re Dawson* [1966] 2 NSWR 211, 216. See *Markwell Bros Pty Ltd v. CPN Diesels (Qld) Pty Ltd* (1982) 7 ACLR 425, especially at 427 per Thomas J for the origins of the jurisdiction. See too *Duke Group Ltd (in liq.) v. Pilmer* (1999) 17 ACLC 1329, 1469 *et seq.* Reversed [2001] HCA 31.
8   Lipton and Herzberg, *op. cit.,* p. 327.
9   s. 1317H of the Corporations Act.
10   *Paul A. Davies (Aust) Pty Ltd (in liq.) v. Davies (No 2)* [1983] 1 NSWLR 337.
11   *Cook v. Deeks* [1916] 1 AC 554.
12   *Linter Group Ltd v. Goldberg* (1992) 10 ACLC 739.

Injunction

Where the director is proposing to act in breach of duty the remedy of injunction may be more appropriate.[13]

Tracing

Tracing into the hands of a third party, who is not a bona fide purchaser for value without notice, is possible and is a useful remedy where the director or third party is bankrupt. Tracing is lost where money is used to repay a debt owed to the third party.[14]

Non-equitable remedies

Compensation orders can be made under section 1317H of the Corporations Act in respect of damage suffered by the corporation where a person has contravened a civil penalty provision in relation to the corporation.

Where a director is liable in common law negligence the remedy will be damages.

Where a director has received a bribe it can be recovered in an action for money had and received in restitution as well as constructive trust.[15]

Certain self-interested transactions can be reopened as voidable transactions and the like in winding up under Part 5.7B Division 2 of the Corporations Act[16] or sections 292 to 301 of the New Zealand Act.[17]

---

13   *Pacifica Shipping Co. Ltd v. Anderson* [1986] 2 NZLR 328.
14   *Linter Group Ltd v. Goldberg* (1992) 10 ACLC 739.
15   See P. Davies, *Gower's Principles of Modern Company Law*, 6th edn, Sweet & Maxwell, London, 1997, pp. 655–6.
16   s. 588FA, unfair preferences; s. 588FB, uncommercial transactions; s. 588FC, insolvent transactions; s. 588FD unfair loans to a company.
17   Voidable transactions (s. 292); voidable charges (s. 293), transactions at undervalue (s. 297), transactions for inadequate or excessive consideration with directors and certain other persons (s. 298), certain securities and charges (s. 299), no proper accounts (s. 300), repayment of money or property (s. 301).

CHAPTER 18

Holding Directors Accountable: Minority Shareholder Remedies[1]

Minority shareholders who wish to seek a remedy against the directors face a number of obstacles. Often the transactions are of a complicated nature, and difficult to unravel. The board, if questioned at a general meeting,[2] may refuse to disclose any information on the basis that the matter is a confidential one, unsuitable for discussion at a public meeting. In any event, it is very difficult to overcome the judiciary's traditional reluctance to question the business judgment of the directors.[3] Then there is the attitude of the innocent directors, who are more anxious not to rock the boat than they are to adopt an active policing role.[4] Nor is removing the directors always the attractive option that it theoretically appears to be. In any event, the control which directors have of the proxy machinery, and in smaller companies, their close identification with the majority shareholders, normally ensure that the required resolution will not be passed. Added to all this are the large costs involved in bringing a case to court.[5] The failure of our law until recently to allow for derivative actions and the continuing uncertainty over a system of contingent fees, has caused minority shareholders' rights to receive less attention than in the USA, for example.

---

1   This chapter is based in part on chapters in J. H. Farrar and B. Hannigan, *Farrar's Company Law*, 4th edn, Butterworths, London, 1998; and J. H. Farrar and M. Russell, *Company Law and Securities Regulation in New Zealand*, Butterworths, Wellington, 1985. For a useful comparative study see L. Griggs and J. P. Lowry, 'Minority Shareholder Remedies: A Comparative View' [1994] JBL 463.

2   As to shareholders' rights see ch. 7.

3   See *Burland v. Earle* [1902] AC 83, 92, per Lord Davey; *Hogg v. Cramphorn* [1967] Ch 254, 268 per Buckley J.

4   See for instance *Prudential Assurance Co. Ltd v. Newman Industries Ltd (No 2)* [1982] Ch 204.

5   However, in *Wallersteiner v. Moir (No 2)* [1975] QB 373 the English Court of Appeal provided for a minority shareholder to be indemnified by the company for his costs where he prosecuted an action on behalf of the company in circumstances where it was reasonable to do so. This has now been replaced by the statutory derivative action procedure in Australia and New Zealand.

169

It is because of all these impediments that actions against directors tend to occur only where there has been a family squabble between the directors themselves, or a change of control. Accordingly, the court often finds itself adjudicating upon a dispute motivated more by personal passions than by a desire to heighten business morality.

It is not surprising that many shareholders simply prefer to sell their shares if they are unhappy with the actions of management. If the company is a listed company, this is relatively easy. In the case of a small firm, however, the market for the shares will be much smaller, if there is one at all. The company's constitution may also contain restrictions on the right to transfer shares.

Before examining the rule in *Foss v. Harbottle*, which historically has been the chief procedural bar to the minority shareholder, some terminology should be clarified with regard to the different types of action that a shareholder can bring. There are three types: first, a shareholder may bring a personal action, where some personal right has been infringed. Second, he or she may bring a representative action, which is really in many ways a multiple personal action. The individual shareholder sues on behalf of themselves and other shareholders who have suffered the same damage to their personal rights. There are limitations on the remedies that can be sought in a representative action.[6] The third form of action is called a derivative action. This sort of action is brought by a shareholder, on behalf of their company, enforcing the company's rights, where the wrongdoers are in control of the company, and prevent it from suing in its own name. In this case the entire benefit of the proceedings goes to the company.[7] Because it is really the company that is suing, the shareholder can sue in respect of the wrongs that occurred even before he or she became a member.[8] At common law a derivative action could only be brought if one of the so-called exceptions[9] to the rule in *Foss v. Harbottle* was applicable. The matter is now governed by new statutory procedures in Australia and New Zealand.

The remedies now available to a minority shareholder are:

1 An action under the personal rights exceptions to the rule in *Foss v. Harbottle*[10] or section 169 of the New Zealand Act.

2 A statutory minority shareholders action under section 232 of the Corporation Law or section 174 of the New Zealand Act.

3 An application for winding up by the court:
   (a) on the just and equitable ground

---

6 For more detail on representative actions, see R. R. Pennington, *Pennington's Company Law*, 6th edn, Butterworths, London, 1995.

7 In the old case law procedure, the company was joined as a co-defendant to enable it to take advantage of any judgment in its favour. Shareholders benefited through recovery by the company by reason of enhancement of the value of their shareholding.

8 *Seaton v. Grant* (1867) 2 Ch App 459. A shareholder could join a derivative suit and representative action in the same action: *Prudential Assurance v. Newman Industries Ltd (No 2)* [1982] Ch 204, although the latter action might be dismissed if the shareholder had already received indirect recompense by means of an award of damages to the company in the derivative action.

9 Some of the 'exceptions' are in reality cases where the rule does not apply of its nature.

10 (1843) 2 Hare 461.

(b) in Australia on the ground of oppression or unfairly prejudicial conduct

(c) in Australia on the ground of directors acting in their own self-interest.

4   A statutory derivative action under Part 2F.1A of the Corporations Act or section 165 of the New Zealand Act.

In addition, minority shareholders are given power to apply to the court under sections 247A to 247D for an order for inspection of the books of the company and they have *locus standi* under section 1324 to apply for an injunction or damages for a breach of the Corporations Act. Section 197 of the New Zealand Act is similar to section 274A. New Zealand has no exact equivalent of section 1324 but sections 164, 170 and 172 of the New Zealand Act are an approximate equivalent. New Zealand also has a North American appraisal remedy in sections 110–115 of the 1993 Act which confers buy-out rights in certain circumstances. We refer to this at the end of the chapter.

The rule in *Foss v. Harbottle*

The rule in *Foss v. Harbottle* established that, in the case of a wrong done to a company, the company was the proper person to sue and not individual shareholders.

Although the rule was thus capable of being expressed in this singular way, there were in fact two bases for it. The first basis was simply that if a wrong was done to the company, then it was the company which should sue.[11] The second basis could be called the 'internal management' rule. This was expressed succinctly by Lord Justice Mellish in *MacDougall v. Gardiner*[12] as follows:

> If the thing complained of is a thing which in substance the majority of the company are entitled to do, or if something has been done irregularly which the majority of the company are entitled to do regularly, or if something has been done illegally which the majority of the company are entitled to do legally, there can be no use in having litigation about it, the ultimate end of which is only that a meeting has to be called, and then ultimately the majority gets its wishes.[13]

In *Edwards v. Halliwell*[14] Lord Justice Jenkins explained the relationship between the two bases of the rule: if the alleged wrong was capable of being ratified, a suit by a minority shareholder would not lie since either the majority would approve of the

---

11   *Burland v. Earle* [1902] AC 83, 93 per Lord Davey.

12   (1875) 1 Ch 13, 25. See also *Burland v. Earle*, *ibid.*; K. W. Wedderburn, 'Shareholders' Rights and the Rule in *Foss v. Harbottle*', (1957) CLJ 194; (1958) CLJ 93.

13   The cases have produced a long list of instances in which the courts have refused to interfere on this ground, e.g. proper appointment and removal of directors: *Foster v. Foster* [1916] 1 Ch 532; *Re Inderwick & Snell* (1850) 2 Mac & G. 216; remuneration of directors: *Normandy v. Ind Coope & Co.* [1903] 1 Ch 84; making of calls: *Gregory v. Patchett* (1864) 33 Beav. 595, 606; payment of dividends: *Gregory v. Patchett*; the setting up of reserves: *Burland v. Earle* [1902] AC 83; the reduction of capital: *Re MacKenzie & Co.* [1916] 2 Ch 450; creation of new classes of shares: *Andrews v. Gas Meter Co.* [1897] Ch 361; the issue of bonus shares: *Mills v. Mills* (1938) 60 CLR 150. This list is by no means exhaustive.

14   [1950] 2 All ER 1064, 1066.

wrong, in which case no wrong had been done to the company, and no action could lie; alternatively, if the majority opposed what had been done, there was no reason why action should not be brought by the company itself.

There were a number of advantages to the rule. First, it was more convenient that the company should sue, instead of having any number of suits started and subsequently discontinued by individual shareholders.[15] It eliminated vexatious actions started by troublesome minority shareholders trying to harass the company.

But there was a major drawback. The rule said that the company was the proper person to sue, but a company could only act through its human agents, usually the board of directors, and they might well be the actual wrongdoers. They might, therefore, decide not to sue, a decision which might be approved by the company in general meeting, where the wrongdoers might similarly control a majority of the votes. The outcome would be that the wrongdoers would go unpunished and the minority shareholders would be at the mercy of the majority, who could loot the company with impunity.[16] This could not be tolerated. Therefore exceptions were developed whereby, notwithstanding the rule, a minority shareholder might sue.

Before looking at these exceptions, a preliminary observation might be made. It is clear that the application of the rule was marked out by the boundaries of the majority's power of ratification. In principle, then, the exceptions to the rule did not apply where the wrong complained of was one that was capable of ratification.[17]

Exceptions to the rule[18]

There were five main exceptions (although some are not so much exceptions as merely instances where the rule does not apply):

(i)   where the transaction was *ultra vires* or illegal;
(ii) where the transaction required the sanction of a special majority;
(iii) where the personal rights of the shareholders were infringed;
(iv) where the 'fraud on the minority' or derivative action exception applies;
(v)   whenever the interests of justice required the rule not to apply.

With the advent of a statutory derivative action (i), (ii), (iv) and (v) have been abolished with effect from 1 July 1994 in New Zealand and 13 March 2000 in Australia. Only the personal action exception remains and in New Zealand this now has statutory form in section 169 of the 1993 Act. However, since the general law rules may still be of

---

15   The argument that any relaxation of the rule would open the floodgates seems to ignore the Court's discretion to strike out proceedings as abuses of process: see *Re Bellador Silk Ltd* [1965] 1 All ER 667.
16   See *Wallersteiner v. Moir (No 2)* [1975] QB 373, 396 per Lord Denning MR.
17   See P. Davies, *Gower's Principles of Modern Company Law*, 6th edn, Sweet & Maxwell, London, pp. 664–8, 708–9.
18   See *Edwards v. Halliwell* [1950] 2 All ER 1064, 1066–67 per Jenkins LJ.

some relevance for legal proceedings based on breaches of duty before the commencement of the new provisions and for considering when a derivative action should be
allowed, these are summarised below.[19]

(i) *Ultra vires* or illegal

It was quite clear that a majority in general meeting could authorise the company to act
in a way which was *ultra vires* or illegal.[20] A personal action might, therefore, be brought
by a shareholder to restrain an *ultra vires* transaction.[21] However, the significance of
ultra vires diminished with reforms which limited it generally to internal effect and
specified the nature of internal redress available. There were few cases of illegality in
practice. The derivative action based on this has now been abolished.

(ii) Special majorities

The rule did not apply where the matter was one which could validly be done or sanc-
tioned not by a simple majority of the members but by some special majority. This
exception covered the situation where the constitution specified the procedure which
had to be followed in respect of a particular transaction. If that procedure was not followed, the majority could ratify such conduct, for that would be to deny the minority
the protection afforded by the initial provision. The only option open to the majority in
such a case was to follow the procedure laid down in the constitution or, alternatively,
to alter the constitution.[22] Where the majority simply purported to ratify the transaction by an ordinary resolution, the minority shareholder could bring an action to
restrain them, as in *Edwards v. Halliwell.*[23] There, two members of the trade union
successfully restrained an attempt by the delegate meeting to increase the members'
contribution without obtaining the two-thirds majority required under their rules.
Similarly in *Salmon v. Quin and Axtens,*[24] where the articles of association provided that
certain transactions could not be entered into without the consent of both of the managing directors. In this instance one of the managing directors dissented, but the company in general meeting nevertheless tried to authorise the transaction without the
director's consent. It was held that they could not ratify the transaction. It was an
attempt to alter the terms of the contract between the parties by an ordinary resolution

---

19   See the interesting ex tempore judgment by Santow J in *Karam v. ANZ Banking Group Ltd* (2000) 18
     ACLC 590. See also *Chapman v. E-Sports Club Worldwide Ltd* (2001) 19 ACLC 213; *Advent Investors Pty Ltd
     v. Goldhirsch* (2001) 19 ACLC 580.
20   *Simpson v. Westminster Palace Hotel Co.* (1860) 8 HLC 712.
21   *Russell v. Wakefield Waterworks Co* (1875) LR 20 Eq 474; *Hawkesbury Development Pty Ltd v. Landmark
     Finance Pty Ltd* [1969] 2 NSWR 782, 793–94.
22   *Automatic Self-Cleaning Filter Syndicate v. Cuninghame* [1906] 2 Ch 34; *Salmon v. Quin & Axtens Ltd* [1909]
     AC 442.
23   [1950] 2 All ER 1064.
24   [1909] AC 442.

instead of by special resolution.[25] The derivative action based on this has now been abolished.

(iii) Personal rights

Obviously, if a member can point to the infringement of some personal right[26] then he or she need not be concerned with *Foss v. Harbottle* at all. Here the wrong will be done to them and not to the company and the rule will not apply.

The crucial question then is to decide what are the membership rights which will give rise to a personal action if infringed? Membership rights can arise in a number of ways, from the constitution, from statute, or from a separate shareholders' agreement. But it is primarily rights arising from the constitution that cause concern, for this is the grey area where the conflict between shareholder protection and majority rule is most acute.

To determine the extent of the membership rights under the constitution, it is of course necessary in Australia to consider the effect of section 140(1) of the Corporations Act. Does a member have a personal right to have all the articles observed? The answer seems to be 'no', according to Justice Young in the New South Wales case of *Stanham v. The National Trust of Australia (NSW)*.[27] Membership rights are more limited than that,[28] but include such rights as the right to have a vote recorded,[29] to have a dividend paid in cash if the constitution so specifies,[30] to enforce a declared dividend as a legal debt,[31] and to have the constitution observed if it specifies a certain procedure to be followed in a particular instance.[32] However, a member does not have a right to have a poll taken,[33] nor to have accounts prepared in accordance with the requirements of the Corporations Act,[34] nor apparently to have directors retire in accordance with the constitution,[35] nor do they have the right not to have the value of their shares reduced by the wrongdoing of the directors, where that wrong-

---

25 But note the inconsistency here between these cases and *Grant v. UK Switchback Railway Co.* (1888) 40 ChD 135; and *Irvine v. Union Bank of Australia* (1877) 2 App Case 366, where the mandate was altered by ordinary resolution.

26 There is some overlap here with the 'special majorities' exception. Some cases speak of the shareholders' personal right to have the articles complied with, see *Salmon v. Quin & Axtens Ltd* (supra). See K. W. Wedderburn, 'Shareholders' Rights and the Rule in *Foss v. Harbottle*' (1957) CLJ 194, 209–215.

27 (1989) 7 ACLC 628, 631

28 See in New Zealand, *Black, White & Grey Cabs Ltd v. Gaskin* [1971] NZLR 552; *Nathan v. Kiwi Life & General Mutual Assurance Co. Ltd* (1982) 1 NZCLC 98, 503.

29 *Pender v. Lushington* (1877) 6 ChD 70.

30 *Wood v. Odessa Waterworks Co.* (1889) 42 Ch D 636.

31 *Mosely v. Koffyfontein Mines Ltd* [1904] 2 Ch 108.

32 *Edwards v. Halliwell* [1950] 2 All ER 1064.

33 *MacDougall v. Gardiner* (1875) 1 ChD 13.

34 *Devlin v. Slough Estates Ltd* (1982) *Times*, 11 June.

35 *Mosley v. Alston* (1847) 1 Ph 790.

doing has caused damage to the company and the shareholder's loss is only conse-quential to that.[36]

It has been held in Australia that a shareholder has a personal right not to have his or her shareholding diluted by an issue for an improper purpose. This was held by Chief Justice King in the South Australian case of *Residues Treatment and Trading Co. Ltd v. Southern Resources Ltd.*[37] This is grounded on equitable principles and is ultimately consistent with the recognition of shareholder proprietary rights in *Gambotto v. WCP Ltd.*[38] The essential characteristic of personal rights seems, however, somewhat elusive.

A finding by the courts, then, that a personal right of a shareholder has been infringed is very useful, enabling as it did the 'controversial obscurities' of the rule in *Foss v. Harbottle* to be bypassed. But it is clear that drawing the line between what is an internal irregularity capable of ratification and what is an infringement of a personal right, is very difficult. Many commentators have argued for a liberalisation of the personal rights category[39] since ultimately that would have made the rule in *Foss v. Harbottle* redundant. One suggestion was that all the articles should be regarded as con-ferring personal rights on the shareholders, except for those articles which have already been clearly identified by the case law as concerning internal procedures only.[40] Another suggestion was to regard any breach of a director's fiduciary duty as giving a shareholder a personal cause of action.[41] It seems clear, however, from the remarks of the English Court of Appeal in *Prudential Assurance Co. v. Newman Industries Ltd*[42] that the courts will not look favourably on any extension of the personal action.

In New Zealand, section 169 of the *Companies Act 1993* deals with the matter by expressly giving shareholders a right of action against directors in respect of duties owed to shareholders. It excludes damages for diminution of the value of shares caused by a wrong done to the company and the mainstream directors' duties, but specifies the statutory duties which are owed to shareholders. These are supervision of the register, disclosure of interests and disclosure of share dealings (sections 169(2) and (3)). What the relationship of this section is to the common law and equity is not clear. The section is not a codification so it is strongly arguable that the common law and equitable per-sonal rights still subsist.

---

36 *Prudential Assurance Co. Ltd v. Newman Industries Ltd (No 2)* [1982] Ch 204, although such conduct may found a derivative action. To found a personal action, the shareholder's loss must be separate and distinct from that of the company.
37 (1988) 6 ACLC 1160. Compare *Christiansen v. Scott* [1996] 1 NZLR 273 for possible personal right in guarantor/shareholders to sue professional advisers for negligence but see also *Stein v. Blake* [1998] BCC 316 and *Johnson v. Gore Wood & Co.* [1999] BCC 474 for a contrary view.
38 (1995) 13 ACLC 342.
39 S. Beck, 'The Shareholders' Derivative Action' (1974) 52 Can Bar Rev 159, 171–2; Davies, *op. cit.* footnote 18 supra, pp. 660 *et seq.*
40 K. W. Wedderburn, 'Shareholders' Rights and the Rule in *Foss v. Harbottle*' (1957) CLJ 194, 214–15.
41 Beck, *op. cit.*, pp. 171–2.
42 [1982] 1 All ER 354, 367.

(iv) Fraud on the minority

As with the other exceptions to the rule, the breach constituting fraud on the minority had to be one that could not be ratified by a simple majority of the company in general meeting. If the breach was capable of being ratified, then an action would not lie, since there was no objection to directors using their votes to exculpate themselves in such circumstances.[43] It was necessary that the breach could not be ratified. It was also necessary to show that the wrongdoers were in control of the company. It should be pointed out that the label 'fraud on the minority' was somewhat misleading, since we are concerned here with injuries to the company.

Fraud

The requirement that the breach in question was not capable of being ratified was traditionally expressed in terms of 'fraud'.[44] Again, however, this was a rather misleading term to use. Fraud in this context included not only fraud at common law but also equitable fraud, which is much broader. In one case, it was categorised as 'an abuse or misuse of power'.[45] In fact, it was always been difficult to draw the line between those breaches which could and those which could not be ratified. Some cases were clear, but there was a substantial grey area.

It was clearly established that misappropriation of company assets was not capable of being ratified.[46] Directors holding a majority of votes were not, therefore, permitted to make a present of company assets to themselves.[47]

A similar view was taken in *Estmanco Ltd v. GLC*[48] where the court held that the action of the company in voting to discontinue proceeding against the GLC for breach of an agreement to sell council properties to their tenants amounted to fraud on the minority. The company had been set up to manage flats which the council was in the process of selling to their tenants. Its members comprised the GLC and former tenants who had completed the purchase of their flats. All voting rights in the company were vested in the GLC until such time as all sixty flats were sold. After twelve of the flats had been sold, the GLC changed its policy and discontinued selling. In reality then, the decision of the majority to discontinue proceedings was the decision of the GLC not to proceed against itself. This the court would not permit.

---

43   *NW Transportation Co. Ltd v. Beatty* (1887) 12 App Cas 589. Even if a ratifying resolution is impeachable as not having been passed bona fide for the benefit of the company as a whole, the remedy in respect of this would presumably only require that the resolution be passed bona fide. The breach which was sought to be ratified would not be the subject of a remedy on this ground alone.

44   See *Burland v. Earle* [1902] AC 83, 93 per Lord Davey.

45   *Estmanco Ltd v. GLC* [1982] 1 All ER 437, 445.

46   *Burland v. Earle* [1902] AC 83, 93; *Menier v. Hooper's Telegraph* (1874) LR 9 Ch App 350.

47   *Cook v. Deeks* [1916] 1 AC 554, 565; *Millers Invercargill Ltd v. Maddams* [1938] NZLR 490, where a director who had exercised his majority control to vote himself excessive fees was ordered to repay them at the suit of the minority shareholder. See also *Ngurli v. McCann* (1953) 90 CLR 425, 447 (High Ct).

48   [1982] 1 All ER 437.

Fraud on the minority also extended to a decision by the majority to expropriate a minority shareholder when this was not for a proper purpose and was unfair. This was held by the Australian High Court in *Gambotto v. WCP Ltd.*[49] Mere tax advantages or greater administrative efficiency are not 'proper' for this purpose. Expropriation of a competitor or compliance with regulations in an area such as broadcasting and media rules would be proper.

It has already been noted that the making of incidental profits, by directors, as in *Regal (Hastings) Ltd v. Gulliver*[50] was apparently capable of ratification by the company in general meeting.[51] This was inconsistent with the approach in *Cook v. Deeks*[52] but could be explained on the basis of the incidental nature of the profits and the bona fides of the directors.

It seems that mere negligence on the part of the directors was insufficient to found a derivative action. In *Pavlides v. Jensen*[53] a shareholder complained that corporate assets had been sold at a gross undervalue. He alleged negligence on the part of the directors, but no bad faith. Justice Danckwerts held that the negligence could be ratified.

However, in *Daniels v. Daniels*[54] the directors negligently sold a company asset to one of their number at an undervalue. He resold the asset at a substantial profit. Justice Templeman (as he then was) refused to say that a derivative action could not proceed in these circumstances. In characteristically trenchant terms he stated:[55]

> To put up with foolish directors is one thing; to put up with directors who are so fool-ish that they make a profit of £115 000 odd at the expense of the company is something entirely different.

It would seem, then, that self-serving negligence with corresponding benefits could not be ratified. The decision enlarged one of the exceptions to the rule in *Foss v. Harbottle* to such an extent as to consume it.[56] The case could simply be seen as one which involved the appropriation of corporate assets.[57] However, a similar formulation was put forward by Justice Vinelott in *Prudential Assurance Ltd v. Newman Industries Ltd*[58] at first instance. For him, a derivative action lay whenever directors (albeit bona fide) 'are guilty of a breach of duty to their company (including their duty to exercise proper care) and as a result of that breach obtain some benefit'. The criticism which can be

---

49   (1995) 13 ACLC 342
50   [1942] 1 All ER 378.
51   See chs 11 and 12 above.
52   [1916] 1 AC 554.
53   [1956] Ch 565.
54   [1978] Ch 406.
55   At 414.
56   See D. D. Prentice, '*Wallersteiner v. Moir*: The Demise of the Rule in *Foss v. Harbottle*' (1980) 40 Conv 47.
57   K. W. Wedderburn, 'Derivative Actions and *Foss v. Harbottle*' (1981) 44 MLR 202, 205.
58   [1980] 2 All ER 841, 869. Reversed in part on appeal [1982] 1 All ER 354, although the Court of Appeal did not have to comment on this part of Vinelott J's judgment.

made of this is that it included breaches of duty which had hitherto been thought capable of ratification; ratification and *Foss v. Harbottle* traditionally went hand in hand.

Another difficult area which had to be considered was where directors act otherwise than bona fide in the interests of the company as a whole, or for a collateral purpose. Certainly a *mala fide* exercise of their powers for a collateral purpose could not be ratified by the company[59] whereas a bona fide exercise of powers for a collateral purpose could be: *Hogg v. Cramphorn*[60] and *Bamford and Bamford*.[61]

One final point in relation to ratification is the question of voting: could a wrongdoing director vote, as a shareholder, to ratify his or her misconduct? The answer seemed to be that he or she could, for:

> Every shareholder has a perfect right to vote upon any such question, although he may have personal interest in the subject-matter opposed to or different from the general or particular interest of the company.[62]

If the matter could be ratified then the director could vote. Ratification did not mean ratification by an independent majority.[63] Voting, however, to deprive the company of an asset, as in *Menier v. Hoopers Telegraph Works*[64] and *Estmanco Ltd v. GLC*[65] was in itself a fraud on the minority. Ratifying one's own wrongdoing could in any event amount to unfairly prejudicial conduct within section 232 and section 174.

Control

The second element that, prior to the recent reforms, had to be established before a member could come within the fraud on the minority exception was control by the wrongdoers that prevented the company itself bringing an action in its own name.[66] This control existed if the wrongdoers had a majority of the votes, or the majority had actually approved a fraud on the minority, or the company had otherwise shown that it was not willing to sue.[67] It was, therefore, necessary to make some attempt to persuade the company to sue; it was not sufficient simply to allege that the wrongdoers were in control.

In *Eromanga Hydrocarbons NL v. Australis Mining NL*[68] Chief Justice Malcolm described the essence of control as 'a reference to those who command a majority of the

---

59 *Cook v. Deeks* [1916] 1 AC 554.
60 [1967] Ch 254.
61 [1970] Ch 212. Approved by New South Wales Court of Appeal in *Winthrop Investments Ltd v. Winns Ltd* [1975] 2 NSWLR 666.
62 *North-West Transportation Co. v. Beatty* (1887) 12 App Cas 589, 598.
63 Possibly it should, see R. Baxt, 'Judges in Their Own Cause: The Ratification of Directors' Breaches of Duty' (1978) 5 Monash LR 16. The general meeting would then have greater control over the directors. Vinelott J suggested that there should be an independent majority, in the *Prudential* case at 862, but this view has its difficulties, see K. W. Wedderburn note (1981) 44 MLR 202, 208–9.
64 (1867) LR 5 Eq 464.
65 [1982] 1 All ER 437.
66 See J. H. Farrar and B. Hannigan, *Farrar's Company Law*, 4th edn, Butterworths, London, 1998, p. 458.
67 *ibid.*
68 (1988) 14 ACLR 486 at 489.

votes at an ordinary general meeting of the company'. This proposition was accepted in *Biala PL v. Mallina Holdings Ltd (No 2)*[69] by Justice Ipp. In that case it was argued that the plaintiffs should be able to bring their action on the basis of fraud on the minority. To satisfy the requirements of this exception the plaintiffs needed to be able to show that at the time of trial the majority of shareholders would have voted against establishing proceedings against the wrongdoers. However, Justice Ipp decided that the evidence was not clear enough and therefore the exception was not established. He said:

> Accordingly the plaintiffs have not been able to satisfy me that more than 50 per cent of the shareholders of Mallina would at the date of trial, have voted against commencing or proceedings with the action. This, of course, is not a finding that less than 50 per cent of the shareholders would have voted in favour of the action. It is a finding that the plaintiffs have not established their case as regards the allegations.[70]

It is not altogether clear whether the courts recognised de facto control, or whether legal control had to be established. Justice Vinelott in *Prudential Assurance Co. v. Newman Industries Ltd*[71] was prepared to allow the minority to proceed even though the two directors whose conduct was challenged did not hold a majority shareholding and the rest of the board was apparently independent. This was put on the basis that control existed if there was no real possibility that the issue would ever be put to the shareholders in a way which would enable them to exercise a proper judgment on the issue. The exception, in his opinion, applied wherever the defendants were shown to be able, by any means, to manipulate their position in the company to ensure that an action is not brought by the company.[72] The Court of Appeal,[73] while stating that they did not consider *Atwool v. Merryweather*[74] (which Justice Vinelott had relied upon) to have established the proposition the judge considered it had,[75] did not, however, proceed to identify what is the proper control test. They pointed out that control embraces a broad spectrum extending from an overall, absolute majority of votes at one end, to a majority of votes at the other end made up of those likely to be cast by the delinquent himself plus those voting with him through apathy.[76] This suggested a broad approach to the problem.

Before leaving the rule in *Foss v. Harbottle*, note must be made of a vital procedural point which was raised by the English Court of Appeal in *Prudential Assurance Ltd v. Newman Industries Ltd*.[77] It was there held that, as a preliminary point, the shareholder had to establish a *prima facie* case

---

69   (1993) 11 ACSR 785
70   *ibid.*, at 843.
71   [1980] 2 All ER 841.
72   *ibid.*, at 875.
73   [1982] 1 All ER 354.
74   (1867) LR 5 Eq 464.
75   [1982] 1 All ER 354, 362.
76   *ibid.*, at 364.
77   [1982] 1 All ER 354.

(i) that the company was entitled to the relief claimed; and

(ii) that the action fell within the proper boundaries of the Rule.[78]

In the lower court Justice Vinelott had refused to try the issue as a preliminary point. The Court of Appeal pointed out the problems in 'subjecting the company to a thirty-day action … in order to enable [the judge] to decide whether the plaintiffs were entitled in law to subject the company to a thirty-day action'.[79] To allow this would be to subvert the rule in *Foss v. Harbottle*, which was partly aimed at preventing a multiplicity of actions.

However, as was pointed out in *Hurley v. BGH Nominees Pty Ltd*,[80] sometimes it is reasonable to consider the question of standing on the basis of certain facts, which are assumed, but equally, evidence will sometimes have to be heard to provide a factual foundation upon which the court may make a decision. The court retains a discretion to adopt whatever course is just and convenient in the circumstances.

The general law and procedure on fraud on the minority has now been abolished with the introduction of statutory derivative actions in both countries.

(v) Interests of justice

Although there was some English authority in favour of this exception, it was rejected by the English Court of Appeal in *Prudential Assurance Ltd v. Newman Industries (No 2) Ltd*.[81]

It was, however, recognised in Australia in a number of cases starting with *Hawkesbury Development Co. Ltd v. Landmark Finance Pty Ltd*[82] and *Biala Pty Ltd v. Mallina Holdings Ltd (No 2)*.[83] In *Biala Pty Ltd v. Mallina Holdings Ltd (No 2)* Justice Ipp clearly recognised the interests of justice as an exception to the rule in *Foss v. Harbottle*. The overall effect of this exception was that it allowed minority shareholders to bring an action in their name with the result that any benefit from the action went to the company. The essence of this exception was elaborated by Justice Ipp where he said:

> it seems to me to be contrary to principle to require wronged minority shareholders to bring themselves within the boundaries of the well-recognised exceptions and to deny jurisdiction to a court of equity even where an unjust or unconscionable result may otherwise ensue … I consider it to be desirable to allow a minority shareholder to bring a derivative claim where the justice of the case clearly demands that such a claim be brought, irrespective of whether the claim falls within the confines of the established exceptions.[84]

78   *ibid.* at 366.
79   *ibid.* at 365.
80   (1982) 1 ACLC 387.
81   [1982] Ch 204.
82   [1969] 2 NSWR 782.
83   (1993) 11 ACLC 1082.
84   *Biala Pty Ltd v. Mallina Holdings Ltd (No 2)* (1993) 11 ACLC 1082 at 1102.

These cases were followed in a number of later Australian cases.[85] The derivative action based on this exception has now been abolished with the introduction of the statutory derivative action.

Applications under section 232 of the Corporations Act and section 174 of the New Zealand Act

The difficulties associated with the rule in *Foss v. Harbottle* caused alternative remedies to be devised, which are intended to avoid many of the technical obstacles that faced the minority shareholder at common law.

Legislative provisions giving to minorities a means of redress have been appearing since section 210 of the *Companies Act 1948* was enacted in the United Kingdom. Since then many other common law jurisdictions have adopted similar provisions. Legislation in both Australia and New Zealand was originally similar in most respects to the UK Act. However, since the 1980s there have been substantial changes in the provisions.

Section 232 of the Corporations Law provides that the court shall have power to make an order if:

(a) the conduct of a company's affairs; or

(b) an actual or proposed act or omission by or on behalf of a company; or

(c) a resolution, or a proposed resolution, of members or a class of members of a company;

is either

(d) contrary to the interests of the members as a whole; or

(e) oppressive to, unfairly prejudicial to, or unfairly discriminatory against, a member or members whether in that capacity or in any other capacity.

Section 174 of the New Zealand *Companies Act 1993* is substantially similar.

Before examining the key terms in the section, reference should be made to defects in the earlier sections which were eliminated by the reforms.[86]

1 Previously, the courts had held that a shareholder must have been affected in their capacity as a member. Therefore, if a member who was also a director was dismissed from their post as director, they would have no remedy under the section.[87]

---

85 R. Teele, 'A Fifth Exception to the Rule in *Foss v. Harbottle* (1995) 13 C&SLJ 329 at 330; *Aloridge (prov. liq. apptd) v. West Australian Gem Explorers (prov. liq. apptd)* (1995) ACSR 645 at 651; *Cope v. Butcher* (1996) 20 ACSR 37; *Mesenberg v. Card Industrial Recruiters Pty Ltd* (No 1 & 2) (1996) 19 ACSR 483; *Rycorp Consulting Pty Ltd v. Pynary Pty Ltd* (1996) 21 ACSR 161; *Nece Pty Ltd v. Riteck Inc.* (1997) 24 ACSR 38, 44.

86 See J. H. Farrar and M. Russell, *Company Law and Securities Regulation in New Zealand*, Butterworths, Wellington, 1985, p. 266. See generally M. Berkahn, *The Role of the Oppression Remedy in New Zealand Company Law*, Occasional Paper No. 4, Department of Business Law, Massey University, Palmerston North, 1999.

87 *Re Lundie Bros Ltd* [1965] 2 All ER 692.

This was particularly harsh if all company profits were channelled into directors' remuneration. A member may now sue in respect of alleged wrongs to them in any capacity.

2   It had been held that the acts complained of must be continuing at the time of the presentation of the application.[88] Isolated or completed acts were not included. Therefore, potentially damaging transactions might go untouched, for instance, oppressive alterations to the constitution. Now, however, the application may be in respect of past, or indeed, future acts, as well as a continuing course of action.

3   The old sections allowed redress only in cases of 'oppression'. This term was narrowly construed by the courts as requiring some dishonesty, bad faith, or lack of probity by those concerned.[89] Mere negligence, however gross, would not be sufficient on this interpretation.[90] The section now includes the terms 'unfairly prejudicial' and 'unfair discriminatory conduct'. The plain intent, therefore, is to widen the scope of the section;

4   There was some doubt as to the right of personal representatives of shareholders to make an application.[91] This is now specifically provided for in the sections.

The concept of unfair prejudice/discrimination

Unfortunately, the legislature has given no guidelines as to the interpretation of these key terms. Perhaps clear definitions of them were either impossible, or inadvisable because they might lead to narrow restrictions being placed on the courts' power to intervene, in line with previous interpretations.[92] The consensus is, however, that the term 'unfairly prejudicial' has potentially a wider scope than 'oppression'.

The dictionary meaning of 'prejudice' is 'damage or detriment to interest'. However, prejudice is inherent in all corporate decision making. The principal issue thus becomes one of fairness. The meaning of 'unfair prejudice' may come to be found by the courts upon an examination of principles which the common law has developed with relation to the rights of minority shareholders. The common law favoured the majority. For instance, in the context of alteration to the constitution, all that is required is that the majority vote consistently with the constitution and avoid oppression and in the case of expropriation, for a proper purpose and fairly.[93] Mere damage to

---

88   *Re Jermyn St Turkish Baths Ltd* [1971] 3 All ER 184, 198.

89   *Scottish Cooperative Wholesale Society v. Meyer* [1959] AC 324, 342 per Lord Simmonds; *Elder v. Elder & Watson Ltd* [1952] SC 49; K. W. Wedderburn, 'Oppression of Minority Shareholders' (1966) 29 MLR 321, 324.

90   *Re Five Minute Car Wash Ltd* [1966] WLR 745.

91   See the contrasting view in *Re Jermyn St Turkish Baths Ltd* [1970] 3 All ER 374, 385 per Plowman J at first instance and *Re Mayer Douglas Pty Ltd* [1965] VR 638, 654–5.

92   For a useful analysis of the court's jurisdiction see Spigelman CJ in *Fexuto Pty Ltd v Bosnjak Holdings Pty Ltd* (2001) 37 ACSR 672 at 674–5. This case contains an Australian discussion of Lord Hoffmann's speech in *O'Neill v Phillips* [1999] 1 WLR 1092.

93   *Gambotto v. WCP Ltd* (1995) 13 ACLC 342.

the interests of the minority is not enough. Indeed, the minority accept the possibility of damage when they take up their shares, and this is part of the wider principle of majority rule.

Again, the principle that a shareholder may vote in their own interests added to the minority's difficulties. This was particularly evident in the context of ratification, see *North-West Transportation Ltd v. Beatty.*[94]

Both of these principles may still have some relevance in interpreting the new section, in that they are partly grounded in the priority afforded to majority rule. This latter principle should remain unaffected for the most part so that, for example, the court would probably be very reluctant to regard 'independent' ratification by the company in general meeting to be unfairly prejudicial conduct, while ratification by the company in general meeting, which has been brought about by the votes of the wrong-doers, would be seen as unfairly prejudicial conduct, involving the imposition of further restraints on the shareholder's proprietary right to vote as he or she pleases.

While it is clear that the principle of majority rule will still be a great influence, there are cases in which it will be given less weight. For instance, in small companies, which are in substance little more than incorporated partnerships, the members of the company will be bound together largely by trust and confidence, as is the case with partnerships. There will also be certain underlying expectations,[95] which will not necessarily appear in the constitution. The courts, in the context of winding up, have shown that they will in such cases control the exercise of majority rule so as to give effect to these expectations.[96] The same approach is adopted under the sections in defining the term 'unfairly prejudicial'.[97]

Basically, the whole issue remains very much undecided. The New Zealand Court of Appeal, however, considered the section in *Thomas v. HW Thomas Ltd.*[98] This was a case where the substance of a petitioning shareholder's complaint was that he had inherited shares. He found that he was locked into a company which was allegedly paying insufficient dividends to the shareholders. The petitioner claimed that this, coupled with a refusal by the other members to purchase his shares, amounted to oppression, unfair prejudice, or unfair discrimination.

The Court of Appeal, upholding Justice Ongley, dismissed the petition. However, the court took the opportunity to make some observations on what was then the new section 209 of the *Companies Act 1955*. It was thought first, that since the court was empowered by section 209(2) to grant relief where it considered it 'just and equitable'

---

94   (1887) 12 App Cas 589, 593.

95   For example, a right to participate in management, a pre-emptive right to shares of retiring members, sharing in profits, and so on.

96   *Ebrahimi v. Westborne Galleries Ltd* [1973] AC 360 (HL) at 379 per Lord Wilberforce. See in New Zealand *Re Gerard Nouvelle Cuisine Ltd* (1981) 1 NZCLC 98, 148 for a classic example; see also *Re North End Motels (Huntly) Ltd* [1976] 1 NZLR 446.

97   See *O'Neill v. Phillips, Re a Company (No 00709 of 1992)*, [1999] 1 WLR 1092 (HL). See also *Diligenti v. RWMD Operations Ltd* (1976) 1 BCR 36; see especially at 51 per Fulton J.

98   (1984) 2 NZCLC 99, 148.

to do so, the considerations underlying the exercise of jurisdiction in winding up on the ground that it is just and equitable, have some bearing on the exercise of the jurisdiction under section 209(2). Second, the court acknowledged that the inclusion of 'unfairly discriminatory or unfairly prejudicial' afforded petitioners a wider base on which to found a complaint.

The case was followed by the High Court of Australia in *Wayde v. NSW Rugby League Ltd.*[99] As Justice Brennan said, 'The operation of [the section] may be attracted to a decision made by the directors which is made in good faith for a purpose within the directors' powers but which reasonable directors would think to be unfair'.

Thus unfairness is the key concept. Some prejudice or detriment may be inevitable in share ownership. What is ruled out is *unfair* prejudice or discrimination. Fairness is not to be assessed in a vacuum. Its content depends upon the context in which it is being used. Justice Richardson in *Thomas* said:

> Fairness cannot be assessed in a vacuum or simply from one member's point of view. It will often depend on weighing conflicting interests of different groups within the company. It is a matter of balancing all the interests involved in terms of the policies underlying the companies legislation in general and [the section] in particular: thus to have regard to the principles governing the duties of a director in the conduct of the affairs of a company and the rights and duties of a majority shareholder in relation to the minority; but to recognise that s 209 is a remedial provision designed to allow the court to intervene where there is a visible departure from the standards of fair dealing; and in the light of the history and structure of the particular company and the reasonable expectations of the members to determine whether the detriment occasioned to the complaining member's interest arising from the acts or conduct of the company in that way is justifiable.[100]

These dicta have been followed in Australia.[101] However, somewhat narrower views were expressed by Lord Hoffmann in the recent House of Lords case of *O'Neill v. Phillips*[102] where *Thomas* does not appear to have been cited. There Lord

---

99 (1985) 3 ACLC 99.

100 (1984) 2 NZCLC 99, 148.

101 See *Wayde v. NSW Rugby League* (supra); *Gjergjat & Atco Controls Pty Ltd v. Cooper* (1986) 4 ACLC 359; *Morgan v. 45 Flers Avenue Pty Ltd* (1987) 5 ACLC 222; *The Phosphate Cooperative Co. of Australia v. Shears* (1988) 6 ACLC 124; *Darvall v. North Sydney Brick and Tile Co. Ltd* (1989) 7 ACLC 659; *Residues Treatment and Trading Co. Ltd v. Southern Resources Ltd (No 2)* (1989) 7 ACLC 1, 130; *Re Spargos Mining NL* (1990) 8 ACLC 1, 218; *Re Enterprise Gold Mines NL* (1991) 9 ACLC 168; *Jenkins v. Enterprise Gold Mines NL* (1992) 10 ACLC 136; *ASC v. Multiple Sclerosis Society of Tasmania* (1993) 11 ACLC 461; *Parker v. NRMA* (1993) 11 ACLC 866; *Re Bountiful Pty Ltd* (1994) 12 ACLC 902; *Gray Eldsdell Timms v. Combined Auctions* (1995) 13 ACLC 965; *Re DG Brims & Sons Pty Ltd* (1995) 16 ACSR 559; *Martin v. Australian Squash Club Pty Ltd* (1996) 14 ACLC 452; *Re Polyresins Pty Ltd* (1998) 16 ACLC 1674; *Raymond v. Cook* (2000) 1 QdR 65.

102 [1999] 1 WLR 1092. Cited in *Fedorovitch v. St Aubins Pty Ltd* (1999) ACLC 1558, 1560 and *Fexuto Pty Ltd v Bosnjak Holdings Pty Ltd* (2001) 37 ACSR 672. Noted by J. Payne and D. D. Prentice (1999) 115 LQR 587, R. Goddard [1999] CLJ 487 and A. J. Boyle (2000) 21 Co. Law 253. See also G. Shapira, 'The Hand that Giveth is the Hand that Taketh Away—*O'Neill v. Phillips* and Shareholder Legitimate Expectations' (2000) 11 Aust Jnl of Corp Law 260.

Hoffmann, with whom the other law lords agreed, said the context and background are very important and the background has two features. First, the company is an association of persons for an economic purpose usually entered into with legal advice and some degree of formality. The manner in which the affairs of the company may be conducted is closely regulated by agreed rules. Second, the way company law has developed seamlessly from the law of partnership, which was treated by equity as a contract of good faith. Thus unfairness may consist of a breach of the rules or in using the rules in a manner which equity would regard as contrary to good faith. His Lordship gave a narrow interpretation to unfairness and retreated from his earlier references[103] to legitimate expectations. The latter should not have a life of its own and there should not be any no fault divorce concept.

His Lordship thought that where the majority shareholder wishes to put an end to the association unfairness did not lie in exclusion alone but exclusion without a reasonable offer to buy the minority shareholder's shares or make some other fair arrangement. Where litigation has already been commenced this should probably include an offer of costs as well.

His Lordship said the court has to strike a balance between the breadth of the discretion given to it and the principle of legal certainty. This, with respect, seems confusing. If the legislature has given the court a broad discretion what right has the court to seek to cut it down? Further, legal certainty is not a legal principle, it is simply a policy. What right has a conservatively minded court to use policy to curtail legislation in this way? It is a pity that *Thomas* was not cited, as Justice Richardson's views are a more thorough review of the various issues of principle and policy involved.

In *Thomas* the petition was dismissed because the petitioner had not explored all possible avenues as regards the sale of his shareholding, and also because the court was not prepared to give adverse weight to the policy of low dividend payments, neither was it prepared to say that the majority were wrong in preferring to retain the company's real property, rather than sell it and distribute the proceeds. These questions involved commercial judgment with which the court would not normally interfere. It was said, however, by Sir Thaddeus McCarthy, that a total failure to pay dividends might give rise to a successful petition.[104]

Examples of unfairly prejudicial conduct

In the light of the cases, the following may be regarded in the circumstances as evidence of unfairly prejudicial or oppressive conduct:

(a) exclusion from management
(b) excessive remuneration payments

---

103 See *Re Saul D Harrison & Sons Plc* [1995] 1 BCLC 14; J. Hill, 'Protesting Shareholders and Reasonable Expectations' (1992) 10 C&SLJ 86. See now *Fexuto Pty Ltd v Bosnjak Holdings Pty Ltd* (2001) 37 ACSR 672, 683, 723–4, 743, 784.
104 See *Thomas v. H. W. Thomas Ltd* (1984) 2 NZCLC 99, 148 at 99, 159. Cf. *Roberts v. Walker Developments Proprietary Ltd* (1997) 15 ACLC 882.

(c) unfairly restricted dividend policy

(d) overbearing or irregular conduct of meetings

(e) issues of shares to water down the minority interest

(f) self-interested transactions

(g) diversion of business.

Orders

Section 233(1) and section 174(2) give the court complete freedom to make such order as it considers appropriate. There are, however, certain types of order which are specified, although they do not limit the generality of the court's power. These are as follows:

(i) The court may make an order regulating the conduct of the company's affairs in the future

A classic example of this type of order is that made in the English case of *Re Harmer Ltd*.[105] Here the court order involved a sweeping reorganisation of the company's management structure. The court ordered that the eighty-year-old founder director who had run the company in an autocratic and tyrannical fashion, ignoring the requirements of the articles and the wishes of the board, should be made president of the company, without any rights, duties or powers and that the company should contract for his services as a consultant for life. The court also ordered him not to interfere in any aspect of the management of the company save in accordance with the decisions of the board. This was a remarkable order amounting to a considerable intrusion in the affairs of the company and one which can only be justified by the exceptional circumstances of the case. Other typical orders under this heading might include the appointment or removal of directors,[106] the reduction of capital, the alteration of the constitution and the calling of meetings.[107]

(ii) The court may require the company to refrain from doing or continuing an act complained of by the applicant or to do an act which the applicant has complained that it has omitted to do

Under this provision the court can compel the payment of dividends or order the company not to carry into effect a proposed alteration to the constitution or it can order the cessation of payment of excessive salaries to directors.

---

105 [1958] 3 All ER 689.

106 See *Re Spargos Mining NL* (1990) 8 ACLC 1218.

107 For an example of the types of orders which might be made, see *Re Peterson and Kanata Investments Ltd* [1976] 1 BCLR 36 where the court orders included ordering the controlling shareholder to sell his shares back to the company at the price he originally paid for them, enjoining a special meeting of shareholders called to approve the sale of the company's only substantial asset and appointing a receiver–manager to manage the affairs of the company pending a general meeting.

(iii) The court may order the purchase of a member's shares by other members or by the company itself and, where the purchase is by the company itself the reduction of the company's capital accordingly

This provision was regarded as somewhat novel at the time it was enacted, as companies were then prohibited from purchasing their own shares. An order for the purchase of their shares is probably the relief most commonly sought by shareholders with these disputes, as usually they have no wish to remain further in the company and their only concern is to have their shares purchased at a fair price. A purchase order was in fact made under the original section by the House of Lords, in *Scottish Co-operative Wholesale Society v. Meyer.*[108] There, the majority shareholder was ordered to purchase the minority's shares at the price at which they stood before the oppressive conduct which rendered the shares valueless. The House of Lords emphasised that the purchase is at fair value, not necessarily market value. This seems to include the possibility of some compensation although Justice Young did not think so in the recent case of *Fedorovitch v. St Aubins Pty Ltd.*[109]

(iv) The court may direct the company to conduct specified proceedings, or may authorise a member or members to do so in the name and on behalf of the company

This is intended as a statutory form of derivative action. Inclusion of this form of order in section 233(1) means that prejudice to a member may be treated as, in effect, a corporate cause of action, whereas previously, courts have been reluctant to allow the rule in *Foss v. Harbottle* to be circumvented by means of a personal action.[110] It could, however, be argued that the intent was to define a shareholder's personal rights more widely than was the case at common law. The position then under section 233 is that acts that damage the company are also accepted as being capable of indirectly damaging a shareholder's interest by way of a diminution in the value of the shares held. However, it might have been better had the section more clearly delineated the line between shareholders' personal rights and corporate rights as the New Zealand legislation does in

---

108 [1959] AC 324; *O'Neill v. Phillips* [1999] 1 WLR 1092. Compare *Fedorovitch v. St Aubins Pty Ltd* (1999) 17 ACLC 1558. In *Re Bird Precision Ltd* [1984] 2 WLR 869, Nourse J held that in considering the fair price to be paid for minority shares upon the making of an order for their purchase, there was no rule of universal application as to whether the price paid should be fixed on a pro rata basis, or on a discount basis (i.e. a discount reflecting the fact that the holding is only a minority one). However, he also held that there was a general rule that, where the purchase order is in respect of shares in a 'quasi-partnership', where the majority has been guilty of prejudicial conduct towards the minority, or there has been an agreement that a fair price be determined by the court, without any admission by the majority as to the existence of such prejudicial conduct, the fair price should be determined on a pro rata basis. The discount basis might, however, be applicable where the minority has deserved its exclusion from the company. See too *Holden v Architectural Finishes Ltd* (1996) 7 NZCLC 260, 976 and *Yovich v M Yovich & Sons Ltd* (2000) 8 NZCLC 262, 317.

109 (1999) 17 ACLC 1558, 1562. For a useful article on valuation see S. Sirianos, 'Problems of Share Valuation under s. 260 of the *Corporations Law*' (1995) 13 C&SLJ 88.

110 *Prudential Assurance Co. Ltd v. Newman Industries Ltd* [1982] 2 WLR 31, 48 CA.

section 169. Consequently section 174 of the New Zealand Act which deals with prejudiced shareholders does not include this kind of order.

This part of section 233 and the derivative action procedure in Part 2F.1A and section 165 of the New Zealand Act might well render *Foss v. Harbottle* superfluous. It could avoid the defects of the rule, while at the same time ensuring that one of its objects, the avoidance of a multiplicity of actions, is preserved.

Empirical study of use of the statutory remedy

A valuable empirical study of the use of the remedy in Australia has been recently carried out by Professor Ian Ramsay.[111] His main findings are:

1   The courts have tended on balance to find against applicants
2   There has been a significant rise in the use of the remedy
3   It is mainly used in disputes concerning small incorporated firms
4   Often all or most of the shareholders are involved in management in the companies concerned
5   There has been a broad range of allegations in the cases but the most common is exclusion from management
6   The courts are reluctant to wind up the companies
7   The courts have employed a range of tests but ultimately this is a test-driven jurisdiction, by which he means that the section confers jurisdiction based on broad principles to be applied to the totality of the facts in a given case.

Winding Up

(a) On the ground that it is just and equitable

Winding up under section 461 is the most drastic remedy available to shareholders. Early attempts to restrict it *ejusdem generis* with earlier paragraphs[112] (which list a number of instances where the court can order that a company be wound up) have been rejected,[113] and the courts now regard it as providing a wide discretionary jurisdiction.[114] The equivalent section in the New Zealand Act is section 241(4)(d).

It is necessary to examine first, the procedural requirements of the section and second, the grounds upon which the court may order a company to be wound up.

---

111   I. M. Ramsay, 'An Empirical Study of the Use of the Oppression Remedy' (1999) 27 ABLR 23. For useful comparison see M. Berkahn, 'Public and Private Enforcement of Company Law in New Zealand 1986–1998', unpublished paper, Deakin University (1999).
112   *Re Suburban Hotel Co.* (1887) LR 2 Ch App 737.
113   *Re Yenidje Tobacco Co.* [1916] 2 Ch 426.
114   See Smith J in *Re Wondoflex Textiles Ltd* [1951] VR 458 and Lord Wilberforce in *Ebrahimi v. Westbourne Galleries Ltd* [1972] 2 All ER 492, 495.

Procedural matters

Section 462(2)(c) of the Corporations Act permits an application to the court for a winding up order to be made by a contributory. This is defined in section 9 to mean every person liable to contribute to the assets of the company in the event of its being wound up. Section 9 also includes the holders of fully paid shares in the definition. The term 'contributory' no longer appears in the New Zealand legislation.

Once individual members can establish a tangible interest then they can apply for winding up notwithstanding the fact that their particular shareholdings are very small ones. This was the case in *Bryanston Finance Ltd v. De Vries*[115] where the petitioner held a mere 62 shares out of some 7.5 million issued shares. However, the amount the applicant hopes to recover in a liquidation is likely to be appreciable in relation to the size of his or her shareholding.[116] If the *de minimis* principle applies then the court may regard the application as an abuse of process and throw it out of court. The jurisdiction under section 461(1)(k) and section 241(4)(d) of the New Zealand Act, after all, is an equitable one and the court will require the applicant to come before it with clean hands. If the breakdown in the conduct of the company's affairs is a result of the applicant's own misconduct,[117] or the applicant has acquiesced in the conduct which is the subject of complaint,[118] or if the applicant is merely trying to put pressure on the company,[119] then the court will refuse an order. If, however, the applicant can establish sufficient grounds, the fact that there is also an ulterior, perhaps personal motive for pursuing the matter does not render those grounds insufficient.

A contributory is not, however, entitled to apply unless the contributory's shares have been so held for at least six months before the commencement of the winding up, unless the number of shareholders has fallen beneath the statutory minimum, or the contributory is an original allottee of the shares, or a person to whom the shares have devolved on the death of a former holder. While this provision was designed to prevent individuals from purchasing shares with a view to winding up a company, the six-month period seems inadequate for this purpose. There is now no longer an equivalent to this under New Zealand law.

It was at one time a requirement that the applicant had to show that the conduct complained of affected them in their capacity as a member of the company and not as a director or employee or any other capacity. This has now been rejected by the House of Lords in *Ebrahimi v. Westbourne Galleries Ltd*[120] and a member is entitled to rely on any circumstances of justice or equity which affect them in their relations with the company or with the other shareholders.[121]

---

115 [1976] Ch 63.
116 [1976] Ch 63 at 75, per Buckley LJ and see also *Re Rica Gold Washing Co* (1879) 11 ChD 36 at 43 per Jessel MR.
117 *Ebrahimi v. Westbourne Galleries Ltd* [1973] AC 360 at 387, per Lord Cross.
118 *Re Fildes Bros Ltd* [1970] 1 All ER 923.
119 See *Bryanston Finance v. De Vries* [1976] Ch 63 at 75.
120 [1973] AC 360.
121 [1973] AC 360 per Lord Wilberforce. A 'qua member' requirement would unduly limit the instances in which a shareholder, particularly in the smaller private companies, could obtain relief.

Under section 467(4) the court cannot grant a winding up order on the ground that it is just and equitable if there is some alternative remedy available to the applicant, for example an injunction or an action for breach of contract, and the court finds that the applicant is acting unreasonably in not pursuing that alternative remedy. Another common alternative will be an application under sections 232 or 174. In *Re A Company*[122] the offending parties offered to purchase the petitioner's shares at a fair value to be determined by an independent expert. The petitioner refused to accept this: the court said this was unreasonable and the petition was struck out. This means, therefore, that 'remedy' in section 467(4) is not confined to a statutory, or even a legal remedy, but includes an extra-legal solution to the applicant's problem. There is now no longer an equivalent to section 467(4) in the New Zealand Act.

It should be noted that the right of a contributory to apply for a winding up is one conferred on him or her by statute and it cannot be taken away or restricted by the constitution.[123]

Grounds for the application

Various attempts have been made in the past to categorise the grounds on which an application will be granted, but this has been criticised, most notably by Lord Wilberforce, in the leading case *Ebrahimi v. Westbourne Galleries Ltd*,[124] where the view was taken that general words must remain general and should not be reduced to the sum or particular instances.[125] Certainly the categories of conduct within the phrase 'just and equitable' are not and should not be regarded as closed but there are nevertheless certain well-recognised headings which can usefully be relied on when attempting to determine the scope of the just and equitable provision. It is proposed to examine first, in brief, some of these 'old' headings, in particular the quasi-partnership, lack of probity and loss of substratum cases; second, to examine in detail the decision in the *Ebrahimi* case; and finally to attempt to determine the extent of the jurisdiction in light of that decision.

Quasi-partnership

One of the most important grounds for winding up was where the court decided that the company in question was really an incorporated partnership or quasi-partnership. Generally the company in question would have a small number of shareholders, most, if not all of whom, would participate in the management of the company and were prevented by restrictions in the articles from freely transferring their shares. Where the company possessed these characteristics, the court looked to see if grounds existed for winding up such a 'partnership', in particular, whether the personal relationship, so important to the continued existence of the partnership, was still intact, The classic

---

122 [1983] 2 All ER 854.
123 *Re Peveril Gold Mines* [1898] 1 Ch 122; *Re American Pioneer Leather Co.* [1918] 1 Ch 556.
124 [1973] AC 360.
125 [1973] AC 360 at 374.

example of this category is *Re Yenidje Tobacco Co.*[126] Here the relationship between the two shareholders (who were also the directors) had completely broken down. They refused even to talk to one another and all communications were through a third party. The court found that the company was in essence a partnership and that there was such a state of animosity between the parties as to preclude all reasonable hope of reconciliation and/or friendly cooperation. In such circumstances the court would order that it be wound up.

It was sometimes argued that a separate ground for winding up was deadlock, but as it mainly arose in the quasi-partnership cases, where it clearly signified the breakdown of the personal relationship between the parties,[127] it is convenient to include it here. It was unlikely to be accepted as a ground for winding up companies that did not fall within the quasi-partnership category, since in those companies, the general meeting would be in a position to exercise its residual powers to resolve any deadlock that might arise.[128]

Lack of probity

The classic statement of lack of probity is to be found in the Privy Council case of *Loch v. John Blackwood Ltd*:[129]

> It is undoubtedly true that at the foundation of applications for winding up on the 'just and equitable rule' there must lie a justifiable lack of confidence in the conduct and management of the company's affairs. But this lack of confidence must be grounded on conduct of the directors, not in regard to their private life or affairs, but in regard to the company's business. Furthermore the lack of confidence must spring not from dissatisfaction at being outvoted on the business affairs or on what is called the domestic policy of the company. On the other hand, whenever the lack of confidence is rested on a lack of probity in the conduct of the company's affairs, then the former is justified by the latter and it is, under the statute, just and equitable that the company be wound up.[130]

Here the directors failed to hold general meetings or submit accounts or recommend a dividend. Instead, the major shareholder treated the business as if it were his own and ran it down with a view to forcing the minority shareholder to sell out at an undervalue.[131] The court ordered that it be wound up.

---

126 [1916] 2 Ch 426, although the first case to rely on this ground was *Syminton v. Syminton Quarries Ltd* (1906) 8 Sess Cas 121; see also *Re Davis and Collet* [1935] Ch 693; *Re Wondoflex Textiles Pty Ltd* [1951] VLR 458.

127 Deadlock, however, was not a required factor, see *Re Davis and Collett* [1916] 2 Ch 426.

128 See B. McPherson, 'Winding Up on the Just and Equitable Ground' (1964) 27 MLR 282, also *Barron v. Potter* [1914] 1 Ch 895; *Foster v. Foster* [1916] 1 Ch 532.

129 [1924] AC 782.

130 [1924] AC 782 at 788 per Lord Shaw.

131 See also *Re Bleriot Manufacturing Co.* (1916) 32 TLR 253; *Re Newbridge Sanitary Steam Laundry* (1917) 1 IR 67; *Thomas v. Drysdale* (1925) SC 311.

Loss of substratum

Basically here, the position is that, if at the time of the formation of the company it was or it thereafter became impossible or illegal to achieve the main objects for which the company was formed, then the company would be wound up.[132] The theory was that where a member had subscribed to the company on the basis of its carrying on a particular business and the company proposed to pursue some other object, then as that member had not agreed to his money being used for that purpose, or his being subjected to the risk of loss in that venture, he was entitled to recover it by having the company wound up. Thus in *Re German Date Coffee Co.*[133] a company formed to produce coffee under a German patent was wound up when they failed to obtain the patent, even though they were successfully producing coffee made under a Swedish patent, and even though the majority of the shareholders were in favour of continuing the business.[134] The fact that the company, while formed for a particular purpose, has sufficient powers to carry on some other business will not prevent the company from being wound up if that particular purpose fails.[135]

Loss of substratum should be distinguished from the question of *ultra vires*. In the case of the former, the court is concerned with questions of equity as between the shareholders, and will not be confined to an examination of the literal wording of the constitution. Even where there is a *Cotman v. Brougham* clause in the constitution which treats each object as separate and independent, the court will nevertheless determine the main objects of the company, and will wind it up if they have been abandoned.[136]

Ebrahimi v. Westbourne Galleries Ltd[137]

This was a case of the truth of the old adage, 'Two is company. Three is a crowd'. In 1958 E and N, having originally traded as a partnership, selling oriental carpets, decided to form a company to take over the business. They became the only directors and shareholders, each holding 500 shares. Shortly afterwards, N's son A joined the business and E and N each transferred 100 shares to him. He also became a director. Eventually the parties fell out and E was removed from the board by N and A, as they were entitled to do by means of an ordinary resolution under the UK Companies Act, and excluded from the day-to-day management of the company. As all the profits in the company were distributed by way of directors' remuneration and not by way of dividend, he was

---

132 The doctrine originated in *Re Suburban Hotel Co* (1867) LR 2 Ch App 737; see also *Re Haven Gold Mining Co* (1882) 20 ChD 169; *Re Red Rock Gold Mining Co* (1889) 61 LT 685; *Re Baku Consolidated Oilfields Ltd* [1944] 1 All ER 24.
133 (1882) 20 ChD 169.
134 See also *Re Haven Gold Mining Co* (1882) 20 ChD 151.
135 *Re Baku Oilfields* [1944] 1 All ER 24; *Re Kitson and Co. Ltd* [1946] 1 All ER 435.
136 *Cotman v. Brougham* [1918] AC 514, 520 per Lord Parker. See also *Re National Portland Cement Co. Ltd* [1930] NZLR 564.
137 [1973] AC 360.

now deprived of any return on his investment. He petitioned for a winding up order on the just and equitable ground[138] and eventually succeeded in the House of Lords.

The House of Lords found that as a matter of law N and A had acted completely within their rights, within the provisions of the articles and the Companies Act in removing E in this way. But the just and equitable jurisdiction is not limited to proven cases of bad faith, and the legal correctness of their conduct did not make it unassailable. In certain instances the courts would subject the exercise of legal rights to equitable considerations, that is, considerations of a personal character arising between one individual and another that might make it unjust or inequitable to insist on strict legal rights or to exercise them in a particular way.

In this instance E and N had together formed the company on the basis that the character of the association would, as a matter of personal relation and good faith, remain the same.[139] N and A were not therefore, in all the circumstances, entitled to exercise their undoubted legal power to remove E as a director.[140] Once they had done so the only just and equitable course was to dissolve the association.

This is not to say that every exercise of majority power will now be restrained by the imposition of equitable considerations. In the vast majority of cases, compliance with the acts and the constitution will ensure the validity of the act (in the absence of bad faith or fraud or any other invalidating ground). But there will be some instances where the rights of the members will not be exhaustively defined in the articles.

It is, then, of crucial importance to majority shareholders to know precisely those instances when mere compliance with the legal requirements may not be sufficient.

It is obviously not enough that the company be a small or private one. There are thousands of small companies that are not of the Westbourne Galleries mould and which are run on strictly commercial lines. Lord Wilberforce suggested that one or more of the following factors should be present:[141]

1 that it be an association formed or continued on the basis of a personal relationship, involving mutual confidence;
2 that there be an agreement that all or some of the shareholders shall participate in the management of the business; and
3 that there are restrictions on the transfer of the members' interest in the company.

---

138 Ebrahimi also petitioned under s. 210 of the 1948 Act (UK), the alternative remedy in cases of oppression but he failed, because of the restrictive approach adopted by the courts to that provision, in particular their insistence that the petitioner be oppressed qua member, which Ebrahimi was not since his complaint was about being removed as a director, see *Re Westbourne Galleries Ltd* [1971] Ch 799.
139 [1973] AC 360 at 380.
140 [1973] AC 360 at 375. The court emphasised that the fact that he was not affected qua member was irrelevant to a petition under s. 217(f). Instead a member was entitled to rely on any circumstances of justice and equity that affected him in his relations with the company or with the other shareholders.
141 [1973] AC 360 at 379, see Prentice, note (1973) 89 LQR 107 at 114 where he suggested a fourth criterion, which is that profits are distributed by way of directors remuneration and not as dividends.

In these instances equitable considerations may come into play.

It would seem that most of the old headings, in particular the quasi-partnership, deadlock and the lack of probity cases, could all be subsumed within a more general *Ebrahimi* category, as indeed could the loss of substratum cases, on the basis that they involve the destruction of some underlying, fundamental obligation upon which the company was based.

The *Ebrahimi* approach was applied in *Re A & BC Chewing Gum Ltd.*[142] Here, minority shareholders, including in fact an American public company, were entitled under the articles *and* by virtue of a separate shareholders' agreement to appoint one director to the board, yet the majority refused to give effect to their appointment. Justice Plowman, relying on *Ebrahimi*, held that the company should be wound up, as the majority had repudiated the minority's right to participate in the management of the company, a right which was the underlying basis of their participation in the company.

A New Zealand decision has taken *Ebrahimi* even further. In *Re North End Motels (Huntly) Ltd*[143] the court, relying on *Ebrahimi*, ordered a company to be wound up where a minority director was being consistently outvoted[144] at board meetings and so had little say in the running of the company. The court found that while it was true that a minority director accepts and runs the risk of being consistently outvoted, in this case the petitioner had had no outside advice before joining the company and had little business experience. Moreover, were he to sell his shareholding, the majority shareholder was to be the final arbiter of their value. In the circumstances the court felt a winding up order was warranted.

One issue which has generated some debate has been whether the decision in *Ebrahimi* has ramifications for majority rule in areas outside winding up proceedings. Judicial support[145] for extending its application can be found in two cases, in particular, *Pennell v. Venida Investments*[146] and *Clemens v. Clemens Bros Ltd.*[147]

In *Pennell's* case the court found that the parties had entered into an understanding that the share ratio would remain at 51:49 and that there would be no increase in share capital without the plaintiff's consent. Justice Templeman found that the company was a quasi-partnership founded on mutual trust and confidence, and any attempt to alter the agreement, through an increase in capital and an ensuring rights issue, would be restrained by an injunction. Similarly in *Clemens*[148] an attempt to issue additional

---

142 [1975] 1 All ER 1017.

143 [1976] 1 NZLR 446. See also *Re Gerard Nouvelle Cuisine Ltd* (1981) 1 NZCLC 98, 148.

144 It will be recalled, see *Loch v. John Blackwood* [1924] AC 782, that mere dissatisfaction at being outvoted was not justification for making an order under the old headings although here the Court seemed to find the entire transaction something of an unconscionable bargain, see Shapira, Note (1977) 93 LQR 22.

145 For academic support see B. Rider, 'Partnership Law and its Impact on Domestic Companies' [1979] CLJ 148.

146 Unreported (1974) Templeman J, ChD noted at length in S. Burridge, 'Wrongful Rights Issues' (1981) 44 MLR 40.

147 [1976] 2 All ER 268.

148 [1976] 2 All ER 268, 282.

shares, which was designed to reduce a particular member's holding, was set aside using the *Ebrahimi* principle.

However, these extensions of the doctrine to cases where the company is a going concern and no winding up application has been made, have been criticised.[149] The orthodox position is that taken in *Bentley-Stevens v. Jones*[150] in which the court took the view that where a director was removed from his position, he could not call into play the *Ebrahimi* principles in the absence of a winding up petition.[151] The court said that the decision in *Ebrahimi* did not make it illegal for the majority to exercise their undoubted powers to remove a director, but simply said that if they did so, they may be subject to a winding up order.[152]

Ebrahimi's case clearly strengthened the position of the minority shareholder at least in the context of winding up. Majority shareholders in exercising their legal powers, be it as owner to remove someone as a director, or a power to refuse to register a transfer of shares or the power to issue shares, must now bear in mind that, notwithstanding the absence of bad faith, or that it was done bona fide for the benefit of the company as a whole, there is the risk that the aggrieved minority may obtain a winding up order under section 461(1)(k) or section 241(4)(d). The minority shareholders may not really wish to have the company wound up. They will normally prefer to realise their investment and quit the company, but as has been pointed out previously, it is not easy to obtain a purchaser for their shares. Now, however, given the serious possibility that a shareholder may succeed under the section, the majority may decide to purchase the minority's shares at fair value rather than run the risk. The impact of the obiter dicta in the House of Lords decision in the statutory minority shareholder action case of *O'Neill v. Phillips*[153] in this area is at the moment uncertain.

(b) Oppression and unfairly prejudicial conduct

Section 461(1)(f) and (g) of the Corporations Act provides for compulsory winding up on grounds which overlap with sections 232 and 174. These provisions no longer appear in the New Zealand Act. Apart from the just and equitable ground and inability to pay debts the only other grounds under section 241(4) of the New Zealand Act are persistent or serious failure to comply with the Act or non-compliance with section 10.

Under section 461(1), the court may order the winding up of a company if:

> (f) affairs of the company are being conducted in a manner that is oppressive or unfairly prejudicial to, or unfairly discriminatory against, a member or members or in a manner that is contrary to the interests of the members as a whole;

---

149 See Burridge, *op. cit.*, p. 55.
150 [1974] 2 All ER 653.
151 Lord Grantchester QC, in *Re A Company* [1983] 2 All ER 36, took an equally restrictive view.
152 [1974] 2 All ER 653 at 655.
153 [1999] 1 WLR 1092. For the dubious view that the just and equitable jurisdiction is no wider than s. 232 see *Re Guidezone Ltd* [2000] 2 BCLC 321.

(g) an act or omission, or a proposed act or omission, by or on behalf of the company, or a resolution, or a proposed resolution, of a class of members of the company, was or would be oppressive or unfairly prejudicial to, or unfairly discriminatory against, a member or members or was or would be contrary to the interests of the members as a whole …

(c) On the grounds of directors acting in own self-interest

Section 461(1)(e) of the Corporations Act provides that an order can be made where the directors have acted in affairs of the company in their own interests rather than in the interests of the members as a whole, or in any other manner whatsoever that appears to be unfair or unjust to other members. There is now no equivalent in New Zealand.

In *Re Cumberland Holdings Ltd*[154] Chief Justice Bowen in Equity made the following points on this ground:

(i) it is not limited to cases where the board has acted as a whole;

(ii) the words 'the affairs of the company' are not limited to trade or business matters, but encompass capital structure, dividend policy, voting rights, consideration of takeover offers, etc;

(iii) directors may be held to have acted in their own interests if they act in the interest of another company of which they are directors and shareholders;[155]

(iv) the nature of the injustice or unfairness, and the extent to which this prejudices members are matters for the court to consider in the exercise of its discretion.[156]

There is obviously some overlap here with the just and equitable jurisdiction[157] as there is with sections 232 and 174.

Statutory derivative actions

(a) Australia

We saw earlier in this chapter that it was possible to bring a derivative action under the case law but this was problematic in concept and procedure and the tendency has been to follow Canadian experience and to deal with the matters by statute. New Zealand did this in 1993 and Australia in the *Corporate Law Economic Reform Program Act 1999* operative since March 2000.

The purposes of the new provision are:

1 to overcome the problems associated with the rule in *Foss v. Harbottle*, especially the impact of ratification

---

154 (1976) 1 ACLR 361.
155 *Re National Discounts Ltd* (1951) 52 SR (NSW) 244.
156 *Re Weedmans Ltd* [1974] Qd R 377.
157 See, for example, *Re William Brookes & Co. Ltd* [1962] NSWR 142.

2   to clarify the procedure and financing of derivative actions

3   to reconcile such actions with the new Business Judgment Rule and to achieve accountability

4   to shift the role of corporate enforcer back to the private sector.

Politically, the new derivative action provision was the price to be paid for the introduction of the Business Judgment Rule.

The relevant Australian provisions are now set out in Part 2F.1A of the Corporations Act.

The nature of a derivative action

Section 236(1)(a) allows the court to grant leave for an authorised person:

(a) to bring proceedings on behalf of a company

(b) intervene in any proceedings in which the company is a party to take responsibility on behalf of the company

(c) to take a particular step in the proceedings, for example to compromise or settle them.

A person referred to in section 236(1)(a) is

(i) a member, former member, or person entitled to be registered as a member of the company or a related body corporate;

(ii) an officer or former officer of the company.

This is reasonably wide *locus standi*. The proceedings must be brought in the company's name (section 236(2)).

The case law derivative action is abolished (section 236(3)) but it may still be possible in an appropriate case to bring a personal action.

Procedure for applying for and granting leave

Under section 237(2) the court must grant the application if it is satisfied that:

(a) it is probable that the company will not itself bring the proceedings, or properly take responsibility for them, or for the steps in them; and

(b) the applicant is acting in good faith; and

(c) it is in the best interests of the company that the applicant be granted leave; and

(d) if the applicant is applying for leave to bring proceedings—there is a serious question to be tried; and

(e) either:

(i) at least 14 days before making the application, the applicant gave written notice to the company of the intention to apply for leave and of the reasons for applying; or

(ii) it is appropriate to grant leave even though subparagraph (i) is not satisifed.

The use of 'serious question to be tried' in section 237(2)(d) differs from the Canadian and New Zealand provisions. The latter, however, includes a requirement of 'the likelihood of proceedings succeeding' so there is probably no great difference between them. However, the criteria in section 237(2)(a), (b), and (c) seem tighter than the New Zealand requirements.

Section 237(3) provides a rebuttable presumption that granting leave is not in the best interests of the company and arises if it is established that:

(a) the proceedings are:
    (i)   by the company against a third party; or
    (ii) by a third party against the company; and
(b) the company has decided:
    (i)   not to bring the proceedings; or
    (ii) not to defend the proceedings; or
    (iii) to discontinue, settle or compromise the proceedings; and
(c) all of the directors who participated in that decision:
    (i)   acted in good faith for a proper purpose; and
    (ii) did not have a material personal interest in the decision; and
    (iii) informed themselves about the subject matter of the decision to the extent they reasonably believed to be appropriate; and
    (iv) rationally believed that the decision was in the best interests of the company.

The directors' belief that the decision was in the best interests of the company is a rational one unless the belief is one that no reasonable person in their position would hold. This wording echoes the Business Judgment Rule in section 180(2) and is not present in the New Zealand and Canadian legislation.

Section 237(4) clarifies who is a third party for the purposes of section 237(3). A person is a third party if the company is a public company and the person is not a related party of the company, or where the company is not a public company and the person would not be a related party if it were a public company.

Section 238 allows substitution of another person for the person granted leave.

An important question is the effect of ratification by members. This is dealt with in section 239 which provides that it does not prevent the applicant from applying for a derivative action but the court may take it into account in deciding what order to make. The court must have regard to how well informed the members were about the conduct when deciding to ratify the conduct and whether those who voted for it were acting for proper purposes.

The court can appoint an independent investigator to report to the court (section 241). This is not in the New Zealand or Canadian legislation. Unlike the USA there is no reference to independent directors. In the USA independent directors have a role in the special litigation committees either at the demand stage or where demand is excused in derivative litigation.

The court's permission is necessary for any discontinuance or settlement (section 240).

The court has wide general powers including a power to require mediation. It has wide powers also to make orders in respect of costs and can order the company to pay the applicant's costs (section 242).

(b) New Zealand

In New Zealand the matter is now governed by section 165 of the *Companies Act 1993*, which is in Part IX Enforcement. Section 164 deals with injunctions, section 165 with derivative actions, section 169 with personal actions, section 173 with representative actions and section 174 with unfairly prejudiced shareholders.

Like the Australian procedure, section 165 supersedes the case law remedy[158] (section 165(6)).

A shareholder and director have *locus standi* (section 165(1)). There is no reference to former shareholders or prospective shareholders or former directors. The proceeding is one in the name of or on behalf of the company or a related company (section 165(1)(a)) or to intervene in proceedings to which the company or any related company is a party (section 165(1)(b)).

Leave may only be granted if the court is satisfied that:
(a) the company or related company do not intend to bring proceedings or take appropriate action; or
(b) it is in the interests of the company that the conduct of the case should not be left to the directors or the shareholders (section 165(3)).

Unlike the case law there is no requirement of establishing control by the wrong-doers or limitation of the type of case.

Section 165(2) lists the factors which the court must take into account in granting leave:
(a) the likelihood of the proceedings succeeding;
(b) the costs;
(c) any action already taken by the company or related company to obtain relief;
(d) the interests of the company or related company in having proceedings commenced, continued, defended or discontinued as the case may be.

Unlike the Australian and Canadian legislation, the New Zealand legislation does not deal clearly with the effect of ratification. It has a general provision in section 177 which allows ratification and preserves the case law. The impact of this on the derivative action is unclear. The better view is probably that this provides evidence for the

---

158 See M. Berkahn, 'The Derivative Action in Australia and New Zealand: Will the Statutory Provisions Improve Shareholders' Enforcement Rights?' (1999) 10 Bond LR 74, 90 et seq.

purposes of section 165(3)(a) of the fact that the company does not intend to bring an action.[159]

The costs will be ordered against the company unless the court considers it would be unjust or inequitable (section 166).[160]

The court is given wide powers to make orders or directions under section 167 and any compromise, settlement or withdrawal must be done with the leave of the court (section 168).

The first statutory derivative action brought under the *Companies Act 1993* was the decision in *Vrij v. Boyle*.[161] In this decision the 'prudent business person' test was used in relation to whether the action should have been brought.[162] It has been argued that this represents a conservative approach to this type of action especially considering that there is no regulatory body in New Zealand that could bring the action.[163] However, in this case the application was allowed because there would only be a small amount of costs associated with the application.[164] This type of reasoning limits the significance of this decision because a vast number of cases would not involve small incorporated partnerships linked to trading partnerships as in this case; and therefore the costs involved would be significantly higher.[165] It has been argued that a further limitation on the significance of this decision lies in the fact that the applicant had 'access to information'; in many cases this would not be possible and therefore it is suggested that this decision may be likely to give a false impression on the ease of using this remedy.[166]

The following year the case of *Techflow (NZ) Ltd v. Techflow Pty Ltd*[167] was decided. This confirmed that the test to be applied when deciding whether proceedings should be allowed to be brought 'should be judged by the standard of a prudent businessman in the conduct of his own affairs'.[168] However in this case the action was not allowed to continue since the costs greatly exceeded the benefit of litigation.[169] Justice Elias said

---

159 See L. Taylor, 'Ratification and the Statutory Derivative Action in the *Companies Act 1993*' (1998) 16 C&SLJ 221, 224.

160 For discussion of the costs issue see A. Fraser, 'The *Companies Act 1993*: Shareholders' Remedies' (1994) 7 Auckland University LR 739, 742; P. Fitzsimons, 'The *Companies Act 1993*: A New Approach to Shareholder Litigation in New Zealand' (1997) 18 Co Law 306; Berkahn, *op. cit.*, 95–7.

161 (1995) 1 NZCLC 280, 846. This has been followed in a number of unreported cases.

162 Based on *Smith v. Croft* [1986] 1 WLR 580. See G. R. Walker and A. Borrowdale, 'Overseas Notes' (1996) 14 C&SLJ 184. For a valuable recent discussion of the new remedy see L. Taylor, 'The Derivative Action in the *Companies Act 1993*' (1999) 7 Canterbury LR 314.

163 Walker and Borrowdale, *op. cit.*; P. Fitzsimons, Note, [1995] CSLB 128, 129–30.

164 Walker and Borrowdale, *op. cit.*, 189.

165 ibid.

166 *ibid.*, 190.

167 (1996) 7 NZCLC 261, 138; See also *Mcfarlane v. Barlow* (1997) 8 NZCLC 261, 470; *Porrit v. Weir* High Court, Wellington CP 307/97 12 March 1998 Master Thomson; *McKay v. PHC Holdings* High Court, Auckland M 225/97, 19 May 1998, Master Anne Gambrill; *Thorrington v. McCann* High Court, Auckland M 1289/97, 2 March 1998, Laurenson J.

168 *Techflow (NZ) v. Techflow Pty Ltd* (1996) 7 NZCLC 261, 138 at 261, 138.

169 *ibid.* 261, 142.

that the significant matter was whether the proceedings were in the best interests of the company. The advantage to the shareholder was at best a fringe concern.[170]

Conclusion

Australian courts have shown greater flexibility than UK courts in dealing with minority shareholder remedies.[171] Recognition continued for the interests of justice exception to the rule in *Foss v. Harbottle* until the recent changes and a more liberal approach has been shown to the concept of personal rights. Indeed the latter seems broader than the New Zealand provision in section 169 of the *Companies Act 1993*. Greater flexibility has been shown on questions of standing and in the procedures.

The new statutory derivative action procedures are to be welcomed as they clarify and reform the law and increase *locus standi*. However, there are still some technical problems of distinguishing personal from corporate actions in Australia[172] and an odd drafting error in section 237(4) of the Corporations Act which seems to create a rebuttable presumption that litigation against a former director who resigned more than six months earlier is not in the best interests of the company.[173]

It is interesting to see that the Canadian[174] and New Zealand[175] reforms of derivative actions have led to relatively few cases. The statutory minority shareholder remedy for oppression and unfairly prejudicial conduct remains popular with small incorporated firms[176] although many cases are actually settled out of court.[177] There are few publicly listed companies that are the subject of this remedy.[178]

One must face the fact that law is an expensive and blunt instrument to deal with corporate governance problems. New Zealand, following the North American model,

---

170   *ibid.* 261, 141.

171   See I. Ramsay, 'Corporate Governance, Shareholder Litigation and the Prospects for a Statutory Derivative Action' (1992) 15 UNSWLJ 149.

172   See P. Hanrahan, 'Distinguishing Corporate and Personal Claims in Australian Company Litigation' (1997) 15 C&SLJ 21; J. Poole and P. Roberts, 'Shareholder Remedies—Corporate Wrongs and the Derivative Action' [1999] JBL 99; H. A. J. Ford, R. P. Austin and I. Ramsay, *An Introduction to the CLERP Act*, 1999, Butterworths, Sydney, para. 2.54–5.

173   See Ford, Austin and Ramsay, *op. cit.*, para. 2.55.

174   See B. Cheffins, 'Reforming the Derivative Action: The Canadian Experience and British Prospects' (1997) 1 *Company Financial and Insolvency Law Review* 227.

175   See above.

176   See Ramsay, *op. cit.*, footnote 111 supra. For useful comparison see M. Berkahn, 'Public and Private Enforcement of Company Law in New Zealand 1986–98', unpublished paper, Deakin University, 1999.

177   Conversation with Professor Bruce Welling of the University of Western Ontario which confirms the author's experience with New Zealand.

178   See *Re Spargos Mining NL* (1990) 8 ACLC 1218; *Re Blue Arrow Plc* [1987] BCLC 585. See further Ramsay, *op. cit.* 31. He lists 6.8 per cent listed public companies in his survey of Australian oppression remedy cases. This contrasts with 7.27 per cent private companies. There were four cases involving 'widely held companies' in New Zealand in the period 1986–98. See Berkahn, *op. cit.*, footnote 176 supra 35, 40. For a discussion of the categories used see *op. cit.* 33.

opted in 1993 for the introduction of an additional remedy in the form of appraisal or buy-out rights.[179] The essence of the remedy is a right for a shareholder who dissents on changes to the constitution affecting the activities of the company,[180] a major transaction,[181] or amalgamation,[182] or certain changes to rights affecting shares,[183] to have their shares 'appraised at fair and reasonable price'[184] and bought out at that price. It is not necessary to prove any unfair prejudice and it does not bar a personal action.[185] The Act sets out a procedure. It does not need an application to the court. A company, however, can apply to the court for exemption on certain limited grounds.[186] In 1997 the English Law Commission recommended the introduction of exit right articles into Table A.[187] This is a similar concept but depends on voluntary adoption by the company. A further proposal for arbitration and mediation articles was dropped due to a negative response from the legal profession. So far nothing has been done but the whole subject of reform of the Companies Acts is under consideration. There is currently no plan to reform the Australian law along any of these lines.[188] The case for such rights is strongest in relation to small incorporated firms. In public listed companies one can always sell one's shares.

---

179 Sections 110–15 *Companies Act 1993*. For useful discussion see L. Taylor, 'Minority Buy-out Rights in the *Companies Act 1993*' [1996] 6 Cant LR 539. D. O. Jones, *Companies Law in New Zealand: A Guide to the Companies Act 1993*, Butterworths, Wellington, 1993, ch. 8; A. Beck and A. Borrowdale, *Guidebook to New Zealand Companies and Securities Law*, 6th edn, CCH New Zealand, Auckland, 1998, para. 567 *et seq.* For criticism of this right in US laws see B. Manning, 'The Shareholder's Appraisal Remedy: An Essay for Frank Coker' (1962) 72 Yale LJ 223 and a response by M. A. Eisenberg in *The Structure of the Corporation—A Legal Analysis*, Little Brown & Co, Boston, 1976, ch. 7. See also F. Easterbrook and D. Fischel, *The Economic Structure of Corporate Law*, Harvard University Press, Cambridge, 1991, ch. 6. For recent discussion see A. R. Pinto and D. M. Branson, *Understanding Corporate Law*, Matthew Bender, New York, 1999, para. 6.06. For useful Australian discussion see V. Mitchell, 'The US Approach Towards the Acquisition of Minority Shares: Have We Anything to Learn?' (1996) 14 C&SLJ 283.
180 See s. 106(1)(1).
181 Sections 106 (1)(b) and 129(2).
182 Sections 106 (1)(c) and 221.
183 Sections 116–18.
184 Sections 112(1)(a) and 112(b).
185 *Hinton v Heartland Prime Meat (NZ) Ltd* (1999) 8 NZCLC 261, 885.
186 Section 114. This allows exemption by the court where the purchase would be disproportionately damaging to the company, where the company cannot reasonably be required to finance the purchase or it would not be just and equitable to require it to purchase the shares. The company may, however, arrange for some other person to purchase the shares: see sections 111(2)(b) and 113.
187 Law Commission Report 246, *Shareholder Remedies*, Part V.
188 See Mitchell, *op. cit.* footnote 179 supra.

CHAPTER 19

The Role of the Auditor and Audit Committee in Corporate Governance

Public regulation of companies and their management often takes the form of disclosure requirements. Disclosure of information by companies is one of those topics in company law which are dominated by detailed statutory requirements. Let us first briefly consider the general arguments for and against disclosure in this context since disclosure is a means rather than an end in itself.[1] Disclosure to the public also acts as a way of monitoring management performance and discourages fraud. From the investors' point of view, it achieves a broad egalitarianism since all investors have equal access to the information and can react accordingly. The main counter arguments centre on the disproportionate cost and uselessness of much of the information and the need to maintain confidentiality in certain circumstances. Time factors enter into it also. Legal requirements of disclosure are of hard rather than soft data, for example, facts rather than forecasts. This lends a bias towards historical data, whereas many investors are more concerned with the future prospects of a company. On the other hand, premature disclosure may raise expectations which are not fulfilled and lead to an irrational reapplication of resources. A balance has to be struck somewhere as a matter of policy. Debate is necessary, in which increasingly economic considerations feature, sometimes in conflict with the traditional intuitive and institutional values of lawyers. Unfortunately such limited empirical research about the efficacy and efficiency of the legal requirements as has been done[2] has been strongly criticised and the status of its findings is problematic.[3]

---

1   See R. B. Stevenson Jr, *Corporations and Information—Secrecy, Access and Disclosure*, Johns Hopkins University Press, Baltimore, 1980, ch 6; W. M. H. Grover and J. C. Ballie, *Proposals for a Securities Market Law for Canada*, vol. 3—Disclosure Requirements. See M. B. Fox, 'Required Disclosure and Corporate Governance (1999) 62 *Law and Contemporary Problems* 113.

2   See the material by G. Benston and G. Stigler cited by Stevenson, *op. cit.*, p. 210.

3   Stevenson, *op. cit*, p. 210.

Disclosure of information has been part of the scheme of corporate governance from the earliest English legislation of the nineteenth century.[4] The obligation is on the company and its directors to disclose information and the most important disclosure obligation is financial reporting. The detailed rules have emerged out of a combination of accounting and auditing requirements of the companies legislation supplemented by Stock Exchange Listing Rules. The policy behind this is linked originally with the idea of incorporation as a privilege which was granted on certain terms. In other words, disclosure is part of the price paid for the privilege of incorporation. As Justice Louis D. Brandeis of the US Supreme Court once wrote, 'Sunlight is said to be the best of disinfectants; electric light the most efficient policeman …'[5]

The principal concerns were originally business failure and fraud. Later the emphasis was more on directors' stewardship of assets and funds and the protection of investors and creditors. Later still has been emphasis on the role of information in making investment decisions.[6]

Sources of information

The legislation mandates:

- financial records, reports and audit
- continuous disclosure (in Australia)
- prospectuses for fundraising
- substantial shareholder disclosure.

These requirements are supplemented by the Stock Exchange Listing Rules.

Financial reporting

The general obligations of the company are:

- to maintain adequate financial records
- to prepare an annual financial report or statement and directors' report
- to have the financial report or statement audited
- to send both reports to members
- to lodge them with ASIC or the Registrar of Companies in New Zealand and the Stock Exchange, if listed
- to lay them before the annual general meeting except in Australia where this is dispensed with
- (in Australia) to prepare a half-yearly report

4   See P. Taylor and S. Turley, *The Regulation of Accounting*, Basil Blackwell, Oxford, 1986, pp. 34–5.
5   *Other People's Money*, Stokes, New York, 1932, p. 92.
6   Taylor and Turley, *op. cit.*

- to have it audited or reviewed by the auditor and lodge it with ASIC and the ASX, if listed.[7]

The obligations extend to groups of companies or other entities. There are accounting privileges granted to small proprietary companies in Australia and exempt companies in New Zealand. These cover preparation of the annual financial statements, audit requirements, sending copies to members and ASIC or the Registrar in New Zealand.

Since this is a book about corporate governance and not about accounts we will concentrate on the contribution of audited financial disclosure to corporate governance.

Statutory duties to comply with accounting standards and to give 'a true and fair view'

The Australian position

The Australian Corporations Act is now quite explicit on the obligations on the company to comply with accounting standards and for the accounts to give a true and fair view of the company or group's financial position and performance.

Section 296(1) requires financial reports for a financial year to comply with accounting standards of the AASB except in the case of a small proprietary company, where the members have dispensed with this requirement. According to Ford,[8] if the accounting standard is inconsistent with the Corporations Act, the latter prevails but there is an argument that an accounting standard prevails over an inconsistent regulation. An even more difficult question is whether the accounting standards prevail over the obligation for the accounts to give a true and fair view.

The latter obligation arises under section 297 and now extends to the company's financial position and performance. The UK *Joint Stock Companies Act 1844* required a presentation of a full and fair balance sheet. After this various formulae were employed before the term 'true and fair view' was adopted in the United Kingdom *Companies Act 1948* and the *Victorian Companies Act 1958*.[9]

The New Zealand position

The matter is now dealt with in New Zealand by the *Financial Reporting Act 1993*. Financial statements have to comply with 'general accepted accounting standards' (section 11(1)).

---

7   See H. A. J. Ford, R. P. Austin and I. M. Ramsay, *Ford's Principles of Corporations Law*, 10th edn, Butterworths, Sydney, 2001, ch. 10; *Morison's Company and Securities Law*, Butterworths, Wellington, 1998, vol. 2, ch. 39.

8   *Op. cit.* paras 10, 170 *et seq.*

9   Taylor and Turley, *op. cit.*, ch. 3.

This means applicable accounting standards as approved by the Accounting Standards Review Board or where none is applicable, policies appropriate to the company's circumstances which have authoritative support in the accounting profession (section 3).

Where this will not present a true and fair view of the company's affairs, additional information must be provided (section 11(2)). The emphasis is now on intelligibility to shareholders.

The position is thus broadly similar to Australia.[10]

The obligations of directors

Formerly the obligations were on the directors. Now in Australia they are on the company *and* the directors. The obligation of the directors is to take all reasonable steps to comply or secure compliance, which seems to imagine the possibility of something like a due diligence defence. The obligation under section 344 in Australia is a civil penalty provision but the obligations to assist the auditor under sections 314, 323 and 232B are subject to criminal sanctions. New Zealand imposes the obligation on the board of directors and non-compliance is an offence (section 194(1) and (4) of the New Zealand Act).

The role of auditors

Auditors were provided for in section 38 of the first UK *Companies Act 1844*. Australia and New Zealand legislation followed suit.

In Australia, unless a company is a small proprietary company whose members opt out, or the ASIC otherwise directs, financial reports have to be audited. The auditor has an obligation to prepare an audit report to the members of the financial report. Section 307 requires the auditor to form an opinion about:

  (a) whether the financial report is in accordance with the Corporations Act, including:
      (i) section 296 or 304 (compliance with accounting standards); and
      (ii) section 297 or 305 (true and fair view); and
  (b) whether the auditor has been given all information, explanation and assistance necessary for the conduct of the audit; and
  (c) whether the company, registered scheme or disclosing entity has kept financial records sufficient to enable a financial report to be prepared and audited; and
  (d) whether the company, registered scheme or disclosing entity has kept other records and registers as required by the Corporations Act.

---

10   See generally *Morison's Company and Securities Law, op. cit.*, vol. 2, ch. 39.

The auditor must report on annual and half-yearly financial reports in accordance with sections 308 and 309.

The auditor has power to obtain information under section 310 and a duty to report to ASIC if he or she has reasonable grounds to suspect a contravention of the Corporations Act that has not been adequately dealt with by commentary in the auditor's report or by bringing it to the attention of the directors.

Section 1289 gives the auditor qualified privilege in respect of statements made in an audit report or in the course of his or her duties.

An auditor is under no obligation to report on imprudent business judgments.

Auditors may be liable in contract to the company and in tort to third parties for breach of statutory duty or negligence.[11]

Auditors may apply to the court for relief if they have acted honestly and ought fairly to be excused. They can also apply for a specific exception order from ASIC and get relief from all or specified requirements of the Corporations Act. The application under section 340 is made by the company (section 340(3)). ASIC has power under section 341 to make a class order of exemption.

In New Zealand there is a general requirement of auditing (section 15 of the *Financial Reporting Act 1993*). However, companies (other than public issuers) may decide by unanimous resolution not to appoint an auditor (section 196(2) of the Companies Act 1993). Companies controlled by foreign interests are not permitted to do so (section 196(3)).

There are similar provisions to sections 307 and 310 of the Corporations Act in the *Financial Reporting Act 1993* sections 16 and 17.

Audit committees and the importance of audit to corporate governance

Self-regulation regimes

The UK Cadbury Report stated at 5.1 that 'The annual audit is one of the cornerstones of corporate governance ... The audit provides an external and objective check on the way in which the financial statements have been prepared and presented, and it is an essential part of the checks and balances required. The question is not whether there should be an audit, but how to ensure its objectivity and effectiveness.'

The committee was critical of the looseness of some accounting standards and the lack of a shareholder link with the auditors. It was also mindful of intense competition for audit work and the pressures put on auditors by the companies. It thought that there was something of an 'expectation gap' about the nature and significance of audited accounts.

---

11   See Ford, *op. cit.*, para. 10.540 *et seq.*; *Morison's*, para. 39.22 *et seq.*

It thought that the answers lay in professional objectivity through improved standards and the use of audit committees of at least three non-executive directors.

It did not favour quarantining of audit from other services or rotation of auditors but in its Code of Best Practice said that the board should ensure that an objective and professional relationship is maintained with the auditors.

The *Combined Code* now states in Principle C3 that the board should establish formal and transparent arrangements for considering how they should apply the financial reporting and internal control principles, and for maintaining an appropriate relationship with the company's auditors.

Code Provision D.3.1 requires the establishment of an audit committee with a majority of independent non-executive directors. Provision D.3.2 states:

> The duties of the audit committee should include keeping under review the scope and results of the audit and its cost effectiveness and the independence and objectivity of the auditors. Where the auditors also supply a substantial volume of non-audit services to the company, the committee should also keep the nature and extent of such services under review, seeking to balance the maintenance of objectivity and value for money.

In Australia *Corporate Practices and Conduct* contains similar recommendations as do the IFSA Guidelines and the Institute of Directors in New Zealand *Code of Proper Practice for Directors*.

The ASX Indicative List of Corporate Governance Matters requires disclosure of the main procedures for:

(i)   the nomination of external auditors; and
(ii) reviewing the adequacy of existing external audit arrangements, with particular emphasis on the scope and quality of the audit.

If any of these procedures involves an audit committee it requires a summary of the main responsibilities and core rights of the committee, and the names of the committee members. If one or more members are not directors of the company, it requires a statement of their positions in the company.

Corporate Practices and Conduct thought that a listed company board of more than four members should appoint an audit committee with at least a majority of non-executive directors and a non-executive director chairperson who is preferably not the chairperson of the board.

It should have unrestricted access to the chief financial officer, chief executive officer (CEO) and the internal and external auditors, and the internal and external auditors should have access to the audit committee. It should have power to consult experts at the company's expense.

It thought that the primary functions of the committee should include reviewing:

• the nomination and performance of the external auditors. Where necessary, the audit committee should recommend to the board the name of the audit firm to be put before shareholders

- external audit engagements, including any audit tenders, with particular emphasis on the scope and quality of the audit
- effectiveness of the annual audit, ensuring emphasis is placed on areas where the committee, management or the auditors believe special attention is necessary
- coordination of audit approach between internal and external auditors
- effectiveness of the internal audit function
- all areas of significant financial risks and the arrangements in place to contain those risks to acceptable levels
- effectiveness of management information and other systems of internal control
- accounting policies adopted, or any changes made or contemplated
- significant transactions which are not a normal part of the company's business
- financial statements with both management and the external auditors
- contracts, arrangements and undertakings that may involve related parties
- interim financial information
- any letter of resignation from the company's auditors.

The report recognised that the establishment of an effective audit committee did not remove the need for the external auditors to meet the board as a whole on at least one occasion each year.

Smaller boards might choose alternative methods but these should be fully disclosed. The IFSA Guidelines state that the audit committee:

- should be chaired by an independent director and be composed entirely of non-executive directors a majority of whom should be independent directors;
- should be composed of directors with the mix of skills, experience and other qualities appropriate for its role;
- should assist the board to discharge its responsibilities in connection with the financial management, financial performance and financial reporting of the company, including corporate risk assessment and the system of internal control, preparing the company's financial statements and the independence of the company's auditors, and the quality of their audit; and
- should have written terms of reference which include core matters to be dealt with by the committee and core rights of the committee.

The guidelines state that an audit committee composed of non-executive directors is free, and would be well advised to involve company executives, including executive directors, in its business, and it can do so by inviting the appropriate participation of those executives. However, it will also be appropriate for the audit committee to discuss matters with the external and internal auditors in the absence of management, including executive directors. This is so that external and internal auditors are not inhibited by the presence of senior management from raising matters with the committee.

The appointment of an audit committee comprised entirely of non-executive directors with the requisite mix of skills, experience and other qualities achieves all of these objectives.

In addition there is a *Best Practice Guide* issued in 1997 jointly by the Australian Accounting Research Foundation, Institute of Internal Auditors, and the Australian Institute of Company Directors.

The New Zealand *Code of Proper Practice for Directors* paragraph 9 provides:

9.0 Audit committees

9.1 The audit committee should be formally constituted to ensure its relationship with the board is clear and it should have written terms of reference agreed by the board including the review of all financial statements to be released by the company and the regular review of compliance with internal systems and controls and with statutory and regulatory requirements.

9.2 The audit committee should normally meet at least three times a year and a statement to this effect should be recorded in the annual report.

9.3 The audit committee ideally should comprise only non-executive directors.

9.4 There should be clear lines of communication between the audit committee and the external auditors. The audit committee should meet with the external auditors at least once a year and for at least part of that meeting no executive directors or other employees of the company should be present.

9.5 There should also be clear lines of communication between the chairman of the audit committee and the head of any internal audit function.

According to Korn/Ferry International's survey *Boards of Directors in Australia and New Zealand 1999* around one-third of audit committees in both countries had been in existence for ten years or more. Eighty-nine per cent of Australian companies and 80 per cent of New Zealand companies surveyed now had an audit committee. In the writer's own survey of the top 100 Australian listed companies 93 per cent of the companies had an audit committee. The latter percentage may in fact be higher since 93 per cent takes into account failure to respond. On average according to the Korn/Ferry survey audit committees met four times a year for two to three hours. They typically consist of four people. In Australia 54 per cent did not have an executive director on the committee. Thirty-four per cent had one and 7 per cent had two.

Conclusion

It can be seen from this chapter that disclosure has been a well-established part of corporate governance for over 150 years. Central to this is financial disclosure by the company and its board. This is monitored by the auditor and is regulated by the Corporations Act or the New Zealand acts, and accounting standards. In addition to self-regulation by professional accounting bodies, ASIC plays an important legal role in the overall scheme as a public repository of information, regulator and source of exemptions and relief. In New Zealand similar roles are played by the Registrar of Companies and the Securities Commission. The courts also play a residual role in giving relief for honest breach of duty that ought fairly to be excused.

Some economists challenge the wisdom of the overall disclosure policy on cost/benefit grounds. Auditors are subject to economic pressures, faced with intense competition, and mounting costs of insurance due to potential negligence liability. These affect performance. ASIC and the New Zealand Securities Commission are arguably underfunded to execute their complex roles effectively. The protection given by the disclosure policy may, therefore, tend to be somewhat illusory. However, the modern practice of audit committees as self-regulation is a step in the right direction to ensure the efficacy and transparency of the system at moderate cost.

Nevertheless, one is left with the impression of auditors being subject to pressures from the board which conflict with their duties to the shareholders and to the regulators.

Their appointment is in the hands of the board and shareholders merely ratify it and authorise the payment of their fees. Although shareholders in theory can seek their removal, in practice they do not do so. Shareholders also have little information about consultancy work done by other arms of the accounting firm. To this extent they are compromised and their constructive role in corporate governance diminished.[12]

Michael Power of the London School of Economics[13] has argued that auditing is a 'political technology'. 'It is a technology which is demanded by a regulatory regime which presupposes its own effectiveness and thereby the possibility of effective auditing'. As a political technology it constantly responds to demands put upon it.

The Cadbury Report envisaged that auditors should review companies' statements of compliance with the Code of Best Practice. However, the Hampel Report thought that the primary responsibility of good corporate governance rested with the directors. The statutory role of auditors was to provide shareholders with independent and objective assurance on the reliability of the financial statements and certain other information provided. 'Auditors ... do not have an executive role in corporate governance. If the directors fall short of high standards of corporate governance, the auditors may be able to identify the deficiency, they cannot make it good.'[14] The committee, therefore, did not recommend any additional requirements on auditors to report on governance issues. It thought that auditors were inhibited from going beyond their present functions by concerns about legal liability.

Any extension of the auditors' role will require consideration of all the pressures upon them and reform of the law of professional negligence as it applies to them. The question of potential liability for members of an audit committee is considered in Chapters 14 and 28.

---

12 The matter is currently being considered by the SEC in the USA. See D. Parker, 'Independence Day' (2000) draft guidance on ethical considerations for auditors <www.ifac.com> and the CPA/ICAA response see <www.cpaonline.com.au>.

13 M. Power, 'Auditing and the Politics of Regulatory Control in the UK Financial Services Sector', in J. McCahery, S. Picciotto and C. Scott (eds), *Corporate Control and Accountability*, Clarendon Press, Oxford, 1993, pp. 187, 202.

14 *Report of the Committee on Financial Aspects of Corporate Governance*, Gee and Co., London, 1992, para. 6.2.

CHAPTER 20

The Australian Securities and Investments Commission, Statutory Penalty Regime and Disqualification of Directors in Australia and New Zealand

We have seen in Chapter 11 that Australia was the first jurisdiction to criminalise breach of the basic duties of directors. This step was taken before the development of administrative regulation of corporate affairs. This further step was first taken in 1978 by the development of a cooperative national companies and securities scheme and the setting up of the National Companies and Securities Commission. In 1989 there was a more comprehensive attempt to introduce a national scheme with the setting up of the Australian Securities Commission, now renamed the Australian Securities and Investments Commission (ASIC), which absorbed the state bodies into a coherent national scheme of companies registration and securities regulation. This was vulnerable to constitutional challenge in the High Court.

The objectives of ASIC are now set out in section 1(2) of the *Australian Securities and Investments Commission Act 2001* (the ASIC Act). This provides that in performing its functions and exercising its powers ASIC must strive:

(a) to maintain, facilitate, and improve the performance of the financial system and the entities within that system in the interests of commercial certainty, reducing business costs, and the efficiency and development of the economy; and

(b) promote the confident and informed participation of investors and consumers in the financial system; and

(c) [(c) has been deleted and replaced by detailed provisions in the ASIC Act]; and

(d) administer the laws that confer functions and powers on it effectively and with a minimum of procedural requirements; and

(e) receive, process, and store, efficiently and quickly, the information given to the Commission under the laws that confer functions and powers on it; and

(f) ensure that information is available as soon as practicable for access by the public; and

(g) take whatever action it can take, and is necessary, in order to enforce and give effect to the laws that confer functions and powers on it.

ASIC acts as a Registrar of Companies and maintains a national data base about companies, ASCOT. It is also the main authority responsible for regulating the securities and futures industries and takeovers. It has powers of inspection and investigation and powers to bring legal proceedings. Included in the latter is the power to bring proceedings for penalties under the Corporations Act.

ASIC is given discretionary powers to intervene in corporate affairs under section 50 of the ASIC Act, and sections 234(d) and 1324 of the Corporations Act. Section 50 allows it to bring civil proceedings in the name of any person where, as a result of an investigation or examination, it appears to be in the public interest. These can be brought for the recovery of damages or property and fall outside the Rule in *Foss v. Harbottle:* see *ASC v. Deloitte Touche Tohmatsu.*[1] Section 234(e) enables ASIC to nominate a person to bring proceedings under the statutory minority shareholder remedy where it thinks it appropriate as a result of investigations into the company's affairs or matters connected with them. Section 1324 enables ASIC to apply for an injunction in respect of a contravention of the Corporations Act.

In the Report of the Cooney Committee there were recommendations that criminal liability in company law should not apply in the absence of the normal tests of criminality and that a new regime of civil penalties be introduced where there was no criminality involved.

In the *Corporate Law Reform Act 1992* steps were taken to implement these recommendations. This Act introduced the concept of civil and criminal penalties. Civil penalties result in a financial penalty and possible disqualification. If there are extra elements of criminal intention present, criminal penalty proceedings can be brought resulting in a possible fine or imprisonment.

Civil penalty sections of the Corporations Act

Until 30 June 1998 the following were designated civil penalty provisions:

- duty of company officer to act honestly
- duty of company officer to exercise reasonable care and diligence
- duty of company officer not to make improper use of information
- duty of a company officer not to make improper use of position
- giving prohibited benefits to a related party of a public company
- contraventions in relation to company accounts
- duty of director not to have company trade while insolvent.

1   (1996) 138 ALR 655.

As from 1 July 1998 the following were added to the list:

- contravention of requirements regarding redemption of redeemable preference shares
- contravention of requirements regarding capital reductions
- contravention of restrictions on company acquiring its own shares and taking security over its own shares
- contravention of restriction on company providing financial assistance in connection with the acquisition of its shares
- contravention of duties and obligations imposed on those involved in the management of managed investment schemes.

Now as a result of the *Corporate Law Economic Reform Program Act 1999* reforms and renumbering, the list is as follows:

- Section 180(1)—duty of a company officer to exercise reasonable care and diligence
- Section 181(1)—duty of a company officer to act in good faith in the best interests of the company and for a proper purpose
- Section 182—duty of a company officer and employee not to make improper use of position
- Section 183—duty of a company officer and employee not to make improper use of information
- Section 209—giving prohibited benefits to a related party of a public company
- Section 254L—contravention of requirements regarding redemption of redeemable preference shares
- Section 256D—contravention of requirements regarding capital reductions
- Section 259F—contravention of restriction on company acquiring its own shares and taking security over its own shares
- Section 260D—contravention of restriction on company providing financial assistance in connection with the acquisition of its shares
- Section 344—contravention in relation to company accounts
- Section 588G—duty of company director not to have company trade while insolvent
- Sections 601FC, 601FD, 601FE, 601G and 601JD—contravention of duties and obligations imposed on those involved in management of managed investment schemes.

Limited *locus standi*[2]

Under section 1317J(1) ASIC can apply to the court for a declaration of contravention, a pecuniary penalty order, or a compensation order. A shareholder or creditor does not have the *locus standi* to apply but the corporation itself can apply for a compensation order and may intervene in proceedings for a declaration of contravention or pecuniary penalty order.

2   s. 1317J does not exclude the power of the DPP under the *Director of Public Prosecutions Act 1983*.

The nature of civil penalty proceedings

Section 1317L provides that in hearing proceedings for a declaration of contravention or pecuniary penalty order, the court must apply the rules of evidence and procedure for civil matters. This means that the standard of proof is the civil standard, not the criminal standard of proof beyond reasonable doubt. It is enough for the case to be proved on a balance of probabilities. The Law Council of Australia objected to this on the basis that a civil penalty is still, in its nature, penal.

The court may order a person to pay a pecuniary penalty of up to $200 000 if

(a) a declaration of contravention by the person has been made under section 1317E; and
(b) the contravention
    (i) materially prejudices the corporation or its members; or
    (ii) materially prejudices the corporation's ability to pay its creditors; or
    (iii) is serious (section 1317G(1)).

A pecuniary penalty is a civil debt payable to ASIC on the Commonwealth's behalf and ASIC or the Commonwealth can enforce the order as if it were an order in civil proceedings and the debt is taken to be a judgment debt (section 1317G(2)).

Section 1317H(1) provides for compensation orders by a person who has contravened a civil penalty provision and caused damage. The damage includes profits made by the person (section 1317H(2)). This too can be enforced as if it were a judgment debt (section 1317H(5)).

There is a time limit of six years after the contravention (section 1317K).

No proceedings can be brought if there has been a criminal conviction for conduct substantially the same as the contravention (section 1317M). On the other hand criminal proceedings may be started after the civil penalty proceedings (section 1317P).

Evidence in the penalty proceedings is not admissible in the criminal proceedings if they cover substantially the same ground unless the criminal proceedings are in respect of false evidence given by the person in the earlier proceedings (section 1317Q).

Section 1317R(3) *et seq.* deals with ASIC requiring third parties to assist in criminal proceedings.

ASIC can require a person to give assistance in connection with an application for an order if it thinks that they have relevant information (section 1317R).

Criminal proceedings

Criminal intention is now no longer dealt with under a general provision in section 1317FA(2) but in specific offences in the Corporations Act. Thus section 184 deals with new criminal offences in connection with breaches of the duty of good faith and abuse of position or information. These contain classic elements of guilt in criminal law such as intention and recklessness.

The maximum penalty is a fine of $200 000 or five years imprisonment or both. (Schedule 3 of the Corporations Act).

Discretionary relief

Under section 1317S the court can grant relief from liability for contravention of a *civil* penalty provision if the person has acted honestly and ought fairly to be excused. This is dealt with in Chapter 16.

Practical effect of this regime

In a report the writer prepared for the Business Council of Australia and the Australian Institute of Company Directors in 1992,[3] he drew attention to the fact that Australia is the only developed country which criminalised a breach of the basic directors' duties. Malaysia and Singapore, which based themselves on the *Uniform Companies Act 1962*, also adopted the provision. The so-called decriminalisation of 1992 still retained a penal trait in the legislation. Observations and inquiries since then revealed very few cases where the new provisions had been used. Now, a very useful survey carried out at the University of Melbourne, *Regulating Directors' Duties: How Effective are the Civil Penalty Sanctions in the Australian Corporations Law?*[4] has demonstrated the ineffectiveness of this regime. The authors, Helen Bird, Dr George Gilligan and Professor Ian Ramsay, show that only fourteen cases have been brought and none in New South Wales, itself an astonishing fact.

The reasons are said to be: first, a number of alternative remedies that are more viable especially ASIC's summary power of disqualification under section 206F; second, reservations about the handling of cases by the courts; third, the fact that relevant staff tend to have a criminal prosecution background and prefer criminal proceedings, with which they are familiar; and fourth, the difficulties and delays that arise from the necessity to liaise with the Director of Public Prosecutions over significant enforcement matters. We look at this in Chapter 23.

The steps taken in 1992 were intended to reform Australian law and make it less penal. The effect seems to have been more cosmetic and rhetorical than real. The fundamental question is whether any useful purpose is served by the retention of the regime.

New Zealand retains a Registrar of Companies and has a separate Securities Commission. It does not have a statutory penalty regime. Although there are some criminal

---

3   *Modernising Australian Corporations Law*, August 1992.
4   Centre for Corporate Law and Securities Regulation, University of Melbourne, Melbourne, 1999. For a powerful but unbalanced critique see A. Ferguson, 'The Watchdog No One Fears', *Business Review Weekly*, 1 September 2000, p. 58.

penalties and disqualification provisions in the New Zealand Act, the Act is based on a model of private, rather than public enforcement in practice.

The disqualification regime

Disqualification falls within the civil and criminal penalty regimes in Australia as we have just seen but there are also general provisions in the Corporations Act that deal with it.[5] These were reorganised in a more coherent manner by the *Corporate Law Economic Reform Program Act 1999*. The relevant provisions are in Part 2D.6 of the Corporations Act.

There is a general provision in section 206A that a disqualified person must not manage a corporation. Section 206B provides for automatic disqualification for criminal convictions or bankruptcy, or entering into deeds of arrangement or compositions with creditors. Section 206C gives the court power to disqualify for a contravention of a civil penalty provision. Section 206D gives the court power to disqualify in cases of involvement in two or more business failures within the last seven years and section 206E extends to repeated contraventions of the Corporations Act. Sections 206C, 206D and 206E all require applications to the court.

There is no equivalent in the Corporations Act of the UK general ground of unfitness. This was a new ground introduced in the *Insolvency Act 1985* and now contained in the *Company Directors Disqualification Act 1986*. Unfitness requires the court to have regard to a list of specified factors.[6] Dr Andrew Hicks, in a research report for the Association of Chartered Certified Accountants, describes the broad thrust of unfit conduct as follows:[7]

* General long-term recklessness prejudicing creditors, and failure to minimise losses in the run up to closure
* dishonest misuse of company assets
* irregular treatment of the company's interest (loans, excess benefits, inter-company transfers, etc.) prejudicing creditors
* improper treatment of individual creditors
* non-compliance with legislation.

---

5   See generally J. Corkery, 'Convicted Offenders and Section 227 of the National Companies Code; Restrictions on Persons Managing Companies', (1983) 1 C&SLJ 153; J. Cassidy, 'Disqualification of Directors under the Corporations Law', (1995) 13 C&SLJ 221. For the UK see A. Hicks, *Disqualification of Directors: No Hiding Place for the Unfit*, Certified Accountants Educational Trust, London, 1998; A. Walters and M. Davis-White, *Directors' Disqualification: Law and Practice*, Sweet & Maxwell, London, 1999; A. Mittani and S. Wheeler, *Disqualification of Company Directors*, Butterworths, London, 1996; L. S. Sealy, *Disqualification and Personal Liability of Directors*, 4th edn, CCH, London, 1993; J. Dine, 'Disqualification of Directors', (1991) 12 Co Law 6; V. Finch, 'Disqualification of Directors: A Plea for Competence', (1990) 53 MLR 385; A. Hicks, 'Disqualification of Directors: Forty Years On', (1988) JBL 27.
6   See the lists in Parts I and II of Schedule 1 to the *Company Directors Disqualification Act 1986*.
7   Hicks, (1998) *op. cit.* pp. 39–40.

A particularly difficult question is whether incompetence constitutes unfit conduct.

Section 206F deals with ASIC's power of disqualification by administrative orders.

A person disqualified may apply to the court for leave to manage a corporation or corporations under section 206G.

In New Zealand the relevant provisions are sections 382 to 386. Section 382 prohibits certain persons from managing companies. Section 383 deals with the court's powers to disqualify directors. Section 384 imposes personal liability for breaches of sections 383. This is in addition to the criminal offences specified by those sections. Section 385 deals with the Registrar's power to prohibit persons from managing companies and section 386 imposes personal liability for breach of section 385 in addition to the criminal offence specified in section 385(9).

Applications for disqualification typically focus on one or more of the following factors:

• poor accounting records
• continued trading while insolvent without regard to creditors' interests
• self-dealing including excessive remuneration.

Let us deal with these provisions in more detail.

The Australian provisions

Disqualified persons not to manage corporations

Under section 206A (1) a person who is disqualified from managing[8] corporations under Part 2D.6 commits an offence if:

(a) they make, or participate in making, decisions that affect the whole, or substantial part, of the business of the corporation; or

(b) they exercise the capacity to affect significantly the corporation's financial standing; or

(c) they communicate instructions or wishes to the directors of the corporation:

    (i) knowing that the directors are accustomed to act in accordance with the person's instructions or wishes; or

    (ii) intending that the directors will act in accordance with those instructions or wishes.

Item (c) applies to instructions or wishes other than advice given by the person in the proper performance of functions attaching to the person's professional capacity or their business relationship with the directors or the corporation.

---

8   As to the case law on the meaning of managers in the earlier legislation see *CAC (Vic) v. Bracht* [1989] VR 821; *Cullen v. CAC* (NSW) (1988) 14 ACLR 789. See generally *Byrnes v. ASIC* (2000) 34 ACSR 320 (AAT).

It is a defence to the contravention if the person had permission to manage the corporation under either section 206F or 206G and their conduct was within the terms of that permission.

Under section 1274AA, ASIC is required to keep a record of persons disqualified from managing corporations.

Section 206A(2) provides that a person ceases to be a director, alternate director or a secretary of a company if:

(a) the person becomes disqualified from managing corporations; and

(b) they are not given permission to manage the corporation under section 206F or 206G.

If a person ceases to be a director, alternate director or a secretary under subsection (2) the company must notify ASIC (section 205B(1)).

Automatic disqualification

Convictions

Under section 206B(1) a person becomes disqualified from managing corporations if the person:

(a) is convicted on indictment of an offence that:

    (i) concerns the making, or participation in making, of decisions that affect the whole or substantial part of the business of the corporation ; or

    (ii) concerns an act that has the capacity to affect significantly the corporation's financial standing; or

(b) is convicted of an offence that:

    (i) is a contravention of the Corporations Act and is punishable by imprisonment for a period greater than twelve months; or

    (ii) involves dishonesty and is punishable by imprisonment for at least three months; or

    (iii) is convicted of an offence against the law of a foreign country that is punishable by imprisonment for a period greater than twelve months.

The offences covered by paragraph (a) and subparagraph (b)(ii) include offences against the law of a foreign country.

The period of disqualification under section 206B(1) starts on the day the person is convicted and lasts for:

(a) (if the person does not serve a term of imprisonment) five years after the day on which they are convicted; or

(b) (if the person serves a term of imprisonment) five years after the day on which they are released from prison (section 206B(2)).

In *Chew v. NCSC*[9] it was held that the policy of the legislation was to deter people from offending and to protect the public rather than punish the convicted person. The court considers:

- the nature of the offence
- the nature of the convicted person's involvement
- the person's general character
- the companies of which he may be a director
- the risk to the company and the public.[10]

Bankruptcy, deed of arrangement or composition with creditors

Under section 206B(3) and (4) a person is disqualified from managing corporations if:

(a) the person is an undischarged bankrupt under the law of Australia, its external territories or another country.

(b) the person has executed a deed of arrangement under Part X of the *Bankruptcy Act 1966* (or a similar law of an external territory or another country) and the terms of the deed have not been fully complied with; or

(c) the person's creditors have accepted a composition under Part X of the *Bankruptcy Act 1966* (or a similar law of an external territory or another country) and final payment has not been made under the composition.

Court power of disqualification

Contravention of civil penalty provision

Under section 206C(1), on application by ASIC, the court may disqualify a person from managing corporations for a period that the court considers appropriate if:

(a) a declaration is made under section 1317E (civil penalty provision) that the person has contravened a civil penalty provision; and

(b) the court is satisfied that the disqualification is justified.

The purpose of this power is to protect the public. The protective and compensatory aspects should be dealt with before the question of penalty. Attention needs to be focused on the likely capacity of the person concerned to do harm to the public. Age can enter into it.[11]

In determining whether the disqualification is justified, the court may have regard to:

(a) the person's conduct in relation to the management, business or property of any corporation; and

(b) any other matters that the court considers appropriate (section 206C(2)).

---

9   [1985] WAR 337. For the UK courts' approach see Walters and Davis-White, *op. cit.*, pp. 23–36.
10   *Re Record Leather Manufacturers (Aust) Pty Ltd* (1980) 5 ACLR 19.
11   *ASC v. Forem-Freeway Enterprises Pty Ltd* (1999) 17 ACLC 511, 521–3.

In *ASC v. Donovan*[12] the court thought that the criteria were the applicant's prior conduct, present activities, the likelihood of a repetition of the behaviour, whether the applicant showed contrition and the extent to which he or she benefited personally from the misconduct.

Court power of disqualification

Insolvency and non-payment of debts

Under section 206D(1) on application by ASIC, the court may disqualify a person from managing corporations for up to ten years if

(a) within the last seven years, the person has been an officer of two or more corporations when they have failed; and

(b) the court is satisfied that:
   (i) the manner in which the corporation was managed was wholly or partly responsible for the corporation failing; and
   (ii) the disqualification is justified.

Section 206D(2) provides that a corporation fails if:

(a) a Court orders the corporation to be wound up because the court is satisfied that the corporation is insolvent; or

(b) the corporation enters into voluntary liquidation and creditors are not fully paid or are unlikely to be fully paid; or

(c) the corporation executes a deed of company arrangement and creditors are not fully paid or are unlikely to be fully paid; or

(d) the corporation ceases to carry on business and creditors are not fully paid or are unlikely to be fully paid; or

(e) a levy of execution against the corporation is not satisfied; or

(f) a receiver, receiver and manager, or provisional liquidator is appointed in relation to the corporation; or

(g) the corporation enters into a compromise or arrangement with its creditors under Part 5.1; or

(h) the corporation is wound up and a liquidator lodges a report under subsection 533(1) about the corporation's inability to pay its debts.

To satisfy paragraph (h), a corporation must begin to be wound up while the person is an officer or within twelve months after the person ceases to be an officer.

In determining whether the disqualification is justified, the court may have regard to:

(a) the person's conduct in relation to the management, business or property of any corporation; and

(b) any other matters that the Court considers appropriate (section 206D(3)).

---

12   (1998) 28 ACSR 583. Cf. the UK law: see Walters and Davis-White, *op. cit.*, chs. 4 and 5.

Repeated contravention of the Act

Section 206E(1) provides that on application by ASIC, the court may disqualify a person from managing corporations for the period that the court considers appropriate if:

(a) the person:

    (i) has at least twice been an officer of a body corporate that has contravened this Law while they were an officer of the body corporate and each time the person has failed to take reasonable steps to prevent the contravention; or

    (ii) has at least twice contravened this Law while they were an officer of a body corporate; or

    (iii) has been an officer of a body corporate and has done something that would have contravened subsection 180(1) or section 181 if the body corporate had been a corporation; and

(b) the Court is satisfied that the disqualification is justified.

In determining whether the disqualification is justified, the court may have regard to:

(a) the person's conduct in relation to the management, business or property of any corporation; and

(b) any other matters that the Court considers appropriate (section 206E(2)).

See too *Re Gold Coast Holdings Pty Ltd (in liq)* (2000) 35 ACSR 107, 111.

ASIC's administrative power of disqualification

Power to disqualify

Under section 206F(1) ASIC may disqualify a person from managing corporations for up to five years if:

(a) within seven years immediately before ASIC gives a notice under paragraph (b)(i):

    (i) the person has been an officer of two or more corporations; and

    (ii) while the person was an officer, or within twelve months after the person ceased to be an officer of those corporations, each of the corporations was wound up and a liquidator lodged a report under subsection 533(1) about the corporation's inability to pay its debts; and

(b) ASIC has given the person:

    (i) a notice in the prescribed form requiring them to demonstrate why they should not be disqualified; and

    (ii) ASIC is satisfied that the disqualification is justified.

Grounds for disqualification

In determining whether disqualification is justified, ASIC:

(a) must have regard to whether any of the corporations mentioned in subsection 533(1) were related to one another; and

(b) may have regard to:
   (i) the person's conduct in relation to the management, business or property of any corporation; and
   (ii) any other matters that ASIC considers appropriate (section 206F(2)).

Notice of disqualification

If ASIC disqualifies a person from managing corporations under this section, ASIC must serve a notice on the person advising them of the disqualification. The notice must be in the prescribed form (section 206F(4)).

Start of disqualification

The disqualification takes effect from the time when a notice referred to in subsection (3) is served on the person (section 206F(4)).

ASIC power to grant leave to manage

ASIC may give a person whom it has disqualified from managing corporations under this Part of the Corporations Law, written permission to manage a particular corporation or corporations. The permission may be expressed to be subject to conditions and exceptions determined by ASIC (section 206F(5)).

Appeals

Appeal lies from ASIC to the Administrative Appeals Tribunal under Part 9.4A. It is a *de novo* hearing.[13]

Court power to grant leave to manage corporations

Under section 206G(1) a person who is disqualified from managing corporations may apply to the court for leave to manage:

a corporations; or
b a particular class of corporations; or
c a particular corporation;
   if the person was not disqualified by ASIC.

The person must lodge a notice with ASIC at least twenty-one days before commencing the proceedings. The notice must be in the prescribed form (section 206G(2)).

The order granting leave may be expressed to be subject to exceptions and conditions determined by the court (section 206G(3)).

---

13   See further Ford's *Principles of Corporations Law*, 10th edn, H. A. J. Ford, R. P. Austin and I. M. Ramsay (eds), Butterworths, Chatswood, NSW, 2001, para [7.91] and the loose leaf edition.

The person must lodge with ASIC a copy of any order granting leave within fourteen days after the order is made (section 206G(4)).

On application by ASIC, the court may revoke the leave. The order revoking leave does not take effect until it is served on the person (section 206G(5)).

The court can only grant leave to manage one or more specified companies, not companies generally (*Re Schneider* (1996) 22 ACSR 497).

Territorial application of Part 2D6

Part 2D6 does not apply in respect of an act or omission by a person while they are managing a corporation that is a foreign company unless the act or omission occurred in connection with:

(a) the foreign company carrying on business in Australia; or

(b) an act that the foreign company does, or proposes to do, in Australia; or

(c) a decision by the foreign company whether or not to do, or refrain from doing, an act in Australia (section 206(H)).

Section 206HA also limits its application in respect of registrable Australian bodies.

The New Zealand provisions[14]

Disqualified persons not to manage companies

Section 382 of the *Companies Act 1993* prohibits the following from managing companies:

a   persons convicted on indictment of any offence in connection with the promotion, formation or management of a company

b   persons convicted of offences involving dishonesty under sections 377 to 380 or any crime involving dishonesty as defined in the *Crimes Act 1961* or

c   persons against whom a judgment has been obtained for insider trading under Part 1 of the *Securities Amendment Act 1988*.

The prohibition is for five years from conviction or judgment and is from being concerned 'directly or indirectly' or taking part in the management of a company unless the person has leave of the court.

What constitutes the relevant behaviour is ultimately a question of fact. Some sort of responsibility is necessary but not necessarily ultimate responsibility.[15]

The purpose of the section is to protect the public rather than to punish the person.[16]

---

14   See A. Beck et al. (ed.), *Morison's Company and Securities Law*, Butterworths, Wellington, 1998, vol. 2, pp. 237 *et seq.*; A. Beck and A. Borrowdale, *CCH Guidebook to New Zealand Companies and Securities Law*, CCH, Auckland, 6th edn, para. 328 *et seq.*

15   *R v. Neath* [1974] 2 NZLR 760; *CAC (Vic) v. Bracht* (1988) 14 ACLR 728.

16   *Re Minimix Industries Ltd* (1982) 1 NZCLC 95-043

As to the question of obtaining leave of the court, the onus is on the applicant to show good ground and absence of harm to the public. The court considers a wide range of factors.[17]

Disqualification by the court

Section 383 gives the court power to order disqualification for a period not exceeding ten years on the following grounds:

- any ground upon which a person is automatically disqualified under section 382;
- commission of an offence under Part XXI of the *Companies Act 1993*;
- persistent failure as a director to comply with the Companies Act or the *Securities Act 1978* or to take reasonable steps to ensure compliance by the company with those statutes;
- fraud in relation to the company, or breach of duty to the company or a shareholder;
- reckless or incompetent performance of duties as a director;
- unsound mind.

In *First City Corporation Ltd v. Downsview Nominees Ltd*[18] the court held that the purpose of the section was to deal with conduct which is dishonest or a serious failure to meet the standards required.

Applications can be made by the Registrar, Official Assignee, liquidator or a shareholder or creditor. A high standard of proof is required.[19]

Disqualification by the Registrar

Section 385 contains a power similar to that of ASIC under section 206F of the Corporations Act. It is a power by notice to prohibit a person from being involved in the management of a company for a period not exceeding five years. The power applies in relation to a company:

(a) that has been put into liquidation because of its inability to pay its debts as and when they became due;

(b) that has ceased to carry on business because of its inability to pay its debts as and when they became due;

(c) in respect of which execution is returned unsatisfied in whole or in part;

(d) in respect of the property of which a receiver, or a receiver and manager, has been appointed by a court or pursuant to the powers contained in an instrument, whether or not the appointment has been terminated;

---

17   *Ramsay v. Sumich* [1989] 3 NZLR 628, 633.
18   *(No 2)* (1989) 4 NZCLC 65, 192.
19   *ibid.*

(e) in respect of which, or the property of which, a person has been appointed as a receiver and manager, or a judicial manager, or a statutory manager, or as a manager, or to exercise control, under or pursuant to any enactment, whether or not the appointment has been terminated;

(f) that has entered into a compromise or arrangement with its creditors.

It is exercisable where the Registrar is satisfied that the persons have within the previous five years been directors of a concern or taken part in the management of a company in the circumstances specified in (a)–(f) whether the management is wholly or partly responsible for the state of affairs or where the person was similarly involved in two or more such companies (section 385(4)).

The Securities Commission must authorise the exercise of the power and the person concerned must be allowed to make representations prior to it doing so (section 385(5)(b)).

Consequences of breach of sections 382, 383 and 385

There are criminal consequences under sections 382(4), 383(6) and 385(9). There is personal liability for unpaid debts under sections 384 and 386. The liability is to the liquidator or any creditors. The latter provisions are potentially more stringent than those in section 588G of the Corporations Law.

CHAPTER 21

Use and Abuse of Corporate Groups[1]

Salomon v. Salomon & Co. Ltd[2] was not a case involving a group of companies. It was about the legitimacy of the de facto one-person company. It predates the modern law of insolvency and the growth of corporate groups. The main motivation behind the House of Lords' recognition of the legitimacy of the de facto one-person company seems to have been, first, a logical approach to the interpretation of the legislation and, second, a recognition of freedom of contract or freedom of transactions. Since 1897 when the case was reported there has been a significant rise in the number of corporate groups. The principle of *Salomon's* case has been applied to corporate groups with a few exceptions in the case law.

As Justice Rogers AJA said in *Briggs v. James Hardie & Co. Pty Ltd*:[3]

> The proposition that a company has a separate legal personality from its corporators survived the coming into existence of the large numbers of fully owned subsidiaries of companies and their complete domination by their holding company ... There was continued adherence to the principle recognised by *Salomon*, notwithstanding that for a number of purposes, legislation recognised the existence of a group of companies as a single unit.

His honour later[4] referred to the fact that the law pays scant regard to commercial reality when referring to the phenomenon of corporate control in a group. The courts in the British Commonwealth have generally applied the principle of separate legal personality and adopted a reasonably strict approach to directors' duties and authority in

---

1   An earlier version of this chapter appeared as 'Legal Issues Involving Corporate Groups' (1998) 16 C&SLJ 184. For a recent study see J. Dine, *The Governance of Corporate Groups*, Cambridge University Press, Cambridge, 2000.
2   [1897] AC 22.
3   (1989) 16 NSWLR 549 at 576. See R. Goode (ed.), *Group Trading and Lending Banker*, Sweet & Maxwell, London.

a group situation. However, there are some inconsistencies in judicial attitudes about piercing the corporate veil, consideration of the group interest, and the applications of authority principles to the group context. The increasingly broad range of the statutory minority shareholder's remedy has enabled some of these matters to be subject to equitable scrutiny and the extension of the statutory definition of 'director' has enabled the courts to consider recently whether a parent company can be subject to fiduciary duties as a shadow director in the absence of a coherent doctrine of duties on controlling shareholders.

Just as *Salomon* lent itself to abuse, so has the extension to corporate groups. As a result, in spite of judges' traditional reluctance to pierce the corporate veil in favour of creditors, *Salomon's* principle has now been modified by statutory reform in New Zealand and more recently Ireland and Australia.[5] New Zealand and Ireland allow the court discretion to make contribution orders and pooling orders in the case of related companies.

Currently, Australia merely provides that a parent company can be made liable for the debts of an insolvent subsidiary in certain circumstances. It has also encouraged the growth of group guarantees in the case of closed groups. The New Zealand legislation on pooling is under consideration and there is new legislation dealing with asset stripping in groups to the detriment of employee entitlements. Only in the United Kingdom and Canada is *Salomon* applied to corporate groups in the old form. The US Bankruptcy Law recognises consolidation of corporate groups as well as equitable subordination of group debts.[6]

The approach of the law to corporate groups often seems accidental or casuistic. The recognition of corporate groups has preceded a rational consideration of their merits and demerits. In this chapter we shall attempt an examination of the emerging trends in the case law that sometimes seem contradictory. We shall examine common abuses that arise from the group relationship and the reasons why these occur. We shall then review the current statute law and practice on group insolvencies in Australia and New Zealand, making brief comparions with the USA. Finally, we shall examine questions of principle and policy behind reform of this area and consider whether they necessarily entail some recognition of group legal personality or responsibility.

---

4   (1989) 16 NSWLR at 576. See also his remarks in *Qintex Australia Finance Ltd v. Schroders Australia Ltd* (1990) 3 ACSR 267 at 269. See too his extracurial comments in 'Corporate Groups—Problems for Outsiders'; in M. Gillooly (ed.), *The Law Relating to Corporate Groups*, The Federation Press, Leichhardt, 1993, ch. 5. Cf. R. Baxt, 'The Need to Review the Rule in *Salomon's* Case as it Applies to Groups of Companies' (1991) 9 C&SLJ 185, 186–7 and S. Fridman, 'Removal of the Corporate Veil: Suggestions for Law Reform in *Qintex Australia Finance Ltd v. Schroders Australia Ltd* (1991) 19 ABLR 211. For a recent thorough analysis see I. Ramsay, 'Allocating Liabilitiy in Corporate Groups: An Australian Perspective' (1999) 13 *Connecticut Journal of International Law* 329. This *inter alia* gives useful statistics of Australian groups and piercing the veil cases.

5   See J. H. Farrar and A. B. Darroch, 'Insolvency and Corporate Groups—the Problem of Consolidation', in J. P. G. Lessing and J. F. Corkery (eds), *Corporate Insolvency Laws*, Bond University, Gold Coast, 1995, p. 231. See too J. O'Donovan, 'Grouped Therapies for Group Insolvencies', in Gillooly, *op. cit.*, ch. 3.

6   See Farrar and Darroch, *op. cit.*, pp. 250 *et seq.*

First of all, we shall address two topics of case law: (a) piercing the corporate veil and (b) directors' duties in the group context. As a subset of (b) we will consider the shadow director cases.

The emerging trends in corporate group cases

Piercing the veil cases

The orthodox approach to the application of *Salomon* to groups is that the parent company and each subsidiary is a separate legal person and is, as a necessary consequence, solely responsible for its own debts.

There are a number of exceptional cases where the courts have pierced the veil either as a facade or on the basis of what they conceived to be the reality of the group enterprise as a single economic entity.[7] The facade cases have usually been at one end of the spectrum and the enterprise cases at the other. Facade is used as a category of illusory reference to express the courts' disapproval of the use of the corporate form to evade obligations and the courts have failed to identify a clear test based on pragmatic considerations such as undercapitalisation or domination.[8] The main group enterprise cases have been compulsory acquisition cases where the courts see no harm in the arrangements and it would be unjust for the court to rely too heavily on technicalities.[9] Whereas the facade cases, which represent no clear principle, have generally been approved of, the group enterprise cases, which are clearer if unorthodox, now represent a backwater. One is reminded of the Oscar Wilde aphorism 'If one tells the truth, one is sure, sooner or later, to be found out'.[10]

The orthodox modern approach is reflected in the English Court of Appeal decision in *Adams v. Cape Industries Plc*[11] in 1990 where the piercing the veil argument was used to attempt to bring an English public company, which was the parent company of a group that included subsidiaries in the USA, within the jurisdiction of the courts of the USA. The Court of Appeal rejected the single group entity argument and held that it was a legitimate use of the corporate form to use a subsidiary to insulate the remainder of the group from tort liability. There was no evidence to justify a finding of agency or facade. The Court of Appeal followed the House of Lords in the Scottish appeal in *Woolfson v. Strathclyde Regional Council*[12] which had rejected the earlier reasoning in the English Court of Appeal in *DHN Food Distributors Ltd v. Tower Hamlets LBC.*[13]

---

7   See H. A. J. Ford, R. P. Austin and I. M. Ramsay, *Ford's Principles of Corporations Law*, 10th edn, Butterworths, Sydney, 2001, para. 4.140 *et seq.*

8   See J. H. Farrar and B. Hannigan, *Farrar's Company Law*, 4th edn, Butterworths, London, 1998, p. 74.

9   See *Smith, Stone & Knight Ltd. v. Birmingham Corporation* [1939] 4 All ER 116; *DHN Food Distributors Ltd. v. Tower Hamlets LBC* [1976] 1 WLR 852.

10   'Phrases and Philosophies for the Use of the Young', *The Chameleon*, December 1894.

11   [1990] Ch 433

12   (1978) 38 P&CR 521

13   [1976] 1 WLR 852

However, the court felt that earlier authorities provided sparse guidance as to the principles that should guide the court in determining whether or not the arrangements of a corporate group involved a facade. Counsel had argued that the court should lift the veil where the corporate structure attempts to evade (a) limitations imposed on conduct by the law; (b) such rights of relief as third parties already possess; (c) such rights of relief as third parties might in the future require. On the basis of the authorities it would be safe only to accept (a) and (b). Case (c) seems to go beyond the present law.

By contrast, in two cases involving the granting of injunctions, the courts have been more inclined to take a more flexible approach. Thus in *Aiglon Ltd and L'Aiglon SA v. Gau Shan Co. Ltd.*[14] the court granted an injunction against a company in connection with a liability owed by its affiliate where there was evidence of transactions at undervalue. Also in *TSB Private Bank International SA v. Chabra*[15] Justice Mummery was prepared to countenance that a company was the alter ego of its controlling shareholder and granted an injunction against it in respect of a claim by the shareholder.

Australian authority has generally followed the UK authorities in spite of the increasing awareness of judges such as Andrew Rogers of the need for reform to bring the law into contact with commercial reality. Thus in *Pioneer Concrete Services Ltd. v. Yelnah Pty Ltd*[16] we have a useful review by Justice Young of the English, New Zealand and Australian authorities, in the context of construction of a complex commercial agreement. In *Briggs v. James Hardie & Co. Pty Ltd.*[17] Justice Rogers referred to the unity of enterprise theory in cases such as *DHN* and thought that its adoption may have been foreclosed to Australian courts below the High Court as a result of the decision in *Industrial Equity Ltd. v. Blackburn.*[18] In that case the High Court held that where a parent company had full and effective control over the funds of a subsidiary and the way they dealt with them, the profits to which it could look for the purposes of the declaration of dividends were confined to those already within the parent company. Similarly in *Walker v. Wimborne*[19] Justice Mason emphasised the principle of separate legal personality of members of a group and the need for directors of each company to consult its interests and its interests alone in deciding whether to make payments to other companies.

There have been similar conservative trends in New Zealand[20] and Canadian[21] case law which stand in stark contrast to the greater willingness of US courts to pierce the

---

14   [1993] BCLC 1321
15   [1992] 1 WLR 231
16   (1986) 5 NSWLR 254
17   (1989) 16 NSWLR 549
18   (1977) 137 CLR 567
19   (1976) 137 CLR 1
20   See *Re Securitibank Ltd (No 2)* [1978] 2 NZLR 136.
21   See B. Welling, *Corporate Law in Canada—The Governing Principles*, 2nd edn, Butterworths, Toronto, 1991, pp. 122 *et seq.*

veil on a number of different doctrinal bases which include domination, unity of enterprise and undercapitalisation.[22]

The courts' approaches to directors' duties and authority in the group context

It was accepted by the English Court of Appeal in *Lindgren v. L. and P. Estates Ltd*[23] that directors of a parent company do not owe duties to protect the interests of subsidiaries where these have independent boards, although oppression or unfairly prejudicial conduct may be the subject of relief under the statutory minority shareholder remedy, and it has been suggested in Australia that both parent and subsidiary boards owe a duty of good faith to each other.[24]

The most conservative approach to directors' duties in a subsidiary is that demonstrated by Justice Mason in *Walker v. Wimborne*[25] where he emphasised the need for directors of a subsidiary to consult its interests and its interests alone while recognising the possibility of derivative benefits. In *Northside Developments Pty Ltd v. Registrar General & Ors*[26] Justice Brennan likewise recognised derivative benefits. This differs from the more flexible approach demonstrated by Justice Pennycuick in the English case of *Charterbridge Corp. Ltd v. Lloyds Bank*[27] where his lordship recognised that the directors need not necessarily have considered the separate interests of the subsidiary if an honest and reasonable director would have considered the transaction to be for the good of the company. A stricter view was taken by Justices Clarke and Cripps in the New South Wales Court of Appeal in *Equiticorp Finance Ltd. (in liq.) v. BNZ*[28] where they said that the preferable view was that the directors had committed a breach of duty but if the transaction was objectively viewed in the interests of the company then no consequences would flow from the breach. However, Justice

22 See for example *Gibraltar Savings v. LD Brinkman* 860 F 2d 1275 (USCA 5th Circuit), 1286–9 (1988). See generally P. Blumberg, *The Multinational Challenge to Corporation Law*, Oxford University Press, New York, 1993, ch. 4 and his magisterial five volume treatise *The Law of Corporate Groups*, Little Brown, Boston, 1987. For a simple overview of the US position see T. W. Cashel, 'Groups of Companies—Some US Aspects', in C. Schmitthoff and F. Wooldridge (eds), *Groups of Companies*, Sweet & Maxwell, London, 1991, ch. 2.
23 [1968] Ch 572.
24 See Joske J in *Re Associated Tool Industries Ltd* [1964] ALR 73, 82 citing Lord Keith of Avonholme in *Scottish Ltd v. Meyer* [1959] AC 324 at 361.
25 (1976) 137 CLR 1, 6–7. See generally R. Austin, 'Problems for Directors within Corporate Groups', in Gillooly, *op. cit.* footnote 4 supra, ch. 6; and P. Redmond, 'Problem for Insiders' in Gillooly, *op. cit.*, ch. 8.
26 (1989–1990) 170 CLR 146.
27 [1970] Ch 62. This has been applied many times: see e.g. *Reid Murray Holdings Ltd* (1971–3) CLC 40–075; *Australian National Industries v. Greater Pacific Investments Pty Ltd (in liq.) (No 3)* (1992) 7 ACSR 176; *Linton v. Telnet Pty Ltd* (1999) 17 ACLC 619.
28 (1993) 11 ACLC 952 at 1019.

Pennycuick's view was followed by the New South Wales Court of Appeal in the recent case of *Linton v. Telnet Pty Ltd*.[29]

The strict approach contrasts with the legislative reforms in sections 131(2) and (3) of the New Zealand *Companies Act 1993* which enable contracting out of the strict duty in the articles of a wholly owned subsidiary, and by vote in general meeting in the case of a partly owned subsidiary. Section 131(2) provides that a director of a wholly owned subsidiary may, if expressly permitted by the constitution of the company, act in a manner which he or she believes is in the best interests of the parent company, even though it may not be in the best interests of the subsidiary. Section 131 (3) provides that where the subsidiary is not wholly owned, a director, if expressly permitted by the constitution and with the prior agreement of the shareholders (other than the parent company), acts in a like manner.

Section 187 of the Corporations Act now adopts the approach of section 131(2) but not section 131(3). However, the wording of section 187 is more restricted. It provides that the director is to be taken to act in good faith in the best interests of the subsidiary if:

(a) the constitution of the subsidiary expressly authorises the director to act in the best interests of the holding company;

(b) the director acts in good faith in the best interests of the holding company; and

(c) the subsidiary is not insolvent at the time the director acts and does not become insolvent because of the director's act.

The main differences are that (b) is probably objective and omits the words 'even though it may not be in the best interests of the company' which appear in section 131(2) of the New Zealand Act and (c) does not appear in the New Zealand section.

Contrasting with the previous strictness of the Australian courts to the question of duty is the greater laxity in the case of the authority of a group CEO in the *Equiticorp* case. In spite of a vigorous and well-reasoned dissent by President Kirby, Justices Clarke and Cripps held that Alan Hawkins had general authority to manage the affairs of the group and 'to whom was deferred, whether or not after consultation with the more senior members of management, decisions of significance'. With respect, this goes too far. As President Kirby said,[30] to accept inferences of a 'unanimous albeit informal agreement' of the company members

> would set at nought the separate identity of corporations and the duties which are owed in each case separately to the company as a whole, even by directors who hold office in a number of corporations in a corporate group. The requirement concerning ratification of otherwise unauthorised conduct to the shareholders of a company is not a mere technicality. It is a rule which imposes on companies the beneficial discipline of the law for the protection of investors and creditors and, through them, of the community which is so dependent upon corporations for its economic well-being.

---

29 (1999) 17 ACLC 619, 625. Compare also *Pascoe Ltd (in liq.) v. Lucas* (1999) 33 ACSR 357.

30 *Equiticorp Finance Ltd (in liq.) v. BNZ* (1993) 11 ACLC 952 at 979–80.

Shadow directors

An important question which has assumed some prominence in recent cases is that of shadow directors. The question in the context of groups is whether a parent company, while disqualified by statute from being appointed a director of a subsidiary, can nevertheless be held to be a director because of the wide definition in section 9 of the Corporations Act or section 126 of the New Zealand Act. Notwithstanding earlier Privy Council authority to the contrary, Justice Hodgson held in *Standard Chartered Bank v. Antico*[31] that a company, falling short of legal control so as to be technically a parent company, was still capable of being regarded as a shadow director under the section where it had demonstrated some measure of de facto control in relation to accounts. In the English case of *Re Hydrodam (Corby) Ltd*[32] and the New Zealand cases of *Kuwait Asia Bank v. National Mutual Life Nominees Ltd*[33] and *Dairy Containers Ltd v. NZI Bank Ltd*,[34] such arguments were unsuccessful on the facts.

Abuses of the group relationship

In a valuable recent UK study,[35] Dr Andrew Muscat has classified the main types of abuse as follows:

(a) the subservient subsidiary
(b) the undercapitalised subsidiary
(c) the integrated economic enterprise
(d) the group persons' situation

In the case of (a) the subsidiary is not allowed to act as an independent profit centre. This usually arises because of domination by the parent company, which leads to group profit maximisation, transfer pricing, diversion of corporate opportunities, and manipulation of assets or shell subsidiaries. Manipulation of assets takes the form of commingling of assets, movement of funds, draining of assets, financial support of the group or the operation of the subsidiary without a profit motive. Situation (b) raises

---

31 (1995) 13 ACLC 1381. See too *ASC v. AS Nominees Ltd* (1995) 18 ACSR 459; N. Campbell, 'Liability as a Shadow Director' [1994] JBL 609; M. Markovic, 'The Law of Shadow Directorships' (1996) AJ of CL 331; P. Koh, 'Shadow Director, Who Art Thou' (1996) 14 C&SLJ 340; K. Sutherland, 'Shadow Boxing', unpublished LLM research paper, University of Melbourne, 1997.
32 [1994] 2 BCLC 180
33 [1990] BCLC 868
34 (1995) 13 ACLC 3211
35 *The Liability of the Holding Company for the Debts of Its Insolvent Subsidiaries*, Dartmouth, Aldershot, 1996, ch. 5, 6, 7 and 8. See J. Landers 'A Unified Approach to Parent, Subsidiary and Affiliated Questions in Bankruptcy' (1975) 42 U Chi L Rev 589; R. Posner, 'The Legal Rights of Creditors of Affiliated Corporations: An Economic Approach' (1976) 43 U Chi L Rev 499. Landers, in a later reply to Posner 'Another Word on Parents, Subsidiaries and Affiliates in Bankruptcy' (1976) 43 U Chi L Rev 527, identifies the dangers faced by creditors of a multicorporate enterprise to which law and economics fail to provide practical solutions.

issues of appropriate financing for the debt burden carried by the subsidiary and the position of the parent company as an ordinary or secured creditor. Sometimes this is exacerbated by the use of 'creditor proof' devices such as leasing assets and bookkeeping devices such as management charges. Situation (c) involves abusive integration which goes beyond normal patterns of economic integration. This involves an artificial division of a unitary enterprise into separate subsidiaries. Situation (d) involves an element of misrepresentation or holding out of a single entity, which misleads creditors.

Such abuses are more likely to be found in the case of the smaller groups which are less subject to the monitoring by markets than larger corporate groups. Proprietary groups are not participating in the markets for investment capital and their management is often less responsive to the market for management, which to some extent monitors unethical behaviour. There is inadequate empirical research being done on these causes of corporate collapse.

These problems are increased when some of the affiliated companies are in different jurisdictions. The English courts in recent years have encountered a growing number of such cases. Even in the European Union progress towards a Bankruptcy Convention has been slow and international insolvency represents a costly legal nightmare for creditors. Currently the matter is under review by the United Nations Commission on International Trade Law (UNCITRAL).

Many of the problems in this area arise from a confusion of separate legal personality with limited liability. One does not necessarily entail the other as historical experience shows. The rise of corporate groups, coupled with a strict application of *Salomon*, has created the possibility of limited liability within limited liability, which arguably goes beyond the intention of the legislature. Faced with abuses of the kind listed above and unacceptable consequences of strict application of *Salomon* the legislatures in Australia and New Zealand have reformed the law and modified *Salomon's* principle as it affects creditors.

Review of Australian and New Zealand law

The Australian position

Australian corporations law originally followed the UK model on group liability. There was potential in the sections on preventing insolvent trading, as there is in the UK wrongful trading provisions, to impose liability on a parent company for debts incurred by a subsidiary under its control. An attempt to argue liability for fraudulent trading in England failed in *Re Augustus Barnett & Sons Ltd.*[36] Liability under sections 592 and 593 of the Corporations Act required the parent company to be treated as a director or person who had taken part in the management of the company. A parent

---

36 [1986] BCLC 170

company could be a shadow director under the wide provisions of the statutory definition of director.

Group debt situations might fall within the voidable preference (section 565) or defective floating charges (section 566) provisions and the provisions on recovery of excess profits on sales to or by a company (section 567), as well as the related party provisions introduced by Part 3.2A in 1992.

Group debt is also dealt with in the Australian Securities and Investments Commission's 'Class Order: Wholly Owned Subsidiaries' 98/1418 which superseded earlier ASC (Australian Securities Commission) and NCSC (National Corporate and Securities Commission) class orders. This is dealt with below.

Exceptional cases of intermingling

In the United Kingdom and Australia there has from time to time been found the need for consolidation of assets and creditors of a group of companies in cases where there has been such intermingling of the business affairs of the companies that it is difficult or impossible to ascertain the financial position of the respective companies.

In *Re Trix Ltd*,[37] Justice Plowman in the English Chancery Division refused to approve a compromise agreement and said that the proper method of dealing with the problem was a scheme of arrangement. This is, however, often too cumbrous and expensive. Since then, the experience of the English courts of dealing with the cases involving the Bank of Credit and Commerce International SA has caused them to be more flexible with 'exceptional cases' of intermingling. See *Re BCCI (No 3)*.[38] In the New South Wales case of *Dean Willcocks v. Soluble Solution Hydroponics Pty Ltd*,[39] Justice Young, faced with what was nearly a unanimous shareholder resolution in favour of consolidation in a case of commingling, was prepared under section 447A of the Corporations Act to direct the liquidator to treat the resolution as valid. All of these are extreme cases of intermingling.

The ALRC proposals

In its *General Report on Insolvency*,[40] the Australian Law Reform Commission proposed in 1988 that the court should be given discretion to order a company which is or has been a related company, to pay to the liquidator all or any part of an amount that is an admissible claim in the winding up 'if it is satisfied that it is just'. Three specific criteria were proposed to which the court should have regard. These were:

---

37   [1993] BCLC 106; [1992] BCC 1490.
38   [1992] BCC 1490
39   (1997) 15 ACLC 833.
40   1988, vol. 1, para. 334.

(a) the extent to which the related company took part in the management of the company
(b) the conduct of the related company towards the creditors of the company
(c) the extent to which the circumstances that gave rise to the winding up of the company are attributable to the actions of the related company.

The commission's proposals were supported by a number of submissions but were attacked by the Law Council of Australia on four grounds. These were:

(1) They would contradict the separate entity principle.
(2) They would interfere with project financing.
(3) They would give rise to uncertainty.
(4) They would complicate company accounts.

The commission did not find the Law Council's reasoning compelling. The proposals in section 13 strongly resembled the New Zealand provisions, but also drew on the European experience. The proposals have recently been revisited by the Companies and Securities Advisory Committee (CASAC) and we discuss this later.

The *Corporate Law Reform Act 1992*

The *Corporate Law Reform Act 1992* did not implement these proposals but contained a less radical provision enabling a liquidator of an insolvent company to sue the company's holding company if the holding company had allowed the subsidiary to trade when the holding company knew or should have known that the subsidiary was insolvent. The relevant wording was enacted as Division 5 of Part 5.7B of the Corporations Act.[41]

Basis of liability

Section 588V(1) of the Corporations Act now provides that a corporation which is a holding company contravenes the section if the subsidiary of the holding company incurs a debt when the subsidiary is insolvent, or the subsidiary becomes insolvent by incurring the debt, and (a) there are reasonable grounds at the time for suspecting that the subsidiary is insolvent or will become insolvent; and (b) either the holding company or one or more of its directors is aware of grounds for suspecting insolvency or, having regard to the nature and extent of the corporation's control of the subsidiary's affairs, it is reasonable to expect that the corporation would have been aware of those grounds or that one or more of the holding company's directors would have been aware

41   For useful comment on these provisions, see R. P. Austin, 'The Corporate Law Reform Bill—Its effect on liability of holding companies for debts of insolvent subsidiaries' (18 March 1992) BCLB [103], I. Ramsay, 'Holding Company Liability for the Debts of an Insolvent Subsidiary: A Law and Economics Perspective' (1994) 17 UNSWLJ 520; I. Ramsay, *op. cit.*, footnote 4 supra, pp. 360–76; see too D. Murphy, 'Holding Company Liability for Debts of its Subsidiaries—Corporate Governance Implications' (1998) 10 Bond LR 241.

of those grounds. Thus, the test involves an assessment both of whether there are reasonable grounds to *suspect* the subsidiary's insolvency and whether the holding company or one of its directors was aware or a reasonable person would *expect* that they would have been aware, of those grounds.

'Insolvent' is defined in section 95A. A company is insolvent if it is not solvent, that is, if it is not able to pay its debts when they become due and payable. Only debts are covered and there is considerable case law on the meaning of debts and when they fall due.[42]

There must be reasonable grounds for suspecting that the subsidiary is insolvent or will become insolvent. The requirement of 'reasonable grounds to *suspect*' is identical to the equivalent section dealing with directors' liability for insolvent trading. Thus, the new test is higher than the old test of 'expect'. The Australian Law Reform Commission Report paragraph 304 explains the justification for a higher test. This was based on a requirement for continual monitoring. If directors suspect that a company may be trading while insolvent, they should examine its affairs to ascertain whether there are reasonable grounds to expect that it will be able to pay its debts. There is some justification for imposing this test on the directors of the subsidiary. The imposition of the duty on the holding company by the 1992 Act is questionable.

The provisions employ a combination of actual knowledge and an objective standard based on whether, having regard to the nature and extent of the corporation's control over the subsidiary's affairs, a reasonable person would expect that the holding company, or one or more of its directors, would have been aware that there were reasonable grounds to suspect the subsidiary's insolvency.

Consequences

Contravention of this section results in civil liability but not a civil penalty or a criminal offence. This is in line with the Australian Law Reform Commission's proposals. The civil liability falls on the corporation and not the directors personally. Section 588W deals with recovery of compensation for loss resulting from insolvent trading. A liquidator of the subsidiary may take proceedings against the holding company for recovery of loss or damage suffered by unsecured creditors as a result of the contravention. The recovery is subject to a limitation period of six years from the relevant date. Certain presumptions apply. These include (a) the presumption that, if a corporation has been proved to be insolvent on a particular date during the twelve months prior to the relation back date, then the corporation is presumed insolvent from that time until the relation back date (section 588E(4)(i)); and (b) a presumption that, where the corporation has failed to keep adequate accounting records as required by section 289(1) and (2), the corporation was insolvent for the period to which the inadequacy or absence of records relates (section 588E(4)(ii)). These presumptions can be rebutted by evidence to the contrary (section 588E(9)).

---

42   See e.g. *Hawkins v. Bank of China* (1992) 10 ACLC 588.

Defences

Section 588X sets out a number of defences to an action under section 588W. These are similar to those for section 588G. The defences are (1) when the debt was incurred, the holding company and each relevant director had reasonable grounds to expect and did expect that the corporation was solvent at the time and would remain so; (2) when the debt was incurred, the holding company and each relevant director had reasonable grounds to believe that a competent and reliable person was responsible for providing to the holding company adequate information about whether the subsidiary was solvent and that the person was fulfilling that responsibility; or (3) the corporation took all reasonable steps to prevent the corporation from incurring the debt. In addition, the section also provides that when a particular director did not take part in the management of the holding company at the time the subsidiary incurred the debt because of illness or other cause, the fact that the director was aware of the subsidiary's insolvency is to be disregarded.

These provisions represent a limited piercing of the corporate veil but will give rise to concern where the holding company is not the principal operating entity. The risk of liability of the holding company for a subsidiary's operations will be a cause for concern among the boards of large corporations, who will be required to monitor the affairs of subsidiaries more closely. Where the ultimate holding company is in an overseas jurisdiction there may be practical difficulties with meeting these requirements.

NCSC and ASIC class orders

Wholly owned subsidiaries

Closed groups of companies have been exempted by the NCSC and ASIC from the need to prepare audited accounts and directors' statements for each wholly owned subsidiary.[43] The main qualification is that each company and the holding company in the group have entered into a deed approved by the NCSC or ASIC. Under the deed (of cross guarantee), the holding company covenants with the subsidiaries to pay the liquidator any shortfall of liabilities over assets. There is a cross guarantee by the subsidiaries in respect of the holding company's shortfall.

Debts covered by the deed are those that are admissible to proof in a winding up. This now includes damages in tort, and thus is wider than sections 588G and 588V. The

---

43 See Wholly-owned Subsidiaries: Class Order and Revocation (98/1418). See the case law on the earlier class order cross guarantee: *Re JN Taylor Holdings Ltd (in liq.) (No 7)* (1991) 9 ACLC 1483; *Westmix Operations Pty Ltd (in liq.) v. Westmix Ltd (in liq.)* (1992) 10 ACLC 1179; (1994) 12 ACLC 106 (NSWCA); and the more recent case of *Re Egnia Pty Ltd (in liq.)* (1992) 10 ACLC 185. For extensive and valuable discussion of such orders, see G. Dean, P. Luckett and E. Houghton, 'Notional Calculations in Liquidations Revisited: The Case of ASC Class Order Cross Guarantees' (1993) 11 C&SLJ 449; their unpublished paper 'ASC Class Order Deed of Cross Guarantee and Negative Pledge Instruments: Preliminary Analysis of Deregulation in Corporate Group Finance and Group Liquidation', University of Sydney; J. Hill, 'Corporate Groups, Creditor Protection and Cross Guarantees: Australian Perspective' (1995) 24 CBLJ 321; and D. Murphy, *op. cit.* footnote 41 supra.

deed can be revoked or released in certain circumstances. If the shares in a group company are sold by an insolvency administrator, or enforcement of a security interest, or on a bona fide sale for fair and reasonable consideration, it is treated as if the deed had never been executed by the sold company and its subsidiaries. The companies in question can be released from all their obligations under the deed. Each other group company is released from its obligations in respect of the debts of the companies sold. These results depend on certain procedural steps being taken, and notification to ASIC of a sale to persons who are not associates of any of the group companies. There are other more onerous provisions for revocation of deeds.

The 'carve out' in respect of hiving off subsidiaries seems inherently problematic. Damian Murphy has made some serious criticisms of this practice.[44] He argues that in one sense it is very practical, because it permits a corporate group to readily dispose of shares in subsidiaries, and the purchaser of those shares may rely on the creditors of the purchased entity being only those creditors who in the first place were creditors of the purchased entity without regard to its obligation under the Deed of Cross Guarantee. However, in another sense it cuts across the entire purpose of the deed, which is to provide creditors of all group companies with access to all the assets of all group companies. It may be argued that the remaining creditors have access to the proceeds of sale. But this misses the point. The creditors of the purchased entity will more than likely now be fully paid out, since a person does not usually buy a company with the view of letting it fail in the short term. The purchase price of shares in the entity will reflect this and will be reduced to take account of existing liabilities. Accordingly, the proceeds of the sale will be 'net' the liabilities to the existing creditors. So, in the very circumstances that the Deed of Cross Guarantee was intended to cover, it is able to be frustrated. Murphy argues[45] that this reflects a conceptual confusion. The class order sought to replace regard to the financial position of separate entities with regard to the financial position of the entire group, so there was no longer any reason to have individual accounts. Yet it is clear that for a creditor to accurately assess their financial position, access to the individual accounts is required. It is not the position of the creditors of the entity being sold, since in all likelihood they are better off. Rather, it is the position of the remaining creditors who will be left with a much reduced asset base to access for payment. At the time of extending credit, notwithstanding the existence of a Deed of Cross Guarantee, they need to assess the financial position of the group and its prospects as well as assess which companies in the group may be sold in their entirety, and so reduce the assets available upon a group insolvency. This is a very complicated assessment and probably represents a backwards step. The position of the creditors of other group companies is thrown into relief when emphasis is given to there being no notification requirement upon a sale. This is to be contrasted with the position when a

---

44   Murphy, *op. cit.* footnote 41 supra, pp. 268 *et seq.*
45   *ibid.,* p. 269.

Deed of Cross Guarantee is revoked. These criticisms seem very convincing and point to serious flaws in the scheme.

Murphy also refers to the corporate governance implications of entering into a Deed of Cross Guarantee.[46] The first question is whether it can be said to be for the corporate benefit of each company. This must be very debatable. The second question is the possible extension of the duties of directors of one group company to monitor other group companies out of self-interest.

To sum up, there are two very important things to notice about such Deeds of Cross Guarantee. The first is that they go much further than either the ALRC proposal or the *Corporate Law Reform Act 1992* (Cwth), in that there is automatic liability and this is undertaken by subsidiaries as well as the holding company. It seems that this approach was developed without any reference to the two reform proposals.

Second, the arrangements are contractual, with all the resulting complications of guarantees, rights of indemnification and subrogation, as well as awkward questions of corporate benefit. A legislative solution would be better. This is an odd method of law reform and it bears an uneasy relationship with sections 588G and 588V.

The New Zealand position

Contribution and pooling orders in respect of related companies

We will now examine the question of consolidation of group debts in the New Zealand legislation. Since the approach is a radical departure from *Salomon* we need to examine it closely. In essence, the New Zealand legislation allows the court to make a contribution order on broad grounds in the case of insolvency of a related company and also provides for pooling orders in respect of insolvent related companies. US bankruptcy law allows joint bankruptcy administration, equitable subordination and substantive consolidation of group indebtedness, but not contribution orders as such. There are similarities between US consolidation and the New Zealand provisions and it will be possible to use the US case law in the New Zealand courts, although to date this has not been done. Recently there has been a number of New Zealand cases on the interpretation of the relevant sections.

New Zealand courts have a wide discretionary power under the Companies Acts to deal with related companies once *one* of the companies is placed into liquidation. The court can order that a related company contribute to the assets available for winding up or, if there is more than one related company in liquidation, the court can wind them up as if they were one company.[47]

---

46   *ibid.*, pp. 269 *et seq.*
47   Originally added as sections 315A and 315B of the Companies Act 1955 (now sections 245–6) and see also sections 271–2 of the *Companies Act 1993*. This part of the chapter is based on A. Darroch's LLM Research Paper, written under my supervision in the Corporate Insolvency class at Victoria University of Wellington in 1991.

It is clear that a pooling order is not merely an administrative or procedural order but is one which affects the substantive rights of those parties interested in the winding up of any company subject to such orders.[48]

The courts, in considering making a pooling order, must determine whether it is 'just and equitable' to make the order. Although the legislature has provided a number of factors for the court to consider, the circumstances which will amount to just and equitable are unclear. The case law involving the pooling sections provides some guidelines, but the extent and circumstances in which an order will be granted are still unclear.

Related companies

The *Companies Amendment Act 1980* introduced the concept of 'related companies' into the *Companies Act 1955*. The court is empowered to make pooling orders affecting 'related' companies.

The term 'related' is now defined in section 2(3) of the *Companies Act 1993* as follows:

A company is related to another if:

(a) The other company is its holding company or subsidiary; or

(b) More than half of the issued shares of the company, other than shares that carry no right to participate beyond a specified amount in a distribution of either profits or capital, is held by the other company and companies related to that other company (whether directly or indirectly, but other than in a fiduciary capacity); or

(c) More than half of the issued shares, other than shares that carry no right to participate beyond a specified amount in a distribution of either profits or capital of each of them is held by members of the other (whether directly or indirectly, but other than in a fiduciary capacity); or

(d) The businesses of the companies have been so carried on that the separate business of each company, or a substantial part of it, is not readily identifiable; or

(e) There is another company to which both companies are related; and 'related company' has a corresponding meaning.

The definition includes reference to the definitions of 'holding' and 'subsidiary' company, and to the holding of majority shares, but also goes wider than the Corporations Act by the fact-based provision where the businesses of the companies have been intermingled.

The legislation

The legislative provisions relating to contribution and the pooling of assets of related companies are contained in sections 245–246 (formerly sections 315A, 315B and 315C) of the *Companies Act 1955*. These provisions were introduced by the *Companies*

---

48   See *Stewart Timber and Hardware Ltd (in liq.)* (1991) 5 NZCLC 67, 137.

Amendment Act 1980. The new provisions are now contained in sections 271–272 of the *Companies Act 1993.*

Origin

The MacArthur Report[49] recommended that the court be given the power to make orders that would require a company to pay all or part of its related company's liability to creditors if it went into liquidation.

The committee had been referred by the New Zealand Society of Accountants to abuses by companies with the same controlling shareholders. It was said that creditors of one company in a group (which was a failing company) lost money as a result of assets being transferred from that company to another company in the same group for inadequate consideration. The examples of two well known but unnamed companies were cited for having abandoned subsidiaries in this way. It was considered inequitable that the holding company could take the benefit of tax advantages accruing from the subsidiary and then leave the creditors of the same subsidiary to a reduced payout in the winding up.

The recommendations[50] resulted in pooling provisions being placed in the Companies Amendment Bill containing a broad equitable power either to require a contribution from a company to its related company (section 315A) or, if both are insolvent, to wind them up as if they were one company (section 315B). The power was to be exercised whenever the court considered it 'just and equitable' to do so.

As the Bill passed through Parliament, a large number of submissions complained that the powers were expressed in terms that were too wide and that no criteria were specified to guide the court as to when it should exercise its discretion.[51] In particular, submissions outlined concern that all too often, creditors who had lost money would rely on the excuse that they had invested in or traded with a company on the basis that another company was a shareholder in it. It was feared that a vocal group of creditors could persuade the court that they invested or traded solely because of the involvement of the other company and that, consequently, they should be reimbursed.

The volume and argument of the submissions led to the drafting and inclusion of section 315C, which provided criteria for the guidance of the court and expressly precluded a court order if the only ground for the order was the fact that creditors relied on the relationship between the companies.

Contribution orders under section 271(1)(a)

Section 271 of the *Companies Act 1993* confers powers on the court in the following terms:

---

49   *Report on the Reform of Companies* (MacArthur chairman) New Zealand Government Printer, 1977.
50   MacArthur Report, *ibid.,* para. 405.
51   Hansard Parliamentary Debates, Second Reading, Companies Amendment Bill 1980.

271— Pooling of assets of related companies

(1) On the application of the liquidator, or a creditor or shareholders, the court, if satisfied that it is just and equitable to do so, may order that:

    (a) A company that is, or has been, related to the company in liquidation must pay to the liquidator the whole or part of any or all of the claims made in the liquidation; and

    (b) Where two or more related companies are in liquidation, the liquidations in respect of each company must proceed together as if they were one company to the extent that the court so orders and subject to such terms and conditions as the court may impose.

(2) The court may make such other order or give such directions to facilitate giving effect to an order under subsection (1) of this section as it thinks fit.

Although the heading to the section now reads 'Pooling of Assets' it covers both contribution orders and pooling.

Section 271(1)(a) confers an extremely wide discretion on the court to make orders requiring a company to contribute towards the assets of the related company that is being wound up. The benefits of such an order to creditors and shareholders of the company in liquidation are obviously to increase the size of any dividend of surplus assets that they might receive. It is, therefore, important for those persons to be aware of what types of circumstances will amount to 'just and equitable' and to judge whether to make an application for such orders. Equally, the management of a company should be aware of the types of transactions that may render their company liable to a contribution where a related company goes into liquidation. Creditors and shareholders of the solvent company should also be aware that such an order may affect their substantive rights by weakening the company with which they are involved.

An applicant must first prove that the company, from whom the contribution is sought, is related to the company in liquidation and then adduce evidence that it is just and equitable to make an order.[52] There is no presumption that an order should be made solely on the basis of creditor reliance on the relationship of the companies. Some further evidence is required to justify the order being made.[53]

It seems that a creditor or shareholder who succeeds in an application under section 271 is limited to benefiting from an increased dividend in the winding up, as the contribution resulting from a successful application is directed to be paid to the liquidator. Although the section allows the court to make the order on such terms and conditions as it thinks fit, it is submitted that this would not allow the court to improve the priority of any creditor or shareholder.

---

52   *Rea v. Barker* (1988) 4 NZCLC 64, 312.

53   s. 315C(3) of the *Companies Act 1955*. This has, however, since been deleted but presumably the same principle applies.

Just and equitable

In a judgment concerning the words 'just and equitable' in the *Companies Special Investigations Act 1958*, Justice Casey stated that there was little authority to guide him on the interpretation of the words 'just' and 'equitable' and commented that:

> Obviously, it contemplates a departure from the priorities laid down in the Companies Act 1955. I think Parliament intended the Court to have the broadest discretion to effect a result which accords with common notions of fairness in all the circumstances, bearing in mind the cardinal principle of insolvency administration, that there shall be equality among creditors of the same standing.[54]

Justice Casey stated that pooling provisions demonstrated the legislative acceptance of the importance of equality in the distribution of an insolvent company's assets.[55]

The power to intervene is expressed in extremely wide language, but is tempered by the equitable basis of the section and the flexibility to place conditions on the orders to ensure that equity is done. In exercising the broad discretion conferred by the section, the court is directed to take into account the guidelines outlined in section 272(1). These are:

(a) the extent to which the related company took part in the management of the company in liquidation
(b) The conduct of the related company towards the creditors of the company in liquidation
(c) The extent to which the circumstances that gave rise to the liquidation of the company are attributable to the actions of the related company
(d) Such other matters as the court thinks fit

The presence or absence of any of these factors is not decisive. In *Rea v. Barker*[56] the requirements of the section were discussed in the context of an application to strike out a party to which the section would have applied. The question before the court was whether there was an arguable case that an order should be made.

The liquidator established that the two companies were related by their common shareholders and adduced two possible grounds on which a contribution order could be made:

1   Evidence that one company, Altherm Auckland, had given its related company, Altherm Waikato, orders without payment at a time when Altherm Waikato must have know that Altherm Auckland could not afford to do so.

    The court found that the action of accepting Altherm Auckland's order, while being aware that it could not afford to give assets away, could render Altherm

---

54   *Re Home Loans Funds (NZ) Ltd (in group liq.)* (1983) 1 NZCLC 95 073 at 95, 583.
55   *ibid.* at 95, 583–4.
56   (1988) 4 NZCLC 64, 312.

Waikato liable to contribute to Altherm Auckland's assets in its winding up. It was stated that, depending on the scale of such orders, this could be seen as conduct towards Altherm Auckland's creditors.

2   Stocks of Altherm products commonly used by both companies were offered for sale by Altherm Auckland to Altherm Waikato. Altherm Waikato refused to purchase the stock.

The refusal to purchase the stock was also considered *arguably* to be possible conduct towards the creditors of Altherm Auckland, despite the lack of any contractual obligation to purchase the stock.

The fact that the stock was offered by the *liquidator* of Altherm Auckland to Altherm Waikato was not considered to remove it from the court's consideration. It held that actions of a company after the liquidation of its related company could still be seen as conduct towards the creditors of that company in liquidation.[57]

Such other matters as the court thinks fit

Two interlocutory decisions discussing the section have included reference to the *ability* of the related company to contribute to the assets of the company being wound up.[58] In the first case, *Lewis v. Poultry Processors*,[59] there was evidence that a contribution might threaten the solvency of the related company. Justice Tipping commented that,

> I doubt very much whether [the section] is intended to prejudice the position of bona fide unsecured creditors of the related company. If the related company is fully solvent then there is no problem. The contrasts between [the contribution and pooling provisions] suggest [a contribution] order will only run against the balance of assets in the related company's hands after it has satisfied its bona fide indebtedness.

The second case, *Re Liardet Holdings Ltd*,[60] confirmed this view, stating that it was considered doubtful that any order to contribute under the section would be made because there was evidence that nothing would be left after that company paid its own creditors.

If the contribution sought from a related company threatens that company's solvency, then the court must consider the equities involved affecting the creditors of that company. These creditors will rely on arguments that they had relied on the separate assets of the company when trading with it and should not be denied a full payout because of that company's relationship with another company.

The comments in *Lewis v. Poultry Processors* and *Liardet Holdings* make it clear that such equities will have significant input to the court's decision to make an order but will not necessarily be decisive. The court is faced with balancing the equities of two sets of

---

57   *ibid.* at 64, 312.
58   *Lewis v. Poultry Processors* (1988) 4 NZCLC 64, 508; *Re Liardet Holdings Ltd* (1983) BCR 604.
59   (1988) 4 NZCLC 64, 508.
60   (1983) BCR 604.

creditors who have dealt with two separate companies. It is submitted that the expression 'bona fide unsecured creditors' of the company mentioned by Justice Tipping, could be limited to those creditors who have clearly dealt with the company as a separate commercial entity and not the combined companies. This may be a difficult decision for a court to make and may mean ascribing to creditors, motives that were not clear at the time of the trading.

Pooling orders under section 271(1)(b)

This subsection deals with pooling and provides:

> Where two or more related companies are in liquidation, the liquidations in respect of each company must proceed together as if they were one company to the extent that the court so orders and subject to such terms and conditions as the court may impose.

Justice Hardie Boys in *Re Pacific Syndicates (NZ) Ltd*[61] described this provision as a valuable remedial measure designed to facilitate the task of liquidation and the general interests of all concerned.

'Wound up together as if they were one company'

In a decision dealing with the same wording under the Companies Special Investigation Act, Justice Cooke stated that winding the companies up together, as if they were one, caused the assets to form a common pool which was available to meet the claims of all unsecured creditors.[62] In more complex group situations, inter-company debts and liabilities may also be involved in the winding up, in addition to the assets of the companies. The question will be whether the liabilities of the related companies are to be merged as one and whether the inter-company debts will disappear as the assets and liabilities merge.

In *Re Dalhoff & King*[63] Justice Gallen indicated that the difficulty in establishing the precise nature of the inter-company debts was a factor to be taken into account in making a pooling order. A creditor of one company submitted that the guarantee obtained for its debt from one of the other related companies should be preserved, despite the pooling order. If no pooling order was made, this creditor was entitled to prove something in the winding up of both the companies, up to a dividend of 100 cents in the dollar. Justice Gallen rejected this submission and stated that the obligations as well as the assets of the related companies would merge and that it was inappropriate to allow the creditor to retain a position which involved the retention of the separate identity of two of the companies within the group.

---

61   (1989) 4 NZCLC 64, 757
62   *Re Grazing and Export Meat Company Ltd* (1984) 2 NZCLC 96, 021
63   (1991) 5 NZCLC 66, 959

The result is that the creditor that had attempted to secure its trading position by requiring inter-company guarantees was placed with other unsecured creditors in the winding up. It might be argued that this is inequitable, as it deprives a diligent creditor of the additional security gained and places it with other creditors who were not as diligent in arranging their terms of trade.

A different result was reached in *Re Stewart Timber & Hardware Ltd.*[64] The liquidators in that case obtained an *ex parte* order pooling the assets of the related companies. The question of a set-off with a third party arose and the liquidators returned to court and argued that the order made to pool the assets had the consequence of also pooling the liabilities. This was rejected by Justice Doogue, who stated that the order did not relate to liabilities and, therefore, they were excluded. It was clear that the order had been granted in terms of the application made by the liquidators, but it is not certain why mention of the liabilities was omitted.

The differing interpretations taken by these decisions, regarding the expression 'wound up together as if they were one company' in the wording of the old section, are not easily reconciled. The new wording reads 'proceed'. The courts have taken the view that this expression could be interpreted to include only assets, or may extend to include liabilities as well. A more consistent interpretation would be that assets and liabilities are combined, except to the extent that the court places conditions on the order to the contrary by its power in section 271(2). This would achieve the same flexibility but give some certainty to the interpretation of being wound up as one company.

Ex parte application

The *ex parte* application in *Re Stewart* should also be mentioned to point out the substantive effect it had on the rights of the creditors of a major shareholder of both the companies in liquidation. In support of the order, the liquidators adduced evidence that these creditors would only be affected to the extent of 1.2 cents in the dollar by the pooling orders, leaving them with a payout in the region of 98 cents in the dollar. The end result was substantially different, with their dividend being a maximum of 28 cents in the dollar. Other than pointing out that the court would prefer the application to have been made on an inter-party basis, Justice Doogue noted that no application on behalf of these creditors had been made. Whether this should be taken as acquiescence to the pooling order is not clear, but it demonstrated the danger of not being involved in the argument and, further, the danger of *ex parte* applications.

Factors to be considered

In deciding whether it is just and equitable to make a pooling order, the court is required to have regard to the guidelines under section 272 (2). These are:

---

64   *Re Stewart Timber & Hardware (Whangarei) Ltd (in liq.) and Stewart Timber & Hardware Ltd (in liq.)* (1991) 5 NZCLC 67, 137.

(a) The extent to which any of the companies took part in the management of any of the other companies

(b) The conduct of any of the companies towards the creditors of any of the other companies

(c) The extent to which circumstances that gave rise to the liquidation of any of the companies are attributable to the actions of any of the other companies

(d) The extent to which the businesses of the companies have been combined

(e) Such other matters as the court thinks fit

In *Re Dalhoff & King Ltd*[65] the liquidators of three companies in liquidation sought pooling orders to wind them up as one. A major shareholder of one company opposed the order, as it would have the effect of reducing the dividend payable to the shareholders in the winding up from 28 cents in the dollar to zero. Justice Gallen considered each of the factors in turn.

'Intermingled management'

Evidence was brought that the management operated the interrelated group of companies as one entity, using whichever corporate body was convenient for the business operation in hand. A combined board meeting was held for the companies and one bank account was maintained for all three. This practice was continued by the receivers and the liquidators. This factor was found to be a significant but not decisive consideration by Justice Gallen.[66] It appears to have aided the arguments of creditors who had relied on the group as a whole, without distinguishing the specific entity with which they had been trading.

'Conduct towards creditors'

This factor was treated by Justice Gallen largely as the degree of confusion of the creditors of the companies as to which company they had been dealing with. The creditors included employees who were unsure which company was their employer. The amount of confusion led Justice Gallen to the view that the fault for the confusion must be due in some part to the conduct of the companies. The shareholders, in opposition, argued that, in comparison to the total amount of debts in the winding up of the three companies, the amounts in confusion were small and determinable. Justice Gallen considered the *number* of people confused, rather than the *amount* involved in the confusion.[67] He held that, while particular instances may not of themselves have been of great significance, taken together they demonstrated a greater degree of responsibility for confusing conduct on the part of the companies. This conduct led to the situation where the conduct of the companies may be said to have given rise to concerns that the section was dealing with. In effect, Justice Gallen was stating that the creditors were entitled to rely

---

65   (1991) 5 NZCLC 66 959.
66   *ibid.* at 66 964–5.
67   *ibid.* at 66 967.

on the group assets, as the legal boundaries of the companies had become blurred, and that the management had encouraged creditors to treat the companies as a single entity.

'Actions of one leading to the liquidation of another'

Justice Gallen decided, as a matter of fact, that the three companies stood or fell together and that the liquidity of one must have affected the others.[68] It seems clear that the legislative intent of this subsection is directed towards the intertwining of transactions between the group, with the actions of one pulling the others down into liquidation.

'Intermingled business'[69]

Not only were the creditors unaware of the separate identities of the companies, there was evidence that there was even some confusion in the minds of the shareholders of the companies. There was not a great deal of discussion on this point as much of the similar evidential factors were considered in the discussion of the intermingled management of the companies.

'Other matters'

The existence and extent of inter-company debts between the companies in the group was an additional factor taken into account by Justice Gallen. He stated that, to resolve the inter-company debts, it would be necessary to initiate legal proceedings and that, therefore, funds available for the creditors would be unjustifiably depleted. Justice Hardie Boys in *Re Pacific* also considered this to be a relevant factor in justifying the making of a pooling order in that case.

The cancelling out of inter-company debts, by the making of a pooling order, may have the effect of removing any action against a director of one of the companies under section 135, for transactions between the companies constituting reckless trading. Such avoidance may not be seen as equitable and could be taken into account in determining whether an order should be made.

Shareholders versus creditors

In *Re Dalhoff & King*[70] Justice Gallen had to consider the rights of the creditors of the companies against those of the opposing shareholders of one of the companies.

He held that, generally, the rights of creditors tend to weigh more heavily than those of shareholders when a company is insolvent. It was significant that creditors would be better off if a pooling order were made. It was also significant that, if a pooling order were not made, it would allow shareholders to recover at the expense of the creditors of the rest of the companies.

---

68   *ibid.* at 66 968.
69   (1991) 5 NZCLC 66 959.
70   *ibid.* at 66 971.

The finding accords with the general view that, as the insolvency of companies increases, so the duty to creditors and the interests of the creditors in the company's assets increases, to the detriment of the shareholders.[71] The shareholders in *Re Dalhoff & King* argued that creditors were better able to protect their own position by requiring additional security and altering their conditions of trade, whereas shareholders did not have such controls. Justice Gallen did not accept this and stated that shareholders had the advantage of making their own inspection of the company and its management before investing in it and had the continuing opportunity to attend annual general meetings, an opportunity denied to creditors.

Conclusion

The lack of contested proceedings concerning contribution and pooling means that there is still doubt as to what situations will justify orders being made. Arguments based on the factors set out in the legislation have not indicated any particular weight and ordering of the factors. It is submitted that arguments developed in connection with the American doctrine of substantive consolidation may prove useful in resolving these questions.[72]

The main policies behind *Salomon* lay in the logic of the original statutory scheme of the companies legislation and a freedom of contract or freedom of transactions approach. This arguably tipped the pendulum too far away from creditor protection and exposed involuntary creditors at least to excessive risk. This approach neglected the fundamental principles of the law as stated by Justinian in relation to Roman law nearly two thousand years ago, '*Honeste vivere, alterum non laedere, suum cuique tribuere*'[73] (The purposes of the law are to cause people to live honestly, not to harm others and to give to each their due). As a consequence, the strict application of *Salomon* to groups of companies, coupled with limited liability, has led to a system of limited liability within limited liability which was never countenanced by the early legislation, and has facilitated abuses of the kind specified above. The extremes of this approach were demonstrated in the waterfront dispute.[74]

Of the existing reforms, New Zealand law has the advantage of boldness, generality and flexibility. The Australian reform is more limited in scope and will easily lend itself to evasion through assets being transferred to a subsidiary rather than being retained by the parent company. The advantage of the Australian law over the New Zealand law is greater certainty. The New Zealand law nevertheless is closer to the equitable case law in US Bankruptcy Law which has generally been developed in a conservative fashion. The New Zealand provisions have been considered by the Australian Companies and Secu-

---

71   See, e.g. *Nicholson v. Permakraft (NZ) Ltd* [1958] 1 NZLR 242 (CA) which recognised that the directors owe an increasing duty to consider the rights of creditors of the company as it becomes insolvent.
72   See Farrar and Darroch *op. cit.* footnote 5 supra.
73   *Justinian's Institutes*, Book I-1-3.
74   See generally H. Trinca and A. Davies, *Waterfront—The Battle that Changed Australia*, Doubleday, Sydney, 2000.

rities Advisory Committee[75] which recommended pooling by liquidators where all the creditors agree or by order of the court but not a general power to make contribution orders. Recently amendments have been to the Corporations Act to penalise asset stripping to the detriment of employees.[76]

An alternative not considered by Australia and New Zealand is to adopt a more relativist approach to reform, based on the types of abuse we have considered. Thus where the subsidiary is not allowed to act as an independent profit centre, the US case law on domination as a subset of piercing the veil jurisprudence could be followed. Similarly, it could be used with the undercapitalised subsidiary. The abuse of integration through artificial division of a unitary enterprise could be developed as a legitimate extension of entity theory case law. All of these would be rational developments of the existing case law and would be more justifiable in terms of principle than much of the existing case law. Misrepresentation is probably covered by the existing case law or the statutory provisions on misleading and deceptive conduct. In Australia we also need to examine the extent to which the related party provisions in Chapter 2E of the Corporations Act deal with the first of these abuses in the case of subsidiaries which are not wholly owned.

There is an increasing awareness in both jurisdictions that there is little to be learned from UK experience in dealing with these problems. Until the United Kingdom is forced, through membership of the European Union, to consider root and branch reform of corporate groups it is likely to languish as a backwater of reform. The latest indication, however, is that the proposed Ninth Directive on Corporate Groups, which was based on German Law, has stalled. In the meantime the Irish Republic, showing greater initiative, has opted for the New Zealand model.

A pragmatic program of statutory reform would:

1   spell out the nature of directors' duties in group situations
2   provide for the consequences of inadequate financing of subsidiaries
3   provide for judicial discretion in respect of contribution orders and pooling orders in the case of related companies or cases of a 'group persona'. Clear criteria need to be specified.

A radical solution to (2) would be in effect to abolish wholly owned subsidiaries by deeming them to be branches of the parent company. Such a radical reform has been put forward by Professors Clarke, Dean and Oliver in their recent work, *Corporate Collapse: Regulatory, Accounting and Ethical Failure.*[77] The experimentation with such a reform in the form of a requirement for cross guarantees by the NCSC and ASIC in the exercise of their administrative regulatory discretion, has been inherently problematic. It seems to be a disproportionate exercise of the discretion. It only deals with some groups. It can

---

75   CASAC, Discussion Paper Corporate Groups, Recommendations 22 and 23, Final Report, July 2000; Draft Proposals, October 1999; Final Report May 2000, Recommendations 22 and 23. See J. H. Farrar, 'Corporate Group Insolvencies, Reform and the US Experience', (2000) 8 *Insolvency Law Journal*, 148.
76   *Corporations Law Amendment (Employee Entitlements) Act 2000.*
77   Cambridge University Press, Cambridge, 1997, p. 225.

prejudice some creditors and can lead to complex results. That having been said, the underlying proposal is worth consideration as a matter of statutory reform.

A more fundamental reform of enterprise liability based on some concept of group legal personality or automatic group responsibility would probably create as many problems as it would solve. Since we are currently seeking to escape from the strait jacket of separate legal personality[78] it seems a mistake to seek refuge in a larger concept of group legal personality or responsibility, enticing though this may be because of its apparent reflection of commercial reality. 'Commercial reality', however, is not the simple and clear phenomenon we might think it is, and a thorough going interest analysis, within the framework of fundamental principle stated above, must precede any further reform.

---

78   See H. Collins, 'Ascription of Legal Responsibility to Groups in Complex Patterns of Economic Integration' (1990) 53 MLR 731. For a thorough review of the alternatives see A. Nolan, 'The Position of Unsecured Creditors of Corporate Groups: Towards a Group Responsibility Solution Which Gives Fairness and Equity a Role' (1993) 11 C&SLJ 461. This article also critically reviews the New Zealand sections.

CHAPTER 22

Insider Trading

Insider trading represents the dirty washing of corporate governance and influences public opinion about the efficacy of the present system. We hear a lot about insider trading in the media yet there is persistent looseness in usage of the concept and uncertainty about the underlying policy. The essence of insider trading is improper trading in securities on the basis of price-sensitive information that is not available to the public in order to make a profit or avoid a loss.[1] The main reason for the confusion lies in why it is necessary to single out this kind of behaviour for special treatment since, as Montaigne once wrote, 'No profit can be made except at another's expense'.[2] The answers lie in the nature of the transaction, its context, and the basis of possession of the inside information.

The history of insider trading regulation

The common law in Australia and New Zealand did not prohibit insider trading in the absence of a specific fiduciary obligation. At common law, a director owes his or her duties to the company, not to individual shareholders.[3] US case law recognised the special facts doctrine which allowed the recovery by the shareholder where the director owed fiduciary duties because of the peculiar circumstances of the case.[4] This authority has been cited in cases in New Zealand and Australia since 1977.[5]

---

1   Compare P. Anisman, *Insider Trading Legislation for Australia: An Outline of the Issues and Alternatives*, AGPS, Canberra, 1986, p. 1.
2   M. de Montaigne, *The Complete Essays*, trans. M. A. Screech, Penguin Books, 1991, p. 48 cited by Anisman *ibid.*
3   *Percival v. Wright* [1902] 2 Ch 421.
4   *Strong v. Repide* 213 US 419 (1919).
5   *Coleman v. Myers* [1977] 2 NZLR 255; *Hurley v. BGH Nominees Pty Ltd (No 2)* (1984) 2 ACLC 497; *Glandon Pty Ltd v. Strata Consolidated Pty Ltd* (1993) 11 ACLC 895; *Brunninghausen v. Glavanics* (1999) 17 ACLC 1247.

The USA developed legislation and regulations on insider trading from the 1930s onwards. Section 16(a) and (b) of the *Securities Exchange Act 1934* were designed to combat the practice. Section 16(a) required disclosure of dealings to the Securities and Exchange Commission (SEC) and the Stock Exchanges on which the securities were listed. Section 16(b) prohibited short swing profits. However, these were limited provisions and the major developments took place under section 10(b) and Rule 10b—5. Section 10(b) prohibited manipulative or deceptive devices or contrivances contrary to SEC rules and regulations. Rule 10b—5 provides as follows:

Rule 10b—5 Employment of manipulative and deceptive devices

It shall be unlawful for any person, directly or indirectly, by the use of any means or instrumentality of interstate commerce, or of the mails or of any facility of any national securities exchange:

(a) to employ any device, scheme, or artifice to defraud,

(b) to make any untrue statement of a material fact or to omit to state a material fact necessary in order to make the statements made, in the light of the circumstances under which they were made, not misleading, or

(c) to engage in any acts, practice, or course of business which operates or would operate as a fraud or deceit upon any person, in connection with the purchase or sale of any security.

These provisions have now been supplemented by Rule 14e—3, which relates to possession of non-public information at the time of a takeover bid; the *Insider Trading Sanctions Act 1984*, which allows recovery of treble damages; and *the Insider Trading and Securities Fraud Enforcement Act 1988*, which increased penalties and allows recovery from insiders.

In Australia the first provision was section 128 of the Securities Industry Code but this was limited in effect. Reform eventually followed as a result of the House of Representatives Standing Committee on Legal and Constitutional Affairs report *Fair Shares for All: Insider Trading in Australia* issued in October 1989[6] ('Fair Shares for All').

The first New Zealand legislation specifically on insider trading was enacted in the *Securities Amendment Act 1988* as a result of the report of the Securities Commission.[7]

Policy arguments for and against insider trading regulation[8]

The arguments in favour of regulation are:

---

6   AGPS, Canberra, 1989. See too Anisman *op. cit.* footnote 1 supra.

7   *Insider Trading—Report to the Minister of Justice by the Securities Commission*, vol. 1 and 2, 1987 ('New Zealand Report').

8   See e.g. Anisman, *op. cit.*, p. 10; *Fair Shares for All: Insider Trading in Australia*, AGPS, Canberra, 1989 , p. 13; New Zealand Report vol. 1; H. Manne, 'In Defence of Insider Trading' (1966) 44 Harv L Rev 113; L. Semaan, M. Freeman and M. Adams, 'Is Insider Trading a Necessary Evil for Efficient Markets? An International Comparative Analysis' (1999) 17 CVSLJ 220.

1   Insider trading is inherently unfair. There should be equal access to information for all market participants. This is the equal access theory and forms a basis for the fraud on the market argument.
2   It damages investor confidence in the integrity of the stock market.
3   It involves misappropriation of a corporate asset, namely the information.
4   It involves either a breach of fiduciary duty or a logical extension of existing law.

Arguments against regulation are:

1   Insider trading signals information to the market about the price of shares.
2   Regulated disclosure is not efficient.
3   Insider trading provides an incentive to provide information to the market.
4   It rewards entrepreneurism.

While the arguments in favour of regulation are not individually compelling, the arguments against regulation are conspicuously weak. In essence insider trading provides perverse incentives for management.

Insider trading law in Australia[9]

Overview
Australia now has a plethora of statutory provisions directly and indirectly dealing with insider trading. This supplements the common law. It is important to consider these provisions in discussing the adequacy of Australia's insider trading laws. The following is a summary of these provisions:

1   Criminal and civil liability for insider trading in securities (Division 2A of Part 7.11 (section 1002, section 1102A to section 1002U), section 1005 and section 1013 to section 1015 of the Corporations Act).
2   Criminal and civil liability for insider trading in futures contracts over securities (Part 8.7—Divisions 1 and 2).
3   Criminal and civil liability for insider trading in superannuation interests in section 175 to section 191 of the *Superannuation Industry (Supervision) Act 1993*.
4   The continuous disclosure provisions (section 1001A to section 1001D of the Corporations Act and ASX Listing Rule 3.1). These provisions underpin the equal access theory in Australia.
5   Section 205G of the Corporations Act, which requires a director of a listed company to disclose to ASX the director's interest[10] in the company or a related body corporate. Disclosure must be made within fourteen days of any change in a

9   This is based on the unpublished LLM paper done under my supervision by A. Bulman, 'A Comparative Analysis of Australia's Insider Trading Provisions', University of Melbourne, 1998. See too M. Ziegelaar, 'Insider Trading in Australia' in G. Walker (ed.), *Securities Regulation in Australia and New Zealand*, 2nd edn, LBC Information Services, Sydney, 1998, ch. 16.
10 For a definition of 'interest' for this purpose see s. 205G(1)(a) and (b).

director's interest. This provision is similar to section 16(a) of the US *Securities Exchange Act 1934* and derives from the first attempt in the United Kingdom to regulate insider trading, recommended by the Cohen Committee.[11]

6   The substantial shareholding provisions (Chapter 6C of the Corporations Act).[12]

7   The prohibition against self-acquisition (Chapter 2J.2).[13]

8   Section 183(1) of the Corporations Act which provides that a director or other officer or employee of a corporation, or a former director, officer or employee of a corporation, must not improperly use information acquired by virtue of his or her position as such director, other officer or employee to gain an advantage for themselves or someone else or to cause detriment to the corporation.

9   Section 182(1) which provides that a director, secretary, other officer or employee of a corporation must not improperly use their position to gain an advantage for themselves or someone else or to cause detriment to the corporation.

In this chapter we will concentrate on the provisions in Part 7.11 Division 2A of the Corporations Act, which are the main provisions in force in Australia, before turning to the New Zealand provisions.

The elements of the offence under section 1002G of the Corporations Act are:

(a) A person is in possession of information not generally available.

(b) If the information were generally available, a reasonable person would expect it to have a material effect on the price or value of the securities of a body corporate.

(c) The person does a prohibited action in connection with the securities or the information.

The key concepts in section 1002G are:

- 'insider',
- 'securities of a body corporate',
- the prohibited actions
- 'possesses information',
- information which is not generally available and
- 'material effect on the price or value of securities'.

---

11   (1945) Cmd 6649 at para. 86.

12   The UK Jenkins Report (Cmnd 1749 of (1962)), para. 142 suggests that a major reason for these provisions was so that shareholders, the company and the public should know who has a beneficial substantial interest in the company.

13   See Companies and Securities Law Review Committee, Report to the Ministerial Council, A Company's Purchase of Its Own Shares, September 1987, [16]. The prohibition against self-acquisition was re-enacted by the *Company Law Review Act 1988*.

Who is an insider under section 1002G of the Corporations Act?

Section 1002G(1) extends the insider trading prohibition as it relates to securities to any person who:

(a) possesses information that is not generally available but, if the information were generally available, a reasonable person would expect it to have a material effect on the price or value of securities of a body corporate (section 1002G(1)(a)); and

(b) the person knows, or ought reasonably to know, that the information is not generally available and if it were generally available, it might have a material effect on the price of the value of those securities (section 1002G(1)(b)).

These persons are defined to be 'insiders' for the purposes of the prohibition. This definition is very wide and covers people who are not conventionally regarded as corporate insiders and information which does not emanate from the company at all.

There has been little detailed case law on the interpretation of these broad provisions.[14] In fact the only comprehensive decision on the issue has put their wide application in doubt. In *Exicom Pty Ltd v. Futuris Corporation Ltd*[15] Exicom required new equity capital. It approached X, Y and Z, asking these three companies to subscribe for shares in Exicom. In approaching these companies, Exicom provided the companies with information. X (the first and second defendants) allegedly used this information to purchase Exicom shares on the market. Exicom obtained court orders preventing X from taking advantage of the shares purchased. Y dropped out of the picture. Z was about to enter into an agreement with Exicom to subscribe for shares in Exicom at par value to be agreed. X sought orders that the orders made against it be removed on the basis of Exicom's dealings with Z (applying the 'sauce for the gander' rule) or that an injunction be granted restraining Exicom from dealing with Z.

In considering whether an injunction be made against Exicom and Z, Justice Young thought that there were difficulties in construing the provisions:

There are real problems in construing the division sensibly if one adopts strict traditional methods of construction, construing each word in its ordinary grammatical sense. Accordingly, one should approach the construction in a purposive way. However, that again leads into trouble. The division is one which can be dealt with criminally by extremely harsh penalties (see section 1311). There is also significant civil liability (see section 1013). Where a harsh criminal penalty is imposed on conduct, consideration of the liberty of the subject requires one to construe provisions strictly. On the other hand, the division shows an intention to protect members of the public

---

14 See *Keygrowth Ltd v. Mitchell* (1991) 9 ACLC 260; *Exicom Pty Ltd v. Futuris Corporation Ltd* (1995) 16 ACSR 404; *Ampolex Ltd v. Perpetual Trustee Co. (Canberra) (No 2)* (1996) 14 ACLC 1514; *R v Kruse*, District Court (NSW) 2 December 1999, No 98/11/0908; *R v Evans and Doyle* [1999] VSC 488; *R v. Hannes*, (2001) 36 ACSR 72; *R v Firns* [2001] NSWCCA 191.

15 (1995) 18 ACSR 404.

who are in the securities market, who are not 'insiders'. Protective legislation of that nature should be construed beneficially.[16]

Justice Young held that the application should be dismissed. The agreement with Z did not fall within the insider trading provisions. A company itself was not an insider, unissued shares did not come within the definition of security, and the information in question could not have had a material effect on the price of the securities.

The decision has been criticised[17] as not being consistent with the recommendations of the Standing Committee but the Court of Appeal refused to review it.[18]

Which securities are covered by the prohibition?

There was a concern expressed by the Standing Committee that section 128 of the Securities Industry Code did not cover insider trading in prescribed interests, exchange trade options, and convertible securities, and recommended that these securities be included.[19] This recommendation was adopted by the government.[20]

Section 1000G(1) refers to 'securities of a body corporate'. Securities in relation to a body corporate are defined in section 1002A(1) as:

(a) shares in the body corporate;

(b) debentures (including convertible notes) issued by the body corporate;

(c) interests in a managed investment scheme[21] made available by the body corporate;

(d) units of shares referred to in (a); or

(e) an option contract under which a party acquires from another party an option or right, exercisable at or before a specified time, to buy from, or sell to, that other party a number of securities of a kind referred to in paragraphs (a), (b), (c) or (d) at a price specified in, or to be determined in accordance with, the contract.[22]

This definition includes exchange traded options over issued shares (under paragraph (e)) and warrants over issued shares (under paragraph (e) and possibly if they are covered warrants under paragraph (d). However, options issued by a company to sub-

---

16 *ibid.*, p. 407.
17 See J. Mannolini, 'Insider Trading—The Need for Conceptual Clarity' (1996) 14 C&SLJ 151; Ziegelaar, *op. cit.*, p. 576; Bulman, *op. cit.*
18 The Court of Appeal refused to review the decision on the basis that it is only in exceptional circumstances that an appeal court will interfere with interlocutory orders—see *Futuris Corporation Ltd v. Exicom Ltd* (1995) 18 ACSR 413.
19 *Fair Shares for All, op. cit.*, 4.6.10 (Recommendation 6).
20 See Government Response to the Report of the House of Representatives Standing Committee on Legal and Constitutional Affairs entitled 'Fair Shares for All: Insider Trading in Australia', p. 9 and Explanatory Memorandum to the Corporations Legislation Amendment Bill 1991, para. 316–24.
21 Securities would also be taken to include prescribed interests offered by a body corporate, which remain prescribed interests pursuant to the transitional provision of the *Managed Investments Act 1988* (Sections 1451–65).
22 Share ratio contracts are included pursuant to Reg 1.2.04 of the Corporations Regulations.

scribe for shares are not covered as they are options to subscribe for shares rather than options to buy and sell.[23] There seems to be no reason why options over unissued shares should be excluded from the definition.[24]

It follows from this that index options and index warrants would be excluded. Ford, Austin and Ramsay, and Ansell argue that this is sensible because, in Ford's words, 'their value depends on the movement of an index which is unlikely to present opportunity for gains arising from the possession of inside information'.[25] Presumably these authors distinguish these securities from interests in managed investment schemes in that the shares that make up an index are transparent, while it is possible to have insider information as to the investments in a managed investment scheme and the performance of those investments. However, it is possible that a person may be able to make a profit from trading in index warrants or options when in possession of information which would materially affect the price of a company which has a large presence in that index.

Section 1002A(2) applies the terms 'securities of a body corporate' to include securities issued 'by a government, an unincorporated body or any other person'.

The definition of 'securities' in section 1002A(1) does not include a futures contract or an excluded security. As noted above, insider trading in futures over shares is prohibited under Part 8.7 of the Corporations Act.

Sections 175 to 191 of the *Superannuation Industry Supervision Act 1993* are modelled closely on the insider trading provisions relating to securities. They apply to 'superannuation interests' which are defined to be beneficial interests in a regulated superannuation fund, an approved deposit fund, or a superannuation trust.[26]

What actions are prohibited by section 1002G(2)?

An insider for the purposes of section 1002G must not, in relation to the body corporate of which he or she is an insider:

(a) subscribe for, purchase[27] or sell, or enter into an agreement to subscribe for, purchase or sell, any securities of the body corporate (section 1002G(2)(a));

(b) procure another person to subscribe for, purchase or sell, or to enter into an agreement to subscribe for purchase or sell (section 1002G(3)(a));[28] and

---

23 See *Calvert v. MacKenzie* [1937] NZLR 966, 979; *Re VGM Holdings Ltd* [1942] 1 All ER 224; *ASC v. Burns & Ors* (1994) 12 ACLC 545; and *Exicom Pty Ltd v. Futuris Corporation Ltd* (1995) 18 ACSR 404.
24 Bulman, *op. cit.* footnote 9 supra.
25 *Op. cit.* para. [9.650].
26 See definitions of 'superannuation interest' and 'superannuation entity' in s. 10(1) of the *Superannuation Industry (Supervision) Act 1993*. It would appear, paradoxically, that insider trading in non-complying funds would not be covered by these provisions.
27 The terms 'purchase' and 'sell' are given specific meanings in the case of option contracts s. 1002A(1).
28 The expression 'procure' includes situations where an insider 'incites, induces, or encourages an act or omission by another person', s. 1002D(2).

(c) in the case where the securities are traded on a stock market of a securities exchange,[29] communicate, either directly or indirectly, the information, or cause the information to be communicated, to another person if the insider knows, or ought reasonably to know, that the other person will engage in the activity described in paragraphs (a) and (b) (section 1002G(3)).

In *Exicom Pty Ltd v. Futuris Corporation Ltd*, Justice Young took the view that shares which were not yet issued were not 'securities' for the purposes of section 1002A(1). He made the point, correctly, that the term 'subscription' refers to the issue of shares and 'purchase' refers to the acquisition of already issued shares.[30] However, he rejected the submission by counsel that as section 1002G refers to subscription, unissued shares 'are to be included within securities'. Justice Young said that he did not consider this submission as valid, as the Explanatory Memorandum to the provisions shows that the legislature had in mind 'prescribed interests, units and options rather than unissued shares'.[31] Therefore, as he considered that the shares to be allotted were not securities, section 1002G did not apply. This seems, with respect, a somewhat narrow view.

The provision against tipping in section 1002G(3) appears too broad in its scope in that it catches all communications of price sensitive information where the insider knows, or ought reasonably to know, that the person would or would be likely, to purchase or subscribe for (or procure another person to purchase or subscribe for) the securities. There is no defence to this provision that the insider held a reasonable belief that the information would become generally available before the person traded.[32] This can have serious repercussions in relation to corporate governance.

Suppose, for example, a director of a company informed the board that he or she intended to make a takeover offer for the company. Section 1002G(3) would possibly limit the ability of the company to brief the director with price-sensitive information, even if they could be assured that it would be disclosed in a Part A statement, or ensure that it was included in a Part B statement and knew that the director was not going to purchase shares on market in the interim. The situation becomes even more problematic when the director proposes to make a takeover bid when another takeover bid is already afoot, in that arguably the director has a duty to advise the board in relation to his or her views on the takeover.

---

29 s. 1002D(1) states that the securities are still traded on a stock market for the purposes of s. 1002G(3), even if they had been suspended by either the exchange or ASIC pursuant to s 775(2).

30 (1995) 18 ACSR 404, 407.

31 (1995) 18 ACSR 404, 408. The only part of the Explanatory Memorandum which explicitly discussed the meaning of the word 'subscription' was the discussion in relation to s. 1013 which appeared to suggest that the inclusion of the word 'subscription' was designed to correct the anomaly in the previous law, which Young J noted in *Hooker Investment Pty Ltd v. Baring Bros Halkerston & Partners Securities Limited and others* (1986) 10 ACLR 462, 467 that dealing in securities did not include subscription. See Ziegelaar, *op. cit.* footnote 9 supra, pp. 576 *et seq.*

32 *Australian Corporations Law*, Butterworths Looseleaf Service, June 1997, [7.3.0110]. The commentary also questions why the provision is limited to listed securities only.

Possession of information

Section 1002G(1) refers to an insider who 'possesses information'.

> 'Information' is defined in section 1002A(1) to include:
> (a) matters of supposition and other matters that are insufficiently definite to warrant being made known to the public; and
> (b) matters relating to the intentions, or the likely intentions, of a person.

The Explanatory Memorandum states that a broad definition was given to the term 'information' because it was feared that a narrow interpretation might be placed upon the expression. This was despite a broad interpretation being given to the expression in *Commissioner for Corporate Affairs v. Green*[33] and in *Hooker Investments Pty Ltd v. Baring Bros Halkerston & Partners Securities Limited and others.*[34]

In *Ampolex Ltd v. Perpetual Trustee Company (Canberra) Ltd and Others,*[35] GPG and County Natwest had determined that there was a doubt over the conversion ratio of Ampolex's convertible notes. Ampolex maintained that it was a conversion ratio of 1 share for 1 note. However, GPG attempted to convert the notes with Ampolex on a 6.6 to 1 basis. Justice Rolfe held that the intention to disclose that they were to convert the notes on that basis to the ASX was information for the purposes of section 1002G.[36] Profit forecasts have also been held to be information for the purposes of the insider trading provisions.[37]

There seems to be no reason why the word 'possess' should not be given a broad meaning to include information that a person has overheard in a public place or information which the person has generated from the person's own efforts.[38]

Section 1002E(1) provides that a body corporate is taken to possess any information that one of its officers possesses and that came into the officer's possession in the course of the performance of the officer's duties. In addition, where an officer of a body corporate knows or ought reasonably to know of any matter or thing because he is an officer of the body corporate, 'it is to be presumed that the body corporate knows or ought reasonably to know that matter or thing' (section 1002E(2)). Section 1002F applies the same logic to partnerships.

Information that is generally available

Information is defined to be generally available under section 1002B(2) if:

> (a) it consists of readily observable matter;[39] or

---

33 [1978] VR 505, 515.
34 (1986) 10 ACLR 462, 467.
35 (1996) 20 ACSR 649.
36 *ibid.*, 659.
37 *ICAL Ltd v. County Natwest Securities Aust Ltd & Anor* (1988) 13 ACLR 129, 166.
38 See generally *Australian Corporations Law*, Butterworths Looseleaf Service, North Ryde, June 1997, [7.3.0120].
39 As to whether a court decision is such matter see *R v Firns* [2001] NSWCCA 191.

(b) without limiting the generality of paragraph (a), both the following subparagraphs apply:

  (i) it has been made known in a manner that would, or would be likely to, bring it to the attention of persons who commonly invest in securities of bodies corporate of a kind whose price or value might be affected by the information; and

  (ii) since it was so made known, a reasonable period for it to be disseminated among such persons has elapsed.

Section 1002B(3) states that information is also generally available if it consists of deductions, conclusions or inferences made or drawn either or both from:

• the information referred to in section 1002B(2)(a); or
• the information made known as referred to in section 1002B(2)(i).

The Explanatory Statement argues that these provisions exclude from the insider trading provisions an observation that the body corporate had excess stocks in its yard or deductions or conclusions 'which investors, brokers or other market participants may make based on independent research of generally available information'.[40]

The Explanatory Statement also stated that section1002B(2)(b)(ii) was designed to prevent a person in possession of information 'getting an unfair head start on other market participants'.[41]

For the purposes of section 128 of the Securities Industry Code, Justice Connolly in *Kinwat Holdings v. Platform*[42] held that disclosure to the stock exchange, coupled with a news story detailing the information, was enough to make information 'generally available'.[43]

The qualification of 'generally available' has been considered to be a relevant factor in determining whether an injunction should be granted. In *ICAL v. County Natwest*,[44] Justice Bryson refused to grant an injunction on the basis that the price sensitive information had already been disclosed in a public hearing and that there was nothing stopping the party seeking the injunction from making the information publicly available. In *Darvall v. Lanceley*,[45] a competing bidder alleged that the defendant possessed price sensitive information and sought an injunction to prevent the defendant from sending out its offers. Justice McLelland accepted the defendant's undertaking that the price sensitive information would be sent out to shareholders and refused to grant an injunction.

---

40   Explanatory Memorandum to the Corporations Legislation Amendment Bill 1991, para. 326 and 327.
41   *ibid.*, para. 328., section 1102B(2)(b)(ii) should be read in conjunction with sections 1002T(2)(a) and 1002T(3)(a) which provided a defence from prosecution if a person only become aware of the information as a result of section 1002B(b)(i).
42   (1982) 6 ACLR 398, 400.
43   This was supported by the NCSC's submission to the Standing Committee. See *Australian Corporations Law*, Butterworths Looseleaf Service, North Ryde, June 1997, [7.3.0140]. For brokers' reports to private clients see *Leadenhall Aust Ltd v Peptech Ltd* (1999) 33 ACSR 307.
44   (1988) 13 ACLR 129, 167.
45   (1986) 10 ACLR 893, 896.

This expanded definition is likely to create uncertainty as to what are deductions, conclusions or inferences made or drawn from publicly available information. It is arguable that a discovery or an invention which may have a material effect on the price of securities, because it makes its major product obsolete, is generally available information for the purposes of section 1002B. The words 'deductions, conclusions, or inferences' are not defined and it is difficult to know whether it would encompass all internally generated information based on generally available information and if not, where the line should be drawn. It is also difficult to know how the factual elements of a scientific discovery could be proved to be 'readily observable matter'. In the case of insider trading based on a discovery, it is quite likely for the purposes of a prosecution that a court would read these words broadly.

However, it is arguable that in terms of the integrity of the market, while such behaviour should not be criminal, a person should not be able to use their scientific discoveries to make profits on the market for shares, warrants or options where it would constitute price sensitive information in relation to a company's securities. This is different from information created by market analysts as generating this information is open to the whole community of analysts. Although such examples are likely to be rare, scientific discoveries may be used to make considerable trading profits where there is asymmetric information between market participants.

A reasonable person would expect the information to have material effect on the price or value of securities

Section 128 of the Securities Industry Code left the expression 'material effect on the price or value of securities' undefined. The NCSC in its submission to the standing committee argued that this resulted in the prosecution having to call expert witnesses to prove that the relevant information had a material effect on the price or value of securities.[46] The standing committee recommended that a statutory definition of 'materiality' be included in the new legislation.[47] It would appear that they were in part influenced by the definition of materiality in the US Supreme Court case of *TSC Industries Inc. v. Northway*:[48]

> An omitted fact is material if there is a substantial likelihood that a reasonable shareholder would consider it important in deciding how to [act] ... Put another way, there must be a substantial likelihood that the disclosure of the omitted fact would have been

---

46   *Fair Shares for All: Insider Trading in Australia, op. cit.* para. 4.4.3.

47   *ibid.*, 4.4.17 (Recommendation 3).

48   426 US 438 (1976). It appears on interpreting similar wording to s. 128 of SIC, the courts in Singapore have also judicially enunciated a reasonable investor test—see *Public Prosecutor v. Allan Ng Poh Meng* [1990] 1 MLJ quoted in C. T. Swee Kian and R. Chandran, 'Singapore and Malaysia—Recent Developments—insider trading laws' (1995) 16 *The Company Lawyer* 188, 189. See also *Coleman v. Myers* [1977] 2 NZLR 255 at p. 334.

viewed by the reasonable investor as having significantly altered the 'total mix' of the information made available.

Section 1002G(1) states 'a reasonable person would expect it [the information not generally available] to have a material effect on the price or value of securities of a body corporate'. This phase is defined further in section 1002C as being where 'the information would, or would be likely to, influence persons who commonly invest in securities in deciding whether or not to subscribe for, buy or sell' the securities.

In *Ampolex v. Perpetual Trustees*,[49] Justice Rolfe held that the intention to disclose that they were to convert the notes on that basis to the ASX was such that a reasonable person would expect it to have a material effect on the price or value of securities of a body corporate. In *ICAL v. County NatWest*,[50] Justice Bryson held that a commitment from a shareholder that he would not sell down his 20 per cent holding in the company for a year was price sensitive information, as was the company's own profit projections. It also appears that Justice Nathan held that an offer to purchase a shareholder's substantial shareholding at a premium to market price was price sensitive information in *Keygrowth Ltd v. Mitchell*.[51]

In *Exicom Pty Ltd v. Futuris Corporation Ltd*, Justice Young accepted Exicom's argument that, as the price of the placement to Z was fixed and known to both parties, this was not a situation where Z ought reasonably to know that the information would have a material effect on price.[52]

Justice Young also stated that as Z and Exicom possessed the information, 'we do not have a situation where an insider is making use of information in a market to gain an advantage over an outsider'. It would appear that Justice Young is saying that while the price sensitive information would have a material effect on the securities as traded on the ASX, the shares in question were not in the rubric of 'such securities' for the purposes of section 1002G(2). It is unlikely that the legislature intended this distinction.[53]

Defences

There are various defences to the insider trading provisions as they relate to securities. They are found in section 1002H to section 1002T of the Corporations Act and Regulation 7.11.01 of the Corporations Regulations. The following is a discussion in relation to four of these defences. These four are the most important defences in practice.

---

49 (1996) 20 ACSR 649, 659.
50 (1988) 13 ACLR 129, 166.
51 (1990) 3 ACSR 478.
52 A similar conclusion was reached by McHugh JA (as he then was) in *Hooker Investments Pty Ltd v. Baring Bros Halkerston & Partners Securities Ltd & Ors (No 2)* (1986) 10 ACLR 524, 528, where he said that for the purposes of s. 128 of SIC that the preclusion is limited in dealing in 'those securities' in respect of which the information 'would be likely materially to affect price'. Therefore as the underwriting price was fixed the defendant was not precluded from dealing in those securities.
53 This conclusion has been criticised by M. Whincop, 'Towards a Property Rights and Market Microstructural Theory of Insider Trading Regulation' (1996) 7 Jnl of Banking and Finance Law and Practice 212, 222.

Chinese Walls

Section 1002M and section 1002N provide a defence to companies and partnerships respectively, if a person (A) has price sensitive information if:

(a) the transaction or agreement were undertaken by another person (B);

(b) the company or partnership had in place arrangements that could reasonably be expected to ensure that the information was not communicated to B and that no advice was given by A to B in respect of the transaction; and

(c) no communication or advice was given from A to B.

This exception has been subject to some criticism, primarily on the basis that it gives a great deal of scope for abuse, for there 'has never been a Chinese Wall that does not have a grapevine growing over it'.[54] Many of the opponents of the defence base their arguments on the several cases relating to firms of solicitors acting for one or more clients.[55] However, the issue at stake in these cases is the danger that justice may be perverted if a solicitor acts for one party when his partner may possess prejudicial material in relation to the opposing party. In the case of insider trading the provisions are there to ensure that the provisions in sections 1002E and 1002F do not adversely affect the business of the firms in question.[56] In addition, a part of the defence is that the defendant corporation is required to prove that the information was not communicated or the advice was not given (sections 1002M(c) and 1002N(1)(c)).

Underwriting

The standing committee saw that the exception for underwriters was necessary as a consequence of broadening the application of the insider trading provisions. Section 1002J(1) allows an underwriter to subscribe for securities, enter into an agreement for securities, and sell those securities subscribed for.[57] There is also a similar exception to section 1002G(2) in relation to communicating information in relation to underwriting and sub-underwriting or placing shares under an underwriting agreement.

A person's own intentions or activities

Section 1002P provides an exception from section 1002G(2) if the information consists of the person knowing that 'he or she proposed to enter into, or has previously entered into, one or more transactions or agreements in relation to securities of that body

---

54   *Fair Shares for All: Insider Trading in Australia, op. cit.,* para. 4.9.5 quoting Professor Tomasic, although the original phrase was that of Professor L. C. B. Gower. See generally R. Tomasic, 'Insider Trading Law Reform in Australia' (1991) 9 C&SLJ 121; V. R. Goldwasser, 'Recent Developments in the Regulations of Chinese Walls and Business Ethics—In Search of a Remedy for a Problem that Persists' (1993) 11 C&SLJ 227; Ziegelaar, *op. cit.* footnote 9 supra, pp. 584–7.

55   See *D&J Constructions P/L v. Head and others trading as Clayton Utz* (1987) 9 NSWLR 118; *Re a firm of solicitors* [1992] 1 All ER 353; and *Mallesons Stephen Jaques v. KPMG Peat Marwick* (1991) 4 WAR 357.

56   A. J. Black, 'The Reform of Insider Trading Law in Australia' (1992) 15 UNSWLJ 214, 248–9.

57   *Fair Shares for All: Insider Trading in Australia, op. cit.,* para. 4.3.4.

corporate'. Section 1002Q and section 1002R apply the same exception in relation to bodies corporate and officers of bodies corporate.

In *Ampolex v. Perpetual Trustees*,[58] Justice Rolfe considered that section 1002Q and section 1002R only applied in relation to an intention to acquire or deal in further securities. As the relevant information in this case was the intention to disclose to the ASX that conversion was sought of notes at a particular conversion ratio, his Honour held that the sections did not apply.

Where both parties to the transaction have access to the price sensitive information

Section 1002T(2)(b) states that it is a defence to a prosecution under section 1002G(2) if the court is satisfied that the other party to the transaction or agreement knew, or ought reasonably to have known, of the information before entering into the transaction or agreement. Section 1002T(3)(b) states that it is defence to a prosecution under section 1002G(3) if the court is satisfied that the other person knew, or ought reasonably to have known, of the information before the information was communicated.

Many of the difficult cases which have arisen in insider trading in recent years would not have arisen if this were a defence in all cases. *Exicom v. Futuris*[59] and *Ampolex v. Perpetual Trustee Company*[60] were examples of cases where a third party attempted to prevent, or seek damages for, a transaction where both parties to the transaction had the relevant information. There have also been two cases (one of which went on appeal) that involved the question of whether a contract made between two parties who both possessed price sensitive information which was not generally available, was void, voidable or unenforceable.[61]

It is arguable that this defence could be extended to become a general defence. This would stop some of the commercial claims in the courts that do not appear to have much to do with the principles underlying insider trading. It would also appear that the exception does not derogate from any of the theories in relation to insider trading. The fraud on the market theory is not contravened as there has been no market trading on the price sensitive information.

There would also be no need for an underwriting defence, as the company and the underwriter would both possess the price sensitive information. The defence

---

58 (1995) 20 ACSR 649, 661.
59 (1995) 18 ACSR 404.
60 (1996) 20 ACSR 649.
61 *Crafter & Anor v. Singh* (1990) 2 ACSR 1; *Singh v. Crafter* (1992) 10 ACLR 1, 365; and *CLC Corporation v. Cambridge Gulf Holdings NL and Ors* (1997) 25 ACSR 296. In *Cambridge Gulf*, Carr J stated (331): 'I was not referred to any authority to the effect that the insider trading provisions of the Corporations Law would invalidate a contract made between two parties both of which were fully appraised of the very information said to be 'inside information'. Nor have I found any such authority. Penale and Holdings, through Mr Conway, knew everything known to the applicant. Even the civil remedy of damages provided by s. 1013 of the Corporations Law, is premised on a contract made between an insider and an innocent third party. I do not consider that the case based on insider trading has been made out.'

would also cover sub-underwriting if the same information were passed on to the sub-underwriters.

It may be argued that there would still be an issue with the offence of communicating price sensitive information 'if the insider knows, or ought reasonably to know, that the other person would or would be likely to' enter into a transaction with the insider or to trade (section 1002G(3)). However, it could be a defence to that provision that the information was communicated on the written undertaking that it would be only used for the purposes of the transaction. Contravening the written undertaking would be evidence of a guilty intent for the purposes of the tippee's liability.

Penalties and remedies

Criminal penalties

The criminal penalty for a contravention of section 1002G is a fine of up to $200 000 or imprisonment of up to five years or both.[62] The penalty for a body corporate is a fine up to $1 000 000.[63]

Civil remedies

In terms of interim relief, an injunction may be granted pursuant to either section 1114 or section 1324 of the Act. The court also has a variety of powers under section 1002U. These powers were recommended by the standing committee and are based on similar powers which are granted to the Corporations and Securities Panel pursuant to section 734(2).[64]

There are a number of provisions in section 1013 which relate to civil recovery. Section 1013(2) gives the company the right to recover in relation to a subscription made where the subscriber is in contravention of section 1002G. Section 1013(3) provides a right of recovery for a purchaser of securities where the other party has contravened section 1002G. Section 1013(4) gives a similar right to the seller of securities. Section 1013(5) gives a right to the company to recover from an insider, while section 1013(6) allows ASIC to recover on behalf of the company pursuant to section 1013(2) or section 1013(5). Section 1013(8) gives a right of recovery to the responsible entity or ASIC in relation to registered managed investment schemes. The basis for recovery is the difference between the value the securities were bought or sold at and the value if the information had been generally available.

---

62   s. 1311(2) & (3), Schedule 3 of the Act.
63   s. 1312 of the Act. In relation to jurisdiction, the insider trading provisions as they relate to securities are:
    a)   acts and omissions within this jurisdiction in relation to securities of any body corporate, whether formed or carrying on business in this jurisdiction or in Australia or not; and
    b)   acts and omissions outside this jurisdiction, whether in Australia or not, in relation to securities of a body corporate that is formed or carries on business in this jurisdiction (s. 1002 of the Act).
64   *Fair Shares for All: Insider Trading in Australia, op. cit.*, para. 4.13.15 and Explanatory Memorandum to the Corporations Legislation Amendment Bill 1991, para. 374.

Sections 1013(3) and (4) do not apply where the other person possessed the price sensitive information. This is not the case in relation to section 1013(2) or section 1013(5). From this it could be gathered that these rights of recovery are designed for a situation where the company has informed the subscriber of the price sensitive information in breach of its fiduciary duties.

The right for the other party to seek recovery pursuant to section 1013(3) or section 1013(4) does not adequately uphold any of the theories relating to insider trading. It is only a matter of chance that a person trading on the day traded with the insider, giving the person a remedy.

Section 1005 provides a general right to civil recovery for any contravention of Parts 7.11 and 7.12, and gives a limitation period to make a claim of six years after the day on which the cause of action arose. In *Ampolex v. Perpetual Trustee*,[65] Justice Rolfe was of the preliminary view that section 1005 did not have any independent operation from the specific recovery provisions found in section 1013. He based this view on the words 'subject to this Division' in section 1005(1). On the basis of statutory construction and the recommendations of the standing committee, it is likely that his interpretation is correct. This is unfortunate as it precludes the rights of other aggrieved persons, such as a takeover bidder, seeking recovery from being harmed by insider trading.

The standing committee considered the issue of penalties. They did not adopt submissions seeking civil penalties, based on a multiple of the profit gained or the loss avoided. The Attorney-General's Department also submitted to the standing committee that civil liability should not be extended to compensate others 'beyond the parties to the transaction', as such a move 'could be considered punitive and inconsistent with the common law principles underpinning the assessment of damages'.[66]

The standing committee did suggest that pecuniary penalty for an insider trading conviction should be twice the profit gained or the loss avoided.[67] The government rejected this submission, saying that this may limit the ability of traders affected by the crime seeking damages from the offender.[68]

There is scope for law reform debate on whether civil recovery should be broadened to include contemporaneous traders, as in the USA, and other persons who are damaged by insider trading, such as takeover bidders. There is also scope for the use of civil penalties, which could be proved on the balance of probabilities, being used to deter insider trading. Civil penalties should be used where the conduct is not inherently 'criminal' in nature, but is still a threat to market confidence. In this sense they can be justified, irrespective of general arguments against civil penalties for breach of directors' duties.

---

65 (1996) 20 ACSR 649 662.
66 *Fair Shares for All: Insider Trading in Australia, op. cit.* para. 4.13.3 to 4.13.9.
67 *ibid.,* para. 4.12.20.
68 Government Response to the Report of the House of Representatives Standing Committee on Legal and Constitutional Affairs *Fair Shares for All: Insider Trading in Australia,* p. 3.

Insider trading law in New Zealand[69]

The *Securities Amendment Act 1988* was designed to deal with insider trading in securities listed on the New Zealand Stock Exchange. As in Australia, the basic principle is that an insider who obtains price sensitive information by virtue of his or her position as an insider should be prohibited from dealing in securities or tipping until the information is published or otherwise reflected in market prices. Unlike Australia, insider trading is not made a criminal offence, but the insider is liable to pay damages to the party with whom he or she deals and the gain made or loss avoided, plus a penalty to the company.

Who is an insider?

The legislation envisages three levels of insider; what commentators have called primary, secondary and tertiary insiders. (The terms are not used in the Act.)[70]

A primary insider is the company itself (section 3(1)(a)); this differs from Australia); a person who by reason of being a principal officer, employee or company secretary or a substantial security[71] in the company has inside information about the company on another company (section 3(1)(b)).

A secondary insider is a person who receives inside information in confidence from a primary insider (section 3(1)(c)).

A tertiary insider is a person who receives inside information in confidence from a secondary insider (section 3(1)(e)).

What is inside information?

Section 2 defines inside information as information about a listed company which is not publicly available and would or would be likely to affect materially the price of the securities of the company if publicly available.[72] According to the Court of Appeal in *Re Wilson Neill Ltd; Colonial Mutual Life Assurance Society Ltd v. Wilson Neill*[73] 'likely' refers to a real or substantial risk and not a mere possibility that the information

---

69   See P. Fitzsimons, 'Insider Trading in New Zealand', in G. Walker (gen. ed.), *Securities Regulation in Australia and New Zealand*, 2nd edn, LBC Information Services, Sydney, 1998, ch. 17 for a very detailed discussion. See also his 'Enforcement of Insider Trading Laws by Shareholders in New Zealand' (1995) 3 Waikato LR 101; 'Enforcement of Insider Trading Laws in New Zealand', in C. Rickett and R. Grantham (eds), *Essays on Securities Regulation and Insider Trading*, Brooker, Wellington, 1997, p. 206; E. H. Abernathy, '*Securities Amendment Act 1988*—The Regulators' Prespective', unpublished speech, July 1996; and 'The Uncertainties of Insider Trading Law', unpublished speech, 11 March 1999.

70   See A. Beck and A. Borrowdale, *Guidebook to New Zealand Companies and Securities Law*, 6th edn, CCH (NZ) Ltd, Auckland, para. 602; Fitzsimons in Walker, *op. cit.*, pp. 612–13.

71   Defined in s. 2 as a person who has an interest in 5 per cent or more of the voting securities of the company.

72   See Fitzsimons in Walker, *op. cit.*, p. 601.

73   [1994] 2 NZLR 152 at 161.

could materially affect the price.[74] In that case nominee directors who had extensive board papers which they had not analysed were held to have objective possession. The test was not subjective knowledge.

Insider liability for dealing

The insider is liable to:

    (a) the purchaser or seller of the securities (section 7(2)(a) and(b)); and

    (b) the company itself (section 7(2)(c)).

The insider is liable in (a) for the loss suffered and in (b) for the gain *and* any amount which the court considers to be an appropriate pecuniary penalty (section 7(2)(c)(i) and (ii)).

There are limits to the liability for loss and penalty. Excluding the penalty, the insider's liability cannot exceed the greater amount for which the insider is separately liable in (a) or (b).

The limit on the penalty is the price of the securities or three times the gain made or loss avoided (section 7(4)(b) and (b)).

In *Wilson Neill*[75] the Court of Appeal indicated that the absence of moral fault has no bearing on liability under sections 7 or 9.

Exceptions

1   Company Officers—Approved Procedures

    These procedures are under the approved procedures for company officers authorised by Section 8(1) of the Act and set out in the *Insider Trading (Approved Procedure for Company Officers) Notice 1993.*

2   Takeovers

    'Takeovers' refers to a takeover bid in accordance with section 4 of the *Companies Amendment Act 1963.*

3   Chinese Walls[76]

    Chinese Walls are dealt with in section 8(3).

Insider liability for tipping[77]

Tipping is dealt with in section 9 and covers (1) advising or encouraging A to buy or sell or (2) advising or encouraging A to advise or encourage B to buy or sell or (3) commu-

---

74   As to materiality see Fitzsimons in Walker, *op. cit.*, pp. 605–11.

75   [1994] 2 NZLR 152, 162.

76   See Fitzsimons in Walker, *op. cit.*, pp. 628–9; *Re Bank of New Zealand; Kincaird v. Capital Markets Equities (No 2)* (1995) 7 NZCLC 260, 718, 260, 734. For examples see E. Abernathy et al. (eds), *Anderson's Company and Securities Law Service*, Brooker, Wellington, 1991, para. SA8.10.

77   See Fitzsimons in Walker, *op. cit.*, pp. 621–5; *Colonial Mutual Life Assurance Society Ltd v. Wilson Neill (No 2)* [1993] 2 NZLR 657, 675 per Heron J.

nicating information knowing that A or B will buy or sell or advise another person to buy or sell.

The insider is liable to the innocent buyer or seller for any loss (section 9(2)) and to the company on the same basis as under the dealing provisions (section 9(2)(g)(i)(ii) and (iii)). The Chinese Wall exception can apply here (section 10).

Where a company is liable as a tippee a director of the company who is also a director (and hence an insider) of the company whose shares are in question can also be held separately liable for tipping.[78]

Dealing and tipping in respect of shares in other companies

Liability is extended by sections 11 and 13 to conduct in respect of inside information about company B acquired as an insider of company A.

Shareholder proceedings[79]

Unlike the Australian legislation, the New Zealand legislation is exclusively civil and facilitates shareholder proceedings by:

(a) enabling a shareholder with the consent of the Securities Commission to require the company at its expense to get a legal opinion on whether the *company* can sue (section 17(1));[80] and

(b) enabling derivative proceedings to be taken under section 18.[81]

Applications under (b) were unsuccessful in *Re Wilson Neill Ltd* (supra) and successful in *Re Bank of New Zealand; Kincaird v. Capital Market Equities Ltd* [1994] 3 NZLR 738.

In *Wilson Neill* the company itself had already commenced action and a proposal by the shareholders to broaden the scope of the action was regarded as unwise. In the *BNZ* case the court considered a report of the Securities Commission itself which was not strictly an opinion under section 17(1)).

Conclusion

As can be seen there are significant differences between the insider trading laws of the two countries. Australian law is both criminal and civil whereas New Zealand law is exclusively civil, but with a penal element and provision to facilitate shareholder redress. The Australian provisions are broader in scope both in respect of the concept of insider and the source of the information. Neither country has been particularly successful in its enforcement of the law. To some extent this may be due to the nature of

---

78 *Re Bank of New Zealand; Kincaird v. Capital Markets Equities Ltd (No 2)* (1995) 7 NZCLC 260, 718.
79 See Fitzsimons in Walker, *op. cit.*, pp. 636 *et seq.*
80 *ibid.*, pp. 638–41.
81 *ibid.*, pp. 641 *et seq.*

insider trading itself. Insider trading is difficult to detect and prove: the regulators' resources are limited; the legislation is complex; and the courts have not worked out a clear and principled approach to interpretation and application of the legislation.[82] The result is that we have a few 'flagship' prosecutions in Australia, such as Hannes,[83] in order to set an example, and desultory shareholder initiatives in New Zealand, the Securities Commission choosing not to seek an enforcement role.

---

82   Ziegelaar, *op. cit.* footnote 9 supra, pp. 589–94.

83   R. v. Hannes (2001) 36 ACSR 72. For recent consideration see Companies and Securities Advisory Committee, *Insider Trading Draft Issues Paper*, November 2000 and A. White, 'Insider Trading Laws Toughen', *The Australian*, Business section, 13 July 2001, p. 22.

Investigation of Serious Fraud[1]

Introduction

Serious fraud is a subset of white collar crime that represents the inner core of the legal part of corporate governance. The term 'white collar crime' may 'be defined approximately as a crime committed by a person of respectability and high social status in the course of his occupation'.[2] The term was coined in the late 1930s[3] and is an expression used to denote an array of fraudulent offences such as insider trading, securities violations, embezzlement, forgery and corruption.[4] White collar offences traditionally have been committed by individuals against companies. These days, however, corporate crime includes criminal conduct committed by companies or their agents against members of the public in areas of 'environmental protection, product safety and consumer protection'.[5] Corporate crime includes a broad range of 'non-violent offences'[6] where manipulation, dishonesty and corruption within the financial and corporate sectors are the central elements.

---

1 This chapter is partly based on a useful unpublished LLM research paper by Lara Lukich at Bond University done under my supervision.

2 E. Sutherland, 'White-Collar Crime' Holt, Rinehart and Winston, New York, 1949, p. 9; see also G. Geis, 'White-Collar Crime: What is It?' (1991) 3 *Current Issues in Criminal Justice* 7 at 12.

3 The term 'white-collar crime' was first introduced in 1939 by E. H. Sutherland during his presidential address to the American Sociological Society in Philadelphia: see Geis, *op. cit.,* p. 11.

4 A. Cromie, 'NCA Changes tack on Corporate Crime', *Business Review Weekly,* 2 October 1992, p. 66.

5 *ibid.*

6 For some, white-collar crime is not viewed as a 'crime' at all because of its non-violent nature. There is a commonly held view that 'crimes of violence and invasion of space and property are the real destroyers of the community'. White-collar crime can, however, create the greater havoc. White-collar crimes 'are economically more significant and have the capacity to undermine faith in the basic institutions of society': J. H. Farrar, 'The ASC and the Criminal Process' (1993) 67 *Law Institute Journal* 603 at 603.

In recent years, the subject of white collar crime has received increasing attention in the United Kingdom and Australia. The 1980s were, without doubt, a financial disaster for Australia. There were major frauds being perpetrated on shareholders which largely were going unchecked. Asset and income concealment, false bank accounts, insider trading and tax evasion were rife. Illegal and unethical behaviour by some Australian companies occurred as regulatory and prosecutional agencies failed to act. Australia, however, was not alone. The United Kingdom had its share of unethical behaviour. Barlow Clowes, Blue Arrow, Polly Peck International, Robert Maxwell, and BCCI are a few of the big fraud cases that rocked the City of London. Maxwell alone was responsible for embezzling a staggering $A1.25 billion out of his employees' pension funds. New Zealand had a number of cases; prominent among these was the Equiticorp group collapse which involved fraud of $NZ440 million. This chapter examines white collar crime, which was prevalent in the 1980s, as evidenced by some of the cases. It focuses on the approach taken by the relevant regulatory and prosecutional authorities in regulating corporate activity and combating serious fraud. Moreover, it examines the nature of serious fraud with reference to experience in Australia, the United Kingdom, and New Zealand.

The nature of corporate fraud

George Staple, former Director of the UK Serious Fraud Office, in a lecture published in 1993,[7] argued that company fraud is cyclical. In boom conditions when share prices are high, people use their company's paper to take over other companies and take steps to enhance the market price of their securities. This leads to schemes of market manipulation in one form or another. Some of these schemes involve the company's assets being improperly used to finance the purchase of its shares.

Conversely, in times of recession, bull markets become bear markets and takeover activity declines. People have grown used to high standards of living and some, in order to sustain this, engage in deception, false accounting and trading when insolvent, while others resort to outright theft.

Specialist criminal lawyers recognise that fraud is different from other crimes. Rowan Bosworth-Davies, in his book on fraud in the City of London,[8] quotes an unnamed successful solicitor specialising in defence of white collar criminals as follows:

> Now, a fraudsman's different. For a start, the issues involved are much more complex. In a lot of cases, the Director of Public Prosecutions (DPP) won't prosecute at all, because of the complexity and the costs involved. Robbery, by and large, is a very

7   G. Staple, 'Serious and Complex Fraud: A New Perspective' (1993) 56 MLR 127. For an earlier discussion see R. Bosworth-Davies, *Fraud in the City: Too Good to be True*, Penguin Books, London, 1988. For an Australian discussion see P. Grabosky (ed.), *Complex Commercial Fraud*, Australian Institute of Criminology, Canberra, 1992.

8   *op. cit.* 21.

simple matter and, in most cases, it boils down to whether the jury believe the police evidence, but fraud cases contain a wealth of possibilities. For a start, your client is almost invariably on bail. In most cases, there is so much documentary evidence that you can almost always find something the police have overlooked and use this fact to suggest that they haven't done their job thoroughly. The trials last much longer and are usually fairly uninteresting to the average onlooker. I suppose the chances of conviction are much the same as the other offences, in the end, but the big plus factor from your client's point of view is that he is very unlikely to receive a custodial sentence, even if he is convicted. If he does go to prison, he is most unlikely to receive the same sort of sentence he would get for a robbery. The fraudsman will always give it a run, because he has nothing to lose by fighting a charge and everything to gain.[9]

It is easy for the ordinary person to view the prosecution of serious fraud with a degree of cynicism. There seems to be one law for the rich and another for the poor but, like nearly everything else, it comes down to a question of resources and priorities in law enforcement. It also involves effective case management by lawyers and the courts, something which they are not necessarily good at.

Corporate crime in Australia

The 1980s saw one of the largest upsurges in corporate crime in Australia's history. The decade was one market by 'greed, recklessness and abandonment of procedures and codes of conduct'.[10] Corporate high flyers such as Bond, Connell and Yuill, who enjoyed enormous wealth, power and prestige, merely received 'a slap on the wrist' for their corporate crimes. The Australian Institute of Criminology estimated that their unethical behaviour cost the Australian economy approximately $13 billion a year.[11]

It was no secret that the 'corporate cowboys' were after money for its own sake.[12] Laurie Connell's merchant bank—Rothwell's Ltd—at one time had assets totalling $740 million. Approximately two-thirds of those assets, however, were loans or investments to Connell himself and various associates. Similarly, Brian Yuill defrauded GPI Leisure of $100 million in an attempt to prop up his Spedley Group. Shareholders were required to approve the transaction after the money had disappeared. No former

---

9   For an interesting Australian discussion see M. Rozenes QC, 'Issues in the Defence of Charges Relating to Fraud', in Grabosky, *op. cit.*, p. 155. Since then Victoria has reformed its criminal procedure: see *Crimes (Criminal Trials) Act 1993* (Victoria). See also M. Rozenes' address to the 28th Australian Legal Convention on 'The New Procedures for the Prosecution of Complex Fraud—Will They Work?' <http://www.cdpp.gov.au/cdpp/speeches>.

10   S. Miller, 'Corporate Crime, the Excesses of the 80s and Collective Responsibility: an Ethical Perspective' (1995) 5 *Australian Journal of Corporate Law* 139 at 141–2; see too R. Tomasic and S. Bottomley, *Directing the Top 500—Corporate Governance and Accountability in Australian Companies*, Allen & Unwin, Sydney, 1993, p. 63.

11   Cromie, *op. cit.* footnote 4 supra, p. 66.

12   T. Sykes and A. Sampson, 'A Nation of Crooks?', *Australian Business Monthly*, March 1993, 26.

corporate high flyer, however, attracted more attention than Alan Bond. More than a billion dollars of Bell Resources' funds were moved into the Bond empire without the knowledge or approval of Bell shareholders while it was under Bond Corp. control.[13]

Ignorant and small investors were not the only victims of the 1980s excesses. Banks and professional investors who should have been aware of the risks they were taking fell victim.[14] Total write-offs by banks and financial groups amounted to $28 billion. Australia's three largest investment banks had to be rescued by their parents.[15] Two of Australia's state banks suffered enormous losses.[16] The four major commercial banks had to write billions of dollars off their loan books.[17] The 1980s were, indisputably, devastating.

While unethical conduct took place within Australia's corporate community, it should be borne in mind that relatively few business people were involved. Henry Bosch, the former chairman of the National Companies and Securities Commission, states:

> Unquestionably, dreadful things happened during the long boom. They ought be, and they have been, condemned. But we need to remember that there are some 10 000 public companies in Australia of which nearly 1500 are listed on the stock exchange. Of these not more than 100, and probably not more than 50, were involved in the practices now so rightly condemned. The vast majority of Australian companies are and always have been behaving both legally and ethically.[18]

The responsibility for the corporate disasters of the 1980s extends beyond the unethical and corrupt practices of the corporate high flyers. It even extends beyond the bankers and the financial community. For the most part, it is contended that responsibility lies with the regulatory agencies—the Australian Securities and Investments Commission (ASIC), the Director of Public Prosecutions (DPP), and the National Crime Authority (NCA).

The Australian Securities and Investments Commission and the Commonwealth Director of Public Prosecutions

As we saw in Chapter 20, the Australian Securities and Investments Commission (ASIC) is an independent body established by the *Australian Securities and Investments*

---

13   *ibid.*
14   *ibid.*
15   The three investment banks were Tricontinental, Partnership Pacific, and Elders Finance; cited in Miller, *op. cit.* footnote 10 supra, p. 139.
16   These were the State Bank of Victoria and State Bank of South Australia: *ibid.*
17   The four major banks are: Westpac, National Australia Bank, Commonwealth, and ANZ: *ibid.*
18   Quoted in Sykes and Sampson, *op. cit.* footnote 12 supra, p. 26.

Commission Act 2001 and superseded the National Companies and Securities Commission (NCSC). The commission is a specialist regulatory agency with administrative and enforcement responsibility for the Corporations Act in the Commonwealth, states and territories. ASIC is the primary investigative body in relation to complex criminal matters involving corporate law. It ensures fair play in business, protects investors and consumers, and prevents corporate wrongdoing. The commission takes a pro-active stance in its approach to corporate regulation. It plays an important role in maintaining Australia's reputation in the international markets and is closely involved in everyday commercial life, litigating perceived breaches of the corporate law.[19]

In performing its functions and exercising its powers, the commission strives:

- to ensure that information is available as soon as practicable for access by the public;
- to maintain, facilitate and improve the performance of the financial system and the entities within that system in the interests of commercial certainty;
- to register, supervise and discipline a range of intermediaries such as securities dealers, stock exchanges and auditors; and
- to be an enforcement agency, with civil, criminal and administrative capacities.[20]

As the primary investigative body for offences involving serious corporate wrongdoing, section 13 of the Act confers very wide powers on the commission to conduct formal investigations. The commission has power, for the 'due administration of the corporations legislation (other than excluded provisions)', power to investigate suspected contraventions of Commonwealth law, or laws of a state or territory that involve the management of affairs of a corporation, a body corporate or a securities or futures contract.

As the specialist regulatory body, ASIC concentrates on serious breaches of corporate law.[21] Deciding what constitutes 'serious' is a matter of public policy and in so doing, the commission pays regard not only to the nature of the breach, but also the detriment suffered by shareholders and creditors of the company and the breadth of the suffering.[22]

Where a breach of the law occurs, the commission will commence an investigation. The commission seeks to conduct investigations in an efficient and cost effective way, resulting in expeditious and timely prosecutions. Although the commission has the

---

19   S. Menzies, 'The Australian Securities Commission and the Prevention of Fraud', published in *Complex Commercial Fraud* (Proceedings of a conference held 20–23 August 1991), Australian Institute of Criminology, Canberra 1991, 29 at 30.
20   Australian Securities and Investments Commission, 'About ASIC' (available online at <http://www.asic.gov.au/page-201.html>).
21   The commission concentrates solely on breaches of the Corporations Act. Where breaches of criminal law are discovered, the commission refers the matter to the Federal Police, the state police or the NCA. Furthermore, pursuant to s. 16(1) of the Act, the Australian Securities and Investments Commission has a statutory duty to report to the Attorney-General when, in its opinion, a serious contravention of a Commonwealth or state law has been perpetrated: Menzies, *op. cit.* footnote 19 supra, p. 35. For strong criticism of ASIC's record see A. Ferguson, 'The Watchdog No One Fears', *Business Review Weekly*, 1 September 2000, p. 58.
22   Menzies, *op. cit.*

278 The Legal Core

power to prosecute problems arising under the Corporations Act,[23] major offences are generally prosecuted by the Commonwealth (DPP) in accordance with a memorandum of understanding between the DPP and ASIC. The commission's preference in enforcement and prosecution is, however, the use of civil litigation to recover money on behalf of and for the benefit of the members and creditors of a company. The primary emphasis is placed upon recovery or compensation to those who have been injured by corporate illegality rather than taking the time-consuming course of criminal action.[24] This is a sore point in relations between ASIC and the DPP.

The DPP's office was established by the *Director of Public Prosecutions Act 1983* with the office beginning operations in 1994. Michael Rozenes, former DPP, said in an unpublished address on 'The Role of the DPP in the Investigation and Prosecution of Complex Fraud':[25]

Perhaps the most important principle underlying the creation of the Office was to separate the role of the prosecutor from that of the investigator and give the prosecutor independence from the political process. This has had the effect of injecting objectivity into the prosecution process. While the merit of a separate and independent prosecutor should not be overlooked, the severance of the investigating function from the prosecuting functions can, on occasions, create tensions.

In that context it should perhaps be mentioned that the relationship between ASIC and the DPP is not that of solicitor and client. As an independent prosecuting agency we have statutory responsibility in relation to the matters that are brought before the criminal courts.

Accordingly, while there must be close cooperation and mutual understanding of the respective roles of the ASIC and the DPP the ultimate decision in relation to whether a prosecution of a matter of any substance should proceed must and does remain with the DPP.

The DPP acknowledges that there is a role for civil remedies in the prosecution of corporate crime but strongly argues that civil action cannot in the case of serious fraud or dishonesty be an adequate and effective deterrent.[26] Also ASIC's record in bringing civil penalties under the Corporations Act is not particularly impressive and there are significant differences between states.

The differing attitudes of ASIC and the DPP have, in the past, resulted in relations between the two organisations becoming strained. ASIC regards its character as commercial and professional, clearly having an affinity with commerce. This is very differ-

---

23 See s. 49 of the *Australian Securities and Investments Commission Act 1989* and s. 1315 of the Corporations Act.
24 An example of the commission using a civil remedy to right a corporate matter was in relation to the Victorian Inland Meat Company. Henry Rosens, a former director, was ordered to repay $249 000 to the receivers–managers, as well as a court-imposed fine of $230 000: Cromie, *op. cit.* footnote 4 supra, p. 66.
25 ASIC/Law Council Enforcement Conference, Perth, 16 September 1994.
26 *ibid.*

ent to the legal culture existing at the Director of Public Prosecutions, whose primary role is criminal law investigations and prosecutions. As a result, tensions between the two bodies reached crisis proportions in September 1992.[27] It led to the intervention of the Attorney-General, who recognised that the regulator will focus on 'enforcement action'[28] it views appropriate in response to the nature of the activity undertaken, while the prosecutor will focus solely on criminal law investigation and prosecution. Consequently, both organisations were provided with direction to develop and implement policies for the exercise and discharge of their respective functions and powers.

The guidelines

Michael Rozenes, then Commonwealth DPP, in a speech on 'The Role of the DDP in the Investigation and Prosecution of Complex Fraud',[29] described the practice under the guidelines as follows:

> The guidelines focus on the processes involved in investigating a matter. The guidelines recognise that it is for ASIC to primarily decide which matters it will investigate. In ASIC's case something like 8000 to 9000 complaints are received each year. ASIC does not have resources to investigate each of those complaints so it undertakes its own internal procedure to prioritise which matters are to be investigated.
>
> Once ASIC devotes resources to that investigation it develops an investigation plan which will be modified as the matter progresses.
>
> The investigation plan provides for assessment stages. In the first of those stages ASIC decides which direction that investigation will follow. The investigation may have civil (including disciplinary action) or criminal aspects or both.
>
> At this stage ASIC will provide the DPP with details of any investigation which ASIC considers as criminal aspects. This is provided for information. The DPP will not normally be expected to provide advice to ASIC at this stage but is available to advise ASIC, especially in large or important matters.
>
> At a point in the investigation ASIC will take an informed decision as to whether criminal or civil or both processes are to be seriously contemplated. Where ASIC is considering criminal proceedings it will at that stage consult with the DPP.
>
> It is also during this stage of the investigation that the DPP may provide advice to ASIC as to the use of search warrants and criminal investigative techniques.
>
> If the DPP considers that, having regard to the entirety of the evidence and the available material, it is unlikely it will form a view that the prosecution is in the public

---

27 Farrar, *op. cit.* footnote 6 supra, p. 603.

28 Whether civil, criminal, or administrative. Under T. Hartnell, however, the Australian Securities Commission's first priority was to take civil action to preserve property and otherwise obtain civil remedies in cases of public interest where private litigants were unable to do so. Its policy in respect of criminal matters was to concentrate on major investigations of national priority: *ibid.*

29 See the website cited in footnote 9 above.

interest, the DPP will advise ASIC in writing of that decision and its reasons. Of course, during that process the DPP will give close consideration to ASIC's views.

When ASIC has decided that criminal proceedings should in its opinion be instituted and has gathered substantial evidence to enable it to support that view, ASIC is required to request in writing the DPP's view as to whether the matter should be referred to DPP for the purposes of criminal proceedings. This process is referred to as the 'hand-over process'.

The DPP then certifies that the matter is appropriate for hand-over. It will only do so if it believes that there is sufficient evidence to enable it to form the view that there is a real prospect of the commencement of criminal proceedings.

The investigation is usually substantially complete at the hand-over stage although there may remain some outstanding investigative tasks. From the hand-over date ASIC is obliged to devote the resources that it is reasonably able to provide for the purpose of finalising the matter.

Rozenes added:

> The arrangements between ASIC and DPP reflect a certain maturity and development in the traditional investigator/prosecutor role. As previously indicated there are dangers in prosecutors becoming investigators. Those most often cited include the potential for lack of objectivity, the potential for lawyers to become witnesses and, not least, the potential for friction to arise between the investigators and lawyers. However, it was felt at least in relation to the ASIC/DPP relationship that we could no longer afford the luxury of sitting back and waiting for a complete brief of evidence to arrive. It was important that the prosecutors be much more active in the investigation process.

He referred to past cases where further investigation had been required or plans to prosecute had to be dropped. He added that in practice it may be that the DPP's involvement in smaller investigations is not as crucial as in the larger ones. Nevertheless there should in every case be a general awareness by the DPP of the investigations, the type of allegations, and the expected referral dates.

Undoubtedly, a balance should be struck between the use of civil remedies and the imposition of criminal penalties. There needs to be a distinction between behaviour which should invoke a sanction because it is against the public interest, but not criminal, and behaviour which should incur criminal penalty.[30] In other words it should be a crime for a director to act dishonestly but it should not be a crime for a director to act unreasonably. The new Business Judgment Rule introduced by the *Corporate Law Economic Reform Program Act 1999* reflects this kind of philosophy. Professor Roman Tomasic submits that few perceive the purposes of the Corporations Act in terms of traditional criminal law goals such as retribution or deterrence. Moreover, in general terms the Corporations Act is seen as a mechanism for achieving ethical conduct

---

30 K. Farrell, 'Corporate Crime: Complex Criminal Trials the ASC Perspective' (1994) 5 *Current Issues in Criminal Justice* 256 at 258.

within the business community. Corporate law is something to be invoked rather than imposed and as a consequence, emphasis should be placed upon civil remedies.[31] Tomasic states:

> there is a dominant civil law culture operating in regard to the *Corporations Act* and this serves to moderate or deflect the impact of criminal law inspired strategies for dealing with criminal breaches of this Law. Even the victims of corporate law breaches … would prefer compensation rather than retribution.[32]

The experiences of the 1980s demonstrated that contraventions of corporate law are frequently committed under the guise of legitimate commercial transactions.[33] Consequently, ASIC has a very important role to play in combating serious breaches of the Corporations Act. It is submitted that civil remedies have a legitimate place as an end product of investigations. They provide greater advantages[34] to those who have been injured by corporate illegality. That protection cannot be matched in the criminal process. As such, criminal penalties for corporate offences should be reserved for acts of gross dishonesty, negligence and fraud.

The National Crime Authority

The National Crime Authority (NCA) was founded in 1984 following the Moffit, Williams, Costigan, and Stewart royal commissions, which levelled criticisms at Australia's effort to combat organised crime.[35] Under its general functions, the authority investigates criminal activities as specified in the *National Crime Authority Act 1984*. The Act makes no reference to organised crime but states that the authority may conduct investigations and inquiries into relevant criminal activity.[36]

---

31 R. Tomasic, 'Corporate Crime in a Civil Law Culture' (1994) 5 *Current Issues in Criminal Justice* 244 at 248.
32 *ibid.* at 249.
33 Farrell, *op. cit.* footnote 30 supra, p. 262.
34 For a general discussion see Tomasic, *op. cit.* footnote 31 supra, p. 251.
35 Cromie, *op. cit.* footnote 4 supra, p. 67.
36 A relevant offence is defined in s. 4. It requires that an offence subject to investigation by the NCA:
   • involve two or more offenders and substantial organisation;
   • involve the use of sophisticated techniques and methods;
   • is an offence that is committed or is of a kind that is ordinarily committed with offences of a like kind; and
   • is an offence that involves, inter alia, 'theft, fraud, tax evasion, currency violations … obtaining financial benefits by vices engaged in by others, corruption, bankruptcy and company violations or matters of the same general nature as one or more of the forgoing'.
   Furthermore, the authority applies two additional criteria in focusing on the investigation of serious and complex matters. They are: that the conduct under investigation involves criminal behaviour crossing jurisdictional boundaries; and that the matter under consideration is not suited to investigation by normal police exercising normal powers: G. Livermore, 'The National Crime Authority and the Investigation of Fraud', published in *Complex Commercial Fraud* (Proceedings of a conference held 20–23 August 1991), Australian Institute of Criminology, Canberra, 1991, pp. 122–3.

The NCA holds a unique position in Australian law enforcement, with special investigative powers and multijurisdictional focus. Its aim is 'to take effective action to reduce the incidences and impact of organised crime in Australia'.[37] As such, the Act arms the authority with special powers beyond those enjoyed by other criminal law enforcement agencies.[38] The NCA has a number of special powers. These cover hearings, including compulsory appearances and production of documents, imposition of penalties, warrants for search and seizure, for arrest, and for interception of communications.[39] The NCA, however, has no prosecutional function and is purely an investigative agency. As such, pursuant to the Act, the NCA has responsibility to provide admissible evidence assembled by it to the relevant prosecutional authorities.[40]

The NCA conducts its investigations by way of multidisciplinary investigative teams. Its objective is to bring together different professions, disciplines and expertise to carry out its functions. As a result, it is structured to ensure its teams are composed of a mix of lawyers, accountants, intelligence officers, police, computer and word-processing staff.[41] The multidisciplinary approach places it in a superior position to tackle serious fraud investigations. It is with these resources that the NCA has undertaken work with other law enforcement agencies and establishes and coordinates task forces involving a variety of federal and state criminal offences.[42]

Since its inception, the NCA has conducted a number of investigations involving drug and fraud related offences. This has been its core business. Under the chairmanship of Justice Stewart the NCA was focused on investigating sophisticated organised crime. This meant drugs and semi-organised thuggery. At that time, this reflected prevailing community concerns. In more recent times, the authority has placed considerable emphasis on white-collar criminal activity. Under Peter Faris, QC, the NCA

---

37 R. Galbally, 'Corporate and Commercial Crime: The New Emphasis' (1991) 65 *Law Institute Journal* 826 at 827.

38 A 'special investigation' involves the use of the NCA's coercive powers. These powers include: the power to compel a person to appear at a hearing before the authority; the power to compel any such person to produce documents, take an oath or affirmation, and answer any questions put to him or her; the power to appoint specialist consultants to assist in investigation; and the power and obligation to cooperate with similar international agencies. These provision abrogate the right to silence in hearings before the NCA, but retain the privilege against self-incrimination. As a consequence, a special investigation can only be conducted under a reference from either the Commonwealth Attorney-General, or his state counterparts, Any notice referring the matter to the NCA must include, among other things, the general nature of the circumstances or allegations constituting the relevant criminal activity. The limitations prevent the NCA 'from being able to roam at will over the whole field of its jurisdiction, without having to justify its investigations to those politically accountable': Commonwealth, Hansard, House of Representatives (1984) 7 June 3094 (Michael Duffy, Minister for Communications); cited in A. Palmer, 'R v. Elliot' (1997) 21 *Melbourne University Law Review* 331 at 332.

39 For detailed discussion see A. Leaver et al., *Investigating Crime—A Guide to the Powers of Agencies Involved in the Investigation of Crime*, LBC Information Services, Sydney, 1997, ch. 9.

40 Livermore, *op. cit.* footnote 36 supra, p. 122.

41 J. Buxton, 'The National Crime Authority: Its Role in Investigating Fraud' (1998) 56 *Canberra Bulletin of Public Administration* 98 at 99.

42 *ibid.*

branched out from its more traditional drug-related investigations into the corporate crime area. The NCA recognised, and responded to, the far-reaching damage done to Australia by corporate and securities industry defalcation during the 1980s.[43] The appointment of Justice Phillips to the NCA in 1991 saw a more aggressive pursuit of corporate and white collar crime. In a move responding to criticisms levelled at the authority by Frank Costigan, QC,[44] Justice Phillips made it clear that they would give greater priority to investigating white collar crime, and thus, a 'package' of new directions was announced. The proposed reforms involved:

- a shift from drug related investigations to 'white collar' crime
- a shift from 'competitor' to 'partner' in law enforcement
- a shift from secrecy to more open procedures
- a more active role in law reform.[45]

The fundamental principle underlying the shift from drug-related offences to corporate criminal activity was the determination of the NCA to act as a 'partner' to other law enforcement agencies.[46] The significance of this shift was that it signalled a new approach to investigating and prosecuting organised crime. The NCA was eager to be seen as capable of supplying complementary services to other agencies in the investigation of complex matters that crossed jurisdictional boundaries and that could only be effectively handled by the NCA.[47] In this regard, it was said that the NCA intended to 'place optimum effort on attacking the profit motive in crime and in particular to target serious fraud offenders whose criminal conduct is based solely upon greed and the accumulation of wealth'.[48]

The new direction of the NCA did not mean it abandoned drug trafficking investigations. It is still the 'only agency capable of investigating highly complex multi-jurisdictional drug related offences'.[49] Instead, the NCA thought that its role in successfully investigating and prosecuting fraudulent high fliers would help restore

---

43   Livermore, *op. cit.* footnote 36 supra, p. 125.

44   '… there has been a failure to recognise and acknowledge that when Paul Keating opened the financial deregulation doors and failed to keep in place proper monitoring mechanisms, he prepared the ground for the financial vandalism which we had seen in recent years … And when the NCA walked away from the job it was set up to do, the National Companies and Securities Commission was without proper resources in its area, we were left without the protection we were entitled to expect': Costigan, QC, 'Anti-Corruption Authorities in Australia 1990', unpublished address to Labour Lawyers Conference, Brisbane, 22 September 1990, at 16–17 cited in C. Corns, 'New Directions for the NCA' (1991) 16 *Legal Service Bulletin* 113 at 113.

45   *ibid.*

46   As stated by Justice Phillips: 'Essentially, I envisage the Authority as a body which should act as a partner to the other law enforcement agencies. It should not be—or appear to be—a competitor. Rather, it should follow the roles of a coordinator and an agency offering complementary service to other agencies' in Corns, *op. cit.* footnote 44 supra, p. 114.

47   Livermore, *op. cit.* footnote 34 supra, p. 130.

48   *ibid.*, pp. 130–1.

49   Corns, *op. cit.* footnote 44 supra, p. 114.

'confidence in bona fide companies within Australia and in the Australian capital markets generally'.[50]

Despite the new approach taken by the NCA, in recent times it came under fire for its continued secrecy, limited accountability and unfettered powers. The prosecution of John Elliott and three other Elders executives certainly raised a few eyebrows. In late 1996 Elliott and three former executives were acquitted of charges following an investigation relating to an alleged $66 million foreign exchange scam involving the Equiticorp group in New Zealand. Justice Vincent in the Victorian Supreme Court rendered inadmissible virtually the entire prosecution case. His Honour made two crucial rulings: that evidence taken during confidential hearings was inadmissible as it went beyond the original government authorisation of the investigation; and hence, any evidence gained with its formidable coercive powers was tainted and inadmissible.[51] The prosecution and acquittal of Elliott and the other executives were an unmitigated disaster for the NCA. The Victorian Court of Appeal disagreed with Justice Vincent and the High Court refused to grant leave to appeal,[52] but the NCA came under siege as never before. Elliott sued the NCA in civil proceedings in the Federal Court, which he subsequently dropped.[53] Jeff Kennett, then the Victorian Premier, called for the NCA's abolition. A former Liberal Party state director, Petro Georgiou, called for a royal commission. The federal parliamentary joint committee overseeing the NCA launched its own investigation.[54] Never before had the future of the NCA been under such threat.

Since then the NCA has dropped its investigations into serious fraud except in the areas of organised crime in the region, crimes against the Commonwealth involving tax, and criminal networks. Its references are set by the Intergovernmental Committee. In spite of these criticisms it is submitted that the NCA has been effective in combating organised and corporate crime. Indisputably, the NCA has a real and valuable role in investigating major organised crime within Australia. Looking back at the 1980s, it is clear that 'no single agency has the capacity, resources or expertise to properly undertake investigations and assemble evidence to prosecute offenders in serious fraud cases'.[55] The Elliott saga has, however, raised many complex and serious issues. The powers of ASIC and the NCA are in need of reform, possibly along the lines of the United Kingdom Serious Fraud Office which has been copied in New Zealand.

---

50 Livermore, *op. cit.* footnote 36 supra, p. 125.
51 G. Greens, 'Under Siege: Can the NCA Survive the Acquittal of John Elliott?' (1996) 31 *Australian Lawyer* 28 at 29. See also D. Elias, 'How Hearing Unveiled Dark Secrets of the NCA', <http://theage.com.au/news/agenewe/deelli3.htm>.
52 *R v. Elliott and others*, per Vincent J, unreported, 2 February 1996; 137 ALR 419.
53 See *Elliott v. Seymour* [1999] FCA 976 (19 July 1999).
54 Elias, *op. cit.*
55 Livermore, footnote 36 supra, p. 125.

The handling of serious fraud in the United Kingdom[56]

The Roskill Report

In November 1983, the British government appointed a committee under the chairmanship of Lord Roskill to consider in what ways the conduct of criminal proceedings in England and Wales, arising from fraud, could be improved. It also considered what 'changes in existing law and procedure would be desirable to secure the just, expeditious, and economical disposal of such proceedings'.[57] The resulting report made the following observation:

> The public no longer believes the legal system in England and Wales is capable of bringing the perpetrators of serious frauds expeditiously and effectively to book. The overwhelming weight of the evidence laid before us suggests that the public is right. In relation to such crimes, and to the skilful and determined criminals who commit them, the present legal system is archaic, cumbersome and unreliable. At every stage, during investigation preparation, committal, pre-trial review and trial, the present arrangements offer an open invitation to blatant delay and abuse.[58]

The report, covering the investigative, prosecution and trial stages of fraud cases, made 112 recommendations, only one of which was not implemented. The greatest controversy in the report was caused by the proposal for a Fraud Trials Tribunal. The committee made recommendation that in 'complex fraud cases'[59] a trial by jury should be replaced by a Fraud Trials Tribunal. Under tribunal procedure, either the prosecution or defence counsel would be entitled to apply to a High Court judge for the accused to be tried before the tribunal. The tribunal was to be composed of a High Court or a circuit judge and two lay members who should be 'elected from a panel of persons who have skill and expertise in business generally and experience of complex business

---

56 See B. Widlake, *Serious Fraud Office*, Warner Books, London, 1996, p. 24; M. Killick, *Fraudbusters—The Inside Story of the Serious Fraud Office*, Victor Gollancz, London, 1998.

57 Fraud Trials Committee Report (1986) HMSO; cited in M. Levi, 'The Future of Fraud Prosecutions and Trials: Reviewing Roskill' (1996) 7 *The Company Lawyer* 139 at 140.

58 *ibid.*

59 'Complex fraud' as defined by the committee: 'A complex case is not necessarily one in which enormous sums of money are involved, or one in which the documentation is copious, or the list of witnesses long, although it would be normal if some—if not all—of these ingredients were present. It is a fraud in which the dishonesty is buried in a series of interrelated transactions, most frequently in a market offering highly-specialised services, or in areas of high finance involving (for example) manipulation of the ownership of companies.

'The complexity lies in the fact that the markets, or areas of business, operate according to concepts which bear no obvious similarity to anything in the general experience of most members of the public, and are governed by rules, and conducted in a language, learned only after prolonged study by those involved.' See Levi, *op. cit.* footnote 57 supra, p. 144.

transactions'.[60] This was, however, politically unacceptable. Despite the fact the committee was attempting to address the issue of complexity, critics felt that such a tribunal smacked of elitism. Widlake states:

> while it seemed obvious that comprehension of complex evidence would be at a much higher level if the tribunal procedure were adopted, it was equally obvious that members of the general public would think that the system was a fix, based on class, education and experience.[61]

Serious fraud cases are complex and, hence, difficult to try within the traditional adversarial jury trial system. The committee therefore identified three major areas that needed improvement or attention. They include:

- the competence of judges and counsel
- the misuse of committal proceedings
- the use of preparatory hearings.[62]

The Roskill Committee questioned the competence of judges to try serious fraud cases and of counsel to appear in them. The committee concluded that an overwhelming portion of fraud cases in the Crown Court were tried by circuit judges.[63] Further, the committee established that between 1979 and 1983 only three out of 129 fraud cases were tried by a High Court judge.[64] Widlake offers two reasons. First, there is a limited supply of High Court judges and as a result it is very much a case of 'doing without'. Second, the High Court judges have heavy and burdensome workloads.[65] Thus the committee recognised the impossibility of High Court judges trying serious and complex fraud cases at all times and that 'circuit judges would have to be selected on the basis of an informal rating of aptitude'.[66]

In addition, Roskill recognised that an immense number of fraud cases have been handled by inexperienced counsel. Roskill argued that, having the requisite skills to prosecute crimes including murder and rape did not imply that counsel had the necessary skills and competence for prosecuting serious fraud.[67] As a result, the committee submitted that a list of 'appropriate' counsel be compiled and kept under review by judges experienced in trying serious and complex fraud cases. Roskill, however, went even further, recommending compulsory training in accountancy and information technology for all barristers. Roskill was of the view that 'accountancy should be a

---

60 *ibid.*
61 Widlake, *op. cit.* footnote 56 supra, p. 25.
62 Levi, *op. cit.* footnote 57 supra, pp. 141–3. See also L. Fleming, 'The Serious Fraud Office' (1995) 49 *Australian Police Journal* 216 at 216.
63 Circuit judges are judges ranking below those who sit in the High Court.
64 Widlake, *op. cit.* footnote 56 supra, p. 28.
65 *ibid.*
66 *ibid.*, p. 29.
67 *ibid.*

compulsory subject in training for the bar, either at the bar examinations stage or during pupillage'.[68]

The committee criticised the use of committal proceedings 'which very seldom lead to discharge, are very expensive, are not within the competence of most magistrates, but which can cause serious delays'.[69] The committee recognised that:

> fraudsters and sometimes their advisers are skilful in exploiting delaying tactics and throughout that time fraudsters are free to continue their operations to the detriment of the public.[70]

Consequently, the report recommended that abolition of committal proceedings for some frauds. Alternatively, any fraud cases viewed as 'suitable' by the prosecuting authorities should be issued a 'transfer certificate' that would allow the case to be tried in a Crown Court and be dealt by a 'judge with appropriate special experience'.[71] From this procedure there is no right of appeal, but an accused 'should be able to apply to the nominated judge for a preparatory hearing in open court at which he would have the right to make an application for discharge'. Additionally, in order to prevent delaying tactics, ploys and abuse, the accused should not be permitted to 'embark upon a prolonged hearing of issues which should properly be examined during the trial'.[72]

To make fraud trials less time-consuming, less obscure and more effective, the report emphasised the importance of preparatory hearings. A preparatory hearing takes place before the jury enters the picture and is designed to identify the material issues, familiarise the judge with them, and help the jury understand.[73] The committee strongly recommended that pre-trial reviews are viewed as preparatory hearings and are to be treated as the trial process itself. In a preparatory hearing both defence and prosecution would be required to disclose the outlines of their cases in advance. The committee made the point that this should 'assist comprehension, and should inhibit the development of irrelevant lines of arguments in the hope of causing maximum obfuscation and uncertainty over guilt'.[74] In addition, the report suggested that attendance by counsel at preparatory hearings should be an obligation unless there are clearly defined and 'compelling' reasons to the contrary.[75]

The most significant suggestion the Roskill Committee made was the 'formation of a single, unified organisation responsible for all the functions of detection,

---

68   *ibid.*
69   Levi, *op. cit.* footnote 57 supra, p. 142.
70   *ibid.*
71   *Report of the Committee on Fraud Trials*; cited in Levi, *op. cit.* footnote 57 supra, p. 142.
72   *ibid.*
73   Fleming, *op. cit.* footnote 62 supra, p. 220.
74   Levi, *op. cit.* footnote 57 supra, p. 143.
75   *ibid.*

investigation and prosecution of serious fraud'.[76] The advantages of such an organisation include:

- fewer serious and complex frauds escaping prosecution;
- investigations leading to more effective prosecutions;
- greater efficiency and reduction in delays;
- less overlapping of resources;
- the removal of restrictions on the disclosure of information between departments; and
- full powers of investigation.[77]

The Serious Fraud Office (SFO) was created by section 1 of the *Criminal Justice Act 1987* and came into operation in April 1988.

The Serious Fraud Office

The Serious Fraud Office[78] differs substantially from the model recommended by the Roskill Committee. First, the SFO is required to investigate and prosecute fraud but not, as the report suggested, to detect fraud. Detection was dropped from its ambit and left to the Department of Trade and Industry, the police, the regulatory bodies, the public, the media and other interested parties. Second, Roskill envisaged an umbrella organisation tackling all serious and complex fraud in the United Kingdom. Removing work from other government departments in that area, however, was not politically practicable. Widlake states:

> Whitehall departments instinctively oppose any diminution in their powers and fight vigorously to retain them. There was never any likelihood that the SFO would take over the investigation and prosecution roles of the Inland Revenue, Customs and Excise or the Department of Trade and Industry.[79]

Despite these exceptions, the SFO is committed to tackling serious and complex fraud. It is a separate government department having jurisdiction in England, Wales and Northern Ireland. Furthermore, it is responsible for all the functions of investigation and prosecution of serious or complex fraud offences. This authority is provided by the *Criminal Justice Act of 1987* which specifies it to be 'an Act to make further provisions for the investigation of and trials for fraud; and for connected purposes'.

---

76 Widlake, *op.cit.* footnote 56 supra, p. 30.
77 *ibid.,* p. 30.
78 The Serious Fraud Office is responsible only to the Attorney-General. It does not refer to the Director of Public Prosecutions, who conducts all investigations through the Fraud Investigation Group (which is part of the Crown Prosecution Service). The Serious Fraud Office supplements the Fraud Investigation Group, which continues to handle between 700 and 800 cases of less serious fraud at any one time: Fleming, *op. cit.* footnote 62 supra, p. 216.
79 Widlake, *op. cit.* footnote 56 supra, pp. 41–2.

For the SFO to assume responsibility for an investigation there must be some significant matter in relation to the alleged offence that categorises the fraud as either serious or complex or both. In deciding whether to accept fraud cases, the SFO has regard to three major factors:

- the facts and/or the law are of great complexity;
- the sums of money at risk are substantial;[80] and
- there is great public interest and concern.[81]

In general terms, an investigation by the SFO is carried out in the same manner as an investigation by any other authority. However, there are two significant features which distinguish the SFO. These are the multidisciplinary approach to the investigation and prosecution of serious fraud—which is central to its operation—and the use of the special powers in the Criminal Justice Act. Together they provide for efficient and successful investigation into the complexities of serious fraud offences.

The powers given to the SFO are requisite and effective investigatory tools. Serious or complex fraud involves an intricate web of financial transactions known only to the perpetrator. The Roskill Committee recognised that:

> There is a paramount need for those charged with investigation of fraud to be able to move swiftly from the first moment that there is suspicion of fraud … it is time wasting and administratively unsatisfactory for one body to have to seek the assistance of another.[82]

Consequently, Parliament saw fit to implement tough investigatory powers to combat the complex transactions of fraudsters.

The most significant power is given by section 2 of the Act which enables the director (and any person designated by the director) by written notice to any person, to require any person under investigation, or any other person who may have relevant information, to answer questions and furnish information relevant to the investigation.[83] A written notice may also be served requiring the production of documents. The SFO can take copies or extracts and explanations may be sought.[84] It is an offence to refuse or fail to comply with a notice or to do so in a false or misleading way.

There are exceptions to the section 2 provisions. First, a person cannot be required to produce documents which are legally privileged between himself and his solicitor in regard to High Court proceedings. Second, a person is not required to furnish documents or information of a 'banking nature' unless permission is obtained from the person to whom the obligation of confidentiality is owed or, unless the director, the

---

80   At the time of its inception this was deemed to be £1 million. This was however quickly outdated by the rapid growth in the size of serious fraud cases. It was increased in May 1992 to £5 million.
81   Fleming, *op. cit.* footnote 62 supra, p. 218.
82   Fraud Trials Committee Report (1986) HMSO; cited in Fleming, *op.cit.* footnote 62 supra, p. 217.
83   s. 2(2).
84   s. 2(3).

deputy director or the chief accountant of the SFO specifically authorise 'the bank' to provide such information.[85]

The powers for compulsory interview and production of documents effectively abrogate the common law right of a citizen to refuse to answer questions from anyone, thereby breaking the right to silence and the allied privilege against self-incrimination. However, a safeguard is provided in the Act. Self-incriminating statements are not admissible as evidence against the accused in a prosecution for an offence, except where the person gives evidence which is not consistent with his section 2 statement. In such circumstances the section 2 evidence becomes admissible.[86]

A series of high profile failures

Barlow Clowes[87]

Barlow Clowes was the ultimate 1980s financial scam. The Barlow Clowes group consisted of a number of companies all owned or controlled by Peter Clowes. The major companies included the UK partnership, which carried out investment management of gilt-edged securities until mid 1986, the UK company Barlow Clowes Gilt Management Ltd, which carried out similar work after that date, and the offshore partnership Barlow Clowes International, based originally in Jersey, then Geneva and later in Gibraltar.

The Barlow Clowes investment group professed to offer a secure investment with capital growth or an income plus the guarantee of the return of the investment on demand. Using newspaper advertisements promising miraculous returns from British government securities ('gilts'), the investment group robbed investors of £150 million. The scam involved using 'new' investment money to pay 'returns' on existing customers' investments, which had gone offshore and were used for the benefit of Peter Clowes. Typically, investors' money would be diverted through an elaborate network of offshore entities controlled by Clowes. The 'disbursement of client funds was deliberately complicated, with multiple transactions involving payments passing through a number of different bank accounts in the names of different entities and often in different countries.'[88]

Clowes owed much of his continued existence and success to the incompetence, omission and inertia of the authorities.[89] They stood him in good stead for a number of

85   Fleming, *op.cit.* footnote 62 supra, pp. 217–18.
86   *ibid.*
87   The following discussion is based on the information contained in: Widlake, *op. cit.* footnote 56 supra, p. 93; B. Singleton-Green, 'If Its Not Plausible, Don't Accept It', *Accountancy*, August 1995, p. 25; Anonymous, 'Three Expelled Over Barlow Clowes', *Accountancy*, May 1995, p. 13; A. Verity, '18,500 Investors Lost £190m', *Money Marketing*, 29 February 1996, p. 5.
88   Fleming, *op. cit.* footnote 62 supra, p. 222.
89   Widlake, *op. cit.* footnote 56 supra, p. 102.

years. Even when a liquidator acting for the Stock Exchange was appointed to Hedder-wick Stirling and Gunbar,[90] and discovered that the firm was running a gilts gambling syndicate of which Clowes was a part, the authorities turned a blind eye. The liquidator also noticed that Clowes was trading illegally without a licence, and thus reported the firm to the Department of Trade and Industry's licensing unit. The department left much to be desired in terms of competence and failed to follow up the 'discoveries' passed to it by the liquidator for the Stock Exchange. It was not until late 1987 that the Department of Trade and Industry appointed inspectors to look at the UK entity. The department found sufficient procedural and control problems with the company to notify the Securities and Investments Board, which successfully petitioned for the winding up of Barlow Clowes Gilt Management Ltd.

When Barlow Clowes International collapsed in 1988, it had liabilities of £115 mil-lion, and only £1.9 million in gilts. It was estimated that a further £23 million was in rolled up interest. The rest of the money had been stolen and used by Peter Clowes, his family, and a number of close associates. The money had been spent on other compa-nies, consumer luxuries such as cars, houses and yachts, and 'on making payments to the UK Barlow Clowes business to make it appear falsely profitable when merged with a public limited company'.[91]

The scenario was perfect for the SFO. Approximately £140 million had gone miss-ing and, as Widlake pointed out:

> Clowes was no City Slicker, with a public school background and respectable parents in
> the Home Counties, but an out-and-out crook, fat, short and unattractive, who ate,
> dreamed and slept other people's money and spent it like water. Clowes was one of
> those operators who didn't need to be charged with anything: he looked like a walking
> indictment for fraud and should have been locked up on sight.[92]

Four individuals were charged and prosecuted. The trial took 112 days and heard 113 witnesses, and the SFO only managed to secure the conviction of two of the four accused.[93] For years Clowes had been stealing his clients' money, lying successfully to the authorities and spending lavishingly on a lifestyle designed to impress people and enhance his prestige.[94] As a result, he faced twenty charges of theft and falsely promising to invest in government securities. Clowes was convicted and sentenced to ten years in jail.[95] Peter Naylor, Clowes' business associate, who received eighteen months, 'claimed

---

90 Hedderwick Stirling and Gunbar were well known gilt dealers acting on Clowes' instructions. As Clowes was not a member of the Stock Exchange, he used the firm to invest money in gilts on his behalf. Hed-derwicks was placed in liquidation in April 1981.
91 Fleming, *op. cit.* footnote 62 supra, p. 222.
92 Widlake, *op. cit.* footnote 56 supra, p. 93.
93 Anonymous, 'Fraud: Marginal Returns', *Economist*, 15 February 1992, p. 90.
94 Widlake, *op. cit.* footnote 56 supra, p. 106.
95 It should be noted that Clowes served only four years of his ten-year sentence. In early 1996, Clowes was freed on parole.

that he believed that he had been transferring Clowes' own money; that his purchase of a home was a bonus he had earned; and that a large amount drawn from a client's account was an agreed loan rather than theft'.[96] Guy von Cramer, a key figurehead in the Buckley Brewery takeover, was acquitted. Christopher Newman, the financial director at Barlow, was a heavy drinker, and produced the defence that he was intoxicated during the three years that he was with the firm and was thus not responsible for what went on around him. He too was acquitted.

The Barlow Clowes fraud was achieved because the facts were skilfully concealed over a considerable period of time; auditors, solicitors, merchant bankers and other advisers were deliberately misled as to the true state of affairs; and at the least, there was acquiescence if not collusion on the part of a number of directors and employees, without which the underlying frauds would not have remained undetected for so long. In addition, all evidence relating to the offshore operations of Barlow Clowes was concealed from the Department of Industry and Trade inspectors investigating Barlow Clowes Gilt Management Ltd. However, allowing Barlow Clowes to continue trading after the department was continuously warned of its activities was negligent, and hence the government reimbursed investors.

Blue Arrow[97]

To date the Blue Arrow scandal is one of the worst failures of the SFO. The investigation and prosecution of County NatWest Bank for its role in the takeover of an American employment company cost British taxpayers an estimated £40 million for the four advisers who were initially found guilty but had their convictions quashed on appeal. It was the most complex of cases, dealing with market manipulation, disclosure rules and share ramping.

In mid 1987, Blue Arrow, a British employment agency, decided to take over Manpower, the world's largest temporary employment agency. County NatWest, the merchant bank which advised Blue Arrow, agreed to provide £837 million to buy out the Manpower shareholdings. Blue Arrow would finance the takeover by a rights issue of new shares to existing shareholders. The £837 million issue was Britain's largest non-bank rights issue at that time. The issue, however, was unsuccessful. Blue Arrow shareholders had taken up their rights to only 38 per cent of the shares on offer. If County NatWest were to require sub-underwriters to take the remainder, the issue would have been seen for the failure it was and the share price would fall.

96   Fleming, *op. cit.* footnote 62 supra, p. 222.
97   For a general discussion on Blue Arrow see the following: Widlake, *op. cit.* footnote 56 supra, p. 194; Anonymous, 'Blue Arrow: Everyone's a Loser', *Economist*, 22 February 1992, p. 70; Anonymous, 'The Blue Arrow Affair: The Buck Stops Where?', *Economist*, 7 March 1992, p. 23; Anonymous, 'Where Will the Blue Arrow Land?', *Institutional Investor* (International Edition), February 1989, p. 122; Anonymous, 'The City after County', *Economist*, 29 July 1989, p. 17.

A scheme was hatched to mislead the market into thinking that the rights issue had been a success. It was announced that 49 per cent of the issue had been taken up and the remainder sold in a placing. In fact, the adviser—County NatWest, Phillips and Drew (the broker on the deal) and Dillon Read (Blue Arrow's American advisers)—purchased the shares. County NatWest took onto its books 4.9 per cent of Blue Arrow and its market-making subsidiary, County NatWest Securities, another 4.6 per cent, and was protected by an indemnity offered by County NatWest that would cover any fall in the value of shares. Similarly, County NatWest gave an oral indemnity to its market-maker. As a result, County NatWest had a 13.5 per cent interest in Blue Arrow worth £150 million.

The Companies Act required that any stake of more than 5 per cent (currently 3 per cent) be disclosed. County NatWest argued that as a whole it was under no legal obligation to abide by the Companies Act requirement that investors disclose any stake of 5 per cent or more in a British company. It based its argument on two beliefs. First, that it did not own the 4 per cent held by Union Bank of Switzerland. Second, that section 209 of the Act exempts market-makers from the disclosure requirements assuming any shares are acquired 'in the normal course of business'. County NatWest Securities, however, felt under pressure in order to avoid a disaster to purchase the shares and had kept them on a 'back book' that its traders did not know about. The shares were not held by County NatWest Securities for the purposes of its market-making business.

At the end of 1998, Department of Industry and Trade inspectors were appointed to conduct an inquiry into the affairs of Blue Arrow. The inspectors determined that by concealing the true take-up rate and buying shares after the closure of the rights issue, County NatWest and its associates intentionally misled the markets. The inspectors concluded:

> The events referred to in this report give rise to concern. The market was misled. Provisions of the Companies Act 1985 were not complied with. There was no justification for what happened ... In its written submission, the NWB [National Westminster Bank] group informed us that all possible steps were being taken to ensure that all investment banking activities within the NWB group would be carried out to high standards of integrity and priority. The matters referred to in this report disclose a highly unsatisfactory state of affairs.[98]

Their report was passed to the SFO, whose central argument was 'that there was a unified conspiracy between the accused to rig the market to create a situation which enabled the market to trade in the shares in Blue Arrow in ignorance of those steps that had been taken to enable the rights issues to be completed and to enable the market to believe that there were voluntary takers for the shares at the rights issue price or above'.[99]

98   Wldlake, *op. cit.* footnote 56 supra, p. 214.
99   Fleming *op. cit.* footnote 62 supra, p. 223.

The defendants were charged with conspiring together to fraudulently induce other persons to enter into agreements for acquiring securities, namely shares in Blue Arrow. The second charge was that the defendants conspired together to defraud the other person who had or might have had an interest in dealing in shares in Blue Arrow, National Westminster Bank, or in dealing on the Financial Times Stock Exchange 100 Shares Index.[100]

The jury found the four defendants guilty. Their convictions, however, were quashed on appeal. Justice McKinnon made it clear that the length and complexity of the trial placed considerable strain on all involved. His Lordship also made clear that the prosecution deserved the majority of the blame. The prosecution spun its case out in elaborate detail calling approximately one hundred witnesses. His Lordship pointed out that the prosecution might have done better to concentrate on essential issues of market manipulation and lack of disclosure. The long, expensive and unsuccessful Blue Arrow trial indicated that the SFO's approach to prosecution of corporate fraud left a lot to be desired.

Polly Peck International[101]

Polly Peck International was a 1980s success story. The company owned hotels, a large fruit and packaging business, and a Japanese electronics company, and for 'many years had been a stock market darling'.[102] Polly Peck was the 'hot' stock of the 1980s; £1000 invested in the issue in 1980 would have become £1 million by the end of the decade. At the end of 1990, however, Polly Peck experienced a collapse as dramatic as its rise. The company collapsed owing debts totalling £1.4 billion. Asil Nadir, the former chairman and chief executive, faces thirteen charges of false accounting and theft. The prosecution alleges that transfers totalling £383 million were made from the bank accounts of Polly Peck International and from accounts held by its wholly owned subsidiary, Unipac. The funds were moved to a variety of locations for the benefit of Naidir, his family and associates.

Trouble for Polly Peck commenced in 1990, when there were a number of 'bear' raids on Polly Peck shares in July and August initiated, as Nadir believes, by the Greeks. As Widlake states,'Byzantine plots and dark intrigues have always been a part of the Nadir ethos'.[103] Added to that, news slipped out that Polly Peck and Nadir were being

---

100   Widlake, *op. cit.* footnote 56 supra, p. 216.
101   Refer to the following information for the discussion on Polly Peck International: Widlake, *op. cit.* footnote 56 supra, p. 112; T. Hindle, 'Free, Fit and Fighting: Polly Peck International PLC owner Asil Nadir' (1994) 1 (10) *Eurobusiness* 18; J. Brown, 'On the Run with Asil Nadir', *Institutional Investor* (International Edition), October 1993, p. 67; Anonymous, 'Don't let it get you down', *Accountancy*, December 1994, p. 10; Anonymous, 'Polly Peck International: Whose Nadir?', *Economist*, 12 November 1994, p. 100; Anonymous, 'Nadir Plans Comeback to the UK', *Independent*, 14 January 1996 (available on http://www.krivinskas.u-net.com/6.htm); Robert Verkaik, 'Nadir Lawyer Calls for Inquiry', *Times*, 20 October 1995 (available on <http://www.krivinskas.u-net.com/5.htm>).
102   Widlake, *op. cit.* at 114.
103   *ibid.*, p. 118.

investigated by the Inland Revenue in relation to offshore dealings in Polly Peck shares. The Inland Revenue were convinced that Nadir was using offshore companies for dealing in Polly Peck shares and not declaring his taxable profits. Thus, Nadir instigated a management buy-out only to withdraw the plan a few days later knowing it would seriously damage his credibility and harm the company. As a result, Polly Peck International shares crashed.

The stock exchange commenced an inquiry into Polly Peck International. The report criticised Nadir for his timing and lack of preparation. The board was criticised for allowing the buy-out disclosure to go ahead, despite the fact that the directors had been urged to do so by their advisers. Nadir was also criticised for convening a board meeting at only twenty-four hours' notice. The stock exchange made clear that it was passing the report to the Department of Industry and Trade and the SFO.[104]

The stock exchange report led the SFO to believe that Nadir's private investment company, South Audley Management, was being used as a share support operation for his Polly Peck business empire. After further investigation into Polly Peck, the SFO brought fraud and theft charges against Nadir totalling £30 million. However, in early 1993 Nadir jumped bail and fled to the Turkish Republic of Cyprus, which is not recognised by the international community and has no extradition treaties with the United Kingdom. Nadir's consultant and tax adviser, Elisabeth Forsyth, also moved to Cyprus. Forsyth, however, voluntarily returned to the United Kingdom to face charges of handling stolen funds worth nearly £400 000. In early 1995, Forsyth had her conviction quashed. In light of the quashing of the Forsyth conviction, Nadir is gathering evidence to prove that he was the victim of a complicated plot to pervert the course of British justice. Nadir is preparing an application to have the charges against him dropped alleging abuse of process by the SFO.

The Maxwell affair[105]

Shortly after the mysterious demise of British media tycoon Robert Maxwell in November 1991, the Maxwell group of companies collapsed. Investigations revealed that approximately £420 million had been misappropriated from the pension funds of two of his public companies, Mirror Group Newspapers and Maxwell Communications Corporation. Six individuals involved with the Maxwell empire were prosecuted by the SFO and acquitted.

There were three parts to Robert Maxwell's empire: Mirror Group Newspapers; Maxwell Communications Corporation; and some 400 private companies based in Liechtenstein, all owned or controlled by Maxwell. The pension funds, many of which were held in a common investment fund, were managed by Bishopsgate Investment Management, a subsidiary of the Maxwell Charitable Trust, which was controlled by

104 *ibid.*, p. 221.
105 The following discussion is based on the information contained in: Widlake, *op. cit.* footnote 56 supra, p. 221; Anonymous, 'The Maxwell Affair: Trying Times', *Economist*, 27 January 1996, p. 65; G. Vinten, 'The Maxwell Interview' (1993) 8 *Managerial Auditing Journal* 22.

Maxwell himself. Maxwell was obviously faced with a conflict of interest. He was effectively trustee and investment manager. It was, however, in his capacity as trustee that Maxwell took control of investment funds and dealt with them in fundamental breach of his duties. The pension funds were used to bail out Maxwell's private companies, knowing the private companies were unlikely to repay the funds.

In 1993 the SFO laid charges against six individuals. Kevin Maxwell, former chief executive of Maxwell Communications Corporation, faced two charges of conspiracy. The first alleged that he conspired with his father to defraud Maxwell pensioners of £100 million over dealings with Scitex Corporation, an Israeli computer imaging company. The second alleged that he, his brother Ian (former chief executive of Mirror Group Newspapers), Larry Trachtenburg and Robert Bunn conspired to defraud pensioners in dealings related to shares worth £122 million in Teva Pharmaceutical Industries, another Israeli firm. The other accused were Michael Stoney, former treasurer of Mirror Group Newspapers and Albert Fuller, the former Maxwell Communications Corporation treasurer. Both were charged with conspiracy to defraud and false accounting. The defendants strenuously denied the charges.

The trial lasted eight months and in spite of the best efforts by the SFO, the jury acquitted the defendants after eleven days of deliberation. Once again, the SFO failed to secure a high profile conviction. Once again, the cost of prosecuting a high profile fraud case had been astronomical. The Maxwell trial was, without doubt, a bitter blow.

The tide turns

The BCCI frauds[106]

The collapse of the Bank of Credit and Commercial Investments (BCCI) involved the world's biggest fraud and investigations by fraud squads and regulatory authorities round the world.

The SFO was involved in the prosecution of Syed Akbar for false accounting, Mohammed Baqi and Nazmudin Virani for conspiring to furnish false audit information slips to the auditors, Imran Iman for overcharging management fees and concealing guarantees, Abdul Chiragh for dishonestly providing information to the auditors, and Abbas Gokal for conspiring to defraud.

The SFO was successful in all these cases. In all of them there was a single defendant in each case and the evidence cut down to a minimum necessary for a jury to understand the case.[107] These successes greatly improved the SFO's reputation.

The latest score[108]

The conviction rate in cases brought by the SFO remained fairly constant for the first four years, fluctuating between 62 per cent and 75 per cent. In mid 1992 this deterio-

106 See Killick, *op. cit.* footnote 56 supra, ch. 10.
107 *ibid.*, p. 208 referring to comments by Chris Dickson, formerly of the SFO.
108 See Killick, *op. cit.* footnote 56 supra, p. 237 *et seq.* on which this relies.

rated to just over 50 per cent and was reflected in negative reporting of the performance in the small number of high profile cases.

There was a recovery in mid 1994 and the success has continued. However, since the SFO prosecutes so few cases, statistical anomalies can easily arise.

The Graham and Davie Reports[109]

The Graham Report in March 1994 recommended consideration of establishing a new organisation combining the SFO and the handling of serious or complex cases by the Fraud Investigation Group of the Crown Prosecution Service. This was followed by the Davie Report which ruled out a merger of the two bodies and recommended an increase in the workload of the SFO. The Davie Report recommendations were accepted by the UK Parliament in 1995 and the SFO has undertaken a larger caseload.

Serious fraud in New Zealand[110]

New Zealand followed the UK model in 1990 by passing the *Serious Fraud Office Act*. This gave the director the most extensive powers that have ever been granted in the case of criminal investigation in New Zealand. If the director has reasonable grounds to believe that an offence involving serious or complex fraud has been committed, he has power to demand that any other person under investigation or any other person believed to possess the information, appear before him to answer questions, supply information or produce documents (sections 9 and 5).

While lawyers can still claim client privilege, this is strictly defined and excludes communication involving furtherance of a fraud (section 24(3)). The SFO can take over investigations from the police and where necessary obtain search warrants and use reasonable force to enter property to execute such warrants (sections 6 and 10).

Any decision made by the director to investigate or prosecute cannot be challenged in court (section 20). If any challenge is made, the power can continue to be exercised until a final decision is given (section 21 as explained by Justice Thomas in *Hawkins v. Sturt* (1990) 5 NZCLC 66,606 at 66,610). Refusal to answer questions or providing false information is a criminal offence and overrides the right to silence.

The SFO was set up with Charles Sturt as director and Judge Dennis Pain as deputy. It aimed at establishing a multidisciplinary unit made up of lawyers, accountants and investigators but was handicapped by tight budgetary restraints. Its major work involved the successful prosecution arising out of the collapse of the Equiticorp group.[111] The SFO was also involved in investigation of the mysterious 'H' fee paid by Elders and investigated by the NCA.[112]

---

109 Killick, *op. cit.* footnote 56 supra, ch. 11.
110 See C. Sturt, *Dirty Collars*, Reed Books, Auckland, 1998; Serious Fraud Office, Annual Reports.
111 Sturt *op. cit.*, ch. 7.
112 Sturt *op. cit.*, ch. 8.

In addition to the Equiticorp case, the SFO had to handle a number of high profile cases and was the subject of unjustified attacks by prominent members of Parliament under the protection of absolute privilege. One series of attacks centred around the so-called Wine Box allegations which led to a long inquiry by Sir Ronald Davison which exonerated the SFO and its director.[113] There was also some degree of infighting among the staff. Sturt, the victim of overwork and vicious personal attacks, eventually resigned due to ill health. His account of his experiences at the hand of the politicians in *Dirty Collars* makes sobering reading.

After Sturt resigned Judge Ron Jamieson was acting director until the appointment of D. J. Bradshaw, an experienced government lawyer. One now has the impression of a quieter, more settled time.

Something which is noticeable from the Annual Reports is that the SFO is given precise performance targets such as 'to present properly prepared and well researched prosecution cases, achieving a minimum of 85 per cent successful prosecution' and 'to achieve at least an 80 per cent Senior Counsel satisfaction rating for the quality of the case investigation, and preparation and prosecution'. The results seem successful although one has the impression that the number of serious fraud cases in New Zealand is now relatively small.

There is useful information about the SFO's policy of acceptance of cases, referral of cases, and handling of cases, in the Report for the year ended 30 June 1998, pp. 45–47. Detailed statistics of the cases are given in the Annual Reports.

Conclusion

The term 'white collar crime' comprehends fraud, embezzlement, price fixing, insider trading and many more offences. It is often committed by educated persons of above average wealth and standing. Generally, the crime is non-violent and involves the manipulation of the corporate and financial sectors. In many cases the crime can be quite deliberate, or it can arise from recklessness, negligence or inattention to detail.

Throughout the years, white collar crimes have increased in number and size. As a result, it was necessary for governments to step in and take action. In 1983, the British government appointed the Roskill Committee to look at the problem. One of its recommendations was for the introduction of a unified organisation which was to be responsible for the investigation and prosecution of fraud. The result was the Serious Fraud Office.

The establishment of the office indicated the government's commitment to fight corporate crime. The office was given special powers of investigation to aid it in its fight against corporate offenders. Despite these powers, the office lost some very important headline cases: Blue Arrow, Barlow Clowes, Maxwell and Polly Peck International. The

113 *op. cit.*, ch. 14–18.

tide began to turn with the BCCI prosecutions. The SFO has an important role to play in investigating and prosecuting corporate offenders. As the only office specifically established to fight corporate crime, it has the capacity, resources and expertise to undertake investigations and instigate prosecutions against serious fraud offenders.

New Zealand followed the UK model and set up an SFO, which has been reasonably successful but was the subject of attack by unscrupulous politicians under the protection of absolute privilege. It has now entered into a more settled period.

In Australia, like the United Kingdom, the 1980s saw an upsurge in white-collar crime offences. Corporate high flyers such as Bond, Connell and Yuill cost the Australian economy during this period approximately $13 billion a year for their involvement in illegal and unethical behaviour.

The Australian Securities and Investments Commission and the National Crime Authority are the primary investigative bodies in relation to complex criminal matters involving serious fraud. Their preferences in enforcement and prosecution differ in that ASIC favours persuasion and the use of civil litigation while the NCA prefers taking criminal action but has recently narrowed its focus. Perhaps because of these differing approaches, the commission and the authority have failed to play an important role in combating corporate crime.[114] Their most spectacular failures have been in the Elders prosecutions and the investigations of Bond and Coles Myer. Moreover, neither organisation has the resources and expertise to tackle white collar crime effectively. No doubt, clarification and refinement with regard to the role the two organisations play will continue, and we may eventually see a Serious Fraud Office in Australia. The relationship between the Commonwealth DPP and ASIC was problematic at the start but has gradually settled down. However, one is left with the impression that Australia has too many bodies involved in the process of handling serious fraud cases.

---

114 See Ferguson, *op. cit.* footnote 21 supra, for strong and at times unfair criticism.

THE SELF-REGULATION PENUMBRA AND OTHER CONTEMPORARY ISSUES IN CORPORATE GOVERNANCE

CHAPTER 24

Key Relationships

Chairperson, managing director/CEO, company secretary and the board

In Part 2 we have dealt with the legal core of corporate governance. The law only provides a basic framework of procedure and accountability. Good corporate governance goes beyond this. The success of any company depends on good working relationships and certain relationships are the key to this success.

The chairperson is a director whom the board of directors elect to chair their meetings and sign the minutes of meetings. This person will usually also chair meetings of members.

The managing director, alternatively known as the chief executive officer or CEO, is the person in charge of the day-to-day management of the company. This person has such powers and authority as the board delegates to them.

There may be other executive directors on the board but the modern tendency in Australian and New Zealand listed companies is to reduce the number of them.[1] The other members of the board are non-executive directors. Some of these can be regarded as independent directors. We examine the precise meaning of these terms in Chapter 27.

The company secretary serves the board in an administrative capacity and is not a member of it. The chairperson relies on the secretary for servicing the board and the successful board has a good working relationship between the chair, and CEO and the company secretary.

---

1 See Korn/Ferry International, *Boards of Directors in Australia and New Zealand 2000*, Korn/Ferry International, Sydney, 2000.

The role of the chairperson and the CEO

Strictly speaking, the chairperson is chair of the board, not chair of the company. The law only recognises the role in relation to meetings but this is a misleading view of the modern role of public company directors in fact. The office is becoming of greater importance in the development of good corporate governance.

The legal powers and obligations of the chair in respect of board meetings and general meetings have been discussed in Chapter 7 and we have discussed delegation by the board to a managing director in Chapter 8. Otherwise, what particular authority the chairperson and CEO have, depends on the constitution and delegation by the board. How they work together depends on modern conceptions of the respective roles and individual perceptions of them.[2]

Sir Adrian Cadbury in his book *The Company Chairman*[3] identified the modern role of the chairperson as ensuring the following:

• that the board provides leadership and vision;
• that the board has the right balance of membership;
• that the board sets the aims, strategy and policies of the company;
• that the board monitors the achievements of those aims;
• that the board reviews the resources of people in the company;
• that the board has the information it needs for it to be effective.

He identified the chair's external responsibilities as:

• reporting financial results
• corporate representative
• guardian of the corporate character and conduct
• arbiter of internal and external disputes.[4]

Cadbury stresses the important role of the chair in dealing with shareholders, especially institutional investors, and the media.

Henry Bosch in his useful Australian book *Conversations Between Chairmen*[5] describes the role of the chairperson as making the board work effectively and acting as representative and spokesperson for the board.

He states that the most important part of the role is to manage the relationship with the CEO.[6] First, both must understand that their roles are different.[7] The chairper-

---

2   Consider the difficult relationship which developed in 1999–2000 in AMP Ltd.
3   Sir Adrian Cadbury, *The Company Chairman*, 2nd edn, Director Books, Hemel Hempstead, 1995, p. 16.
4   *ibid.*, pp. 18 *et seq.*
5   H. Bosch, *Conversations Between Chairmen*, AICD, Sydney, 1999. See also Institute of Directors in New Zealand Inc., Best Practice Statements 1997/6 Duties of the Chairman Best Practice for New Zealand Directors; and H. Parker, *Letters to a New Chairman*, Director Publications, London, 1979. Reprinted 1990.
6   Bosch, *op. cit.*, conversation 4.
7   *ibid.*, p. 26.

son manages the board and the CEO manages the company, under the authority delegated by the board.[8]

Second, the CEO reports to the board, not simply to the chairperson.[9]

Third, the CEO position is lonely and exposed and this necessitates a close working relationship between the chairperson and the CEO. The chairperson should seek to maintain the relationship between the board and the CEO.[10]

Fourth, in spite of questions of personal loyalty, the chairperson's ultimate responsibility is to the board and the company.[11]

Corporate Practices and Conduct,[12] the *IFSA Guidelines,*[13] and the New Zealand *Best Practice Statement,*[14] following the UK Cadbury Report, recommend the separation of the chair from the chief executive position. Where this is not done there is a need for a strong independent element on the board with a lead director. Ideally the separate chair should be filled by a non-executive director.

The chairperson and the company secretary[15]

Originally the company secretary was a mere clerk or servant with no authority to bind the company.[16] However, times have changed. Now the company secretary has clear legal and administrative responsibilities and often carries out routine management functions.[17] The ever increasing volume of legislation affecting companies requires constant attention, although New Zealand, with mistaken enthusiasm for gratuitous reform, abolished the office in 1993. However, it is still possible for companies to retain them.

Company secretaries are often the first port of call for advice by the chairperson and the board.[18]

The chairperson usually relies on the company secretary to consider the items on the agenda and any relevant precedents and policies.[19]

They also need to consult over the minutes of meetings and the implementation of decisions.[20]

---

8   ibid., pp. 26 et seq.
9   ibid., p. 26.
10   ibid.
11   ibid., p. 27.
12   *Corporate Practices and Conduct*, 3rd edn, H. Bosch (ed.), F T Pitman Publishing, Melbourne, 1995. See pp. 15 et seq.
13   See appendix.
14   See footnote 5 supra.
15   Bosch, op. cit., conversation 5.
16   *Barnett, Hoares & Co. v. The South London Tramways Co* (1887) 18 QBD 815, 817 per Lord Esher MR. See also *George Whitechurch Ltd v. Cavanagh* [1902] AC 117, 124; *Ruben v. Great Fingall Consolidated* [1906] AC 439.
17   *Panorama Developments (Guildford) Ltd v. Fidelis Furnishing Fabrics Ltd* [1971] 2 QB 771 at 716 G-H-717A per Lord Denning MR
18   Bosch, op. cit., p. 32.
19   ibid.
20   ibid.

The company secretary is responsible for board papers and ensuring that they reach members in time. He or she also arranges the logistics of telephone, fax, and video conferencing of meetings.[21]

The company secretary's responsibility is ultimately to the board as a whole. Obviously this presents particular problems when there are splits on the board. The company secretary needs to be able to provide information and assistance to each member of the board.[22]

Sir Adrian Cadbury[23] in his book on chairmanship quoted Ralph Vaughan Williams, the composer, on the role of conductor of an orchestra:

> All their art and all their skill are valueless without that corporate imagination which distinguishes the orchestra from a fortuitous collection of players.

It is essential for the chairperson, in cooperation with the CEO and assisted by the company secretary, to achieve the imagination and corporate spirit that characterise the best kind of corporate enterprise. This includes but goes beyond accountability.

---

21   *ibid.*, p. 34.
22   *ibid.*, p. 35.
23   Cadbury, *op. cit.* footnote 3 supra, p. 208.

CHAPTER 25

Determining the Appropriate Roles of the Board and Management

We saw in Chapter 8 how the modern legal definition of the role of the board is to manage or direct or supervise the management of the company. This still leaves the matter somewhat up in the air and it is desirable for the working relationship to be more closely defined in practice. The main ways in which this can be done are in relation to responsibilities for what is currently called conformance, or compliance with regulations, and for performance.

AWA

In *AWA Ltd v. Daniels*[1] Justice Rogers at first instance had this to say on the topic:

> [M]any companies today are too big to be supervised and administered by the board of directors except in relation to matters of high policy. The true oversight of the activities of such companies resides with the corporate bureaucracy. Senior management and, in the case of mammoth corporations, even persons lower down the corporate ladder, exercise substantial control over the activities of such corporations involving important decisions and much money. It is something of an anachronism to expect non-executive directors, meeting once a month, to contribute anything much more than decisions on questions of policy and, in the case of really large corporations, only major policy. This necessarily means that, in the execution of policy, senior management is, in the true sense of the word, exercising the powers of decision and of management which in less complex days used to be reserved for the board of directors.

---

1   (1992) 10 ACLC 993, 998. See too *Accountability*, a paper prepared by the Corporate Governance Committee of the Australian Institute of Company Directors, August, 1993. See also P. F. Kocourek, *Measuring Board Performance*, AICD, Sydney, 1993.

This was criticised on appeal by the majority of the New South Wales Court of Appeal.[2] Unfortunately their honours did not greatly elucidate the matter. We have already dealt with their judgment in Chapter 13 and contrasted it with the position under US laws. As Henry Bosch has indicated, what we do not need are boards that meddle in matters better left to management, while neglecting the important things that the directors alone can do.[3]

Current thinking

Corporate practices and conduct

The Bosch committee in *Corporate Practices and Conduct*[4] thought that the division of responsibilities, terms of reference, and delegations to management, should be put in writing and reviewed periodically, probably annually. The IFSA Guidelines agreed.

According to *Corporate Practices and Conduct* in most cases the board's functions would include:

- taking steps to protect the company's financial position and its ability to meet its debts and other obligations as they fall due
- adopting a strategic plan for the company, including general and specific goals and comparing actual results with the plan
- adopting an annual budget for the financial performance of the company and monitoring results on a regular basis
- adopting clearly defined delegations of authority from the board to the CEO or a statement of matters reserved for decision by the board
- agreeing on performance indicators with management
- ensuring that systems are in place that facilitate the effective monitoring and management of the principal risks to which the company is exposed
- determining that the company has instituted adequate reporting systems and internal controls (both operational and financial) together with appropriate monitoring of compliance activities
- establishing and monitoring policies directed to ensuring that the company complies with the law and conforms with the highest standards of financial and ethical behaviour
- determining that the company accounts are in conformity with Australian Accounting Standards and are true and fair
- determining that satisfactory arrangements are in place for auditing the company's financial affairs and that the scope of the external audit is adequate
- selecting and recommending auditors to shareholders at general meetings

---

2   *Daniels v. Anderson* (1995) 13 ACLC 614.
3   See H. Bosch, *Conversations with a New Director*, AICD, Sydney, 1997, p. 16.
4   H. Bosch (ed.), *Corporate Practices and Conduct*, 3rd edn, FT Pitman Publishing, Melbourne, 1995, pp. 8–9.

- selecting and, if necessary, replacing the chief executive, setting an appropriate remuneration package, ensuring adequate succession, and giving guidance on the appointment and remuneration of other senior management
- ensuring that the company has in place a policy that enables it to communicate effectively with its shareholders, other stakeholders and the public generally
- adopting formal processes for the selection of new directors and recommending them for the consideration of shareholders at general meetings with adequate information to allow shareholders to make informed decisions
- reviewing its own processes and effectiveness, and the balance of competence on the board.

This long list was influenced by overseas practice including the formulation in the American Law Institute's *Principles of Corporate Governance.*[5]

The UK reports

The UK reports on corporate governance surprisingly did not deal with the matter in much detail.

The Cadbury Report's Code of Best Practice[6] 1.4 said that the board should have a formal schedule of matters reserved to it for decision. The notes state that this should include acquisition and disposal of assets that are material to the company, investments, capital projects, authority levels, leasing policies and risk management policies. The Hampel Report[7] paragraph 3.11 thought that the prime responsibility was to determine the broad strategy of the company and to ensure its implementation. The Consultation Document from the Company Law Review Steering Committee, *Developing the Framework*, paragraph 3.10, March 2000, states boldly that the relationship between a company and its management is generally for the parties to define in the constitution, for contractual arrangement between company and directors and for developing practice in the markets.

Strictly Boardroom

Professors Hilmer and Tricker in *Strictly Boardroom* see the role of the board (see Figure 25.1)[8] as five-fold:[9]

1 appointing and rewarding the chief executive
2 ensuring accountability
3 strategic thinking

---

5   *Principles of Corporate Governance: Analysis and Recommendations,* American Law Institute, Philadelphia, 1992, para. 3.02.
6   A. Cadbury, *The Financial Aspects of Corporate Governance: A Report of the Committee on Corporate Governance,* Gee & Co., London, 1992.
7   R. Hampel, *Committee on Corporate Governance: Final Report,* Gee & Co., London, 1998.
8   F. G. Hilmer, *Strictly Boardroom,* 2nd edn, Information Australia, Melbourne, 1998, p. 31.
9   *ibid.,* p. 31.

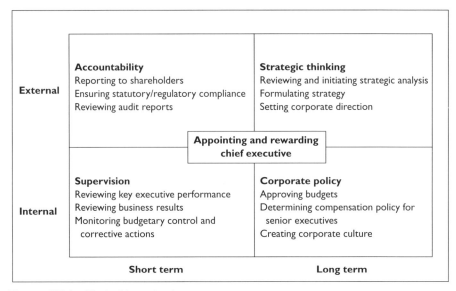

	Short term	**Long term**
External	**Accountability** Reporting to shareholders Ensuring statutory/regulatory compliance Reviewing audit reports	**Strategic thinking** Reviewing and initiating strategic analysis Formulating strategy Setting corporate direction
	Appointing and rewarding chief executive	
Internal	**Supervision** Reviewing key executive performance Reviewing business results Monitoring budgetary control and corrective actions	**Corporate policy** Approving budgets Determining compensation policy for senior executives Creating corporate culture

Figure 25.1 Typical board roles

4   supervision
5   corporate policy.

Future direction

In a useful work carried out for the Australian Institute of Company Directors, Dr Ivor Francis[10] set out the six important functions of the board of directors as follows:

1   to set policies in regard to purpose, partnerships and ethical behaviour
2   to manage the directors' agenda, appointment, accountabilities and communications
3   to determine strategic and tactical directions and alliances
4   to assume the capability of the company's operational and financial management functions
5   to constructively oversee the company's operating performance and improvement
6   to ensure corporate learning, renewal, evolution and succession.

In Figure 25.2 he analysed the above in more detail.

This is an analytical summary that is also very practical. It is significant that Dr Francis has been chairman of the Deming Centre International. The approach is similar to the Tasks of the Board and Indicators of Good Practice in the UK Institute of Directors' *Standards for the Board*.

---

10   I. Francis, *Future Direction—The Power of the Competitive Board*, FT Pitman Publishing, Melbourne, 1997, p. 78. See also his comparative table at pp. 74–5.

Set policies in regard to purpose, partnership, and ethical behaviour	Manage the directors' agenda, appointments, accountabilities, and communications	Determine strategic and tactical directions and alliances	Ensure the capability of the company's operational and financial management functions	Constructively oversee the company's operating performance and improvement	Ensure corporate learning, renewal, evolution and succession
Set broad parameters of the business: purpose, domain of the business, mission	Manage the board's agenda, meetings, information, access to management, support	Review and improve long-term and medium-term strategic directions	Secure an understanding of the company's system of creating value and key measure of peformance, conformance, and potential	Establish a disciplined regime for management to report financial and operational performance	Maintain a collective knowledge of trends in industry, competition, technology, the economy, social environment
Set policies in regard to the structure of the bus ness; for example, diversified, integrated alliances, suppliers, etc.	Appoint the CEO; establish accountabilities; review and reward	Approve financial and investment policies, debt, dividends, alliances, acquisitions, takeover defences	Maintain a relationship of understanding, trust, and support with management	Receive, verify and monitor results on the key measures of performance, conformance, and potential	Examine the company's structure, vitality, adaptability, intellectual assets, and potential; explore scenarios
Set policies in regard to culture, values, ethics, risk, environmental and safety; assure compliance	Ensure the development and succession of executive management	Approve strategic plans, medium-term tactical plans, and annual plans, and budgets	Assign accountabilities of directors, committees and auditors for assuring management functions	Support the CEO with advice and consent, in improving performance, conformance, and management systems	Strengthen and evolve the management organisation and director succession
	Oversee board communications and company secretarial functions		Ensure the capability of the financial reporting and control functions		
	Manage the appointment, education, and succession of directors; evaluate performance of board and directors		Ensure the capability of the management and of all essential operational management functions		

Figure 25.2 The six important functions of the board of directors

An important question is the relative responsibilities of the chairperson on behalf of the board and the chief executive officer. Bob Garratt in his book *The Fish Rots from the Head*[11] provides a simple sharing model in respect of accountability, policy formulation, supervising management and strategic thinking.

The Korn/Ferry International Survey of Boards of Directors in Australia and New Zealand 2000

The 2000 survey by Korn/Ferry International[12] listed the following as the objectives for directors:

* financial and operating performance
* long-term strategy
* responsibility to shareholders
* responsibility to external stakeholders
* reviewing CEO performance.

In New Zealand responsibility to shareholders was the most important objective for publicly listed companies and government boards. This was followed by financial and operating performance. Australian boards ranked equal priority to financial and operating performance and long-term strategy, followed by responsiblities to shareholders.

Survey of the top 100 listed Australian companies

In a survey which the author conducted based on 1999 annual reports, the following results were obtained regarding disclosure of the role of the board:

Role of the board specified	82%
Review of strategy	75%
Monitoring management	78%
Review of capital expenditure	48%
Review of CEO	71%
Review of compliance	36%

This contrasted sharply with the limited information given by UK companies listed on the ASX.

The New Zealand *Code of Proper Practice for Directors* simply states in para 4.1 that the board must meet regularly to monitor and control the performance of manage-

---

11   *The Fish Rots from the Head: The Crisis in Our Boardroom: Developing the Crucial Skills of the Competent Director*, HarperCollins Business, London, 1997, p. 49.
12   Korn/Ferry International, *op. cit.*, footnote 1 supra.

ment. Paragraph 4.3 states that there should be a clearly accepted division of responsibility at the head of the company.[13] The top listed companies in New Zealand generally specify the respective roles of the board and management. Telecom New Zealand Ltd is particularly explicit.

Particular roles

Supervision and monitoring

Supervising and monitoring involves reviewing the performance of the CEO and other key executives by a disciplined system of reporting and monitoring performance.

The board needs to review business results, especially financial performance. The UK-based multinational GEC Plc does this on the basis of seven financial ratios and twelve trendlines (see Figures 25.3 and 25.4).

Figure 25.3   GEC Plc's seven financial ratios

---

13   The Institute of Directors Best Practice 1996/2 recommends the setting up of advisory boards which may resolve the matter.

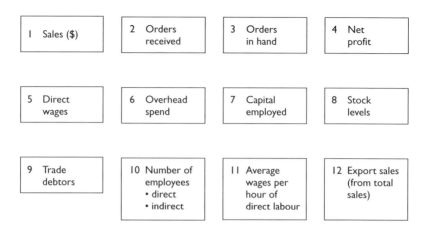

Figure 25.4 GEC Plc's trendlines

These are very much based on accounting data and are concerned with economic efficiency. They do not address aspects of quality management concerned with customer satisfaction and need to be complemented by appropriate quality control criteria.

A key element in supervision is monitoring. References to monitoring have been common in the USA for the last twenty years and occasionally, as we saw in earlier chapters, it is reflected in case law. Professor Hilmer identifies the factors affecting the type of monitoring in Figure 25.5.[14]

This shows that normally the board relies on its papers and questioning of the CEO. It also shows that sometimes there is a need to go beyond this and to request further reports and to question the appropriate executives.

Some companies provide for project management as part of a move towards decentralisation. This is particularly useful with joint ventures and strategic alliances.

Risk analysis and risk management are increasingly important aspects of supervision.

Strategic thinking

Strategy involves either initiating long-term and medium-term strategic analysis or reviewing and approving management's proposals. The board's function here should be the latter, concentrating on goals, performance and critical appraisal of the strategy proposals and rarely, if ever, developing the details. A longer range task of the board is to evaluate the calibre of senior executives' strategy-making and strategy-implementing skills.[15]

---

14 Hilmer, *op. cit.*, p. 40.
15 Hilmer, *op. cit.*, p. 45. See also A. A. Thompson and A. J. Strickland, *Strategic Management Concepts and Cases*, 9th edn, Irwin McGraw-Hill, Boston, 1995, p. 19; T. Clarke and S Clegg, *Changing Paradigms*, HarperCollins, London, 1998, ch. 4.

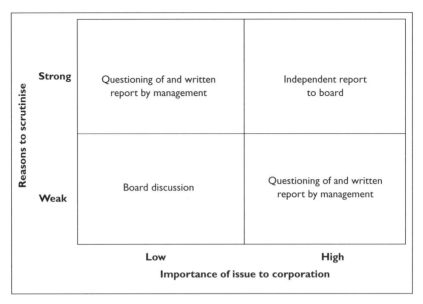

Figure 25.5   Factors affecting types of monitoring

Directors can contribute to dealing with the complexity and uncertainty associated with strategic decisions. They possess problem solving expertise which they can apply in a variety of contexts.[16]

The board should also either foster an appropriate corporate culture or sign off on it where appropriate, paying particular attention to ethical standards.[17]

In formulating an appropriate strategy, Professor Michael Porter puts forward the five forces model, which shows the interaction of five forces or variables (see Figure 25.6).[18]

Prahalad and Hamel[19] list the following as factors creating pressure for radical rethinking of strategy:

- global competititon
- deregulation
- structural changes
- excess capacity
- mergers and acquisitions
- environmental concerns

16   See V. Rindova, 'What Corporate Boards have to do with Strategy: A Conjunctive Perspective' (1999) 36 *Journal of Management Studies* 953.
17   Hilmer, *op. cit.*, p. 45.
18   M. Porter, *Competitive Advantage*, Free Press, New York, 1980.
19   C. D. Prahalad and G. Hamel, 'Strategy as a Field of Study: Why Search for a New Paradigm?' (1994) 15 *Strategic Management Journal*, 5 at 7; Clarke and Clegg, *op. cit.*, p. 196.

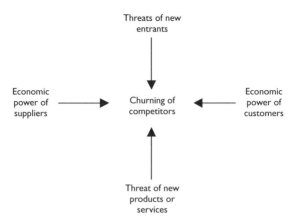

Figure 25.6 Michael Porter's five forces model

- less protectionism
- changing customer expectations
- technological discontinuities
- emergence of trading blocs

Strategy involves such issues as business rationalisation in a changing and increasingly competitive environment, quality improvement and business process re-engineering, and innovation and regeneration.

Policy formulation

Policy, like strategy, is a very general concept and consequently can overlap with it. Policy involves identification of the purpose, vision and basic values of the company.

It also involves the establishment of particular policies on key issues including matters such as risk management and compensation for senior executives and compliance with such policies. Many of these matters are delegated to specialist committees which then report back to the board.

Policies should be fair, clear, adequately publicised and followed. Compliance should be monitored like other management activities.

Accountability[20]

Accountability refers to the important areas of shareholder relations and statutory and regulatory compliance. It also includes the appointment of auditors and oversight of the audit process. We have dealt with this in Chapter 19.

---

20   Hilmer, *op. cit.* footnote 6 supra, p. 47; Australian Institute of Company Directors, *Accountability*, a paper prepared for the Corporate Governance Committee of the Australian Institute of Company Directors, AICD, Sydney, August 1993.

While the board has overall responsibility, the immediate question of dealing with shareholder relations is often referred to the chairperson. Issues of regulatory compliance are often handled by management and specialist committees. We deal with this in Chapter 28.

All major listed companies now have audit committees and many have specific compliance programs in place for matters such as competition law and health and safety at work laws. We examine these in Chapter 28.

Monitoring the board's own effectiveness

The board itself needs to be the subject of critical review, both as a board and as the performance of individual members is concerned. Following General Motors Guidelines on Significant Corporate Governance Issues,[21] many top companies are instituting procedures to these ends. Included in this exercise is a review of the relationship between the board and management.

---

21   para. 15. This provides for an annual report by the Committee on Director Affairs to be discussed by the full board. See also IFSA Guideline 7—Performance Evaluation.

The Role of Institutional Investors in Corporate Governance[1]

Institutional investors have been holders of debt capital for over a century. Merchant banks and insurance companies needed to have this kind of investment to satisfy their own needs and the needs of their constituents. However, since World War II there has been a rise of investment by institutions in shares and in the last twenty years we have seen the growth of international institutional investment. These facts all have a very significant impact on corporate governance.

In this chapter we will first consider the definition of 'institutional investor' and the nature of their relationship with their own constituents. Second, we will look at the factors which have led to increased institutional investment in shares. Third, we shall consider how this fits into the Berle and Means analysis of ownership and control and

---

1   The literature on this since 1985 has been prolific. For a sample see J. H. Farrar and M. Russell, 'The Impact of Institutional Investment on Company Law' (1984) 5 Co Law 107; and J. H. Farrar, 'Legal Restraints on Institutional Investor Involvement in Corporate Governance', unpublished report for the Australian Investment Managers Association, 1993, on which some of what follows is based. For an outstanding study see G. P. Stapledon, *Institutional Shareholders and Corporate Governance*, Oxford University Press, Oxford, 1996. See also G. P. Stapledon, 'The Structure of Share Ownership and Control: The Potential for Institutional Investor Activism' (1995) 18 UNSWLJ 250 and P. Davies, 'Institutional Investors: A UK View' (1991) 57 Brooklyn L Rev 129 and P. Davies, 'Institutional Investors in the United Kingdom', in D. D. Prentice and P. R. J. Holland (eds), *Contemporary Issues in Corporate Governance*, Oxford University Press, Oxford, 1993, p. 69. See also J. C. Coffee Jnr, 'Institutional Investors as Corporate Monitors: Are Takeovers Obsolete?', in J. H. Farrar (ed.), *Takeovers, Institutional Investors and the Modernisation of Corporate Laws*, Oxford University Press, Melbourne, 1993, ch. 2. See Report of Joint Committee on Corporations and Securities (Commonwealth of Australia) on the Role of Institutional Investors in Australia's Capital Markets, 1994; N. G. Maw et al., *Maw on Corporate Governance*, Dartmouth, Aldershot 1994, ch. 8. For a useful recent discussion, see R. A. B. Monks and N. Minow, *Corporate Governance*, Blackwell, Oxford, 1995, pp. 124–77. This contains a good bibliography of US material. For further valuable US data, see M. J. Roe, 'The Modern Corporation and Private Pensions', 1993, 41 *UCLA L Rev* 75 and his *Strong Managers, Weak Owners—The Political Roots of American Corporate Finance*, Princeton University Press, Princeton, 1994. See also I. M. Millstein, 'Distinguishing "Ownership" and "Control" in the 1990s' in Monks and Minow *op. cit.* Appendix 7.

modern law and economics theories. Fourth, we will consider legal and other restraints on institutional investor activism and fifth, we will examine some initiatives that institutions have taken in corporate governance. Last, we shall consider briefly their role in the promotion of global corporate governance. We return to this last topic in Chapter 34.

Definition of institutional investor[2]

'Institutional investor' is a broad term that encompasses pension and superannuation funds, investment companies, mutual funds and unit trusts, insurance companies, banks and charitable foundations. It also includes funds managers, who are professionals managing investments on behalf of other institutional investors.[3] Institutional investors are thus not a monolithic whole with one investment objective. They are not all subject to the same degree of competition or internal monitoring by their own constituents. There are, however, certain underlying similarities which make it unrealistic to regard them as separate unconnected investors, and increasingly, they act under the umbrella of what is now the Investment and Financial Services Association (IFSA) in Australia.

The rise of institutional investment

Figure 26.1 gives details of ownership of the Australian share market June 1991 – June 1998. Table 26.1 details as at 30 June 1998.[4]

Table 26.1   Ownership of listed Australian equities at 30 June 1998[5]

Owner	%
Life insurance and superannuation funds	24.1
Other financial institutions	9.3
Banks and deposit taking institutions	3.5
Foreign investors	31.7
Other companies	8.3
Private domestic investors	23.0
Government	0.1
Total	100

2   See Farrar and Russell, *op. cit.*; J. H. Farrar, 'Legal Restraints on Institutional Investor Involvement in Corporate Governance', unpublished paper for the AIMG, 1993.
3   For an interesting recent discussion of funds management in the City of London see T. Golding, *The City: Inside the Great Expectation Machine*, Pearson Education Ltd, London, 2001.
4   Taken from *ASX Fact Book 1999*, The Equities Market.
5   *ibid.*; cf. G. Stapledon, 'Australian Sharemarket Ownership' in G. Walker (gen. ed.), *Securities Regulation in Australia and New Zealand*, 2nd edn, Law Book Company, Sydney, 1998, p. 244.

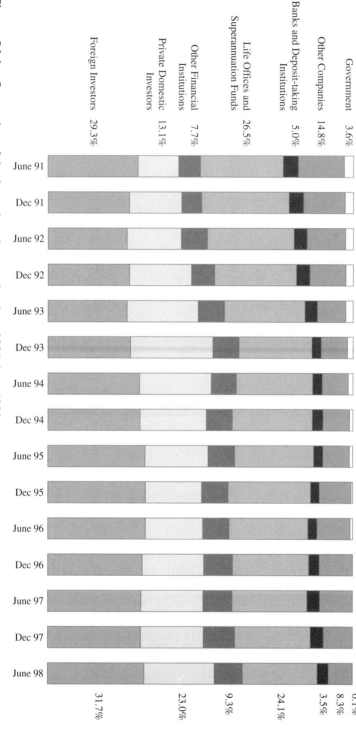

Figure 26.1 Ownership of the Australian sharemarket June 1991–June 1998

Source: Adapted from ASX Fact Book 1999, The Equities Market.

Table 26.1 indicates that Australian institutions owned 36.9 per cent of Australian equities. Overseas investors, of which about one-third were institutions, held 31.7 per cent. This probably underestimates the correct percentage of share ownership by institutions due to the fact that many shares are held by nominees, and Australia, unlike other jurisdictions, seems less able to penetrate this barrier effectively for the purpose of keeping proper statistics.

In the United Kingdom approximately 60 per cent of shares in listed companies are held by local institutions with a further 20 per cent held by overseas institutions. These percentages are very high. The percentages are lower in the USA—about 50 per cent held by local institutions—but the percentage rises to 60 per cent for the top 1000 companies.

The reasons for the rise since 1945 are:[6]

- the growth of superannuation and pension funds
- the relaxation of trustee investment rules
- the rise of insurance-linked investment schemes
- the rise of managed investment schemes.

It is interesting to note that none of these reasons is company oriented. The company is simply the outlet for these investment urges.

Ownership and control issues

As we saw in Chapter 5, Berle and Means, in their original study,[7] showed how, as listed corporations grew, ownership and control began to separate and shares became diffused among a large number of shareholders. Management power grew in importance in the absence of a counterveiling power.

Later, in 1959, Berle restated his theory, taking into account the increasing role of pension funds.[8] He emphasised their essentially passive role and his former research student Dr Paul Harbrecht talked about 'the paraproprietal society' in which the majority of investors were divorced from the corporations in which their funds were ultimately invested.[9]

More modern theories in law and economics have emphasised agency problems in the listed company and the problems of collective action.[10] Agency costs arise due to

---

6   See J. H. Farrar and B. Hannigan, *Farrar's Company Law*, 4th edn, Butterworths, London, 1998, p. 579.
7   A. Berle and G. Means, *The Modern Corporation and Private Property*, Revised edn, Harcourt Brace, New York, 1968.
8   A. Berle, *Power Without Property*, Sidgwick & Jackson, London 1960, pp. 55–6.
9   P. Harbrecht, 'Pension Funds and Economic Power: The Paraproprietal Society', preface to D. J. Baum and N. B. Stiles, *The Silent Partners: Institutional Investors and Corporate Control*, Syracuse University Press, Syracuse, New York, 1965. For a modern discussion see J. Gates, *The Ownership Solution—Towards a Shared Capitalism for the Twenty-First Century*, Penguin Books, London, 1998, ch. 4.
10 See these discussed in G. P. Stapledon, 'Disincentives to Activism by Institutional Investors in Listed Australian Companies' (1996) 18 Sydney LR 152, pp. 177–9.

shirking, slacking and rorting, and the consequent need to monitor and bond management to their companies to ensure performance.

As we saw in Chapter 5, management is monitored by the various markets in which the company participates. The regrouping of ownership interests through the phenomenon of increased institutional investment creates the possibility of restoration of a counterveiling power to management. However, as Harbrecht realised, we need to evolve a new conception of property to accommodate these developments and as we shall see, there are still a number of factors limiting institutional investor activism.

Legal and other restraints

The main legal constraints that limit activism by institutional investors are:[11]

- problems centred around control
- problems about conflict of interest
- problems of access to inside information and insider trading
- possible problems centred on fiduciary and statutory obligations.

Let us deal with these in turn.

Problems centred around control

There is a statutory obligation under Part 6.7 of the Corporations Act and the New Zealand *Securities Amendment Act 1988* to disclose a substantial shareholding that is triggered by entitlement to 5 per cent or more of the voting shares. There is also a basic prohibition, in section 606 of the Corporations Act, on acquisition of relevant interests in voting shares in a listed company or an unlisted company with more than 50 members or on increasing a holding between 20 per cent and 90 per cent. The latter is subject to the exceptions set out in section 611 which include a takeover bid.

The real risk here is for institutional investors to be treated as associates by merely liaising with other institutions in a takeover bid situation. To alleviate the risk, ASIC has made a Class Order granting conditional relief to enable institutions to liaise with each other and enter into an agreement to vote collectively at particular company meetings.[12] ASIC indicates when they will consider that institutions have or have not entered into a relevant agreement about voting.

The relief under the Class Order is only available when:

---

11 See Farrar and Russell, *op. cit.* footnote 1 supra; Stapledon, *op. cit.* footnote 9 supra; I. Ramsay, G. P. Stapledon and K. Fong, 'Corporate Governance: The Perspective of Australian Institutional Shareholders' (2000) 18 C&SLJ 110, pp. 127–34. This largely follows the earlier Stapledon article on these points.

12 See Class Order 98/649 Collective Action by Institutional Investors; J. Lessing, 'Institutional Investors: Will We See Greater Cooperation Between Them Regarding Corporate Governance?' (1998) 10 Bond LR 376.

(a) the agreement is publicly announced in the prescribed manner;

(b) no consideration (other than a promise to exercise a vote in a particular way) passes between any of the relevant institutuions or other parties in connection with, or as a result of, the agreement;

(c) the agreement relates to voting in a particular way, on a particular issue, or abstaining from voting, at a specified or proposed meeting of a company in which the institutions have a relevant interest in the voting shares of that company;

(d) any party to the agreement is able to terminate its participation in the agreement at will;

(e) the agreement specifies that it will terminate at the close of the relevant meeting;

(f) an institution would, but for the operation of the Class Order, have an entitlement to 5 per cent or more of the voting shares of the company whose meeting is the subject of the voting agreement; and

(g) the parties to the voting agreement would not, apart from the Class Order, be collectively entitled to 20 per cent or more of the voting shares in the company which is the subject of the voting agreement, excluding shares which are:

  (i) held by a party to the agreement, or its associate, on trust for, as agent of, on behalf of or for the benefit of persons to whom the party owes a fiduciary duty; or

  (ii) held for a statutory fund for a registered life insurance company in respect of investment-linked products.

In New Zealand the matter is governed by the *Takeovers Act 1993* but this is not yet fully in force. The New Zealand Stock Exchange (NZSE) Listing Rules apply.

Quite apart from takeover-related activity there is a risk of an institution being regarded as a shadow director if it becomes too active in the affairs of a particular company.[13]

Problems about conflict of interest

In theory, shareholders may vote in their own self-interest, even if that does not coincide with the company's interests. At the same time, however, it is established that a majority of shareholders are subject to equitable restraints,[14] when voting, for example on a proposed alteration to the constitution. The relationship between these two apparently conflicting principles is not an easy one in theory or in practice. For our purposes it is sufficient to note that power accruing to institutional shareholders as members of a majority must be exercised for a proper purpose and fairly, without oppression. Any duty which an institution owes to its investors ranks behind that owed to the company in which the institution holds shares, at least as far as company law is concerned.

Clearly, therefore, the potential exists for what might colloquially be termed a 'no-win' situation. A similar sort of dilemma faced trustees in the case of *Re Holders'*

---

13   See ch. 9 of this book.
14   See *Gambotto v. WCP Ltd* (1995) 182 CLR 432.

Investment Trust Ltd[15] where Justice Megarry (as he then was) refused to confirm a proposed reduction of capital, on the ground that the trustees, who held preference shares, had voted, at a class meeting of preference shareholders, not in the best interests of that class as a whole, but rather to benefit their total holdings in the company which included large holdings of equity shares. Justice Megarry thereby affirmed that the trustees' first duty as members of the class was to act bona fide in the interests of the general body of members of that class, and not simply in the interests of the trusts as a whole.

Two principles compete here:

1   Institutions owe it to their constituent investors, as a matter of fiduciary principle or contract or at least legitimate expectation based on their documentation, to safeguard returns, providing either wealth maximisation or steady income. The trust deed or contract will usually proscribe unlimited freedom to *dispose* of securities but will not envisage subjecting the investors to the possibility of reduced returns pending solution of the corporate problems in issue, or to increased risk in the event that a solution is not achieved.

2   Institutions must act, as part of the majority, for a proper purpose fairly and without oppression. This is sometimes linked with a wider social responsibility of institutions. Some institutions would no doubt argue that their interest is exclusively financial.

Access to inside information and insider trading

Any major shareholder may have advantages over small shareholders in respect of unpublished, price-sensitive information about the share market. In the case of the institutions, much of this may derive simply from expertise in the financial markets. Some may come from closer contract with portfolio companies, roadshow presentations and brokers' lunches. Some of it may also derive from nominees appointed to the board of directors or interlocking directorships, although such appointments are rare in Australia and New Zealand.[16]

The biggest risk is probably from 'pre-marketing' of a transaction.[17]

Possible problems centred on fiduciary and statutory obligations

In an unpublished report to what was then Australian Investment Managers Group (AIMG)[18] the author raised the risk of fiduciary and statutory restraints. These centre

---

15   [1971] 2 All ER 289.

16   There are other possible advantages to be gained from having a nominee on the board, for example, knowledge of a company's intention to make a takeover offer for shares of a target company. Information about negotiated acquisitions can, of course, be particularly sensitive. The New Zealand Securities Commission has stated that there should be no disclosure of such information by a nominee director to his appointor where it is not publicly available. See *Review of the Law and Practice of Company Takeovers*, vol. 2, New Zealand Securities Commission, Wellington, 1983, pp. 19 *et seq.*

17   Stapledon, *op. cit.* footnote 9 supra., p. 171.

18   See Farrar, *op. cit.*

on the inability of a fiduciary to fetter its discretion and to delegate essential functions such as the basic investment decisions and statutory restrictions or prudential guide-lines on particular investments or proportions of holdings.

In so far as this is simply a matter of delegation, although the Trustee Acts envisage limited delegation, it has been suggested that it is sufficient if the trust deed gives the necessary power.[19] Although this is common practice it does not seem right since public policy restricts contracting out of the basic fiduciary duties and fettering discretion.[20] This is certainly so in the case of an existing fiduciary duty. The matter should be clari-fied by amendment to the Trustee Acts.

Economic and other restraints

In addition to legal restraints there are a number of economic restraints. Each institu-tional investor has its own investment needs and strategies and the prevailing use of funds managers links the matter inexorably to their investment performance. This compounds the problems of collective action and free riders[21] which inhibit increased activism from a simple cost/benefit point of view.

Added to this is the increased use of indexed funds, essentially a passive investment technique.[22]

There are also a host of practical considerations such as lack of relevant informa-tion, inadequate time for consultation, and lack of homogeneity and coordination among institutional investors in spite of the IFSA.[23] There is also fear of a political or public relations backlash to increased activism as evidenced by the criticism aimed at AMP Ltd for its actions over Arnotts Ltd and GIO and its own failure recently to get its own corporate governance house in order.[24]

Examples of institutional investor activism

Passive and discrete role

In the past, institutions have been relatively passive investors.[25] They have sometimes been accused of short-termism, since they lack management expertise and manifest a

---

19 Stapledon, *op. cit.* footnote 9, p. 173.
20 See A. Anderson, 'Conflicts of Interest: Efficiency, Fairness and Corporate Structure' (1978) 25 UCLA Law Rev 738, 755–6; J. Glover, *Commercial Equity—Fiduciary Relationships*, Butterworths, Sydney, 1995, pp. 212–13.
21 Stapledon, *op. cit.* footnote 9, p. 177; H. Short and K. Keasey, 'Institutional Shareholders and Corporate Governance in the United Kingdom', in K. Keasey *et al.* (eds), *Corporate Governance: Economic, Manage-ment and Financial Issues*, Oxford University Press, Oxford, 1997, pp. 18, 26 *et seq.*
22 Stapledon, *ibid.*, p. 185.
23 *ibid.*, p. 188 *et seq.*
24 See Farrar and Russell *op. cit.* footnote 1 supra. See for instance the *Weekend Australian*, 27–28 May 2000, pp. 33, 36.
25 For a valuable discussion see Stapledon, 1996, *op. cit.* footnote 1 supra, ch. 8. Compare his discussion of the United Kingdom.

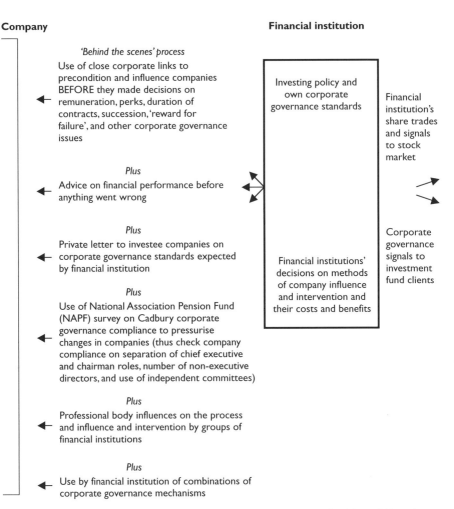

Figure 26.2   Model of the corporate governance process in the United Kingdom

rational apathy because of collective action problems.[26] This is further compounded by the rise of specialist funds managers[27] who lack motivation for shareholder activism. This particularly manifests itself in non-voting of proxies, which is complicated by the question of appropriate delegations and the use of custodians.[28]

---

26   Economic Planning and Advisory Council, *Short-termism in Australian Investment*, AGPS, Canberra, 1995.
27   See Stapledon, 1996, *op. cit.* footnote 1 supra, ch. 3.
28   See G. Stapledon et al., *Proxy Voting in Australia's Largest Companies*, Centre for Corporate Law and Securities Regulation, University of Melbourne, Melbourne 2000. See especially Figure A. See also *Corporate Governance: The Role of Superannuation Trustees*: A Report prepared by Institutional Analysis and the Centre for Corporate Law and Securities Regulation for the Australian Institute of Superannuation Trustees, December 2000. See <www.institutionalanalysis.com>

Institutional investors have had behind-the-scenes consultation with management and sometimes applied public pressure through the media but in the end they have often operated on the basis of 'the Wall Street Walk', which is if in doubt, sell. Their most important role has been their pivotal role in takeovers.

A very detailed and useful study of Australian and UK practices was carried out by Dr Geof Stapledon for his Oxford doctorate. This is now published in *Institutional Shareholders and Corporate Governance*.[29] Another useful study is by Professor John Holland in his report *The Corporate Governance Role of Financial Institutions in Their Investee Companies*,[30] which contained a diagram showing a model of the corporate governance process in the UK reproduced in Figure 26.2. This shows the range of activities undertaken by institutional investors. Let us look at particular examples.

Thalidomide[31]

In the United Kingdom, Distillers Ltd defended a class action by a number of the victims of the drug Thalidomide which caused birth defects when prescribed for pregnant mothers. This occasioned very bad publicity for the company, which began to affect its share price significantly. At this point the institutions convened a meeting with management, which ultimately led to a more generous settlement.

Litigation[32]

The Prudential Assurance Co Ltd, which has long been regarded as a or the leading UK institutional investor, litigated in personal, representative and derivative action form against directors of Newman Industries Ltd, a small listed company in a case of self-dealing. This was against the wishes of the independent directors. It won a pyrrhic victory and incurred some sharp criticism from the English Court of Appeal.[33] The fault, however, probably lay as much with the trial judge who failed to control what should have been brief interlocutory proceedings at first instance. Since then, institutions have seemed reluctant to litigate.

Australia

In Australia there have been a number of instances of behind-the-scenes discussions on company-specific issues documented by Stapledon.[34] Leigh Hall, recently retired from AMP, was particularly active in this respect, sometimes to the irritation of management. He also took a leading role in public debate of corporate governance

---

29   Clarendon Press, Oxford, 1996.
30   Research Report 46 for the ACCA 1995. For current information in respect of directors' views of these consultations in Australia and New Zealand see Korn/Ferry International, *Survey of Boards of Directors in Australia and New Zealand 2000*.
31   See Farrar and Russell, *op. cit.* footnote 1 supra.
32   *ibid.*
33   *Prudential Assurance Co. v. Newman Industries Ltd (No 2)* [1982] Ch 204.
34   Stapledon, 1996, *op. cit.*, ch. 8.

through the Australian Investment Managers Group, later the Australian Investment Managers Association (AIMA), and now the Investment and Financial Services Association (IFSA). It is ironic that since his departure, AMP itself has undergone some corporate governance problems, which have not been handled well and have occasioned institutional investor disquiet.

The institutions were particularly active in opposing News Ltd's attempt to persuade the ASX to waive its one share, one vote rule for listed companies in favour of Supershares.[35] They publicly opposed it and lobbied the federal Attorney-General, Michael Lavarch, who set up a panel of experts that recommended against the waiver.[36]

Other recent cases of intervention have been Coles Myer's Yannon transaction and buy-back of shares from K-Mart, ANI's board restructuring, and Crown Ltd's proposal to buy the management rights of Melbourne's Crown Casino from Hudson Conway Ltd.

The possibility of some forms of collective action in takeovers has increased with Class Order 98/649 Collective Action by Institutional Investors issued on 8 May 1998.[37]

The IFSA (in its various forms) has been vocal on particular issues such as differential voting rights, continuous disclosure, disclosure of directors' share dealings, board composition and executive remuneration. The IFSA (in its earlier forms) was not an active participant in the drafting of *Corporate Practices and Conduct* but supported them and drafted its own guidelines in 1995. The latest version is presented as appendix 2 to this book.

Guidance Note 2.00 of the IFSA's Guidelines for Investment Managers provides that investment managers should vote on all material issues at all Australian company meetings where they have the voting authority and responsibility to do so.

In a survey carried out in 1998 by Professor Ian Ramsay, Dr Geof Stapledon and Kenneth Fong on *Institutional Investors' Views on Corporate Governance* for the Centre of Corporate Law and Securities Regulation, the authors found inter alia:

(a) a number of institutions do not exercise their voting rights routinely, only voting on issues of major significance;
(b) most did not support compulsory voting;
(c) reasons for intervention commonly revolve around the share price and the size of the institution's holding and interventions have been infrequent in Australia.

Further research by the Melbourne Centre has shown that Australian institutions exercise their votes much less than their UK and US equivalents. This may call for investigation by the government in its new found enthusiasm for improving corporate governance.

---

35 ASX Discussion Paper, *Differential Voting Rights*, November 1993.
36 Report of the Committee of Experts, 1994.
37 See Lessing, *op. cit.* footnote 11 supra.

Impact of increased activism

The evidence on the effect of increased institutional investor activism on corporate performance is inconclusive.

Professor Bernard Black of Stanford[38] has identified six areas where institutional investor activism is likely to improve corporate performance. These are:

1 through the promotion of the practice of independent directors
2 through opposing unwise diversification
3 through involvement in takeovers—for and against particular takeovers
4 through opposition to management protection devices such as golden parachutes and poison pills
5 through opposition to cash retention and unnecessary investments
6 through opposition to excessive management compensation.

Point 1 seems debatable and points 2–6 seem somewhat self-evident.

International action

There is increased international investment and close contact between representative bodies of institutional investors round the world. Also certain key institutions such as Calpers are highly vocal and tend to travel to speak at institutional investor conferences round the world.

The institutions have been influential together with the OECD and the World Bank in promoting global corporate governance. We talk about this in Chapter 34.

Conclusion

There has been

• a rise in institutional investment in equities since 1945
• a rise in international institutional investment in the last two decades
• increased institutional activism which has taken a variety of forms against a background of some impediments to collective action
• a growth of national systems of self-regulation in a number of countries including Australia and New Zealand

---

38   B. S. Black, 'Shareholder Activism and Corporate Governance in the United States', in P. Newman (ed.), *The New Palgrave Dictionary of Economics and the Law*, Stockton Press, New York, 1998, Vol 3, p. 459; See also C. K. Brancato, *Institutional Investors and Corporate Governance*, Irwin Professional Publishing, Chicago, 1997, ch. 3 and 6. For Australian discussion see Ramsay, Stapledon and Fong, *op. cit.* footnote 10 supra.

• the recent development of global corporate governance.

The future role of institutions is complex. They are professional investors whose own performance is increasingly closely monitored. They have not the time, will or expertise for a more active role in the day-to-day management of companies. Their most creative role is probably in the promotion of sophisticated benchmarks of good corporate governance. Institutional investor activism is thus only one of several mechanisms to monitor the performance of management.[39]

---

39   I, Ramsay, G. Stapledon, K. Fong, *Institutional Investors' Views on Corporate Governance*, CCLSR, Melbourne, 1998, p. 41, now published as 'Corporate Governance: The Perspective of Australian Institutional Investors' (2000) 18 C&SLJ 110.

CHAPTER 27

Systems of
Self-regulation

We saw in Chapter 1 that legal regulation represents the core of corporate governance but that core is surrounded by a penumbra of systems of self-regulation of differing degrees of 'hardness' and 'softness'.

Closely related to legal regulation and now given some legal recognition in the legislation, are the Stock Exchange Listing Rules and the Statements of Accounting Practice. Beyond them lie *Corporate Practices and Conduct*,[1] the Australian equivalent of the UK Cadbury, Greenbury or Hampel reports, *Corporate Governance: A Guide for Investment Managers and Corporations*[2] of the AIMA, now the IFSA, and the Institute of Directors in New Zealand Inc's Code of Practice for Directors and Best Practice Statements. Beyond these lies business ethics. This can be reduced to a Venn diagram as shown in Figure 27.1.[3] With this can be contrasted Figure 27.2, which presents similar information in pyramid form.

There are cases to be made for and against self-regulation. The main arguments are set out below.

Arguments for a system of self-regulation:[4]

1   The persons concerned with a system of self-regulation are experts in the field.
2   The system is not expensive; the costs are borne by the market.
3   It has speed and flexibility because of the absence of legal procedures and detailed technical rules.

---

1   Third edn, H. Bosch (ed.), FT Pitman Publishing, Melbourne, 1995.
2   Third edn, July 1999.
3   Figure 27.1 drafted by Henry Bosch and the present author.
4   This summary is based on the City Capital Markets Committee's pamphlet 'Supervision of the Securities Market', June 1974; the Panel on Takeovers and Mergers pamphlet with the same title, July 1974; see B. A. K. Rider and E. J. Hew, 'The Regulation of Corporation and Securities Law in Britain—the Beginning of the Real Debate' (1977) 19 Mal LR 144 at 168 *et seq.* See also Review of Investor Protection, Cmnd 9125 (1984). For a recent discussion see D. Branson, 'Teaching Comparative Corporate Governance: The Significance of "Soft Law" and International Institutions' (2000) 34 Georgia L Rev 669.

Figure 27.1   Legal and self-regulation of corporate governance

4   The rules are easily amended.

5   There is emphasis on the spirit rather than the letter of rules and consequent discouragement of evasion.

6   The responsibility of participating in a system of self-regulation produces greater professional integrity and discipline within the various professions operating in the securities industry.

7   Law by its nature is concerned with the minimum necessary standards and operates at the margin whereas it is argued that self-regulatory norms operate from a higher threshold.

8   Self-regulation avoids a 'them' and 'us' feeling which arguably arises with the establishment of another government agency.

9   A system of self-regulation operates with greater informality and there is the possibility of preliminary rulings.

10   Sanctions of disapproval and damaged reputation are far stronger than legal sanctions in this field.

11   It avoids superfluous litigation.

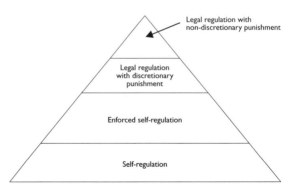

Figure 27.2   Pyramid of enforcement strategies

Arguments against self-regulation:

1 Self-regulators seem to the public to act as judge and jury in their own cause.
2 The sanctions are either too draconian (for example, expulsion) or ineffective.
3 There is a lack of legal powers, particularly powers of investigation.
4 Since a system of self-regulation is based on consent, it is both objectionable and impracticable to extend it to those who have not consented.
5 Difficulties arise because of the vague jurisdictional basis if the position of self-regulatory agencies is challenged in the courts.
6 There is uncertainty as to whether such agencies have qualified privilege from liability in defamation.
7 Self-regulatory systems can result in unnecessary duplication.
8 There is a lack of public accountability.
9 There are likely to be gaps in self-regulatory frameworks.
10 Self-regulatory systems are arguably less certain and predictable.

We shall now look at the different types of self-regulation.

The Stock Exchange Listing Rules

Companies whose securities are listed on the Australian Stock Exchange ('ASX') must comply with the ASX Listing Rules.[5] The ASX rules operate as a matter of contract although they are also given statutory recognition.[6] Non-compliance may result in sanctions by the ASX and possible civil and criminal liability under sections 777 and 1001A of the Corporations Act. Section 777 deals with the Listing Rules and 1001A with continuous disclosure liability. Liability under section 1001A arises if the company contravenes the rule by intentionally, recklessly or negligently failing to notify ASX of information which is (a) not generally available and (b) that a reasonable person would expect, if it were generally available, to have a material effect on the price or value of the securities. A criminal offence only arises if the contravention is intentional or reckless.

Included in the Listing Rules is Listing Rule 4.10.3 which requires each listed company to include in its annual report a statement of the main corporate governance practices that the company had in place during the reporting period. There is an indicative list of corporate governance matters in Appendix 4A of the Listing Rules. This provides as follows:

1 If the entity of a body corporate, whether individual directors, including the chair, are executive or non-executive directors (in the case of a trust, whether individual

---

5 New Zealand listed companies must comply with the New Zealand Listing Rules. There are no statutory sanctions.
6 *Chapmans Ltd v. ASX* (1996) 14 ACLC 1297.

directors of the management company, including the chair, are executive or non-executive directors).

2 The main procedures the entity has in place for:
   (a) devising criteria for membership of the entity's governing body;
   (b) reviewing the membership of that body; and
   (c) nominating representatives to that body.

   If a procedure involves a nomination committee, set out, or summarise, the committee's main responsibilities, the names of committee members and their positions in relation to the entity (for example, director of the company).

3 The policies relating to the appointment and retirement of non-executive directors (in the case of a trust, non-executive directors of the management company).

4 The main procedures by which the governing body or individual members of it can seek independent professional advice, at the entity's expense, in carrying out their duties.

5 If the entity is a body corporate, the main procedures for establishing and reviewing the compensation arrangements for:
   (a) the chief executive officer (or equivalent), and other senior executives of the governing body, and
   (b) non-executive members of the governing body.

   If a procedure involves a remuneration committee, set out, or summarise, the committee's main responsibilities and rights, and the names of committee members. If a member of the committee is not a member of the entity's governing body (for example, directors of the company), state that person's position.

6 If the entity is a trust, the main procedure for establishing and reviewing the compensation arrangements for the governing body.

   If a procedure involves a remuneration committee, set out, or summarise, the committee's main responsibilities and rights, and the names of committee members. If a member of the committee is not a member of the entity's governing body (for example, director of the company), state that person's position.

7 The main procedures the entity has in place for the nomination of external auditors, and for reviewing the adequacy of existing external audit arrangements (particularly the scope and quality of the audit).

   If a procedure involves an audit committee, set out, or summarise, the committee's main responsibilities and rights, and the names of committee members. If a member of the committee is not a member of the entity's governing body (for example, director of the company), state that person's position.

8 The governing body's approach to identifying areas of significant business risk, and to putting arrangements in place to manage them.

9 The entity's policy on the establishment and maintenance of appropriate ethical standards.

Compliance

In a study by Professor Ian Ramsay and Richard Hoad of the University of Melbourne, *Disclosure of Corporate Governance Practices by Australian Companies*[7] in 1997 based on 268 listed companies, the authors concluded *inter alia*:

- Many companies are now disclosing detailed information about a range of corporate governance practices. Such disclosure may assist shareholders and other stakeholders in companies in monitoring directors and may also cause directors to reflect upon the appropriateness and adequacy of the corporate governance practices of their companies.
- The extent of quality of disclosure is typically better for larger companies than for smaller companies.
- When industry classification was examined, more detailed disclosure was made by companies in the banking and finance industry while some of the shortest disclosure was made by companies in the gold mining, media, and investment and financial services industries.
- There was substantial scope for improvement in disclosure of corporate governance practices. A number of important issues were not discussed by many companies. For example, 25 per cent of the companies surveyed did not discuss criteria for board membership, whether the chairperson is executive or non-executive, or whether directors are able to obtain their own independent advice at the company's expense.
- Twenty-three per cent of the companies did not discuss management remuneration. A particularly noticeable finding was that 65 per cent of the companies did not discuss procedures for reviewing the performance of managers and directors. Only 41 per cent of companies classified as large stated that they regularly reviewed the performance of management.
- Another area for improvement is the failure of the vast majority of the companies surveyed to distinguish between non-executive and independent directors and non-executive and independent chairpersons. It would be desirable for the ASX to address this issue in its indicative list of corporate governance matters contained in Appendix 4A.

Since that survey was carried out the *Company Law Review Act 1998* introduced a special rule for specific companies in section 300(10) and for listed companies in section 300(11). These dealt with qualifications, experience and responsibilities of directors and their attendance rate and particulars of interests and options in shares. In addition, section 300A requires the directors' reports of listed Australian companies to

---

7   Centre for Corporate Law and Securities Regulation, University of Melbourne, Melbourne, 1997.

include discussion of broad policy[8] for determining remuneration of senior executives and the link between pay and performance.

The present author carried out research[9] for the purpose of this book into the practices of the top 100 Australian listed companies in 1999 and the main findings were:

- There is still inadequate discussion in most companies about the process for board appointments.
- All companies surveyed now disclosed whether the chair is an executive or non-executive. Out of a response of seventy-three, twelve were executive directors, sixty-one were non-executives.
- All companies surveyed disclosed whether directors were executive or non-executive. The average board size was 9.6 comprised of 2.2 executive directors and 7.4 non-executive directors.
- Most companies discussed management remuneration procedures and criteria but many in the vaguest terms. This was often token compliance with section 200A of the Corporations Act.
- There is inadequate disclosure of risk management practices in many companies. Only 16 per cent of the companies that responded had risk management committees as such.

We discuss other aspects of the survey in the next chapter.

Australian Accounting Standards Board standards

A company's financial statements made in compliance with its annual reporting obligations have to be prepared in accordance with applicable accounting standards. In Australia these may be made by the Australian Accounting Standards Board (AASB) which is now overseen by the new Financial Reporting Council. AASB was established by section 226 of the *Australian Securities and Investments Commission Act 2001*. Its functions and powers are set out in section 227 of that Act.

Compliance with the accounting standards is envisaged by a number of provisions of the Corporations Act. Thus, under section 295(4), the directors' declaration in the annual financial report includes a statement that the financial statements and notes comply with the accounting standards and section 296 imposes a statutory duty on the company, compliance with which must also be declared by the directors in section 295(4)(d)(i). Small proprietary companies which comply with section 293 are exempted from compliance.

Section 297 imposes a duty for the financial statements and notes to give a true and fair view of the financial position and performance of the company or the group. Section 305 imposes a similar duty for half-yearly accounts.

---

8   Effective from 1 July 1998.
9   Based on Annual Reports for 1999. For Disclosure of Corporate Governance Practices in New Zealand see *Best Practices 1998/2*.

The auditor's report under section 307 must also state an opinion as to compliance with the accounting standards and true and fair view. The auditor must quantify the effect of non-compliance under section 308(2).

Similar information has to be provided in the concise report under section 314(2)(a).

There is something of an equation of the two obligations because AASB Release 100 describes 'true and fair view' in terms of 'agreed framework of broad accounting concepts'.

Section 228 requires a purposive interpretation of AASB standards. The courts usually accept proof of compliance with AASB standards as compliance with the statutory obligation and evidence of this is strong but not conclusive evidence of an auditor's compliance with a duty of care in contract and tort.

Section 226(4A) provides that AASB must, so far as is reasonably practicable, ensure that the New Zealand authority is consulted in the course of the development of possible accounting standards and the review of possible accounting standards. AASB has the duty to participate and contribute to the development of a single set of accounting standards for worldwide use (section 227(1)(d)).

The *Corporate Law Economic Reform Program Act 1999* set up an advisory body, the Financial Reporting Council, to oversee the standard-setting process and to ensure that the process is more responsive to the needs of preparers and users of the financial statements. AASB has been reconstituted to fit into this framework.

Australia will continue to harmonise its accounting standards with International Accounting Standards Committee (IASC) standards.

Corporate Practices and Conduct

We now move to an area of softer regulation. *Corporate Practices and Conduct* (CPC) 3rd edition is the report of a working group chaired by Henry Bosch, former chairman of the National Companies and Securities Commission (NCSC) (the predecessor of ASIC), and an experienced business executive. The working group was chosen from the Australian Institute of Company Directors, Australian Society of Certified Practising Accountants, the Business Council of Australia, the Business Law Section of the Law Council of Australia, the Institute of Chartered Accountants in Australia, and the Securities Institute of Australia.The first edition appeared in 1991.

Henry Bosch has described the thinking behind the original initiative as follows:

> Behind the initiative lay two considerations. The honest majority of the business community had been shocked by the revelations that had emerged about a small number of companies that had become very prominent in the late 1980s. They perceived that damage had been done to the reputation of the business community as a whole and they wished to restore that reputation and prevent a repetition of the excesses. It was

recognised that the general acceptance of a set of principles would raise the standard of conduct and make it easier to identify unacceptable behaviour at an early stage.

At the same time there was widespread concern about the Government's legislative program. The new Corporations Law, which was in the last stages of its passage, had been described by the Attorney-General as the largest legislative undertaking in the history of the Commonwealth and, in addition to it a great volume of additional 'reform' was being proposed. Conscious that detailed blackletter law raises the cost of doing business for the honest while often providing a road map for the unscrupulous, a large part of the business community was anxious to slow the Attorney-General's rush to legislate.

In this they had been encouraged by a parliamentary committee which had recently held hearings and produced findings on 'Company Directors' Duties'. It had concluded that, while a basic legal framework was necessary for the fair and efficient operation of the business community, 'The degree to which the law will need to intervene in the corporate sector beyond the provision of this framework depends on the degree to which the corporate sector can effectively regulate itself'.

The four objectives of the report[10] are:

1 to assist listed companies in making the declarations that are required by Australian Stock Exchange (ASX) Listing Rules
2 to assist the directors and officers of companies and other comparable organisations, and their professional advisers, in understanding recent developments in best practice in corporate governance in Australia and overseas, and to assist directors and officers in considering whether any changes are needed in the way their organisations are governed
3 to assist investors to assess the quality of governance in the companies in which they invest
4 to spread and reinforce high standards of corporate conduct.

The report was the subject of close consultation with business leaders and many listed companies expressed support for and compliance with it.[11] The AIMG expressed its support and recommended that its members give preference to investment in companies which complied with it.

Corporate Practices and Conduct (CPC) sets out guidelines, not rigid standards, and does not purport to give specific legal advice.

The third edition of CPC was drawn up in the light of the AIMA Guidelines and overseas reports from the United Kingdom, Canada, the USA, and Hong Kong.[12]

The structure of CPC is:[13]

---

10   *ibid.*, p. 1.
11   H. Bosch, *Corporate Practices and Conduct*, 3rd edn, FT Pitman Publishing, Melbourne, 1995.
12   *ibid.*, 3–4.
13   *ibid.*

- a review of board functions
- matters raised by ASX
- other governance matters, which cover guidelines for conduct of directors, the company secretary and shareholders.

A discussion of recommendations of CPC is contained in the relevant parts of this book and the text of Parts I, II and III are set out in Appendix 1 to this book, with permission from the Business Council of Australia.

The main interest in CPC lies in its review of board functions, the guidance it gives for compliance with ASX requirements and the practical advice it gives to directors and the secretary on a number of matters.

IFSA Guidelines[14]

IFSA is the representative association for the major investment management organisations in Australia and successor to the AIMG and AIMA. It publishes *A Guide for Investment Managers and Corporations*. AIMG was formed in December 1990.

The guidelines for investment managers are for the use of IFSA members in determining their approach to corporate governance, voting, and other issues proposed by public companies in which they invest. The structure of the guidelines is:

(a) guidelines for investment managers
(b) guidelines for corporations.

The guidelines for investment managers deal with:

- communication between investment managers and companies
- voting
- proxy voting policy and procedures
- reporting to clients.

The guidelines for corporations provide a series of guidelines for public companies over a range of corporate governance issues. They provide the framework for a sound approach to corporate governance from the point of view of the investment community.

The guidelines for corporations deals with:

- annual disclosure
- composition of the board of directors
- chairperson to be an independent director
- board committees generally
- key board committees
- appointment of non-executive directors (NEDs)

---

14   See footnote 2 above. IFSA, *Corporate Governance: A Guide for Investment Managers and Corporations.*

- performance evaluation
- equity participation by NEDs
- respective roles of the board and management
- board and executive remuneration policy and disclosure
- company meetings
- disclosure of beneficial shareholder information
- major corporate changes
- company codes of ethics.

A number of these guidelines are discussed in relevant parts of this book and the text is set out in Appendix 2 of this book with kind permission of IFSA.

New Zealand Code of Proper Practice for Directors and Best Practice Statements

The Institute of Directors in New Zealand (Inc.) has produced a code of proper practice to provide guidance to directors to assist them to carry out their duties effectively and in accordance with the highest professional standards. This is more elaborate than the Australian institute's code and is presented as Appendix 3 in this book. It is supplemented by a set of Best Practice Statements, which cover a wide range of topics. The following is a list of contents.

New Zealand Best Practice Statements

1996/1	Directors' and officers' liability insurance and indemnities—a checklist
1996/2	Advisory boards
1996/3	Conflicts of interest
1996/4	Audit committees
1996/5	Evaluation
1996/6	Induction and development
1997/1	Guidelines for non-executive director remuneration
1997/2	Planning the board's workload
1997/3	Committees of the board
1997/4	Successional planning and selection
1997/5	Guidelines for a board in setting a CEO's contract
1997/6	Duties of the chairman
1997/7	Providing business or other professional services to your company
1998/1	Board composition and mix
1998/2	Disclosure of corporate governance practices
1998/3	The solvency test
1998/4	Should executive directors hold non-executive appointments in other entities?
1998/5	Key competencies for non-executive directors

1998/6	Before accepting non-executive board appointments
1998/7	Effective board meetings
1999/1	The conduct of annual meetings
1999/2	The tenure and termination of board appointments
1999/3	Evaluation of the CEO
1999/4	Shareholdings by non-executive directors in their companies

Business ethics

Dr Elaine Sternberg in her useful book *Just Business: Business Ethics in Action*[15] writes: 'All businesses have systems which are simply organised ways of doing things. Like everything else within business, systems are ethical to the extent that they aim at maximising long-term value while respecting distributive justice and ordinary decency.' This stresses the aim of maximising shareholder value while recognising other moral ends. Increasingly, businesses find it useful or convenient to promote accountability through a code of conduct.

Both CPC[16] and the IFSA Guidelines[17] provide that listed companies should have a company code of ethics that is adopted by the board and is available to shareholders on request. In addition, these companies may belong to trade associations which adopt voluntary codes of business ethics. We deal with business ethics in Chapter 33.

The question of business ethics has become something of an international issue and we set out in Appendix 5 the Caux Round Table *Principles for Business*, which deal with relationships with stakeholders, the economic and social impact of business, the spirit of trust going beyond the letter of the law, avoidance of illegal and corrupt operations, support for multilateral trade, and respect for the environment.[18]

---

15   Warner Books, London, 1994, p. 222.
16   CPC, *op. cit.*, Part II para. 8.
17   IFSA, *op. cit.*, Guideline 14.
18   See ch. 32 of this book.

CHAPTER 28

Current Issues in Corporate Governance of Listed Public Companies

In this chapter we will consider five significant practical issues in corporate governance of listed public companies. These are: independent, non-executive directors; board committees; directors' remuneration; takeovers and management buy-outs; and risk management. All five are central to the modern corporate governance debates. Let us look at each in turn.

Independent directors

The idea of independent directors, which is a subset of non-executive director, has been fashionable in the last thirty years[1] and has been a theme song of the Securities and Exchange Commission (SEC) and many corporate governance advocates.[2]

---

1   The idea can perhaps be traced to the *US Investment Company Act 1940* which required the board of a registered investment company to be comprised of at least 40 per cent 'disinterested' persons. This was a measure aimed at potential conflicts of interests.

2   There is extensive literature on this. See for instance M. A. Eisenberg, *The Structure of the Corporation—A Legal Analysis*, Little, Brown & Co, Boston, 1976, pp. 170 *et seq*; L. van den Berghe and L. de Ridder, *International Standardisation of Good Corporate Governance—Best Practices for the Board of Directors*, Kluwer, Dordrecht, Boston, 1999, ch. 10; S. M. Bainbridge, 'Independent Directors and the ALI Corporate Governance Project' (1993) 61 Geo Wash L Rev 1034; J. Cox, 'The ALI, Institutionalisation and Disclosure: the Quest for the Outside Director: An Agenda for Institutional Investors' (1991) 43 Stan L Rev 863; L. Lin 'The Effectiveness of Outside Directors as a Corporate Governance Mechanism: Theories and Evidence' (1996) 90 Northwestern L Rev 898. As to the complex question of the link between such directors and performance see Lin, *op. cit.*; A. Klein, 'Firm Performance and Board Committee Structure' (1993) 41 JL & Econ 275; S. Bhagat and B. Black, 'The Uncertain Relationship Between Board Composition and Firm Performance' (1999) 54 Bus Lawyer 921; J. Lawrence and G. Stapledon, 'Do Independent Directors Add Value?' Research Report, CCLSR, University of Melbourne, 1999.

Some favour all the board, except the CEO, being made up of independent directors but most favour a majority of independent directors. Thus Principle A3 of the Combined Code in the United Kingdom now provides: 'The board should include a balance of executive and non-executive directors (including independent non-executives) such that no individual or small group of individuals can dominate the board's decision taking.'

The Hampel Report[3] thought that it was difficult for non-executive directors to be effective if they made up less than one-third of the board and the Combined Code A3.1 provides: 'The board should include non-executive directors of sufficient calibre and number for their view to carry significant weight in the board's decisions. Non-executive directors should comprise not less than one-third of the board.'

The IFSA 'Guidelines for Corporations'[4] recommend that the boards of listed companies should be constituted with a majority of independent directors and chaired by an independent director and this is supported by 'Corporate Practices and Conduct'.[5]

The idea is tied up with the role of the board as monitoring the performance of management.[6] In this model of the board, as we have seen, the board does not manage but chooses senior management, oversees major plans and policies, reviews performance and holds management accountable.[7] This model is also linked with the role of specialist board committees.

This idea is based on Berle and Means' theory of separation of ownership and control and the need to monitor management performance. Independent directors can also play a useful role in relation to strategic planning and matters such as risk management. However, a super majority of independent directors may result in less effective decision making in these areas.[8]

Problems of definition of independence

Given that independent directors are non-executive directors, the question remains of what constitutes independence.

Corporate Practices and Conduct, Guideline 1.1, states that independence is more likely to be assured if the director:

---

3   Committee on Corporate Governance, *Final Report*, Gee Publishing Ltd, London, 1998, Para. 3.14.
4   Guidelines 2 and 3. As to institutional investor views on this see I. Ramsay, G. P. Stapledon and K. Fong, 'Corporate Governance: The Perspective of Australian Institutional Shareholders' (2000) 18 C&SLJ 110, 115–16.
5   H. Bosch (ed.) *Corporate Practices and Conduct*, 3rd edn, F T Pitman, Melbourne, 1995, pp. 14 and 16. Compare the lower key approach of the New Zealand *Code of Proper Practice for Directors*, para. 4.4.
6   As to this see Eisenberg, *op. cit.*, p. 162.
7   See also *Principles of Corporate Governance: Analysis and Recommendations*, ALI, Philadelphia, 1992, para. 3.02 *et seq.*
8   See Bhagat and Black, *op. cit.*, p. 951 and materials cited.

(i)   is not a substantial shareholder of the company
(ii) has not been employed by the company within the last few years
(iii) is not retained as a professional adviser by the company
(iv) is not a significant supplier to or customer of the company and
(v)   has no significant contractual relationship with the company otherwise than as a director.

The IFSA Guidelines Note No 2.00 is a little more explicit and provides:

- An independent director is a director who is not a member of management (a non-executive director) and who:
- is not a substantial shareholder of the company or an officer of or otherwise associated directly or indirectly with a substantial shareholder of the company
- has not within the last three years been employed in an executive capacity by the company or another group member or been a director after ceasing to hold any such employment
- is not a principal of a professional adviser to the company or another group member
- is not a significant supplier or customer of the company or another group member or an officer of or otherwise associated directly or indirectly with a significant supplier or customer
- has no significant contractual relationship with the company or another group member other than as a director of the company
- is free from any interest and any business or other relationship which could, or could reasonably be perceived to, materially interfere with the director's ability to act in the best interests of the company.

The UK Cadbury Report[9] said that, apart from directors' fees and shareholdings, the non-executive directors should be independent of management and free of any business or other relationship which could materially interfere with exercise of their independent judgment. It is for the board to decide whether this definition is met in particular cases. Information about their relevant interests should be disclosed in the directors' report.

There are similar but less specific definitions in the General Motors Board Guidelines, the Calpers Guidelines, the French *Vienot* Report and the Toronto Stock Exchange Report.[10]

---

9   Paras 4.1 *et seq.* Cf. Calpers, 1997 *Guidelines on Fundamentals*, for what is probably the widest definition.
10   See *Corporate Practices and Conduct*, 3rd edn, FT Pitman Publishing, Melbourne, 1995, p 12. See also Best Practice for New Zealand Directors BP 1998/1 para. 2.4.

Advantages of independent directors

Various arguments are put forward for the practice of appointing independent directors. Thus Professor R. I. Tricker[11] lists the following:

- to give access to relevant external information
- to provide an independent appraisal and check on management
- to strengthen the board
- to give new perspectives on the company's direction
- to provide status
- to provide a counterweight to managerial power
- to provide public accountability and credibility.[12]

Independent directors bring to the board a possible diversity of skill and experience and wider networks. They can also play a useful role in resolution of conflicts of interest, consideration of social issues and the protection of shareholder interests. Overall, they are capable of exercising an independence and objectivity of judgment which it may be difficult for executive directors to achieve or maintain.

Lawrence and Stapledon, in their research report 'Do Independent Directors Add Value?',[13] explain the rationale for independent directors as follows:

- The use of independent directors to monitor the performance of the executive management is one element of a broader tapestry of monitoring devices and rules which serve to reduce the divergency between the interests of shareholders and management ('agency costs').

- It appears that those who advocate an increase in the proportion of independent directors on company boards are implicitly, if not explicitly, suggesting that such a development would bring about a net reduction in agency costs.

- A related—but subtly different—rationale for independent directors has emerged from the OECD's project of preparing corporate governance guidelines aimed particularly at developing countries. The OECD advocates 'good' corporate governance structures and practices, such as including independent directors on the board, on the basis of access to international capital markets.

Three areas where independent directors have proved useful have been takeovers, directors' remuneration, board succession and improving the quality of financial reporting. We examine the first two in more detail later in this chapter.

---

11 R. I. Tricker, *The Independent Director: A Study of the Non-Executive Director and of the Audit Committee*, Tolley Publishing Co. Ltd, Croydon, Vic., 1978, p. 46
12 Cf. *Corporate Practices and Conduct, op. cit.*, p. 11.
13 Centre for Corporate Law and Securities Regulation, University of Melbourne, 1999, Executive Summary.

Disadvantages

Professor Nicholas Wolfson[14] wrote: 'The fundamental design of the reform is to place control over the corporation in the hands of the people whose major interests are elsewhere. Stated so accurately and baldly the proposition sounds fairly idiotic but it is … the most widely accepted reform effort of the past decade.'

He argues first that the empirical underpinnings of the proposals are non-existent. Research had failed to show any significant difference between companies with and those without a majority of independent directors.

Second, he argues that as their main interests are elsewhere, they have no economic incentives to make the company a success. They will be most disposed to protect their reputation by pleasing government regulators and 'private do good reform groups'.

Third, they will most likely enhance the power of the CEO, on whom they will closely rely.

Fourth, they are likely to pursue conservative disclosure philosophies which understate income and overstate expenses.

In an Australian study,[15] Dr Geof Stapledon and Jeffrey Lawrence in 1996 listed six disadvantages:

1   Some independent directors are not sufficiently independent. They are too closely allied to management.
2   On many boards they are outnumbered by executive directors or non-independent directors.
3   Their position is weakened where the chairperson is not an independent director.
4   They have limited time to spend on the directorship.
5   They lack detailed knowledge of the company's business.
6   They are insufficiently linked with shareholders.

Do independent directors add value?

In their 1999 research report with the above title[16] Lawrence and Stapledon said that the US and UK studies have produced mixed results on this question. As regards Australia, their own researches indicated that independent directors do not appear to have added value in the period 1985 to 1995. They stress the need to consider local environmental factors in assessing the relevance of overseas studies. They conclude that there is no sound body of empirical evidence in Australia supporting mandatory corporate governance requirements.

---

14   N. Wolfson, *The Modern Corporation—Free Markets Versus Regulation*, The Free Press, New York, 1984, p. 83.
15   *Corporate Governance in the Top 100*, Research Report, CCLSR, University of Melbourne, Melbourne 1999.
16   *ibid.*, pp. vii–viii.

Conclusion

According to the Korn/Ferry Report for 2000,[17] across Australia and New Zealand boards typically had seven directors. In Australia this was made up of an average of five non-executive and two executive directors. In New Zealand there was an average of only one executive director. In Australia a majority of publicly listed companies had only six directors whereas in New Zealand the figure was seven. Government boards tended to only have one executive—the CEO. Fifteen per cent of Australian non-executive directors were accountants. For New Zealand the figure was 14 per cent. In Australia 10 per cent of directors were women. For non-executive directors the percentage was 13.7. For executive directors the figure was 2.9 per cent, still very low. In New Zealand 13.7 per cent of all directors are women, 16.6 per cent of non-executive directors were women, a significant decline from the previous year. The Korn/Ferry survey is based on a sample of public listed and unlisted and private companies, and government enterprises.

The author's own survey in 1999 of the top 100 listed Australian companies using 1998 data showed an average size of 9.6 with 7.4 non-executive and 2.2 executive directors. There was an average of 0.7 women. What this shows graphically is that the top companies are slow to appoint women directors, particularly as executive directors.

Board committees[18]

Corporate Practices and Conduct[19] page 17 states:

> While properly structured committees can increase board effectiveness, they cannot reduce the responsibility of the board as a whole and care should be taken to ensure that all concerned understand their functions. The Working Group considers the following arrangements to be good practice:
>
> - written terms of reference for each committee, which should deal adequately with its authority and duties, including whether, and in what areas, it can act on behalf of the board, or whether it can only investigate, consider and recommend
> - procedures for reporting to the full board, both orally and in writing

---

17 Korn/Ferry International, *Boards of Directors in Australia and New Zealand* 2000, Korn/Ferry International, Sydney, 2000, p. 8. For a valuable study see M. Fox and G. Walker, 'Boards of Directors and Board Committees in New Zealand: International Comparisons' (1998) 10 Bond LR 341. Fox and Walker report a consistently smaller board size than the Korn/Ferry survey. The mean size for 1996 was 6.

18 See N. Calleja, 'To Delegate or Not to Delegate: Board Committees and Corporate Performance in Australia's Top 100 Companies' (1999) 21 Sydney LR 5; Fox and Walker, *op. cit.*, footnote 17 supra; L. Braiotta Jr and A. A. Sommer Jr, *The Essential Guide to Effective Corporate Board Committees*, Prentice Hall, Englewood Cliffs, NJ, 1987.

19 Third edn, H. Bosch (ed.), F T Pitman Publishing, Melbourne, 1995.

- agreed arrangements for staffing the committees, for providing adequate access to relevant company executives, and agreed procedures for obtaining independent external advice at the cost of the company.

    Where it is particularly important that boards exercise, and are seen to exercise, independent judgment, such as in the areas of company accounts, remuneration practices and the selection of board members, the independence and objectivity of the judgments can be enhanced by the appointment of appropriate committees.

    It is good practice for the membership of committees to be set out in the company's annual report, and consideration should be given to the disclosure of a summary of the terms of reference and other arrangements that have been put in place.

The IFSA Guidelines 4 and 5 (of the Guidelines for Corporations) make similar recommendations and recommend an audit committee, a remuneration committee and a nomination committee.

The arguments for board committees are:[20]

1 they make it more likely that the matter will receive adequate attention.
2 by having proper terms of reference they make it more likely that the matter will be decided objectively and after appropriate in-depth discussion.
3 the committee will bring more independent judgment to bear on the decision.
4 they make it easier to handle sensitive or technical matters.

The arguments against excessive use of committees are:

1 it can lead to erosion of the board's authority
2 it can duplicate work
3 it can freeze out other directors
4 it can lower the level of board proceedings

As to the difficult question of whether membership of such a committee increases the standard of care expected of a director, see Chapter 14. It is imperative that the terms of reference of such committees be realistically drafted with this in mind.

Current Australian and New Zealand practice

According to the 2000 Korn/Ferry survey[21] 91 per cent of Australian and 83 per cent of New Zealand boards operated through one or more formal committees. All Australian and New Zealand top listed public companies operated through committees compared with 44 per cent of Australian and 50 per cent of New Zealand private companies.

Eighty-nine per cent of Australian companies and 80 per cent of New Zealand companies surveyed had an audit committee and 57 per cent of boards in both

---

20   Cf. Calleja, *op. cit.*, pp. 21 *et seq*; Braiotta and Sommer, *op. cit.*, pp. 40–2; van den Berghe, *op. cit.*, ch. 13.
21   Pp. 22–3. Cf. Fox and Walker, *op. cit.*, footnote 17 supra, pp. 345–6. See also Best Practice for New Zealand Directors BP 1997/3.

countries had a compensation committee. Sixteen per cent of Australian companies had a nomination committee but only 6 per cent of New Zealand companies did. Ten per cent of boards in both countries had a risk management committee.

In the author's survey of the top 100 Australian listed companies 93 per cent stated that they had an audit committee and 60 per cent a remuneration committee.

Audit committees

Audit committees were first introduced in the USA in 1978 as a general requirement as a result of the recommendation of the New York Stock Exchange and the SEC. Although they were little heard of in Australia and New Zealand until 1980, they are now common, as we have seen.

The Cadbury Report[22] stated their rationale as follows:

> The Committee believes that boards should appoint audit committees, rather than aiming to carry out their functions themselves. A separate audit committee enables a board to delegate to a sub-committee a thorough and detailed review of audit matters, it enables the non-executive directors to contribute an independent judgement and play a positive role in an area for which they are particularly fitted, and it offers the auditors a direct link with the non-executive directors. The ultimate responsibility of the board for reviewing and approving the annual report remains undiminished by the appointment of an audit committee, but it provides an important assurance that a key area of a board's duties will be rigorously discharged.

This is supported by ASIC, the IFSA Guidelines, *Corporate Practice and Conduct,* and the New Zealand Code of Proper Practice for Directors and Best Practice Statements.[23]

The IFSA Guidance Note No 2.00, Guideline 12, paragraph 6.1 provides:

The audit committee:

- should be chaired by an independent director and be composed entirely of non-executive directors, a majority of whom should be independent directors
- should be composed of directors with the mix of skills, experience and other qualities appropriate for its role
- should assist the board to discharge its responsibilities in connection with the financial management, financial performance and financial reporting of the company, including corporate risk assessment and the system of internal control, preparing the company's financial statements and the independence of the company's auditors, and the quality of their audit

---

22   A. Cadbury, *The Financial Aspects of Corporate Governance: A Report of the Committee on Corporate Govern-ance,* Gee & Co, London, 1992, para. 4.35 and appendix 4.

23   See e.g. IFSA Guidelines 5 para. 12.6.1; *Corporate Practices and Conduct, op. cit.,* footnote 10 supra, pp. 32–6; New Zealand *Code of Proper Practice for Directors,* para. 9.0; New Zealand BP 1996/4.

- should have written terms of reference which include core matters to be dealt with by the committee and core rights of the committee.

An audit committee composed entirely of non-executive directors is free, and would be well advised, to involve company executives, including executive directors, in its business, and it can do so by inviting the appropriate participation of those executives. However, it will also be appropriate for the audit committee to discuss matters with the external and internal auditors in the absence of management, including executive directors. This is so that external and internal auditors are not inhibited by the presence of senior management from raising matters with the committee.

The appointment of an audit committee comprised entirely of non-executive directors with the requisite mix of skills, experience and other qualities achieves all of these objectives.

Remuneration or compensation committees

Corporate Practices and Conduct[24] recommends remuneration or compensation committees for listed companies and proposes that they should review:

- the remuneration arrangements of the chief executive and other senior executives (including incentive plans, share options and other benefits) and service contracts
- the remuneration policies and practices for the company generally
- the recruitment and termination policies and practices of the company
- any company share schemes or other incentive schemes
- company superannuation arrangements
- the remuneration arrangements for members of the board.

The IFSA Guidance Note 2.200 [AQ1], paragraph 12.6.2, provides:

The remuneration committee:

- should be chaired by an independent director and at least a majority of the committee should be independent directors
- should be responsible for reviewing the remuneration of directors and senior management and advising the full board whether the remuneration, in the case of non-executive directors, realistically reflects the responsibilities and risk involved in being an effective director, and in the case of senior management, promotes the long-term growth of shareholder values and is reasonable in comparison with industry or other yardsticks
- should have written terms of reference which include core matters to be dealt with by the committee and core rights of the committee.

24   H. Bosch (ed.) *op. cit.*, pp. 24 *et seq.* See New Zealand BP 1997/1, Guidelines for Non-Executive Remuneration, para. 2.2 (such committees 'can be a useful mechanism').

Nomination committees

The Cadbury Report recommended:[25]

> Given the importance of their distinctive contribution, non-executive directors should be selected with the same impartiality and care as senior executives. We recommend that their appointment should be a formal matter for the board as a whole and that there should be a formal selection process which will reinforce the independence of non-executive directors and make it evident that they have been appointed on merit and not through any form of patronage.

Corporate Practices and Conduct[26] recommends that the main functions of such a committee should be:

- assessing the performance of the CEO annually
- assessing the performance of the board as a whole or making arrangements for the board to assess its own performance
- assessing the contribution of individual directors or arranging for the board to do so
- selecting the nominating candidates for board membership when necessary
- reporting and making recommendations to the board as a whole.

The IFSA Guidance Note No 2.00 paragraph 12.6.3 provides:

The nomination committee:

- should be chaired by an independent director and at least a majority of the committee should be independent directors
- should be responsible for proposing new nominees to the board (after taking into account the other directorships held by candidates), for advising the board on the procedures for assessing existing directors' performance and generally for advising the board on the company's policies on the employment of non-executive directors. This would include the appropriate mix of skills, experience and other qualities, especially the core competencies of the independent directors and the maximum period of service and retirement age proposed by the company
- should be responsible for preparing appropriate disclosure in the company's annual report of its performance of that responsibility
- should have written terms of reference which include core matters to be dealt with by the committee and core rights of the committee.

The 1998 Statement on Corporate Governance from the UK funds management group Hermes, which is more explicit about constitution, recommended that:

- The nomination committee should comprise a minimum of three directors, a majority of whom should be independent non-executive directors. Membership of the committee should be disclosed in the annual report.

---

25   Cadbury, *op. cit.*, paras 4.15 and 4.30.
26   Bosch, *op. cit.*, p. 31. See also IFSA, Guideline 5, para. 12.6.3; and New Zealand BP 1997/4, para. 2.3.

- The chairman of the company and the senior independent NED should always be members of committee.
- The nomination committee should be formally constituted as a subcommittee of the main board to whom it is answerable and to whom it should report. It should be given written terms of reference which deal adequately with its membership, authority and duties.
- The chairman of the remuneration committee should normally be a fully independent NED.
- Hermes recommends that the nomination committee be responsible, after consultation with other directors, for finalising the candidate specification for all board appointments and for approving the process by which suitable candidates are identified and shortlisted, including choosing a third party advisor where appropriate. Confirmation of the appointment should be the responsibility of the board as a whole.
- The nomination committee should ensure that all board appointees undergo an appropriate induction programme.

Conclusion

As Henry Bosch stated in his useful book *The Director at Risk*,[27] 'the mere establishment of a committee is no guarantee that it will make an effective contribution'.

In an interesting recent survey, Nicole Calleja found that companies with audit, remuneration and nomination committees tended to perform better than companies without those types of committees.[28] However, questions of causation of this kind are notoriously difficult to establish and it may be that the existence of such committees is just part of a profile of a better managed, more successful enterprise.

Directors' remuneration

There is a general consensus in the Cadbury Code, Toronto Guidelines, IFSA Guidelines and *Corporate Practices and Conduct* that as a matter of principle the level and form of remuneration should be approved by independent persons acting in the interests of the shareholders and in the case of non-executive directors by the shareholders. This predicates a remuneration or compensation committee as we have seen earlier.

In Australia the rules for listed companies are now quite strict. The remuneration of directors is to be determined in Australia by the company under section 202A of the Corporations Act but this is a replaceable rule. Section 202B deals with shareholders requesting information and provides for 5 per cent or at least 100 members entitled to vote having a right to seek such information. This is a lower threshold than previously.

---

27   H. Bosch, *The Director at Risk*, F T Pitman Publishing, Melbourne, 1995, p. 175.
28   Calleja, *op. cit.* footnote 18 supra, p. 28. Compare the debate on independent directors referred to above, especially Bhagat and Black, *op. cit.*, footnote 2 supra.

In New Zealand the matter is governed by section 161 of the 1993 Act and there is no equivalent of section 202B of the Corporations Act but a general requirement of fairness to the company (section 161(2)).

In Australia excessive remuneration will be caught by the related-party provisions. In Australia the *Company Law Review Act 1998* enacted new disclosure rules for listed companies incorporated in Australia.

These require the directors' report to include:

(a) discussion of broad policy for determining remuneration

(b) discussion of the relationship between such policy and performance

(c) details of the nature and amount of each element of the emoluments paid to each director and each of the five highest paid officers (section 300A(1) of the Corporations Act).

Guidelines produced by the Australian Institute of Company Directors (AICD)[29] recommend the establishment of a remuneration policy and the setting up of remuneration committees. The guidelines set out terms of reference for remuneration committees which include an annual review of the board's own remuneration. The AICD believe that the independence of independent directors should not be compromised by participation in share or options plans for executives or by payments of consultancy fees.

The question of executive and employee share and option schemes has been addressed by IFSA Guidance Notes 12 and 13 of May 2000 [AQ2]. These have also been endorsed by the Australian Institute of Company Directors, Australian Shareholders Association, and the Australian Employee Ownership Association.

The matter was thoroughly reviewed by the UK Greenbury[30] and Hampel Committees[31] Reports. Principle B1 of the UK Combined Code[32] now provides the following on 'The Level of and Makeup of Remuneration':

B.1.1 Remuneration committees should provide the packages needed to attract, retain and motivate executive directors of the quality required but should avoid paying more than is necessary for this purpose.

B.1.2 Remuneration committees should judge where to position their company relative to other companies. They should be aware of what comparable companies are paying and should take account of relative performance. But they should use such comparison with caution, in view of the risk that they can result in an upward ratchet in remuneration levels with no corresponding improvement in performance.

---

29   See *Non-Executive Director Remuneration Guidelines*, AICD, Sydney, October 1996. See also IFSA Guideline 10, Board and Executive Remuneration Policy and Disclosure and Guidance, Note No 2.00, para. 12.11; and New Zealand BP 1997/1, Guidelines for Non-Executive Director Remuneration.

30   *Directors' Remuneration*, Report of a Study Group Chaired by Sir Richard Greenbury, Gee Publishing Ltd, London, 17 July 1995

31   Committee on Corporate Governance, *Final Report*, Gee Publishing Ltd, London, January 1998.

32   Committee on Corporate Governance, *The Combined Code*, Gee Publishing Ltd, London, June 1998.

B.1.3 Remuneration committees should be sensitive to the wider scene, including pay and employment conditions elsewhere in the group, especially when determining annual salary increases.

B.1.4 The performance related elements of remuneration should form a significant proportion of the total remuneration package of executive directors and should be designed to align their interests with those of shareholders and to give these directors keen incentives to perform at the highest levels.

B.1.5 Executive share options should not be offered at a discount save as permitted by paragraphs 13.30 and 13.31 of the Listing Rules.

B.1.6 In designing schemes of performance related remuneration, remuneration committees should follow the provisions in schedule A to this Code.

The emerging best practice is further reflected in the UK Department of Trade and Industry's Consultative Document, *Directors' Remuneration.*[33]
This provides *inter alia*:

1 All quoted companies should be required to set up a remuneration committee of independent non-executive directors.
2 The best practice framework should be strengthened by its stating that:
(a) the chairman of the board should be a member of the committee;
(b) the chairman of the board should ensure that the remuneration committee has access to professional advice from outside the company;
(c) if the committee wishes to seek advice from outside consultants, the committee should itself choose and appoint the consultants;
(d) the committee should not employ remuneration consultants who are also employed by the company's executive management.

Linkage to performance

3 The general framework on linkage to performance should be strengthened by amending the disclosure requirements so that companies are required to make more informative disclosures on linkage to performance.

New provisions should ensure simplified and improved disclosure, particularly the linkage between pay and performance.

Other important corporate governance issues aired by the Consultative Document include:

• whether shareholders of listed companies should have an annual vote on the board's remuneration report
• whether listed companies should be required to have a remuneration policy and whether this should be subject to annual stakeholder approval

---

33 DTI, London, July 1999.

• whether shareholders rather than the board should elect members of the remuneration committee.

In conclusion, it seems that companies are beginning to be held more accountable in respect of their remuneration policy. At present in Australia, at least the rules are stricter, there is greater disclosure, and the practice of remuneration or compensation committees is developing, but in the future, institutional investors may push for the remuneration policy to be voted on at the annual general meeting. New Zealand seems to have opted for a less strict legal regime. This is not necessarily reflected in the rates of remuneration actually paid. According to Korn/Ferry International the average remuneration for non-executive directors in listed companies in Australia was $A52 760. In New Zealand it was $NZ39 130. The rates for non-listed companies were lower.[34]

Takeovers and management buy-outs

In the USA, the role of independent directors in tender offers and mergers is more clearly defined than in Australia and New Zealand.

Takeovers in Australia are closely regulated by the Corporations Act whereas until recently the only detailed regulation in New Zealand has been under the *Companies Amendment Act 1963* and the listing rules. The *Takeover Act 1993*, which introduces a panel and a code, came into force on 1 July 2001. Takeover defences are more restricted in Australia and New Zealand because of the proper purpose doctrine. In Australia this has survived the introduction of a Business Judgment Rule because of the presence of proper purpose in the statutory conditions to be fulfilled.

The most significant area for independent director involvement in Australia and New Zealand is likely to be in a management buy-out where the executive directors have a clear conflict of interest.[35] Independent directors will also play a useful role where the company is in play. This may also arise where there is an outside bid for the company and this is countered by a management buy-out proposal. In these cases the setting up of a committee of independent directors, although not obligatory, would be desirable.

It was held in the New Zealand case of *Trounce v. NCF Kaipoi Ltd*[36] that directors of a target company who were also directors of a bidding company, could not be excluded from the board deliberations but would be answerable if they acted in breach of their fiduciary duties. With respect, this is a naïve and unworkable rule in practice. A stricter

---

34   For best practice in New Zealand see Guidelines for Non-Executive Director Remuneration BP 1997/1. See the Korn/Ferry Survey *Boards of Directors in Australia and New Zealand 2000* Korn/Ferry International, Sydney, 2000.

35   See *Coleman v. Myers* [1977] 2 NZLR 225; *Glandon Pty Ltd v. Strata Consolidated Pty Ltd* (1993) 11 ACLC 895; *Brunninghausen v. Glavanics* (1999) 17 ACLC 1247.

36   (1985) 2 NZCLC 99, 423. This seems questionable in principle but the rule in s. 144 of the New Zealand Act is very lax. Compare US practice: see Braiotta and Sommer, *op. cit.*, footnote 16 supra, pp. 112–15, although the discussion is now slightly dated in the light of more recent Delaware case law.

rule may apply in Australia by virtue of sections 182 and 183 of the Corporations Act and in any event it is always open to directors to voluntarily elect not to participate in the meetings and give their reasons for doing so if they consider that is in the best interests of the company and its shareholders.

The case pays insufficient attention to the risk not only of a conflict of interest but also of a conflict of duty and duty. It may not always be sufficient to disclose one's interest, abstain from voting and absent oneself from the meeting during discussion of the impugned business in this kind of situation. The circumstances may require proactive conduct to identify clearly the perceived conflict and to suggest a course of action to limit the possible damage. This may put the director in a no-win situation through a conflict of duty and duty situation.[37]

Corporate Practices and Conduct[38] deals expressly with directors' duties in a management buy-out as follows:

> In the case of management buy-outs, directors must ensure that shareholders are fully informed and able to make an informed and independent decision on any substantial management buy-out. As there is a greater possibility of conflicts of interest during management buy-out situations, it is important that management buy-outs of any substantial part of the company's business should be subject to shareholder approval. Further:
>
> • non-executive directors should ensure that they make available to all shareholders, as far as possible, all information that is available to the proposed purchaser
>
> • shareholders should be provided with independent expert advice with the independent advisers having access to all information necessary to enable them to give a fully informed opinion as to the merits of the offer.

In the USA a board's duty in such circumstances is not necessarily to produce an auction but to maximise shareholders' return for the board must be fully informed and each director must act free of any disabling personal interest.[39]

In the US Delaware Supreme Court decision in *Mills Acquisition Co. v. Macmillan Inc*,[40] the court confronted an auction process where the board had favoured a bidder preferred by management. This resulted in the favoured bidder being informed of the terms of the rival bid. The court held that this had skewed the process improperly in favour of the preferred bidder. The occasion called for 'intense scrutiny and participation' in the process by the independent directors. Their failure to exercise this amounted to the 'virtual abandonment of the oversight functions', constituting a breach of the fundamental duties of loyalty and care.

---

37 See *Permanent Building Society v. Wheeler* (1994) 12 ACLC 674; *State of South Australia v. Marcus Clarke* (1996) 14 ACLC 1019; *Fitzsimmons v. R* (1997) 15 ACLC 666, 668; *Duke Group Ltd (in liq.) v. Pilmer* (1999) 17 ACLC 1329, 1437–9; reversed on other grounds sub. no. *Pilmer v Duke Group Ltd* [2001] HCA 31.

38 H. Bosch (ed.), *op. cit.*, p. 48.

39 For a useful discussion see A. R. Pinto and D. M. Branson, *Understanding Company Law*, Matthew Bender, New York, 1999, pp. 317 *et seq.*

40 559 A2d 1261 (Del 1989).

This was reaffirmed in *Paramount Communications Inc. v. QVC Network Inc,*[41] where the court held that:

> The Paramount directors had the obligation: (a) to be diligent and vigilant in examining critically the Paramount-Viacom transaction and the QVC tender offers; (b) to act in good faith; (c) to obtain, and act with due care on, all material information reasonably available, including information necessary to compare the two offers to determine which of these transactions, or an alternative course of action, would provide the best value reasonably available to the stockholders; and (d) to negotiate actively and in good faith with Viacom and QVC to that end.

The American Bar Association's *Fundamentals of Corporate Governance: A Guide for Directors and Corporate Counsel*[42] states:

> Three principles can be deduced from *Revlon* and its progeny. First, if called upon to make decisions regarding the sale of the corporation, the sole object of the directors' activities should and must be geared toward generating the highest possible return to shareholders. Second, in a sale of the enterprise, the directors' duty of oversight is heightened. Delaware law appears to encourage, if not require, the board to be actively involved in the design and execution of the sale. The board should not be content merely to delegate the conduct of the sale to others and receive periodic reports. Instead, the board should be prepared to give 'intense scrutiny' to the process and, where appropriate, to participate in its execution. Third, except as they may enhance the value ultimately received by shareholders, defensive devices are likely to be subject to close scrutiny in connection with the sale of the company.

How much of this is applicable to Australian and New Zealand law? The answer seems to be that the first two principles would apply on the basis of current law but directors in Australian and New Zealand have less discretion over takeover defences because of the proper purpose test. As we have seen earlier, this will survive in Australia, notwithstanding the adoption of a statutory Business Judgment Rule.

Risk management

All companies face risk. Indeed the modern company developed as a method of spreading the risk of business failure. Modern financial management is aimed at protecting the company against risk in the areas of interest rates, credit, currency and liquidity. Nevertheless the modern concept of risk management extends beyond financial management to risks of legal liability under such matters as health and safety, public

---

41   637 A2d 34; 48 (Del (1994).
42   G. Varallo and D. Dreisbach, *Fundamentals of Corporate Governance: A Guide for Directors and Corporate Counsel*, p. 44. In order to evade *Revlon*, practitioners sometimes try to structure the transaction as a merger of equals: see *Paramount Communications Inc. v. Time Inc.* 571 A2d 1140 (Del 1989).

liability, trade practices, property, and environment protection legislation. Risk management here extends to operating adequate compliance systems. Any system of risk management needs to balance risk and control.

Risk management is, therefore, another area of corporate governance because:[43]

- directors and management are operating in an increasingly complex legal environment
- failure to attend to risk can lead to extensive corporate and personal liability and criminal sanctions
- defending the consequences of unmanaged risks is costly.

The choices open to management and the board are:[44]

- to accept the risk
- to institute adequate control systems and compliance programs to guard against the risk
- to terminate the conduct in question
- to transfer the risk to another by contract such as insurance or outsourcing.

The fundamental requirements of an adequate risk management system have been identified by the *CCH Corporate Governance—Directors' Handbook*[45] in relation to New Zealand as follows:

1   identification of the main risks
2   training of key employees
3   development of relevant documentation and procedures
4   incorporation of the program into the company's business plan and strategy.

The Australian/New Zealand risk management standard[46] provides a general framework for risk management and sets out procedures which involve:

- establishing the context
- identifying the risks
- analysing the risks
- evaluating the risks
- dealing with the risks
- monitoring and reviewing the risk management program
- communicating and consulting with relevant shareholders.

---

43   M. McSweeney et al., *Corporate Governance: A Directors' Handbook*, CCH NZ Ltd, Auckland, 1999, ch. 19. Appendix I of this sets out a useful checklist. This chapter by M. McSweeney is an excellent treatment of the subject and has been heavily relied on here. See also R. Kendall, *Risk Management for Executives*, Financial Times, London, 1999; for a recent article see R. Ward, 'Managing your Risks @ E-Speed', *Company Director*, March 2000, p. 28. This sets out a risk management continuum ranging from compliance and prevention, through operating performance to shareholder value enhancement. The latter seems to transcend the concept of risk and move into the area of value-based management.
44   McSweeney, *op. cit.*, p. 364.
45   *ibid.*, p. 365.
46   AS/NZS 4360:1999. See Standards Australia, *An International Guide to Best Business Practice—Risk Management*, Standards Australia International Ltd, Strathfield, NSW, 1999.

Although few listed companies in Australia and New Zealand have specific risk management committees they have risk management programs. Often these are part of the board's responsibilities but in an increasing number of companies risk management is dealt with by the audit committee or a compliance committee. References to risk management feature prominently in annual reports. Another development is the shift in perspective among some of the major auditing firms to a strategic risk approach to auditing. This enables them to make themselves more relevant to their clients and to expand the range of additional assurance services they offer.

Corporate Governance in Small and Medium-sized Enterprises

Small and medium-sized enterprise is a vital part of the economy. In Australia there were over a million small businesses in 1996 to 1997. These employed 3.5 million people. They accounted for 97 per cent of all private sector business and more than 50 per cent of all private sector employment.[1] Small and medium-sized enterprises (SMEs) have distinct corporate governance needs.

Definitional questions

What a small or medium-sized enterprise is raises difficult questions of definition. We are talking here about SMEs which are incorporated, not sole traders or partnerships.[2]

The UK Bolton Report in 1971 had this to say about attempting to define a small firm:

> First, in economic terms, a small firm is one that has a relatively small share of its market. Second, an essential characteristic of a small firm is that it is managed by its owners or past owners in a personalised way, and not through the medium of a formalised management structure. Third, it is also independent in the sense that it does not form part of a larger enterprise and that the owner-managers should be free from outsider control in taking their principal decisions.[3]

---

1   See Australian Bureau of Statistics, *Small Business in Australia*, Canberra, 1997, p. 1.

2   M. Robertson and E. Monkhouse, 'The Promise of SMEs', in T. Clarke and E. Monkhouse (eds), *Rethinking the Company*, Pitman Publishing, London, 1994, p. 210.

3   J. E. Bolton, *Small Firms—Report of the Committee of Inquiry on Small Firms*, Cmnd 4811, HMSO, London, 1978, p. 1. Cf. the definition in Australian Bureau of Statistics, *op. cit.*, p. 1.

The first part of this definition is problematic today since through technology a number of SMEs can produce turnover in volumes which were unheard of in 1971. Small firms in niche but lucrative markets can command a large market share in those markets.

The European Union in Eurostat[4] classified enterprises by number of employees as follows in 1992:

Table 29.1 European Union classification of enterprises by number of employees, 1992

	Number of enterprises %	Employment share %
Micro (1–9 employees)	92.1	29.8
Small and medium (10–500)	7.8	41.3
Large (over 500 employees)	0.1	28.9

Many SMEs are family companies and for the purposes of this chapter we shall take such companies as the typical SME.

Family owned business accounts for 83 per cent of all business and employs approximately 50 per cent of the private sector workforce in Australia. Just under 80 per cent are proprietary companies and 1.9 per cent are public companies listed on ASX. In the UK over 76 per cent of companies are family owned. In the USA 90 per cent of companies are family owned with over 30 per cent of the *Fortune* 500 companies being family owned or controlled. Family companies employ more than 60 per cent of the workforce.[5]

Bond University 1993 survey of managing and controlling family owned businesses[6]

A survey carried out by Professor Ken Moores and Associate Professor Joseph Mula of the Bond University Business School addressed the question of how family owned businesses (FOB) survive and grow in Australia.

The survey involved 341 firms, which represented a low response rate.[7]

Definition

The survey took as its definition of family owned business:

4   Cited by Robertson and Monkhouse, *op. cit.*, p. 211. The Australian Bureau of Statistics defines small business as employing fewer than 100 employees in the manufacturing industries and less than 20 in non-manufacturing.
5   (1995) 11 *Company Director* 21.
6   K. Moores and J. Mula, *Managing and Controlling Family Owned Businesses—A Life Cycle Perspective of Australian Firms*, Bond University School of Business, Queensland, July 1993.
7   *ibid.*, Table 5.1.

- a grouping of people related by blood or marriage (family)
- who own the organisation either by controlling 20 per cent or more of the shares or having 25 per cent or more of the family in senior management positions or control 50 per cent or more of the governing group, that is, board of directors, partners or trustees
- where the *business* is one or more legal entities closely held by the family group.

The survey concentrated on those family businesses that had been operating for more than five years with at least the second generation involved in the business.[8]

The following are the main findings relevant for our purposes.

Size

- Fifty per cent of Australian FOBs generated sales in the $5 million to $20 million region as reported for the financial year ended June 1992. The largest firm reported sales over $500 million.
- Fifty per cent of FOBs employed more than 100 employees. Average firm size was 171 but the most common size was 50 employees with the largest firm reporting 4600 staff.
- More than a third of firms indicated that they marketed within a single state while another third reported that they sold their products in six or more Australian states and territories. Forty-two per cent indicated that they sold their products in one or more overseas markets.
- A majority of firms (71 per cent) reported that they had offices/factories in more than one location and in some cases these additional sites were overseas.
- Family firms were widely distributed throughout Australia in much the same way as other small and medium-sized firms. FOBs were represented in a wide cross-section of industries.

Ownership, governance and the family

- The average age of an Australian family business was approximately 50 years. Some families, however, had been in business for more than 100 years, the oldest was in its 143rd year of continuous operation.
- Of those family businesses that have survived beyond the first generation, close to 90 per cent were managed by a second and third generation family member. One firm was in its sixth generation.
- Sixty per cent of family owned businesses were structured as proprietary companies. Less than 5 per cent were public companies.
- Most families owned 50 per cent or more of the firm's shares.
- Family members, on average, made up 80 per cent of the board of directors.
- At least 25 per cent of senior managers were family members.
- Less than 10 per cent of all the staff employed by FOBs were family members.

---

8   *ibid.*, pp. 7–8.

Structure

- FOBs had modest levels of structural complexity as would be expected in closely controlled firms.
- Family firms exhibited a relatively high level of structure centred around specific products and services.
- The chief executive officer was most commonly the senior family member.

Management and control

- Family firms used conventional financial reports to control their businesses.
- Historically based profit and loss statements and balance sheets, largely prepared using computerised systems, were the primary controls used by FOBs.
- Moderate use was made of more modern management techniques.
- Long-term planning was only moderately used.
- The importance of speed and delivery of a diverse set of information was relatively important, indicating that family businesses tended to value information that is broadly based and supplied relatively quickly.

Succession

- About 60 per cent of FOBs had succession plans in place.
- Eighty per cent of those with succession plans intended to appoint a family member as the next chief executive officer.

Monash University 1996 survey of family business

A study by Professor Claudio Romano and Dr Kosmas Smymios of Monash University,[9] using criteria similar to previous overseas studies, took the following as the definition of family business for inclusion in their study:

- more than 50 per cent of the ownership is held by a single family
- more than 50 per cent of the ownership is held by more than one family
- a single family group is effectively controlling the business
- a significant proportion of the senior management is drawn from the same family.

The study sampled 5000 businesses randomly selected from Dun and Bradstreet's national data base (1994) and the Victorian Employers Chamber of Commerce and Industry (1994).

---

9   C. Romano and K. Smymios, 'Family Business Survey Findings', in *Family Business*, BLEC, Sydney, 1996, p. 1.

Ownership

The survey found:

- 76.3 per cent of respondents identified their ownership through one family
- 15.2 per cent through more than one family
- 5.6 per cent rated majority of management as their owners
- In 2.9 per cent the family exerted significant control.

Lifespan

The average age of the owner was fifty-two years. There was a strong preference for majority ownership and 81.7 per cent of the respondents stated that the family owner-ship was important, 50.8 per cent preferred ownership to remain in the family, whereas 49.2 per cent had no specific policy at the present time.

The average period of establishment was 30.8 years with a range from 1 year to 158 years. The period was less than the Bond survey but no doubt reflects the samples used. The average life cycle of a UK family business is 24 years, which reflects the average career of the founder. The Australian period of establishment showed an interesting difference in both surveys.

Board structure

- 51.4 per cent of family owned businesses had two directors
- 19.2 per cent had three directors
- 16 per cent had four directors
- 63.6 per cent had no non-family members on the board
- 16.5 per cent had one non-family members on the board
- 9.5 per cent had two non-family members of the board
- 36.6 per cent held monthly directors meetings but
- 35.7 per cent met only annually or every six months.

The majority of management positions were held by members of the family.

Business policy and financing

Only 37.2 per cent of family owned businesses had a business plan in place. The Aus-tralian Bureau of Statistics *Small Business in Australia 1997*[10] survey showed that only 21 per cent did.

As regards finance the five most important sources were:

- retained profits (24 per cent)
- shareholder funds (21 per cent)

---

10   *Op. cit.,* p. 88.

- cash flow (18 per cent)
- bank loans (12 per cent)
- overdrafts (11 per cent).

Leasing and equity finance ranked lowest.

The Australian Bureau of Statistics survey[11] in 1997 showed that three-quarters of small businesses in Australia were established by using personal savings or borrowings.

For advice outside the company, 70.6 per cent relied on accountants, only 5.7 per cent on lawyers, 24.2 per cent relied on none.

Succession policy

Succession and retirement presented a problem: 40.8 per cent of family businesses survived to the second generation but only 11.3 per cent to the third.

The nature of family business inevitably involves dual roles and family issues can affect business decisions but 72.7 per cent of respondents stated that where there was conflict business objectives prevailed.

Economic issues in SMEs[12]

As both surveys showed there tends to be less separation of ownership and control in family owned SMEs. SMEs tend to have few managers and these are the largest residual claimants.[13] There is thus not the specialisation that one gets in a listed public company.[14] The investors usually have a larger percentage of their wealth tied up in one firm and lack access to capital markets. They lack the advantage of diversification. The monitoring costs are, however, lower because of active involvement by the owners.[15]

Nevertheless the dual roles involved in family owned SMEs give rise to some agency problems which are exacerbated by death, divorce or retirement of the founder or key person.[16]

There is lack of a liquid market for the shares. This can make valuation difficult, create problems over distribution policies, preclude reliance on public monitoring, and discourage involvement by outsiders.[17] Also, the lack of a liquid market makes share options and share participation schemes for employees less attractive than in a listed public company.[18]

---

11   *ibid.*, p. 89.
12   See F. Easterbrook and D. Fischel, *The Economic Structure of Corporate Law*, Harvard University Press, Cambridge, Mass., 1991, ch. 9.
13   *ibid.*, p. 228.
14   *ibid.*, p. 229.
15   *ibid.*
16   *ibid.*, pp. 299–330.
17   *ibid.*, p. 230.
18   *ibid.*, p. 231.

Specific corporate governance issues[19]

Common problems

Common challenges faced by family owned SMEs are:[20]

- failure to find capital for growth without diluting the family's equity (total ownership control being a sacrosanct principle for many families)
- an inability to balance the family's need for liquidity and the business's need for cash
- poor estate planning and the inability of the next generation to pay inheritance taxes
- unwillingness on the part of the older generation to 'let go' of ownership and management power at the appropriate moment
- An inability to attract and retain competent and motivated family successors
- unchecked sibling rivalry with no consensus on the chosen successor
- an inability to attract and retain competent senior non-family managers
- unmanaged conflict between the cultures of the family, the board, and the business and an inability to develop appropriate governance structures that assign optimal roles to each of the governance institutions or bodies.

It is important to notice here the predominance of factors relating to the question of ownership and management succession which mark the fragility of family SMEs.

Christopher Goldsworthy, in a postgraduate research paper on 'Corporate Governance in Family and Closely Held Enterprises' done in 1998 under the author's supervision at Bond University, listed the following as characteristics of a family firm that can create difficulties and emphasised that the list was not exhaustive:[21]

- family firms are usually managed by the people who own them
- the ability of family members may not necessarily face the same scrutiny as in public companies before appointment to management positions and there may be no allowance for the differing abilities of family members and the influence he or she may have on what business decisions are taken
- asymmetries of remuneration may exist, for example, length of service versus actual position of seniority. This often leads to a culture of friction and apathy
- allocation of management positions among family members may be done on an *ad hoc* basis instead of conforming to actual performance criteria
- the criteria for business decisions in a family firm may result from an individual preference rather than being evaluated on a more formalised basis.

---

19   For an excellent study of the problems of such companies under the New Zealand *Companies Act 1993* see R. Dugan, P. McKenzie and D. Patterson, *Closely Held Companies—Legal and Tax Issues*, CCH New Zealand Ltd, Auckland, 2000.

20   F. Neubauer and A. G. Lank, *The Family Business: Its Governance for Sustainability*, Macmillan Press Ltd, Basingstoke, 1998, p. 17.

21   C. Goldsworthy, *Corporate Governance in Family and Closely Held Enterprises*, MBL Individual Study, Law School, Bond University, 1998, pp. 6–7.

- while conforming to imposed regulation there may be scant attention paid to corporate governance issues, for example, the way meetings of family shareholders are conducted, how decisions are taken within those meetings and the use of committees
- the use of executive share ownership and its implications for remuneration
- strategic business decisions may be made on an emotional level instead of agreed rates of return on investment/equity. This is especially so if the decision involves divestiture of part of the founding business.

Formalising the relationship with the family

There is a need for agreement on the relationship between the family and the company. As families get bigger or go into the second generation it may be necessary to have something like a family council. The policy of the family in relation to the company needs to be determined.

The corporate constitution needs to be carefully drafted to take into account the policies of the family. It may need to be amended over time in the light of changing circumstances.

The question of minority shareholders will assume greater significance as the family goes into the second and third generations. Steps may need to be taken to avoid the risk of deadlock in decision making.

From a consideration of the majority interest it may be desirable to spell out more matters in the constitution since the courts may otherwise engage in a broader based equitable enquiry in exercise of their statutory powers under sections 232 (statutory minority shareholders' remedy) or 461(1)(e), (f), (g) or (k) (solvent winding up by the court) or their New Zealand equivalents.

Structure and role of the board

Matters such as choice of the members of the board of directors, the appointment of a CEO, buy-out rights and internal dispute resolution mechanisms are all matters which can usefully be covered in the constitution or a shareholders agreement.

There is a need for regular board meetings and consideration should be given to the appointment of at least one outside director. Such a person can perform a number of useful roles in a family SME. These include:[22]

- *Arbitrator*—capable of handling family disagreements, hostilities, and other emotional stresses or conflicts.
- *Gap-filler*—when owners lack time or expertise to cope with the difficulties of managing a family firm in a dynamic environment.

---

22   R. Mueller, 'Differential Directorship: Special Sensitivities and Roles for Serving the Family Business Board' (1988) 1 *Family Business Review* 3.

- *Resource* to the board or top management, who can supplement internal resources and provide freedom from group and insider thinking when key decision makers are advocates of a particular view or beneficiaries of a particular action.
- *Father confessor* with whom owner, directors, and managers can talk confidentially and share concerns, hopes, or troubles.
- *Devil's advocate*, who can pinpoint the defects in the evidence or presentation when a family-dominated board needs a champion of the worst cause or case.
- *Catalyst* and agent of change who can provoke the need for significant shifts in conduct or objectives of the enterprise. Going public, making a divestment or an acquisition, or changing top personnel are all examples of this kind of catalytic action.
- *Image builder* who as a talented or distinguished person adds credibility to the firm by his or her association and identification with the enterprise.
- *Corporate networking agent* whose network of potential sources of capital, new business, technology, information on economic trends, international contacts, and connections in industry, government, and education can benefit the family firm.

In the case of family SME boards there are broadly four scenarios. First, it may have little or no influence. This is a very dangerous situation and board members face potential legal liability for their passivity. Second, it may be protective of the family. There are dangers here if this is at the expense of the minority shareholders or creditors. Third, it may play a role in strategy and the hiring of key management and, fourth, it may actually run the business.[23]

Other key governance issues are: determining an appropriate retirement and succession plan; and other business strategies for the future which may involve a sale, merger or going public.

Good corporate governance is developmental and changes over time. Just as the needs of a family change over time, so too do the needs and imperatives of a business. The two do not necessarily coincide. Good corporate governance in an SME involves striking the appropriate balance.[24]

The impact of recent reforms on corporate governance in SMEs

The major legal reforms that affect corporate governance in SMEs are:

- the introduction of the single-person company
- the possibility of unanimous shareholder consent
- in New Zealand the use of section 42 of the Act which authorises the board of directors to issue shares as it thinks fit
- the facilitation of shareholder agreements in New Zealand.

---

23 Neubauer and Lank, *op. cit.*, pp. 101 *et seq.*
24 R. Narva, *The World of Family Business*, GT ONLINE Assurance and Governance, <www.gt.com/content/ic840.asp> 1996.

Both Australia and New Zealand now recognise the single-person company.[25] The main corporate governance issue here is the protection of creditors.[26]

The express statutory recognition of unanimous shareholder agreements in proprietary companies in section 249(A) of the Corporations Act[27] was probably based on earlier case law and unanimous shareholder agreements in North American laws.[28] However, the North American provisions remove the necessity for a board and allow the shareholders to run the business. The Australian and New Zealand provisions do not do so.

Section 107 of the New Zealand Act is more complex than the Australian provision.[29] It only applies to matters listed in section 107(1), (2) and (3). Section 107(1) and (2) deals with matters relating to share capital. Section 107(3) deals with dispensing with the limited formalities required for self-interested transactions by directors. A shareholder is allowed to withdraw his or her consent under section 107(6). A section 107 assent is subject to a solvency requirement under section 108.

In the New Zealand Act section 42, probably by accident, seems to defeat some of the protection of the Act and confers on the board powers to issue shares without corresponding protection for minority shareholders.[30] The problem is likely only to arise in companies where there is a person holding more than 25 per cent but less than 51 per cent of the votes.[31] In the case of a listed company any abuse is addressed by the listing rules which require shareholder approval for most new issues.[32]

Shareholder agreements have been less common in Australia and New Zealand than in North America in the past except in relation to joint ventures.[33] Now New Zealand law, having abolished private companies, and following the North American practice, envisages a greater role for shareholder agreements in the case of SMEs.[34] Shareholder agreements can be particularly useful for defining the relationship between the company and a particular family.

Both the Corporations Act and the New Zealand Act remain, notwithstanding these reforms, unsuitable frameworks for SMEs. Both are primarily aimed at a situation characterised by a separation of ownership and control. They are not well suited, therefore, to the majority of companies which do not have these characteristics.

---

25   Sections 135(1), 198E, 201F and 202C of the Corporations Act; s. 10 of the New Zealand Act.
26   See s. 249A, introduced in 1998 and amended in 1999. This provides for the circulation and signature of one or more copies of a written resolution.
27   However, for other practical issues involving such companies in New Zealand, see the thorough discussion in R. Dugan, P. McKenzie and D. Patterson, *Closely Held Companies—Legal and Tax Issues,* CCH New Zealand Ltd, Auckland, 2000, ch. 12.
28   See *ibid.,* ch. 7.
29   *ibid.,* p. 134.
30   *ibid.,* ch. 8.
31   *ibid.,* p. 182.
32   *ibid.,* p. 182; New Zealand Stock Exchange Listing Rules, Rule 7.3.
33   See J. H. Farrar and M. W. Russell, *Company Law and Securities Regulation in New Zealand,* Butterworths, Wellington, 1985, ch. 9.
34   See Dugan, McKenzie and Patterson, *op. cit.,* ch. 9.

As Dugan, McKenzie and Patterson say in relation to the New Zealand Act:[35]

> The statute requires the gathering and dissemination of information that has little value for those affected by the business, complicates the making of decision and the implementation of common transactions, poses liability traps for the unwary and turns honest business people into involuntary offenders. The rules raise the cost of using the corporate form without providing any offsetting benefit except to those involved in the compliance industry.

They recommend the adoption of a limited liability company act along the lines of US laws. These provide for a kind of incorporated limited partnership and contain a minimal mandatory core necessary for the corporate form while allowing members the same freedom to regulate their affairs by agreement as they enjoy in respect of other commercial arrangements. There is much to be said for the adoption of uniform trans-Tasman legislation along these lines. US experience shows the efficacy of this legislation and does not demonstrate any significant abuse.[36]

---

35   *ibid.*, p. 733.
36   *ibid.*, p. 738.

CHAPTER 30

Corporate Governance in
Not for Profits

In this chapter we shall look at corporate governance problems of not for profit corporations (NFPs), which are a distinct type of organisation. We are concentrating on incorporated bodies and do not consider those that are unincorporated.

Distinctive characteristics of not for profits

In a useful article on Australia's non-profit sector in *Year Book Australia 1999*, Associate Professor Mark Lyons of the University of Technology, Sydney described the range of NFPs as follows:[1]

> Many well-known organisations are non-profit organisations, for example: Opera Australia and the Australian Football League, the ACTU and the Business Council of Australia; the Australian Jockey Club and the Surf Lifesaving Association; the Melbourne Club and the Returned Services League, the Brotherhood of St Laurence and the Salvation Army; the Australian Labor Party and Pauline Hanson's One Nation Party; the Australian Medical Association and Greenpeace; Geelong Grammar School and the Workers Educational Association. Many more non-profits constitute the fabric of local communities, for example: local play groups and child care centres, sporting clubs and associations, recreation clubs and societies, churches and church groups, residents' associations, and service clubs.
>
> Non-profit organisations are many and varied, but together they constitute a separate, distinct class of organisations, neither government nor business, with their own distinctive rules and characteristics.

---

1   Australian Bureau of Statistics, *Year Book Australia 1999*, Canberra, 1999, pp. 536–41. See also his recent work *Third Sector*, Allen & Unwin, Crows Nest, NSW, 2001.

371

Professor Lyons describes the distinctive characteristics as the following:[2]

- NFPs are organisations with their own set of rules.
- NFPs are private organisations.
- NFPs operate on a not for profit basis.
- NFPs involve some degree of voluntary commitment of time.
- NFPs are member owned or owned by other NFPs, for example church-based social welfare organisations such as the Blue Nurses.
- The financing of NFPs is generally more complicated than government or the private sector organisations.

NFPs make a significant contribution to the economy, particularly the service economy, and also play an important social and political role.[3]

The size of Australia's non-profit organisations is indicated in Table 30.1, based on 1995 to 1996 data. The table shows operating expenditure and number of employees.

Table 30.1 Australia's non-profit organisations, by field of activity, 1995 to 1996

Field of activity	Operating expenditure (a) $m	Number of employees (b) No.
Health	4 200	111 000
Education and research	6 600	137 000
Community services	3 700	132 000
Other human services (including housing, legal services, employment services)	400	12 000
Religion	900	17 000
Arts and culture	400	5 000
Leisure (including sport, recreation and social clubs)	5 900	94 000
Interest organisations (including business, trade and professional associations, trade unions, political parties, lobby and advocacy organisations)	3 000	47 000
Other (including accommodation such as university colleges, school parents organisations, emergency service organisations, charitable trusts).	1 400	16 000
Total	26 500	571 000

(a) Rounded to nearest $100 million. (b) Rounded to nearest 1000 at the end of June 1996.
Source: CACOM estimates based on published and unpublished ABS data. Taken from *Year Book Australia 1999*, 538.

---

2 *ibid.*, pp. 536–7.
3 *ibid.*, p. 540. For a recent discussion of the more active NFPs see D. Bagnall, 'The Influence Epidemic', *Bulletin*, 9 May 2000, p. 26.

We shall concentrate on sporting organisations, churches and universities, each of which have very distinctive characteristics, but before we do so, we will look at the purpose of NFP and how this is related to questions of taxation. NFPs are a subset of Non-Government Organisations or NGOs.

Purpose

All NFPs by definition exist for a purpose other than profit. That is not to say that they cannot or do not make a profit. It simply means that they cannot return it to investors. The purpose may include the promotion of some sport, the mission of a particular church or some educational objectives.

Some NFPs are charities or, to put it more accurately, charitable corporations.

The constitution of the particular NFP defines its purpose both by inclusion and exclusion.

The drafters of the US Non-Profit Guidebook make an interesting comment:[4]

It has been said that all organisations exist to maximize *something* for *somebody*: the non-profit corporation is no exception. Defining the *something* and the *somebody* is a duty of every non-profit board and every director.

The consequences of failure to bear in mind the purpose may expose the board or other governing body to an internal claim for *ultra vires,* or subject the body to taxation, or lose the body its tax exempt status under section 50-5 or 50-45 of the *Income Tax Assessment Act 1997.*

The fundamental purpose, therefore, is not to make a profit but to advance a purpose. For those members of the board or governing body accustomed to the private sector there is a steep learning curve.

There is usually no question of significant ownership interests and no clearly defined residual claimants and control often rests as a consequence with the officers, subject to loose constraints by the board or other governing body. Sometimes difficult questions of financing new ventures have to be considered, and not for profits often have a weak accounting and financial function which can exacerbate the risk for board members.

NFPs fall between the public and private sectors and are thus subject neither to many of the disciplinary forces which apply to the private sector nor to the public sector controls. They are, however, free to resolve some of the contractual problems associated with specific economic activities more effectively.[5]

---

4   Cited in A. Davis, *A Strategic Approach to Corporate Governance,* Gower, Aldershot, 1999, p. 61.
5   See R. Hirshhorn, 'The Governance of Non Profits', in R. Daniels and R. Morck (eds), *Corporate Decision-Making in Canada,* University of Calgary Press, Calgary, 1995, p. 591.

Property rights, contracts and governance of NFPs

In the public sector the residual claimants are at least well defined and mechanisms exist for bureaucratic and political controls.[6]

NFPs lack these controls as well as the constraints of the private sector which emanate from clearly defined ownership rights.

At the same time, NFPs operate in markets and the question arises as to their rationale in such markets. Hansmann[7] explains this in terms of market failure as well as the special characteristics of charitable donations. Another rationale is the ability of NFPs to operate in respect of public functions such as employee recruitment, free of political constraints which inhibit experimentation, particularly with new services.[8] It has also been argued that NFPs may economise on transaction costs of monitoring and enforcing contracts.

In the case of charities, donors and recipients act as some kind of equivalent of residual claimants.[9] The risk of staff capture of benefits in NFPs is also met to some extent by the motivation of management and employees of some NFPs to serve the mission of the NFP. This is true of bodies such as churches, less true of universities and many of the larger sporting organisations.

Four cultures of governance

In a recent UK report by the Ford Partnership, *Under Pressure: Trends in the Governance of Large Charities for the 21st Century*,[10] four cultures of governance were identified:

1   trust culture
2   membership culture
3   stakeholder culture
4   strategic culture

The first is the legalistic culture appropriate for those bodies that are actually trusts, particularly charitable trusts. It is not necessarily appropriate for those that are not and tends to lead to more conservative decision making.

The second involves membership control and can lead to political systems and mandates that may be incompatible with charity laws. Membership culture is particularly present in mutuals.

The third is appropriate for those bodies providing services and is characterised by a fluid consensus.

---

6   *ibid.,* p. 595.
7   H. Hansmann, 'The Role of Non-Profit Enterprise' (1980) 89 Yale LJ 835.
8   Hirshhorn, *op. cit.,* p. 595.
9   *ibid.,* p. 596.
10 Compare Lyons *op. cit.* (2001) cited in footnote 1 at pp. 126–31. See also P. D. Steane and M. Christie 'Non-rofit Boards in Australia: A Distinctive Governance Approach' (2001) 9 Corporate Governance. An International Review 48.

The fourth is a private sector approach concentrating power in the board and the CEO. The aim is professionalism. The problem is ensuring accountability, particularly since most boards will be staffed by volunteers.

The problem with the larger sporting NFPs is that they are becoming very large businesses increasingly governed by the strategic culture while getting the benefits of tax exemptions. It is to these we now turn.

Corporate governance in sporting organisations

In Australia incorporated sporting NFPs will either be incorporated associations under state legislation, usually one of the Associations Incorporation Acts, or companies limited by guarantee under the Corporations Act. Thus the Queensland Rugby Union Inc. is an incorporated association but the Australian Rugby Union Limited is a company limited by guarantee. Australian Rugby Football League and Soccer Australia Limited are all companies limited by guarantee.

Both types of organisation will usually have a written constitution which operates as a contract.[11] Management of an incorporated association rests with a committee who, in Queensland, are deemed to be its agents and it is assumed that they are subject to some of the basic duties of directors. This is expressly recognised in Part IV of the South Australian Act and Part 5 of the Victorian Act but not by other state statutes, although section 38 of the NSW Act contains an insolvent trading offence. The committee is, however, expressly made subject to judicial review and to the rules of natural justice[12] in most states. We show the differences between the state and ACT acts in Table 30.2.

There is a real need for harmonisation of the legislation and for the expression of provisions equivalent to the basic fiduciary duties for the committees and officials of such bodies in all the states. Currently, they are probably subject to the basic duties of agents or employees.

Companies limited by guarantee are public companies under the Corporations Act and are subject to the rules discussed in earlier chapters.

From a tax point of view the main purpose of the NFP must be the encouragement of the relevant game or sport. All of the club's features have to be weighed up to ascertain its main purpose.

The society, club or association must not be carried on for the purposes of gain to its individual members. There needs to be an express prohibition in the constitution.

The concept of encouragement of a game or sport can occur directly through coordinating activities, training participants, and improving standards or indirectly by marketing, research and development.

---

11 This is expressly stated by the NSW, Victoria, Queensland and South Australia legislation. As to a company limited by guarantee see s. 140(1) of the Corporations Act.
12 See *Associations Incorporation Act 1981* (Qld), sections 71(2) and (3); AIA 1985 (SA), s. 40; AIA 1981 (Vic), s. 14B.

Table 30.2 Incorporated associations: a comparison of legislative provisions[1]

Jurisdiction	VIC[2]	WA[3]	SA[4]	ACT[5]
Duties of committee members	Section 29 A Duties of committee members (1) A member or former member of the committee of an incorporated association must not knowingly or recklessly make improper use of information acquired by virtue of his or her position in the incorporated association so as to gain, directly or indirectly, any pecuniary benefit or material advantage for himself or herself or any other person, or so as to cause a detriment to the incorporated association. Penalty: 60 penalty units. (2) A member of the committee of an incorporated association must not knowingly or recklessly make improper use of his or her position in the incorporated association so as to gain, directly or indirectly, any pecuniary benefit or material advantage for himself or herself or any other person or so as to cause detriment to the incorporated association. Penalty: 60 penalty units. (3) If a person is found guilty of an offence against this section, the court, in addition to imposing any penalty, may order the person to pay a sum specified by the court to the incorporated association as compensation. (4) An order made under sub-section (3) must be taken to be a judgment debt due by the offender to the incorporated association and payment of any amount remaining unpaid under the order may be enforced in the court by which it was made.		Section 39A Duties of officers, etc. (1) An officer of an incorporated association must not, in the exercise of his or her powers or the discharge of the duties of his or her office, commit an act with intent to deceive or defraud the association, members or creditors of the association or creditors of any other person or for any fraudulent purpose. Maximum penalty: $20 000 or imprisonment for four years. (2) An officer or employee of an incorporated association, or former officer or employee of an incorporated association, must not make improper use of information acquired by virtue of his or her position in the association so as to gain, directly or indirectly, any pecuniary benefit or material advantage for himself or herself or any other person, or so as to cause a detriment to the association. Maximum penalty: $20 000 or imprisonment for four years. (3) An officer or employee of an incorporated association must not make improper use of his or her position as such an officer or employee so as to gain, directly or indirectly, any pecuniary benefit or material advantage for himself or herself or any other person, or so as to cause a detriment to the association. Maximum penalty: $20 000 or imprisonment for four years. (4) An officer of a prescribed association must at all times act with reasonable care and diligence in the exercise of his or her powers and the discharge of the duties of his or her office. Maximum penalty: $1250. (5) A person who contravenes a provision of this section is liable to the association for any profit made by him or her and for any damage suffered by the association as a result of that contravention.	

Table 30.2 Incorporated associations: a comparison of legislative provisions *(Continued)*

Jurisdiction	VIC	WA	SA	ACT

Disclosure of interest	**Section 29 B Disclosure of interest**
	(1) A member of the committee of an incorporated association who has any direct or indirect pecuniary interest in a contract, or proposed contract, with the incorporated association:
	  (a) Must, as soon as he or she becomes aware of his or her interest, disclose the nature and extent of his or her interest to the committee; and
	  (b) Must disclose the nature and extent of his or her interest in the contract in the statement submitted under section 30(3) by the incorporated association to its members at the next annual general meeting of the incorporated association.
	10 penalty units.
	(2) Sub-section (1) does not apply in respect of a pecuniary interest that exists only by virtue of the fact:
	  (a) That the member of the committee is an employee of the incorporated association; or
	  (b) That the member of the committee is a member of a class of persons for whose benefit the incorporated association is established; or
	  (c) That the member of the committee has the pecuniary interest in common with all or a substantial proportion of the members of the incorporated association.
	(3) If a member of the committee of an incorporated association discloses a pecuniary interest in a contract, or proposed contract, in accordance with this section, or his or her interest is not such as need be disclosed under this section:
		Section 21 Disclosure of interest
		(1) A member of the committee of an incorporated association who has any direct or indirect pecuniary interest in a contract, or proposed contract, made by, or in the contemplation of, the incorporated association:
		  (a) Must, as soon as he becomes aware of his interest, disclose the nature and extent of his interest to the committee.
		Penalty: $500.
		(2) Subsection (1) does not apply in respect of a pecuniary interest that exists only by virtue of the fact:
		  (a) that the member of the committee is an employee of the incorporated association; or
		  (b) that the member of the committee is a member of a class of persons for whose benefit the association is established.
		(3) Where a member of the committee of an incorporated association discloses a pecuniary interest in a contract or proposed contract in accordance with this section, or his interest is not such as need be disclosed under this section:
		  (a) the contract is not liable to be avoided by the association on any ground arising from the fiduciary relationship between the member and the incorporated association; and
		  (b) the member is not liable to account for profits derived from the contract.
		(4) An association shall cause every disclosure made under this section by a member of the committee to be recorded in the minutes of the meeting of the committee at which it is made.
			Section 31 Disclosure of interest
			(1) A member of the committee of an incorporated association who has any direct or indirect pecuniary interest in a contract, or proposed contract, with the association:
			  (a) must, as soon as he or she becomes aware of his or her interest, disclose the nature and extent of his or her interest to the committee; and
			  (b) must disclose the nature and extent of his or her interest in the contract at the next annual general meeting of the association (if an annual general meeting is required to be held by the association).
			Maximum penalty: $5000.
			(2) Subsection (1) does not apply in respect of a pecuniary interest that exists only by virtue of the fact:
			  (a) that the member of the committee is an employee of the association; or
			  (b) that the member of the committee is a member of a class of persons for whose benefit the association is established; or
			  (c) that the member of the committee has the pecuniary interest in common with all or a substantial proportion of the members of the association.
			(3) Where a member of the committee of an incorporated association discloses a pecuniary interest in a contract, or proposed contract, in accordance with this section, or his or her interest is not such as need be disclosed under this section:
				Section 65. Disclosure of committee member's interest
				(1) Where a member of the committee of an incorporated association has any direct or indirect pecuniary interest in a contract or proposed contract to which the association is or may be a party, the committee member shall:
				  (a) as soon as the interest becomes apparent to him or her, disclose the nature and extent of the interest to the committee; and
				  (b) disclose the nature and extent of the interest at the next general meeting of the association.
				Penalty: $2000.
				(2) A member of the committee of an incorporated association who has an interest in a contract or proposed contract referred to in subsection (1) shall not take part in making any decision with respect to the contract or proposed contract, but may, subject to this section and section 66, participate in any deliberations of the committee with respect to the contract or proposed contract.
				Penalty: $2000.
				(3) Subsection (1) does not apply in relation to a member of the committee of an incorporated association in respect of an interest in a contract or proposed contract that arises only because the committee member is an employee of the association.
				(4) Where a member of the committee of an incorporated association discloses an interest in a contract or proposed contract in accordance with subsection (1), or has an interest in a contract or proposed contract of the kind referred to in subsection (3):
				  (a) the contract is not liable to be avoided by the association on any ground arising from the fiduciary relationship between the committee member and the association; and

Table 30.2 Incorporated associations: a comparison of legislative provisions *(Continued)*

Jurisdiction	VIC	WA	SA	ACT
	(a) The contract is not liable to be avoided by the incorporated association on any ground arising from the fiduciary relationship between the member and the association; and (b) the member is not liable to account for profits derived from the contract.		(a) the contract is not liable to be avoided by the association on any ground arising from the fiduciary relationship between the member and the association; and (b) the member is not liable to account for profits derived from the contract.	(b) the committee member is not liable to account for any profits derived by him or her from the contract or proposed contract. (5) A person who contravenes a provision of this section is liable to the association for any profit made by that person or any other person, and any damage or loss suffered by the association, as a result of that contravention.
Voting on a contract in which committee member has an interest	Section 29 C Voting on contract in which committee member has interest (1) A member of the committee of an incorporated association who has any direct or indirect pecuniary interest in a contract, or proposed contract, with the incorporated association must not take part in any decision of the committee with respect to that contract but may, subject to the provisions of this Part, take part in any deliberations with respect to that contract. 10 penalty units. (2) Sub-section (1) does not apply in respect of a pecuniary interest: (a) that exists only by virtue of the fact that the member of the committee is a member of a class of persons for whose benefit the incorporated association is established; or (b) that the member of the committee has in common with all or a substantial proportion of the members of the incorporated association.	Section 22 Voting on a contract in which a committee member has an interest (1) A member of the committee of an incorporated association who has any direct or indirect pecuniary interest in a contract, or proposed contract, made by, or in the contemplation of, the committee, shall not take part in any deliberations or decision of the committee with respect to that contract. Penalty: $500. (2) Subsection (1) does not apply in respect of a pecuniary interest that exists only by virtue of the fact that the member of the committee is a member of a class of persons for whose benefit the association is established.	Section 32 Voting on a contract in which a committee member has an interest (1) A member of the committee of an incorporated association who has any direct or indirect pecuniary interest in a contract, or proposed contract, with the association must not take part in any decision of the committee with respect to that contract (but may, subject to complying with the provisions of this Division, take part in any deliberations with respect to that contract). Maximum penalty: $5000. (2) Subsection (1) does not apply in respect of a pecuniary interest: (a) that exists only by virtue of the fact that the member of the committee is a member of a class of persons for whose benefit the association is established; or (b) that the member of the committee has in common with all or a substantial proportion of the members of the association.	

1 There are no relevant provisions for the following acts: *Associations Incorporation Act 1984* (NSW); *Associations Incorporation Act 1981* (Qld); *Associations Incorporation Act 1963–78* (NT); *Associations Incorporation Act 1964* (TAS); *Incorporated Societies Act 1908* (NZ).
2 *Associations Incorporation Act 1981* (Vic).
3 *Associations Incorporation Act 1987* (WA).
4 *Associations Incorporation Act 1985* (SA).
5 *Associations Incorporation Act 1991* (ACT).

Justice Hill in *St Mary's Rugby League Club Ltd v. The Commissioner for Taxation* dated 8 July 1997,[13] described the overall position of such clubs as follows:

[M]any, if not all, sporting clubs commence in a small way and in circumstances where there can be no doubt as to the characterisation of the club as a sporting club. A consequence of the exemption of the income of that club from tax is often that the club grows and prospers. Particularly, if it engages in activities which are designed to raise money to be used to further the sporting activities. Activities so undertaken may include poker machines, liquor sales, bingo games and the like. There may … come a time when these other activities take on a life of their own. From being merely concomitant or incidental to the activities of sport, they become an end in themselves. That was the case in Cronulla–Sutherland. It has not happened to the Terranora Lakes Country Club. As each of those cases demonstrate and the present facts reinforce, the line to be drawn will be a difficult one. To determine on what side of the line the club falls … it is necessary to have regard … to the constitution, activities, history and control of the body seeking the exemption.

The states take little or no action to police the associations incorporation legislation. ASIC generally adopts a passive role in policing the rules, leaving the matter to the Commissioner of Taxation. The commissioner needs to take a closer look at the bigger players. The fact is that, despite adopting NFP structures, bodies such as the AFL are now big businesses and should be regulated and taxed as such.[14]

In New Zealand these are now no longer companies limited by guarantee so the only possibilities are incorporation under the *Incorporated Societies Act 1908* or as a company limited by shares under the *Companies Act 1993*.

Churches[15]

Christianity had a hard time getting established in the early history of Australia. The first church was burned down by convicts. Religion generally fared better in New Zealand. Churches that are incorporated are set up by statute or incorporated as associations or limited companies. In addition, religion tends to spawn a host of unincorporated bodies but we are not concerned with them here. The larger churches resemble some loose kind of conglomerate and are currently entering the employment recruitment business in Australia, supported by the Commonwealth government.

13   (1997) 97 ATC 4528 at 4529–4530.
14   For excellent discussions see S. Lipe, 'Corporate Governance in Non-Profit Organisations', unpublished University of Melbourne LLM paper, 1999; K. Levy, 'The Australian Football League: Is it time for the Siren to Blow?' in M. McGregor-Lowdes, K. Fletcher and A. S. Sievers (eds), *Legal Issues for Non-Profit Associations*, Law Book Company, Sydney, 1996, p. 95.
15   For statistics on religious affiliations see Australian Bureau of Statistics, *Year Book Australia 1999*, ABS Canberra, 1999, p. 99. For the history see I. Breward, *A History of the Australian Churches*, Allen & Unwin, Sydney, 1993.

In so far as a church is created or recognised by statute, the statute must be interpreted against the background of the common law and equity. In so far as the church is incorporated as an incorporated association or company limited by shares or guarantee, the position is basically the same as we have stated in relation to sporting organisations.

Certain churches are also subject to systems of Canon Law peculiar to that church.

Corporate governance issues faced by churches are centred on the unique mission of the church and how this can be implemented through fallible human organisations. Few priests have received any management training. The constitutions of most churches are often badly drawn and this can cause or aggravate disputes. Religious people seem to have a talent for dissension over matters of belief and difficult questions such as the proper role of the laity and women have raised problems for those in authority.

Most churches have the equivalent of parish councils or elders. These are often supplemented by parish meetings or forums. In addition there are special committees or groups who report to one or more of the main bodies. The Anglican and Uniting churches have synods which are large and unwieldy bodies, something like a more democratic version of parliament without a party system.

Churches with bishops have a clearer line of authority and the role of priests is usually more clearly defined.

There is a need in all churches to monitor the expenditure of scarce resources and to actively raise funds.

Universities[16]

Universities represent a complex form of NFP. Universities in Australia and New Zealand are usually set up or recognised by legislation which gives them some tax exempt status. Some universities and university colleges or halls may be set up as companies limited by shares or guarantee. Only the former is now possible in New Zealand. Bond University is a company limited by guarantee which is the subject of two Queensland statutes.

Universities have been explained in different ways in the literature.[17] One approach is to see the public universities as akin to public enterprises subject to market and regulatory constraints. The problem with this is the pattern of financing of public universities which creates a surrogate market situation where the consumer does not pay directly. A second approach focuses on internal control mechanisms while a third uses the model of labour-managed cooperatives. None of these is satisfactory for explaining the nature of universities in Australia and New Zealand.

The main corporate governance questions are the definition of the powers of the university or other body, its management, and membership. Most universities have large and unwieldy councils which in the past have acted as parliaments rather than boards and have been a very ineffective monitor of university management. The chair is

---

16   Compare Lyons *op. cit.* (2001) Ch. 6. For statistics on government outlays on tertiary education see Australian Bureau of Statistics, *op. cit.*, p. 292.

17   See Hirshhorn, *op. cit.*, p. 612 and literature cited.

called chancellor and the CEO is the vice-chancellor. The registrar is the senior admin-istrator. Sometimes he or she is given a more grandiose title. Membership of the univer-sity is usually defined in the university's act or constitution. It often includes all university staff and graduates, which again makes it a large and unwieldy body that is an ineffective deliberative body.

Since universities are NFPs which are also educational charities, there is much to be said for the imposition of fiduciary duties, not only on officers and university councils but also on the members. Universities are public bodies with a very privileged position in society and, at the moment, are not sufficiently accountable for their actions. Even so-called private universities such as Bond University and the University of Notre Dame are recognised by state legislation and given tax exemption. They too are NFPs and charities. Steps should be taken to ensure that the membership, as well as the man-agement, of all universities behave in a fiduciary way and not out of self-interest. Staff can often capture NFPs, including universities.

A committee chaired by David Hoare in 1995 recommended a more rational system of management of the public sector universities.[18] The report recommended as follows:

1   The governing body of higher education institutions should have ultimate respon-sibility for strategic direction and development of the university and external and internal accountability, including monitoring and review of institutional strategic performance. It should also ensure that:
    (a) accountability for implementation is appropriately delegated;
    (b) there is an appropriate body to monitor academic policy and standards and protect academic freedom;
    (c) there are adequate and effective separate fora available to determine stakehold-ers' opinions, particularly for those of staff and students; and
    (d) it reports on progress against strategic directions.
2   The role of Vice-Chancellor should be to exercise stewardship of the institution on behalf of the governing body, and he or she should be formally accountable to the governing body for performance according to an agreed set of objectives, and arrangements and criteria.
3   Governing bodies should, on a regular basis, review their own role and perfor-mance, and that of the Vice-Chancellor.

The report also considered the role of the federal government and thought that:

The Minister for Employment, Education and Training, through appropriate Com-monwealth and State/Territory bodies, should recommend that States amend univer-sity enabling legislation.

---

18   *The Higher Education Management Review*, AGPS, Canberra, 1995; See P. Coaldrake and L. Stedman, *On the Brink: Australia's Universities Confronting their Future*, University of Queensland Press, St Lucia, Qld, 1998, ch. 7.

The aim should be to ensure *inter alia* that:

(a) the primary responsibilities and roles of governing bodies and their members are made explicit;

(b) members elected or appointed to the governing body have fiduciary responsibility and must disclose interests in matters under consideration;

(c) the size of the governing body is typically between ten and fifteen members;

(d) the governing body is able to co-opt members;

(e) external independent members outnumber internal members.

In spite of its eminently sensible recommendations the report was successfully resisted by the public universities and nothing has come of it.

As Coaldrake and Stedman state:[19]

> The point to be made, of course, is that while universities tend to emphasise how different they are from other organisations in the community, they are no different from either the corporate or public sector in their need for direction and monitoring, and their obligation to satisfy the community at large that they are operating effectively.

While the debate rages, in Australia public universities continue to grow as corporate juggernauts absorbing public and private funds without effective management accountability or a proper system of financial disclosure.

In New Zealand, the public sector reforms have been carried through to the educational sector and reforms have been carried out to university constitutions and the role of councils and vice-chancellors. Whether there has been any significant improvement in substance as opposed to form is debatable.

Specific corporate governance problems

The absence of conventional investors and pursuit of a purpose other than profit in such bodies makes corporate governance potentially more complex.

Management and the board or other governing body owe duties to the body and possibly to its members in appropriate cases. However, the corporate objectives tend to be defined more by its purpose than by its membership.

The public also has an interest in all three types of organisation and in so far as they are charities the Attorney-General of the particular state may have a residual role on behalf of the Crown as *parens patriae*.

Beyond charity law, the lack of clear norms of behaviour in incorporated associations and the lack of harmonisation of legislation between the states makes monitoring management difficult. It seems that a director of a charitable corporation is not subject

---

to charitable trusts although he or she is subject to fiduciary obligations that may equate to them.

Even in the case of an incorporated association it appears that the director will be subject to the fiduciary restraints, imposed on agents, that rule out conflict of interest.

The basic tasks of governance are to ensure good financial management including risk management, implementing and safeguarding the mission, and balancing the stakeholders within an appropriate system of accountability.

There is a need for greater accountability to their stakeholders and the public. Openness and disclosure of information should be essential operating principles of all NFPs.

At present the main systems of accountability are:

Fundraising legislation
This is a state matter and differs from state to state.

State associations incorporation legislation
This differs between states. There is a need for harmonisation as we have seen.

Incorporation under the Corporations Act
This legislation is too complex for this kind of body and there is a need for special not for profit provisions and possibly modified duties for directors of such bodies.

Incorporation under a specific act of parliament
Sporting bodies such as the Grand Prix and the Sydney Organising Committee for the Olympic Games, churches, and public universities fall into this category. The legislation varies greatly although there has been a tendency in some states to have similar university statutes.

Voluntary accountability
Voluntary accountability is achieved by means of annual reports, newsletters and functions. There are problems of lack of consistent data collection processes, public access to information and lack of standardisation of financial reporting and other information.

Industry Commission 1995 proposals
In a useful report on *Charitable Organisations in Australia*,[20] in Report No. 45 of 16 June 1995, the Industry Commission considered several strategies for improving accountability. These were:

• a voluntary code of reporting
• the establishment of a supervisory body
• improving fundraising legislation

---

20   Industry Commission, *Charitable Organisations in Australia*, Report No. 45, 16 June 1995, AGPS, Melbourne.

- uniform state associations incorporation acts
- requiring such bodies to be incorporated as public companies under the Corporations Act.

The commission reviewed each of these but opted for a two-stage reform package:

1   sector-specific accounting standards
2   a modified form of incorporation under the Corporations Act.

It was thought that this would overcome problems at state level and, although it would result in increased costs, it would lead to greater benefits in the form of heightened accountability, better management practices, and increased public confidence.

CHAPTER 31

Corporate Governance in Corporatised Enterprises[1]

In the course of the past two decades, the public sector in Australia and New Zealand has been subject to increasing commercialisation. The commercialisation process involves the application of private sector management techniques and structures to government departments, government trading enterprises and statutory corporations that were previously subject to rigid central control. The restructured entities have been given greater authority over the management of their affairs and in particular have been allowed to exercise more control over finances (including levels of investment) and staffing. In some cases, government trading enterprises have been sold either wholly or in part.

Commercialisation can be seen as part of a general policy of micro-economic reform. In carrying out micro-economic reform, governments have taken steps to promote more competitive markets in goods and services by removing barriers to entry and enhancing the effectiveness of competition laws, taken steps towards industrial relations reform, and engaged in structural reform, for example on the waterfront. As part of this same process, governments have come under pressure to consider ways in which the services that they provide can be delivered more efficiently.[2] High budget deficits and community perceptions of waste in the public sector have prompted policy-makers to look to the private sector for guidance.[3]

---

1   This is based substantially on J. H. Farrar and B. McCabe, 'Corporatisation, Corporate Governance and the Deregulation of the Public Sector Economy' (1995) 6 PLR 24.

2   The need to extend micro-economic reform to business activities carried on by the public sector was made clear in the Hilmer Report (*Report of the Independent Committee of Inquiry into National Competition Policy*, 1993). Hilmer cited statistics showing that government business enterprises accounted for 10 per cent of gross domestic product (p. 129). See also Parliament of Victoria Public Bodies Review Committee Discussion Paper on Corporatisation, October 1991, p. 12.

3   P. Allan, Secretary to the New South Wales Treasury, 'Corporatisation: The NSW Experience', National Accountants in Government Convention 1989—Privatisation and Corporatisation, 2–4 March 1989, Southern Cross Hotel, Melbourne, p. 2.

The term 'commercialisation' covers the policies of corporatisation and privatisation and certain other deregulatory policy changes. Corporatisation involves retention of public ownership, but otherwise it is the establishment of an operating environment for appropriate public sector enterprises that replicates, as far as possible, the internal and external conditions faced by successful private enterprises.[4] Telstra, Australia Post and a number of public utilities have all been corporatised. Privatisation involves the transfer of ownership of the enterprise into private hands. Privatisation has found favour in New Zealand and the United Kingdom but has been less popular in Australia at the federal level (although several major enterprises such as the Commonwealth Bank, Qantas and part of Telstra have been sold off).[5] A number of enterprises owned by state governments have also been sold.

This chapter aims to consider the political and historical framework within which corporatisation has occurred. It examines the process in the light of modern writing on the theory of the firm and identifies practical corporate governance issues that are raised by the corporatisation process. An attempt will then be made to sum up, considering the extent to which solutions to the problems still require public ownership and the application of public law techniques.

The political and historical framework of corporatisation and the development of the current model

The public sector has played an important role in economic development in Australia and New Zealand since the beginning of European settlement. Throughout the nineteenth century, for example, Australia had a low ratio of capital and labour to resources which had to be addressed through imports. In the early twentieth century the public sector consistently contributed over 50 per cent of total gross domestic capital formation and even today central government is still the biggest industry in Australia.[6] From 1880 onwards, Australia and New Zealand pioneered the extension of the state into service-oriented business enterprises and then, at the turn of the century, the development of public corporations, which are statutory corporations under their own legislation. These moves were justified expressly or by implication on the basis of market failure. They removed ministers from direct control and resulted in decision-making less likely to be influenced by political considerations.[7] The tendency was less pro-

---

4   *ibid.*, p. 4.
5   Also a number of smaller Commonwealth government enterprises, such as the Snowy Mountains Engineering Corporation, have been sold in their entirety.
6   P. Botsman, '"The Moscow Papers"—Privatisation, Corporatisation and Commercialisation: The Australian Experience', a paper for the Academy of National Economy, USSR Council of Ministers, Moscow, December 1990, p. 59.
7   See generally, Parliament of Victoria Public Bodies Review Committee, Discussion Paper on Corporatisation, October 1991, pp. 15–16.

nounced in New Zealand where more matters remained in the hands of government departments until even as late as the 1980s.

Nationalisation did not form a significant part of the Australian and New Zealand experience. Most of the enterprises had never been in private ownership. To this extent the Antipodean experience differs from the post-World War II UK experience. To such corporations can be added the occasional case of the state-owned limited liability company such as Qantas.

In more recent times, in both Australia and New Zealand, there have been 'Think Big' projects. These have often involved the use of state corporations to promote economic and social objectives (consider, for example, the role of some of the state banks in promoting economic development).

The corporatisation process has focused on state-owned trading organisations,[8] the regulatory functions having been hived off.[9] Managers are required to run them as successful business enterprises. The New Zealand *State-Owned Enterprises Act 1986* epitomises this approach. It was introduced:

> to promote improved performance in respect of government trading activities and, to this end, to (a) specify principles governing the operation of state enterprises; and (b) authorise the formation of companies to carry on certain government activities and control the ownership thereof; and (c) establish requirements about the accountability of state enterprises, and the responsibility of ministers.[10]

The aims of the New South Wales legislation[11] are expressed more tersely: the preamble of the *State-Owned Corporations Act 1989* states that the Act is intended 'to provide for the establishment and operation of Government enterprises as state-owned corporations'.

---

8   Although (as the discussion in 'Corporatisation and the Theory of the Firm' suggests—see below) the corporatisation process can apply to other more 'traditional' public sector organisations that perform social welfare or regulatory functions. The entity need not be a profit-seeking business in order to enjoy the efficiency gains available from corporatisation: see text accompanying n 21 in the main body of text below. The most obvious application of the process, however, will be to government enterprises that trade in a commercial or quasi-commercial environment.

9   The separation of regulatory and commercial functions was endorsed by the Hilmer Report, *op. cit.*, pp. 217–18.

10   I. Duncan and A. Bollard, *Corporatisation and Privatisation—Lessons from New Zealand,* Oxford University Press, Auckland, 1992, p. 11.

11   For useful discussion of the New South Wales experience see NSW Treasury, *Framework for Effective Corporate Governance of GTEs and SOCs,* October 1996. For an overview of the Australian legislation see A. Reynolds and P. von Nessen, 'The Government Owned Corporations and State Owned Corporations Statute', in B. Collier and S. Pitkin (eds), *Corporations and Privatisation in Australia,* CCH Australia Ltd, Sydney, 1999, ch. 5. For a discussion of directors' duties see B. Doyle and C. Moller, 'Government Owned Enterprises—Duties and Liabilities of Directors', in Collier and Pitkin (eds) *op. cit.* ch. 11; and for accountability see S. Pitkin and D. Farrelly, 'Government Owned Corporations and Accountability: the Realm of the New Administrative Law?', in Collier and Pitkin (eds), *op. cit.*, ch. 9.

Section 9 of the New South Wales Act deals with the status of state-owned corporations and provides that a state-owned corporation or any of its subsidiaries:

(a) is not and does not represent the state except by express agreement with the voting shareholders of the corporation; and

(b) is not exempt from any rate, tax, duty or other impost imposed by or under any law of the state merely because it is a state-owned corporation; and

(c) cannot render the state liable for any debts, liabilities or obligations of the corporation of any of its subsidiaries

unless this or any other Act otherwise expressly provides.

Section 10 deals with the directors. The directors are to be persons who, in the opinion of those appointing them, will assist the corporation to achieve its principal objective. Under section 10(2) the board is accountable to the voting shareholders in the manner set out in the Act and in the memorandum and articles of the corporation. Schedule 2 sets out provisions to be included in the memorandum and articles of state-owned corporations. Schedule 3 sets out provisions to be in the memorandum and articles of subsidiaries of state-owned corporations. Included in the requirements to go into articles is the requirement that only eligible ministers may hold shares in the corporation for and on behalf of the state.

Part 4 of the Act deals with accountability. It requires statements of corporate intent which have to be laid before Parliament together with a copy of the memorandum and articles. There are provisions for half-yearly reports and annual reports and accounts. These are supplemented by special reports of the Auditor-General. Section 26 sets out the information to be laid before Parliament.

The structure of the Queensland *Government-Owned Corporations Act 1993*,[12] one of the newest of the state corporatisation acts, states the objectives and how they are to be achieved (Chapter 1 Part 5); mechanisms for creating and altering types of government-owned corporations (GOCs) (Chapter 2) and the detailed requirements for GOCs (Chapter 3). Chapter 3 deals *inter alia* with the two types of GOC—statutory and company—the application of the Corporations Act; shares and shareholding ministers; memorandum and articles; board of directors; the CEO; the corporate plan and statement of corporate intent; community service obligations; the general reserve powers of the shareholding ministers; reports; duties and liabilities of directors and other officers; legal capacity and powers; acquisition and disposal of assets; and employees. Detailed rules about the board of a statutory GOC are set out in Schedule 1 and audit is dealt with in Schedule 3. The Queensland Act is more detailed than the other acts.

The Australian and New Zealand legislation appears to have been strongly influenced by the model developed by Herbert Morrison in the United Kingdom in the

12 See *Corporatisation in Queensland—Policy Guidelines*, a Queensland Government White Paper 1995; D. McDonagh, *Government Owned Corporations in Queensland*, SJD dissertation, Bond University; and A. Rentoul, 'Corporate Governance and Company GOCs', unpublished paper, 27 July 1999.

postwar Labour government. The main distinguishing features of the typical UK public corporation established under that model are as follows:[13]

1   The public corporation is a body corporate established by statute with its own legal existence.
2   It is free to manage its affairs without detailed supervision by Parliament.
3   The minister has the power to give directions (a) of a general character as to the exercise and performance of the functions of the corporation and (b) with regard to specified matters of special importance; for example, major expenditure programs.
4   The minister appoints the whole or a majority of the board.
5   The corporation is financially independent in the sense that it has powers to maintain its own reserves and to borrow within limits laid down by Parliament.

As Professor George Jones of the London School of Economics said in a seminar held in Wellington, New Zealand, on 3 September 1987:

> Morrison was a socialist. He didn't like private ownership, he didn't like profit. He didn't want a department running state public enterprise. He felt there'd be too much political interference and he felt that the dead hand of bureaucracy would stifle enterprise. He didn't want the United States system either. He didn't want the system of private ownership and public regulation through independent regulatory agencies. He thought that would inhibit management, and there was always the possibility of capture of the regulatory agency by the entity being regulated. So he wanted bodies, boards ... imbued if you like, with the notion of a public trust.[14]

The aim of the United Kingdom public corporation was thus to combine freedom of management from government supervision of day-to-day operations with public control of the broader policies of the enterprises. In the words of Professor W. A. Robson in *Nationalised Industry and Public Ownership:*

> The public corporation is based on the theory that a full measure of accountability can be imposed on a public authority without requiring it to be subject to ministerial control in respect of its managerial decisions and multitudinous routine activities, or liable to comprehensive parliamentary scrutiny of its day-to-day working. The theory assumes that policy, in major matters, can be distinguished from management or administration; and that a successful combination of political and managerial freedom can be achieved by reserving certain powers of decision in matters of major importance to ministers answerable to Parliament and leaving everything else to the discretion of the public corporation acting within its legal competence. The Government is further

---

13   J. Vickers and G. Yarrow, *Privatisation: An Economic Analysis*, MIT Press, Cambridge, Mass., 1988, ch. 5, pp. 123–4.
14   G. Jones, Corporatisation and Privatisation: Completing the Revolution, seminar held in Wellington, New Zealand, 3 September 1987.

endowed with residual powers of direction and appointment which mark its unquestionable authority.[15]

Professor Jones argues that the Morrison model has been a failure.[16] He claims that ministers and their departments were not prepared to leave management of the enterprises to their managers. Rather than developing broad guidelines and general directions for management to follow, politicians and bureaucrats intervened repeatedly, making *ad hoc*, short-term decisions that damaged the commercial viability of the enterprises and management morale.

The tension over goals and objectives continues under the New Zealand and Australian legislation. Section 4 of the *State-Owned Enterprises Act 1986* (NZ) made it clear that the principal objective of a state-owned enterprise should be to operate as a successful business, being:

(a) as profitable and efficient as comparable businesses that are not owned by the Crown;

(b) a good employer; and

(c) an organisation that exhibits a sense of social responsibility by having regard to the interests of the community in which it operates by endeavouring to accommodate these when able to do so.

In short, state-owned enterprises are expected to perform their function in a socially responsible fashion but with due regard to the bottom line. These objectives will often be inconsistent.[17] The difficulties have been highlighted in *New Zealand Maori Council v. Attorney-General*.[18] The Privy Council held that the social objectives referred to in section 4 of the New Zealand Act were as important as the commercial goals.

The New South Wales legislation has tacitly recognised the potential for conflict by providing a mechanism to compensate the corporation when it has to diverge from its commercial objectives.[19] Section 11 of the New South Wales Act deals with non-commercial activities. Section 11(1) provides that if a minister wishes a state-owned corporation to perform activities or to cease to perform activities or not to perform activities in circumstances where the board considers it is not in the commercial interests of the corporation to do so, that minister, with the approval of the Treasurer, may by written

---

15 W. A. Robson, *Nationalised Industry and Public Ownership*, Allen & Unwin, London, 1960.

16 Jones, *op. cit.* footnote 14 supra.

17 The Bible reminds us of the difficulties inherent in serving two masters. F. Easterbrook and D. Fischel in *The Economic Structure of Corporate Law*, Harvard University Press, Cambridge, 1991, p. 38, explain the dangers of conflicting goals as follows: 'a manager told to serve two masters (a little for the equity holders, a little for the community) has been freed of both and is answerable to neither. Faced with a demand from either group, the manager can appeal to the interests of the other.' For a general discussion of questions of social responsibility, see B. McCabe, 'Are Corporations Socially Responsible? Is Corporate Social Responsibility Desirable?' (1992) 4 Bond LR 1.

18 [1994] 1 NZLR 513.

19 The NSW legislation builds on the more skeletal provisions in the *State-Owned Enterprises Act 1986* (NZ), s. 7.

notice to the board, direct the corporation to do so in accordance with any require-ments set out or referred to in the notice. Under section 11(3) the corporation is enti-tled to be reimbursed, from money advanced by the Treasurer or appropriated by Parliament for the purpose, an amount equal to reimbursement of the cost of compli-ance. The Queensland Act is less explicit but does consider the impact of community service obligations on a GOC's solvency.

Provisions of directors' duties differ between the various statutes and so far none have been updated in the light of the new form of corporate constitution introduced by the *Company Law Review Act* 1998 and the corporate governance reforms of the Cor-porate Law Economic Reform Program in Australia. Care has been taken in section 32 of the *Queensland Government-Owned Corporations Act 1993* to exempt ministers from the risk of being shadow directors but these may not be wide enough to cover liability in respect of joint-venture companies set up by corporatised enterprises and the private sector, which are not subsidiaries.

Corporatisation can be viewed from one perspective as the extension of the drive for efficiency within the public sector while retaining ownership within the public sec-tor. The other perspective is that corporatisation is simply a poor man's privatisation.[20] In Australia, the former view has prevailed with the Commonwealth, New South Wales, Queensland, South Australian, Tasmanian, Victorian, Western Australian and the ACT governments maintaining that corporatisation is an end in itself, designed to achieve more efficient use of resources, an appropriate return on public capital, and more effi-cient management. Thus, in 1988, the Commonwealth government corporatised the largest dozen government business enterprises.[21] In the states and the ACT there were a number of green papers, often followed by white papers, recommending the corporat-isation of a range of state government activities. These included electricity, ports, water, gas, works, public transport, gambling and finance. The minister would not have day-to-day control over the enterprises but their performance would be monitored by the Treasury or Finance ministry. In practice, the corporatisation process in Australia has concerned itself with 'government activities which are business oriented, routine in nature, self-contained in administration, heavily focused on service delivery, and phys-ically easier to separate'.[22]

Looking at the Australian legislation overall, one has the impression of a retention of greater political control and *ad hoc* intervention that demonstrates many of the weaknesses of the UK public corporation experiment. To some extent, corporatisation in Australia seems a cosmetic exercise, getting the worst of both worlds. There is the appearance of the application of private sector techniques but these are emasculated by the retention of extensive political controls, and the ultimate question of accountability

20   K. Wiltshire, 'Privatisation and Corporatisation', in R. G. Stewart (ed), *Government and Business Relations in Australia,* Allen & Unwin, Sydney, 1994, pp. 202–17.
21   See Joint Committee of Public Accounts and Audit Report 372, *Corporate Governance and Accountability for Arrangements for Commonwealth Government Business Enterprises,* AGPS, Canberra, December 1999.
22   Wiltshire, *op. cit.,* p. 218.

is diffused. The result, despite some improvements, is continuing inefficiency and lack of proper accountability.

Corporatisation and the theory of the firm

In the corporatised entity, as in any other corporation, there is at least a theoretical separation of ownership from control. In the public sector organisation, the 'ownership' is in the hands of the state[23] while control (in the corporatisation model described above) lies with the management of the entity subject to a number of restrictions. In an economic sense, the managers are the agents of the state in that they run the enterprise on its behalf. It is appropriate, then, to examine the implications of the relationship using agency cost analysis.[24]

An agency cost analysis of corporatisation

We have referred to the agency theory of the firm in Chapter 3.

Agency cost analysis is valuable because it provides a means of assessing the efficiency of a firm. Efficiency does not necessarily equate with profit: profitability is the usual standard against which the success of a private sector organisation is measured, but it is possible to nominate alternative goals and assess whether they are being pursued in an efficient manner.[25]

Agency cost

Jensen and Meckling explained that agency costs are the costs that arise in every relationship where one party is entrusted with the power to act on behalf of others.[26] The model can be applied to any team relationship, similar to that which exists between shareholders and managers in a company, or between partners. But the analysis is not limited to commercial contexts:[27] agency problems can occur wherever someone is put into a position in which they are expected to act in the interests of somebody else.

The agency problem arises because the interests of principal and agent are not identical. The principal, for its part, hopes to extract some sort of surplus from the agent's activities. (The principal would only countenance the relationship were it expected to gain.) The agent, in turn, hopes to capture for itself a larger share of the surplus in value

---

23 Thus the NSW *State Owned Corporations Act* 1989 for example provides that the Treasurer and other relevant ministers are to be the 'voting shareholders' in the corporation.

24 See generally R. Romano, *Foundations of Corporate Law*, Oxford University Press, New York, 1993, pp. 3–5.

25 P. Milgrom and J. Roberts, *Economics, Organisations and Management*, Prentice Hall, Englewood Cliffs, NJ, 1992, pp. 39–42.

26 M. Jensen and W. Meckling, 'Theory of the Firm: Management Behaviour, Agency Costs and Ownership Structure' (1976) 3 J Fin Eco 305 at 308.

27 *ibid.*, p. 309.

that it generates. It does this by seeking higher remuneration; but it can also seek out 'on the job' benefits, especially where the principal does not pay generously. [28]

An agent might consume a range of non-pecuniary 'on the job' benefits. They might be less diligent in the discharge of their duties than they would be if they were working on their own account ('slacking'); alternatively, they could attempt to avoid their share of the workload ('shirking'). There is also the danger that agents might divert the resources of the organisation for their own ends ('rorting' or theft). The cost to the principal of slacking, shirking and rorting is known as residual cost, which is a component of agency cost. [29]

Principals are generally aware of residual cost and are naturally concerned to reduce it. This can be done in several ways. The parties might incur the cost of implementing measures that demonstrate the agent's fidelity to the interests of the principal. This expense, known as a bonding cost, also forms part of the agency cost. [30] Bonding strategies, such as performance-related pay and other incentive schemes, are designed to ensure that the interests of the principal and the agent converge. The parties will incur bonding costs whenever they expect that they will be more than offset by a reduction in residual cost, leading to a reduction in overall agency cost.

The principal might also take steps to monitor the performance of agents more closely to ensure that they do not rort, slack or shirk. The costs of these measures—which are designed to make agents more accountable—are known as monitoring costs. [31] Ordinarily, the principal will only incur the cost of monitoring when it leads to a decrease in residual cost that is great enough to justify the expense. [32]

There is a vast range of monitoring arrangements available to the principal. Some are more costly that others and they operate in different ways. The modern company structure incorporates a number of monitoring devices as a matter of course, for example, the board of directors, the independent auditor, and the requirement that directors report to the annual general meeting. Principals constantly search for ways to make these mechanisms work better. Some advocate the appointment of independent, non-executive directors to company boards [33] while others favour the adoption of codes of conduct. [34] Other internal monitoring mechanisms can be established at the discretion of the board. Reporting systems, internal audits and other procedures can help to contain residual cost.

---

28   *ibid.*, p. 308. See also A. Alchian and H. Demsetz, 'Production, Information Costs and Economic Organisation' (1972) 62 Am Eco Rev 777 at 780–1.

29   Jensen and Meckling, *op. cit.* footnote 26 supra, p. 308.

30   *ibid.*

31   *ibid.* See also Easterbrook and Fischel, *op. cit.* footnote 17 supra, p. 10.

32   In a publicly owned organisation, however, it is conceivable that political considerations might compel the principal to insist on monitoring even where it is not justified by equivalent reductions in residual cost. The introduction of political objectives can lead to inefficient outcomes.

33   See G. Pease and K. McMillan, *The Independent Non-executive Director*, Pro Ned Australia, Longman Professional, Melbourne 1993.

34   See e.g. H. Bosch, *Corporate Practices and Conduct*, 3rd edn, FT Pitman Publishing, Melbourne, 1995.

Scholars from the law and economics school have recognised that the principal can also attempt to harness external monitors in the fight against residual cost. Commercial organisations are typically affected by the operation of one or more markets. All enterprises operate in a product market: they have to convince consumers to purchase their output. Posner argues that where the product market is active and competitive, it disciplines the managers of the enterprise:[35] if they do not manage effectively and contain costs, the enterprises will falter or even fail and they can expect to lose their positions. In this way, an active product market helps to reduce residual cost. Best of all, it does so at very low cost to the principal. Once the product market has been established, market forces do the rest.

The operation of some of the other external markets that impact on the enterprise can have a similar effect on residual cost. Fama and Jensen argue that the market for managerial services is a particularly important source of discipline.[36] Managers compete for relatively scarce management jobs by demonstrating that they are more efficient (and thus more desirable employees). In effect, the market acts as a low-cost monitor of managers.

The capital market can also monitor the management of commercial enterprises as they perform their role of providing debt and equity capital. Easterbrook and Fischel point out that enterprises which labour under high levels of residual cost will find it harder to raise finance.[37] New investors will demand concessions and discounts before purchasing equity in an inefficiently managed organisation. In the debt markets, lenders will insist on a higher rate of interest or other safeguards before they will extend credit. The scrutiny of the capital markets is virtually free to the principal. So, too, is the scrutiny of the market for corporate control, which consistently haunts company managers with the spectre of takeover. Managers of the firm know that any want of efficiency on their part will be reflected in the market price for the stock. A low share price might excite the interest of a predator who will seek to replace the incumbent management team.[38]

In each case, the object of the monitoring arrangements—whether internal or external—is to reduce residual cost in a cost-effective way. After all, the aim is to mini-

---

35   R. Posner, *Economic Analysis of Law*, 5th edn, Little, Brown & Co, Boston, 1998, p. 419. See also M. Jensen, 'The Modern Industrial Revolution, Exit, and the Failure of Internal Control Systems' (1993) 48 J Fin 831 at 850.

36   E. Fama and M. Jensen, 'Separation of Ownership and Control' (1983) 26 J Law and Eco 301 at 310–11.

37   Easterbrook and Fischel, *op. cit.* footnote 17 supra, pp. 46–7 and 114. Interestingly, Posner suggests that the cost of this greater difficulty in raising finance will be borne by the original shareholders in the entity (because their interest in the enterprise is diluted) rather than the managers themselves: Posner, *op. cit.* footnote 35 supra, p. 410.

38   Jensen, *op. cit.* footnote 35 supra at 850; D. Fischel, 'Efficient Capital Markets Theory, the Market for Corporate Control, and the Regulation of Cash Tender Offers' (1978) Texas L Rev 1 at 9. See also R. A. Booth, 'Is There any Valid Reason Why Target Managers Oppose Tender Offers?' (1987) 14 Sec Reg LJ 43 at 49. See generally R. J. Zeckhauser and M. Horn, 'The Control and Performance of State-Owned Enterprises', in P. W. MacAvoy, W. T. Stanbury, G. Yarrow and R. J. Zeckhauser (eds), *Privatisation and State-Owned Enterprises: Lessons from the United States, Great Britain and Canada*, Kluwer Academic Publishers, Boston, 1989, pp. 37–8.

mise agency costs, not simply to reduce residual cost at any price. The principle is best served by that combination of bonding and monitoring arrangements that maximises efficiency, although the circumstances in which the organisation operates will naturally affect the choice of arrangements.

Analysing agency cost in the public sector

The wide range of organisations in the public sector makes it difficult to generalise about their agency cost efficiency. Some entities are closely integrated into the government apparatus and perform administrative or even social welfare functions, for example, public hospitals; others operate in a quasi-commercial environment, although they may be protected against competition (like the power and water utilities, the railways and Australia Post). Governments also own or part-own organisations such as Telstra which are expected to trade in competitive markets as if they were private enterprises. Some of this group of businesses have either been partially privatised or are ripe for sale to the private sector. Of those that remain, almost all are candidates for corporatisation.

This section of the chapter discusses the gains to be had from corporatising government-controlled businesses.[39] It concludes that corporatisation can yield real gains in efficiency. In other words, corporatisation tends to reduce agency cost. The chapter goes on to argue, however, that in most cases the extent of the reduction in agency cost will not be as great as the case in which the organisation is privatised. Ownership *does* matter.

The agency cost benefits of corporatisation[40]

The corporatisation process involves a restructuring of the internal governance arrangements of the organisation which will enjoy (at least notionally) a greater measure of independence from the government. In many cases, these arrangements will mirror those that have long been a feature of private enterprises, for example, a board, an independent auditor and separate legal personality. An agency cost analysis suggests that internal monitoring devices of this nature should have the effect of reducing residual cost. But will the monitoring be as cost effective as it would be in private enterprise?

There is a risk that government-controlled entities will be monitored more closely than their counterparts in the private sector. This danger arises because the incentives of governments are different to those of private owners who wish to maximise their financial return. A private owner will not insist on extra monitoring if the

---

39   Although this chapter focuses on the agency cost implications of corporatising government businesses, an agency cost analysis could also be done on agencies that provide non-commercial services. As noted above, the agency cost approach can be applied to virtually any relationship where power is exercised on behalf of others. It follows that bodies at the core of the public service might benefit from agency cost analysis. The task, however, is beyond the cope of this chapter.

40   See Australian National Audit Office, *Corporate Governance in Commonwealth Authorities and Companies— Principles and Better Practices*, Discussion Paper, 1998.

cost of implementing and administering the arrangements outweighs the likely benefits. A government, however, has other priorities: in particular, it is concerned to minimise the risk of political scandal which might result in the event of any waste being uncovered, even waste that would not be pursued in the private sector because of the enforcement of costs. Political considerations might compel the government to insist on higher standards of accountability in the entities that it controls notwithstanding the cost of doing so.[41]

Cultural factors must also be taken into consideration. Auditors, for example, might be more diligent in examining the books of a public body out of sense of duty to the taxpayers whose money is at stake. This sense of duty might be particularly well entrenched where the entity is required to use auditors based on the public sector.[42] While more stringent accounting standards would be welcomed by some in light of the rash of legal actions against auditors in the wake of the 1980s, it is nonetheless true that public sector organisations will be disadvantaged by higher costs—both in terms of auditors' fees and because of the reduced flexibility of the balance sheet—if the auditors really are more diligent.

The real obstacle to cost-effective monitoring comes from the fact that state-owned enterprises have greater difficulty in obtaining access to low-cost external monitors. Where organisations are prevented from harnessing the forces of some of the markets referred to earlier, they will be forced to rely more heavily on relatively costly internal monitoring devices. Agency costs will be harder to contain as a result.

Competition between managers for jobs in the market for managerial services should act as an effective monitor in state-owned enterprises (although the market's efficiency might be impaired if the enterprise is subject to an industrial relations regime similar to that typically operated in the public sector).[43] Assessing the impact of competition in the product market is more complicated. Where the enterprise trades in a market without competition, for example, due to a statutory monopoly, or because of the market's failure to provide the goods or services in question at an acceptable price, then the product market will not exert any discipline over the management of the entity. Where competition exists, however, the impact of the market forces is more likely to be felt. If the market is highly competitive, the pressures that it generates may be effective in restraining management from acting in a self-interested fashion. Of course, that assumes that managers of state-owned enterprises are more exposed to all of the consequences of failing to compete effectively in a competitive product market: will the organisation be allowed to survive, for example, if it fails to prosper? At first glance, it seems

---

41   See Zeckhauser and Horn, *op. cit.* footnote 38, p. 19.

42   *ibid.*, pp. 28–9.

43   Under the traditional industrial relations mode, the state enjoyed less flexibility in determining rates of pay and conditions. Dismissal was also a more complicated affair in many cases than it would have been in the private sector. See also Zeckhauser and Horn, *ibid.*, p. 18.

unlikely that a government would stand by while the entity was liquidated,[44] assuming that such a process were even possible.

The reality, of course, is that most state-owned enterprises do not operate in highly competitive markets (although the same could be said of many private enterprises in Australia). It follows that it is unlikely that the product market will be a completely effective means of monitoring the management of public sector organisations at low cost. What of the other external monitors?

With the exception of a few partially privatised entities, state-owned corporations are not traded on the stock exchange. The government through ministers is usually the only shareholder. It follows that state-owned enterprises tend to have little exposure to the scrutiny of the equity market. The absence of monitoring by the equity market is likely to lead to increased agency costs[45]—a conclusion which is supported by evidence that restrictions on the trading of equity (regardless of the identity of the shareholder) will lead to poorer financial performances.[46]

What about debt markets? Many of these entities borrow money. Where the debt issued by the enterprise is effectively guaranteed by the state, however, the risk assessment process in the debt markets becomes distorted. Creditors are less inclined to scrutinise a debtor's finances and operation where the loan is backed by the state.[47] It follows that the capital markets are likely to make more stringent demands on private enterprises than they would on their counterparts in the public sector. To the extent that creditors do take an easier line, it is likely that the state-owned enterprises will be faced with higher agency costs.

---

44 Parliament of Victoria Public Bodies Review Committee Discussion Paper on Corporatisation, *op. cit.* footnote 2 supra, p. 13.

45 See, e.g. M. Jensen and W. Meckling, 'Rights and Production Functions: An Application to Labour-managed Firms and Co-determination' (1979) 52 J Bus 469. The authors observed (at 485): 'The existence of a well-organised market in which corporate claims are continually being assessed is perhaps the single most important control mechanisms affecting management behaviour.' See also F. Easterbrook, 'Two Agency Costs Explanations of Dividends' (1984) 74 Am Eco Rev 650; M. Jensen, 'Agency Cost of Free Cash Flow, Corporate Finance, and Takeovers' (1986) 76 Am Eco Rev (Papers and Proceedings) 323.

46 See J. M. Karpoff and E. M. Rice, 'Organisational Form, Share Transferability, and Firm Performance: Evidence from the ANCSA Corporations' (1989) 24 J Fin Eco 69. This was a study of the performance of corporations established under the *Alaska Native Claims Settlement Act 1971* (ANCSA), the shares of which could not be traded. The authors noted that the corporations were characterised by poor financial performance and were subject to a high incidence of control contests and a high level of management turnover. The study concluded that the difficulties were caused by the restrictions on the organisational form, most notably the absence of trading.

47 The guarantee may be a formal, legal, binding arrangement, but even without a formal agreement, state ownership will often be regarded in the market as a de facto guarantee because a government would find it politically difficult to avoid bailing out a state-owned enterprise—witness the travails of the Commonwealth government in relation to the Australian National Line. It is difficult to envisage a government minister being sued under the insolvent trading legislation in the event that the creditors of a state-owned enterprise were to wind up the enterprise—assuming that such an action were possible. In fact statutes tend to exclude ministers from the category of director.

What of the market for corporate control? There is a substantial body of evidence that suggests the market for corporate control is an effective monitor.[48] It disciplines managers with the threat of replacement; if they fail to contain residual cost, control can be transferred to a more efficient management team. A corporatised entity is not ordinarily subject to these rigours.

Thus absence of a market for corporate control is a serious disadvantage for corporatised entities because takeovers do more than just exert discipline. They also provide a cost-effective means of expanding into[49] and exiting from a product market.[50] The absence of a takeover market makes business less flexible over time, which diminishes the wealth of taxpayers and the community as a whole.

In summary, then, it has been argued that the corporatisation process does offer the prospect of gains in efficiency through reductions in residual cost, although the magnitude of the gains is undermined by the barriers to use low-cost external monitors—which means that monitoring cost is not likely to be as low in most cases as it is in private enterprise. This conclusion is supported by evidence that shows ownership and organisational form do make a difference to productive efficiency.[51]

Some practical governance issues

Five principles of corporatisation

Having considered some theoretical perspectives, let us examine corporatisation in practice. In an address to the National Accountants in Government Convention in Melbourne in 1989 entitled 'Corporatisation: the NSW Experience', Percy Allan, Secretary of the New South Wales Treasury, identified the five principles of corporatisation in practice. These were:

1   clear objectives
2   managerial autonomy
3   performance evaluation

---

48   See e.g. M. Jensen and R. S. Ruback, 'The Market for Corporate Control: The Scientific Evidence' (1983) 11 J Fin Eco 5; G. Jarrell, J. A. Brickley and J. M. Netter, 'The Market for Corporate Control: The Empirical Evidence Since 1980' (1988) 2 Jnl of Eco Perspectives 49; J. R. Franks and R. S. Harris, 'Shareholder Wealth Effects of Corporate Takeovers' (1989) 23 J Fin Eco 225; F. M. Scherer, 'Corporate Takeovers: The Efficiency Arguments' (1988) 2 Jnl of Eco Perspectives 69; see also F. McDougall and D. Round, 'The Determinants and Effects of Takeovers in Australia 1970–1981' in *The Effects of Mergers and Takeovers in Australia*, Australian Institute of Management, Melbourne, 1986; J. Pound, 'The Information Effect of Takeover Bids and Resistance' (1988) 22 J Fin Eco 207; cf. M. Sullivan, *Contests for Corporate Control, Corporate Governance and Economic Performance in the United States and Germany*, Oxford University Press, Oxford, 2000.

49   Acquiring assets through the medium of a takeover can be relatively cheap compared to the option of purchasing the same assets directly or building them from the start.

50   See Jensen, *op. cit.* footnote 35, p. 831.

51   See generally H. Demsetz and K. Lehn, 'The Structure of Corporate Ownership: Causes and Consequences' (1985) 93 J Pol Eco 1, 155; see also J. A. Brickley and F. Dark, 'The Choice of Organisational Form: The Case of Franchising' (1987) 18 J Fin Eco 401 at 402.

4   rewards and sanctions

5   competitive neutrality.

Let us examine each of these in turn.

Clarity of objectives

Clarity of objectives involves not only defining objectives but distinguishing between social and regulatory objectives on the one hand and commercial objectives on the other, so that each can be pursued for its own sake. Modern management recognises the importance of clarity of goals for an organisation. These act as a focus for management. The underlying aim is to assist the corporation to achieve a commercial level of performance commensurate with that achieved by private sector organisations with similar risk characteristics. One way of achieving a reconciliation between the commercial objectives and the social objectives is for the government specifically to contract with the corporation to provide the community service in return for a fee.[52] By disclosing the true costs of subsidy, society is able to make its own cost–benefit evaluation. It is also thought that these entities should not themselves engage in regulatory activities but these should be determined by an independent authority.[53]

Managerial authority

Managerial authority involves giving boards of directors and management clear responsibility and authority for accomplishing the commercial and social objectives set by government. It is regarded as essential that the organisation's important decisions should be taken by those persons who have strong incentives to maximise the value of the organisation. The minsters and public servants lack the requisite information and organisation-specific knowledge. Also, externally imposed controls stifle management creativity and innovation, and frequently the result is that nobody is held accountable. These concepts apply equally to the performance of non-commercial goals.

Management autonomy can be safeguarded by ensuring that ministers sign commercial and social contracts with boards and these should outline precisely the commercial and social objectives expected of the corporation. In the Morrison model in the United Kingdom it was envisaged that such guidelines should be given but this was often not done. In Australia and New Zealand attempts have been made to do so but the legislation as a whole erodes this principle somewhat by the retention of too many controls in the ministers.

Performance monitoring

Performance monitoring involves improving accountability by subjecting the corporations to rigorous external monitoring and assessment by independent expert analysis. Even the most commercial of public corporations is still subject to less market-based

---

52   See text accompanying footnote 19 supra. See also Zeckhauser and Horn, *op. cit.* footnote 38 supra at 30–1.

53   See footnote 9 supra.

performance monitoring than private sector organisations. Therefore, it is necessary for government to develop surrogate monitoring and incentive mechanisms. The most important mechanism is the provision of a reliable flow for monitoring performance.[54]

Rewards and sanctions

Rewards and sanctions involves introducing a market-based system of rewards and sanctions for directors and management, closely tied to individual and corporate performance. As far as possible this system should reflect private sector practices. It should include the level and structure of remuneration, the basis for income review and the criteria for terminating employment.

Competitive neutrality

Competitive neutrality involves creating a 'level playing field' *vis-à-vis* the private sector, by removing special advantages and disadvantages that apply to public corporations by virtue of government ownership. Competitive neutrality impacts directly on allocative efficiency, particularly through the price charged for goods and services, and the interest charged on loan funds. Losses in allocative efficiency may occur because either (a) the prices charged may not cover the value to society of the resources and alternative uses or (b) the corporation possesses a significant degree of monopoly power in the market for its goods and services and special access to low-cost funds through the state's central borrowing authority.

Practical problems of the corporatisation process

Experience of corporatisation in both Australia and New Zealand has been described as 'best viewed as a variety of processes rather than a single predefined step'.[55] The standard technique is to set up an establishment board or steering committee to oversee the transitional arrangements and to prepare the ground for the state enterprise. Thus there have been different paths and different speeds used in the transition in different cases. An important question is whether radical restructuring has occurred before or after corporatisation. Another important question is whether industry deregulation has taken place before or after transition. A third important factor is whether the enterprise has been seen as a long-term operation or in transition for sell-off.[56]

---

54 It is interesting to note in this regard the debate over whether corporatised entities should be subject to freedom of information legislation. The Victorian Parliament's Public Bodies Review Committee referred in its report to the view that government business enterprises 'as custodians of taxpayers' funds, with community service responsibilities, and in many cases the potential for monopoly power, have special obligations for meeting stricter standards of disclosure than [are] used in the private sector': Parliament of Victoria Public Bodies Review Committee Discussion Paper on Corporatisation, *op. cit.* footnote 2 supra, p. 29. See also Report of the Government Administration Committee on the Inquiry into the State-Owned Enterprise Government Property Services Ltd, May 1990, App 16A.

55 Duncan and Bollard, *op. cit.* footnote 10 supra, p. 21.

56 *ibid.*, ch. 2.

Establishment of an appropriate monitoring regime

A major problem has been the establishment of an appropriate monitoring regime.[57] In the past, state trading departments and corporations have pursued mixed objectives. It was the intention of the corporatisation process that this should be replaced by clearer specification of commercial objectives. This policy may have been frustrated by the conjunctive drafting of the legislation that defines the goals of corporatisation. In *New Zealand Maori Council v. Attorney-General*,[58] Lord Woolf, delivering the judgment of their Lordships, said that there was nothing to suggest that the different goals 'are not to be treated as being of the same weight'. His Lordship went on to say that '[t]he creation of profit is of no greater importance than the other objectives identified in the subsection'.[59]

In most cases, the aim has been to operate a successful business with measures such as return on capital and the necessity to maintain an agreed capital structure. In the case of some corporations, however, there has been a necessity to continue to pursue mixed objectives. For example, government-owned airlines have had to pursue objectives relating to safety, efficiency and equitable pricing as well as complying with international air traffic obligations and the like.

Another important factor in the process of transition has been the change of control. This has involved difficult questions regarding the extent of continuing ministerial and bureaucratic involvement.[60]

There are fundamental decisions that have to be made with regard to accountability regimes.[61] This is a question of determining whether the traditional methods of accountability (such as the auditor-general or parliamentary committees) will be used for corporatised bodies. Some overseas governments have taken the view that performance agreements are sufficient. This seems a short-sighted approach since government will often be responsible for actions of the corporation unless there is specific provision in legislation to the contrary. Such provisions appear in the legislation of Commonwealth, the various states and the ACT.

Government-appointed directors

Extensive use has been made of non-executive directors from the private sector although political considerations influence appointments too much. Executive directors have seldom been used. The attitude towards the appointment of the chief executive officer has differed between organisations. In some cases public servants have been chosen, usually with experience in or aptitude for private sector management. In other cases private sector management has been directly recruited.

---

57   *ibid.*, p. 23.
58   [1994] 1 NZLR 513 at 519. The Privy Council decided that the *State-Owned Enterprise Act 1986* did not relieve the government of its obligation to pursue appropriate social objectives.
59   *ibid.*
60   Duncan and Bollard, *op. cit.* footnote 10 supra, pp. 26 *et seq.*
61   *ibid.*, pp. 27–8.

All directors must act bona fide for the benefit of the company as a whole and for a proper purpose. This means they must give priority to the company's interest. This overriding equitable duty is also now stated in the corporate legislation.[62] A government appointed director must therefore exercise independent judgment and not simply act on the instruction of the minister unless this takes the form of a statutory direction and even here the director must have regard to the effect of compliance on the solvency of the company.

In the United Kingdom the role of nominee directors received close attention after the collapse of the De Lorean Company. A report from the Public Accounts Committee revealed that the legal position of nominee directors is not clear, although guidelines were issued in 1985.[63]

Industrial relations

In the case of the public sector, many management practices have been in the past determined by rules set down by centralised authorities such as the Public Service Board. In areas of personnel management, management has not been free to hire and fire or to pay by performance and result.[64] In industrial relations, a public service body controls the major negotiations. The Australian Council of Trade Unions (ACTU), however, argues that public sector workers do not enjoy more favourable conditions than their counterparts in the private sector. The pay and conditions of many public sector workers have declined relative to the pay and conditions of the private sector workers. Public sector workers have less industrial bargaining power than some unionists in the private construction, mining, transport and manufacturing sectors. With tight budgetary constraints it is often more difficult to achieve concessions from government than from individual employers in the private sector. Also, the Prices and Incomes Accord and the centralised wage-fixing system ensured that public sector pay and conditions could not move in advance of those in the private sector of the economy in Australia. The aim of corporatisation in this, as in other areas, is to approximate more closely the private sector, but the legislation differs between the states. The impact of union power on pay and conditions has been greatest where there has been complete privatisation. The managerial structures and industrial relations of the corporations

62 See Corporations Act, s. 181(1). The *Companies Act 1993* (NZ) also imposes duties on directors. While the provisions overlap with the Australian legislation, they are not identical. See generally Doyle and Moller, *op. cit.* footnote 11 supra; *Committee of Public Accounts Report on the Role and Responsibilities of Nominee Directors*, HM Treasury, London, November 1985.

63 See *Committee of Public Accounts Report, ibid.*

64 The advent of enterprise bargaining may result in considerably increased flexibility in public sector organisations. Many of the gains in productivity which have been achieved in corporatised entities in recent years may in fact be realisable in the public sector as a result of a more flexible industrial relations environment. See, for example, the Overview Statement of the ACTU Congress, September 1993, which promotes (at cl. 5.1) the role of industry and enterprise agreements. See J. J. Catanzariti, 'Corporatisation, Privatisation and Employment Relations', in Collier and Pitkin (eds), *op. cit.* footnote 11 supra, ch. 16.

have given rise to difficult questions for the public service and the unions. The solutions have tended to be generous remuneration outside the public sector norms. On the other hand, these have been accompanied by more rigorous conditions of employment. Where redundancies have been necessary these have usually been on generous terms.

Accounting and finance

In preparing for corporatisation, an important question has been the appropriate form of the accounts. This has given rise to a number of balance sheet issues. Debt and capitalisation have been major issues in the restructuring process. This has involved difficult questions of valuation. The method of valuation, repayment of debt, and financial autonomy have had an important effect on performance.[65] Professor Wiltshire states:

> Amazing though it may seem, there is still no universal methodology available from accountants or auditors for the valuation of public assets. Indeed many governments do not even have a complete inventory of their assets. This is a crucial deficiency since so much of the corporatisation regime depends on such valuations because they are the main basis for performance indicators and evaluation of various kinds.[66]

In many cases the underlying assets are unique in the sense that they have been developed for a limited function. There is, for example, only one railway system in New Zealand. The determination of the property rights of the underlying enterprise has often proved surprisingly difficult and there has been untidiness in the public sector conveyancing at times.

It has been argued that governments have a tendency to provide minimum equity for their business enterprises and to take money out as dividends, weakening the enterprise in relation to competitors. This also creates uncertainty for management and hinders long-term planning.[67] This is contrary to the normal justification for state-owned enterprises.

The competitive advantage with regard to government guarantee of debt raised by state-owned enterprises or government trading enterprises (GTEs) has also been identified as a problem but this can be handled by an independent credit rating organisation's examination on the basis of no government guarantee.

There has been, particularly in the early period, a lack of adequate yardsticks to monitor performance. In some cases there has been no comparable business with which to match up. The underlying problems of agency have sometimes been acute in particular sectors. These have been compounded by the mixed objectives of state-owned enterprises.

---

65   Duncan and Bollard, *op. cit.*, footnote 10 supra, p. 25.
66   Wiltshire, *op. cit.* footnote 20 supra, p. 220.
67   Duncan and Bollard, *op. cit.* footnote 10 supra, p. 25.

It seems generally agreed that corporatisation should be accompanied by accrual accounting, but governments resist this and prefer the traditional accounting methods with the line item accountability system.[68]

A criticism which can be levied at corporatisation and, even more so, privatisation, wherever they have occurred, is the high cost of professional fees. Merchant banks, solicitors, accountants and valuers have all had a bonanza from government policy. In many cases this has proved to be an over-generous subsidy of a learning process, and public servants and politicians have not been particularly effective monitors of these services, or their cost, to the public.

Corporatisation, privatisation and the public/private distinction

Issues of corporatisation and privatisation raise in an acute form the public/private distinction and the question whether it is sustainable in modern conditions. If one concentrates on ownership it is a meaningful distinction. If, however, one engages in a wider ranging analysis, it is increasingly problematic. It is possible to approach such an analysis in different ways, by reference to function, organisation or financing, as well as ownership. Professor Stephen Bottomley, in a useful article,[69] divides up the functions of corporatised enterprises into commercial, social services or administrative, advisory or supervisory functions, and argues that, given that corporatised enterprises are by nature hybrids, some are more public than others because of their function. In the case of commercial functions it is easier to see a case for a private sector approach. In the case of social services the argument tends to favour a public approach. In the case of the third category the arguments are more evenly balanced. An analysis by reference to present organisation structure or financing rather begs the question of whether this is the best form.

Another complication is the increasing tendency of Australian, but not New Zealand, corporate law towards a public law approach.[70] While this is perhaps inevitable with a system of securities regulation, this is not so with company law as such, but constitutional complication in Australia has led to the present composite regime with its obese legislation and general regulatory bias. While this point has been raised by commentators, it seems, if anything, to indicate an eventual blurring of the public/private distinction.

---

68 Wiltshire, _op. cit._ footnote 20 supra, p. 220.
69 S. Bottomley, 'Regulating Government-Owned Corporations: A Review of the Issues' (1994) 53 AJPA 521, 530. See also the valuable paper by M. Taggart, 'Corporatisation, Privatisation and Public Law', Legal Research Foundation, Auckland, 1990.
70 See M. J. Whincop and M. E. Keyes, 'Corporatisation, Contract, Community: An Analysis of Governance in the Privatisation of Public Enterprise and the Publicisation of Private Corporate Law' (1997) 25 Federal LR 51. See also the earlier discussion in J. H. Farrar, 'Fuzzy Law, the Modernisation of Corporate Law, and the Privatisation of Takeover Regulation', in J. H. Farrar (ed.), _Takeovers, Institutional Investors and the Modernisation of Corporate Laws_, Oxford University Press, Auckland, 1993, ch. 1.

Going to the substance of the distinction, there are innate differences between the public and private sectors in a number of key areas. These are:[71]

* Markets in the public sector, if they exist, are often a different kind.
* Public services have been traditionally financed more by taxation than user pays.
* Some public agencies provide a service where government seeks to control costs while others such as prison services and social work actually impose consumption on people. Education and health are 'merit' goods rather than private goods.
* Public organisations are created for collectivist purposes and are accountable to political representatives.
* Criteria of success differ and are measured as much by equity, availability and access as achievement of economic goals.
* Whereas the private sector has the primary objective of making a profit, the public sector is more often focused on providing a certain level of service within a set budget.
* The ultimate question of accountability is more complex. The issue of relevant stakeholders is more complicated: user, community, taxpayers, and government (with trial by media regularly taking place). While financial accountability is the main focus in the private sector, in the public sector this is subordinate to political accountability.

Conclusion

Corporatisation is part of a policy of commercialisation which in its turn is part of a policy of liberalisation or deregulation of the economy. It uses the private sector as the model of efficiency and aims to replicate as far as possible the corporate firm in the private sector. Yet the replication can go only so far: the absence of low-cost monitors and political interference means that corporatised entities are almost inevitably less efficient in agency-cost terms than their counterparts in the private sector.

If governments are serious about increasing the efficiency of the economy, they must be prepared to give more consideration to privatisation in appropriate cases. Only private enterprises can access the full range of low-cost monitors and thereby reduce the agency cost of their operations. However, there are areas where privatisation will be inappropriate or politically unacceptable.

Of course, even privatisation may not be enough in some instances: as Margaret Thatcher said in *The Downing Street Years*, '[P]rivatisation itself does not solve every problem ... though ... it certainly exposed hidden problems which could thus be tackled'.[72] A government that pursued a comprehensive privatisation program would need

---

71   This is based on the useful chapter by L. Ashburner, 'Corporate Governance in the Public Sector: The Case of the NHS', in K. Keasey, S. Thomson and M. Wright (eds), *Corporate Governance: Economic, Management and Financial Issues*, Oxford University Press, Oxford, 1997, ch. 13.

72   HarperCollins, London, 1993, p. 677.

406 Self-regulation and Contemporary Issues

to think carefully about the way in which the privatised entities should be regulated. Australia has much to learn from the difficulties encountered in the United Kingdom and New Zealand in this regard.[73] Where the privatised entities retain significant market power, it may be appropriate to create a powerful independent regulator like Oftel in the telecommunications industry in the United Kingdom. Alternatively, the government might unbundle vertically and horizontally integrated entities and expose their various functions to effective competition. Promoting competition may necessitate the encouragement of foreign ownership of competing firms.[74]

Unlike New Zealand, governments in Australia have hesitated to embrace privatisation in a wholehearted fashion. In most cases, they have settled for corporatisation or limited outsourcing as substitutes. At first glance, this is puzzling: why stop there if the object is to reform the economy? One explanation is that politicians and bureaucrats remain firmly wedded to the notion of a strong public sector. While they are prepared to countenance reforms that will make public sector entities operate more efficiently, they are not prepared to accept a diminished role for government and political accountability. Perhaps the most important task is to address the basic question of the role of the modern state.[75]

In the interim, governments must sort out their priorities in relation to corporatised entities. If the entities are expected to perform social service functions, means must be found to make the cost of those activities more explicit.[76] The activities themselves should be identified more clearly. An obligation to be 'socially responsible' or to be a 'good employer' is worse than meaningless: it may provide a cover for inefficiency.

Further thought should be given to the role of minsters and public servants.[77] Is it politically realistic to expect that corporatised entities will enjoy independence, regardless of the formalities? To the extent that ministers are responsible for the activities of an entity, there will be an incentive to interfere, based on short-term political considerations. Governments should aim to develop control arrangements that destabilise the enterprise as little as possible and that are reported publicly.[78]

The disclosure obligations must also be given careful consideration. How much disclosure should be expected from a government-owned enterprise? The fact that cor-

---

73   See N. Lawson, *The View from No. 11*, HarperCollins, London, 1992, ch. 19; see also C. Veljanovski, *Selling the State*, Weidenfeld & Nicolson, London, 1987, ch. 8; see also Duncan and Bollard, *op. cit.* footnote 10 supra, pp. 63–9.

74   K. Wiltshire, 'Privatisation, Regulation and the Public Interest: Britain and Australia', in B. Head and E. McCoy (eds), *Deregulation or Better Regulation?*, University of Queensland Press, Brisbane, 1991, p. 36. See generally Lawson, *op. cit.*, p. 239.

75   K. König and H. Siedentopf, 'An International Perspective II: Privatisation and Institutional Modernisation in Asia and Europe', in I. Thynne and M. Ariff (eds), *Privatisation: Singapore's Experience in Perspective*, Longman, Singapore, 1988, pp. 185–6. See generally S. Bottomley, 'Regulating Government-owned Corporations: A Review of the Issues' (1994) 53 AJPA 521.

76   Zeckhauser and Horn, *op. cit.* footnote 38 supra, pp. 31–2.

77   For a useful recent discussion of how corporate governance applies to state government enterprises see *Corporate Governance—Beyond Compliance*, Auditor-General of Queensland Report No. 7 (1998–99).

78   Wiltshire, *op. cit.* footnote 74 supra, p. 38.

poratised entities are ultimately the property of the state and its taxpayers, militates in favour of a freedom of information regime similar to that which applies elsewhere in the public sector. Disclosure is, however, costly and can make commercial operations less efficient. Perhaps each entity needs to be considered separately: in some cases, the need for information will be great (particularly where the enterprise is a monopoly)[79] while in others it will not be necessary or appropriate to provide more information than that provided by the private sector.

The reform process which has seen the growth of corporatisation in Australia is far from over. Governments must clarify for themselves and others, the objects of reform. They must be prepared to reconsider the role of the public sector in the larger economy. That debate has only just begun in Australia.

---

79   *ibid.*, pp. 37–8.

CHAPTER 32

Business Ethics

In Chapter 1 we saw that at the outer penumbra of the concept of corporate governance lies business ethics. Business ethics is rapidly becoming a subject in its own right and all that is attempted in this chapter is to give an outline.

The word ethics comes from the Greek words *ethos* and *ethikos* which refer to character and traditions.[1] The *Oxford Dictionary* gives a number of definitions including 'the department of study concerned with the principles of human duty'. An equivalent Latin word is *mos* which is the origin of our word 'morality'.

A distinction can perhaps be drawn between ethics as the customary norms and ways of behaving, and morality as the reflection upon those norms and the development of principles to explain and influence them.[2]

The term 'business ethics' is wide enough in one sense to accommodate the whole of corporate governance but we are using it here in a narrower sense to cover those principles that are not the subject of law or voluntary institutional codes of conduct.[3]

Characteristics of business ethics

The three main characteristics of ethics in general are:[4]

---

1   See D. Grace and S. Cohen, *Business Ethics: Australian Problems and Cases*, 2nd edn, Oxford University Press, Melbourne, 1998, p. 3. This is an excellent book and this chapter relies on it substantially. Other books of significance are E. Sternberg, *Just Business: Business Ethics in Action*, Warner Books, London, 1994; C. A. J. Coady and C. J. G. Sampford (eds), *Business Ethics and the Law*, The Federation Press, Annandale, 1993; and R. D. Francis, *Ethics and Corporate Governance*, UNSW Press, Sydney, 2000.
2   Georg Wilhelm Friedrich Hegel cited by Grace and Cohen, *op. cit.*, p. 3, without reference. Grace and Cohen think that by and large there is no reason to make the distinction: *op. cit.* p. 4.
3   Even the latter part of this definition is problematic due to the eclecticism of some voluntary codes. See e.g. T. Renton, *Standards for the Board*, 2nd edn, Institute of Directors, London, 1999.
4   Compare Grace and Cohen, *op. cit.*, pp. 4–5.

- the need to go beyond self-interest.
- the possibility of the decision being universalised, that is, capable of general application, for example, Kant's categorical imperative, 'So conduct yourself that the maxim of your conduct can be the maxim of universal action',[5] which is a more abstract version of 'Love your neighbour as yourself'.[6]
- the need for the ethical opinion to be defended by rational responses so that it is not a mere bias or preference.

Ethical matters can be assessed by reference to absolute standards or relative standards. One measure that perhaps lies in between is consequentialism, which is conduct being assessed by reference to its consequences. One form of relative standards is Utilitarianism, a system of ethics based on the greatest happiness of the greatest number, which was fashionable and influential in the nineteenth century.

So far we have spoken about ethics in general as opposed to business ethics. Business has been described as the oldest profession but some would deny its professional status. Business is predicated on rational pursuit of self-interest in a market situation. Adam Smith in the eighteenth century argued that rational pursuit of self-interest in markets led them as if by an invisible hand to the common good.[7] In other words the existence of markets serves the public good. Smith has been misrepresented by some later commentators.[8] In his *Theory of Moral Sentiments*[9] he recognised that reciprocity was a prerequisite of markets. The question is, how far does this go? Does it necessitate social responsibility?

The Chicago economist Milton Friedman has argued that not only does business not have a duty to practise social responsibility, it has a duty *not* to have an eye to social responsibility.[10] Its sole duty is to maximise profits. This is a plausible exaggeration. A market is an elaborate information system. All that markets do is to facilitate exchange transactions by providing information about the cost and availability of resources necessary for particular ends. They do not determine what the ends are. Similarly, markets do not set objectives. Nevertheless, a business needs objectives. A firm is not solely a creature of markets. It is a social institution as we saw in Chapter 3.

Some modern writers argue that good ethics is good business on the following grounds:[11]

- They may overlap in fact.
- Bad ethical behaviour may attract external regulation.

---

5   See the discussion on this between Geoffrey Warnock and Bryan Magee in B. Magee, *The Great Philosophers*, Oxford University Press, Oxford, 1987, p. 184.

6   Mark 12:13. Also Leviticus 19:18.

7   *An Inquiry into the Nature of Causes of the Wealth of Nations*, Modern Library, New York, 1937 (1st edn 1776), p. 423.

8   See ch. 3 of this book.

9   Clarendon Press, Oxford, Pt 3, s. 3, para. 7; Pt 2, s. 2, ch. 3, para. 1.

10   M. Friedman, 'The Social Responsibility of Business is to Increase its Profits', *New York Times Magazine*, 13 September 1970.

11   See e.g. Grace and Cohen, *op. cit.* footnote 1 supra, pp. 26–32.

- Good publicity can be attracted by good ethical behaviour, bad publicity by bad ethical behaviour.
- Good ethical conduct leads to a greater sense of professionalism among the work force. People like to work for the 'best companies in Australia'.

Long-termism and the stakeholder concept

As we saw in Chapter 3, some commentators have emphasised the role of long-term thinking in the investment policies and management decision making in countries such as Germany and Japan and have compared these with short-termism in countries such as the USA and the United Kingdom.[12] More recently we have seen the resurgence of the stakeholder concept which emphasises that corporations exist to serve a number of stakeholders and not just shareholders.[13]

The problem with the concept of 'stakeholder' is to move from the acceptable proposition that a person or group has an interest in the corporation, to the idea that they have enforceable rights. Clearly, employees have an interest in the corporation but their rights are determined by contract and employment law. Similarly, consumers have an interest but their rights are governed by contracts of sale of goods and consumer protection laws. If one moves beyond this, one is talking about ethics and moral rights and this raises the sense in which the word 'right' is being used.

We have seen how countries such as Germany and Japan have a different scale of values and give differing degrees of recognition to stakeholders. In the case of Germany this has included co-determination and worker representation on supervisory boards. Even the United Kingdom now accepts that directors can take into account the interests of employees and a number of states in the USA have passed constituency statutes that allow consideration of a broad range of stakeholders.[14]

There is arguably a need to revisit the role of employees in the corporation and to move away from the present adversarial culture.

Primary norms of business ethics

Although a number of values have been recognised in the literature, the following have been identified by Mary Guy as core values:

---

12   See for instance the discussion in J. Charkham, *Keeping Good Company*, Oxford University Press, Oxford, 1994; H. Short and K. Keasey, 'Institutional Shareholders and Corporate Governance in the United Kingdom', in K. Keasey, S. Thompson and M. Wright (eds), *Corporate Governance—Economic, Management and Financial Issues*, Oxford University Press, Oxford, 1997, pp. 13, 43–5.

13   There is growing literature on this but see Grace and Cohen, *op. cit.* footnote 1 supra, ch. 3; T. Clarke and S. Clegg, *Changing Paradigms—The Transformation of Management Knowledge for the Twenty-First Century*, HarperCollins Business, London, 1998, ch. 6. For acute criticism of the concept see Sternberg, *op. cit.* footnote 1 supra, pp. 49–52, pp. 170 *et seq.*

14   See the discussion in chapter 3 of this book.

- caring—respect for the individual
- honesty—operating in good faith
- accountability—responsibility for one's actions
- promise keeping—one's word is one's bond
- pursuit of excellence—ensuring quality
- loyalty—to employees and persons with whom one has dealings
- fairness—treating people properly and not taking advantage of them
- integrity—avoiding conflicts of interest
- respect for others—in the workforce and as suppliers and consumers
- responsible citizenship—obeying the law and behaving in an upright fashion.[15]

Application of the primary norms

Many of the primary norms can be seen as aspects of broader concepts of distributive justice and basic good faith.[16] As such they can be applied in decisions regarding employees, finance and trading. The most difficult questions probably arise in the context of trading.

Australian and New Zealand law contains provisions aimed against misleading and deceptive conduct[17] and these are gradually giving rise to a large and complex case law although the underlying principle seems clear enough.

The kind of tactics practised by British Airways on Virgin Atlantic Airways which led to an eventual settlement[18] would probably be unlawful in both countries.

While falling short of such tactics, the managerial errors committed by Western Mining in connection with the purchase of a half share in a Western Australian gold mine, Lady Bountiful, were later regretted by the company and led to a heightened awareness of ethical issues.[19]

Advertising is an area where ethical issues are often raised. This is governed by the *Trade Practices Act 1974* and industry codes of advertising ethics.[20]

Codes of ethics[21]

The established professions have long operated with codes of conduct or practice. Recently, however, we have seen a significant increase in voluntary codes being adopted

---

15 These are based on M. Guy, *Ethical Decision Making in Everyday Work Situations*, Quorum Books, New York, 1990. See also the other approaches in Grace and Cohen, *op. cit.* footnote 1 supra, appendix 1.
16 See Sternberg, *op. cit.* footnote 1 supra, pp. 79 *et seq.*
17 *Trade Practices Act 1974* (Cwth) s. 52; *Fair Trading Act 1986* (NZ) s. 9.
18 See Grace and Cohen, *op. cit.* footnote 1 supra, pp. 77–8
19 *ibid.*, pp. 79–80.
20 *ibid.*, ch. 5.
21 *ibid.*, ch. 10.

by Australian and New Zealand companies. Both *Corporate Practices and Conduct*[22] and the IFSA Guidelines for Corporations[23] recommend the adoption of company codes of ethics, and that they should be available to shareholders on request.

To some extent the adoption of such codes is brought on by the enlightened sense of self-interest: either we do this or we face yet more legal regulation. This kind of attitude is often expressly encouraged by government. Also the adoption of such codes can give rise to publicity and advertising claims. Further, an increasing number of managers see positive advantages in having codes as a form of education and training for staff.

The kind of things covered by such codes typically include:[24]

- a general statement of the values of the organisation and its guiding principles
- definitions of what constitutes both ethical and corrupt conduct in the organisation
- competence requirements and professional standards
- directives on personal and professional behaviour
- affirmations of fairness, equity, equal opportunity and affirmative action
- rules on gifts and conflicts of interest
- restrictions on use of the company's facilities for private purposes
- guidelines on confidentiality, public comment, whistle-blowing, and use of company information
- identification of different stakeholders and other interested parties, and their rights
- commitment to occupational health and safety
- commitment to the environment and social responsibility
- mechanisms for enforcing the code, including sanctions for violations
- advice on interpreting and implementing the code.

In order to have an effective code it is not necessary to have employee consultation although it may well be advisable.[25] A code is not a survey of employees' ethical attitudes. It is something which should be produced by management under the supervision of the board of directors. A code which is not supported by the board is unlikely to be adopted. It should also be promulgated and publicised.

Although it is possible to have an unwritten set of ethical principles it can hardly be called a code. There are distinct advantages in having a written code: it identifies key principles; it serves as an educative medium; it signals the company's commitment to ethical standards; and it can be used as a method of monitoring managerial and employee misconduct. The main disadvantage is a tendency, particularly in Australia, to excessive legalism and overelaboration of technical detail. Lawyers are often the worst people to draft codes of conduct.

---

22 H. Bosch (ed.), *Corporate Practices and Conduct*, 3rd edn, FT Pitman Publishing, Melbourne, 1995, pp. 38–41.
23 Guideline 14.
24 *ibid.*, pp. 168–9. See also H. Bosch (ed.), *op. cit.*, pp. 40–1
25 See Sternberg, *op. cit.* footnote 1 supra, p. 244.

According to Korn/Ferry International's report *Boards of Directors in Australia and New Zealand 2000,* 62 per cent of Australian respondents and 43 per cent of New Zealand respondents had a written code of ethics. In Australia 69 per cent of the public listed companies, 50 per cent of private companies and 33 per cent of government boards surveyed had them. In New Zealand 55 per cent of public listed companies had them but only 25 per cent of private companies did. By contrast, 54 per cent of government boards had them.

The ethics of lobbying[26]

Lobbying is seeking to influence government policy by making representations to ministers, members of parliament and government officials. It is about avoiding or promoting legislation or other government regulatory action and getting a share of resources.

As an industry it has developed substantially in Australia and New Zealand in the last twenty years. Bodies such as the Business Council of Australia, the Australian Institute of Company Directors and the ACTU are all involved in lobbying. Lobbying constitutes an integral part of the democratic process and usefully supplements the advice given by public servants. At its best it facilitates consultation and open government.

The dangers are the domination of the public debate by key interest groups with adversarial positions on the one hand and the practice of sham consultation by government, particularly with tight deadlines for submission, on the other hand.

A model for ethical conduct in the lobbying process is contained in the Queensland *Public Sector Ethics Act 1994,* based on the report of the Electoral and Administrative Review Commission. This sets out in section 4 a declaration of basic principles of ethics. These are:

* respect for the law and the system of government
* respect for persons
* integrity
* diligence
* economy and efficiency.

These are declared by section 4(1) to be fundamental to good public administration. The content of each principle is defined in sections 7–11.

Provision is made for codes of conduct, additional responsibilities of chief executive officers and disciplinary action. Part 7 sets up an integrity commissioner whose role is to advise on conflict of interest questions and to contribute to public understanding of public integrity standards.

---

26 See S. Tongue, 'The Virtues and Vices of Lobbying', in G. L. Clark, E. P. Jonson and W. Caldow (eds), *Accountability and Corruption—Public Sector Ethics,* Allen & Unwin, St Leonards, NSW, 1997, ch. 8.

Although the above principles were drafted for public officials they can also serve as an appropriate declaration of relevant principles for the private sector in its lobbying practices.

International business ethics[27]

Ethics reflects the traditions and morals of particular societies. Business ethics is no exception and in fact demonstrates most clearly the significance of cultural differences. The basic question is whether one has a system built up on trust or on competition. Because of a history of adverse external and political factors, countries such as China and Japan have built up business networks based on trust.[28] Countries such as the United Kingdom, Australia, New Zealand, and the USA opt for greater competition. Recently, however, there seems to be greater emphasis on networking although the Western conception seems different from the Asian conception.[29]

A particular issue which is a perennial problem is corruption.[30] What constitutes corruption differs from country to country. Corruption in many Asian countries takes the form of bribes that are justified on the basis of low wages in the public service.

In a survey in the *Journal of Business Ethics* in 1992 Australian exporters listed the following as the ten most commonly perceived problems in international business dealing. There were:[31]

- large-scale bribery
- cultural differences
- involvement in political affairs
- pricing practices
- illegal or immoral activities in a host country
- questionable commissions
- gifts or favours
- tax evasion
- inappropriate use of products
- traditional small-scale bribery

There has been increasing awareness of the problems of corruption. International bodies such as the OECD have done work on this topic[32] and there have been private initiatives such as the Sullivan Code, the Caux Round Table and

---

27 See Grace and Cohen, *op. cit.* footnote 1 supra, p. 244.
28 See the fascinating study by F. Fukuyama, *Trust—The Social Virtues and the Creation of Prosperity*, Penguin Books, London, 1995.
29 On this see Fukuyama, *op. cit.* and Clark and Clegg, *op. cit.* footnote 13 supra, pp. 29–34.
30 See Grace and Cohen *op. cit.* footnote 1 supra, pp. 188 *et seq.*
31 R. Armstrong, 'An Empirical Investigation of International Marketing Ethics: Problems Encountered by Australian Firms' (1992) 11 *Journal of Business Ethics* 161–71.
32 See AnCorR WEB, Anti-corruption Hotline.

Transparency International.[33] The Sullivan Code was the product of Leon Sullivan, a black minister of religion from Philadelphia and member of the board of General Motors. This was an attack on the system of apartheid.

The Caux Round Table aimed to encourage business to contribute to global economic and social development. The two basic ethical values are working together for the common good, summed up in the Japanese word *kyosei*, and respect for human dignity. The Caux Round Table produced its principles for business in 1994 as a 'world standard against which business behavior can be measured'. These are set out in Appendix 5 to this book.

Transparency International (TI) was formed in 1993 and is well known for its annual Corruption Perception Index. Australia is represented on TI by Henry Bosch, former chairman of the NCSC.

The relationship of international business ethics to issues such as human rights and environmental protection is controversial. Developing countries tend to see emphasis on these as latter day colonialism. Western countries, it is argued, developed free of such constraints so it is unfair for them now to seek to impose them on developing countries. This itself raises an interesting ethical question.

---

33   See further Grace and Cohen, *op. cit.* footnote 1 supra, pp. 202–5.

CHAPTER 33

Comparative Corporate Governance Systems: An Overview[1]

Historical phases

Corporate governance has traditionally operated within a particular national ethos. Even where the imperial model was adopted, it operated in accordance with the local business culture. In Chapter 2 we saw that there have been different systems in place at different periods of history and in different countries. There were, however, certain dominant themes in Western countries. These have been classified by Professor Lutgart van den Berghe and Liesbeth De Ridder[2] as:

- entrepreneurial capitalism
- banking capitalism
- managerial capitalism
- institutional capitalism
- reference shareholding
- the evolving democratic corporate model.

The first represents the earliest modern phase.[3] The second[4] a phase that describes early development in countries such as the USA, Australia and New Zealand, and

---

1   See generally J. Charkham, *Keeping Good Company—A Study of Corporate Governance in Five Countries*, Clarendon Press, Oxford, 1994; K. J. Hopt and E. Wymeersch (eds), *Comparative Corporate Governance— Essays and Materials*, Walter de Gruyter, Berlin, 1997; D. H. Chew, *Studies in International Corporate Finance and Governance Systems—A Comparison of the US, Japan and Europe*, Oxford University Press, New York, 1997; K. J. Hopt, H. Kandar, M. J. Roe, E. Wymeersch and S. Prigge, *Comparative Corporate Governance—The State of the Art and Emerging Research*, Oxford University Press, Oxford, 1999.
2   *International Standardisation of Good Corporate Governance—Best Practices for the Board of Directors*, Kluwer Academic Publishers, Dordrecht, 1999, ch. 4.
3   *ibid*, p. 29.
4   *ibid.*, pp. 29–30.

modern Germany where banks play a prominent role. The third[5] represents the managerial revolution characterised by the separation of ownership and control described by writers such as Berle and Means. The fourth[6] is the stage that we are at in the USA, the United Kingdom, Australia and New Zealand where institutional investors play an ever increasing role. Reference shareholding[7] describes the situation prevalent in countries such as France, Belgium and Italy with long-term shareholders. In Australia and New Zealand we have a number of listed companies controlled by other listed companies although the holdings are not necessarily long term. The last[8] represents a new model emerging with knowledge-based companies where there is a power shift to the workforce where the enterprise becomes an end in itself, not simply the instrument of the shareholders. Asian countries do not fit easily into these categories.

Broad classifications

A basic distinction is sometimes made between corporate governance and other forms of governance. Thus corporate governance is distinguished from political governance or governance in general. Again it is sometimes distinguished from social governance which is a broader based concept referring to how a given society orders itself. This takes into account a whole range of factors—political, economic and cultural. Discussion of the Japanese system sometimes draws a distinction between corporate governance and overall contractual governance of which corporate governance is a subset. Contractual governance can in turn be seen as a subset of social governance.

Turning to corporate governance specifically, Professor Colin Mayer[9] has broadly classified corporate governance systems into two: outsider-based and insider-based systems. Into the first category come the Anglo-American models such as exist in Australia and New Zealand. Into the second come Japan, Germany and other Western European systems. The classification can be represented as shown in Figure 33.1.

The first depends on active external markets for shares which include the market for corporate control through takeovers. The second does not depend on these but has more stable long-term shareholder relationships with other companies holding shares in cross shareholdings. Banks play a central role in corporate relationships. Professor On Kit Tam of Monash University, in his excellent monograph on China,[10] distinguishes the insider-based model from insider *control* systems developing in Eastern Europe's transitional economies, where there is a vacuum filled by existing management.

---

5   *ibid.*, pp. 30–1.
6   *ibid.*, pp. 31–32.
7   *ibid.*, pp. 33–5.
8   *ibid.*, pp. 35–7.
9   C. Mayer, 'Stock Markets, Financial Institutions and Corporate Performance', in N. Dimsdale and M. Preveser (eds), *Capital Markets and Corporate Governance*, Clarendon Press, Oxford, 1994, p. 179.
10 On Kit Tam, *The Development of Corporate Governance in China*, Edward Elgar, Cheltenham, UK, 1999, p. 32.

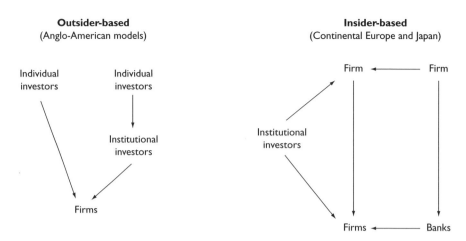

Figure 33.1   The two main corporate governance systems

Professors Clarke and Clegg in their interesting book *Changing Paradigms*[11] distinguish between three types of capitalism, as represented in Table 33.1.

Table 33.1   Three major types of capitalism

Europe	US/UK	Japan
stakeholder capitalism	shareholder capitalism	collective capitalism

We have made some reference to the stakeholder concept in Chapters 2 and 3 and will return to it later in this chapter.

To this system one can add the People's Republic of China, which has a communist system undergoing complex transition to a market economy.[12]

In the light of the above it can be seen that the dichotomy of Mayer may be over simple as an attempt to summarise the main systems. Before we attempt to describe the dominant characteristics of the main models we must first say a word about method.

The search for an appropriate methodology

In the film *Amadeus* the Archduke makes the seemingly foolish remark to Mozart, 'Too many notes, Mozart, too many notes', but maybe he had a point. In comparative law we often seek to catalogue other people's laws and then to attempt some kind of tentative

---

11   HarperCollins Business, London, 1998, p. 297.
12   See On Kit Tam, *op. cit.* footnote 10 supra.

generalisation. The better scholars seek to do this in a broader fashion, not only taking account of law but also of history, culture and practice.[13] The difficulty is to be accurate in one's descriptions and generalisations and value-free in one's assessments. This has been described as the conundrum of comparative law.[14]

Another basic approach is to treat comparative law as a form of social science[15] and to seek an appropriate method from that source. One method is to produce models,[16] either reducing the foreign system to a simplified model or producing a composite ideal type as some kind of universal measure. The latter is intrinsically difficult. Another method is to use economic concepts and techniques, measuring systems against the universal criterion of efficiency.

A basic problem here is to apply the criterion to legal systems that pursue other goals and, particularly to apply it to those such as the Japanese and the Chinese where the law in the books does not necessarily reflect the law in action.

A third method under the heading of social science is path dependence.[17] Corporate structures, it is said, depend in part on the structures a country had in earlier times, in particular the structures with which the modern economy started.[18] These structures also bias the legal rules in terms of what is efficient in any given country and the interest-group politics that determine which rules are chosen.[19]

Professors Bebchuk and Roe[20] identify two sources of path dependence: structure driven; and rule driven. The structures of an economy depend on what went before and determine what is efficient for a particular corporation and this affects motivation for change. Corporate rules affect structures and yet depend on them.

To some extent this is an application to law and economic phenomena of a metaphor taken from mathematics, physics and the biological sciences. In mathematics for instance 'path dependence structures' means a continuous mapping of a real interval into a space as with lines on a graph.[21] We must be wary of seduction by metaphors. The

---

13   Cf. E. Lambert, 'Comparative Law' in *Encyclopaedia of Social Sciences*, vol. IV, Macmillan, London, 1931, pp. 126 *et seq.*

14   See C. A. Rogers, 'Gulliver's Troubled Travels, or the Conundrum of Comparative Law' (1998) 67 Geo Wash L Rev 149, 189.

15   See M. Schmitthoff, 'The Science of Comparative Law' (1939–41) 7 CLJ 94 but compare A. Watson, *Legal Transplants*, Scottish Academic Press, Edinburgh, 1974, p. 2.

16   D. Dummer, 'The Utility of Comparing Corporate Models', unpublished paper in Contemporary Issues in Corporate Law, April 1999, Bond University.

17   See for example M. Roe, 'Chaos and Evolution in Law and Economics' (1996) 109 Harvard L Rev 641; L. A. Bebchuk and M. J. Roe, 'A Theory of Path Dependence in Corporate Ownership and Governance' (1999) 52 Stanford L Rev 127; G. Walker, 'Reinterpreting New Zealand Securities Regulation', in G. Walker, B. Fisse and I. Ramsay (eds), *Securities Regulation in Australia and New Zealand*, 2nd edn, LBC Information Services, North Ryde, NSW, 1998, p. 88. The chapter by Gordon Walker gives a useful overview at p. 89. See further, R. Lewin, *Complexity—Life on the Edge of Chaos*, Phoenix, London, 1997.

18   Bebchuk and Roe, *op. cit.*, p. 127.

19   *ibid.*

20   *ibid.*

21   Cf. *New Shorter Oxford Dictionary*, vol. 2.

interplay of historical forces which lead to any given state of affairs are often many and complex. This is particularly true of economics.[22] The relationship is not a matter of law being an economic reflex as Marx thought. The relationship is more complex. Take for example the development of separate legal personality and the link with limited liability. Economic forces were pressing for legal reform in the nineteenth century but the *Joint Stock Companies Act 1844*[23] owed as much to the immediate problem of insurance fraud and the personal initiative of William Gladstone as those forces. Gladstone himself had been the innocent victim of business collapse.[24] The development of limited liability is similarly complex.[25] The economic background to recognition of the one-person company in 1897 has not been fully explored,[26] nor has the development of the modern group.[27] Theories of path dependence are suggestive but no more. We need to explore all the variables—dependent and independent—that operated to bring about these changes and to assess their impact. This calls for a richer type of interdisciplinary scholarship than we have so far achieved. This is not to denigrate the work of scholars such as Mark Roe, who have opened up the possibilities of this type of research and offered a number of helpful insights into the development of US and other corporate laws.[28] It is more a plea to transcend the law and economics domination of the debate and to pursue a 'pluralism of paradigms and proper intellectual scepticism'.[29]

The UK and US models[30]

The United Kingdom first developed the modern corporate concepts although at times it was closely paced by France, the USA and later Germany.[31] We traced some of the history of this in Chapters 2 and 3.

Thus the evolution of joint stock, the idea of a general incorporation statute, limited liability, the modern forms of corporate constitution, classes of shares, and flexible debt financing mechanisms were all developed in the United Kingdom. More recently the United Kingdom pioneered the idea of self-regulation. While this has arguably

22 See R. Romano, 'A Cautionary Note on Drawing Lessons from Comparative Corporate Law' (1993) 102 Yale LJ 2021.
23 See R. R. Formoy, *The Historical Foundations of Modern Company Law*, Sweet & Maxwell, London, 1923, part III, s. 1.
24 See R. Jenkins, *Gladstone*, Macmillan, London, 1995, pp. 78–80.
25 See (1855) XXIV *Law Times* 142; see C. A. Cooke, *Corporation, Trust and Company*, Manchester University Press, Manchester, 1950; B. C. Hunt, *The Development of the Business Corporation in England 1800–1867*, Harvard University Press, Cambridge, Mass., 1936, ch. VI; Formoy, *op. cit.*
26 For good attempts see P. Ireland, 'Triumph of the Company Legal Form 1856–1914' and C. R. Rubin, 'Aron Salomon and His Circle', in J. Adams (ed.), *Essays for Clive Schmitthoff*, Professional Books, Abingdon, 1983, pp. 29 *et seq* and pp. 99 *et seq* respectively.
27 See J. H. Farrar and B. Hannigan, *Farrar's Company Law*, 4th edn, Butterworths, London, 1998, ch. 33.
28 See materials cited in footnote 1 supra.
29 R. I. Tricker, Editorial (1994) 2 *Corporate Governance—An International Review* 1, 4.
30 See Charkham, *op. cit.* footnote 1 supra, ch. 5 and 6.
31 See Farrar and Hannigan, *op. cit.*, ch. 2.

failed in the City of London in respect of the securities market and Lloyds, it has succeeded as an idea appropriate for corporate governance and is providing the model for global corporate governance.

The origins of US corporate governance ideas lay in British laws. Each state is a separate jurisdiction. There is no federal chartering.

Consequently there is a market for business corporation acts and corporate governance regimes. In the nineteenth century New Jersey had the most lenient regime. Later Delaware took over as the most liberal and popular regime. It was dominated by a strong corporate bar and specialist judiciary.[32]

US corporate laws developed a number of distinctive features.[33] These include:

- a system based on rigorous laws on self-dealing and a lenient approach to business judgment
- regimes of policing on self-dealing which differ from state to state
- private enforcement by minority shareholders facilitated by derivative actions and contingency fee litigation
- issue of no par value stock and purchase of their own stock by corporations
- bankruptcy legislation which deals with both personal and corporate insolvency and pursues a liberal regime that encourages rehabilitation of business
- flexible merger procedures
- flexible financing techniques.

The USA was the first jurisdiction to develop a comprehensive administrative regulatory approach to securities regulation since 1933. This was a federal system. It later developed a sophisticated law on insider trading.

The UK and US systems are characterised by active stock markets and the separation of ownership and control with some regrouping of ownership interests in the hands of institutional investors.[34] There is a market for corporate control and a preference for boards dominated by non-executive directors.[35]

The separation of ownership and control began after 1918 and is more pronounced in the UK and the USA than in other countries. This was described by Berle and Means as we saw in Chapter 5 and their theory dominated the UK and US corporate governance debates until the advent of law and economic scholarship. In the USA Mark Roe,[36] has argued that the separation of ownership and control developed because of the hostility to bank capitalism and the lack of a nationwide system of branches of banks. Corporations had to seek finance elsewhere and, therefore, turned

32   For a useful historical survey see J. W. Hurst, *The Legitimacy of the Business Corporation*, The University Press of Virginia, Charlottesville, 1970.
33   See for example R. Clarke, *Corporate Law*, Little, Brown, Boston, 1986.
34   See M. Roe, *Strong Managers, Weak Owners: The Political Roots of American Corporate Finance*, Princeton University Press, Princeton, NJ, 1994, ch. 1.
35   See M. von Neumann Whitman, *New World, New Rules—The Changing Role of the American Corporation*, Harvard Business School Press, Boston, 1999, pp. 87 *et seq.*
36   Roe, *op. cit.*, ch. 1, passim.

to stock markets. Conversely, the US laws facilitated mergers and the achievement of economies of scale.

The United Kingdom did not inhibit the development of banks but from an early date restricted equity investment by banks, other than merchant banks.[37] It developed an active stock market from an early period.

However, many significant companies in the United Kingdom remained under family control for longer periods and there were delays in the development of a professional managerial class. This was also affected by the social class system which inhibited development.[38]

At the same time the City of London developed as the world's leading financial centre although it began to face stiff competition from the USA after 1945[39] and is now facing competition from Frankfurt.

Both the USA and United Kingdom have seen the massive rise of institutional investment since 1945.[40] The United Kingdom pioneered the growth of self-regulation of corporate governance by business and the institutional investors which has now been taken up by the USA and promoted on a global basis.[41]

The German model[42]

German corporation law only really developed in its modern form from the end of the nineteenth century and went down a different path from the UK/US model. It developed strong banks and a weak stock market. Bismarck created great banks as engines of national development. These were encouraged to make long-term investments and were necessarily involved in corporate governance.[43] The introduction of stamp duties on transfers encouraged the practice of bank-deposited stock to avoid the tax.[44] Thus the banks were able to control the proxy machinery.[45] Work councils were introduced originally on a voluntary basis as a method of consultation with employees.[46] The overall approach owed more to the idea of a political coalition of interests than corporate governance or agency theories of the firm.[47]

---

37   *ibid.*, pp. 47–8.
38   See generally B. R. Cheffins, 'Putting Britain on the Roe Map: The Emergence of the Berle–Means Corporation in the United Kingdom', unpublished paper, October 1999.
39   See A. Hamilton, *The Financial Revolution*, Free Press, New York, 1986.
40   See chs 2 and 26 above.
41   See ch. 34 below.
42   See generally Charkham, *op. cit.*, footnote 1 supra, ch. 2. See in particular his citation of the speech by Dr Gottfred Bruder to the Royal Society of Arts contrasting the German and the UK systems in operation.
43   See Roe, *op. cit.* p. 215.
44   *ibid.*
45   *ibid.*
46   See the very interesting paper by K. Pistor, 'Codetermination: A Sociopolitical Model with Governance Externalities', in M. M. Blair and M. J. Roe (eds), *Employees and Corporate Governance*, Brookings Institution Press, Washington, DC, 1999, ch. 5.
47   *ibid.*, p. 165.

A Stock Corporation Law was passed under the Nazis in 1937, which provided for minimum capital, increased disclosure, strengthening of management and an emphasis on the interests of the community and the state. In 1951–56, new laws were passed on codetermination which had existed in the iron and steel industries from an earlier period.[48] The modern legislation for public companies is now in the *Aktiengesetz* of 1965. This provides for the public company in a social market economy. It has provision for two-tier boards, worker participation and distinctive provisions on corporate groups.

German codetermination provides for worker participation through works councils and representation on the supervisory board. Codetermination has developed for reasons of social governance, rather than corporate governance, and to reduce employee alienation by involving them in decision making.[49]

The private company was invented by the Germans in 1884 in the form of the GmbH. There have been no major reforms since then.

We shall concentrate on supervisory boards, worker representation and corporate groups.

Supervisory boards[50]

Supervisory boards (SBs) range from three to twenty-one members depending on size and the codetermination rules.[51] As to composition: 43 per cent include a former member of the management board; 70 per cent include bank representatives; and only 5 per cent are women.[52] There is a high incidence of interlocking directorships.[53]

The supervisory board must be called quarterly. There are four meetings per annum in most companies. The average meeting lasts for 3 hours 45 minutes.[54]

The law prescribes obligations for supervisory boards. In practice the following are top priorities:

- meeting financial goals
- business strategy
- improved productivity
- developing foreign business[55]

---

48 For a survey of the relevant history see K. Hopt, 'The German Two-Tier Board (Aufsichtsrat): A German View on Corporate Governance', in K. Hopt and E. Wymeersch (eds), *Comparative Corporate Governance—Essays and Materials*, Walter de Gruyter, Berlin, 1997, pp. 3–6.

49 Pistor, *op. cit.*, p. 164.

50 S. Prigge, 'A Survey of German Corporate Governance', in K. Hopt et al., *Comparative Corporate Governance—The State of the Art and Emerging Research*, Oxford University Press, Oxford, 1999, pp. 943 *et seq.*

51 Prigge, *op. cit.*, p. 955.

52 *ibid.*, p 957.

53 *ibid.*, p. 959.

54 *ibid.*, p. 961.

55 *ibid.*, p. 962.

The main duties are in respect of financial performance, reviewing the CEO and responsibilities to employees.[56]

There is increasing criticism of supervisory boards and attempts to make them compulsory in the European Union have failed. On the other hand the increasing use of independent directors on public company boards resembles the supervisory boards in some respects.[57]

Worker representation[58]

In companies employing more than 2000 people, half the members of the supervisory board are elected by employees. In companies employing fewer than 2000, the proportion is one-third. It should be noted that two-thirds of employees' pension entitlements are retained within the company and represent an important source of internal finance. This helps to explain why the German capital market is less developed.[59]

There is more emphasis in Germany on the long-term interests of the corporation as a firm than in the UK and US models. On the other hand codetermination has added to the cost of governance and strengthened management's hand by enabling them to play off the employee half of supervisory boards against the shareholder half in the larger companies.[60]

Groups[61]

Germany is the only country that has adopted special provisions on groups—the *Konzernrecht*. The rules apply where one company is controlled by or dependent on another firm by virtue of a shareholding, domination contract, or agreement whereby one can take all or part of the profits of another company. Whether the controller is an *Aktiengesellschaft* (AG; a public company), GmbH, partnership or one-man business is immaterial.

Domination agreements must be in writing and there must be rights of appraisal or financial compensation where acts are done that are not in the interests of the controlled company. In the absence of such an agreement, the controller must not cause the controlled company to enter into transactions that are disadvantageous to it. There is a disclosure regime for all important changes.

The attempt to extend the German approach to the European Union has so far failed.

---

56   *ibid.*
57   See Pistor, *op. cit.* footnote 46 supra, and T. Clark and R. Bostock, 'Governance in Germany: The Foundations of Corporate Structure?', in K. Keasey et al., *Corporate Governance—Economic, Management and Financial Issues*, Oxford University Press, Oxford, 1997, ch. 11, pp. 242 *et seq.*
58   See Pistor, *op. cit.* footnote 46 supra, pp. 163 *et seq.*
59   Clarke and Bostock, *op. cit.*, p. 245. See also M. Roe, 'Codetermination and German Securities Markets', in Blair and Roe, *op. cit.* footnote 46 supra, ch. 6.
60   Pistor, *op. cit.* footnote 46 supra, p. 191.
61   See H. R. Hahlo and J. H. Farrar, *Hahlo's Cases and Materials on Company Law*, 3rd edn, Sweet & Maxwell, London, 1987, pp. 53–4.

The Japanese model[62]

In the Meiji period in the nineteenth century, when government by hereditary shoguns acting in the name of the emperor was replaced by government by civil servants acting in the name of the emperor, Japan was increasingly subject to Western influences and sought to modernise in order to defend itself against domination by them.[63]

It was influenced by the German model although it came under US influence after 1945. The result is that Japan has laws that resemble the German model on corporations law and the USA on securities regulation. The reality, however, is different. Japanese corporate practice is not always consistent with the legislative models.

Japan developed privately owned conglomerate corporate relationships in the form of *ziabatsu* before World War II. These were disbanded in 1945 but were effectively replaced by the *keiretsu*.[64] The *keiretsu* is a complex form of group in the broad sense centred around a lead bank and consisting of a number of affiliated companies where there are cross shareholdings and directorships.[65] There is a pattern of intra-group financing and long-term relationships.[66] In the past relationships with employees and consumers have been major priorities. Shareholders rank lower in the priorities unless they are affiliated companies.[67] The Japanese system is perhaps less a system of corporate governance and more a system of contractual governance, geared to the production process.[68]

In the last decade there has been some limited law reform along US lines and there is a growing interest in corporate governance. Recent events in Japan have shown the weakness of the financial system and the effect of secretive, weak and sometimes corrupt governance procedures with inadequate disclosure and accountability.[69]

Japan is increasingly influenced by the US and UK model but is slow to adopt practices such as takeovers.

---

62 See generally Charkham, *op. cit.* footnote 1 supra, ch. 3.
63 See K. Miyashita and D. Russell, *Keiretsu—Inside the Hidden Japanese Conglomerates,* McGraw-Hill, New York, 1996, ch. 2. See too M. Aoki and R. Dore (eds), *The Japanese Firm—The Sources of Competitive Strength,* Oxford University Press, Oxford, 1994.
64 *ibid.*
65 *ibid.*, ch. 4. See also P. Sheard, 'Interlocking Shareholdings and Corporate Governance' in Aoki and Dore, *op. cit.,* ch. 12.
66 *ibid.*
67 See ch. 3 above of this book above and materials cited. On the position of employees in Japanese companies see R. Gilson and M. Roe, 'The Political Economy of Japanese Lifetime Employment' and N. Hiwatari, 'Employment Practices and Enterprise Unionism in Japan', in Blair and Roe, *op. cit.* footnote 46 supra.
68 See R. Gilson and M. Roe, 'Understanding the Japanese Keiretsu: Overlaps Between Corporate Governance and Industrial Organisation' (1993) 102 Yale LJ 871. See too C. Milhaupt, 'The Relational Theory of Japanese Corporate Governance: Contact, Culture and Rules of the Law' (1996) 37 Harvard International LJ 3.
69 See the brief discussion in H. Kanda, 'Notes on Corporate Governance in Japan', in K. Hopt and E. Wymeersh, *op. cit.* footnote 48 supra, pp. 891 *et seq.*

Professor Hideki Kanda,[70] a leading scholar at the University of Tokyo, sums up the position: 'There is no single powerful monitor in Japanese publicly held business corporations. Shareholders, banks, employees, and others are all important. How they provide influence on the firm is not quite clear. Also providing influence does not necessarily mean monitoring management. Empirical studies must be awaited.'

The People's Republic of China model[71]

The People's Republic of China (PRC) model is a corporate governance model for a socialist state. It has been influenced by German, Japanese, and US and UK models. There is, however, a gap between the model and reality. Most corporations are state-owned enterprises. Private ownership is limited. There is provision for two-tier boards but these tend to be ineffective and there is an absence of skilled personnel.

The powers of the board are strictly curtailed in the legislation. Employees are represented in the structure of the corporation and the corporation must allow the presence of the Communist Party.[72]

The basic problem is how to create or simulate appropriate ownership structures and monitoring regimes. At present there is an insider dominated system with the state as the largest shareholder and an absence of arm's length transactions.[73] Gradually an efficient system of courts and other dispute resolution mechanisms is developing but disputes involving high ranking officials or members of the armed forces tend to have a predictable result.[74]

Professor On Kit Tam in a perceptive study, partly based on empirical research, argues that the current failure can be attributed to the serious problem of trying to impose an idealised corporate governance model, based on overseas systems, which is not appropriate to China's present conditions.[75]

Multinational and transnational enterprise[76]

Each of the major models we have considered (other than the PRC) has produced multinational and transnational enterprises, many of which are larger and more economically significant than many nation states.

Such enterprises typically are formed as private corporations in their country of origin and then have subsidiaries in other countries. They are characterised by central-

---

70 H. Kanda, 'Comparative Corporate Governance, Country Report: Japan' in K. Hopt et al. *op. cit.* footnote 48, pp. 921, 941.
71 See On Kit Tam, *The Development of Corporate Governance in China*, Edward Elgar, Cheltenham, 1999.
72 See *Company Act 1993*, articles 15–17.
73 On Kit Tam, *op. cit.* footnote 71 supra, p. 89.
74 The author's own observations and discussions with businessmen and lawyers dealing with the PRC.
75 On Kit Tam, *op. cit.* footnote 71 supra, p. 103.
76 See the discussion in chs. 2 above and 34 of this book.

ised management and integrated production. Because of their size they are able to develop their own distinctive systems of corporate governance which sometimes have an uneasy relationship with those of the host states.

Much research has emphasised the ways in which such enterprises can evade national controls[77] but at the same time they are increasingly subject to an institutional investor presence. Some writers argue that they transcend the traditional concepts of the corporation and the nation state.[78] More recent research, however, emphasises the importance of the country of origin.[79] There is a modern tendency towards more flexible structures, instead of ownership interests and group relationships, and this is particularly the case in the knowledge industries. These are characterised by joint ventures, strategic alliances, and networks. We return to this theme in the last chapter, Chapter 35.

Globalisation, change and convergence?

Each of the major models we have considered has strengths and weaknesses. Clarke and Bostock[80] tabulate the main points as shown in Table 33.2.

Table 33.2   Strengths and weaknesses of the major governance systems

Model	Strengths	Weaknesses
Anglo-Saxon model (US and UK)	• dynamic market orientation • fluid capital • internationalisation extensive	• volatile instability • short-termism • inadequate governance structures
European model (Germany)	• long-term industrial strategy • very stable capital • robust governance procedures	• internationalisation more difficult • lack of flexibility • inadequate investment for new industries
Asian model (Japan)	• very long-term industrial strategy • stable capital • major overseas investments	• financial speculation • secretive, sometimes corrupt governance procedures • weak accountability

Bebchuk and Roe[81] have argued that path dependence sheds light on why major systems differ. They argue that it can explain why, notwithstanding the forces of globalisation and efficiency, key differences have persisted and may well continue. It is

---

77 See the useful discussion in P. N. Doremus et al., *The Myth of the Global Corporation*, Princeton University Press, Princeton, 1999, pp. 18–20. This, however, neglects the full impact of institutional investment on issues of control.

78 See ch. 34 of this book.

79 Doremus, *op. cit.*

80 See T. Clarke and R. Bostock, 'International Corporate Governance: Convergence and Diversity', in T. Clarke and E. Monkhouse (eds), *Rethinking the Company*, FT Pitman, London, 1994.

81 *op. cit.* footnote 17 supra, p. 170.

significant that the company law harmonisation program of the EU has been most successful in the areas of corporate finance and accounts and least successful in the area of corporate governance, where cultural factors are more dominant. Nevertheless some change is inevitable. On the basis of this book we forecast that likely developments in the future will be:

- further growth of multinational and transnational enterprise
- increasing growth of capital markets and institutional investment
- a movement towards more flexible corporate relationships
- further international initiatives in corporate governance.

We pursue these themes in the next two chapters.

CHAPTER 34

Globalisation, the New Financial Architecture and Effective Corporate Governance[1]

The purpose of this chapter is to discuss the impact of globalisation on corporate governance and the latter's place in the new financial architecture. It will examine the meaning of 'the new financial architecture' and 'corporate governance', and the nature and impact of globalisation, particularly on regionalism and reform of national corporate laws. It will review previous attempts to deal specifically with the regulation of multinational and transnational corporations and examine the experience of the European Union in their integrating of laws on corporate governance. Lastly, it will consider the place of a broader concept of corporate governance in the new financial architecture, including the emerging norms of global corporate governance which are of an essentially self-regulatory nature.

The need for a new global financial architecture and effective corporate governance

The use of the word 'architecture' in this context is metaphorical or extended. 'Architecture' literally means a style of building.[2] Here it is being used in the extended sense employed in computer systems where it refers to the conceptual structure and logical organisation of a computer or computer-based system.[3] In this chapter it refers to the

---

1 An earlier version of chapter was published as 'The New Financial Architecture and Effective Corporate Governance' in (1999) 33 *The International Lawyer* 927.

2 *Shorter Oxford Dictionary.*

3 *ibid.* See M. Ebert, 'The Asian Financial Crisis and the Need for a New Global Financial Architecture' (1998) 13 *Butterworths Journal of International Banking and Financial Law* 454; B. Eichengreen, *Towards a New International Financial Architecture*, Institute for International Economics, Washington, 1999; Robert Rubin, Speech on Reform of the International Financial Architecture to the School of Advanced International Studies, 21 April 1999 <http://www.treas.gov/press/releases/pr 3093.htm>.

structure of the evolving global financial services markets or a desirable regulatory structure to encompass them.

We examine below the many and varied factors that are currently swept up in the term 'globalisation'. The principal driving forces have been capital market imbalances, innovations in computer and telecommunication technology, deregulation and the influence of modern finance theory on risk and diversification, hedging and arbitrage.[4] These forces prompt national securities regulators to seek a set of international cooperative measures to facilitate effective regulation of domestic markets.[5] Also they highlight the maze of contradictory regulatory requirements that have evolved for path dependent reasons in different jurisdictions.[6] Of course, diversity in regulation can sometimes serve useful economic ends in the sense of promoting innovation and competition without necessarily leading to a race to the bottom.[7]

The protracted South-East Asian financial crisis and the agreement on financial services through the ratification of the General Agreement on Trade and Services (GATS) have occasioned a call for a *new* financial architecture to improve the level of transparency, accountability and prudential supervision and regulation of the financial services industry.[8] Thus George Soros, in his book *The Crisis of Global Capitalism,*[9] argues that the present system is inherently unstable and he argues against the view that financial markets tend towards equilibrium. His argument is influenced by Karl Popper's philosophy and is based on fallibility, reflexivity and the open society.[10] Others, while not espousing such theoretical assumptions, argue a similar case.[11]

The arguments are for:

1   a common set of objectives
2   the selection of an appropriate supervisory body with
    (a) universal appeal
    (b) the necessary supervisory skills
    (c) enforcement powers.[12]

It has been argued that of the main international bodies, the World Trade Organisation (WTO) seems best suited to this role in relation to financial services, although it has limited dispute resolution powers and a currently frozen budget. The GATS has the

---

4   J. A. Grundfest, 'Internationalisation of the World's Securities Markets: Economic Causes and Regulatory Consequences' (1990) 4 *Journal of Financial Services Research* 349, 360–5.
5   *ibid.*, pp. 367–70.
6   *ibid.*, pp. 367, 370–1.
7   *ibid.*, pp. 367, 371–3.
8   Ebert, *op. cit.* footnote 3 supra.
9   Little Brown & Co, London, 1998.
10   *ibid.*, Preface and ch. 1.
11   See for example R. O'Brien, *Global Financial Integration: The End of Geography*, Royal Institute of International Affairs, London, 1992, pp. 101 *et seq.*
12   Ebert, *op. cit.* footnote 3 supra, pp. 460–2.

support of 102 nations which are committed to integrating their economies to create a new global economic system.[13]

In developing a new system characterised by transparency, accountability and effective regulation of the financial services industry, the promotion of similar virtues in the portfolio companies is arguably a necessary corollary.

However, to understand these trends one needs to see how the present situation has come about. To do this we have to look first at the forces of globalisation that have led to it, and how nation states, regions and international bodies have attempted to deal with some of these forces in the past. In doing so, we can place corporate governance more accurately in an international perspective and see what, if any, lessons can be learned from the past. However, before we do this we must consider the meaning of 'corporate governance'.

As we saw earlier, the concept of corporate governance is somewhat vague. Although many ideas about corporate governance have an international quality, each country has approached it against the background of its own distinctive culture. In Australia, for example, one sometimes has the impression that this lies somewhat uneasily between the culture of the outlaw Ned Kelly and that of his jailer.[14]

If we adopt the position that corporate governance is about the legitimacy of corporate power, corporate accountability, and the standards by which the corporation is to be governed, and by whom, it is obvious that the concept transcends legal standards and liability, perhaps reflecting the fact that the law deals with a minimal morality of obligation rather than a morality of aspiration.[15]

Corporate governance debate is often about the method as opposed to the substance of corporate decision making. Nevertheless, it seems too narrow to limit it exclusively to questions of method and good housekeeping.

A residual question is whether the evolving structure of the financial services markets or the norms of global corporate governance represent a form of global law without a state.[16] Eugene Ehrlich, the Austro-Hungarian sociologist of law, wrote: 'The centre of gravity of legal development ... from time immemorial has not lain in the activity of the state, but in society itself, and must be sought there at the present time.'[17] The idea of a 'living law' that transcends nation states and conventional legal sources and forms, has some appeal in this as in other areas of commercial life.

---

13   *ibid.*, p. 462.
14   See J. H. Farrar, 'Corporate Governance, Business Judgement and the Professionalism of Directors' (1993) 6 *Corporate and Business Law Journal* 1.
15   *ibid.*
16   G. Teubner, 'Global Bukowina: Legal Pluralism and the World Society', in G. Teubner (ed.), *Global Law Without a State*, Dartmouth, Aldershot, 1997.
17   E. Ehrlich, *Principles of the Sociology of Law*, Harvard University Press, Cambridge, Mass., 1936, p. 390.

Globalisation and transition

We live in a complex period of transition and the consequences of dismantling a world order built up in the aftermath of World War II. This is characterised by the following diverse phenomena:[18]

- the breakdown of the World International Monetary Order agreed at Bretton Woods in 1944
- the growth of multinational and transnational corporations and enterprise since 1945
- the rapid development of computers and telecommunications and the resulting reduction in trading costs on international capital markets
- the international financial revolution
- the rise of international institutional investment
- capital market imbalances caused by differences in savings rates and investment opportunities and international trade imbalances such as the Organisation of Petroleum Exporting Countries (OPEC) and later Japanese surpluses
- the collapse of communism in the former USSR and Eastern Europe
- the decline of statism and the growth of corporatisation and privatisation of public enterprise
- the growth of regionalism with such bodies as the European Union (EU) and the North American Free Trade Agreement (NAFTA), and the attempts to activate an Asia–Pacific region through the Asia–Pacific Economic Council (APEC)
- falling trade barriers and increasing international competition
- the rise of some developing countries such as China and India, which have vast economic potential.

Much of this we attempt to sum up in the protean term 'globalisation'. The idea of globalisation is not new. Exploration, trade and migration have always been with us. Similarly, the transmission of information over long distances through trade routes and the like has a long history. Some of the events that we have described are interlinked but sometimes the question of causation is complex. Globalisation is currently the subject of many books and articles. One of these has the suitably ambiguous title *Globalisation*

---

18   See *inter alia* Grundfest, *op. cit.* footnote 4 supra; O'Brien, *op. cit.* footnote 11 supra; T. Dickson and G. Bickerstaffe (eds), *Financial Times Mastering Global Business*, FT Pitman Publishing, London, 1999; P. Hirst and G. Thompson, *Globalisation in Question*, 2nd edn, Polity Press, Cambridge, 1996; K. Ohmae, *The End of the Nation-State: The Rise of Regional Economics*, HarperCollins, London, 1995; D. Held, D. Goldblatt, A. McGrew and J. Perraton, 'The Globalization of Economic Activity' (1997) 2 *New Political Economy* 257; W. Greider, *One World, Ready or Not*, Penguin Books, London, 1998; R. Reich, *The Borderless World: Power and Strategy in the Interlinked Economy*, Collins, London, 1990; R. Reich, *The Work of Nations*, Vintage Books, New York, 1992; J. Wiseman, *Global Nation—Australia and the Politics of Globalisation*, Cambridge University Press, Cambridge, 1998; H. P. Martin and H. Schumann, *The Global Trap: Globalization and The Assault on Prosperity and Democracy*, Pluto Press, Sydney, 1997; *Towards a More Coherent Global Economic Order*, Forward Studies Series, European Communities, Office for Publications of the European Union, Brussels, 1998. See generally the *Global Legal Studies Journal* since 1993.

in Question. In a useful short chapter in the *Financial Times* publication *Mastering Global Business*,[19] Professors Vijay Govindarajan and Anil Gupta define globalisation as 'the growing economic interdependence among countries as reflected in increasing cross-border flows of goods, services, capital and know-how'. They cite the following trends as evidence:

- Between 1989 and 1996 cross-border trade in goods and services grew at an annual average rate of 6.2 per cent.
- From 1980 to 1994 foreign direct investment grew from 4.8 per cent to 9.6 per cent of world gross domestic product (GDP).
- In 1970 cross-border transactions in bonds and equities as a ratio of GDP stood at under 5 per cent in the USA, Germany and Japan. By 1996 the respective figures were 152 per cent, 197 per cent and 83 per cent.[20]

Globalisation can be studied at the level of a specific country or a specific industry or a specific company.[21]

Thus China, for example, globalised its economy much faster than India in the period 1980 to 1994.[22]

In the case of the pharmaceutical industry, worldwide production increased 7.4 per cent, cross-border trade 10.9 per cent and cross-border investment 14.9 per cent per annum in the period of 1980 to 1994.[23]

Toyota is an example of a globalised company with one-third of its global output from affiliates in twenty-five different countries.[24]

What is new about the current processes is the extent to which time and space have been compressed by new technologies, and the impact this has had on the patterns of financing corporations and spreading risk in investment.[25]

Impacts of globalisation

Due to globalisation, an increasing number of countries are adopting the techniques, if not the ideology, of the free market. The advances in technology are constantly improving communications. This interacts with market forces in a similarly complex way. The removal of barriers to trade and investment creates opportunities for national companies in overseas markets but it also opens the door to competitors in domestic markets.[26] The impact of this is affecting labour markets in developed countries. The speed and complexity of change has threatened the capacity of national governments to deal

---

19 Dickson and Bickerstaffe (eds), *op. cit.* p. 5.
20 *ibid.*
21 *ibid.*, pp. 5–7.
22 *ibid.*, p. 6.
23 *ibid.*, p. 6.
24 *ibid.*, p. 7.
25 Grundfest, *op. cit.* footnote 4 supra; O'Brien, *op. cit.* footnote 11 supra.
26 *Mastering Global Business, op. cit.*, p. 9.

with the local impact of change, particularly when this results from events on the other side of the world.[27]

In the past, national governments have mainly encountered globalisation through the activities of multinational and transnational enterprises.

Transnational enterprise has constantly eluded regulation by nation states and even regions in the period since World War II. It would be a mistake to think that all such enterprises are necessarily large, widely held, publicly listed corporations. However, many of the significant players are, and it is to the various attempts to regulate them that we must now turn to see what lessons can be learned.

Past experience in dealing with globalisation— regulating multinational and transnational enterprise[28]

The multinational enterprise represents the latest stage of development of the national company group which evolved from a local corporate enterprise, which, in its turn, evolved from a local non-corporate enterprise. Just as the issues of ownership and control are important in relation to national enterprises, they are crucial in relation to multinational enterprise where the resolution of the question necessarily has a political significance. The multinational enterprise poses additional problems because it is not simply one discrete legal form but many. As the late Wolfgang Friedman wrote:

> It is the complexity of its legal structure, or rather the interplay of legal entities and relationships constituting that structure, no less than the size of its resources or the scale of its operations, which makes its power so elusive and so formidable a challenge to the political order and rule of law. It is therefore inherent in the nature of the multi-national corporation that there is no simple solution for the problem of its relationship to states, the world of states, or an organised world community.[29]

The political and legal regulation of multinational enterprise can be classified under four headings which approximately correspond to stages of historical development. These are:

1 national regulation
2 bilateral regulation
3 regional regulation
4 international regulation

Let us deal with each in turn.

---

27 *ibid.*

28 This is based on J. H. Farrar and B. Hannigan, *Farrar's Company Law*, 4th edn, Butterworths, London, 1998, ch. 44. See also R. Vernon, *In the Hurricane's Eye*, Harvard University Press, Cambridge, Mass., 1998.

29 *Transnational Law in a Changing Society*, Columbia University Press, New York, 1972, pp. 79, 80. For a recent study see M. T. Kamminga and S. Kia-Zarifi (eds) *Liability of Multinational Corporations Under International Law*, Kluwer Law International, the Hague, 2000.

National regulation

It is necessary to distinguish between prescriptive and enforcement jurisdiction. The jurisdiction to make prescriptive laws is very wide, and may be based on territory, nationality, or probably even the fact that particular conduct has effects in the state purporting to exercise jurisdiction.[30] By contrast, the jurisdiction to enforce those laws is narrow, limited to the territory of the state in question. Hence, there are problems with national regulation where the multinational keeps the bulk of its assets outside the state seeking to regulate it: the latter will be unable to access those assets to satisfy judgments. As an additional problem, states may have prescriptive jurisdiction under the effects doctrine (for example, where a multinational competitor engages in export dumping, thereby threatening a state-owned industry), but will not be able to enforce it unless the multinational is present within the state. That is, a state may suffer at the hands of multinational, but may not have any national means of redress open to it.[31]

A liberal regime towards domestic companies by the countries of origin created the economic conditions which favoured the growth of multinational enterprise. The United Kingdom for instance has generally favoured a highly liberal regime compared to those of other European states. To a large extent this has been based on enlightened self-interest since the United Kingdom is the headquarters of a number of multinationals and the City of London has traditionally financed many multinational operations.

For host states, there is often a dilemma of regulating conduct against the national interest yet not discouraging foreign investment. Canada, in the past, has been faced with this dilemma because of its proximity to the USA. On the whole it has favoured the presence of subsidiaries of foreign corporations, although since 1972 it has screened new direct foreign investment.[32]

The main worries, apart from loss of control, that the individual nation has are that multinationals may reduce the effectiveness of national monetary policy, evade taxation and injure labour relations.

The most effective and systematic form of regulation seems to be the control over initial capital investment. Control over later behaviour seems to be more ad hoc, particularly in those host countries without a strong legal tradition.

Bilateral regulation

In the last three decades there has been a growth in bilateral arrangements. These have taken the form of investment protection and promotion treaties and reflect the desire of home country governments to protect the investment of their companies abroad, and the desire of host countries to attract foreign direct investment. Such

---

30   See I. A. Shearer, *Starke's International Law*, 11th edn, Butterworths, London, 1994, ch. 8.
31   P. Bondzi-Simpson, *Legal Relationships Between Transnational Corporations and Host States*, Greenwood, London, 1990, pp. 33–8.
32   R. E. Tindall, *Multinational Enterprise: Legal and Management Structures and Inter Relationship with Ownership, Control, Antitrust, Labor, Taxation and Disclosure*, Oceana, Dobbs Ferry, NY, 1975; J. E. Spero and J. A. Hart, *The Politics of International Economic Relations*, 5th edn, Allen & Unwin, Sydney, 1997, ch. 4.

treaties normally provide for legal protection of foreign direct investment and for foreign subsidiaries and aim to produce a stable environment for development. In the period between 1945 and the mid 1960s, the USA was the first country to seek to achieve its objectives in this manner. Many of the bilateral treaties were concluded with developed countries. The emphasis of the early treaties, however, was more to do with international trade and protection of citizens abroad rather than foreign direct investment. From the 1960s onwards the treaties tended to be more concerned with foreign direct investment and many of these were concluded with developing countries. In this period, the Federal Republic of Germany concluded more than fifty agreements of this kind by the end of 1983. There are today more than 200 such treaties in force and many of these have been initiated between Organization for Economic Cooperation and Development (OECD) countries and developing countries. It should be noted that such treaties do not normally contain obligations on home country governments to promote foreign direct investment. The mere existence of an investment protection treaty is unlikely to lead to increased flows of investment unless there are other inducements. Conversely the absence of such a treaty where there are such other inducements will not necessarily deter foreign investment. The role of such treaties, therefore, is simply marginal in the decision making of the multinational and the host country.[33]

Regional regulation

The USA, Canada and Australia are all federations, yet each effectively operates as one economic unit. Since 1954 there have been a number of looser economic groupings such as the European Free Trade Alliance (EFTA), the European Union (EU) and North Atlantic Free Trade Alliance (NAFTA). Other groupings such as Organization of Petroleum Exporting Countries (OPEC) have been established on the basis of specialised markets.

Of these groupings of states, the most important for our purpose is the EU. Here, the lack of any provision in the Treaty of Rome has hindered progress. The member states have consistently refused to yield any national authority to the EU. In the past, various attempts—the adoption of a regulation of foreign investment in 1965, a commission proposal to protect employees in the event of takeovers, the formulation of common industrial policy and the adoption of a convention on internal mergers—were all unsuccessful.[34] Recently, however, mergers and joint ventures affecting market structure significantly, have to be approved by the commission and multinationals operating in the EU with 1000 or more employees in more than one EU country are

---

33   See *Bilateral, regional and international management on matters relating to transnational corporations. Report of the Secretariat of the UN Economic and Social Council* E/C10/1984/8 6 February 1984 on which this is substantially based.

34   Spero and Hart, *op. cit.* pp. 134–7. See Multinational Undertakings and Community Regulations, EEC Bull Supp 15/73; Industrial Policy in the Community 1970; Draft Convention on International Mergers, EEC Bull Supp 13/73; J. H. Dunning and P. Robson, 'Multinational Corporate Integration and Regional Economic Integration', (1987) 26 JCMS 103.

required to set up European Works Councils. These affect multinational enterprise as do the accounting and auditing changes.

International regulation

The International Monetary Fund (IMF), the General Agreement on Tariffs and Trade (GATT) and the OECD all have some bearing on the activities of multinationals. The IMF provides for convertibility of currency and repatriation of funds. GATT facilitates international production and transfers. Of particular relevance are the two fundamental GATT obligations: most favoured national; and national treatment. In addition, there are multinationals' traditional concerns with trade-related aspects of intellectual property rights and trade-related investment measures. There is also now the GATS agreement on trade in services, which parallels GATT. The OECD facilitates freedom of establishment.

However, the special attempts to deal with multinational enterprise in international law have not been successful. The Havana Charter, which was to have provided for a liberal regime of foreign investment, was later amended by Third World countries to protect host countries and was opposed by the USA.[35]

In 1976, the OECD adopted voluntary guidelines for conduct by multinationals, which were revised in 2000 and reissued.[36] The guidelines are recommendations jointly addressed by the member countries to the multinationals operating within their territories. They are not legally binding. There is no precise definition given of 'multinational', although the guidelines refer to groups that 'comprise companies and other entities having private, public or mixed capital, established in more than one country and linked so that they may be able to exercise a significant influence over the activities of others, their degree of autonomy within the enterprise may vary widely from one multinational enterprise to another. Reference is also made to strategic alliances which blur the boundaries of the enterprise'. The guidelines contain a statement of general policies and then deal with eight topics: disclosure; employment and industrial relations; environment; bribery; science and technology; competition and taxation. Financing has been dropped.

With regard to disclosure, the number and scope of the items of information called for is extensive while at the same time an attempt is made to protect the legitimate requirements of business secrecy.

Matters of finance such as transfer pricing are now dealt with elsewhere.

A third problem is the question of bribes. Here the guidelines draw the line on political contributions at what is legal although even this is questionable since some payments which are legal may still be grossly immoral.

---

35 Spero and Hart, *op. cit.*, p. 138; however, see the *World Bank Guidelines on the Treatment of Foreign Direct Investment* (1992).

36 See *Review of the 1976 Declaration and Decisions on Guidelines for Multinational Enterprises*, OECD, 1979; H. Schwamm, (1978) 12 JWTL 342. See now *The OECD Guidelines for Multinational Enterprises*, OECD, Paris, 2000. See generally M. R. Islam, *International Trade Law*, LBC Information Services, Pyrmont, NSW, 1999, 244 *et seq.*

In the 1970s the United Nations set up a Centre on Transnational Corporations (CTC) to gather and disseminate information on multinationals, and an intergovernmental Commission on Transnational Corporations to act as a forum for discussion of issues relating to them and to supervise the centre.[37] Of these two bodies, the first will probably prove the most practical since ignorance of empirical data impedes rational debate and leads to perpetuation of myth.

From 1977 until 1992, a working group of the commission was engaged in the formation of a code of conduct as its highest priority. It decided against taking the OECD guidelines as its starting point.[38]

The benefits of such a code were considered by the Round Table on the Code of Conduct of Transnational Corporations held in Montreux, Switzerland in October 1986. The round table saw the benefits of a code as follows:

- It would establish a balanced set of standards of good corporate conduct to be observed by multinationals in their operations and of standards to be observed by governments in their treatment of multinationals.
- It would help to ensure that the activities of multinationals were integrated in the development policies of developing countries.
- It would establish *inter alia* the confidence, predicability and stability required for development of foreign direct investment in a mutually beneficial manner.
- It would contribute to a reduction of friction and conflict between multinationals and host countries.
- It would 'encourage positive adjustment through the growth of productive capacities'.

Progress on the code was slow and in 1992 it was announced that no consensus was possible. The CTC was absorbed into the UN Commission on Trade and Development (UNCTAD) in Geneva.

Since 1992 the focus has shifted to environmental protection as a follow-up to the UN Conference on Environment and Development. There has been a recognition of four trends in relation to multinationals and transnationals:

1 the growing role of such entities in sustainable growth;
2 the expansion of corporate environmental management practices;
3 harmonisation of environmental regulations affecting them; and
4 the emergence of voluntary environmental guidelines by such entities.

---

37   See P. D. Maynard, 'The Commission and Centre on Transnational Corporations' (1980) 2 Co Law 226; P. D. Maynard, 'A Code of Conduct for TNCs' (1983) 4 Co Law 103. See the materials collected in N. Simmonds (ed.), *Multinational Corporations Law*, Oceana, New York, 1979.

38   See *The United Nations Code of Conduct on Transnational Corporations*, UNCTC Current Studies, 1988. For some discussion see P. D. Maynard, *op. cit.* (1983) 4 Co Law 103 at 104; P. Sanders, 'Implementing International Codes of Conduct for Multinational Enterprises' (1982) 30 Am J Comp L 241; P. Hansen and V. Aranda, 'An Emerging International Framework for Transnational Corporations' (1990–91) 14 Fordham Int LJ 881.

In addition there has been work done by a number of international institutions, including the Intergovernmental Group of Experts established by the Centre of Transnational Corporations, on the elaboration of international standards of accounting and reporting. Also, there has been the establishment of the Multilateral Investment Guarantee Agency (MIGA) under the aegis of the World Bank. MIGA's main role is to provide insurance coverage for non-commercial work involved in transnational investments.

Over twenty years ago the International Accounting Standards Committee (IASC) and the International Federation of Accountants (IFAC) were set up by the accounting profession to develop international standards for the preparation and verification of corporate information.

The role of IASC is to develop International Accounting Standards (IASs) which are produced by a consultative process. A Standing Interpretations Committee examines urgent issues arising from interpretation of the existing standards or new matters of concern. The role of IFAC is wider. It includes the development of International Standards of Auditing (ISAs) and a code of ethics. IFAC is not involved in the development of accounting standards but simply in assisting in their promulgation.

In December 1996 the meeting of ministers of the World Trade Organisation encouraged the successful completion of international standards in the accounting sector by IFAC, IASC and the International Organisation of Securities Commission. (IOSCO).[39]

Support for these initiatives has come from the Group of Seven, the World Bank and the United Nations.

It is of course easy to dismiss such voluntary codes as unimportant since they are not legally binding. This would, however, be a mistake. Such codes may form the basis of subtle diplomacy by the UN towards a consensus among governments, which in turn will be embodied in national legislation or professional standards. Such a consensus will, in any event, help host countries in negotiating with multinationals, and may assist trade unions in the home countries to oppose outward investment and the host countries to seek regulation of multinational practices against the interests of their members.[40]

---

39   See F. Harding, 'Corporate Credibility—Why a Harmonised Global Accountancy Framework Matters' *Accountancy Ireland*, April 1999, p. 16, on which the above relies.
40   See M. Crawford, 'The Case against Multinationals: The Main Criticism Re-examined', in the EIU Special Report No. 79, *Ten Years of Multinational Business*, Abt Books, Cambridge, Mass., c1982, p. 15. See also the very useful paper by T. H. Reynolds 'Clouds of Codes: The New International Economic Order through Codes of Conduct: A Survey' in N. Simmonds (ed.), *Multinational Corporations Law*, vol. 4, Oceana, New York, 1979; *North–South: A Programme for Survival*, The Report of the Independent Commission on International Development Issues under the chairmanship of Willy Brandt, Pan, London, 1980, ch. 12.

Globalisation, regionalism and national corporate law models

Markets or harmonisation?

The impacts of globalisation motivate developed countries to think about regional trade blocs and harmonisation of laws. They also motivate developing countries to think of adopting new laws based on major Western models.[41]

In the last 150 years there have been a number of dominant Western models of corporate laws and securities regulations. Historically the British imperial model was important until the 1960s. It was adopted in the countries of the Commonwealth and had some influence beyond those boundaries.[42] Germany at the end of the nineteenth century, and in this century, has been a successful innovator in the use of the corporate form. It has contributed the private company, two-tier boards, worker participation and a novel approach to groups.[43] This has had an influence in Western Europe, Japan and Korea. Since at least 1933 the USA has been one of the world's leaders in corporate law and securities regulation.[44]

The USA is a federation and has opted for a market approach to corporate laws.[45] Each state is a separate corporate law jurisdiction with its own business corporations act although much of securities regulation is federal. The extent of the market for corporation law statutes can be exaggerated due to the dominance of Delaware and the *Revised Model Business Corporations Act*, which has been adopted in a number of states.[46]

Canada, since the 1970s, has been increasingly influenced by US corporate law ideas. The US influence was strong on the Ontario reforms of the 1970s and the subsequent Dickerson Report, which led to the *Canada Business Corporations Act*. Canada has a greater degree of similarity between the Ontario, federal and a number of the other provincial statutes than the USA but still lacks uniformity.[47]

Since 1962 Australia has developed uniform laws and an effectively national scheme. *The Uniform Companies Act 1962* provided a model for Malaysia and Singapore.[48]

Since 1973 the United Kingdom has been a member of the EU and been subject to an elaborate scheme of harmonisation of laws, which has recently lost some of its momentum. In the comparative quietus, the United Kingdom is attempting a thorough

---

41 Take for instance the recent examples of the People's Republic of China and Indonesia.
42 See J. H. Farrar and B. M. Hannigan, *Farrar's Company Law*, 4th edn, Butterworths, London, 1998, ch. 42.
43 See H. Wurdinger, *German Company Law*, Oyez Publishing, London, 1975; J. Charkham, *Keeping Good Company: A Study of Corporate Governance in Five Countries*, Clarendon Press, Oxford, 1994, ch. 2; K. Hopt, 'The German Two-Tier Board (Aufsichtsrat): A German View on Corporate Governance,' in K. J. Hopt and E. Wymeersch (eds), *Comparative Corporate Governance—Essays and Materials*, Walter de Gruyter, Berlin, 1997, ch. 1.
44 R. Romano, *The Genius of American Corporate Law*, AEI Press, Washington, DC, 1993, p. 13.
45 Romano, *op. cit.*
46 See C. Jordan, *International Survey of Corporate Law in Asia, Europe, North America and the Commonwealth*, Centre for Corporate Law and Securities Regulation, Melbourne, 1997, part 4.
47 Jordan, *op. cit.*; F. Iaccobucci et al., *Canadian Business Corporations*, Canada Law Book Ltd, Agincourt, 1977, ch. 1.
48 See W. Woon, *Company Law*, 2nd edn, FT Law and Tax Asia Pacific, Singapore, 1997, p. 4.

reform of its Company Law, a project which bears an ill-defined relationship to its EU obligations.[49]

Important questions thus face each nation state as to which models of company law and securities regulation best serve its interests in an era of globalisation. Let us see what can be learned from the experience of the EU since this is the most elaborate attempt to produce harmonised laws on an international basis.

The process of harmonisation of national corporate governance laws in the European Union[50]

Relevant provisions of the Treaty of Rome[51]

Article 2 of the Treaty of Rome sets out the goals of the EU. These include establishment of a common market and an economic and monetary union, progressive approximation of the economic policies of member states, the promotion throughout the community of a harmonious and balanced development of economic activities, and closer relations between the states belonging to it. Article 3 provides that for the purposes set out in article 2, the activities of the EU shall include, *inter alia*, an internal market characterised by the abolition of obstacles to freedom of movement of goods, persons, services and capital, and the approximation of the laws of member states to the extent required for the proper functioning of the common market.

The treaty recognises certain basic freedoms. These include the right of establishment. Article 52 provides for the abolition of restrictions on the freedom of establishment of nationals of a member state in the territory of another. This includes freedom to set up and manage undertakings, in particular companies or firms within the meaning of article 58. Article 58 gives a broad definition of companies or firms. It means companies or firms constituted under civil or commercial law, including cooperative societies, and other legal persons governed by the public or private law, save for those that are non-profit-making. Article 54 provides for the drawing up of a general program for the abolition of existing restrictions on freedom of establishment within the community. Under article 54(3)(g) the council and the commission are instructed to carry out their duties 'by coordinating to the necessary extent the safeguards which, for the protection of the interests of members and others, are required by member states of companies or firms within the meaning of the second paragraph of article 58 with a view to making such safeguards equivalent throughout the Community'.

Article 100 is a general provision on approximation of laws. It provides that the council shall, acting unanimously on a proposal from the commission, issue directives for the approximation of such provisions laid down by law, regulation or administrative action in member states, and directly affect the establishment or functioning of the

---

49   See *Modern Company Law for a Competitive Economy—The Strategic Framework*, Company Law Review Steering Group, DTI, London, 1999.

50   This is partly based on Farrar and Hannigan, *op. cit.* footnote 41 supra, ch. 3. See generally W. Davey, 'European Integration: Reflections on its Limits and Effects' (1993) 1 *Global Legal Studies Journal* 185.

51   See generally W. Davey, 'European Integration: Reflections on its Limits and Effects' (1993) 1 *Global Legal Studies Journal* 185.

common market. The Parliament and the Economic and Social Committee shall be consulted in the case of directives whose implementation would, in one or more member states, involve the amendment of legislation. Articles 100A and 100B which were added by the *Single European Act* [AQ3] provide for qualified majorities in certain cases.

Article 220 provides that member states shall, so far as is necessary, enter into negotiations with a view to securing, *inter alia*, the mutual recognition of companies or firms within the meaning of the second paragraph of article 58, the retention of legal personality in the event of transfer of their seat from one country to another, and the possibility of mergers between companies or firms governed by the laws of different countries; the simplification of formalities governing the reciprocal recognition and enforcement of judgments of courts or tribunals and of arbitration awards. These negotiations led to international treaties which supplement the existing treaties. An example is the 1968 convention on mutual recognition of companies. Article 221 provides for abolition of all discriminatory provisions in the laws of member states with respect to equity participation in companies.

Lastly, article 235 contains sweeping-up provisions. If action by the EU proves necessary to attain one of the objectives of the EU and the Treaty of Rome has not provided the necessary powers, the council, acting unanimously on a proposal from the commission and after consulting the Parliament, will take the appropriate measures.

Patterns of legal integration

The three basic legal techniques of integration used are, therefore:

1 the removal of all restrictions which discriminate on the basis of nationality including restrictions on freedom of establishment
2 the putting into effect of common rules and common policies
3 the approximation of national laws under article 3(h).[52]

The treaty also uses the terms 'harmonisation', which English lawyers tend to prefer, and 'coordination', but there seems to be little consistency in the way in which they are used and there seems to be no meaningful difference between them.[53] All three terms fall short of unification.

The usual pattern is for drafts of proposal to be prepared by the commission. They may then be discussed in a group convened by the commission and consisting of 'experts' (that is, officials) from member states and may be circulated by the Commission to interested outside bodies. After adoption by the commission as formal proposals, they are sent to the European Parliament and the Economic and Social Committee for their opinions. In the light of these opinions the commission may

---

52 See generally R. Buxbaum and K. Hopt, *Legal Harmonisation and the Business Enterprise*, Walter de Gruyter, Berlin, 1988, ch. 3 and 4.
53 On community policy with regard to approximation of laws, see the lecture given by Dr C. D. Ehlermann, Director General of the Legal Service of the commission published in App 3(b) of the Lords Select Committee on the European Communities ('HLSC') (HL 131) (1977–78). See also P. Jan Slot, 'Harmonisation' (1996) 21 EL Rev 378 and B. Lo, 'Improving Corporate Governance. Lessons from the European Community' (1993) 1 *Global Legal Studies Journal* 219.

amend their proposals, before presenting them to the Council of Ministers for discussions in a working group of officials from the various member states. Such discussions are normally chaired by officials from the member state holding the presidency of the Council of Ministers. They are subsequently referred to the Committee of Permanent Representatives (COREPER) which in turn refers them to the Council of Ministers itself for final decision.[54]

Progress to date

Within the EU, some progress has been made on three broad fronts. These are:

1 directives have been prepared under the provisions of article 54(3)(g)
2 treaties have been drawn up under article 220
3 a draft regulation providing a statute for a European company has been drawn up under article 235.

Let us look at each of these in turn.

First, the directives. Although the EU has been successful in harmonisation of share capital, accounting and auditing it has not been particularly successful in the area of corporate governance. The relevant directives are as follows.

The First Directive (68/151/EEC)[55]
The First Directive was adopted on 9 March 1968 and mainly provided for relief against the doctrine of ultra vires and limits of directors' authority as well as providing for some basic publicity. The directive was implemented by the United Kingdom in section 9 of *the European Communities Act 1972* as amended by section 35A of the *Companies Act 1989*.[56]

Draft Fifth Directive[57]
The draft Fifth Directive deals with the important topics of company structure and worker participation and has been the subject of much controversy.[58] The present

---

54 This summary of procedure is taken more or less verbatim from *The Single Market—Company Law Harmonisation* published by the Department of Trade and Industry, London, 1990.
55 20 OJC, L26, 31 January 1977, pp. 1–13.
56 See D. D. Prentice, 'Section 9 of the European Communities Act', (1973) 89 LQR 518; J. H. Farrar and D. G. Powles, 'The Effect of Section 9 of the European Communities Act on English Company Law', (1973) 36 MLR 270; J. G. Collier and L. S. Sealy (1973) 2 CLJ 1. See now *UK Companies Act 1985*, sections 35 and 25A. See Farrar and Hannigan, *op. cit.* footnote 42 supra, ch. 10.
57 This directive was first proposed in 1972; see *Official Journal of the European Communities* 1972 No C 131/49. The current version is that put forward in 1991 (OJC 321/9 of 12 December 1991). See the Green Paper on Employee Participation and Company Structure in the European Communities, EEC Bull Supp 8/75. See C. M. Schmitthoff, 'Commercial Law in a Changing Economic Climate', [1983] JBL 456 and the memoranda of the Law Society's Company Law Committee of March 1984 and April 1990. For useful recent discussions see J. J. Du Plessis and J. Dine, 'The First Draft Directive: A False Dawn [1997] JBL 23.
58 See J. Welch 'The Fate of the Draft Fifth Directive on Company Law: Accommodation instead of Harmonisation' (1983) 8 ELR 83. See also W. Kolvenbach 'EEC Company Law Harmonisation and Worker Participation' (1990) 11 *University of Pennsylvania Journal of International Business Law* 709 at 720–33.

position is that the commission's modified proposal is under consideration by a Council Working Group of officials from the member states and the commission. It is anticipated that discussion of the draft will take several more years. The new draft provides for a distinction between directors of a public limited company who will be responsible for management and those responsible for their supervision. At the end of 1983 the commission announced an alteration so that this distinction could be achieved either through a two-tier board or a conventional one-tier board as in the United Kingdom. On the one-tier board, there would be a division between executive directors who would manage, and non-executive directors who would supervise. The implementation of this distinction as a matter of law would require changes to English law.

Employee participation in corporate decision making would be required to take one of the following forms:

(a) through board representation at the supervisory level;
(b) by means of a works council; or
(c) through collective agreements giving the same rights as (a) or (b).

Further options are included in respect of employee participation in groups of companies.

In addition to these major provisions, the latest draft also includes provision in respect of:

(a) the duties and liabilities of directors;
(b) the power of the general meeting;
(c) the rights of shareholders and in particular minority shareholders;
(d) approval of annual accounts; and
(e) the functions and liability of auditors.

With regard to (a) there is a general provision for personal liability for loss suffered by the company as a result of breaches of the law, the corporate constitution, or other wrongful acts. Liability is to be joint and several which would involve a change in English law and arguably lead to more effective monitoring of management by management. An individual director may be exonerated if he or she can prove that no fault is attributable to him or her personally. The draft does not define the standard of care required of directors although the commission's Explanatory Memorandum to the original proposal in 1972 suggested that 'other wrongful acts' might include negligence and would arguably go further than the current law.

With regard to (b), shareholders are given slightly more rights in respect of the convening of meetings.

As regards (c), articles 16–18 allow a minority shareholder to bring a derivative action on behalf of the company, even where the general meeting has expressly renounced its right to bring proceedings, provided that the plaintiff shareholder voted against the resolution or made objection which was recorded in the minutes. Proceedings can be instituted by a simple majority of the shareholders or in the case of a derivative action by shareholders holding 5 per cent of the issued capital or shares to the value of 100 000 ECUs. An unsuccessful shareholder who fails to establish reasonable grounds for commencing the proceedings may be ordered to pay costs. Under the original article 19, a derivative action could also be brought by a creditor who was unable to obtain payment and such an action would not be affected by any waiver by the company of a breach of duty. This has been deleted and replaced by a vague provision which leaves the matter to be determined by the laws of the member state.

Other important provisions prevent a shareholder from voting on an issue where there is a conflict of interest between the company and him or her personally. This would go further than the existing English law. Another provision renders void shareholder agreements whereby a shareholder undertakes always to vote in a certain way. This would involve an alteration of the English law. There are provisions for compulsory reserves and appropriation of profits. The latter would have the effect of shifting the power to determine dividends to the general meeting. Both of these would involve a change in English law.

We will not comment on the detailed provisions in respect of auditors and accounts.

In addition there is Directive 94/95/EC of 22 September 1994 on the establishment of a European Works Council and also a draft directive on procedures for informing and consulting employees, which overlaps with the Fifth Directive. This is sometimes known as the Vredeling Directive.[59]

Draft Ninth Directive

The draft Ninth Directive, which has never been officially published in the Official Journal, deals with certain aspects of the group relationship.[60] The preliminary draft was greatly influence by the German law relating to groups. A revised text was circulated informally to member states in December 1984. The revised text seeks to provide an organised legal structure for the 'unified management' of a public limited company which is controlled by any other undertaking (whether a company or not) and of that other undertaking. The directive will also set out rules for the conduct of groups that are not subject to 'unified management' although in this case, the rules would apply to the relations between the parent, or dominant, undertaking and those members of the group that are public limited companies. Unless the dominant undertaking formalises its relationship by one of the methods specified in the directive it will be liable for any losses sustained by the dependent company resulting from that influence and attributed to a fault in management or to action which was not in its interests. There are to

---

59   26 OJC 217, 12 August 1983, pp. 3–16.
60   See F. Woolridge, *Groups of Companies*, Sweet & Maxwell, London, 1981; T. Hadden, *The Control of Corporate Groups*, Institute of Advanced Legal Studies, University of London, 1983, p. 42; J. Welch, 'Ninth Draft Directive: The Institute of Directors' Response' (1986) 7 Co Law 112; K. Gleichmann, 'The Law of Corporate Groups in the EC', in D. Sugarman and G. Teubner (eds), *Regulating Corporate Groups in Europe*, Nomos Verlagsgesellschaft, Baden Baden, 1990.

be two methods for constituting a group: the control contract or a unilateral declaration of control. In addition, the directive would leave member states free to introduce other methods of achieving the same result.

The Twelfth Directive[61]

The Twelfth Directive allows private companies with only one member. This was permitted already in a number of jurisdictions.

Proposal for a Thirteenth Directive[62]

The proposed Thirteenth Directive deals with takeovers and is influenced by the City of London Takeover Code. The proposal has been strongly attacked. The UK government is concerned that it is too inflexible and may inhibit takeovers. Other member states have criticised it, however, because it opens the door to hostile takeovers by blocking certain takeover defences. The position regarding takeovers differs between member states. An amended proposal was issued in 1996 and has been discussed by the European Parliament.

International conventions

On 29 February 1968 the original member states of the EU other than the Netherlands signed the convention on the mutual recognition of companies and legal persons.[63] The convention was to apply to all companies incorporated in any member state and would include an English partnership. Recognition was to be accorded when the company has its statutory registered office in one of the member states. This would be subject to certain exceptions based on the principle of the real seat. After much discussion, the member states have now decided to abandon the project. Mutual recognition occurs in practice anyway, without the necessity of a convention.

Bankruptcy, winding-up arrangements, and similar proceedings

A draft convention has been prepared dealing with bankruptcy, winding-up, arrangements, compositions, and similar proceedings.[64] This supplements the convention on

---

61   32 OJC 1989, L 395, 30 December 1989.

62   23 OJC 64, 14 March 1989, pp. 8–14; Amended Proposal (COM(90) 416 final), September 14 1990; OJC 162/5 of 6 June 1996. See L. S. Sealy, 'The Draft Thirteenth EC Directive on Take-overs', in M. Anderras and S. Kenyon-Slade (eds), *EC Financial Market Regulation and Company Law*, Sweet & Maxwell, London, 1993, ch. 9; J. Dine, 'Subsidiarity, Datafin and the DTI', (1996) 17 Co Law 248.

63   EEC Bull Supp 2/69; B. Goldman, *European Commercial Law*, M. Benden, New York, 1973, p. 389; G. K. Morse, 'Mutual Recognition of Companies in England and the EEC' [1972] JBL 195.

64   See Report of the Advisory Committee on the Draft Convention (Cmnd 6602). See also 'Bankruptcy Convention' 26th Report (1980–81) of the HLSC (HL 175) (1980–81). See M. Hunter QC, 'The Draft Bankruptcy Convention of the EEC' (1972) 21 ICLQ 682, 'The European Convention on Insolvency Proceedings and the Administrative Receiver: A Missed Opportunity?' (1976) 25 ICLQ 310; I. Fletcher, 'The Draft EEC Convention: A Further Examination (1977) 2 ELR 15, J. H. Farrar, 'The EEC Draft Convention on Bankruptcy and Winding Up' [1977] JBL 320; F. Dahan, 'The Proposed Community Convention on Bankruptcy and Related Matters' (1996) 17 Co Law 181.

mutual recognition of judgments which has now been given internal effect by legislation.[65] It has undergone a great deal of revision, particularly as a result of UK membership. This in essence provides for the rationalisation of bankruptcy, winding-up, and analogous proceedings in the EU. First, it sets out detailed rules to enable bankruptcy jurisdiction to be vested in a single and appropriate national court. Second, it seeks to secure that the liquidator appointed by the court has extensive authority to administer the insolvent estate, wherever situated in the EU. Third, it aims at simplification of the liquidator's duties in collecting assets and determining claims by a limited measure of harmonisation and identification of applicable law. Fourth, it aims at simplification of the rules and reduction of the costs for a foreign creditor making a claim. The convention is likely to come into effect soon.

Draft regulation for a European company

The last measure to be discussed is the most ambitious. This is the draft regulation for a European company.[66] The proposal goes beyond harmonisation and provides for an additional form of incorporation which will have registration with the EU. It will be available when two or more limited companies merge or form a joint holding or subsidiary company. Much work on this project was done by Professor Pieter Sanders of the Netherlands, although the French claim some responsibility for the paternity of the project. The project has been under debate for thirty years but acquired a momentum as part of the proposals for 1992. The commission adopted an amended draft in April 1996 as a result of the report of a group of experts chaired by Etienne Davignon and this was the subject of a Consultative Document by the UK Department of Trade and Industry in July 1997.

The future of harmonisation within the EU

The tactics employed by the commission have in the past been described as 'salami tactics'. In other words, they approached the matter slice by slice. This approach was criticised on the basis that it was difficult to agree upon any particular directive without knowing, at least in broad terms, what else was to be done. The counter-argument was that elaboration of a complete uniform Companies Act would take a lot of time and bog

---

65   The Convention on Jurisdiction and the Enforcement of Judgements in Civil and Commercial Matters, dated 27 September 1968 and amended on 9 October 1978 (1978) OJC 304, 30 October (1979) OJC 59, 5 March.

66   See *The European Company Statute, A Consultative Document*, July 1997, URN 97/786. See Report of the Select Committee on the EEC, HL. Session 1989–90, 19th Report, HL Paper 81-I; J. Dine Note (1990) 11 Co Law 208. For some earlier discussion see 'Memorandum de la Commission de la CEE sur la création d'une Société commerciale européenne' SEC (66) 1250, 22 April 1966; 'Projet d'un statut des sociétés anonymes européennes' Doc 16. 205/IV 66, December 1966; see generally P. Zonderland (ed.), *Quo Vadis Jus Societatum? Liber Americurum Pieter Sanders*, Kluwer, Deventer, 1972; and Farrar and Hannigan, *op. cit.* footnote 42 supra, ch. 43.

down reform within the EU for a long time. In any event, it has been said that the statute for the European company would provide some sort of blueprint.

In recent years there has been a suspension of work on certain projects and a determination to concentrate on certain key areas. Some real progress was made with company accounts, listing requirements and insider trading.[67] Work on the draft Fifth Directive has continued, although in its nature it is controversial. The key areas on which the commission is currently engaged are disclosure, corporate governance and its relationship to the draft Fifth Directive and the statute for a European company. With regard to disclosure, the commission has participated in the negotiations in the ad hoc expert group on accounting on the United Nations Centre on Multinationals. On groups, the original draft, based heavily on German law, has been the subject of controversy in other member states. This and codetermination have presented obstacles to the implementation of a number of other proposals, including the European Company Proposal. Dorresteijn, Kuiper and Morse in *European Corporate Law*[68] argue that the overall achievements of the harmonisation program have been impressive, particularly when compared with other areas such as taxation, social policy and competition. Nevertheless, there are questions as to how the particular instruments of harmonisation have been used. First, directives tend to be overspecific and sometimes do not fit too well with national laws. Second, some directives, for example the fourth and seventh, contain too many options. Third, the harmonisation so far achieved has mainly related to the external structure of the company. Attempts to coordinate provisions relating to the internal structure have been unsuccessful. The two striking examples are employee participation and the law of groups. In this respect it is interesting to note the fact that the EU has to contend with a market-based outsider model and a representation-based insider model of corporate governance.[69] Attempts to superimpose one over the other have failed for economic as well as social and political reasons.

At the moment it is unclear whether the EU will continue its harmonisation program. The other alternatives are systems of mutual recognition such as have been employed for the financial sector and other less formal methods of unification through the activities of private bodies and systems of self-regulation.

One thing is abundantly clear: the area of least success in the EU program has been corporate governance, due mainly to fundamental differences in national models and the context in which they operate.

---

67 See V. Edwards, *EC Company Law*, Oxford University Press, Oxford 2001, Chapters V–VII, X–XII, and XV.
68 A. Dorresteijn, I. Kuiper and G. Morse, *European Company Law*, Kluwer, Deventer, 1994, pp. 64–6.
69 For a discussion of these two models see *Financial Market Trends*, OECD, Paris, 1995, p. 13 and H. Blommestein, 'The New Financial Landscape and its Impact on Corporate Governance', in M. Balling et al. (eds), *Corporate Governance, Financial Markets and Global Convergence*, Kluwer, London, 1998, ch. 3.

The characteristics of the global corporate landscape

A working paper by three Harvard economists[70] on *Corporate Ownership Around the World* published by the National Bureau of Economic Research in 1998 set out some useful facts on corporate ownership around the world. These include:

The separation between ownership and control in listed public corporations is far from universal.

- Many of the largest firms are controlled by families.
- The widely held corporation is most common in countries with good regimes of shareholder protection.
- Family control is more common in countries with poor shareholder protection.
- State control is common, particularly in countries with poor shareholder protection.
- In family-controlled firms there is little separation between ownership and control.
- Pyramids and deviations from one share, one vote are most common in countries with poor shareholder protection.
- Corporations with controlling shareholders rarely have other large shareholders.

Much of modern corporate governance theory has been premised on the Berle and Means[71] hypothesis of the separation between ownership and control. Berle and Means, writing at the time of the first stock market crash, argued that as companies got larger their shareholdings became diffused and, in the resulting hiatus in significant power blocs, management's power increased. This needed regulation by the courts or legislatures. What the results of the later survey show is that we need to be more diverse and flexible in formulating models of corporations for the purpose of devising corporate governance structures, particularly at an international level. It is neglect of this fact, until recently, that has hampered the EU harmonisation program. Corporate governance necessarily reflects the corporate landscape in which it operates and we must resist a tendency towards ethnocentrism, particularly one centred on the USA simply because of its economic dominance. The USA has a number of path dependent characteristics that characterise its laws and which are not easily exportable or necessarily efficient.[72] It is the economic efficiency of US markets, not necessarily its legal system, that should be emulated.

---

70   R. La Porta, F. Lopez-de-Silanes, A. Shleifer, *Corporate Ownership Around the World*, National Bureau of Economic Research, Working Paper 6625, Cambridge, Mass., 1998.

71   A. Berle Jr and G. Means, *The Modern Corporation and Private Property*, revised edn, Harcourt, Brace & World Inc, New York, 1968. For a more recent study see M. Blair, *Ownership and Control: Rethinking Corporate Governance for the Twenty-First Century*, The Brookings Institution, Washington, DC, 1995.

72   See the valuable analysis by M. Roe, 'Path Dependence, Political Options, and Governance Systems', in K. Hopt and D. Wymeersch (eds), *Comparative Corporate Governance*, Walter de Gruyter, Berlin, 1997, p. 165.

Nevertheless, the South-East Asian financial crisis has exposed the dark side of corporate governance practices in some of the countries involved.[73] Common features include complex systems of family control and the existence of conglomerate structures that often defy economic rationality; little or no effective standards to ensure controlling shareholders and management behave properly to small investors; an absence of transparency and proper auditing practices; inefficient and sometimes corrupt legal systems in some of the countries; a lack of integrity in the regulatory processes (if they exist) and the absence of independent, proactive media. The notable exceptions are Singapore, Hong Kong and, to a lesser extent, Taiwan and Malaysia.

It has been argued[74] that sustained prosperity depends on the following basic rules:

* effective standards of corporate governance
* a high degree of corporate transparency and adequate external auditing
* efficient stock exchanges
* competitive markets
* efficient and transparent legal frameworks
* a clear distinction between regulators and regulated
* independent, transparent and competitive banking systems
* well-resourced, inquisitive and independent media.

The South-East Asian approach sowed the seeds of its own collapse.

The evolution of modern corporate governance and its place in a new financial architecture

Our early ideas of corporate governance have been very much tied in with national models. Thus, in a system characterised by one-tier boards, it makes sense to talk about more independent directors. In a system characterised by two-tier boards, the matter has been substantially catered for by a different mechanism. Nevertheless, in the last twenty years we have seen an extension of the concept of corporate governance beyond national models of corporate laws to encompass systems of self-regulation that differ in degrees of rigour and formality.

Corporate governance does not exist in a vacuum. Modern corporate governance is played out in the context of expanding and increasingly sophisticated capital markets. Within these markets institutional investors are now major players in Western countries and are diversifying into international portfolios.

---

73 For a penetrating recent study see M. Backman, *Asian Eclipse—Exposing the Dark Side of Business in Asia*, John Wiley & Sons (Asia) Pty Ltd, Singapore, 1999. Compare, however, R. Appelbaum, 'The Future of Law in a Global Economy' (1998) *Social & Legal Studies* 171, which argues the contrary.

74 Backman, *op. cit.*, p. 3.

Institutional investors and corporate governance[75]

Extent

Institutional investors increased their market share of UK listed equities from 17.9 per cent in 1957 to 60.4 per cent in 1992, and are acquiring about 2 per cent of the UK equity market each year.[76] Institutions hold over 60 per cent of listed loan capital.[77] These are the highest international percentages but there are similar trends in Australia, New Zealand, Canada and the USA although each country has its own distinctive history.[78] These trends nevertheless potentially revolutionise the concept of corporate governance in those English-speaking countries. Ownership is being regrouped but until recently has been relatively passive. The relationship between institutions and portfolio companies, and between institutions and their constituents, is not uniform and is in fact quite complex in those countries.[79] Whereas the separation of ownership from control is a relatively simple movement, this further stage of a regrouping of ownership and with the potential of control is not so simple. Yet its impact on our understanding of the listed company and the whole conceptual framework of company law is potentially profound. Hence one American writer, Paul Harbrecht, referred to the 'paraproprietal society'.[80] Since Harbrecht's time there has been the massive growth of funds managers who manage funds on behalf of the institutions. This complicates the picture further.

75   This is based on Farrar and Hannigan, *op. cit.* footnote 42 supra, pp. 578 *et seq.* For a magisterial study see J. C. Coffee Jr, 'Institutional Investors as Corporate Monitors: Are Takeovers Obsolete', in J. H. Farrar (ed.), *Takeovers, Institutional Investors and the Modernization of Corporate Laws*, Oxford University Press, Auckland, 1993, ch. 2. See this also for citation of the many US law review articles on aspects of this topic. See also G. P. Stapledon, *Institutional Shareholders and Corporate Governance*, Oxford University Press, Oxford, 1996; I. Ramsay, G. Stapledon, K. Fong, *Institutional Investors' Views on Corporate Governance*, Research Report, Centre for Corporate Law and Securities Regulation, University of Melbourne, Melbourne, 1998; G. Stapledon, 'The Duties of Australian Institutional Investors in Relation to Corporate Governance' (1998) 26 ABLR 331; H. Blommestein, 'The New Financial Landscape and its Impact on Corporate Governance', in M. Balling et al. (eds), *Corporate Governance, Financial Markets and Global Convergence*, Kluwer, London, 1998, ch. 3.

76   R. J. Briston and R. Dobbins, *The Growth and Impact of Institutional Investors*, Institute of Chartered Accountants in England and Wales, London, 1978, p. 24; Stapledon, 1996, *op. cit.* footnote 74 supra.

77   J. Coakley and L. Harris, *The City of Capital*, B. Blackwell, Oxford, 1983, pp. 106–7.

78   See J. H. Farrar and M. Russell, 'The Impact of Institutional Investment on Company Law' (1984) 5 Co Law 107; Coffee in Farrar *op. cit.* footnote 74 supra. For recent surveys see *Australian Stock Exchange Fact Book 1998*, ASX, Sydney, 1998, p. 17; T. Clarke and S. Clegg, *Changing Paradigms—The Transformation of Management Knowledge for the 21st Century*, HarperCollins Business, London, 1998, p. 314. The percentage for the USA was 46 per cent, Japan 45 per cent, Germany 29 per cent. In Japan and Europe a significant percentage was held by non-financial enterprise.

79   Farrar and Russell *op. cit.*; Stapledon, 1996 footnote 74 supra, *op. cit.*, pp. 239 *et seq.*

80   'Pension Funds and Economic Power: The Paraproprietal Society', preface, in D. J. Baum and N. B. Stiles, *The Silent Investors*, Syracuse University Press, Syracuse, New York, 1965.

Reasons for the international growth of institutional holdings

The first reason for the growth of institutional holdings is the growth of pension and superannuation schemes since 1945. Originally in private pension plans, pension obligations were satisfied by the purchase of annuities from life insurance companies. Thus the funds were included in the insurance companies' assets. Later, non-insured plans became popular because of the possibility of investment of the fund in ordinary shares.

A second reason is the relaxation of the trustee investment rules by legislation in many countries that allowed trustees to invest part of the trust funds in equities.

A third reason is the rise of insurance-linked investment schemes to take advantage of insurance tax relief in some countries, although the modern tendency is to withdraw this relief to maintain a level playing field.

A fourth reason is the favourable tax treatment of insurance companies and unit and investment trusts in some countries.

A fifth reason is the deregulation of the banking and securities industries since the early 1980s and the removal of exchange controls in a number of countries.

Last, there has been the impact of technological change and the change in international communications.

It is noticeable how none of these reasons is company-oriented. In other words, the company is simply the outlet for these investment urges. This, combined with the passivity of institutions as shareholders, probably accounts for the fact that until the 1980s such investment caught the corporate world unawares and company lawyers failed to appreciate its full significance. The collapse of the Maxwell empire and the scandals surrounding use of pension funds for corporate purposes have put the spotlight on this legally complex area and led to the Report of the UK Pensions Law Reform Committee chaired by Professor Roy Goode in 1993. The report recommended a new Pensions Act and system of regulation to impose order on the chaos.

The past elusiveness of the institutional role in corporate governance

While the growth of institutional holdings and their potential power is well documented, until the last decade there was little evidence that such power had been exercised in any significant way. One therefore hesitates to talk in terms of control except perhaps in the sense of constraint or power to monitor.[81]

Nowadays, however, there is direct and indirect industry-wide and firm-level monitoring. The direct monitoring is done by analysis of information and regular meetings and dialogue with management. Indirect monitoring is done by investment committees as well as support for non-executive directors.

---

81   E. Herman, *Corporate Control, Corporate Power*, Cambridge University Press, New York, 1981; cf. Stapledon, *op. cit.*, 1996, footnote 74 supra, ch. 4, 5, 9 and 10.

In the United Kingdom, the two best documented cases of institutional intervention are the Thalidomide and the Newman Industries cases. In the former, the management of Distillers Company Ltd foolishly resisted public pressure to settle on more generous terms with the victims. In the end, their shares fell and the institutional investors, together with the company's merchant banks, met senior management on 4 January 1973. Two days later, the company increased its offer from £3.24 million to £21.75 million, which formed the basis of the ultimate settlement.[82] In the Newman Industries case,[83] the Prudential Assurance Co. Ltd litigated in individual, representative and derivative form as a minority shareholder and the costs of the proceedings at the first instance were reported to be £750 000. The case later went on appeal before being eventually settled. The judgment of the Court of Appeal was rather critical of the cost involved in their initiative.

In numerous cases, institutional support has assisted a bidder in a takeover bid. The main aim here has been gain. In the USA, the SEC's Institutional Investor Study Report[84] documented institutional involvement in transfers of corporate control. They instanced the following as the two main strategies that had been adopted:

1 purchase of shares in anticipation of a bid;
2 financial assistance to the bidder.

Among the special inducements that they have received in return for advance information about a bid were a higher price for their shares and assurances of contingent benefits if the bid succeeded. In many countries use of advance information may now be caught by the insider trading provisions.

Dr G. P. Stapledon in *Institutional Shareholders and Corporate Governance*[85] has documented eighteen areas of corporate governance where UK institutional investors or funds managers have been active, usually behind the scenes. These cover a wide range of corporate activity. Usually this monitoring takes the form of direct firm-level monitoring and has taken place through various committees and by the use of non-executive directors.

Nevertheless the prevailing view hitherto has been that the primary responsibility of the institutional investor is simply to achieve maximum investment performance. If this is not present in a portfolio company, the rule has been to sell. This rule has two aspects: first, it denies the existence of any duty to fellow shareholders and other groups such as employees and consumers; and second, it maintains that in any event the overriding duty is to sell rather than incur costs and further risks.[86]

82 See *Times*, 5–6 January 1973; *Economist*, 6 January 1973, p. 9; P. I. Blumberg, *The Megacorporation in American Society*, Prentice Hall, Englewood Cliffs, NJ, 1975, pp. 134–5.
83 *Prudential Assurance Co. Ltd v. Newman Industries Ltd (No 2)* [1982] Ch 204, CA. See also Vinelott J [1980] 3 WLR 543. See also *Sunday Times*, 24 February 1980; *Times*, 19 June 1980, *Times*, 31 July and 1 August 1981.
84 House Doc 64 Pt 5, 92d Cong 1st Session, 2847–9.
85 Stapledon (1996) footnote 74, ch. 4.
86 P. I. Blumberg, *The Megacorporation in American Society*, Prentice Hall, New York, 1975, p. 136.

Institutional investors in the past have been worried about the political consequences of an exercise of power. They eschew public criticism and fear public intervention. Some consider that their expertise is finance and investment rather than
management and this does not necessarily equip them to pursue an interventionist role.
They are also worried about the risks involved. They are also reluctant to offend the
companies in which they invest. There may be more than one relationship between the
company and institutions and in any event the institutions continue to rely on the companies for current information in spite of the new prohibitions on insider trading.

This conservatism of institutions in the exercise of power was criticised by Adolf
Berle Jr in the following terms:[87]

> In effect, the position of the institutional managers is that they will not exercise their
> voting power so as seriously to affect the choice or the policies of corporate manage-
> ments. The individuals for whom the institutions are fiduciaries, holders of rights in
> pension trusts, of shares in mutual funds, or of insurance policies, have surrendered
> their voting power. The institutional managers, therefore, by their policy of non-inter-
> vention, merely insulate the corporate managements from any possible action by or
> influence of the ultimate, beneficial 'owners' of the stock. A policy of non-action by the
> institutions means that the directors and managements of the corporations whose
> stock they hold become increasingly self-appointed and unchallengeable; while it con-
> tinues, it freezes absolute power in the corporate management.

Institutional investor involvement in self-regulation

In the last decade institutional investors have become more organised and have promoted law reform and the development of self-regulation of corporate governance.[88]
Carolyn Brancato[89] has identified five stages in US institutional investor activism:

1   social responsibility investing
2   fighting anti-takeover initiatives
3   pressing for structural governance changes in portfolio companies
4   monitoring performance
5   incorporating non-financial performance issues into indicators of corporate per-
      formances

Institutional investors are important shareholders and debt capital holders that are
themselves subject to increasing monitoring of their investment performance. Their
ever-increasing holdings and increased competition for funds management give them

---

87   A. Berle Jr, *Power without Property*, Harcourt Brace, New York, 1960, pp. 55–6. See also E. Herman and C.
      Stafanda, 'Proxy Voting by Commercial Bank Trust Departments' (1973) 90 Banking LJ 91. Cf. Stapledon
      op. cit. 1996 footnote 74 supra.
88   See C. K. Brancato, *Institutional Investors and Corporate Governance*, McGraw-Hill Companies Inc, Chicago,
      1997, ch. 3.
89   *ibid.*

powerful incentives to take a more proactive role. Despite this, their role is often subject to fiduciary constraints and these is a potential clash between long-term and short-term objectives.

In the USA, the California Public Employees' Retirement System ('Calpers') has taken a leading role. Networks of institutional investors and specialist advisory services have formed in the USA to facilitate institutions exercising their voting duties and organising coalitions on specific policies or issues. In the United Kingdom historically, the Prudential Assurance Company has taken a leading role although not always with conspicuous success. Institutions have been active in the drafting and operation of the City of London Takeover Code and in the Cadbury, Greenbury and Hampel Reports on corporate governance. In Australia, instititions have been represented on the Bosch Committee, which produced *Corporate Practices and Conduct* (see Appendix 1), and the Australian Investment Managers Association (now the Investment and Financial Services Association) have produced guidelines (see Appendix 2).[90] A criticism that is sometimes made about the self-regulation so far evolving is that it concentrates on form rather than substance and puts the emphasis on process rather than the outcome.

A recent UK survey[91] has shown that 'best practice' in corporate governance is generally being followed by institutional investors themselves with most companies having audit and remuneration committees although the incidence of nomination committees is lower than might be desired. Life assurance companies have the highest number of key board committees while the retail bank sector has the highest proportion of non-executive directors.

There is frequent contact between international institutional investors and some degree of cooperation.

Not a universal picture

So far we have concentrated on English-speaking countries. The question arises as to whether this picture is universal. The answer quite simply is 'no'.

Recent studies have shown that institutional investor involvement in corporate governance is relatively recent on the European continent.[92] This is primarily due to the structural factors. In many continental European countries institutional investors are banks or part of a banking group and subject to greater restrictions than institutional investors and investment managers in the countries we have considered.[93]

---

90   See Stapledon *op. cit.* 1996 footnote 74 supra; R. Monks and N. Minow, *Corporate Governance*, Blackwell Publishers Inc, Cambridge, Mass., 1995.

91   See C. Mallin, 'The Role of Institutional Investors in the Corporate Governance of Financial Institutions: the UK case', in Balling, *op. cit.* footnote 10 supra, ch. X. See too Ramsay, Stapledon and Fong, *op. cit.* footnote 74 supra.

92   See E. Wymeersch, 'A Status Report on Corporate Governance Rules and Practices in Some Continental European States', in K. Hopt, H. Kanda, M. Roe, E. Wymeersch and S. Prigge (eds), *Comparative Corporate Governance: The State of the Art and Emerging Research*, Clarendon Press, Oxford, 1998, ch. 12 (d).

93   Wymeersch, *op. cit.*, para. 37.

Also, in countries such as Germany, banks have played a different role in relation to shares in listed companies. Their role has often been more closely involved with major companies than is the case with their English-speaking counterparts due to complex factors including corporate networks. Japan has its own distinctive Keiretsu system where banks are caught up in a spider's web of corporate networks.[94] Both of these factors inhibit shareholder activism and a proactive role in reforming corporate governance.

The recent initiative of the OECD

In 1996 the council of the Organisation for Economic Cooperation and Development (OECD) commissioned a study of corporate governance to review and analyse international corporate governance issues and suggest an agenda and priorities for further OECD initiatives. This led to the setting up of the Business Sector Advisory Group on Corporate Governance, which produced a report, *Corporate Governance: Improving Competitiveness and Access to Capital in Global Markets*, in April 1998. The chairman was Ira Millstein and the other members were Michel Albert, Sir Adrian Cadbury, Robert Denham, Dieter Feddersen, and Nobuo Tateisi.[95]

The following were identified in the report as key areas of common understanding:

- Corporate governance practices constantly evolve to meet changing conditions. There is no single universal model of corporate governance. Nor is there a static, final structure in corporate governance that every country or corporation should emulate. Experimentation and variety should be expected and encouraged.
- Corporate governance practices vary and will continue to vary across nations and cultures. We can learn a great deal from observing experiences in other countries.
- Corporate governance practices will also vary as a function of ownership structures, business circumstances, competitive conditions, corporate life cycle and numerous other factors.[96]

There are, however, a few fundamental parameters:

---

94   See for example K. Miyashita and D. Russell, *Keiretsu—Inside the Hidden Japanese Conglomerates*, McGraw Hill, New York, 1986.

95   *Corporate Governance: Improving Competitiveness and Access to Capital in Global Markets*, A Report to the OECD by the Business Sector Advisory Group on Corporate Governance, OECD, Paris, 1998. For comment see J. C. Coffee, 'The Future as History: Prospects for Global Convergence in Corporate Governance and its Implications' (1999) 93 Nw Univ L Rev 641; L. A. Cunningham, 'Commonalities and Prescriptions in the Vertical Dimension of Global Corporate Governance' (1999) 84 Cornell L Rev 1133.

96   *ibid.*, OECD Report.

1   Increasingly, it is accepted that the corporate objective is maximising shareholder value, which not only requires superior competitive performance but also generally requires responsiveness to demands and expectation of other stakeholders.
2   Increased transparency and independent oversight of management by boards of directors are the central elements of improved corporate governance.
3   Board practice should be subject to voluntary adaptation and evolution, in an environment of globally understood minimum standards.
4   There are certain areas in which the adoption of universal rules is preferable (such as in accounting).[97]

The committee recommended the following agenda:

1   The definition of the mission of the corporation and transparency about non-economic objectives
2   Adaptable corporate governance arrangements
3   The protection of shareholder rights
4   The facilitation of active investing
5   The alignment of shareholder and other stakeholder interests
6   The recognition of societal interests.[98]

As can be seen (1), (5) and (6) are crucially vague and represent something of a political agenda.

The main corporate governance reports to date have addressed such issues as:

1   the structure of the board and board committees and in particular the role of non-executive directors
2   directors' remuneration
3   the conduct of general meetings and managing shareholder relations
4   the role of institutional investors.

The committee set out perspectives for public policy improvement.[99] This would be characterised by:

1   flexibility
2   consideration of regulatory impact
3   regulatory focus centred on
    a   fairness
    b   transparency
    c   accountability
    d   responsibility.

---

97   *ibid.*, para. 8 *et seq.*
98   *ibid.*, para 16 *et seq.*
99   *ibid.*, para 19–23.

The report also refers to clarity, consistency and enforceability and stressed the need for accurate, timely disclosure and protection against litigation abuse, corruption and bribery.

Flexible corporate laws and securities regulation were called for and these were to clearly specify management's responsibilities and protect shareholders' rights. Policy makers should encourage some degree of independence in the composition of company boards, sound audit practices, and a level playing field for institutional investors to ensure competition.[100]

Individual corporations should continue to strive for corporate governance 'best practice'.[101]

The report favoured further OECD efforts:[102]

* to formulate a public policy document setting out minimum standards of corporate governance
* to formulate a code of voluntary 'best practice'
* to encourage common principles of disclosure.

The report was followed recently by the formulation of principles. These are set out in Appendix 5 to this book.

The principles fall under five broad headings.[103] These are:

1   The rights of shareholders
2   The equitable treatment of shareholders
3   The role of shareholders
4   Disclosure and transparency
5   The role of the board.

The principles are built on the foundations of shareholder protection and the residual monitoring role of shareholders. Therefore, minimal protection of shareholders is envisaged to protect the right of participation and exit. Exercise of voting rights is encouraged.

Fair treatment of shareholders is required. In particular self-dealing and insider trading are to be prohibited.

The discussion of stakeholders is well-meaning but necessarily vague. Yes, they have a place but not necessarily legal rights. Disclosure is axiomatic and should be timely and accurate and subject to annual independent audit.

The role of the board is similarly crucial but the OECD countries have diverse structures and practices. Nevertheless the accountability of the board is basic. Various

---

100 *ibid.*, para. 28.
101 *ibid.*, para. 36. See M. Almond and S. Syfert, 'Beyond Compliance: Corruption, Corporate Responsibility and Ethical Standards in the New Global Economy' (1997) 22 NCJ Int'l L & Com Reg 389.
102 *ibid.*
103 See the OECD web site for the latest version of the draft: <http://www.oecd.org//daf/corporate-affairs/governance/index.htm>

responsibilities of the board are discussed including overriding duties to act fairly between different groups of shareholders and stakeholders and to ensure compliance with the law.

The principles went before a meeting of ministers on 26 to 27 May 1999 and were adopted. It was envisaged that there would be intensive collaboration with non-member countries and cooperation with other international organisations, in particular the World Bank. In fact a Memorandum of Understanding was entered into in June between the OECD and World Bank to cooperate by setting up a Global Corporate Governance Forum and World Bank/OECD Policy Dialogue and Development. The Memorandum of Understanding states that:

> The World Bank and the OECD will sponsor the Global Corporate Governance Forum, which will consist of regional development banks and other international organisations and groupings such as APEC, IASC, IOSCO, IMF, Commonwealth Association, private sector participants and institutions as well as donor and developing/transition countries. The Global Corporate Governance Forum will ordinarily meet once a year. It will approve the objectives, policies, and monitoring of the Forum's Secretariat. It will also review the annual work program and the financial plan, as proposed by the Secretariat, with the support of the Private Sector Advisory Group ... The Global Corporate Forum will consult with representatives of non-governmental organisations and stakeholder groups with a specific interest in corporate governance.

In addition the Corporate Governance Private Sector Advisory Group and network of round tables have now been set up jointly with the World Bank.

In a speech given at Seoul, Korea, on 3 March 1999, Ms Joanna Shelton, Deputy Secretary General of the OECD said:

> The OECD Principles could be just one part of a wider dialogue on various aspects of corporate governance, in workshops or conferences that would be organised on a regional basis or possibly in some other ways. We are very open-minded as to the ways in which further dialogue with countries beyond the OECD membership might proceed. Whatever form this cooperation may take, strengthening the corporate governance framework in countries around the world is now recognised as one key element in laying a strong foundation for the resumption of economic growth in Asia and elsewhere and for a more stable international economic system.[104]

The recent announcements clearly envisage the OECD and World Bank playing a leading role in developing norms of international corporate governance. As with the OECD's Guidelines on Multinationals, such an initiative is to be welcomed but the matter needs to be promoted by other international bodies such as the IMF and the

---

104 D. Shelton 'The Importance of Corporate Governance in OECD and non OECD Economies. The Draft OECD Principles', opening remarks: <http://www.oecd.org//daf/corporate-affairs/governance/roundtables/in-Asia/1999/shelton.htm>

WTO because of their broader base. As we have seen the WTO has been suggested for the role of supervision in the new global financial architecture.[105]

The contribution of global corporate governance to new financial architecture

To sum up, the primary goals of global corporate governance are to promote:

- transparency in commercial dealings and financial transactions, especially fund raising
- accountability through more efficient monitoring of management performance
- competition.

Given the present state of a diversity of models of corporate governance, reflected in national laws which may gradually diminish with the growth of regionalism and the impact of globalisation, there is much to be said for the development of voluntary norms of international corporate governance based on an emerging consensus. This can mirror the work already done in respect of international accounting standards.

Sir Ronald Hampel, who chaired one of the recent UK committees, has said: 'I believe an umbrella set of governance principles internationally would be helpful, within which it would be possible for national environments and companies to develop detailed governance structures appropriate to their circumstances.'[106]

The advantages of this approach are:

- It is evolutionary.
- It is more flexible than a more elaborate attempt at harmonisation of laws on a regional basis.
- It transcends the nation state and regions and is evolved by the industry (using that term in a broad sense). It recognises that global convergence is not necessarily inevitable.
- There is an absence of an appropriate international organisation to promote harmonisation or uniform laws. The United Nations has failed in its Code of Conduct for Transnational Enterprise. The OECD has been more successful but its membership is limited and somewhat eclectic.

The dangers of this kind of approach lie in:

- The dominance of the debate by financial institutions in the West and its consequent ethnocentrism.[107]
- The lack of an effective enforcement mechanism.

105 Ebert, *op. cit.* footnote 3 supra.
106 *Company Director*, February 1999, p. 16 (Australia).
107 For an interesting recent discussion of an attempt to export US corporate governance ideas to Germany see T. Andre Jr, 'Cultural Hegemony: The Exportation of Anglo-Saxon Corporate Governance Ideologies to Germany' (1998) 73 Tul L Rev 69.

- The tendency to concentrate on form rather than substance and process rather than outcome.
- The tendency to pursue fashions without any consideration of their efficiency in practice.

We live in a period of complex transition characterised by rapid change and it is difficult to monitor the effects of this change on the existing world order. There are two distinct schools of thought about an appropriate approach to dealing with this. One is a regulatory approach—a projection of national regulation into the international arena. The other is a free market approach—to leave the development to market forces.[108] The evolution of norms of self-regulation of international corporate governance from initiatives such as the OECD's principles represents a possible middle way— a non-legal soft law[109] which can form the basis of a *lex mercatoria*[110] of this area. The Romans said '*Via media, via tuta*' (the middle way is the safe way).

At the present stage of development, to use the language of Jack Nicholson in a recent film, 'This is as good as it gets'.[111]

---

108 See Grundfest, *op. cit.* footnote 4 supra.
109 For a distinction between hard and soft law and legal and non-legal soft law, see C. M. Chinkin, 'The Challenge of Soft Law: Development and Change in International Law' (1989) 38 ICLQ 850, 851.
110 See H-J. Mertens, 'Lex Mercatoria: A Self Applying System Beyond National Law?' in G. Teubner (ed.), *Global Law without a State*, Dartmouth, Aldershot, 1997, ch. 2.
111 For a more pessimistic view of 'soft law' see D. Branson 'Teaching Comparative Corporate Governance: The Significance of "Soft Law" and International Institutions' (2000) 34 Georgia L Rev 669, 695 *et seq.*

CHAPTER 35

Thinking New Thoughts
on Corporate Governance[1]

Corporate governance is ultimately part of social governance. It is the way in which a society operates through its key institutions. The concepts of the corporation and corporate governance are central to social governance since corporations play a vital role in our society. The core of corporate governance is the law of directors' duties and shareholder rights and remedies but there is a developing penumbra of self-regulation which is of growing sophistication. Increasingly, domestic law gives a distorted and dated interpretation to rapidly changing economic reality and attempts are being made to set up minimum standards of corporate governance as global self-regulation.

The new thoughts that have been developing in this book are as follows:

1   Our conceptions of 'corporation' and 'group' are not universal but ethnocentric and are undergoing change.
2   Some of the change is based on politics but other change arises out of the communications revolution, which has affected patterns of corporate finance and is beginning to affect our approach to management and corporate relationships.
3   In an increasing number of cases the emphasis is shifting from corporation to contract and from competition to what is called co-opetition.
4   Corporate governance is becoming international but conceptions of corporate governance in the Anglo-American world, which dominate the corporate governance debates, are based on corporate models which are atypical.
5   In the last two years there has been the birth of global corporate governance through the initiatives of the OECD which have now been supported by the World Bank with the setting up of a Global Corporate Governance Forum. This too is based substantially on the Anglo-American model.

1   This chapter is based on addresses given to the Committee for the Economic Development of Australia Perth, 16 May 2000, Brisbane, 26 July 2000.

6   We have to ask questions about how these various developments affect Australia
    and New Zealand given the fact that the emphasis may be shifting from corporate
    governance to contractual governance and there are some important economic
    facts that distinguish us from the USA and the United Kingdom.

The answers to these questions are quite complex but the questions need to be
asked in view of the increasing globalisation of equity and debt finance and derivatives
and the growing needs of the businesses themselves, faced with increasing international
competition.

Our changing conception of the corporation and corporate group

We saw in Chapter 3 that the corporation provides legal recognition to a natural person
or persons as distinct holders of rights under a collective name with distinct legal consequences. It was firmly established by the House of Lords in the leading case of *Salomon v. Salomon & Co. Ltd*[2] that this collectivity constitutes a separate legal person. The
reasoning in that case was not fully developed in terms of principle and policy and,
combined with limited liability, it has led to abuse, particularly through its later extension to corporate groups, which has led to a system of limited liability within limited
liability, a consequence never originally contemplated by the legislature.

There have been piecemeal legislative reforms which have imposed personal liability on directors for failing to prevent insolvent trading,[3] limited reform of groups[4] and
now there is new Australian legislation to prevent asset stripping to the detriment of
creditors, including employees.[5]

The concept of the corporation as a separate legal person has never been fully
developed and the courts have swung back at times to the earlier concept of the corporation as association. They have never properly developed the idea of the corporation as
a firm. Hence, the narrowness of the Anglo–Australasian concept compared with European, Japanese and even US conceptions which recognise a broader range of stakeholders in the corporation, as we saw in Chapter 3.

Modern law-and-economics scholarship meanwhile sees the corporation as an
elaborate standard form contract or nexus of contracts so the emphasis shifts from legal
person to contract *as a matter of theory*.[6]

The questions then arise as to whether our conception of the corporation as a separate legal person is too narrow and too readily lends itself to abuse in spite of sporadic

---

2   [1897] AC 22.
3   See ch. 14 of this book.
4   See ch. 21 of this book..
5   See ch. 3, 21 and 33 of this book.
6   See ch. 3 of this book.

reform, and whether this is affected (if at all) by the communications revolution, to which we now turn.

The impact of the communications revolution

The transformation of business by technological progress is not a new phenomenon.[7] In their time the steam engine, motor car, aeroplane, transistor and integrated circuit have each overturned the status quo.[8] Some of these changes have been revolutionary. The industrial revolution was such a period of radical change.

The changes in communications now confront us as another revolution. Semi-conductors, computers, information storage and retrieval, and communication are revolutionising business. Advances in other technologies such as laser, xerography, numerical control, voice recognition, computer vision and liquid crystal displays also play a part.[9]

These developments affect data storage and management, the processing of information and the dissemination of information.[10] They are changing the processes of manufacturing, changing the ways companies are managed, and how they are financed. They are beginning to raise fundamental questions about structure.

How the communications revolution affects the activities of a particular company will depend on the sector of industry to which it belongs and what its products are. All companies now make extensive use of computers in terms of the organisation of their business. There is useful computer software for handling most routine accounting and commercial functions. Computers enter into the technological developments in many sectors of manufacturing, often facilitating automation, which leads to redundancies.

The communications revolution, together with the abolition of exchange controls and deregulation, facilitated the international financial revolution. This has promoted capital investment and helped us to apportion and hedge risk by futures and derivatives. It has also led to some fundamental changes in our thinking about corporate finance and corporate strategy.

Twenty years ago diversification was the overwhelming strategy that led to a crop of mergers and acquisitions.[11] By the mid 1980s the urge to diversify by merging was beginning to wane and yet there was no compelling new corporate growth strategy to replace it.[12]

This factor, the existence of a junk bond market, and the arbitrage between the market for securities and the market for assets, led to some of the major transactions of the decade, particularly in the USA, for example, KKR/Beatrice, Pelerman/Revlon,

---

7   See W. H. Davidow and M. S. Malone, *The Virtual Corporation*, HarperCollins Business, New York, 1992, p. 73.
8   *ibid.*, pp. 73–6.
9   *ibid.*, pp. 75 *et seq.*
10   See V. C. S. Yeo, 'Corporate Governance in the Information Age: The Impact of Information Technology and Emerging Legal Issues' (1999) 1 HKLJ 194.
11   See B. Wasserstein, *Big Deal*, Warner Books, New York, 1998, part 1.
12   *ibid.*, ch. 9.

Goldsmith/Crown Zellenbach and Hanson/SCM. In many of these cases the bids were opportunistic, finance driven and not strategic.

Since the 1990s there has been a change of mood. The urge to merge has been replaced by the urge to demerge conglomerate groups and to concentrate on the core business and to build it up. US examples are Union Pacific/Southern Pacific Rail, Time Warner/Turner Broadcasting, and Boeing/Rockwell Aerospace. Australian examples mainly relate to the financial services industry. New Zealand has the experience of Fletcher Challenge Ltd.

Why are there these major shifts in mood? The answer is that in general, in a deregulated, highly competitive global market, a collection of disparate, non-related businesses can no longer compete. It is simply better to concentrate on one's core business and increasing one's market share with resulting efficiencies. Thus it is the blue chip companies themselves that are instigating bids to build up the business, achieve cost savings and create a more powerful competitor. In doing so they are resorting to contract as well as mergers and acquisitions.[13]

The main reasons why all these trends are directly or indirectly related to the communications revolution are:

1 most companies have reached the limit of using re-engineering to fuel growth
2 rapid technological changes are now routine
3 add to (2) deregulation and international competition and one has increased interest in expansion of the core business
4 shareholder activism is high, with increased emphasis on closer monitoring of companies by institutional investors and increased power to smaller investors through the Internet
5 There is a corresponding emphasis on enhancement of shareholder value and an increase in remuneration packages for executives, geared to performance and including stock options.

Transcending our concepts of the corporation and corporate group

The rise of contractual heterarchy

Our modern concept of the corporation evolved as a distinct ownership unit and as a convenient method of raising capital and dealing with the problems of risk and difficulties of communications. It was not the only possible outcome. Other methods were developing but were superseded. One of these methods was contract in the nineteenth century.

The work done by the OECD and the UN Centre for Transnational Enterprise in the last thirty years in attempting to monitor and regulate multinational and transnational

---

13   See M. vN. Whitman, *New World, New Rules—The Changing Role of the American Corporation*, Harvard Business School Press, Boston, 1999, p. 78.

enterprise, have found it necessary to transcend the concepts of the corporation and corporate group.

Thus the OECD guidelines give the following definition:

> A precise legal definition of multinational enterprises is not required for the purposes of the Guidelines. These usually comprise companies or other entities whose ownership is private, state or mixed, established in different countries and so linked that one or more of them may be able to exercise a significant influence over the activities of others and, in particular, to share knowledge and resources with the others. The degree of autonomy of each entity in relation to the others varies widely from one multinational enterprise to another, depending on the nature of the links between such entities and the fields of activity concerned. For these reasons, the Guidelines are addressed to the various entities within the multinational enterprise (parent companies and/or local entities) according to the actual distribution of responsibilities among them on the understanding that they will co-operate and provide assistance to one another as necessary to facilitate observance of the Guidelines. The word 'enterprise' as used in these Guidelines refers to these various entities in accordance with their responsibilities.[14]

This began to broaden the concept. The UN Draft Code took the matter further and provided:

> This code is universally applicable to enterprises, irrespective of their country of origin and their ownership, including private, public or mixed, comprising entities in two or more countries, regardless of the legal form and fields of these entities, which operate under a system of decision-making, permitting coherent policies and a common strategy through one or more decision-making centres, in which the entities are so linked, by ownership or otherwise, that one or more of them may be able to exercise significant influence over the activities of the others and, in particular, to share knowledge, resources and responsibilities with the others. Such enterprises are referred to in this code as transnational corporations.[15]

As part of the process there has been increasing emphasis not so much on ownership and control but on contractual relationships in the form of joint ventures, strategic alliances and networks. This is because ownership matters less in the modern world than access to information and services and a growing awareness of cooperative strategy as an alternative to competition and corporate strategies of expansion, mergers and acquisitions.[16] Some commentators see it is an additional way of competing more effectively. It has even been given a new name—*co-opetition*.[17] This has been defined as a

14   *Guidelines for Multinational Enterprises*, OECD, Paris, 2000, para. 8.
15   UN Economic and Social Council Work on the Formulation of the UN Code of Conduct for Transnational Corporations—Outstanding Issues in the Draft Code of Conduct on Transnational Corporations, E/C10/1985/5/2, 22 May 1985.
16   See J. Rifkin, *The Age of Access*, Penguin Books, London, 2000, and J. Child and D. Faulkner, *Strategies of Cooperation—Managing Alliances, Networks and Joint Ventures*, Oxford University Press, Oxford; 1998.
17   See B. J. Nalebuff and A. M. Brandenburger, *Co-opetition*, HarperCollins Business, London, 1996.

revolutionary mindset that combines competition and cooperation and makes use of game-theory strategy.[18]

Each of the three terms—joint venture, strategic alliance and network—is a little ambiguous and it is possible to take strategic alliance or network as the comprehensive category but there are probably distinguishing characteristics and all three can be subsumed under a general category of cooperative strategy.

A joint venture is either a partnership or something closely allied to partnership although it can take the form of a joint venture company.

There are four main types of joint venture:

1 core business joint venture
2 sales joint venture
3 production joint venture
4 development joint venture.[19]

A core business joint venture is comprehensive whereas the other three are joint ventures in connection with a specific function.

Strategic alliances can cover the same areas as a joint venture but the relationship is looser and resembles more a network relationship. Usually there is no separate company formed. Examples are product swaps, production or development, licences, and technology alliances. These enable the parties to develop new product markets, and share risks and costs.[20]

Although strategic alliances and networks are terms that are often used interchangeably, a network suggests close but non-exclusive relationships.[21] The purpose of a network relationship is:

• to reduce uncertainty in markets
• to provide flexibility
• to provide access to extra capacity
• to provide speed
• to provide access to resources and skills not owned by the company
• to provide industrial intelligence and information.[22]

The latest variation on this theme is the virtual corporation which is 'a loosely coupled enterprise in which the parts are held together through the medium of sophisticated information-technology packages'. Like a network, a virtual corporation can be an equal partner relationship or a dominated relationship.[23] The relationships are dynamic but can be approximately represented, as shown in Figure 35.1.[24]

---

18 *ibid.*
19 See T. Clarke and S. Clegg, *Changing Paradigms—The Transformation of Management Knowledge for the Twenty-First Century*, HarperCollins Business, London, 1998, p. 111.
20 *ibid.*, pp. 111–12.
21 See D. Schiller, *Digital Capitalism: Networking the Global Market System*, MIT Press, Cambridge, Mass., 1999.
22 Child and Faulkner, *op. cit.*, pp. 114–15.
23 *ibid.*, pp. 126 *et seq.*
24 This is influenced by Child and Faulkner, *op. cit.*, and Clarke and Clegg, *op. cit.*

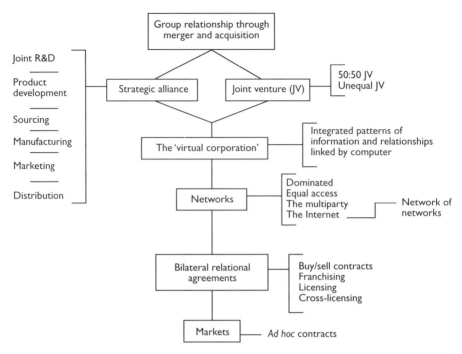

Figure 35.1   Contracts, networks and corporate relationships

What this figure shows is that formal corporate groups are the last stage of a proc-ess of integration, and increasingly the business world is opting for alternatives to hier-archies in corporate relationships which, like modern patterns of financing, are ad hoc, contractual and of a shorter duration. The term 'heterarchy'[25] has been used to describe such structures. This is not to say that the corporation itself is a contract but that increasingly it is necessary to supplement the corporate group with contractual arrangements of this kind in practice.

Global patterns of share ownership and control

Much of modern corporate governance theory has naturally focused on the corpora-tion and has been premised on the Berle and Means hypothesis of the separation of ownership and control. Berle and Means, writing at the time of the first stock market crash, argued that as companies got larger their shareholdings became diffused and in the resulting hiatus in significant power blocs, management's power increased.[26] This needed regulation by the courts or legislatures.

---

25   Clarke and Clegg, *op. cit.*
26   See ch. 5 above of this book.

As we saw in Chapter 34, a working paper by three Harvard economists *Corporate Ownership Around the World*, published by the National Bureau of Economic Research in 1998,[27] demonstrated the following facts about corporate ownership around the world.

- The separation of ownership and control in listed public corporations envisaged by Berle and Means is far from universal.
- Many of the largest firms are controlled by families.
- The widely held corporation is most common in countries with good regimes of shareholder protection.
- Family control is more common in countries with poor shareholder protection.
- State control is common, particularly in countries with poor shareholder protection.
- In family controlled firms there is little separation between ownership and control.
- Pyramids and deviations from one share one vote are most common in countries with poor shareholder protection.
- Corporations with controlling shareholders rarely have other large shareholders.

We have also seen in Chapter 4 that the Berle and Means hypothesis does not accurately describe the current situation in Australia and New Zealand, and we shall return to this later.

The evolution of global corporate governance

We have seen in Chapters 26 and 34 that institutional investors in the USA and the United Kingdom have promoted the development of global corporate governance through national groupings, international networks and, more recently, through international institutions. The latest development has been the work of the OECD in drafting Principles of Corporate Governance which have now been supported by the World Bank. Institutions have been less active in Germany and Japan in this respect although banks in both these countries have historically had closer practical involvement with corporate groups than in the USA and the United Kingdom.

In the development of global corporate governance, there have been a number of tensions. These are:

1   the UK and US models are not typical
2   corporate governance practices vary between countries
3   corporate governance practices constantly evolve
4   the evolution is affected *inter alia* by
   (a)   ownership structures
   (b)   business circumstances
   (c)   competitive conditions
   (d)   corporate life cycles
   (e)   the impact of the communications revolution

---

27   R. La Porta, F. Lopez-de-Silanes, and A. Shleifer *Corporate Ownership Around the World*, National Bureau of Economic Research, Working Paper No 6625, Cambridge, Mass, 1998.

Nevertheless as we saw in Chapter 34 there are certain norms which are emerging. These include:

- maximisation of shareholder value
- responsiveness to other stakeholders
- increased transparency
- voluntary adaptation of best practice
- limited recognition of universal standards in areas such as accounting.

We live in a period of complex transition, characterised by rapid change. It is possible that in this period our basic institutions will undergo some mutation. This will inevitably include the corporation and the corporate group. It may include the state itself. It will probably include our basic conceptions of regulation. Indeed the recent OECD initiative may well herald the future.

The relevance to Australia and New Zealand

What then is the relevance of all this to Australia and New Zealand? Let us first consider some basic facts of economic life:[28]

- In Australia we have a reasonably healthy growth record and recent surveys indicate that it will continue, characterised by low inflation, rapid changes in the structure of industry, and globalisation, but we are different from the USA and the United Kingdom. New Zealand is a more vulnerable economy but shares many features with Australia.
- We have a relatively small population and produce only a small percentage of the world's goods and services.
- The biggest industry in 1998–99 was the central government administration, which probably reflects our colonial origins and the historic shortage of private capital.
- The average profitability of Australian business is 14 per cent (pre-tax profit on shareholder funds) or just over half that of the USA.
- 70 per cent of Australian GDP comes from service industries compared with 51 per cent in 1900.
- 33.5 per cent of listed Australian companies have a substantial shareholder holding of 30 per cent or more, 11.5 per cent had a substantial shareholder holding of 20–30 per cent, 18 per cent had a substantial shareholder with 5–20 per cent and 33.8 per cent had an institution as their largest or only substantial shareholder.
- Of the top forty New Zealand listed companies 30 per cent are under majority control and 57.5 per cent under minority control.
- This is a quite different picture from the US and UK position. There is not the same degree of separation of ownership and control on which their systems of corporate governance are based.

---

28   See J. Kavanagh, 'The State of the Nation', *Business Review Weekly*, 7 April 2000, for some of the statistics in this section of this chapter.

- There is a high percentage of foreign ownership in Australia and New Zealand.
- The average holding of local equities by local institutions is less than in the United Kingdom.
- The biggest area of structural change has been through privatisation and demutualisation rather than through globalisation.
- We have been relatively slow to respond to the communications revolution with our corporate practices.
- Corporate governance in Australia has fallen into the hands of lawyers and politicians. The result is that we have the most complicated system of corporate law and securities regulation in the world. New Zealand has a much simpler system which is perhaps too lax.
- The Australian tax system is also too complex.
- The international perception is that we have a poor record in corporate governance if you take the period 1980 to 2000. We have an image problem based on the 1980s.
- We are getting better at our corporate governance practices but we are largely imitative of the USA and the United Kingdom. We have not taken much initiative with the OECD and the World Bank. We need to continue to improve governance in corporatised enterprises.

Where do we go from here?

What we need to do is:

1   To continue to extend the Corporate Law Economic Reform Program (CLERP) in Australia.
2   To revisit our corporatisation legislation, reduce ministerial controls and consider further privatisation.
3   To go beyond CLERP and consider whether our basic approach to corporate law and corporate governance is still too densely technical and whether it imposes excessive transaction costs on business. In particular, obese legislation and prolix judgments should be avoided.
4   To consider in particular whether our concepts of the corporation and the corporate group are too narrow and if so how, rather than continue making piecemeal and unprincipled amendments, we can adopt modern concepts consistent in principle and policy.
5   To pay more attention to the interests of employees and other stakeholders.
6   To explore the implications for corporate governance of information technology for meetings, voting and shareholder communications.
7   To shift the emphasis from a control-based model to a cooperation model with more emphasis on networks.
8   To learn something from the Asian approach to networks and German and Japanese conceptions of social governance.

9   To set up national think tanks and possibly a trans-Tasman think tank for corporate governance to design a system suited to local conditions and to consider the possibility of uniform legislation and a common stock exchange for Australia and New Zealand.

10   To work within the OECD and World Bank initiatives but ensure that our voice is heard.

To conclude, public companies, together with government, are core institutions of economic power in Australia and New Zealand. In the past, there has been a relatively uncritical public acceptance of business leadership but since the late 1980s, because of the actions of a few, corporate governance has been increasingly politicised in Australia. In New Zealand, until recently, there seemed to have been an opposite trend towards capture of political control of the economy by big business. There have been improvements in corporate governance in both countries since the 1980s. Improved corporate governance ensures compliance or conformance with ever increasing regulation. This is probably a truism and its link with improved economic performance is not yet proven. The jury is still out and the questions of causation are complex. However, it is probably true to say that a company that is performing well will also observe good standards of corporate governance. Also investors seem prepared to pay more for the shares of a well governed company, all other things being equal.[29]

What we now need is a broader conception of corporate governance so that we can devise user-friendly corporate legislation with an appropriate level of regulation.

We must seek an internationally credible system, suited to local conditions, which is open and responsive to rapidly changing circumstances. We need stability, transparency and accountability but we cannot afford to stand still or, even worse, to shoot ourselves in the foot.

We have enjoyed the benefits conferred by the invention and development of the corporate form by our ancestors who were faced with the problems of modernisation caused by the industrial revolution. We now live in what is often described as the postmodern age, characterised by the communications and financial revolutions and globalisation. We need a system of corporate governance capable of meeting these new challenges. This is not the end of the history of corporate governance.[30] It is simply the beginning of a new chapter that we ourselves must write.

---

29   See Editorial, Corporate Governance and the Bottom Line (2001) 9 *Corporate Governance, An International Review*, 77–8 and the materials cited.

30   Compare F. Fukuyama, *The End of History and the Last Man*, Penguin Books, London, 1992; and the unpublished paper by H. Hansmann and R. Kraakman, 'The End of History for Corporate Law', (2001) 89 Georgetown LJ 439.

Appendices

Corporate Practices and Conduct (Extracts)

Part I: Corporate Governance

Corporate governance is the system by which companies are controlled. Shareholders have delegated many of their responsibilities as owners to the directors who oversee the management of the business on their behalf. Directors are accountable to their shareholders and shareholder participation is necessary to make that accountability effective.

Directors should use their best efforts to ensure that the company is properly managed and constantly improved so as to protect and enhance shareholder wealth in perpetuity, and to meet the company's obligations to all parties with which the company interacts — its stakeholders. The essence of any system of good corporate governance is to allow the board and management the freedom to drive their company forward but to exercise that freedom within a framework of effective accountability.

There is no simple universal formula for good governance. Companies vary so greatly in size, complexity, ownership structure and other characteristics that what is ideal in some cases may be inappropriate in others. Moreover, as companies and industries change, ways of governing may need to adapt. Tried and proven structures and processes can help to improve governance, and can play an important role in building shareholder confidence in the soundness of their investments and thus a company's ability to attract capital. However, it is essential that all involved, and particularly boards of directors, should adopt the practices best suited to the good governance of their organisations in their particular circumstances.

BOARD FUNCTIONS

The relationship between management and the board is a partnership that is crucial to the company's long term success. Each has functions which should be clearly defined and understood. The chief executive officer is responsible to the board for the day-to-day management of the company. The board gives direction and exercises judgement in setting the company's objectives and monitoring their implementation.

It is good practice to clarify the allocation of functions in writing. The Cadbury Code requires that 'The board should have a formal schedule of matters specifically reserved to it for

475

decision to ensure that the direction and control of the company is firmly in its hands' and the Cadbury Report recommends that statements be made in company annual reports by the directors which cover their responsibility for the accounts and the effectiveness of the company's system of internal control.

CISCO recognises that the system of corporate governance should not fetter entrepreneurial talent but considers that systems must be established for the consultation of the board before decisions are enacted in relation to certain important areas. It presents a lengthy list of matters that should be decided by the board. It recommends that there should be regular board meetings (normally monthly) to deal with these matters which should be attended by the non-executive directors and which should consider reports on the company's management accounts.

The Toronto Stock Exchange emphasises that the board delegates functions to management and calls for the development of 'position descriptions for the board and for the CEO, involving the limits to management's responsibilities.'

The Working Group considers that whatever mechanism is adopted, there should be no doubt about which matters should be covered specifically in reports to the board. The division of responsibilities, terms of reference or delegations from the board management should be put in writing and reviewed periodically, probably annually.

In most cases, the board's functions would include:

- taking steps designed to protect the company's financial position and its ability to meet its debts and other obligations as they fall due
- adopting a strategic plan for the company, including general and specific goals and comparing actual results with the plan
- adopting an annual budget for the financial performance of the company and monitoring results on a regular basis
- adopting clearly defined delegations of authority from the board to the CEO or a statement of matters reserved for decision by the board
- agreeing performance indicators with management
- ensuring that systems are in place which facilitate the effective monitoring and management of the principal risks to which the company is exposed
- determining that the company has instituted adequate reporting systems and internal controls (both operational and financial) together with appropriate monitoring of compliance activities
- establishing and monitoring policies directed to ensuring that the company complies with the law and conforms with the highest standards of financial and ethical behaviour
- determining that the company accounts are in conformity with Australian Accounting Standards and are true and fair
- determining that satisfactory arrangements are in place for auditing the company's financial affairs and that the scope of the external audit is adequate
- selecting and recommending auditors to shareholders at general meetings
- selecting and, if necessary, replacing the chief executive, setting an appropriate remuneration package, ensuring adequate succession, and giving guidance on the appointment and remuneration of other senior management
- ensuring that the company has in place a policy that enables it to communicate effectively with its shareholders, other stakeholders and the public generally

> • adopting formal processes for the selection of new directors and recommending them for the consideration of shareholders at general meetings with adequate information to allow shareholders to make informed decisions
> • reviewing its own processes and effectiveness, and the balance of competence on the board.

Part II: Matters Raised by the Australian Stock Exchange

1   BOARD STRUCTURE

Item 1 of the ASX *Indicative List of Corporate Governance Matters* suggests disclosure of 'whether individual directors, including the Chairman, are executive or non-executive directors.'

1.1   Categories of Directors

Two categories of directors are generally recognised:

• executive directors who are employees, usually senior managers. They should be of sufficient stature and security of employment to express disagreement, if necessary, with other board members. Executive directors, in addition to their responsibilities as managers, have all the responsibilities of members of the board.
• non-executive directors who are not employees but bring special qualifications, experience, expertise and an independent perspective to the board.

The main functions of non-executive directors are:

• to bring an independent view to the board's deliberations
• to help the board (and the chairman) provide the company with effective leadership
• to foster the continuing effectiveness of the executive directors and management.

The Cadbury Code, written against the UK background in which traditionally most directors were executive, recommended that 'The board should include non-executive directors of sufficient calibre and number for their views to carry significant weight in the board's decisions.' The Cadbury Report comments that 'to meet our recommendations on the composition of sub-committees of the board, all boards will require a minimum of three non-executive directors, one of whom may be chairman of the company...'.

The Cadbury Code further recommended that 'The majority (of non-executive directors) should be independent of management and free from any business or other relationship which could materially interfere with the exercise of their independent judgement...' and the Report recommends that 'it is for the board to decide in particular cases whether this definition is met. Information about the relevant interests of directors should be disclosed in the Directors' Report.'

CISCO acknowledges the problems that smaller companies may have in meeting the Cadbury standards but stresses that 'the appointment of appropriate non-executive directors may nevertheless prove extremely beneficial to the development of the business.' It recommends that 'smaller companies should have at least two non-executive directors as this enables non-executives to liaise and not be isolated or dominated. Most important, to be counted as a non-executive director the individual must be truly independent …'.

The Toronto Guidelines recommend that 'The board of directors of every corporation should be constituted with a majority of individuals who qualify as unrelated directors. An unrelated director is a director who is independent of management and is free from any interest and any business or other relationship which could, or could reasonably be perceived to, materially interfere with the director's ability to act with a view to the best interests of the corporation …'.

The GM Guidelines, and their by-laws, provide that 'there should be a majority of independent directors' on the board. 'GM's By-law defining independent directors was approved by the Board in January 1991. The Board believes there is no current relationship between any outside director and GM that would be construed in any way to compromise any Board member being designated independent. Compliance with the By-law is reviewed annually by the Committee on Director Affairs.'

The GM Guidelines strengthen the position of the outside (non-executive) directors by providing that they will meet in 'Executive Session' three times per year. It is provided that these sessions will include a discussion with the CEO.

The Hong Kong Code seeks to strengthen the position of independent non-executive directors by providing that 'If, in respect of any matter discussed at a board meeting, the independent non-executive directors hold views contrary to those of the executive directors, the minutes should clearly reflect this.'

The AIMA Guidelines recommend that 'the board of directors of every listed company should be constituted with a majority of individuals who qualify as independent directors … An independent director is a director who is not a member of management … and who:

- is not a substantial shareholder of the company or an officer of or otherwise associated directly or indirectly with a substantial shareholder of the company
- has not been employed within the last three years in any executive capacity by the company or any other group member
- is not retained as a professional adviser to the company … or a principal of a firm or company so retained
- is not a significant supplier or customer of the company …
- has no significant contractual relationship with the company …
- is otherwise free from any interest or any business or other relationship which could, or could reasonably be perceived to, materially interfere with the director's ability to act with a view to the best interests of the company.'

The Working Group believes that two important principles underlie concerns about the structure of boards:

- that power without accountability is dangerous
- that no individual or entity should have power of influence which would enable its interests to be preferred over those of the company as a whole.

A separation of power at the top of a company provides a degree of accountability that may reassure shareholders that their interests are being watched over adequately. In companies where all or most shareholders are also directors and managers, these issues may not arise (though the interests of creditors may have to be considered), but when companies raise capital on the market, the directors must accept responsibilities to a fragmented shareholder body. Both directors and shareholders should consider what assurances are being given in respect of adequate accountability and that due regard is being paid to the interests of the company as a whole.

In consequence, the Working group considers that the boards of listed public companies should include a majority of non-executive directors who have an appropriate mix of skills and experience and whose abilities are appropriate to the needs of the company.

It is recognised that some non-executive directors may have a personal or professional association with the company or its officers or a particular shareholder. Such associations should not preclude them from serving as directors, provided they are willing to act in the interests of the general body shareholders rather than of any sectional interest.

However, the majority of non-executive directors should preferably be independent, not only of management but of any other external influence that could detract from their ability to act in the interests of the company as a whole.

Independence is more likely to be assured when the director:
• is not a substantial shareholder of the company
• has not been employed in any executive capacity by the company within the last few years
• is not retained as a professional adviser by the company (either personally or through their firm)
• is not a significant supplier to or customer of the company
• has no significant contractual relationship with the company other than as a director.

It is important that boards include sufficient directors who are generally independent in their views to carry significant weight on the board. Their numbers will vary with the size of the board but it is unlikely that less than two will be able to exercise sufficient influence, and it is desirable that at least one third of the board should be genuinely independent.

It is recognised that the appointment of independent directors will be expensive for smaller companies but the real contributions to performance to be expected from good appointments, and the increased credibility from the standpoint of investors, make it important that a real effort is made to follow these recommendations.

It is recommended that companies indicate in their annual reports any material contacts or relationships, other than membership on the board, which directors have with the company.

1.2   The Chairman

The Cadbury Report recommends 'Given the importance and particular nature of the chairman's role, it should in principle be separate from that of the chief executive. If the two roles are combined in one person, it represents a considerable concentration of power. We recommend, therefore, that there should be a clearly accepted division of responsibilities at the head of a company, which will ensure a balance of power and authority, such that no one individual has unfettered powers of decision. Where the chairman is also the chief executive, it is essential that there should be a strong and independent element on the board.' The Cadbury Code extends this position by recommending that the independent element on the board should have a 'recognised senior member'.

CISCO accepts that 'much of the concern caused by a combination of the roles of chief executive and chairman in one person can be offset by the presence of two independent non-executives. In such cases, it is also considered good practice for one of the two non-executive directors to be appointed chairman.'

In the face of a long established North American practice of appointing executive chairmen, the Toronto Guidelines recognises the problem of concentration of power at the top of companies but leaves the solution open. They state that 'every board should have in place appropriate structures and procedures to ensure that the board can function independently of management'. An appropriate structure would be to:

(i)   appoint a chair of the board who is not a member of management with responsibility to ensure that the board discharges its responsibilities or
(ii)   adopt alternative means such as assigning this responsibility to a committee of the board, such as the governance committee, or to a director sometimes referred to as the 'lead director'.

The GM Guidelines also leave the board free to decide whether the chairman should be executive or non-executive but in practice, the company now separates the roles. The Guidelines stress the need for the board to be able to operate separately from management and make clear that, should the chairman be an executive, a separate lead director will be appointed to chair three 'Executive Sessions' of the non-executive directors each year and to carry out such functions as the non-executive directors decide.

The AIMA Guidelines recommend 'that the chairperson should be an independent director or, if the chairperson is not an independent director, that the independent directors should appoint one of their number to be lead director and to monitor and report to them on issues falling within the normal purview of a non-executive chairperson.'

The Working Group considers that the separation of the roles of Chairman and CEO makes an important contribution to increasing accountability and ensuring that the interests of the shareholders as a whole are given due weight.

The Working Group also considers that the chairman plays a crucial leadership role in ensuring that the board works effectively and that the combination of the roles of chairman and chief executive constitutes a concentration of power that can give rise to conflicts. Except where special circumstances exist, the roles should be separate. Such special circumstances may include:

- wholly owned subsidiaries of overseas parents
- massive restructuring or other major challenges which justify a temporary merging of roles
- small companies which cannot afford the additional cost involved in the separation of roles.

Where the roles are combined, the appointment of an independent non-executive director as Deputy Chairman should be considered (in North America and the UK the term 'lead director' is sometimes used) and it may be necessary to arrange for separate meetings of the non-executive directors or to establish a strong governance or directors' affairs committee made up of independent directors. Since these options make board operations more complex and may undermine the unity and harmonious operation of the board, the separation of the roles of chairman and CEO is strongly preferred.

I.3   Committees of the Board

The effectiveness of the board, and particularly of the non-executive directors, is likely to be enhanced by the establishment of appropriate board committees. They can distribute the board's workload and enable more detailed consideration to be given to important matters and, where sensitive issues (such as the appointment of auditors) have to be considered, an appropriately constituted committee may give independent consideration which will be valuable.

The Cadbury Report, and the Toronto, GM and AIMA guidelines all advocate the appointment of committees and make recommendations on their structure and operations, but all recognise that appropriate committee structures will vary from company to company. Generally, larger companies, and larger boards, will make use of more committees. For instance, GM has six committees — Audit, Capital, Stock, Directors' Affairs, Finance, Incentive and Compensation and Public Policy. It is notable that the allocation of functions between committees is subject to wide variation and that different names are sometimes used to describe committees with similar functions.

While properly structured committees can increase board effectiveness, they cannot reduce the responsibility of the board as a whole and care should be taken to ensure that all concerned understand their functions. The Working Group considers the following arrangements to be good practice:

- written terms of reference for each committee, which should deal adequately with its authority and duties, including whether, and in what areas, it can act on behalf of the board, or whether it can only investigate, consider and recommend
- procedures for reporting to the full board, both orally and in writing
- agreed arrangements for staffing the committees, for providing adequate access to relevant company executives, and agreed procedures for obtaining independent external advice at the cost of the company.

Where it is particularly important that boards exercise, and are seen to exercise, independent judgement, such as in the areas of company accounts, remuneration practices, and the selection of board members, the independence and objectivity of the judgements can be enhanced by the appointment of appropriate committees. Their establishment is particularly important when boards are larger or when executive directors constitute a powerful presence. In such cases, it is very desirable that the membership of the committees is seen to be predominately independent.

It is good practice for the membership of committees to be set out in the company's annual report, and consideration should be given to the disclosure of a summary of the terms of reference and other arrangements that have been put in place.

---

2 BOARD MEMBERSHIP

Item 2 of the ASX *Indicative List of Corporate Governance Matters* suggests that information be disclosed on:

'The main procedures that the company has in place for:
i   devising criteria for Board membership
ii   reviewing membership of the Board
iii nominating directors.

'If any of these procedures involve a nomination committee, a summary of the main responsibilities of the committee, and the names of the committee members. If one or more members are not directors of the company, their positions in the company.'

The Cadbury Code requires that 'Non-executive directors should be selected through a formal process and both the process and their appointment should be a matter for the board as a whole.'

While the Code does not require the establishment of nomination committees, the Cadbury Report regards them as 'good practice'. It recommends that 'A nomination committee should have a majority of non-executive directors on it and should be chaired either by the chairman or non-executive director.'

The Report does not advocate any particular criteria for board membership but it stresses that non-executive directors should be of high calibre and be able to work harmoniously together.

The Cadbury Code does not require a formal process of assessment of either the CEO or the board but the Report identifies 'reviewing the performance of the board and of the executive' as one of the contributions which the non-executive directors should make.

The CISCO Guide recommends that 'Companies should seek to define the role each non-executive director is expected to fulfil, and the specific objectives of that role, as they should for any other senior appointment, in order to ensure that they receive optimum benefit from the appointment. This should be done before starting the selection procedure. The role and the objectives should be redefined whenever the position is vacated, reflecting the changing needs of the company. If necessary, advice may be sought from major shareholders to try and identify those areas of the board's knowledge base and skills that may need strengthening.'

CISCO also suggests that where a company has a board of less than five members, a separate nomination committee is not necessary and the duties may be undertaken by the audit committee.

The Toronto Guidelines sets out the following more detailed and specific recommendations.

> The board of directors of every corporation should appoint a committee of directors composed exclusively of outside, i.e. non-management, directors, with the responsibility of proposing to the full board new nominees to the board and for assessing directors on an ongoing basis.
>
> Every board of directors should implement a process to be carried out by the nomination committee or other appropriate committee for assessing the effectiveness of the board as a whole, the committees of the board and the contribution of individual directors.

The Toronto Report takes the issues associated with board composition further than the Guidelines by:

- recommending that each board should develop its own criteria for selecting board members with the over-riding requirement that there be a majority of unrelated directors. The nomination committee would then apply the criteria laid down by the board. By way of guidance, it stresses the importance of the board functioning harmoniously and as a unit and points to the need for diverse backgrounds and experience, while rejecting the notion of directors representing particular constituencies
- calling on boards to consider which individual directors can be considered 'unrelated' and 'to disclose its analysis of the application of the principles to the circumstances of the board' on an annual basis
- giving more specific attention to the question of the assessment of board performance than Cadbury did. 'Every board of directors will have in place some mechanism for, at least annually, assessing the performance of the CEO. Good governance requires the board to also have in place a mechanism for assessing its own effectiveness as a board and for assessing the contribution of individual directors.'
- taking a similar position in training to that of Cadbury. 'Every corporation, as an integral element of the process for appointing new directors, should provide an orientation and education program for new recruits to the board.' While recognising that company requirements will

vary, the Toronto Report suggests orientation manuals, opportunities to discuss with experts the responsibilities of directors individually and of the board as a whole, the visiting of company facilities and discussions with company officers
- recommending that 'Every board of directors should examine its size and, with a view to determining the impact of the number upon effectiveness, undertake, where appropriate, a program to reduce the number of directors to a number which facilitates more effective decision making.'

The GM Guidelines cover some of the same issues as the Toronto Guidelines. They stipulate that:

- 'The Board itself should be responsible, in fact as well as procedure, for selecting its own members. The Board delegates the screening process involved to the Committee on Director Affairs with direct input from the chairman of the Board as well as the Chief Executive Officer.'
- 'The Committee on Director Affairs is responsible for reviewing with the Board on an annual basis the appropriate skills and characteristics required of Board members in the context of the current make-up of the Board. This assessment should include issues of diversity, age, skills, such as understanding of manufacturing technologies, international background, etc.—all in the context of an assessment of the perceived needs of the Board at that point in time.'
- 'The Committee on Director Affairs is responsible to report annually to the Board an assessment of the Board's performance. This will be discussed with the full Board. This should be done following the end of each fiscal year and at the same time as the report on Board membership criteria.

'This assessment should be of the Board's contribution as a whole and specifically review areas in which the Board and/or Management believes a better contribution could be made. Its purpose is to increase the effectiveness of the Board, not to target individual Board members.'
- 'The full Board (outside directors) should make' a formal evaluation of the CEO annually, 'and it should be communicated to the CEO by the (non-executive) Chairman of the Board or the Lead Director.'

The AIMA Guidelines recommended that 'The board should annually review its required mix of skills, experience and other qualities' and that a nomination committee should be appointed which 'should have the responsibility for proposing to the full board new nominees to the board and for assessing existing directors' performance'. It is further recommended that the nomination committee:

- should be chaired by an independent director and have at least a majority of non-executive members
- should have written terms of reference, which should be minuted by the full board, and which should include certain core matters to be dealt with by the committee and certain core rights of the committee
- should be entitled to obtain independent professional or other advice at the cost of the company
- should be entitled to obtain such resources and information from the company, including direct access to employees of and advisers to the company, as they may require.

The guidelines further recommend that 'the non-executive directors should meet on their own at least once annually to review the performance of the board, the company and management and to discuss any other items raised by any of them. Other directors and/or management may be invited to attend part of the meeting but the business of the meeting should be decided in the absence of such persons.'

The Working Group considers that among the important functions of the board are:

- the determination of the appropriate size and composition of the board
- devising criteria for board membership
- reviewing the effectiveness of management, the board as a whole and the individual members of the board with reference to their contribution to the performance of the company
- reviewing the membership of the board
- nominating directors to the shareholders for election when necessary.

It is essential that these processes be carried out objectively and that independent judgement be seen to be used — selecting directors on the basis of friendship alone is fraught with danger. The board as a whole should discuss these matters and should take the final decision but, since at least some of them are complex and sensitive, it is good practice for the boards of companies listed on the stock exchange to establish committees of independent directors (which might be called nomination committees, corporate governance committees or committees on directors' affairs) and to delegate to them the responsibility for making recommendations in each of these areas.

It is particularly important that nomination committees should have at least a majority of independent non-executive directors, one of whom should be chairman. If the chairman of the board is an independent director, it is appropriate that they chair the nomination committee.

Nomination committee should have written terms of reference which set out their responsibilities and rights. These are likely to include responsibility for:

- assessing the performance of the CEO annually
- assessing the performance of the board as a whole or making arrangements for the board to assess its own performance
- assessing the contribution of individual directors or arranging for the board to do so
- selecting and nominating candidates for board membership when necessary
- reporting and making recommendations to the board as a whole.

To be effective, the nomination committee should have the right to:

- have whatever access it requires to the company's officers and advisers
- obtain whatever information or resources it requires from the company
- obtain whatever independent professional or other advice it requires from outside the company

In some companies, for instance in smaller companies or where a company has a small board, consideration should be given to alternative ways of demonstrating to shareholders that the process of director specification and selection is objective. This may involve the use of external professional advisers and additional disclosures.

3 APPOINTMENT AND RETIREMENT OF NON-EXECUTIVE DIRECTORS

The third item on the ASX *Indicative List of Corporate Governance Matters* calls for disclosure of 'The company's policies on the terms and conditions relating to the appointment and retirement of non-executive directors.'

The Cadbury Code provides that 'Non-executive directors should be appointed for specified terms and reappointment should not be automatic.'

The Cadbury Report amplifies this principle by recommending that directors should receive a letter of appointment which sets out their duties, terms of office, remuneration and its review and it suggests that the letter may cover arrangements for taking professional advice at the company's expense. It also stresses the importance of training for all directors and in particular 'a proper process of induction into a company's affairs for all new directors.' It calls for 'a conscious decision by the board and the director concerned' before any reappointment.

The CISCO Guide recommends that the terms of appointment for non-executive directors of smaller companies should reflect the time and effort expended in finding appropriate directors and the loss of accumulated knowledge when a change is made. It suggests that the period of appointment should be no longer than ten years. It further suggests that the appointment of non-executive directors should be staggered so that they do not retire at the same time.

CISCO further recommends that 'Any non-executive director who resigns from any quoted company should be entitled to communicate (at the company's expense) with its shareholders giving reasons for his resignation and any matters he considers should be brought to their attention. This procedure could also apply when there is fundamental disagreement leading the non-executive directors to vote against resolutions proposed at board meetings.'

The Toronto Guidelines leave the questions of the terms and conditions relating to the appointment and replacement of directors to the boards themselves. The Report specifically rejects the need for guidance on the maximum term which directors should serve or the maximum number of boards on which they should sit. It does, however, strongly recommend that 'each corporation should provide an orientation and education program for new recruits to the board.'

The GM Guidelines pay considerable attention to this area. They reject term limits but provide that the Committee on Director Affairs will review each director's continuation on the board every five years. They also provide for a retirement age of 70 and they require a formal invitation to join the board from the board itself, the chairman and the CEO.

The Hong Kong Code provides that:

- 'Non-executive directors should be appointed for a specific term and that term should be disclosed in the annual report and accounts of the issuer.'
- 'If an independent non-executive director resigns or is removed from office, the Exchange should be notified of the reasons why.'

The AIMA Guidelines recommend that 'the terms of a non-executive director's appointment should be contained in a letter of appointment exchanged between the director/proposed director and the company' and dealing with:

- the director's duties including 'any special skills or experience or other qualities expected to be contributed by the director and the time which the director should expect to devote to the company and, where necessary, should require the director to limit the number of other directorships.'
- the director's rights 'to obtain independent advice, resources and information at the company's expense subject to approval of the chairperson.'

It is recommended that the letter of appointment 'should also record relevant policies of the company such as board, director and CEO evaluation.'

The AIMA Guidelines also call for a formal system of orientation and education for all directors which should be both documentary and practical.

The Working Group considers that all directors should be sent a formal letter of appointment which sets out:

- the term of their appointment (probably three years but renewable)
- if appropriate, the board's policy on the age of retirement
- their remuneration and arrangements for its review
- any special duties or arrangements that may be relevant
- the arrangements by which directors can take advice, at the company's expense, in furtherance of their duties.

Some companies may also consider it appropriate to mention a selection of company policies in the letter of appointment but the Working Group notes that if policies are sent out in letters of appointment, the board may feel that it has reduced its ability to be flexible in the subsequent development of those policies.

The Working Group also believes that it is good practice for companies to establish a system of orientation and training for directors and it may be considered appropriate for it to be discussed with incoming board members. An alternative may be to give each incoming director a director's source book which could include, inter alia, copies of the articles of association, extracts from relevant policies, the executive summary of the corporate plan and other appropriate information.

The Working Group does not believe that it is necessary for any formal limit to be placed on the period of time a director is able to serve, nor on the number of board positions that should be accepted. It doubts the wisdom of indicating in the letter of appointment the special skills and other qualities which an individual director may be expected to bring to the board table.

---

4   DIRECTORS' NEEDS

The fourth item on the ASX *Indicative List of Corporate Governance Matters* suggests disclosure of 'The main procedure(s), if any, by which directors in furtherance of their duties can seek independent professional advice at the company's expense.'

The Cadbury Code provides that:

- 'There should be an agreed procedure for directors in the furtherance of their duties to take independent professional advice if necessary at the company's expense.'
- 'All directors should have access to the advice and services of the company secretary, who is responsible to the board for ensuring that board procedures are followed and that applicable rules and regulations are complied with. Any question of the removal of the company secretary should be a matter for the board as a whole.'

The Cadbury Report takes these principles further by recommending that when occasions arise in which directors have to seek legal or financial advice, they should be able to consult the company's advisers. Any question of taking independent professional advice should be covered by 'an agreed procedure laid down formally, for example in a board resolution, in the articles, or in the letter of appointment.'

The Report further stresses the importance of the role of the company secretary and recommends that it is for the board as a whole to ensure that the secretary remains capable of carrying out the duties which the post entails. It comments that 'The chairman of the board will look to the company secretary for guidance on what their responsibilities are under the rules and regulations to which they are subject and on how those responsibilities should be discharged.'

The Toronto Guidelines provide that 'The board of directors should implement a system which enables an individual director to engage an outside adviser at the expense of the corporation in appropriate circumstances. The engagement of the outside adviser should be subject to the approval of an appropriate committee of the board.'

The Toronto Report stresses the importance of directors having access to adequate information and points to the possibility of a director wishing to dissent from a board decision or being concerned about personal liability. It considers that 'there are any number of circumstances in which an individual director will want to obtain outside advice' and that a director will function better if they know that they have reasonable access to advice.

The GM Guidelines provide that 'Board members have complete access to GM's management. It is assumed that Board members will use judgement to be sure that this contact is not distracting to the business operation of the Company and that such contact, if in writing, will be copied to the chief executive officer (CEO) and the chairman.' The Guidelines provide for managers to come into board meetings to advise the board but they do not cover the question of outside advice.

The Hong Kong Code provides that arrangements shall be made in appropriate circumstances to enable the independent non-executive directors of the board, at their request, to seek separate professional advice at the expense of the issuer.'

The Code also provides:

- for agendas and board papers to be sent to directors in advance of meetings
- for adequate notice of meetings to be given
- for all directors to have access to board papers and materials.

It adds that 'Where queries are raised by non-executive directors, steps must be taken to respond as promptly and fully as possible.'

The AIMA Guidelines provide that board committees should 'be entitled to obtain independent or professional or other advice at the cost of the company; and be entitled to obtain such resources and information from the company, including direct access to employees of and advisers to the company, as they may require.'

The report adds that the rights of a director should include the right to obtain independent advice, resources and information at the company's expense, subject to the approval of the chairman.

The Working Group considers that, as a matter of principle, all directors, including non-executive directors, must have full access to all relevant information. Except where conflicts of interest are involved, there is no matter so secret that it should be withheld from directors. In the case of matters to be considered by the board, directors must insist that full details are made available to them in sufficient time to allow proper consideration.

The board should be satisfied that it has, or has access to, the appropriate levels of skill in all relevant areas of the law and in relation to the business and financial affairs of the company. It is good practice for boards to lay down guidelines covering contacts between non-executive directors and company employees. These are likely to cover requests for information and the provision of resources.

To enable directors to discharge their fiduciary duties properly, it may be necessary for them to be provided with expert advice, particularly on legal and financial matters. Such advice should be objective and as independent as possible. In the first instance, advice is likely to be requested from company officers or advisers but in some circumstances, advice from independent external sources may be appropriate. It is important that an agreed procedure be established which makes clear under what circumstances, with what information and by what method board committees or individual directors can obtain such advice at the company's expense. Where a nomination committee with a majority of independent directors has been appointed, it may be the best mechanism for considering requests.

5 REMUNERATION (COMPENSATION)

The fifth item in the ASX's *Indicative List of Corporate Governance Matters* suggests disclosure of 'The main procedures for establishing and reviewing the compensation arrangements for:

    i   the Chief Executive Officer and other senior executives, and
   ii non-executive members of the Board.

'If these procedures involve a remuneration committee, a summary of the main responsibilities and core rights of the committee, and the names of committee members. If one or more members are not directors of the company, their positions in the company.'

The Cadbury Code provides that 'Executive directors' pay should be subject to the recommendations of a remuneration committee made up wholly or mainly of non-executive directors'. The Report expands on this principle and recommends that:

• 'The overriding principle in respect of board remuneration is that of openness. Shareholders are entitled to a full and clear statement of directors' present and future benefits and how they have been determined.' A statement of benefits should include relevant information about stock options, stock appreciation rights, pension and contributions.
• 'Service contracts should not exceed three years without shareholders' approval.'
• 'Boards should appoint remuneration committees, consisting wholly or mainly of non-executive directors and chaired by a non-executive director, to recommend to the board remuneration of the executive directors in all its forms, drawing on outside advice as necessary ... Membership of the remuneration committee should appear in the Directors' Report.'

The CISCO Guide suggests that where a company has a board of less than five members, a separate remuneration committee may not be necessary and its duties may be performed by the audit committee. The CISCO Guide also recommends that 'non-executive directors should not have share options or any compensation on the termination of their appointment'.

The Toronto Guidelines recommend that 'The board of directors should review the adequacy and form of the compensation of directors to ensure that the compensation realistically reflects the responsibilities and risks involved in being an effective director.'

The Toronto Report notes that the risk and time associated with being a director is increasing and that director accountability is being treated more seriously by the investing public. It recommends that remuneration of directors 'should be appreciable', and it suggests that corporations remunerate directors wholly or partly in shares or options.

The GM Guidelines include an Incentive and Compensation Committee which considers the compensation of the CEO and other executives. Its members are appointed by the Committee on Director Affairs. Board compensation is reviewed annually by the Committee on Director

Affairs on the basis of a report from management on compensation levels in other large US companies. A recommendation is then made to the full board.

The Hong Kong Code provides that 'The director's fees and any other reimbursement or emolument payable to an independent non-executive director shall be disclosed in full in the annual report and accounts of the issuer.'

The AIMA Guidelines recommend that:

- '... the board should annually review, and disclose in the annual report, its policies for remuneration, including incentives, of the board and senior executives. The justification for these policies and their relationship to the performance of the company should be similarly reviewed and disclosed.'
- '... the quantum and components of the remuneration of each director and each of the 5 highest paid executives should clearly be disclosed in one section of the annual report. This should include the existence and length of any service contracts for the CEO.'
- '... the board should establish a policy to encourage non-executive directors to own shares in the company.'
- '... the board should appoint a remuneration committee chaired by an independent director and with at least a majority of non-executive directors.'

The AIMA Report further recommends that the remuneration committee:

- '... should have the responsibility for reviewing the remuneration of directors and senior management and advising the full board whether the remuneration, in the case of non-executive directors, realistically reflects the responsibilities and risk involved in being an effective director and, in the case of senior management, promotes the long term growth of shareholder value and is reasonable in comparison with industry and other relevant yardsticks.'
- '... should have written (minuted) terms of reference which include certain core matters to be dealt with by the committee and certain core rights of the committee' which would include the right to obtain independent or other advice at the cost of the company and the right to obtain resources and information from the company.

The Working Group considers that as a matter of principle, the level and form of remuneration should not be determined by the recipient(s) but should be approved by independent persons acting in the interests of shareholders. The remuneration of non-executive directors, including all benefits such as options, rights and pensions, should be fully disclosed to shareholders and approved by them. The level of remuneration should reasonably reflect the responsibilities and risks of being an effective director.

As a preferred means of implementing this principle, the Working Group recommends that the boards of public companies, and in particular companies listed on the ASX, should appoint remuneration committees with a least a majority of independent non-executive directors. Written terms of reference should be provided to the committee by the board.

The primary functions of the remuneration committee should include matters such as:

- the remuneration arrangements for the chief executive officer and other senior executives (including incentive plans, share options and other benefits) and service contracts
- the remuneration policies and practices for the company generally
- the recruitment and termination policies and practices of the company
- any company share schemes or other incentive schemes
- company superannuation arrangements
- the remuneration arrangements for members of the board

In addition, it may be appropriate for the remuneration committee to review:

- any transactions between the company and directors, or any interests associated with them, to ensure that the transactions are in the interests of shareholders as a whole
- the company's succession planning to ensure that adequate arrangements are in place and that recruitment and training are providing adequate candidates for promotion to senior positions.

The remuneration committee should report to the board regularly and where necessary should make proposals for the board's consideration and decision. Membership of such committees should be set out in the company's annual report.

In companies in which a remuneration committee would not be appropriate, for instance in small companies or where the board is small, consideration should be given to alternative means of demonstrating to shareholders the objective basis of remuneration and related party transactions. This may involve the use of professional advice and additional disclosure.

6 FINANCIAL REPORTING AND AUDITING

The sixth item on the ASX's *Indicative List of Corporate Governance Matters* requests disclosure of 'The main procedures that the company has in place for:

i   the nomination of external auditors, and

ii   reviewing the adequacy of existing external audit arrangements, with particular emphasis on the scope and quality of the audit.

     'If any of these procedures involves an audit committee, a summary of the main responsibilities and core rights of the committee, and the names of the committee members. If one or more members are not directors of the company, their positions in the company.'

The Cadbury Code sets down the following board responsibilities:

- 'It is the board's duty to present a balanced and understandable assessment of the company's position.'
- 'The board should ensure that an objective and professional relationship is maintained with the auditors.'
- 'The board should establish an audit committee of at least three non-executive directors with written terms of reference which deal clearly with its authorities and duties.'
- 'The directors should explain their responsibility for preparing the accounts next to a statement by the auditors about their reporting responsibilities.'

The Cadbury Report emphasises the importance of financial reports. It emphasises that these are the responsibility of the board and that this responsibility should be made clear to shareholders.

The Report also stresses the importance of the annual audit, describing it as 'one of the cornerstones of corporate governance'. 'Audits are a reassurance to all those who have a financial interest in the company, quite apart from their value to boards of directors.' Boards have an essential role in seeing that audits are objective and effective and to that end the Report calls on each listed company to establish 'an audit committee which gives the auditors direct access to the non-executive members of the board.' The written terms of reference should 'deal adequately with their membership, authority and duties, and they should meet at least twice a year.' The Report further recommends that:

- a majority of the members of audit committees should be independent and the names of members should be disclosed in the annual report
- 'The external auditor should normally attend audit committee meetings, as should the finance director. As the board as a whole is responsible for the financial statements, other board members should have the right to attend. The committee should have a discussion with the external auditors, at least once a year, without executive board members being present to ensure that there are no unresolved issues of concern.'
- 'The audit committee should have the resources to investigate any matters within its terms of reference, full access to information and the right to obtain external professional advice.'
- The matters referred to the audit committee should normally include:
  - making recommendations to the board on the appointment of the external auditor, the audit fee, and any questions of resignation or dismissal
  - review of financial statements before submission to the board
  - discussion with the external auditor about the nature and scope of the audit, any problems arising from the audit and any matters the auditor wishes to raise
  - review of the external auditor's management letter
  - review of the company's statement on internal control systems prior to endorsement by the board
  - review of any significant findings of internal audit investigations.
- the chairman of the audit committee should be available to answer questions at the annual general meeting.

The CISCO Guide recommends that for smaller companies 'It is fundamental that an audit committee should be established and that all non-executive directors are members of it, but membership need not be restricted to non-executive directors. A non-executive director should be appointed as chairman of the audit committee. As part of the arrangements, non-executive directors should have meetings (at which the executives are not present) with the company's auditors.'

In Canada, audit committees are required by law and the Toronto Guidelines recommends that 'The audit committee of every board of directors should be composed only of outside directors. The roles and responsibilities of the audit committee should be specifically designed so as to provide appropriate guidance to audit committee members as to their duties. The audit committee should have direct communication channels with the internal and external auditors to discuss and review specific issues as appropriate. The audit committee duties should include oversight reporting responsibility for management reporting on internal control. While it is management's responsibility to design and implement an effective system of internal control, it is the responsibility of the audit committee to ensure that management has done so.'

In the USA, listed companies are required by stock exchange listing rules to establish audit committees and the GM Guidelines do not deal with audit matters in any depth. The Committee on Director Affairs is responsible for the assignment of board members to the committee and the chairman of the audit committee is responsible for determining the frequency and length of meetings together with committee agendas. The committee is required to prepare an annual agenda of matters to be discussed in the ensuing year and to provide it to the board as a whole.

The AIMA Guidelines recommend that the board should appoint an audit committee which:

- 'should be chaired by an independent director and be composed entirely of non-executive directors;

- 'should be composed of directors with a mix of skills, experience and other qualities for its role; and
- 'should assist the board to discharge its responsibilities in respect of the company's financial statements, the company's internal controls and the independence of the company's auditors;
- 'should have written (minuted) terms of reference which include certain core matters to be dealt with by the committee and certain core rights of the committee.'

The AIMA Report further recommends that audit committees should be entitled to obtain independent professional advice at the company's expense and should also have adequate resources, information and access to employees of the company. In addition, it comments that audit committees should be free to involve company executives (including executive directors) in these matters with the external and internal auditors in the absence of management from time to time.

The Working Group considers that the board's duty to present a balanced and understandable assessment of the company's financial position is a fundamental part of its responsibilities and that an effective and objective audit is an essential part of good corporate governance. It is essential that the audit plan be adequate to the company's circumstances and that the independence of the auditors be encouraged and protected. Direct contact between the auditors, the non-executive directors and the board as a whole is important.

Audit committees have become so well established as an effective and recognised means of achieving these objectives that they are widely seen as one of the hallmarks of good governance. In the absence of an audit committee, a board would need to go to considerable lengths to reassure shareholders and potential investors of the quality of the audit and the adequacy of the company's accounts. Where audit committees are established, they should be, and be seen to be, able to operate independently and effectively.

The Working Group therefore considers that each listed company board of more than four members should appoint an audit committee with at least a majority of non-executive directors; the members should preferably be independent. The chairman should be a non-executive director who is preferably not a chairman of the board. Membership of the committee should be published in the annual report. The board must clearly define in writing the terms of reference of the audit committee, and management, internal auditors and external auditors should have a clear understanding of its role.

The audit committee must have unrestricted access to the chief financial officer, the chief executive officer, the internal auditors and the external auditors. Similarly, the internal and external auditors must have access to the committee, particularly to the chairman and the non-executive members. The committee should also be able to consult independent experts as required at the company's expense.

The audit committee's primary functions should include reviewing:

- the nomination and performance of the external auditors. Where necessary, the audit committee should recommend to the board the name of the audit firm to be put before shareholders
- external audit engagements, including any audit tenders, with particular emphasis on the scope and quality of the audit
- effectiveness of the annual audit, ensuring emphasis is placed on areas where the committee, management or the auditors believe special attention is necessary

- co-ordination of audit approach between internal and external auditors
- effectiveness of the internal audit function
- all areas of significant financial risk and the arrangements in place to contain those risks to acceptable levels
- effectiveness of management of information and other systems of internal control
- accounting policies adopted, or any changes made or contemplated
- significant transactions which are not a normal part of the company's business
- financial statements with both management and the external auditors
- contracts, arrangements and undertakings that may involve related parties
- interim financial information
- any letter of resignation from the company's auditors

The audit committee should ensure that the scope of the audit is adequate and should review its scope and cost annually with management.

The independence of the auditors and their value to the company will be enhanced if time is set aside at audit committee meetings to allow for non-executive directors and the auditors to meet separately.

The audit committee is responsible for reporting to the board on all relevant matters within its terms of reference so that the board can take any necessary action.

The establishment of an effective audit committee and its regular contact with the auditors does not remove the need for the external auditors to meet the board as a whole on at least one occasion each year.

Boards of three or four directors should consider whether there are appropriate alternative ways of ensuring that adequate audits are conducted and that the independence of the auditors is maintained. It is important that if the alternative methods are chosen, they be fully disclosed.

7 THE MANAGEMENT OF RISK

The seventh item on the ASX's *Indicative List of Corporate Governance Matters* recommends the disclosure of 'The Board's approach to identifying areas of significant business risk and putting arrangements in place for managing those risks.'

The Cadbury Code provides that:

- 'The directors should report on the effectiveness of the company's system of internal control.
- 'The directors should report that the business is a going concern, with supporting assumptions or qualifications as necessary.'

The Cadbury Report argues that 'an effective system of internal controls is a key aspect of the efficient management of a company' and recommends that the directors' statement on the effectiveness of the control system should be subject to a report by the auditors. As noted above, the Report also recommends that audit committees should review the control systems and it proposes that an internal audit function should be established which would, inter alia, 'undertake investigations on behalf of the audit committee and follow up any suspicion of fraud.'

The Toronto Guidelines identify managing risk as one of the principal responsibilities of the board. 'The board must understand the principal risks of all aspects of the business in which the corporation is engaged and, recognising that business decisions require the incurrence of risk, achieve a proper balance between the risks incurred and the potential returns to shareholders. This requires the board to ensure that there are in place systems which effectively monitor and manage those risks with a view to the long term viability of the corporation.'

The Report also identifies as one of the principal responsibilities of the board 'The integrity of corporate internal control and management information systems.' It recommends that the board should identify control and information systems to monitor the effective discharge of its responsibilities, including the implementation of its strategies, the integrity of the financial data, the compliance of financial information with appropriate accounting principles, the commitment of the corporation's assets to different businesses and action affecting the environment.

As noted in section 6, the Report recommends that the audit committee's duties should include oversight responsibility for management reporting on internal controls.

The AIMA Guidelines recommend that boards of directors, as part of their overall stewardship responsibility, should assume responsibility for 'the integrity of the corporation's internal control and management information system.' It further recommends that the board should ensure that it can 'competently and efficiently monitor management in the organisation and the conduct of management's functions'.

The Working Group considers that the board's functions should include:

- ensuring that the company has identified the principal strategic, operational and financial risks to which it is exposed
- ensuring that systems are in place which facilitate the effective monitoring and management of the principal risks to which the company is exposed
- determining that the company has instituted adequate reporting systems and internal controls (both operational and financial) together with appropriate monitoring of compliance activities
- satisfying itself that the systems for managing risk are working properly
- establishing and monitoring policies directed to ensuring that the company complies with the law and conforms with the highest standards of financial and ethical behaviour.

The Working Group recommends that, as an effective way of discharging some of these responsibilities, boards should delegate to their audit committees the responsibility for reviewing and reporting to the board on:

- all areas of significant financial risk and the arrangements in place to contain those risks to acceptable levels
- effectiveness of management information and other systems of internal control
- significant transactions which are not a normal part of the company's business.

---

8   COMPANY CODES OF CONDUCT

The eighth item in the ASX's *Indicative List of Corporate Governance Matters* recommends disclosure of 'The company's policy on the establishment and maintenance of appropriate ethical standards.'

The Cadbury Code does not cover this area but the Cadbury Report comments that 'It is important that all employees should know what standards of conduct are expected of them. We regard it as good practice for boards of directors to draw up codes of ethics or statements of business practice and to publish them both internally and externally.'

The Toronto Guidelines do not cover this area but the Toronto Report comments that 'In supervising the conduct of the business, the board, through the CEO, sets standards of conduct for the enterprise. These standards include the general moral and ethical tone for the conduct of the business, the corporation's compliance with applicable laws, standards for financial practices and reporting, qualitative standards for products of the business and so on. These standards should reflect the view of the board of directors as to conduct in the best interests of the corporation.'

The Working Group considers that in an economy run on market principles, the freedom allowed by society to the producers of goods and services is dependent on the degree to which the public has confidence in the integrity of the participants. The lower the standard of behaviour, the more regulations are needed.

Company codes of conduct (which have been referred to as codes of ethics, statements of business principles or business practice) have been found to be valuable to companies and to the business community at large. Once understood and recognised, they offer the following benefits:

- they enhance the company's reputation for fair and responsible dealing
- they help to maintain high standards of behaviour throughout the organisation
- they give all employees a clear idea of what the company is setting out to do and how it will do it
- they help to develop pride among staff and to give a focus to the organisation as a whole.

A company code of conduct is a statement of the company's own values. The decision to adopt a code does not mean that the company must accept the values advocated by any particular outside group. While a company code should take the law and general community standards into account, it must be recognised that many different groups are advocating policies that have no general acceptance and are sometimes mutually incompatible. The adoption of a code may well assist the company to resist external pressures and incompatible values.

Elements of Codes of Conduct

If a code of conduct is to have a real meaning, it cannot be imposed from above — it must be developed by each company to meet its own needs and aspirations and must reflect the culture of that company. Ultimately, any code of conduct should be endorsed by the board. Further, there is great variation in the characteristics and needs of different types of businesses.

For these reasons, it is not possible nor desirable to lay down a single model of a code of conduct. However, the following elements are usually found in existing codes and will give some guide to a company developing its own code.

- A general statement signed by the chairman and/or the chief executive officer emphasising the board's, and management's, commitment to the code. It may include an overall statement of the company's objectives, a mission statement or a summary of the company's basic philosophy.

A section dealing with responsibilities to shareholders and the financial community generally. It may include statements on:
  - disclosure of information
  - accounting policies and practices
  - insider trading
  - conflicts of interest.

- A section on relations with customers and consumers which may include reference to:
  - service to customers
  - a commitment to offering quality and fair value
  - safety of goods
  - product recall and related practices
  - pricing policies and practices
  - use of market power.
- A section on relations with suppliers which may include reference to:
  - procurement procedures
  - tendering procedures used, including a commitment to fair and equal treatment of tenders
  - payment procedures.
- A section on employment practices which may include reference to:
  - occupational health and safety
  - equality of employment opportunity
  - the right of all employees to superannuation
  - policy and practice on alcoholism and drug dependence.
- A section on responsibilities to the community which may include references to:
  - environmental policy
  - support for community activities
  - policy and practice on donations.
- A section on personal conduct which may include reference to:
  - bribery, inducements and commissions
  - policy on the giving and receiving of gifts and entertainment
  - use of privileged information
  - the handling of conflicts of interest
  - the misuse of company assets and resources
  - personal conduct outside hours of work, including outside employment.
- A section on the monitoring of compliance and the means to be used in ensuring compliance.

It is recommended that the code of conduct be reviewed regularly and updated when necessary. It is also important that the code of conduct be communicated and is well understood by all employees.

Part III: Other Governance Matters

The ASX Listing Rule 3C (3)(j) requires disclosure of the main corporate governance practices that the company has had in place during the reporting period. *The Indicative List of Corporate Governance Matters* in Appendix 33 to the Listing Rules and used in this document is not necessarily comprehensive and companies may wish to consider the adoption and disclosure of practices which do not fit under the eight headings provided. Some general issues were discussed in Part I of this book. The Working Group considers that there are other matters worthy of board consideration and which might be referred to in a disclosure statement. These are discussed below.

I GUIDELINES FOR CONDUCT OF DIRECTORS

It may be of value for boards to agree on guidelines for the conduct of directors which may be set out in a separate document or incorporated in a company code of conduct. It may be considered appropriate to mention them in the company's annual report and to make them available to shareholders upon request. Matters covered in a set of guidelines for directors might include the following.

1.1 Conflict of Interest

The Cadbury Report identifies the management of conflicts of interest as a matter of major importance and suggests that one of the principal contributions of non-executive directors is to take the lead in resolving conflicts between management and the company.

The Toronto Report points out that Canadian corporate and securities law prescribes a code of conduct to be followed in cases of conflict and stresses that at all times, directors must act in the best interests of the corporation as a whole. It emphasises the distinction between the interests of shareholders generally and the interests of a single shareholder who has nominated the director and makes clear that directors do not have obligations to act in the interests of the nominator but in those of the general body of shareholders.

The Hong Kong Code provides that 'if a matter to be considered by the board involves a conflict of interest for a substantial shareholder or a director, a full board meeting should be held and the matter should not be dealt with by curculation or by committee.'

The Working Group considers that at all times, a director must be able to act in the interests of the company as a whole. The interests of associates, individual shareholders, other companies, and personal interests of the director or the director's family must not be allowed to prevail over those of the company generally.

Where a conflict does or may arise, the director must consider whether to refrain from participating in the debate and/or voting on the matter, whether to arrange that the relevant board papers are not sent, or in an extreme case, whether to resign from the board. In any event, full disclosure of the conflict or potential conflict must be made to the board. In considering these issues, account should be taken of the significance of the potential conflict for the company and the possible consequences if it is not handled properly.

Executive directors must always be alert to the potential for conflict of interest between management interests and their fiduciary duty as directors. Their position will be made easier if the chairman and a majority of directors are non-executive directors.

Directors who are appointed to boards at the instigation of a party with a substantial interest in the company, such as a major shareholder or a creditor, should recognise the particular sensitivity of their positions. Their fiduciary duty requires them to make their contributions in the interests of the company and they have a responsibility to the shareholders as a whole—not only to the interests of those who have nominated them. Where their obligations to other people or bodies preclude an independent position on an issue, they should disclose their position and refrain from participating in the board's consideration of that issue.

1.2 Dissent and Resignation

The CISCO Report recommends that when there is a fundamental disagreement between non-executive directors and management leading to a vote against a resolution, the non-executive(s) should be entitled to communicate with shareholders, at the company's expense, giving their reasons.

The Toronto Report recommends that, with the approval of an appropriate committee of the board, a dissenting director should be allowed to engage outside advisers at the company's expense to enable the director to better understand the proposed board action, the implications of dissent and the various courses open. The Report notes the possibility of resignation or making a public statement as possible outcomes of dissent.

The Hong Kong Code provides that if, in any matter, the non-executive directors hold views contrary to those of the executive directors, the minutes should clearly reflect this. The Code also requires that if an independent non-executive director resigns, the Exchange should be notified of the reasons why.

The Working Group considers that directors should recognise that their responsibilities to their colleagues and to the company as a whole require that where disagreement occurs, every effort be made to resolve the issue and avoid dissention. Resignation from the board, other than for genuine personal reasons, such as health, can be damaging to the company.

Nevertheless, there may be times when directors feel so strongly about a matter of principle that they are unable to acquiesce in a decision of the board. In such a case, the director should consider taking some or all of the following steps:

- making the extent of the dissent and its possible consequences clear to the board as a means of seeking to influence the decision
- asking for additional legal, accounting or other professional advice
- asking that decisions be postponed to the next meeting to allow time for further consideration and informal discussion
- tabling a statement of dissent and asking that it be minuted
- writing to the chairman, or all members of the board, and asking that the letter be filed with the minutes
- if necessary, giving notice of resignation.

Directors who take the serious step of resignation on a point of principle should consider whether their reasons require them to inform shareholders—perhaps through the ASX or the Australian Securities Commission. In deciding whether or not to make public their reasons for resigning and composing any resignation statement, a director should have regard to:

- the fact that a director is under a duty not to disclose confidential information so as to damage the company. However, this duty needs to be balanced with their duty to act bona fide in the interests of the company and, in certain circumstances, it may be proper for them to inform shareholders of their view of a particular proposal, transaction or corporate strategy
- the relevant principles of the law of defamation including the defence of qualified privilege which is available in the absense of malice. Put broadly, qualified privilege applies to communications made by persons with a duty to, or interest in, publishing them to persons with corresponding interest in receiving them. Legal advice should be obtained before taking such steps.

1.3 Directors' Benefits

Directors should ensure that all material benefits received from the company by them, or their relatives or associates, are disclosed to shareholders in the company's annual report. All contracts between directors and the company should also be disclosed. Directors of companies listed on the ASX have additional responsibilities to ensure that the company complies with requirements concerning material benefits received by them whether by way of an issue of shares or a transaction involving assets. In addition, directors should consider whether a benefit to be received is of sufficient magnitude that the approval of shareholders should be sought (even though not required by law) or whether a benefit to be obtained by a director or any associate is such that the director should abstain from exercising voting rights at any general meeting.

1.4 Confidentiality

Directors frequently acquire information not generally known to the public or other businesses such as trade secrets, processes, methods, advertising or promotional programs, sales and statistics affecting financial results. This information is the property of the company and it is improper to disclose it or to allow it to be disclosed to any other person unless the disclosure has first been authorised by the company.

1.5 Insider Trading

The statutory and fiduciary duties of directors require that they do not utilise their position for personal gain or for the gain of any person. Directors must ensure that any information in their possession which is not publicly available and would have a material effect on the price or value of the company's securities is not provided to anyone who may be influenced to subscribe, buy or sell the shares. Such information includes:

- profit forecasts
- proposed share issues
- borrowings
- impending takeovers, acquisitions, mergers, reconstructions, litigation
- significant changes in operations
- new products and new discoveries
- liquidity problems
- major purchases or sales of assets
- management restructuring.

All listed companies should have a policy that regulates any allowable dealing on the part of individual directors and officers in the company's securities, including an agreed time frame in which the buying and selling of the company's securities is permitted.

In developing such a policy, in addition to any legal requirements, the following guidelines should be considered.

- Directors and officers should never engage in short term trading of the company's shares
- Directors and officers should neither buy nor sell at a time when they possess information which, if disclosed publicly, would be likely materially to affect the market price of the company's shares.
- Directors and officers should notify the board in advance of any intended material transactions involving the company's shares (through the chairman or the secretary).

These guidelines should apply to directors (including their nominee companies) and their associates, such as their spouses, dependent children, family trusts and family companies where the transactions are known to the director.

The company's policy on directors and officers dealing in the company's shares should be disclosed in the annual report.

1.6 Management Buy-Outs

In the case of management buy-outs, directors must ensure that shareholders are fully informed and able to make an informed and independent decision on any substantial management buy-out. As there is a greater possibility of conflicts of interest during management buy-out situations, it is important that management buy-out of any substantial part of the company's business should be subject to shareholder approval. Further:

- non-executive directors should ensure that they make available to all shareholders, as far as possible, all information which is available to the proposed purchaser
- shareholders should be provided with independent expert advice with the independent advisers having access to all information necessary to enable them to give a fully informed opinion as to the merits of the offer.

1.7 AICD Code of Conduct

Directors would be well advised to consider the proposed Code of Conduct developed by the Australian Institute of Company Directors which appears in Appendix II.

2 COMPANY SECRETARY

The Cadbury Code stresses the importance of the company secretary. 'All directors should have access to the advice and services of the company secretary, who is responsible to the board for ensuring that board procedures are followed and that applicable rules and regulations are complied with. Any question of the removal of the company secretary should be a matter for the board as a whole.'

The Cadbury Report adds that the secretary has a key role to play in ensuring that board procedures are regularly reviewed and that they should give strong support to the chairman in ensuring the effective functioning of the board. It adds that 'it should be standard practice for the company secretary to administer, attend and prepare minutes of board proceedings.' The board as a whole has the responsibility for ensuring that the secretary remains capable of discharging their duties.

The Hong Kong Code provides that the 'Full minutes shall be kept by a duly appointed secretary of the meeting and such minutes shall be kept open for inspection at any time in office hours on reasonable notice by any director.'

The Working Group considers that the company secretary has an important role in facilitating the proper and effective functioning of the board and ensuring that board procedures are followed and reviewed regularly.

The chairman and the board will look to the company secretary for guidance in fulfilling their responsibilities under the rules and regulations to which they are subject and on how those responsibilities should be discharged. The chairman must have the support of the company secretary in planning and conducting the effective operation of the board. It should be standard practice for the company secretary to administer, attend and prepare a proper record of board proceedings.

All directors should have access to the advice and services of the company secretary whose independence from any individual element on the board should be maintained. The board as a whole is responsible for any appointment to the position and it should be involved in any question of a change.

---

3 SHAREHOLDERS

The Cadbury Report emphasises that shareholders have an important part to play in corporate governance. 'The shareholders as owners of the company elect the directors to run the business on their behalf and hold them accountable for its progress ... [they] have delegated many of their responsibilities as owners to the directors who act as their stewards. It is for the shareholders to call the directors to book if they appear to be failing in their stewardship and they should use this power. While they cannot be involved in the direction and management of their company, they can insist on a high standard of governance ...'.

The Cadbury Report recommends that:

- shareholders and companies seek to increase the effectiveness of annual general meetings
- institutional shareholders maintain regular systematic contact with companies outside general meetings
- institutional shareholders take a positive interest in the composition of the board of directors
- companies ensure that all significant statements about their affairs are made publicly so as to be equally available to all shareholders
- companies should communicate their strategies to their major shareholders who should inform them if there are any aspects of the business which give them cause for concern.

The Toronto Report takes a very similar position. 'Effective governance depends heavily on the willingness of owners to behave like owners and exercise their rights of ownership, to express their views to boards of directors, and to organise and exercise their shareholder franchise if they do not receive a satisfactory response.'

The Report recommends that:

- shareholders exercise their rights to vote
- companies and larger shareholders maintain closer relations between meetings
- greater disclosure be made to shareholders but that care should be taken to provide the same information to all shareholders
- corporations provide more information to shareholders concerning the way they are governed.

The AIMA sets out four recommendations for investment managers:

- 'institutions should encourage direct contact with companies including constructive communication with both senior management and board members about performance, corporate governance or other matters affecting shareholders' interests.'
- 'AIMA members should vote on all material issues ...'
- 'AIMA members should have a formal written policy on the exercising of proxy votes ...'
- '... the investment manager should report back to the client when votes are cast ...'
  In addition, the AIMA recommends that:
- in presenting issues to shareholders for a vote, companies should not combine separate issues
- major corporate changes which may erode share ownership should be submitted to a vote of shareholders.

The Working Group considers that shareholders can play a key role in the good governance of a company. Boards should encourage, where appropriate, full participation of shareholders to ensure a high level of accountability and identification with the company's goals.

Institutional shareholders, because of their increasing influence by virtue of their size, should take an active interest in the governance of the company and develop their own principles of good practice.

As the true proprietors of the company, shareholders have certain rights and obligations which include the following.

- Shareholders should make themselves as informed as possible of the activities of the company.
- Shareholders should see themselves as owners, not just investors. Their responsibility as shareholders increases with the size of their shareholding.
- Shareholders should have made a sufficient analysis to vote in an informed manner on all issues raised at general meetings. Where appropriate, reasons for voting against a motion should be made known to the board beforehand.
- Shareholders in companies listed on the ASX (other than employee shareholders) should not involve themselves in the company's day-to-day operations.
- Shareholders should take a positive interest in the composition of boards of directors with particular reference to
  - concentrations of decision making power which are not formally constrained by checks and balances appropriate to the particular company
  - appointment of a core of non-executive directors of appropriate calibre, experience and independence.
- Shareholders should take a positive interest in the structure of boards, in particular, the appointment of appropriate committees of the board—especially the audit committee.

- Shareholders in listed companies should take a positive interest in the performance of the board and should exercise their votes in the election of directors in an informed manner.
- Shareholders should take a positive interest in the election of auditors and should exercise their votes in an informed manner.
- Shareholders should take a positive interest in the auditor's report and the competence of auditors and where appropriate, be prepared to ask questions of the auditor.
- Shareholders should not seek to receive price sensitive information which is not available to the market generally.

IFSA: *Corporate Governance Guidelines*

Investment and Financial Services Associaton

Corporate Governance: A Guide for Investment Managers and Corporations July 1999 (Extracts)

Main features of this Guidance Note are:

- The first four Guidelines in the Guidance Note provide a series of guidelines for IFSA Members in determining their approach to Corporate Governance, voting and other issues proposed by public companies in which they invest;
- The next fourteen Guidelines in the Guidance Note provide a series of guidelines for public companies in relation to a range of Corporate Governance issues including disclosure, board and board committee composition, non-executive directors, board and executive remuneration policy and disclosure;
- Appendix A to this Guidance Note includes a suggested format for remuneration disclosure and Appendix B a model proxy form.

9 SUMMARY OF GUIDELINES

9.1 Guidelines for Investment Managers

9.1.1 *Guideline 1—Communication*

Investment Managers should encourage direct contact with companies including constructive communication with both senior management and board members about performance, Corporate Governance and other matters affecting shareholders' interests.

9.1.2 *Guideline 2—Voting*

Investment Managers should vote on all material issues at all Australian company meetings where they have the voting authority and responsibility to do so.

504

9.1.3   Guideline 3—Proxy Voting Policy and Procedures

Investment Managers should have a written policy on the exercising of proxy votes that is approved by their board and formal internal procedures to ensure that the policy is applied consistently.

9.1.4   Guideline 4—Reporting to Clients

Wherever a client delegates responsibility for exercising proxy votes, the Investment Manager should report back to the client when votes are cast (including abstentions) on investments owned by the client. Reporting on voting should be a part of the regular reporting process to each client. The Manager should report back to clients whether or not the votes are cast.

The report should include a positive statement that the Investment Manager has complied with its obligation to exercise voting rights in the client's interest only. If an Investment Manager is unable to make this statement without qualification, the report should include an explanation.

9.2   Guidelines for Corporations

9.2.1   Guideline 1—Annual Disclosure

The board of directors of a listed company should prominently and clearly disclose, in a separate section of its annual report, its approach to Corporate Governance. This should include an analysis of the Corporate Governance issues specific to the company so that public Investors understand how the company deals with those issues.

9.2.2   Guideline 2—Composition of the Board of Directors

The board of directors of a listed company should be constituted with a majority of individuals who qualify as independent directors as defined in these Guidelines .... . The board should annually review and disclose in the annual report its required mix of skills, experience and other qualities, including the core competencies, which the independent directors should bring to the board.

9.2.3   Guideline 3—Chairperson to be an Independent Director

The chairperson should be an independent director or, if the chairperson is not an independent director, the independent directors should appoint one of their numbers to be lead director and to monitor and report to them on issues falling within the normal purview of a non-executive chairperson.

9.2.4   Guideline 4—Board Committees Generally

Committees of the board of directors should:

- generally be constituted with a majority who are independent directors;
- be entitled to obtain independent professional or other advice at the cost of the company; and
- be entitled to obtain such resources and information from the company, as they may require.

9.2.5   Guideline 5—Key Board Committees

The board should appoint an audit committee, a remuneration committee and a nomination committee constituted as defined in these Guidelines .... .

9.2.6   Guideline 6—Appointment of non-Executive Directors

Before accepting appointment, non-executive directors should formally be advised of the reasons they have been asked to join the board and given an outline of what the board expects of them.

They should also be advised of their rights as a director, including their access to company employees and access to information and resources. They should also be advised of their entitlement to obtain independent professional or other advice at the cost of the company.

9.2.7 Guideline 7—Performance Evaluation
The board should review its performance and the performance of individual directors, the company and management regularly. As a key part of that process, the independent directors should meet on their own at least once annually to review performance.

9.2.8 Guideline 8—Equity Participation by Non-Executive Directors
The board should establish and disclose in the annual report a policy to encourage non-executive directors to invest their own capital in the company or to acquire shares from an allocation of a portion of their fees.

9.2.9 Guideline 9—Respective Roles of the Board and Management
The board should at least annually review the allocation of the work of the company between board and management.

9.2.10 Guideline 10—Board and Executive Remuneration Policy and Disclosure
The board should disclose in the company's annual report its policies on and the quantum and components of remuneration for all directors and each of the 5 highest paid executives. The disclosure should be made in one section of the annual report in tabular form with appropriate explanatory notes.

9.2.11 Guideline 11—Company Meetings
- Format of Resolutions
  Separate issues should not be combined and presented as a single motion for shareholder vote.
- Form of Proxies
  Companies should adopt the Model Form of Proxy in Appendix B (with appropriate modifications) [*Note: not included in this extract.*]
- Notification Period for Shareholder Meetings
  The annual report, notice of meeting and other documents for all shareholder meetings should be sent to shareholders at least 28 days prior to the meeting.
- Method of Voting
  Voting should be by poll only on the conclusion of discussion of each item of business and appropriate forms of technology should be utilised to facilitate the proxy voting process.
- Disclosure of Voting Results
  In announcing to the ASX the decisions made by shareholders at a general meeting, a listed company should report the aggregate proxy votes validly received for each item of business in the notice of meeting. The report should disclose, in the case of a resolution passed on a show of hands, the aggregate number of proxy votes received in each voting category ('For', 'Against', 'Left to Proxy's Discretion' and 'Abstain') and the aggregate number of votes not exercised by shareholders who submitted proxies ('No Intention'). In the case of a resolution submitted to a poll, the report should disclose both the information specified in the preceding sentence and the aggregate number of votes cast 'For' and 'Against' on the poll.
- Access to Minutes
  Shareholders should be able to authorise an agent to inspect or obtain copies of minutes of shareholders' meetings.

9.2.12   Guideline 12—Disclosure of Beneficial Shareholder Information
Information about beneficial shareholdings obtained by companies in response to their inquiries should be immediately disclosed by them to the market.

9.2.13   Guideline 13—Major Corporate Changes
Major corporate changes, which in substance or effect may impact shareholder equity or erode share ownership rights, should be submitted to a vote of shareholders. Enough time and sufficient information (including a balanced assessment of relevant issues) should be given to shareholders to enable them to make informed judgements on these resolutions.

9.2.14   Guideline 14—Company Codes of Ethics
Listed companies should have a company Code of Ethics that is adopted by the board and is available to shareholders on request.

APPENDIX 3

Institute of Directors in New Zealand (Inc.) Code of Proper Practice for Directors

CODE OF PROPER PRACTICE FOR DIRECTORS

1.0 Introduction and principles

1.1 The purpose of the Code is to provide guidance to directors in New Zealand to assist them to carry out their duties and responsibilities effectively and in accordance with the highest professional standards recognising that wealth creation is the mission of the board.

1.2 The Code is not intended to be an exhaustive statement of a director's obligations. It should be read in conjunction with the law applying to company directors and the provisions contained in the constitution of the company.

1.3 The office of director carries with it both legal and moral responsibilities. The Code offers guidance more on moral and ethical responsibilities than on those imposed by law. It applies to both executive and non-executive directors.

1.4 The Code applies to directors of all companies or corporate entities from those listed on the Stock Exchange to small companies.

1.5 The principles upon which the Code is based include integrity and accountability. These qualities are prerequisites to maintaining confidence and trust in directors.

1.6 The reasons for adhering to the Code are twofold.

First, a clear understanding of moral and ethical responsibilities and strict observance of obligations will assist directors in forming and winning support for their strategies. It will also assist in the efficient operation of capital markets and increase confidence in boards of directors and the general level of confidence in business.

Secondly, if high standards of business conduct are not maintained a greater degree of imposed regulation may result.

1.7 The Code has been approved and adopted by the Council of the Institute of Directors in accordance with the authority conferred on the Council by the Institute's constitution. It is the intention of the Institute to monitor [the] applicability of the Code and as considered necessary to amend or add to it to reflect changes to practice and law.

1.8 In accordance with the provisions of the Institute's constitution the Code is binding on all members of the Institute. Members should make themselves familiar with the content of the Code and observe not only its letter but also its spirit.

2.0 Definitions

'Accountability' means having a duty to answer to another for what is done or not done within an area of responsibility.

'Chairman' is used in a gender neutral sense.

'Company' includes companies registered under the *Companies Act*, state owned enterprises established under the *State Owned Enterprises Act* and corporate entities established under any other Act.

'Director' includes all directors whether executive directors or non-executive directors.

'Executive director' means a director who is also an employee of the company and includes a managing director .

'Independent' is used in the sense of being self reliant and with objectivity unimpaired by outside interests.

'Integrity' means consistent honesty, sincerity and uprightness in all dealings.

'Non-executive director' means a director who is not an executive director.

3.0 Fundamental obligations

3.1 Directors must act honestly and in good faith in what the director believes to be the best interests of the company. Directors must ensure that all shareholders and classes of shareholder are treated fairly according to their different rights.

3.2 Directors must carry out their duties in a lawful manner and use reasonable endeavours to ensure that the company conducts its business in accordance with the law and with a high standard of commercial morality. Directors should refer to the Institute's statements of best practice as part of their decision-making process.

3.3 Directors should avoid conflicts of interest so far as is possible. Where a conflict or potential conflict arises, as a minimum they must adhere scrupulously to the procedures provided by law and by the constitution of the company for dealing with conflicts and with the position of directors having an interest in a particular contract or issue. A director who has a continuing conflict of interest of a material nature should consider resignation as a director of the company, and should also consider the effects of resignation on remaining members of the board and on shareholders.

3.4 Directors should be diligent, attend board meetings and devote sufficient time to make and keep themselves familiar with the nature of the company's business and the environments, including political, legal and social, in which it operates. Directors should be aware of all statutory and regulatory requirements affecting their company including the content of its constitution and, where applicable, the requirements of bodies such as the New Zealand Stock Exchange, and see that such requirements are observed.

3.5 Directors must observe the confidentiality of non public information acquired by them as directors and not disclose it to any other person without the authority of the board. A director who is nominated by, or has a special allegiance to, a particular shareholder or group of shareholders or other stakeholder, may only disclose confidential information to the nominated shareholder or other stakeholder with the authority of the board and in strict compliance with any procedures prescribed by law or the constitution of the company.

3.6   Directors of public issuers should ensure that their company has in place an approved procedure for the buying and selling of share securities in the company by directors or their relatives or associates. Directors should not engage in short term trading in the company's shares or securities. Directors should notify the board in advance of an intended transaction by them or their relatives or associates involving shares or securities in the company.

3.7   Directors must act in accordance with their fiduciary duties. They should comply with the spirit as well as the letter of the law mindful that in addition to purely legal requirements the proper discharge of the duties of a director requires high ethical and moral standards of behaviour.

4.0   Board of directors

4.1   The board must meet regularly to monitor and control the performance of management. It must ensure that appropriate reporting systems are in place and maintained to provide accurate and timely information to the board, and that adequate systems of control are in place. It is responsible for approving and monitoring the company's strategic plan.

4.2   The board should have a formal schedule of matters and authority reserved to it for decision to ensure that the direction and control of the company are in the hands of the board.

4.3   There should be a clearly accepted division of responsibilities at the head of the company to ensure a balance of power and authority and that no one individual has unfettered powers of decision. The board should ensure that independent views on the board are given full and proper consideration and weight.

4.4   The mix of executive directors and non-executive directors will vary from company to company but ideally there should be at least one non-executive director on every board. In the case of companies listed on the Stock Exchange and other companies with diverse and widely spread shareholdings there should be a majority of non-executive directors on the board. The calibre and number of non-executive directors should be such that their views carry significant weight in the decisions of the board. It is the view of the Institute that even small companies would benefit from having a non-executive director with suitable experience and skills on the board.

4.5   It is the duty of the board to present to shareholders a balanced and understandable assessment of the company's performance and position. Often this will involve the provision of information additional to the minimum required by law. In any case of doubt substance and content should prevail over form. The need for reports and accounts to be understood readily by shareholders means that a coherent narrative is necessary as well as figures.

5.0   Chairman

5.1   The board should elect its chairman annually at the first board meeting following the annual general meeting. As a general rule the roles of the chairman and managing director or chief executive officer should be kept separate and not held by one person at the same time.

5.2   The chairman is responsible for the efficient functioning of the board and sets the agenda for board meetings usually in conjunction with the managing director or chief executive officer and the person normally exercising the functions of a company secretary. The chairman should ensure that all directors are enabled and encouraged to play their full part in the affairs of the board and have adequate opportunities to express their views.

5.3   The chairman has primary responsibility for ensuring that all directors, and non-executive directors in particular, receive sufficient timely information to enable them to be effective board members.

5.4   The chairman is the link between the board and the managing director or chief executive officer of the company. It is for the chairman to maintain a proper balance between executive and independent views on the board.

6.0   Non-executive directors

6.1   The principal role of non-executive directors is to provide independent judgement and outside experience and objectivity, not subordinated to operational considerations, on all issues which come before the board.

6.2   Non-executive directors should acquire and maintain a sufficiently detailed knowledge of the company's business activities and on-going performance to enable them to make informed decisions on the issues before the board. At the same time they should recognise the division between the board and management and ordinarily not become involved in management issues or in managing the implementation of board policy.

7.0   Executive directors

7.1   Executive directors have a dual role as employees of the company and as directors. As directors they have responsibilities additional to, and must retain a degree of independence from, their executive position to enable them to carry out those responsibilities effectively. Executive directors should be appointed as individuals and not because of any position they hold. They must always be alert to the potential for conflicts between their management interests and the fiduciary duties of a director.

8.0   Committees

8.1   Companies listed on the Stock Exchange and other companies with diverse and widely spread shareholdings should have an effective committee appointed by the board and, in appropriate circumstances, other board committees to assist with such issues as remuneration, nomination, etc. When a committee is established by the board, its terms of reference and its powers, duties, reporting procedures, membership and duration of office should be clearly recorded. Committee service should be rotational.

8.2   Any non-executive director should be entitled to attend meetings of any board committee provided the director is not specifically excluded for reasons of conflicts of interest, even if the director is not an appointed member of the committee. Executive directors and other employees should attend board committee meetings when requested do so by the committee.

9.0   Audit committees

9.1   The audit committee should be formally constituted to ensure its relationship with the board is clear and it should have written terms of reference agreed by the board including the review of all financial statements to be released by the company and the regular review of compliance with internal systems and controls and with statutory and regulatory requirements.

9.2   The audit committee should normally meet at least three times a year and a statement to this effect should be recorded in the annual report.

9.3   The audit committee ideally should comprise only non-executive directors.

9.4   There should be clear lines of communication between the audit committee and the external auditors. The audit committee should meet with the external auditors at least once a year and for at least part of that meeting no executive directors or other employees of the company should be present.

9.5 There should also be clear lines of communication between the chairman of the audit committee and the head of any internal audit function.

10.0 Trust boards and trustees

10.1 The Code is primarily intended for directors of companies in New Zealand. However, it is also considered to be an appropriate guide for trustees in addition to their specific responsibilities under their particular trust deed and the provisions of the *Trustee Act*.

11.0 Comment

11.1 The following is an example of wording that companies which wish to support the Code may like to include in their annual report:

> 'Your board supports the need for the highest standards of behaviour and accountability from directors and accordingly endorses the principles set out in the Code of Proper Practice for Directors approved and adopted by the Institute of Directors in New Zealand (Incorporated).'

OECD Principles of Corporate Governance

I. THE RIGHTS OF SHAREHOLDERS

The corporate governance framework should protect shareholders' rights.

A. Basic shareholder rights include the right to 1) secure methods of ownership registration; 2) convey or transfer shares; 3) obtain relevant information on the corporation on a timely and regular basis; 4) participate and vote in general shareholder meetings; 5) elect members of the board; and 6) share in the profits of the corporation.

B. Shareholders have the right to participate in, and to be sufficiently informed on, decisions concerning fundamental corporate changes such as: 1) amendments to the statutes, or articles of incorporation or similar governing documents of the company; 2) the authorisation of additional shares; and 3) extraordinary transactions that in effect result in the sale of the company.

C. Shareholders should have the opportunity to participate effectively and vote in general shareholder meetings and should be informed of the rules, including voting procedures, that govern general shareholder meetings:

1. Shareholders should be furnished with sufficient and timely information concerning the date, location and agenda of general meetings, as well as full and timely information regarding the issues to be decided at the meeting.

2. Opportunity should be provided for shareholders to ask questions of the board and to place items on the agenda at general meetings, subject to reasonable limitations.

3. Shareholders should be able to vote in person or in absentia, and equal effect should be given to votes whether cast in person or in absentia.

D. Capital structures and arrangements that enable certain shareholders to obtain a degree of control disproportionate to their equity ownership should be disclosed.

E. Markets for corporate control should be allowed to function in an efficient and transparent manner.

1. The rules and procedures governing the acquisition of corporate control in the capital markets, and extraordinary transactions such as mergers, and sales of substantial portions of corporate assets, should be clearly articulated and disclosed so that investors understand their rights and recourse. Transactions should occur at transparent prices under fair conditions that protect the rights of all shareholders according to their class.

513

2. Anti-take-over devices should not be used to shield management from accountability.

F. Shareholders, including institutional investors, should consider the costs and benefits of exercising their voting rights.

II. THE EQUITABLE TREATMENT OF SHAREHOLDERS

The corporate governance framework should ensure the equitable treatment of all shareholders, including minority and foreign shareholders. All shareholders should have the opportunity to obtain effective redress for violation of their rights.

A. All shareholders of the same class should be treated equally.
   1. Within any class, all shareholders should have the same voting rights. All investors should be able to obtain information about the voting rights attached to all classes of shares before they purchase. Any changes in voting rights should be subject to share-holder vote.
   2. Votes should be cast by the custodians or nominees in a manner agreed upon with the beneficial owner of the shares.
   3. Processes and procedures for general shareholder meetings should allow for equitable treatment of all shareholders. Company procedures should not make it unduly difficult or expensive to cast votes.
B. Insider trading and abusive self-dealing should be prohibited.
C. Members of the board and managers should be required to disclose any material interests in transactions or matters affecting the corporation.

III. THE ROLE OF STAKEHOLDERS IN CORPORATE GOVERNANCE

The corporate governance framework should recognise the rights of stakeholders as established by law and encourage active co-operation between corporations and stakeholders in creating wealth, jobs, and the sustainability of financially sound enterprises.

A. The corporate governance framework should ensure that the rights of stakeholders that are protected by law are respected.
B. Where stakeholder interests are protected by law, stakeholders should have the opportunity to obtain effective redress for violation of their rights.
C. The corporate governance framework should permit performance-enhancing mechanisms for stakeholder participation.
D. Where stakeholders participate in the corporate governance process, they should have access to relevant information.

IV. DISCLOSURE AND TRANSPARENCY

The corporate governance framework should ensure that timely and accurate disclosure is made on all material matters regarding the corporation, including the financial situation, performance, ownership, and governance of the company.

A. Disclosure should include, but not be limited to, material information on:
   1. The financial and operating results of the company.
   2. Company objectives.
   3. Major share ownership and voting rights.
   4. Members of the board and key executives, and their remuneration.

5. Material foreseeable risk factors
6. Material issues regarding employees and other stakeholders.
7. Governance structures and policies.

B. Information should be prepared, audited, and disclosed in accordance with high quality standards of accounting, financial and non-financial disclosure, and audit.

C. An annual audit should be conducted by an independent auditor to provide an external and objective assurance on the way in which financial statements have been prepared and presented.

D. Channels for disseminating information should provide for fair, timely and cost-efficient access to relevant information by users.

V. THE RESPONSIBILITIES OF THE BOARD

The corporate governance framework should ensure the strategic guidance of the company, the effective monitoring of management by the board, and the board's accountability to the company and the shareholders.

A. Board members should act on a fully informed basis, in good faith, with due diligence and care, and in the best interest of the company and the shareholders.

B. Where board decisions may affect different shareholder groups differently, the board should treat all shareholders fairly.

C. The board should ensure compliance with applicable law and take into account the interests of stakeholders.

D. The board should fulfil certain key functions, including:
1. Reviewing and guiding corporate strategy, major plans of action, risk policy, annual budgets and business plans; setting performance objectives; monitoring implementation and corporate performance; and overseeing major capital expenditures, acquisitions and diversitures.
2. Selecting, compensating, monitoring and, when necessary, replacing key executives and overseeing succession planning.
3. Reviewing key executive and board remuneration, and ensuring a formal and transparent board nomination process.
4. Monitoring and managing potential conflicts of interest of management, board members and shareholders, including misuse of corporate assets and abuse in related party transactions.
5. Ensuring the integrity of the corporation's accounting and financial reporting systems, including the independent audit, and that appropriate systems of control are in place, in particular, systems for monitoring risk, financial control, and compliance with the law.
6. Monitoring the effectiveness of the governance practices under which it operates and making changes as needed.
7. Overseeing the process of disclosure and communications.

E. The board should be able to exercise objective judgement on corporate affairs independent, in particular, from management.
1. Boards should consider assigning a sufficient number of non-executive board members capable of exercising independent judgement to tasks where there is a potential for conflict of interest. Examples of such key responsibilities are financial reporting, nomination and executive and board remuneration.
2. Board members should devote sufficient time to their responsibilities.

F. In order to fulfil their responsibilities, board members should have access to accurate, relevant and timely information.

The Caux Round Table
Principles for Business

Principle 1: The Responsibilities of Business: Beyond Shareholders toward Stakeholders

The value of a business to society is the wealth and employment it creates and the marketable products and services it provides to consumers at a reasonable price commensurate with quality. To create such value, a business must maintain its own economic health and viability, but survival is not a sufficient goal.

Businesses have a role to play in improving the lives of all their customers, employees, and shareholders by sharing with them the wealth they have created. Suppliers and competitors as well should expect business to honor their obligations in a spirit of honesty and fairness. As responsible citizens of the local, national, regional and global communities in which they operate, businesses share a part in shaping the future of those communities.

Principle 2: The Economic and Social Impact of Business: Toward Innovation, Justice and World Community

Businesses established in foreign countries to develop, produce or sell should contribute to the social advancement of those countries by creating productive employment and helping to raise the purchasing power of their citizens. Businesses also should contribute to human rights, education, welfare, and vitalisation of the countries in which they operate.

Businesses should contribute to economic and social development not only in the countries in which they operate, but also in the world community at large, through effective and prudent use of resources, free and fair competition, and emphasis upon innovation in technology, production methods, marketing and communications.

Principle 3: Business Behavior: Beyond the Letter of Law Toward a Spirit of Trust

While accepting the legitimacy of trade secrets, businesses should recognise that sincerity, candor, truthfulness, the keeping of promises, and transparency contribute not only to their own credibility and stability but also to the smoothness and efficiency of business transactions, particularly on the international level.

Principle 4: Respect for Rules

To avoid trade frictions and to promote freer trade, equal conditions for competition, and fair and equitable treatment for all participants, businesses should respect international and domestic rules. In addition, they should recognise that some behavior, although legal, may still have adverse consequences.

Principle 5: Support for Multilateral Trade

Businesses should support the multilateral trade systems of the GATT/World Trade Organization and similar international agreements. They should cooperate in efforts to promote the progressive and judicious liberalisation of trade and to relax those domestic measures that unreasonably hinder global commerce, while giving due respect to national policy objectives.

Principle 6: Respect for the Environment

A business should protect and, where possible, improve the environment, promote sustainable development, and prevent the wasteful use of natural resources.

Principle 7: Avoidance of Illicit Operations

A business should not participate in or condone bribery, money laundering, or other corrupt practices: indeed, it should seek cooperation with others to eliminate them. It should not trade in arms or other materials used for terrorist activities, drug traffic or other organized crime.

Index